BUSINESS ETHICS

Fifth Edition

WILLIAM H. SHAW
San Jose State University

THOMSON
™
WADSWORTH

Australia • Canada • Mexico • Singapore • Spain
United Kingdom • United States

THOMSON
—★—
™
WADSWORTH

Publisher: Holly J. Allen
Philosophy Editor: Steve Wainwright
Assistant Editors: Lee McCracken,
　Anna Lustig
Editorial Assistant: Barbara Hillaker
Marketing Manager: Worth Hawes
Advertising Project Managers: Bryan Vann,
　Vicky Wan
Composition Buyer: Ben Schroeter
Print/Media Buyer: Doreen Suruki
Permissions Editor: Joohee Lee

Production Service: Greg Hubit Bookworks
Text Designer: John Odam
Copy Editor: Richard Wingell
Cover Designer: Yvo Riezebos
Cover Image: John Register, *The
Conversation*, 1991, oil on Canvas, 50 ×
70 inches. Courtesy Modernism Inc.,
San Francisco
Compositor: International Typesetting
and Composition
Printer: Transcontinental—Louiseville

Library of Congress Control Number: 2003116109

ISBN 0-534-61972-X

Thomson Wadsworth
10 Davis Drive
Belmont, CA 94002-3098
USA

Asia
Thomson Learning
5 Shenton Way #01-01
UIC Building
Singapore 068808

Australia/New Zealand
Thomson Learning
102 Dodds Street
Southbank, Victoria 3006
Australia

Canada
Nelson
1120 Birchmount Road
Toronto, Ontario M1K 5G4
Canada

Europe/Middle East/Africa
Thomson Learning
High Holborn House
50/51 Bedford Row
London WC1R 4LR
United Kingdom

Latin America
Thomson Learning
Seneca, 53
Colonia Polanco
11560 Mexico D.F.
Mexico

Spain/Portugal
Paraninfo
Calle Magallanes, 25
28015 Madrid, Spain

BRIEF CONTENTS

CONTENTS

Chapter 3 Justice and Economic Distribution   79

PART IV BUSINESS AND SOCIETY   335

Chapter 10 Consumers   336

Chapter 11 The Environment   378

PREFACE

It is difficult to imagine an area of study that has greater importance to society or greater relevance to students than business ethics. As this book enters its fifth edition, business ethics has become a well-established academic subject. Most colleges and universities offer courses in it, and scholarly interest in the field continues to grow.

Yet some people still scoff at the idea of business ethics, jesting that the very concept is an oxymoron. To be sure, recent years have seen the newspapers filled with lurid stories of corporate misconduct and felonious behavior by individual businesspeople. And many suspect that what the newspapers report represents only the proverbial tip of the iceberg. However, these reports should prompt the reflective person not to make fun of business ethics but rather to think more deeply about the nature and purpose of business in our society and about the ethical choices individuals must inevitably make in their business and professional lives.

Business ethics has an interdisciplinary character. Questions of economic policy and business practice intertwine with issues in politics, sociology, and organizational theory. Although business ethics remains anchored in philosophy, even here abstract questions in normative ethics and political philosophy mingle with analysis of practical problems and concrete moral dilemmas. Furthermore, business ethics is not just an academic study but also an invitation to reflect on our own values and our own responses to the hard moral choices that the world of business can pose.

The Organization of the Book
The purpose of this text is fourfold: to expose students to the important moral issues that arise in various business contexts; to provide students with an understanding of the moral, social, and economic environments within which those problems occur; to introduce students to the ethical concepts that are relevant for resolving those problems; and to assist students in developing the necessary reasoning and analytical skills for doing so. Although the book's primary emphasis is on business, its scope extends to related moral issues in other organizational and professional contexts.

Part I, "Moral Philosophy and Business," discusses the nature of morality and presents the main theories of normative ethics and the leading approaches to questions of economic justice. Part II, "American Business and Its Basis," examines the institutional foundations of business, focusing on capitalism as an economic system and the nature and role of corporations in our society. Part III, "The Organization and the People in It," identifies a variety of ethical issues and moral challenges that arise out of the interplay of employers and employees within an organization, including the problem of discrimination. Part IV, "Business and Society," concerns moral problems involving business, consumers, and the natural environment.

Changes in the Fifth Edition
Although instructors who have used the previous edition will find the organization and content of the book familiar, *Business Ethics* has been thoroughly revised. I have updated material throughout the book and tried to enhance the clarity of its discussions

and the accuracy of its treatment of both philosophical and empirical issues. At all times my goal has been to provide students with a textbook that they will find clear, understandable, and engaging.

Thirty-nine case studies now supplement the main text. Six of these are new; many of the others have been revised and updated. The case studies vary in kind and in length, but they are designed to enable instructors and students to pursue further some of the issues discussed in the text and to analyze them in more specific contexts. The case studies should provide a lively springboard for classroom discussions and the application of ethical concepts.

Ways of Using This Book

A course on business ethics can be taught in a variety of ways. Some instructors prefer to treat the foundational questions of ethical theory thoroughly before moving on to particular moral problems; others reverse this priority. Still other instructors frame their courses around the question of economic justice, the analysis of capitalism, or the debate over corporate social responsibility. Some instructors stress individual moral decision making, others social and economic policy.

Business Ethics permits teachers great flexibility in how they organize their courses. A wide range of theoretical and applied issues are discussed; and the individual chapters, the major sections within them, and the case studies are to a surprising extent self-contained. Instructors can thus teach the book in whatever order they choose, and they can easily skip or touch lightly on some topics in order to concentrate on others without loss of coherence.

Acknowledgments

I wish to acknowledge my great debt to the many people whose ideas and writings have influenced me over the years. Philosophy is widely recognized to involve a process of ongoing dialogue. This is nowhere more evident than in the writing of textbooks, whose authors can rarely claim that the ideas being synthesized, organized, and presented are theirs alone. Without my colleagues, without my students, and without a larger philosophical community concerned with business and ethics, this book would not have been possible.

I particularly want to acknowledge my debt to Vincent Barry. Readers familiar with our textbook and reader *Moral Issues in Business** will realize the extent to which I have drawn on material from that work. *Business Ethics* is, in effect, a revised and updated version of the textbook portion of that collaborative work, and I am very grateful to Vince for permitting me to use our joint work here.

*William H. Shaw and Vincent Barry, *Moral Issues in Business*, 9th ed. (Belmont, Calif.: Wadsworth, 2004).

MORAL PHILOSOPHY AND BUSINESS

1

The Nature of Morality

Sometimes the rich and mighty fall. Ask Kenneth Lay, chairman and CEO of Enron until that once mighty company nose-dived and crashed. Founded in the 1980s, Enron soon became a dominant player in the field of energy trading, growing rapidly to become America's seventh-biggest company. Wall Street loves growth, and Enron was its darling, admired as dynamic, innovative, and—of course—profitable. The fact that nobody could quite understand exactly how the company made its money didn't hurt, either. In 1998 the value of Enron stock increased 40 percent. The next year it shot up 58 percent, and in 2000 it went up an unbelievable 89 percent.

After *Fortune* magazine voted it "the most innovative company of the year" in 2000, Enron proudly took to calling itself not just "the world's leading energy company" but "the world's leading company." But when Enron was forced to declare bankruptcy in December 2001—at the time the largest Chapter 11 filing in U.S. history—the world learned that its legendary financial prowess was illusory and the company's success built on the sands of hype. And the hype continued to the end. Even with the company's financial demise fast approaching, Kenneth Lay was still recommending the company's stock to its employees—at the same time that he and other executives were cashing in their shares and bailing out.

Enron's crash cost the retirement accounts of its employees more than a billion dollars as the company's stock fell from the stratosphere to only a few pennies a share. Outside investors lost even more. The reason Enron's collapse caught investors by surprise—the company's market value was $28 billion in October 2001, just two months before its bankruptcy—was that Enron had always made its financial records and accounts as opaque as possible. It did this by creating a Byzantine financial structure of off-balance-sheet special-purpose entities—reportedly as many as 9,000—that were supposed to be separate and independent from the main company. Enron's board of directors condoned these and other dubious accounting practices and voted twice to permit executives to pursue personal interests that ran contrary to those of the company. When Enron was obliged to redo its financial statements for 1997–2000, its profits dropped $600 million and its debts increased $630 million.

Still, Enron's financial auditors should have spotted these and other problems. After all, the shell game Enron was playing is an old one, and months before the company ran aground, Enron Vice President Sherron Watkins had warned Lay that the company could soon "implode in a wave of accounting scandals." Yet both Arthur Andersen, Enron's longtime outside auditing firm, and Vinson & Elkins, the company's law firm, had routinely put together and signed off on various dubious financial deals, and in doing so made large profits for themselves. Arthur Andersen, in particular, was supposed to make sure that the company's public records reflected financial reality, but Andersen was more worried about its auditing and consulting fees than its fiduciary responsibilities. Even worse, when the scandal began to break, a partner at Andersen organized the shredding of incriminating Enron documents before investigators could lay their hands on them. As a result, the eighty-nine-year-old accounting firm was convicted of obstructing justice, and it went out of business. (This was not the first time Andersen had been in trouble, by the way. The year before the Securities and Exchange Commission had fined it $7 million for approving misleading accounts at Waste Management, and it also had to pay $110 million to settle a lawsuit for auditing work it did for Sunbeam before it, too, filed for bankruptcy.)

Enron's fall also revealed the conflicts of interest that threaten the credibility of Wall Street's analysts—analysts who get compensated based on their ability to bring in and support investment banking deals. Enron was known in the industry as the "deal machine" because it generated so much investment banking business—limited partnerships, loans, and derivatives. This may explain why, only days before Enron filed bankruptcy, just two of the sixteen Wall Street analysts who covered the company recommended that clients sell the stock. But the rot doesn't stop there. Enron and Andersen enjoyed extensive political connections, which had helped over the years to ensure the passage of a series of deregulatory measures favorable to the energy company. Of the 248 members of Congress sitting on the eleven House and Senate committees charged with investigating Enron's collapse, 212 had received money from Enron or its accounting firm.[1]

Stories of business corruption and of greed and wrongdoing in high places have always fascinated the popular press, and media interest in business ethics has never been higher. But one should not be misled by the headlines and news reports. Not all moral issues in business involve giant corporations and their well-heeled executives, and few cases of business ethics are widely publicized. The vast majority of them involve the mundane, uncelebrated moral challenges that working men and women meet daily.

Although the financial shenanigans at Enron were complicated, once their basic outline is sketched, the wrongdoing is pretty easy to see: deception, dishonesty, fraud, disregarding one's professional responsibilities, and unfairly injuring others for one's own gain. But many of the moral issues that arise in business are complex and difficult to answer. The topic of business ethics includes not just the question of the moral or immoral motivations of businesspeople, but also a whole range of problems that arise in the context of business. These issues are too numerous to compile, but consider these typical questions:

Is passing a personality or honesty test a justifiable preemployment condition? Are drug tests? What rights do employees have on the job? How should business respond to employees who have AIDS? What, if anything, must it do to improve work conditions?

Should manufacturers reveal all product defects? At what point does acceptable exaggeration become lying about a product or service? When does aggressive marketing become consumer manipulation?

What are businesses' environmental responsibilities? Is a corporation obliged to help combat social problems such as poverty, pollution, and urban decay? Must business fight sexism and racism? How far must it go to ensure equality of opportunity? How should organizations respond to the problem of sexual harassment?

May employees ever use their positions inside an organization to advance their own interests? Is insider trading or the use of privileged information immoral? How much loyalty do workers owe their companies? What say should a business have over the off-the-job activities of its employees?

What obligations does a worker have to outside parties, such as customers, competitors, or society generally? When, if ever, is an employee morally required to blow the whistle?

These questions typify business issues with moral significance. The answers we give are determined largely by our moral standards, principles, and values. What these standards and principles are, where they come from, and how they can be assessed are some of the concerns of this opening chapter. In particular, you will encounter the following topics:

1. The nature, scope, and purpose of business ethics
2. The distinguishing features of morality and how it differs from etiquette, law, and professional codes of conduct
3. The relationship between morality and religion
4. The doctrine of ethical relativism and its difficulties
5. What it means to have moral principles, the nature of conscience, and the relationship between morality and self-interest
6. The place of values and ideals in a person's life
7. The social and psychological factors that sometimes jeopardize an individual's integrity
8. The characteristics of sound moral reasoning

ETHICS

"The word *ethics* comes from the Greek word *ethos*, meaning character or custom," writes philosophy professor Robert C. Solomon.[2] Today we use the word *ethos* to refer to the distinguishing disposition, character, or attitude of a specific people, culture, or group (as in, for example, "the American ethos" or "the business ethos"). According to Solomon, the etymology of *ethics* suggests its basic concerns: (1) individual character, including what it means to be "a good person," and (2) the social rules that govern and limit our conduct, especially the ultimate rules concerning right and wrong, which we call *morality*.

Philosophers generally distinguish ethics from morality. "Morality" refers to a person or group's standards of right and wrong or good and bad, and "ethics" refers to the study and assessment of those standards. Thus, when we reflect critically on our own moral standards or the moral values of the society around us, we are beginning to do ethics. Few people, however, would distinguish a person's "morals" from his or her "ethics," and almost everyone uses "ethical" and "moral" interchangeably to describe people we consider good and actions we consider right, and "unethical" and "immoral" to designate bad people and wrong actions. This book follows that common usage.

Business and Organizational Ethics

The primary focus of this book is ethics as it applies to business. *Business ethics* is the study of what constitutes right and wrong, or good and bad, human conduct in a business context. For example, would it be right for a store manager to break a promise to a customer and sell some hard-to-find merchandise to someone else, whose need for it is greater? What, if anything, should a moral employee do when his or her superiors refuse to look into apparent wrong-doing in a branch office? If you innocently came across secret information about a competitor, would it be permissible for you to use it for your own advantage?

"Business" and "businessperson" are broad terms. "Business" may denote a corner newspaper stand or a multinational corporation that does business in several countries. A "businessperson" may be a gardener engaged in a one-person operation or a company president responsible for thousands of workers and enormous corporate investments. Accordingly, the word *business* will be used here simply to mean any organization whose objective is to provide goods or services for profit. *Businesspeople* are those who participate in planning, organizing, or directing the work of business.

But this book takes a broader view as well. It is concerned with moral issues that arise anywhere that employers and employees come together. That is, it is as much about organizational ethics as business ethics. An *organization* is a group of people working together to achieve a common purpose. The purpose may be to offer a product or service primarily for profit, as in business. But the purpose may also be health care, as in medical organizations; public safety and order, as in law-enforcement organizations; education, as in academic organizations; and so on. The cases and illustrations presented in this book deal with moral issues and dilemmas in both business and nonbusiness organizational settings.

People occasionally poke fun at the idea of business ethics, declaring that the term is a contradiction or that business has no ethics. Such people take themselves to be worldly and realistic. They think they have a down-to-earth idea of how things really work. In fact, despite its pretense of sophistication, this attitude is embarrassingly naive. People who express it have little grasp of the nature of ethics and only a superficial understanding of the real world of business. After you have read this book, you will perhaps see the truth of this judgment.

MORAL VERSUS NONMORAL STANDARDS

Moral questions differ from other kinds of questions. Whether your office computer can download a copyrighted album from the Web is a factual question, not a moral question. On the other hand, whether you should download the album is a moral question. When we answer a moral question or make a moral judgment, we appeal to moral standards. These standards differ from other kinds of standards.

Wearing shorts to a formal dinner party is boorish behavior. Murdering the King's English with double negatives violates the basic conventions of proper language usage. Photographing the finish of a horse race with low-speed film is poor photographic technique. In each case a standard is violated—fashion, grammatical, technical—but the violation does not pose a serious threat to human well-being.

Moral standards are different because they concern behavior that is of serious consequence to human welfare, that can profoundly injure or benefit people.[3] The conventional moral norms against lying, stealing, and murdering deal with actions that can hurt people. And the moral principle that human beings should be treated with dignity and respect uplifts the human personality. Whether products are healthful or harmful, work conditions safe or dangerous, personnel procedures biased or fair, privacy respected or invaded are also matters that seriously affect human well-being. The standards that govern our conduct in these matters are moral standards.

A second characteristic follows from the first. Moral standards take priority over other standards, including self-interest. Something that morality condemns—for instance, the burglary of your neighbor's home—cannot be justified on the nonmoral grounds that it would be a thrill to do it or that it would pay off handsomely. We take moral standards to be more important than other considerations in guiding our actions.

A third characteristic of moral standards is that their soundness depends on the adequacy of the reasons that support or justify them. For the most part, fashion standards are set by clothing designers, merchandisers, and consumers; grammatical standards by grammarians and students of language; technical standards by practitioners and experts in the field. Legislators make laws, boards of directors make organizational policy, and licensing boards establish standards for professionals. In these cases, some authoritative body is the ultimate validating source of the standards and thus can change the standards if it wishes. Moral standards are not made by such bodies, although they are often endorsed or rejected by them. More precisely, the validity of moral standards depends not on authoritative fiat but rather on the quality of the arguments or the reasoning that supports them. Exactly what constitutes adequate grounds or justification for a moral standard is a debated question, which, as we shall see in the next chapter, underlies disagreement among philosophers over which specific moral principles are best.

Although these three characteristics set moral standards apart from others, it is useful to discuss more specifically how morality differs from three things with which it is sometimes confused: etiquette, law, and professional codes of ethics.

Morality and Etiquette

Etiquette refers to the norms of correct conduct in polite society or, more generally, to any special code of social behavior or courtesy. In our society, for example, it is considered bad etiquette to chew with your mouth open or to pick your nose when talking to someone; it is considered good etiquette to say "please" when requesting and "thank you" when receiving and to hold a door open for someone entering immediately behind you. Good business etiquette typically calls for writing follow-up letters after meetings, returning phone calls, and dressing appropriately. It is commonplace to judge people's manners as "good" or "bad" and the conduct that reflects them as "right" or "wrong." "Good," "bad," "right," and "wrong" here simply mean socially appropriate or socially inappropriate. In these contexts, such words express judgments about manners, not ethics.

So-called rules of etiquette that you might learn in an etiquette book are prescriptions for socially acceptable behavior. If you want to fit in, get along with others, and be thought well of by them, you should observe common rules of etiquette. If you violate the rules, then you're rightly considered ill-mannered, impolite, or even uncivilized, but not necessarily immoral.

Rules of etiquette are generally nonmoral in character: "Say 'congratulations' to the groom but 'best wishes' to the bride"; "Push your chair back into place upon leaving a dinner table." But violations of etiquette can have moral implications. The male boss who refers to female subordinates as "honey" or "doll" shows bad manners. If such epithets diminish the worth of female employees or perpetuate sexism, then they also raise moral issues concerning equal treatment and denial of dignity to human beings.

Scrupulous observance of rules of etiquette does not make one moral. In fact, it can camouflage moral issues. A few decades ago in some parts of the United States, it was considered bad manners for blacks and whites to eat together. Those who obeyed the convention and were thus judged well-mannered certainly had no grounds for feeling moral. The only way to dramatize the injustice underlying this practice was to violate the rule and be judged ill-mannered. For those in the civil rights movement of the 1960s, being considered boorish was a small price to pay for exposing the unequal treatment and human degradation that underlay this rule of etiquette.

Morality and Law

Before distinguishing between morality and law, one should understand the term *law*. Basically, there are four kinds of law: statutes, regulations, common law, and constitutional law.

Statutes are laws enacted by legislative bodies. The law that defines and prohibits theft is a statute. Congress and state legislatures enact statutes. (Laws enacted by local governing bodies such as city councils usually are termed *ordinances*.) Statutes make up a large part of the law and are what many of us mean when we speak of laws.

Limited in their knowledge, legislatures often set up boards or agencies whose functions include issuing detailed regulations of certain kinds of conduct—*administrative regulations*. For example, state legislatures establish licensing boards to formulate regulations for the licensing of physicians and nurses. As long as these regulations do not exceed the board's statutory powers and do not conflict with other kinds of law, they are legally binding.

Common law refers to laws applied in the English-speaking world when there were few statutes. Courts frequently wrote opinions explaining the bases of their decisions in specific cases, including the legal principles they deemed appropriate. Each of these opinions became a precedent for later decisions in similar cases. The massive body of legal principles that accumulated over the years is collectively referred to as common law. Like administrative regulations, common law is valid if it harmonizes with statutory law and with still another kind, constitutional law.

Constitutional law refers to court rulings on the requirements of the Constitution and the constitutionality of legislation. The U.S. Constitution empowers the courts to decide whether laws are compatible with the Constitution. State courts may also rule on the constitutionality of state laws under state constitutions. Although the courts cannot make laws, they have far-reaching powers to rule on the constitutionality of laws and to declare them invalid. The U.S. Supreme Court has the greatest judiciary power and rules on an array of cases, some of which bear directly on the study of business ethics.

People sometimes confuse legality and morality, but they are different things. On one hand, breaking the law is not always or necessarily immoral. On the other hand, the legality of an action does not guarantee that it is morally right. Let's consider these points further.

1. *An action can be illegal but morally right.* For example, helping a Jewish family to hide from the Nazis was against German law in 1939, but it would have been a morally admirable thing to have done. Of course, the Nazi regime was vicious and evil. By contrast, in a democratic society with a basically just legal order, the fact that something is illegal provides a moral consideration against doing it. For example, one moral reason for not burning trash in your back yard is that it violates an ordinance that your community has voted in favor of. Some philosophers believe that sometimes the illegality of an action can make it morally wrong, even if the action would otherwise have been morally acceptable. But even if they are right about this, the fact that something is illegal does not trump all other moral considerations. Nonconformity to law is not always immoral, even in a democratic society. There can be circumstances where, all things considered, violating the law is morally permissible, perhaps even morally required.

Probably no one in the modern era has expressed this point more eloquently than Dr. Martin Luther King, Jr. Confined in the Birmingham, Alabama, city jail on charges of parading without a permit, King penned his now famous "Letter from Birmingham Jail" to eight of his fellow clergymen who had published a statement attacking King's unauthorized protest of racial segregation as unwise and untimely. King wrote:

> All segregation statutes are unjust because segregation distorts the soul and damages the personality. It gives the segregator a false sense of superiority and the segregated a false sense of inferiority. Segregation, to use the terminology of the Jewish philosopher Martin Buber, substitutes an "I-it" relationship for an "I-thou" relationship and ends up relegating persons to the status of things. Hence segregation is not only politically, economically, and sociologically unsound, it is morally wrong and sinful. . . . Thus it is that I can urge men to obey the 1954 decision of the Supreme Court,* for it is morally right; and I can urge them to disobey segregation ordinances, for they are morally wrong.[4]

2. *An action that is legal can be morally wrong.* For example, it may have been perfectly legal for the chairman of a profitable company to lay off 125 workers and use three-quarters of the money saved to boost his pay and that of the company's other top manager,[5] but the morality of his doing so is open to debate.

Or, to take another example, suppose that you're driving to work one day and see an accident victim sitting on the side of the road, clearly in shock and needing medical assistance. Because you know first aid and are in no great hurry to get to your destination, you could easily stop and assist the person. Legally speaking, though, you

---

*In *Brown v. Board of Education of Topeka* (1954), the Supreme Court struck down the half-century-old "separate but equal" doctrine, which permitted racially segregated schools as long as comparable quality was maintained.

are not obligated to stop and render aid. Under common law, the prudent thing would be to drive on, because by stopping you would bind yourself to use reasonable care and thus incur legal liability if you fail to do so and the victim thereby suffers injury. Many states have enacted so-called Good Samaritan laws to provide immunity from damages to those rendering aid (except for gross negligence or serious misconduct). But in most states the law does not oblige people to give such aid or even to call an ambulance. Moral theorists would agree, however, that if you sped away without rendering aid or even calling for help, your action might be perfectly legal but would be morally suspect. Regardless of the law, such conduct would almost certainly be wrong.

What then may we say about the relationship between law and morality? To a significant extent, law codifies a society's customs, ideals, norms, and moral values. Changes in law tend to reflect changes in what a society takes to be right and wrong, but sometimes changes in the law can alter people's ideas about the rightness or wrongness of conduct. However, even if a society's laws are sensible and morally sound, it is a mistake to see them as sufficient to establish the moral standards that should guide us. The law cannot cover the wide variety of possible individual and group conduct, and in many situations it is too blunt an instrument to provide adequate moral guidance. The law generally prohibits egregious affronts to a society's moral standards and in that sense is the "floor" of moral conduct, but breaches of moral conduct can slip through cracks in that floor.

Professional Codes

Somewhere between etiquette and law lie *professional codes of ethics.* These are the rules that are supposed to govern the conduct of members of a given profession. Generally speaking, the members of a profession are understood to have agreed to abide by those rules as a condition of their engaging in that profession. Violation of the professional code may result in the disapproval of one's professional peers and, in serious cases, loss of one's license to practice that profession. Sometimes these codes are unwritten and are part of the common understanding of members of a profession—for example, that professors should not date their students. In other instances, these codes or portions of them may be written down by an authoritative body so they may be better taught and more efficiently enforced.

These written rules are sometimes so vague and general as to be of little value, and often they amount to little more than self-promotion by the professional organization. The same is frequently true when industries or corporations publish statements of their ethical standards. In other cases—for example, with attorneys—professional codes can be very specific and detailed. It is difficult to generalize about the content of professional codes of ethics, however, because they frequently involve a mix of purely moral rules (for example, client confidentiality), of professional etiquette (for example, the billing of services to other professionals), and of restrictions intended to benefit the group's economic interests (for example, limitations on price competition).

Given their nature, professional codes of ethics are neither a complete nor a completely reliable guide to one's moral obligations. First, not all the rules of a professional code are purely moral in character, and even when they are, the fact that a rule is officially enshrined as part of the code of a profession does not guarantee that it is a sound moral principle. As a professional, you must take seriously the injunctions of your profession, but you still have the responsibility to critically assess those rules for yourself.

Regarding those parts of the code that concern etiquette or financial matters, bear in mind that by joining a profession you are probably agreeing, explicitly or implicitly, to abide by those standards. Assuming that those rules don't require morally impermissible conduct, then consenting to them gives you some moral obligation to follow them. In addition, for many, living up to the standards of one's chosen profession is an important source of personal satisfaction. Still, you must be alert to situations in which professional standards or customary professional practice conflicts with the ordinary demands of morality. Adherence to a professional code does not exempt your conduct from scrutiny from the broader perspective of morality.

Where Do Moral Standards Come From?

So far you have seen how moral standards are different from various nonmoral standards, but you probably wonder about the source of those moral standards. Most, if not all, people have certain moral principles or a moral code that they explicitly or implicitly accept. Because the moral principles of different people in the same society overlap, at least in part, we can also talk about the moral code of a society, meaning the moral standards shared in common by its members. How do we come to have certain moral principles and not others? Obviously, many things influence us in the moral principles we accept: our early upbringing, the behavior of those around us, the explicit and implicit standards of our culture, our own experiences, and our critical reflections on those experiences.

For philosophers, though, the important question is not how in fact we came to have the particular principles we have. The philosophical issue is whether the principles we have can be justified. Do we simply take for granted the values of those around us? Or, like Martin Luther King, Jr., are we able to think independently about moral matters? By analogy, we pick up our nonmoral beliefs from all sorts of sources: books, conversations with friends, movies, various experiences we've had. The philosopher's concern is not so much with how we actually got the beliefs we have, but whether or to what extent those beliefs—for example, that women are more emotional than men or that telekinesis is possible—can withstand critical scrutiny. Likewise, ethical theories attempt to justify moral standards and ethical beliefs. The next chapter examines some of the major theories of normative ethics. That is, it looks at what some of the major thinkers in human history have argued are the best-justified standards of right and wrong.

But first we need to consider the relationship between morality and religion on the one hand and that between morality and society on the other. Some people maintain that morality just boils down to religion. Others have argued for the doctrine of *ethical relativism,* which says that right and wrong are only a function of what a particular society takes to be right and wrong. Both these views are mistaken.

RELIGION AND MORALITY

Any religion provides its believers with a worldview, part of which involves certain moral instructions, values, and commitments. The Jewish and Christian traditions, to name just two, offer a view of humans as unique products of a divine intervention that has endowed them with consciousness and an ability to love. Both these traditions posit creatures who stand midway between nature and spirit. On one hand, we are finite and bound to earth, not only capable of wrongdoing but born morally flawed (original sin). On the other, we can transcend nature and realize infinite possibilities.

Primarily because of the influence of Western religion, many Americans and others view themselves as beings with a supernatural destiny, as possessing a life after death, as being immortal. One's purpose in life is found in serving and loving God. For the Christian, the way to serve and love God is by emulating the life of Jesus of Nazareth. In the life of Jesus, Christians find an expression of the highest virtue—love. They love when they perform selfless acts, develop a keen social conscience, and realize that human beings are creatures of God and therefore intrinsically worthwhile. For the Jew, one serves and loves God chiefly through expressions of justice and righteousness. Jews also develop a sense of honor derived from a commitment to truth, humility, fidelity, and kindness. This commitment hones their sense of responsibility to family and community.

Religion, then, involves not only a formal system of worship but also prescriptions for social relationships. One example is the mandate "Do unto others as you would have them do unto you." Termed the "Golden Rule," this injunction represents one of humankind's highest moral ideals and can be found in essence in all the great religions of the world:

> Good people proceed while considering that what is best for others is best for themselves. (*Hitopadesa*, Hinduism)

> Thou shalt love thy neighbor as thyself. (*Leviticus* 19:18, Judaism)

> Therefore all things whatsoever ye would that men should do to you, do ye even so to them. (*Matthew* 7:12, Christianity)

> Hurt not others with that which pains yourself. (*Udanavarga* 5:18, Buddhism)

> What you do not want done to yourself, do not do to others. (*Analects* 15:23, Confucianism)

> No one of you is a believer until he loves for his brother what he loves for himself. (*Traditions*, Islam)

Although inspiring, such religious ideals are very general and can be difficult to translate into precise policy injunctions. Religious bodies, nevertheless, occasionally articulate positions on more specific political, educational, economic, and medical issues, which help mold public opinion on matters as diverse as abortion, euthanasia, nuclear weapons, and national defense. Roman Catholicism has a rich tradition of formally applying its core values to the moral aspects of industrial relations and economic life. Pope John Paul II's 1991 encyclical *Centesimus Annus*, the National Conference of Catholic Bishops' pastoral letter *Economic Justice for All*, updated in 1995, on Catholic social teaching and the U.S. economy, and the Pontifical Council for Social Communication's 1997 report on advertising, and its 2002 report on ethics and the Internet stand in this tradition.

Morality Needn't Rest on Religion

Many people believe that morality must be based on religion, either in the sense that without religion people would have no incentive to be moral or in the sense that only religion can provide moral guidance. Others contend that morality is based on the commands of God. None of these claims is very plausible.

First, although a desire to avoid hell and to go to heaven may prompt some of us to act morally, this is not the only reason or even the most common reason that people behave morally. Often we act morally out of habit or simply because that is the kind of person we are. It would just not occur to most of us to swipe an elderly lady's purse, and if the idea did occur to us, we wouldn't do it because such an act simply doesn't fit with our personal standards or with our concept of ourselves. We are often motivated to do what is morally right out of concern for others or just because it is right. In addition, the approval of our peers, the need to appease our conscience, and the desire to avoid earthly punishment may all motivate us to act morally. Furthermore, atheists generally live lives as moral and upright as those of believers.

Second, the moral instructions of the world's great religions are general and imprecise: They do not relieve us of the necessity to engage in moral reasoning ourselves. For example, the Bible says, "Thou shall not kill." Yet Christians disagree among themselves over the morality of fighting in wars, of capital punishment, of killing in self-defense, of slaughtering animals, of abortion and euthanasia, and of allowing foreigners to die from famine because we have not provided them with as much food as we might have. The Bible does not give unambiguous answers to these moral problems, so even believers must engage in moral philosophy if they are to have intelligent answers. On the other hand, there are lots of reasons for believing that, say, a cold-blooded murder motivated by greed is immoral; one need not believe in a religion to figure that out.

Third, although some theologians have advocated the *divine command theory*—that if something is wrong (like killing an innocent person for fun), then the only reason it is wrong is that God commands us not to do it—many theologians and certainly most philosophers would reject this view. They would contend that if God commands human beings not to do something, such as commit rape, it is because God sees that rape is wrong, but it is not God's forbidding rape that makes it wrong. The fact that rape is wrong is independent of God's decrees.

Most believers think not only that God gives us moral instructions or rules but also that God has moral reasons for giving them to us. According to the divine command theory, this would make no sense. In this view, there is no reason that something is right or wrong, other than the fact that it is God's will. All believers, of course, believe that God is good and that He commands us to do what is right and forbids us to do what is wrong. But this doesn't mean, say critics of the divine command theory, that God's saying so makes a thing wrong, any more than your mother's telling you not to steal makes it wrong to steal.

All this is simply to argue that morality is not necessarily based on religion in any of these three senses. That religion influences the moral standards and values of most of us is beyond doubt. But given that religions differ in their moral principles and that even members of the same faith often disagree on moral matters, you cannot justify a moral principle simply by appealing to religion—for that will only persuade those who already agree with your particular interpretation of your particular religion. Besides, most religions hold that human reason is capable of understanding what is right and wrong, so it is human reason to which you will have to appeal in order to support your ethical principle.

ETHICAL RELATIVISM

Some people do not believe that morality boils down to religion but rather that it is just a function of what a particular society happens to believe. This view is called *ethical relativism,* the theory that what is right is determined by what a culture or society says is right. What is right in one place may be wrong in another, because the only criterion for distinguishing right from wrong—and so the only ethical standard for judging an action—is the moral system of the society in which the act occurs.

Abortion, for example, is condemned as immoral in Catholic Ireland but is practiced as a morally neutral form of birth control in Japan. According to the ethical relativist, then, abortion is wrong in Ireland but morally permissible in Japan. The relativist is not saying merely that the Irish believe abortion is abominable and the Japanese do not; that is acknowledged by everyone. Rather, the ethical relativist contends that abortion is immoral in Ireland because the Irish believe it to be immoral and that it is morally permissible in Japan because the Japanese believe it to be so. Thus, for the ethical relativist there is no absolute ethical standard independent of cultural context, no criterion of right and wrong by which to judge other than that of particular societies. In short, what morality requires is relative to society.

Those who endorse ethical relativism point to the apparent diversity of human values and the multiformity of moral codes to support their case. From our own cultural perspective, some seemingly immoral moralities have been adopted; polygamy, pedophilia, stealing, slavery, infanticide, and cannibalism have all been tolerated or even encouraged by the moral system of one society or another. In light of this fact, the ethical relativist believes that there can be no nonethnocentric standard by which to judge actions.

Some thinkers believe that the moral differences between societies are smaller and less significant than they appear. They contend that variations in moral standards reflect differing factual beliefs and differing circumstances rather than fundamental differences in values. But suppose they are wrong about this matter. The relativist's conclusion still does not follow. As Allan Bloom writes, "The fact that there have been different opinions about good and bad in different times and places in no way proves that none is true or superior to others. To say that it does so prove is as absurd as to say that the diversity of points of view expressed in a college bull session proves there is no truth."[6] Disagreement in ethical matters does not imply that all opinions are equally correct.

Moreover, ethical relativism has some unpleasant implications. First, it undermines any moral criticism of the practices of other societies as long as their actions conform to their own standards. We cannot say that slavery in a slave society like that of the American South 150 years ago was immoral and unjust as long as that society held it to be morally permissible.

Second, and closely related, is the fact that for the relativist there is no such thing as ethical progress. Although moralities may change, they cannot get better or worse. Thus, we cannot say that our moral standards today are any more enlightened than they were in the Middle Ages.

Third, it makes no sense from the relativist's point of view for people to criticize principles or practices accepted by their own society. People can be censured for not living up to their society's moral code, but that is all. The moral code itself cannot be criticized because whatever a society takes to be right really is right for it. Reformers who identify injustices in their society and campaign against them are only encouraging people to be immoral—that is, to depart from the moral standards of their society—unless or until the majority of the society agrees with the reformers. The minority can never be right in moral matters; to be right it must become the majority.

The ethical relativist is right to emphasize that in viewing other cultures we should keep an open mind and not simply dismiss alien social practices on the basis of our own

cultural prejudices. But the relativist's theory of morality doesn't hold up. The more carefully we examine it, the less plausible it becomes. There is no good reason for saying
that the majority view on moral issues is automatically right, and the belief that it is
automatically right has unacceptable consequences.

Relativism and the "Game" of Business

In his well-known and influential essay "Is Business Bluffing Ethical?" Albert Carr
argues that business, as practiced by individuals as well as by corporations, has the
impersonal character of a game—a game that demands both special strategy and an
understanding of its special ethical standards.[7] Business has its own norms and rules
that differ from those of the rest of society. Thus, according to Carr, a number of things
that we normally think of as wrong are really permissible in a business context. His
examples include conscious misstatement and concealment of pertinent facts in nego-
tiation, lying about one's age on a résumé, deceptive packaging, automobile companies' neglect of car safety, and utility companies' manipulation of regulators and
overcharging of electricity users. He draws an analogy with poker:

> Poker's own brand of ethics is different from the ethical ideals of civilized human
> relationships. The game calls for distrust of the other fellow. It ignores the claim
> of friendship. Cunning deception and concealment of one's strength and intentions,
> not kindness and openheartedness, are vital in poker. No one thinks any the worse
> of poker on that account. And no one should think any the worse of the game of
> business because its standards of right and wrong differ from the prevailing tra-
> ditions of morality in our society.[8]

What Carr is defending here is a kind of ethical relativism: Business has its own
moral standards, and business actions should be evaluated only by those standards.

One can argue whether Carr has accurately identified the implicit rules of the business world (for example, is misrepresentation on one's résumé really a permissible
move in the business game?), but let's put that issue aside. The basic question is whether
business is a separate world to which ordinary moral standards don't apply. Carr's
thesis implies that any special activity following its own rules is exempt from external
moral evaluation, but as a general proposition this is unacceptable. The Mafia, for
example, has an elaborate code of conduct, accepted by the members of the rival "families." For them, gunning down a competitor or terrorizing a local shopkeeper may be
strategic moves in a competitive environment. Yet we rightly refuse to say that gangsters cannot be criticized for following their own standards. Normal business activity
is a world away from gangsterism, but the point still holds. Any specialized activity or
practice will have its own distinctive rules and procedures, but the morality of those
rules and procedures can still be evaluated.

Moreover, Carr's poker analogy is itself weak. For one thing, business activity can
affect others—such as consumers—who have not consciously and freely chosen to
play the "game." Business is indeed an activity involving distinctive rules and customary ways of doing things, but it is not really a game. It is the economic basis of
our society, and we all have an interest in the goals of business (in productivity and
consumer satisfaction, for instance) and in the rules business follows. Why should
these be exempt from public evaluation and assessment? Later chapters return to the

question of what these goals and rules should be. But to take one simple point, note that a business/economic system that permits, encourages, or tolerates deception will be less efficient (that is, work less well) than one in which the participants have fuller knowledge of the goods and services being exchanged.

In sum, by divorcing business from morality, Carr misrepresents both. He incorrectly treats the standards and rules of everyday business activity as if they had nothing to do with the standards and rules of ordinary morality, and he treats morality as something that we give lip service to on Sundays but that otherwise has no influence on our lives.

HAVING MORAL PRINCIPLES

Most people at some time in their lives pause to reflect on what moral principles they have or should have and on what moral standards are the best justified. (Moral philosophers themselves have defended different moral standards; Chapter 2 discusses these various theories.) When a person accepts a moral principle, when that principle is part of his or her personal moral code, then naturally the person believes the principle is important and well justified. But there is more to moral principles than that, as the philosopher Richard Brandt (1910–1997) emphasized. When a principle is part of a person's moral code, that person is strongly motivated toward the conduct required by the principle, and against behavior that conflicts with that principle. The person will tend to feel guilty when his or her own conduct violates that principle and to disapprove of others whose behavior conflicts with it. Likewise, the person will tend to hold in esteem those whose conduct shows an abundance of the motivation required by the principle.[9]

Other philosophers have, in different ways, reinforced Brandt's point. To accept a moral principle is not a purely intellectual act like accepting a scientific hypothesis or a mathematical theorem. Rather, it also involves a desire to follow that principle for its own sake, the likelihood of feeling guilty about not doing so, and a tendency to evaluate the conduct of others according to the principle in question. We would find it very strange, for example, if Sally claimed to be morally opposed to cruelty to animals yet abused her own pets and felt no inclination to protest when some ruffians down the street set a cat on fire.

Conscience

People can, and unfortunately sometimes do, go against their moral principles, but we would doubt that they sincerely held the principle in question if violating it did not bother their conscience. We have all felt the pangs of conscience, but what exactly is conscience and how reliable a guide is it? Our conscience, of course, is not literally a little voice inside of us. To oversimplify a complex piece of developmental psychology, our conscience evolved as we internalized the moral instructions of the parents or other authority figures who raised us as children.

When you were very young, you were probably told to tell the truth and to return something you filched to its proper owner. If you were caught lying or being dishonest, you were probably punished—scolded, spanked, sent to bed without dinner, denied a privilege. On the other hand, truth telling and kindness to your siblings were probably rewarded—with approval, praise, maybe even hugs or candy. Seeking reward and avoiding punishment motivate small children to do what is expected of them. Gradually, children come to internalize those parental commands. Thus, they feel vaguely that their parents know what they are doing even when the parents are not around. When children do something forbidden, they experience the same feelings as when scolded by their parents—the first stirrings of guilt. By the same token, even in the absence of explicit parental reward, children feel a sense of self-approval about having done what they were supposed to have done.

As we grow older, of course, our motivations are not so simple and our self-understanding is greater. We are able to reflect on and understand the moral lessons we were taught, as well as to refine and modify those principles. As adults we are morally independent agents. Yet however much our conscience has evolved and however much our adult moral code differs from the moral perspective of our childhood, those pangs of guilt we occasionally feel still stem from that early internalization of parental demands.

The Limits of Conscience

How reliable a guide is conscience? People often say, "Follow your conscience" or "You should never go against your conscience," but not only is such advice not very helpful, it may sometimes be bad advice. First, when we are genuinely perplexed over what we ought to do, we are trying to figure out what our conscience ought to be saying to us. When it is not possible to do both, should we keep our promise to a colleague or come to the aid of an old friend? To be told that we should follow our conscience is no help at all.

Second, it may not always be good for us to follow our conscience. It all depends on what our conscience says. Our conscience might reflect moral motivations that cannot withstand critical scrutiny. Consider an episode in Chapter 16 of Mark Twain's *The Adventures of Huckleberry Finn*. Huck has taken off down the Mississippi on a raft with his friend, the runaway slave Jim, but as they get nearer to the place where Jim will become legally free, Huck starts feeling guilty about helping him run away:

> It hadn't ever come home to me before, what this thing was that I was doing. But now it did; and it stayed with me, and scorched me more and more. I tried to make out to myself that *I* warn't to blame, because *I* didn't run Jim off from his rightful owner; but it warn't no use, conscience up and says, every time: "But you knowed he was running for his freedom, and you could a paddled ashore and told somebody." That was so—I couldn't get around that, no way. That was where it pinched. Conscience says to me: "What had poor Miss Watson done to you, that you could see her nigger go off right under your eyes and never say one single word? What did that poor old woman do to you, that you could treat her so mean? . . ." I got to feeling so mean and miserable I most wished I was dead.

Here Huck is feeling guilty about doing what we would all agree is the morally right thing to do. But Huck is only a boy, and his pangs of conscience reflect the principles that he has picked up uncritically from the slave-owning society around him. Unable to think independently about matters of right and wrong, Huck in the end decides to disregard his conscience. He follows his instincts and sticks by his friend Jim.

The point here is not that you should ignore your conscience but that the voice of conscience is itself something that can be critically examined. A pang of conscience is like a warning. When you feel one, you should definitely stop and reflect on the rightness of what you are doing. On the other hand, you cannot justify your actions simply by saying you were following your conscience. Terrible crimes have occasionally been committed in the name of conscience.

Moral Principles and Self-Interest

Sometimes doing what you believe would be morally right and doing what would best satisfy your own interests may be two different things. Imagine that you are in your car hurrying home along a quiet road, trying hard to get there in time to see the kickoff of an important football game. You pass an acquaintance who is having car trouble. He doesn't recognize you. As a dedicated fan, you would much prefer to keep on going than to stop and help him, thus missing at least part of the game. You might rationalize that some-one else will eventually come along and help him if you don't, but deep down you know that you really ought to stop. On the other hand, self-interest seems to say, "Keep going."

Consider another example.[10] You have applied for a new job, and if you land it, it will be an enormous break for you: It is exactly the kind of position you want and have been trying to get for some time. It pays well and will settle you into a desirable career for the rest of your life. The competition has come down to just you and one other person, and you believe correctly that she has a slight edge on you. Now imagine that you could spread a nasty rumor about her that would guarantee that she wouldn't get the job, and that you could do this in a way that wouldn't come back to you. Presumably, circulat-ing this lie would violate your moral code; on the other hand, doing it would clearly be to your benefit.

Some people argue that moral action and self-interest can never really conflict, and some philosophers have gone to great lengths to try to prove this, but they are almost certainly mistaken. They maintain that if you do the wrong thing, then you will be caught, your conscience will bother you, or in some way "what goes around comes around," so that your misdeed will come back to haunt you. This is often correct. But unfortunate as it may be, sometimes—viewed just in terms of personal self-interest—it may pay off for you to do what you know to be wrong. People sometimes get away with their wrongdoings, and if their conscience bothers them at all, it may not bother them that much. To believe otherwise not only is wishful thinking but also shows a lack of understanding of morality.

Morality serves to restrain our purely self-interested desires so we can all live together. The moral standards of a society provide the basic guidelines for cooperative social exis-tence and allow conflicts to be resolved by appeal to shared principles of justification. If our interests never came into conflict—that is, if it were never advantageous for one person to deceive or cheat another—then there would be little need for morality. We would already be in heaven. Both a system of law that punishes people for hurting others and a system of morality that encourages people to refrain from pursuing their self-interest at great expense to others help to make social existence possible.

Usually, following our moral principles is in our best interest. This idea is particu-larly worth noting in the business context. Several recent writers have argued persua-sively not only that moral behavior is consistent with profitability but also that the most morally responsible companies are among the most profitable.[11] Apparently, respect-ing the rights of employees, treating suppliers fairly, and being straightforward with customers pay off.

But notice one thing. If you do the right thing only because you think it will pay off, you are not really motivated by moral concerns. Having a moral principle involves having a desire to follow the principle for its own sake—just because it is the right thing to do. If you do the right thing only because you believe it will pay off, you might just as easily not do it if it looks as if it is not going to pay off.

In addition, there is no guarantee that moral behavior will always pay off in strictly selfish terms. As argued earlier, there will be exceptions. From the moral point of view, you ought to stop and help your acquaintance, and you shouldn't lie about competitors. From the selfish point of view, you should do exactly the opposite. Should you follow your self-interest or your moral principles? There's no final answer to this question. From the moral point of view, you should, of course, follow your moral principles. But from the selfish point of view, you should look out solely for "number one."

Which option you choose will depend on the strength of your self-interested or self-regarding desires in comparison with the strength of your other-regarding desires (that is, your moral motivations and your concern for others). In other words, your choice will depend on the kind of person you are, which depends in large part on how you were raised. A person who is basically selfish will pass by the acquaintance in distress and will spread the rumor, whereas a person who has a stronger concern for others, or a stronger desire to do what is right just because it is right, will not.

Although it may be impossible to prove to selfish persons that they should not do the thing that best advances their self-interest (since, if they are selfish, that is all they care about), there are considerations that suggest it is not in a person's overall self-interest to be a selfish person. People who are exclusively concerned with their own interests tend to have less happy and less satisfying lives than those whose desires extend beyond themselves. This is sometimes called the *paradox of hedonism.* Individuals who care only about their own happiness will generally be less happy than those who care about others. Moreover, people often find greater satisfaction in a life lived according to moral principle, and in being the kind of person that entails, than in a life devoted solely to immediate self-interest. Thus, or so many philosophers have argued, people have self-interested reasons not to be so self-interested. How do selfish people make themselves less so? Not overnight, obviously, but by involving themselves in the concerns and cares of others, they can in time come to care sincerely about those persons.

MORALITY AND PERSONAL VALUES

Some philosophers distinguish between morality in a narrow sense and morality in a broad sense. In a narrow sense, morality is the moral code of an individual or a society (insofar as the moral codes of the individuals making up that society overlap). Although the principles that make up our code may not be explicitly formulated, as laws are, they do guide us in our conduct. They function as internal monitors of our own behavior and as a basis for assessing the actions of others. Morality in the narrow sense concerns the principles that do or should regulate people's conduct and relations with others. These principles can be debated, however. (Take, for example, John Stuart Mill's contention that society ought not to interfere with people's liberty when their actions affect only themselves.) And a large part of moral philosophy involves assessing rival moral principles. This discussion is part of the ongoing development in our moral culture. What is at stake are the basic standards that ought to govern our behavior—that is, the basic framework or ground rules that make coexistence possible. If there were not already fairly widespread agreement about these principles, our social order would not be possible.

But in addition we can talk about our morality in a broader sense, meaning not just the principles of conduct that we embrace but also the values, ideals, and aspirations that shape our lives. Many different ways of living our lives would meet our basic moral obligations. The type of life each of us seeks to live reflects our individual values—whether following a profession, devoting ourselves to community service, raising a family, seeking solitude, pursuing scientific truth, striving for athletic excellence, amassing political power, cultivating glamorous people as friends, or some combination of these and many other possible ways of living. The life that each of us forges and the way we understand that life are part of our morality in the broad sense of the term.

It is important to bear this in mind throughout your study of business ethics. Although the usual concern is with the principles that ought to govern conduct in certain situations—for example, whether a hiring officer may take an applicant's race into account, whether employees may be forced to take an AIDS test, or whether corporate bribery is permissible in countries where people turn a blind eye to it—your choices in the business world will also reflect your other values and ideals—or in other words, the kind of person you are striving to be. What sort of ideal do you have of yourself as a businessperson? How much weight do you put on profitability, for instance, as against the quality of your product or the socially beneficial character of your service?

The decisions you make in your career and much of the way you shape your working life will depend not just on your moral code but also on the understanding you have of yourself in certain roles and relationships. Your morality—in the sense of your ideals, values, and aspirations—involves, among other things, your understanding of human nature, tradition, and society; of one's proper relationship to the natural environment; and of an individual's place in the cosmos. Professionals in various fields, for example, will invariably be guided not just by rules but also by their understanding of what being a professional involves, and a businessperson's conception of the ideal or model relationship to have with clients will greatly influence his or her day-to-day conduct.

There is more to living a morally good life, of course, than being a good businessperson or being good at your job, as Aristotle (384–322 B.C.E.) argued long ago. He underscored the necessity of our trying to achieve virtue or excellence, not just in some particular field of endeavor but as human beings. Aristotle thought that things have functions. The function of a piano, for instance, is to make certain sounds, and a piano that performs this function well is a good or excellent piano. Likewise, we have an idea of what it is for a person to be an excellent athlete, an excellent manager, or an excellent professor—it is to do well the types of things that athletes, managers, or professors are supposed to do.

But Aristotle also thought that, just as there is an ideal of excellence for any particular craft or occupation, similarly there must be an excellence that we can achieve simply as human beings. That is, he thought that we can live our lives as a whole in such a way that they can be judged not just as excellent in this respect or in that occupation, but as excellent, period. Aristotle thought that only when we develop our truly human capacities sufficiently to achieve this human excellence will we have lives blessed with happiness. Philosophers since Aristotle's time have been skeptical of his apparent belief that this human excellence would come in just one form, but many would underscore the importance of developing our various potential capacities and striving to achieve a kind of excellence in our lives. How we understand this excellence is a function of our values, ideals, and worldview—our morality in a broad sense.

INDIVIDUAL INTEGRITY AND RESPONSIBILITY

Previous sections discussed what it is for a person to have a moral code, as well as the sometimes conflicting pulls of moral conscience and self-interest. In addition, we have seen that people have values and ideals above and beyond their moral principles, narrowly understood, that also influence the lives they lead. And we have seen the importance of reflecting critically on both moral principles and moral ideals and values as we seek to live morally good and worthwhile lives. None of us, however, lives in a vacuum, and social pressures of various sorts always affect us. Sometimes these pressures make it difficult to stick with our principles and to be the kind of person we wish to be. Corporations are a particularly relevant example of an environment that can potentially damage individual integrity and responsibility.

The Individual Inside the Corporation

Corporations exact a price for the many benefits they offer their members—jobs, status, money, friendship, personal fulfillment. Sometimes the price of corporate membership amounts to individual conscience, as the experience of David A. Frew, professor of behavioral science, indicates.[12]

Frew interviewed a number of workers at various levels of a corporation known to be a substantial polluter. He discovered that although each person recognized and deplored the organization's polluting activities, each was willing to continue daily activities that contributed to the problem. One respondent even volunteered that it wouldn't be long before the company despoiled the surrounding area. When pressed further about his feelings, he said that he could do nothing but move to a cleaner environment.

Frew was frightened by the "ecologically schizophrenic" behavior he witnessed. But this schizophrenia goes beyond ecological issues. On many fronts—marketing, pricing, competition, contract fulfillment, management practices—the man or woman inside the organization can find it difficult, at times perhaps impossible, to reconcile the dictates of conscience with organizational policy.

One need not study the corporate scene long before observing the bind that people can experience from trying to reconcile two basic roles. The first role is that of the private individual: a decent, responsible person who readily admits the need for moral principles. The second role is that of the organization member: a human being who rarely exhibits, or is expected or encouraged to exhibit, any of the moral sensitivity of the private person. These Jekyll-and-Hyde personalities share little moral ground, and Hyde can often brutalize Jekyll when personal and organizational values collide.

About a century ago, Dan Drew, church builder and founder of Drew Theological Seminary, made a distinction between one's private life and one's business life that can be viewed as a defense of the subordination of the individual to organizational interests. Addressing a group of businessmen, Drew said:

Sentiment is all right up in that part of the city where your home is. But down-town, no. Down there the dog that snaps the quickest gets the bone. Friendship is very nice for a Sunday afternoon when you're sitting around the dinner table with your relations, talking about the sermon that morning. But nine o'clock Monday morning, [such] notions should be brushed aside like cobwebs from a machine. I never took any stock in a man who mixed up business with anything else. He can go into other things outside of business hours, but when he's in the office he ought not to have a relation in the world—and least of all a poor relation.[13]

The many recent cases of corporate misconduct suggest that corporate organizations have frequently embraced Drew's exhortation. While "downtown," the dominant busi-nessperson personality (Mr. Hyde) often is expected to repress the values that the pri-vate individual (Dr. Jekyll) lives by at home. In conflicts, the decent personality is to be sacrificed on the altar of expedience with a prayerful "that's business."

But don't assume that members of corporations would prefer things that way. A basic assumption of this book is that people would rather be Dr. Jekyll than Mr. Hyde, would rather be morally responsible individuals than conscienceless "team players." And yet the structure and function of organizations in general, and corporate organi-zations in particular, require that their members adhere to organizational norms and, in fact, force commitment and conformity to them.

Organizational Norms

One of the major characteristics of an organization, indeed of any group, is the shared acceptance of organizational rules by its members. Acceptance can take different forms; it can be conscious or unconscious, overt or subtle, but it is almost always present, because an organization can survive only if it holds its members together. Group cohe-siveness requires that individual members "commit" themselves—that is, relinquish some of their personal freedom in order to further organizational goals. One's degree of commitment—the extent to which one accepts group norms and subordinates self to organizational goals—is a measure of one's loyalty to the "team."

The corporation's goal is profit. To achieve this goal, top management sets goals for return on equity, sales, market share, and so forth. For the most part the norms or rules that govern corporate existence are derived from these goals. But clearly there's noth-ing in either the norms or goals that necessarily encourages moral behavior; indeed, they may discourage it.

Mounting evidence suggests that most managers experience role conflicts between what is expected of them as efficient, profit-minded members of an organization and what is expected of them as ethical persons. In a series of in-depth interviews with recent graduates of the Harvard MBA program, researchers Joseph L. Badaracco, Jr., and Allen P. Webb found that these young managers frequently received explicit instructions or felt strong organizational pressure to do things they believed to be sleazy, unethical, or even illegal.[14] Another survey found that managers at all levels experience role conflicts because of "pressure from the top" to meet corporate goals and comply with corporate norms. Of the managers interviewed, 50 percent of top managers, 65 percent of middle managers, and 84 percent of lower managers agreed that "managers today feel under pressure to compromise personal standards to achieve company goals."[15]

The young managers interviewed by Badaracco and Webb identified four powerful organizational "commandments" as responsible for the pressure they felt to compromise their integrity:

> First, performance is what really counts, so make your numbers. Second, be loyal and show us that you're a team player. Third, don't break the law. Fourth, don't overinvest in ethical behavior.[16]

Although most corporate goals and norms are not objectionable when viewed by themselves, they frequently put the people who must implement them into a moral pressure cooker. The need to meet corporate objectives, to be a team player, and to conform to organizational norms can lead otherwise honorable individuals to engage in unethical conduct.

Conformity

It is no secret that organizations exert pressure on their members to conform to norms and goals. What may not be so widely known is how easily individuals can be induced to behave as those around them do. A dramatic example is provided in the early conformity studies by social psychologist Solomon Asch.[17]

In a classic experiment, Asch asked groups of seven to nine college students to say which of three lines on a card (right, below) matched the length of a standard line on a second card (left, below):

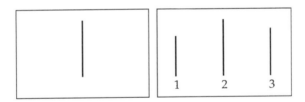

Only one of the subjects in each group was "naive," or unaware of the nature of the experiment. The others were shills of the experimenter, who had instructed them to make incorrect judgments in about two-thirds of the cases and in this way to pressure the naive subjects to alter their correct judgments.

The results were revealing. When the subjects were not exposed to pressure, they invariably judged correctly, but when the shills gave false answers, the subjects changed their responses to conform with the unanimous majority judgments. When one shill differed from the majority and gave the correct answer, naive subjects maintained their position three-fourths of the time. However, when the honest shill switched to the majority view in later trials, the errors made by naive subjects rose to about the same level as that of subjects who stood alone against a unanimous majority.

Why did they yield? Some respondents said they didn't want to seem different, even though they continued to believe their judgments were correct. Others said that although their perceptions seemed correct, the majority couldn't be wrong. Still other subjects didn't even seem aware that they had caved in to group pressure. Even those who held their ground tended to be profoundly disturbed by being out of step with the majority and confessed to being sorely tempted to alter their judgments. Indeed, a subsequent study found that students who stood firm in their judgments suffered more anxiety than those who switched. One student with the strength of his correct convictions was literally dripping with perspiration by the end of the experiment.[18]

In these experiments, which cumulatively included several hundred students, the subjects were not exposed to the authority symbols that people inside an organization face: bosses, boards, presidents, professional peers, established policy, and so on. Nor would their responses entail the serious long-range impact that bucking the system can carry for members of an organization: being transferred, dismissed, frozen in a position, or made an organizational pariah. And of course the students did not bring to these experiments the financial, educational, and other personal investments that individuals bring to their jobs. In comparison, men and women within an organization are under greater pressures to conform than the students in Asch's studies. Unfortunately, conformity can mean the surrender of moral autonomy. It can also result in *bystander apathy* and *groupthink.*

Bystander Apathy   Back in the 1960s a tragic event leaped off the front pages of the newspapers. A young woman named Kitty Genovese was stabbed to death in New York City. The murder was not in itself so unusual. What was particularly distressing was that thirty-eight of Kitty Genovese's neighbors witnessed her brutal slaying. In answer to her pitiful screams of terror at 3 A.M., they came to their windows and remained there for the thirty minutes it took her assailant to brutalize her. Of the thirty-eight, not one attempted to intervene in any way; no one even phoned the police.

Why didn't Kitty Genovese's neighbors help her? One reason, many social psychologists believe, is that an individual's sense of personal responsibility is inversely proportional to the number of people witnessing the event. Thus, the more people who are observing an event, the less likely any of them will feel obliged to do anything. In emergency situations, we seem naturally to let the behavior of those around us dictate our response. This diffusion of responsibility can lead to bystander apathy. Submerged in the group or the crowd, the individual can lose any sense of individuality. Feeling anonymous and thus not responsible, the individual may not even question the morality of his or her actions.[19]

Groupthink   A related phenomenon is what social psychologists call "groupthink." Groupthink happens when pressure for unanimity within a highly cohesive group overwhelms its members' desire or ability to appraise the situation realistically and consider alternative courses of action. Members of the group close their eyes to negative information, ignore warnings that the group may be mistaken, and discount outside ideas that might contradict the thinking or decisions of the group. Group members may have the illusion that the group is invulnerable or that because the group is good or right, whatever it does is permissible. Individuals in the group tend to self-censor thoughts that go against the group's ideas and rationalize away conflicting evidence, and the group as a whole implicitly or explicitly pressures potential dissenters to conform. Groupthink thus leads to irrational, sometimes disastrous decisions, and it has enormous potential for doing moral damage.

Is there anything about the corporate organization that encourages bystander apathy, groupthink, and, more generally, the surrender of individual moral autonomy? Viewed as a massive group, corporations certainly foster these phenomena as much as, and perhaps more than, most groups. Moreover, organizational pressure to produce, make profit, and conform can cultivate, or at least do nothing to inhibit, these propensities. Beyond this, many corporations fail to institutionalize ethics. They don't articulate or communicate ethical standards to their members; they don't actively enforce them; and they retain structures and policies that thwart individual integrity.

Although what is expected of members of a corporation sometimes clashes with their own moral values, they are rarely encouraged to deal with the conflict in an open, mature way. In fact, the more one suppresses individual moral urges in the cause of organizational interests, the more "mature," committed, and loyal one is considered to be. Conversely, the less willing the individual, the less "mature" and the more suspect. For example, when a Beech-Nut employee expressed concerns about the fact that the concentrate the company was producing for its "100% pure" apple juice contained nothing more than sugar water and chemicals, his annual performance review described his judgment as "colored by naïveté and impractical ideals."[20] Or consider the reports of Wall Street analysts pressured by their firms to recommend to clients stocks or bonds the analysts knew to be "junk" or "dogs."[21] Employees frequently have to fight hard to maintain their moral integrity in a showdown with organizational priorities.

Often, however, the problem facing us is not that of doing what we know to be right but rather of deciding what the right thing to do is. In business and organizational contexts, many difficult and puzzling moral questions need to be answered. How do we go about doing that? Is there some reliable procedure or method for answering moral questions? In science, the scientific method tells us what steps to take if we seek to answer a scientific question, but there is no comparable moral method for engaging moral questions. There is, however, general agreement about what constitutes good moral reasoning.

MORAL REASONING

It is useful to view moral reasoning at first in the context of *argument*. An argument is a group of statements, one of which (called the *conclusion*) is claimed to follow from the others (called the *premises*). Here's an example of an argument:

Argument 1

If a person is a mother, the person is a female.

Fran is a mother.

Therefore, Fran is a female.

The first two statements (the premises) of this argument happen to entail the third (the conclusion), which means that if I accept the first two as true, then I must accept the third as also true. Not to accept the conclusion while accepting the premises would result in a contradiction—holding two beliefs that cannot both be true at the same time. In other words, if I believe that all mothers are females and Fran is a mother (the premises), then I cannot deny that Fran is a female (the conclusion) without contradicting myself. An argument like this one, whose premises logically entail its conclusion, is termed *valid.*

An *invalid* argument is one whose premises do not entail its conclusion. In an invalid argument, I can accept the premises as true and reject the conclusion without any contradiction. Thus:

Argument 2

If a person is a mother, the person is a female.

Fran is a female.

Therefore, Fran is a mother.

The conclusion of this argument does not necessarily follow from the true premises. I can believe that every mother is a female and that Fran is a female and deny that Fran is a mother without contradicting myself.

One way to show this is by means of a *counterexample,* an example that is consistent with the premises but is inconsistent with the conclusion. Let's suppose Fran is a two-year-old, a premise that is perfectly consistent with the two stated premises. If she is, she can't possibly be a mother. Or let's suppose Fran is an adult female who happens to be childless, another premise that is perfectly consistent with the stated premises but obviously at odds with the conclusion. If an argument is valid (such as Argument 1), then no counterexamples are possible.

A valid argument can have untrue premises, as in the following:

Argument 3

If a person is a female, she must be a mother.

Fran is a female.

Therefore, Fran must be a mother.

Like Argument 1, this one is valid. If I accept its premises as true, I must accept its conclusion as true; otherwise I will contradict myself. Although valid, this argument is unsound because one of its premises is false—namely, "If a person is a female, she must be a mother." Realizing the patent absurdity of one of its premises, no sensible person would accept this argument's conclusion. But notice why the argument is unsound—not because the reasoning procedure is invalid but because one of the premises is false. *Sound arguments,* such as Argument 1, have true premises and valid reasoning. *Unsound arguments* have at least one false premise, as in Argument 3, or invalid reasoning, as in Argument 2.

Now let's consider some *moral arguments,* which can be defined simply as arguments whose conclusions are moral judgments, assertions about the moral worth of a person, action, activity, policy, or organization. Here are some examples that deal with affirmative action for women and minorities in the workplace:

Argument 4

If an action violates the law, it is morally wrong.

Affirmative action on behalf of women and minorities in personnel matters violates the law.

Therefore, affirmative action on behalf of women and minorities in personnel matters is morally wrong.

Argument 5

If an action violates the will of the majority, it is morally wrong.

Affirmative action on behalf of women and minorities in personnel matters violates the will of the majority.

Therefore, affirmative action on behalf of women and minorities in personnel matters is morally wrong.

Argument 6

If an action redresses past injuries that have disadvantaged a group, it is morally permissible.

Affirmative action on behalf of women and minorities in personnel matters redresses injuries that have disadvantaged these groups.

Therefore, affirmative action on behalf of women and minorities in personnel matters is morally permissible.

Argument 7

If an action is the only practical way to remedy a social problem, then it is morally permissible.

Affirmative action on behalf of women and minorities in personnel matters is the only practical way to remedy the social problem of unequal employment opportunity.

Therefore, affirmative action on behalf of women and minorities in personnel matters is morally permissible.

The first premise in each of these arguments is a moral standard, the second an alleged fact, and the conclusion a moral judgment. *Moral reasoning* or argument typically moves from a moral standard, through one or more factual judgments about some person, action, or policy related to that standard, to a moral judgment about that person, action, or policy. Good moral reasoning will frequently be more complicated than these examples; often it will involve an appeal to more than one standard as well as to various appropriate factual claims. Still, these examples illustrate its most basic form.

Defensible Moral Judgments

If a moral judgment or conclusion is defensible, then it must be supportable by a defensible moral standard, together with relevant facts. A moral standard supports a moral judgment if the standard, taken together with the relevant facts, logically entails the moral judgment and if the moral standard itself is a sound standard. If someone argues that affirmative action for minorities and women is right (or wrong) but cannot produce a supporting principle when asked, then the person's position is considerably weakened. And if the person does not see any need to support the judgment by appeal to a moral standard, then he or she simply does not understand how moral concepts are used or is using moral words like "right" or "wrong" differently from the way they are commonly used.

Keeping this in mind—that moral judgments must be supportable by moral standards and facts—will aid your understanding of moral discourse, which can be highly complex and sophisticated. It will also sharpen your own critical faculties and improve your moral reasoning and ability to formulate relevant moral arguments.

Patterns of Defense and Challenge

In assessing arguments, one must be careful to clarify the meanings of their key terms and phrases. Often premises can be understood in more than one way, and this ambiguity may lead people to accept (or reject) arguments that they shouldn't. For example, "affirmative action" seems to mean different things to different people (see Chapter 9 on job discrimination). Before we can profitably assess Arguments 4 through 7, we have to agree on how we understand "affirmative action." Similarly, Argument 5 relies on the idea of "violating the will of the majority," but this notion has to be clarified before we can evaluate either the moral principle that it is wrong to violate the will of the majority or the factual claim that affirmative action does violate the majority's will.

Assuming that the arguments are logically valid in their form (as Arguments 4 through 7 are) and that their terms have been clarified and possible ambiguities eliminated, then we must turn our attention to assessing the premises of the arguments. Should we accept or reject their premises? Remember that if an argument is valid and you accept the premises, you must accept the conclusion.

Let's look at some further aspects of this assessment process:

1. *Evaluating the factual claims.* If the parties to an ethical discussion are willing to accept the moral standard (or standards) in question, then they can concentrate on the factual claims. Thus, for example, in Argument 4 they will focus on whether affirmative action on behalf of women and minorities is in fact illegal. In Argument 7 they will need to determine whether affirmative action is really the only practical way to remedy the social problem of unequal employment opportunity. Analogous questions can be asked about the factual claims of Arguments 5 and 6. Answering them in the affirmative would require considerable supporting data.

2. *Challenging the moral standard.* Moral arguments generally involve more than factual disputes. The moral standards they appeal to may be controversial. One party might challenge the moral standard on which the argument relies, contending that it is not a plausible one and that we should not accept it. The critic might do this in several different ways—for example, by showing that there are exceptions to the standard, that the standard leads to unacceptable consequences, or that it is inconsistent with the arguer's other moral beliefs.

In the following dialogue, for example, Lynn is attacking Sam's advocacy of the standard "If an action redresses past injuries that have disadvantaged a group, it is morally permissible."

Lynn: What would you think of affirmative action for Jews in the workplace?

Sam: I'd be against it.

Lynn: What about Catholics?

Sam: No.

Lynn: People of Irish extraction?

Sam: They should be treated the same as anybody else.

Lynn: But each of these groups and more I could mention were victimized in the past by unfair discrimination and probably in some cases continue to be.

Sam: So?

Lynn: So the standard you're defending leads to a judgment you reject—namely, that Jews, Catholics, and Irish should be compensated by affirmative action for having been disadvantaged. How do you account for this inconsistency?

At this point Sam, or any rational person in a similar position, has three alternatives: abandon or modify the standard, alter his moral judgment, or show how women and minorities fit the original principle even though the other groups do not.

3. *Defending the moral standard.* When the standard is criticized, then its advocate must defend it. Often this requires invoking an even more general principle. A defender of Argument 6, for example, might defend the redress principle by appealing to some more general conception of social justice. Or defenders might try to show how the standard in question entails other moral judgments that both the critic and the defender accept, thereby enhancing the plausibility of the standard. In the following exchange, Lynn is defending the standard of Argument 5: "If an action violates the will of the majority, it is morally wrong":

Lynn: Okay, do you think the government should impose a national religion on all Americans?

Sam: Of course not.

Lynn: What about requiring people to register their handguns?

Sam: I'm all for it.

Lynn: And using kids in pornography?

Sam: There rightly are laws against it.

Lynn: But the principle you're objecting to—that an action violating the will of the majority is wrong—leads to these judgments that you accept.

Of course, Lynn's argument is by no means a conclusive defense for her moral standard. Other moral standards could just as easily entail the judgments she cites, as Sam is quick to point out:

Sam: Now wait a minute. I oppose a state religion on constitutional grounds, not because it violates majority will. As for gun control, I'm for it because I think it will reduce violent crimes. And using kids in pornography is wrong because it exploits and endangers children.

Although Lynn's strategy for defending the standard about majority rule proved inconclusive, it does illustrate a common and often persuasive way of arguing for a moral principle.

4. *Revising and modifying the argument.* Arguments 4 through 7 are only illustrations, and all the moral principles they mention are very simple—too simple to accept without qualification. (The principle that it is immoral to break the law in all circumstances, for example, is implausible. Nazi Germany furnishes an obvious counterexample to it.) But once the standard has been effectively challenged, the defender of the argument, rather than abandon the argument altogether, might try to reformulate it. For instance, the defender might replace the original, contested premise with a better and more plausible one that still supports the conclusion. For example, Premise 1 of Argument 4 might be replaced by: "If an action violates a law that is democratically decided and that is not morally unjust, then the action is immoral." Or the defender might revise the conclusion of his or her argument, perhaps by restricting its scope. A more modest, less sweeping conclusion will often be easier to defend.

In this way, the discussion continues, the arguments on both sides of an issue improve, and we make progress in the analysis and resolution of ethical issues. In general, in philosophy we study logic and criticize arguments not in order to be able to score quick debating points but rather to be able to think better and more deeply about moral and other problems. Our goal as moral philosophers is not to "win" arguments but to arrive at the truth—or, put less grandly, to find the most reasonable answer to an ethical question.

Requirements for Moral Judgments

Moral discussion and the analysis of ethical issues can take various, often complicated, paths. Nevertheless, the preceding discussion implies certain minimum adequacy requirements for moral judgments. Although there is no complete list of adequacy criteria, moral judgments should be (1) logical, (2) based on facts, and (3) based on sound or defensible moral principles. A moral judgment that is weak on any of these grounds is open to criticism.

Moral Judgments Should Be Logical   To say that moral judgments should be logical implies several things. First, as indicated in the discussion of moral reasoning, our moral judgments should follow logically from their premises. The connection between (1) the standard, (2) the conduct or policy, and (3) the moral judgment should be such that 1 and 2 logically entail 3. Our goal is to be able to support our moral judgments with reasons and evidence, rather than basing them solely on emotion, sentiment, or social or personal preference.

Forming logical moral judgments also means ensuring that any particular moral judgment of ours is compatible with our other moral and nonmoral beliefs. We must avoid inconsistency. Most philosophers agree that if we make a moral judgment—for example, that it was wrong of Smith to alter the figures she gave to the outside auditors—then we must be willing to make the same judgment in any similar set of circumstances—that is, if our friend Brown, our spouse, or our father had altered the figures. In particular, we cannot make an exception for ourselves, judging something permissible for us to do while condemning others for doing the very same thing.

Moral Judgments Should Be Based on Facts   Adequate moral judgments cannot be made in a vacuum. We must gather as much relevant information as possible before making them. For example, an intelligent assessment of the morality of insider trading would require an understanding of, among other things, the different circumstances in which it can occur and the effects it has on the market and on other traders. The information supporting a moral judgment, the facts, should be relevant—that is, the information should actually relate to the judgment; it should be complete, or inclusive of all significant data; and it should be accurate or true.

Moral Judgments Should Be Based on Acceptable Moral Principles   We know that moral judgments are based on moral standards. At the highest level of moral reasoning, these standards embody and express very general moral principles. Reliable moral judgments must be based on sound moral principles—principles that can withstand critical scrutiny and rational criticism. What, precisely, makes a moral principle sound or acceptable is one of the most difficult questions that the study of ethics raises and is beyond the scope of this book. But one criterion is worth mentioning, what philosophers call our "considered moral beliefs."

These beliefs contrast with our gut responses, with beliefs based on ignorance or prejudice, and with beliefs we just happen to hold without having thought them through. As philosophy professor Tom Regan explains, our considered beliefs are those moral beliefs "we hold *after* we have made a conscientious effort . . . to think about our beliefs coolly, rationally, impartially, with conceptual clarity, and with as much relevant information as we can reasonably acquire."[22] We have grounds to doubt a moral principle when it clashes with such beliefs. Conversely, conformity with our considered moral judgments is good reason for regarding it as provisionally established.

This does not mean that conformity with our considered beliefs is the sole or even basic test of a moral principle, any more than conformity with well-established beliefs is the exclusive or even fundamental test of a scientific hypothesis. (Copernicus's heliocentric hypothesis, for example, did not conform with what passed in the medieval world as a well-considered belief, the Ptolemaic view that the earth was the center of the universe.) But conformity with our considered beliefs seemingly must play some part in evaluating the many alternative moral principles that are explored in the next chapter.

SUMMARY

1. Ethics deals with individual character and the moral rules that govern and limit our conduct. It investigates questions of moral right and wrong, duty and obligation, and moral responsibility.

2. Business ethics is the study of what constitutes right and wrong (or good and bad) human conduct in a business context. Closely related moral questions arise in other organizational contexts.

3. Moral standards concern behavior that has serious consequences for human well-being, and they take priority over other standards, including self-interest. Their soundness depends on the adequacy of the reasons that support or justify them.

4. Morality must be distinguished from etiquette (which concerns rules for well-mannered behavior), from law (statutes, regulations, common law, and constitutional law), and from professional codes of ethics (the special rules governing the members of a profession).

5. Morality is not necessarily based on religion. Although we draw our moral beliefs from many sources, for philosophers the issue is whether those beliefs can be justified.

6. Ethical relativism is the theory that right and wrong are determined by what one's society says is right and wrong. There are many problems with this theory. Also dubious is the theory that business has its own morality, divorced from ordinary ideas of right and wrong.

7. Accepting a moral principle involves a motivation to conform one's conduct to that principle. Violating the principle will bother one's conscience, but conscience is not a perfectly reliable guide to right and wrong.

8. Part of the point of morality is to make social existence possible by restraining self-interested behavior. Sometimes doing what is morally right can conflict with one's personal interests. In general, though, following your moral principles will enable you to live a more satisfying life.

9. Morality as a code of conduct can be distinguished from morality in the broader sense of the values, ideals, and aspirations that shape a person's life.

10. Several aspects of corporate structure and function work to undermine individual moral responsibility. Organizational norms, group commitment, and pressure to conform (sometimes leading to bystander apathy or groupthink) can all make the exercise of individual integrity difficult.

11. Moral reasoning consists of forming moral judgments, assessments of the moral worth of persons, actions, activities, policies, or organizations. Moral reasoning and argument typically appeal both to moral standards and to relevant facts. Moral judgments should be entailed by the relevant moral standards and the facts, and they should not contradict our other beliefs. Both standards and facts must be assessed when moral arguments are being evaluated.

12. Philosophical discussion generally involves the revision and modification of arguments; in this way progress is made in the analysis and resolution of moral and other issues.

13. Conformity with our considered moral beliefs is an important consideration in evaluating moral principles. A considered moral belief is one held only after we have made a conscientious effort to be conceptually clear, to acquire all relevant information, and to think rationally, impartially, and dispassionately about the belief and its implications. We should doubt any moral principle that clashes with many of our considered beliefs.

CASE 1.1

Made in the U.S.A.—Dumped in Brazil, Africa, Iraq . . .

When it comes to the safety of young children, fire is a parent's nightmare. Just the thought of their young ones trapped in their cribs and beds by a raging nocturnal blaze is enough to make most mothers and fathers take every precaution to ensure their children's safety. Little wonder that when fire-retardant children's pajamas first hit the market, they proved an overnight success. Within a few short years more than 200 million pairs were sold, and the sales of millions more were all but guaranteed. For their manufacturers, the future could not have been brighter. Then, like a bolt from the blue, came word that the pajamas were killers. The U.S. Consumer Product Safety Commission (CPSC) moved quickly to ban their sale and recall millions of pairs. Reason: The pajamas contained the flame-retardant chemical Tris (2,3-dibromoprophyl), which had been found to cause kidney cancer in children.

Whereas just months earlier the 100 medium and small garment manufacturers of the Tris-impregnated pajamas couldn't fill orders fast enough, suddenly they were worrying about how to get rid of the millions of pairs now sitting in warehouses. Because of its toxicity, the sleepwear couldn't even be thrown away, let alone sold. Indeed, the CPSC left no doubt about how the pajamas were to be disposed of—buried or burned or used as industrial wiping cloths. All meant millions of dollars in losses for manufacturers.

The companies affected—mostly small, family-run operations employing fewer than 100 workers—immediately attempted to shift blame to the mills that made the cloth. When that attempt failed, they tried to get the big department stores that sold the pajamas and the chemical companies that produced Tris to share the financial losses. Again, no sale. Finally, in desperation, the companies lobbied in Washington for a bill making the federal government partially responsible for the losses. It was the government, they argued, that originally had required the companies to add Tris to pajamas and then had prohibited their sale. Congress was sympathetic; it passed a bill granting companies relief, but the bill was vetoed.

While the small firms were waging their political battle in the halls of Congress, ads began appearing in the classified pages of *Women's Wear Daily.* "Tris-Tris-Tris . . . We will buy any fabric containing Tris," read one. Another said, "Tris—we will purchase any large quantities of garments containing Tris."[23] The ads had been placed by exporters, who began buying up the pajamas, usually at 10 to 30 percent of the normal wholesale price. Their intent was clear: to dump* the carcinogenic pajamas on overseas markets.[24]

Tris is not the only example of dumping. There were the 450,000 baby pacifiers, of the type known to have caused choking deaths, that were exported for sale overseas, and the 400 Iraqis who died and the 5,000 who were hospitalized after eating wheat and barley treated with a U.S.-banned organic mercury fungicide. Winstrol, a synthetic male hormone that had been found to stunt the growth of American children, was made available in Brazil as an appetite stimulant for children. DowElanco sold its weed killer Galant in Costa Rica, although the Environmental Protection Agency (EPA) forbade its sale to U.S. farmers because Galant may cause cancer. After the U.S. Food and Drug Administration (FDA) banned the painkiller dipyrone because it can cause a fatal blood disorder, Winthrop Products continued to sell dipyrone in Mexico City.

Manufacturers that dump products abroad clearly are motivated by profit, or at least by the hope of avoiding financial losses resulting from having to withdraw a product from the U.S. market. For government and health agencies that cooperate in the exporting of dangerous products, sometimes the motives are more complex.

For example, when researchers documented the dangers of the Dalkon Shield intrauterine device—among the adverse reactions were pelvic inflammation, blood poisoning, tubal pregnancies, and uterine perforations—its manufacturer, A. H. Robins Co., began losing its domestic market.[25] As a result, the company worked out a deal with the Office of Population within the U.S. Agency for International Development (AID), whereby AID bought thousands of the devices at a reduced price for use in population-control programs in forty-two countries.

Dumping is a term apparently coined by *Mother Jones* magazine to refer to the practice of exporting to other countries products that have been banned or declared hazardous in the United States.

Why do governmental and population-control agencies approve for sale and use overseas a birth control device proved dangerous in the United States? They say their motives are humanitarian. Because the rate of dying in childbirth is high in Third World countries, almost any birth control device is preferable to none. Analogous arguments are used to defend the export of pesticides and other products judged too dangerous for use in the United States: Foreign countries should be free to decide for themselves whether the benefits of those products are worth their risks. In line with this, some Third World government officials insist that denying their countries access to these products is tantamount to violating their countries' national sovereignty.

This reasoning has found a sympathetic ear in Washington, for it turns up in the "notification" system that regulates the export of banned or dangerous products overseas. Based on the principles of national sovereignty, self-determination, and free trade, the notification system requires that foreign governments be notified whenever a product is banned, deregulated, suspended, or canceled by a U.S. regulatory agency. The State Department, which implements the system, has a policy statement on the subject that reads in part: "No country should establish itself as the arbiter of others' health and safety standards. Individual governments are generally in the best position to establish standards of public health and safety."

Critics of the system claim that notifying foreign health officials is virtually useless. For one thing, other governments rarely can establish health standards or even control imports into their countries. Indeed, most of the Third World countries where banned or dangerous products are dumped lack regulatory agencies, adequate testing facilities, and well-staffed customs departments.

Then there's the problem of getting the word out about hazardous products. In theory, when a government agency such as the EPA or the FDA finds a product hazardous, it is supposed to inform the State Department, which is to notify local health officials. But agencies often fail to inform the State Department of the product they have banned or found harmful, and when it is notified, its communiqués typically go no further than U.S. embassies abroad. One embassy official even told the General Accounting Office that he "did not routinely forward notification of chemicals not registered in the host country because it may adversely affect U.S. exporting." When foreign officials are notified by U.S. embassies, they sometimes find the communiqués vague or ambiguous or too technical to understand.

But even if communication procedures were improved or the export of dangerous products forbidden, there are ways that companies can circumvent these threats to their profits—for example, by simply changing the name of the product or by exporting the individual ingredients of a product to a plant in a foreign country. Once there, the ingredients can be reassembled and the product dumped.[26] The United States does prohibit its pharmaceutical companies from exporting drugs banned in this country, but sidestepping the law is not that difficult. "Unless the package bursts open on the dock," one drug company executive observes, "you have no chance of being caught."

Unfortunately for us, in the case of pesticides, the effects of overseas dumping are now coming home. In the United States, the EPA bans all crop uses of DDT and dieldrin, which kill fish, cause tumors in animals, and build up in the fatty tissue of humans. It also bans heptachlor, chlordane, leptophos, endrin, and many other pesticides, including 2,4,5-T (which contains the deadly poison dioxin, the active ingredient in Agent Orange, the notorious defoliant used in Vietnam) because they are dangerous to human beings. No law, however, prohibits the sale of DDT and these other U.S.-banned pesticides overseas, where thanks to corporate dumping they are routinely used in agriculture. In one three-month period, for example, U.S. chemical companies exported 3.9 million pounds of banned and withdrawn pesticides. The FDA now estimates, through spot checks, that 10 percent of our imported food is contaminated with residues of banned pesticides. And the FDA's most commonly used testing procedure does not even check for 70 percent of the pesticides known to cause cancer. With the doubling of exports of Mexican produce to the United States since the signing of the North American Free Trade Agreement (NAFTA), the problem of pesticide-laced food has only grown worse.[27]

Discussion Questions

1. Do you think dumping involves any moral issues? What are they?
2. Complete the following statements by filling in the blanks with either "moral" or "nonmoral":
   a. Whether or not dumping should be permitted is a _____ question.
   b. "Are dangerous products of any use in the Third World?" is a _____ question.
   c. "Is it proper for the U.S. government to sponsor the export of dangerous products overseas?" is a _____ question.
   d. Whether or not the notification system will protect the health and safety of people in foreign lands is a _____ question.
3. Can a moral argument be made in favor of dumping, when doing so does not violate U.S. law? Do any moral considerations support illegal dumping? Speculate on why dumpers dump. Do you think they believe that what they are doing is morally permissible?
4. Defend or challenge the present notification system by appeal to moral principles and facts.
5. What moral arguments can be made against legal and illegal dumping? Should we have laws prohibiting more types of dumping? What is your position on dumping, and what principles and values do you base it on?

CASE 1.2

The A7D Affair

Kermit Vandivier could not have predicted the impact on his life of purchase order P-237138, issued by LTV Aerospace Corporation.[28] The order was for 202 brake assemblies for a new Air Force light attack plane, the A7D, and news of the LTV contract was cause for uncorking the champagne at the B. F. Goodrich plant in Troy, Ohio, where Vandivier worked. Everyone agreed, including Vandivier, that Goodrich had carried off a real coup. Although the LTV order was a small one, it signaled that Goodrich was back in LTV's good graces after living under a cloud of disrepute. Ten years earlier, Goodrich had built a brake for LTV that, to put it kindly, hadn't met expectations. As a result, LTV had written off Goodrich as a reliable source of brakes. So although modest, the LTV contract was a chance for Goodrich to redeem itself, one that the people at the Troy plant were determined to make good.

LTV's unexpected change of heart after ten years was easily explained. Goodrich made LTV an offer it couldn't refuse—a ridiculously low bid for making the four-disk brakes. Had Goodrich taken leave of its financial senses? Hardly. Because aircraft brakes are custom made for a particular aircraft, only the brakes' manufacturer has replacement parts. Thus, even if it took a loss on the job, Goodrich figured it could more than make up for it in the sale of replacement parts. Of course, if Goodrich bungled the job, there wouldn't be a third chance.

John Warren, a seven-year veteran and one of Goodrich's most capable engineers, was made project engineer and lost no time in working up a preliminary design for the brake. Perhaps because the design was faultless or perhaps because Warren was given to temper tantrums when criticized, coworkers accepted the engineer's plan without question. So there was no reason to suspect that young Searle Lawson, one year out of college and six months with Goodrich, would come to think Warren's design was fundamentally flawed.

Lawson was assigned by Warren to produce the final production design. He had to determine the best materials for brake linings and identify any needed adjustments in the brake design. This process called for extensive testing to meet military specifications. If the brakes passed the grueling tests, they would then be flight-tested by the Air Force.

Lawson was under pressure to meet LTV's target date for flight tests, so he lost no time in getting down to work. Because he hadn't received the brake housing and some other parts yet, he used a housing from a brake similar to the A7D's and built a prototype of the four-disk design. What Lawson particularly wanted to learn was whether the brake could withstand the extreme internal temperatures, in excess of 1000 degrees F, when the aircraft landed.

When the brake linings disintegrated in the first test, Lawson thought the problem might be defective parts or an unsuitable lining. But after two more consecutive failures, he decided the problem lay in the design: The four-disk design was simply too small to stop the aircraft without generating so much heat that the brake linings melted. In Lawson's view, a larger, five-disk brake was needed.

Lawson knew well the implications of his conclusion. The four-disk brake assemblies that were arriving at the plant would have to be junked, and more tests would have to be conducted. The accompanying delays would preclude on-time delivery of the production brakes to LTV.

Lawson reported his findings and recommendations to John Warren. Going to a five-disk design was impossible, Warren told him. Officials at Goodrich, he said, were already boasting to LTV about how well the tests were going. Besides, Warren was confident that the problem lay not in the four-disk design but in the brake linings themselves.

Unconvinced, Lawson went to Robert Sink, who supervised engineers on projects. Sink was in a tight spot. If he agreed with Lawson, he would be indicting his own professional judgment: He was the man who had assigned Warren to the job. What's more, he had accepted Warren's design without reservation and had assured LTV more than once that there was little left to do but ship them the brakes. To recant now would mean explaining the reversal not only to LTV but also to the Goodrich hierarchy. In the end, Sink, who was not an engineer, deferred to the seasoned judgment of Warren and instructed Lawson to continue the tests.

His own professional judgment overridden, Lawson could do little but bash on with the tests. Because all the parts for the brake had by this time arrived, he was able to build a production model of the brake with new linings and subject it to the rigorous qualification tests. Thirteen more tests were conducted, and thirteen more failures resulted. It was at this point that data analyst and technical writer Kermit Vandivier entered the picture.

Vandivier was looking over the data of the latest A7D test when he noticed an irregularity: The instrument recording some of the stops had been deliberately miscalibrated to indicate that less pressure was required to stop the aircraft than actually was the case. Vandivier immediately showed the test logs to test lab supervisor Ralph Gretzinger, who said he'd learned from the technician who miscalibrated the instrument that Lawson had requested the miscalibration. Later, while confirming this account, Lawson said he was simply following the orders of Sink and Russell Van Horn, manager of the design engineering section, who according to Lawson were intent on qualifying the brakes at whatever cost. For his part, Gretzinger vowed he would never permit deliberately falsified data or reports to leave his lab.

A month later, the brake was again tested, and again it failed. Nevertheless, Lawson asked Vandivier to start preparing the various graph and chart displays for qualification. Vandivier refused and told Gretzinger what he'd been asked to do. Gretzinger was livid. He again vowed that his lab would not be part of a conspiracy to defraud. Then, bent on getting to the bottom of the matter, Gretzinger rushed off to see Russell Line, manager of the Goodrich Technical Services Section.

An hour later, Gretzinger returned to his desk looking like a beaten man. He knew he had only two choices: defy his superiors or do their bidding.

"You know," he said to Vandivier, "I've been an engineer for a long time, and I've always believed that ethics and integrity were every bit as important as theorems and formulas, and never once has anything happened to change my beliefs. Now this. . . . Hell, I've got two sons I've got to put through school and I just . . ." When his voice trailed off, it was clear that he would in fact knuckle under. He and Vandivier would prepare the qualifying data, then someone "upstairs" would actually write the report. Their part, Gretzinger rationalized, wasn't really so bad. "After all," he said, "we're just drawing some curves, and what happens to them after they leave here—well, we're not responsible for that." Vandivier knew Gretzinger didn't believe what he was saying about not being responsible. Both of them knew that they were about to become principal characters in a plot to defraud.

Unwilling to play his part, Vandivier decided that he, too, would confer with Line. Line was sympathetic; he said he understood what Vandivier was going through. But in the end he said he would not refer the matter to chief engineer H. C. "Bud" Sunderman, as Vandivier had suggested. Why not? Vandivier wanted to know.

"Because it's none of my business, and it's none of yours," Line told him. "I learned a long time ago not to worry about things over which I had no control. I have no control over this."

Vandivier pressed the point. What about the test pilots who might get injured because of the faulty brakes? Didn't their uncertain fate prick Line's conscience?

"Look," said Line, growing impatient with Vandivier's moral needling, "I just told you I have no control over this thing. Why should my conscience bother me?" Then he added, "You're just getting all upset over this thing for nothing. I just do as I'm told, and I'd advise you to do the same."

Vandivier made his decision that night. He knew, of course, he was on the horns of a dilemma. If he wrote the report, he would save his job at the expense of his conscience. If he refused, he would honor his moral code and, he was convinced, lose his job—an ugly prospect for anyone, let alone a forty-two-year-old man with a wife and seven children. The next day, Vandivier phoned Lawson and told him he was ready to begin on the qualification report.

Lawson shot over to Vandivier's office with all the speed of one who knows that, swallowed fast, a bitter pill doesn't taste so bad. Before they started on the report, though, Vandivier, still uneasy with his decision, asked Lawson if he fully understood what they were about to do.

"Yeah," Lawson said acidly, "we're going to screw LTV. And speaking of screwing," he continued, "I know now how a whore feels, because that's exactly what I've become, an engineering whore. I've sold myself. It's all I can do to look at myself in the mirror when I shave. I make me sick."

For someone like Vandivier, who had written dozens of them, the qualification report was a snap. It took about a month, during which time the brake failed still another final qualification test, and the two men talked almost exclusively about the enormity of what they were doing. In the Nuremberg trials they found a historical analogy to their own complicity and culpability in the A7D affair. More than once, Lawson opined that the brakes were downright dangerous, that anything could happen during the flight tests. His opinion proved prophetic.

When the report was finished, copies were sent to the Air Force and LTV. Within a week test flights were begun at Edwards Air Force Base in California. Goodrich dispatched Lawson to Edwards as its representative, but he wasn't there long. Several "unusual incidents" brought the flight tests literally to a screeching halt. Lawson returned to the Troy plant, full of talk about several near crashes caused by brake trouble during landings. That was enough to send Vandivier to his attorney, to whom he told the whole sorry tale.

Although the attorney didn't think Vandivier was guilty of fraud, he was convinced that the analyst/writer was guilty of participating in a conspiracy to defraud. Vandivier's only hope, the attorney counseled, was to make a clean breast of the matter to the FBI. Vandivier did. Evidently the FBI informed the Air Force of Vandivier's disclosure, for within days the Air Force, which had previously accepted the qualification report, demanded to see some of the raw data compiled during the tests.

At this point both Lawson and Vandivier decided to resign from Goodrich. In his letter of resignation, addressed to Russell Line, Vandivier cited the A7D report and stated: "As you are aware, this report contains numerous deliberate and willful misrepresentations which, according to legal counsel, constitute fraud and expose both myself and others to criminal charges of conspiracy to defraud. . . . The events of the past seven months have created an atmosphere of deceit and distrust in which it is impossible to work. . . ."

Vandivier was soon summoned to the office of Bud Sunderman, who scolded him mercilessly. Among other things, Sunderman accused Vandivier of making irresponsible charges and of arch disloyalty. It would be best, said Sunderman, if Vandivier cleared out immediately. Within minutes, Vandivier had cleaned out his desk and left the plant.

Two days later Goodrich announced it was recalling the qualification report and replacing the old brake with a new five-disk brake at no cost to LTV.

Aftermath:

- A year later, a congressional committee reviewed the A7D affair. Vandivier and Lawson testified as government witnesses, together with Air Force officers and a General Accounting Office team. All testified that the brake was dangerous.
- Robert Sink, representing the Troy plant, depicted Vandivier as a mere high school graduate with no technical training, who preferred to follow his own lights rather than organizational guidance. R. G. Jeter, vice president and general counsel of Goodrich, dismissed as ludicrous even the possibility that some thirty engineers at the Troy plant would stand idly by and see reports changed and falsified.
- The congressional committee adjourned after four hours with no real conclusion. The following day the Department of Defense, citing the A7D episode, made major changes in its inspection, testing, and reporting procedures.
- The A7D eventually went into service with the Goodrich-made five-disk brake.
- Searle Lawson went to work as an engineer for LTV assigned to the A7D project.
- Russell Line was promoted to production superintendent.
- Robert Sink moved up into Line's old job.
- Kermit Vandivier became a newspaper reporter for the *Daily News* in Troy, Ohio.

Discussion Questions

1. To what extent did Lawson, Vandivier, and Gretzinger consider the relevant moral issues before deciding to participate in the fraud? What was their reasoning? What led Vandivier to seek legal counsel and then to become a government witness?

2. How did Sink and Line look at the matter? How would you evaluate their conduct?

3. Do you think Vandivier was wrong to work up the qualification report? What moral principle or principles underlie your judgment?

4. Do you think Vandivier was right in "blowing the whistle"? Was he morally required to do so? Again, explain the moral principles on which your judgment is based.

5. Identify and discuss the pressure to conform evident in the A7D episode. Explain the effect of diffusion of responsibility in this case.

6. Do you think the existence of a corporate ethical code, a high-ranking ethics committee, or in-house ethical training might have altered events? What steps could Goodrich take to ensure more ethical behavior in the future?

7. In your opinion, can Goodrich in any way be held morally responsible for the A7D affair, or does the responsibility fall solely on individuals?

Notes

1. For more on the Enron scandal, see Bethany McLean and Peter Elkind, *The Smartest Guys in the Room: The Amazing Rise and Scandalous Fall of Enron* (New York: Penguin, 2003).
2. Robert C. Solomon, *Morality and the Good Life* (New York: McGraw-Hill, 1984), 3.

3. On characteristics of moral standards, see Manuel G. Velasquez, *Business Ethics,* 5th ed. (Upper Saddle River, N.J.: Prentice Hall, 2001), 9–11.

4. Martin Luther King, Jr., "Letter from Birmingham Jail," in *Why We Can't Wait* (New York: Harper & Row, 1963), 85.

5. *Newsweek,* May 26, 1997, 54.

6. Allan Bloom, *The Closing of the American Mind* (New York: Simon & Schuster, 1987), 39.

7. Albert Z. Carr, "Is Business Bluffing Ethical?" *Harvard Business Review* 46 (January–February 1968).

8. Ibid., 145.

9. Richard B. Brandt, *A Theory of the Good and the Right* (New York: Oxford University Press, 1979), 165–170.

10. Baruch Brody, *Beginning Philosophy* (Englewood Cliffs, N.J.: Prentice Hall, 1977), 33.

11. See Tad Tuleja, *Beyond the Bottom Line* (New York: Penguin Books, 1987); Curtis C. Vershoor, "Corporate Performance Is Closely Linked to a Strong Ethical Commitment," *Business and Society Review* 104 (Winter 1999); James E. Post, Anne T. Lawrence, and James Weber, *Business and Society: Corporate Strategy, Public Policy, and Ethics,* 10th ed. (New York: McGraw-Hill, 2002), 104–105; "The Best Corporate Citizens Perform Better Financially," *Business Ethics,* March/April 2002, 13; and "Shares of Corporate Nice Guys Can Finish First," *New York Times,* April 27, 2003 (online).

12. See David A. Frew, "Pollution: Can the People Be Innocent While Their Systems Are Guilty?" *Academy of Management Review,* March 1973.

13. Quoted in Robert Bartels, ed., *Ethics in Business* (Columbus: Ohio State University Press, 1963), 35.

14. Joseph L. Badaracco, Jr., and Allen P. Webb, "Business Ethics: A View from the Trenches," *California Management Review* 37 (Winter 1995): 8.

15. See Milton Snoeyenbos, Robert Almeder, and James Humber, eds., *Business Ethics,* 3rd ed. (Buffalo, N.Y.: Prometheus Books, 2001), 136.

16. Badaracco and Webb, "Business Ethics," 10.

17. See Solomon E. Asch, "Opinion and Social Pressure," *Scientific American,* November 1955, 31–35.

18. M. D. Bogdanoff et al., "The Modifying Effect of Conforming Behavior Upon Lipid Responses Accompanying CNS Arousal," *Clinical Research* 9 (1961): 135.

19. See Malcolm Gladwell, *The Tipping Point* (Boston: Little, Brown, and Co., 2000), 27–28, and John M. Doris, *Lack of Character* (Cambridge: Cambridge University Press, 2002), 28–29, 32–33.

20. Lynn Sharp Paine, "Managing for Organizational Integrity," *Harvard Business Review* 72 (March–April 1994): 108.

21. Barton G. Malkiel, "The Great Wall Street?" *Wall Street Journal,* October 14, 2002, A16.

22. Tom Regan, *Defending Animal Rights* (Urbana: University of Illinois Press, 2001), 45.

23. Mark Hosenball, "Karl Marx and the Pajama Game," *Mother Jones,* November 1979, 47.

24. Unless otherwise noted, the facts and quotations reported in this case are based on Mark Dowie, "The Corporate Crime of the Century," *Mother Jones,* November 1979, and Russell Mokhiber, *Corporate Crime and Violence* (San Francisco: Sierra Club Books, 1988), 181–195. See also Jane Kay, "Global Dumping of U.S. Toxics Is Big Business," *San Francisco Examiner,* September 23, 1990, A2, and Christopher Scanlan, "Danger for Sale," *San Jose Mercury News,* May 19, 1991, 9A, and May 20, 191, 3A.

25. See Mark Dowie and Tracy Johnston, "A Case of Corporate Malpractice," *Mother Jones,* November 1976.

26. Mark Dowie, "A Dumper's Guide to Tricks of the Trade," *Mother Jones,* November 1979, 25.

27. Bernard Gavzer, "We Can Make Our Food Safer," *Parade Magazine,* October 19, 1997, 5–6.

28. The material for this case has been drawn from Kermit Vandivier, "Why Should My Conscience Bother Me?" in Robert Heilbroner, ed., *In the Name of Profit* (New York: Doubleday, 1972). For a discussion skeptical of Vandivier's version of these events, see John H. Fielder, "Give Goodrich a Break," *Business and Professional Ethics Journal* 7 (Spring 1988).

Further Reading for Chapter 1

On Ethics

John Arthur, ed., *Morality and Moral Controversies*, 6th ed. (Upper Saddle River, N.J.: Prentice Hall, 2002) and **William H. Shaw**, ed., *Social and Personal Ethics*, 5th ed. (Belmont, Calif.: Wadsworth, 2005) contain essays in both theoretical and applied ethics.

James Rachels, *The Elements of Moral Philosophy*, 4th ed. (New York: McGraw-Hill, 2003) is an excellent, clear introduction.

George Sher, ed., *Moral Philosophy*, 2nd ed. (San Diego: Harcourt Brace Jovanovich, 1998) and **Louis P. Pojman**, ed., *Ethical Theory*, 4th ed. (Belmont, Calif.: Wadsworth, 2002) offer more advanced readings on various topics in moral philosophy.

Moral Reasoning

Patrick Hurley, *A Concise Introduction to Logic*, 8th ed. (Belmont, Calif.: Wadsworth, 2003) is a good introduction to all the main areas of logic.

Joel Rudinow and **Vincent Barry**, *Invitation to Critical Thinking*, 5th ed. (Belmont, Calif.: Wadsworth, 2004) provides a guide to argument assessment.

Business and Morality

Both **Richard T. De George**, *Business Ethics*, 5th ed. (New York: Macmillan, 1999) and **Manuel G. Velasquez**, *Business Ethics*, 5th ed. (Upper Saddle River, N.J.: Prentice Hall, 2002) contain useful introductions to moral philosophy in relation to business. **Robert E. Frederick**, ed., *A Companion to Business Ethics* (Malden, Mass.: Blackwell, 1999) is a collection of essays by different authors on all aspects of business ethics. Two pertinent discussions of moral conduct in business are **Glenn Martin**, "Once Again: Why Should Business Be Ethical?" *Business and Professional Ethics Journal* 17 (Winter 1998) and **Kevin Gibson**, "Excuses, Excuses: Moral Slippage in the Workplace," *Business Horizons* 43 (November–December 2000). **William H. Shaw**, ed., *Ethics at Work: Basic Readings in Business Ethics* (New York: Oxford University Press, 2003) contains essays on various moral issues that arise in business.

Three good sources of advanced work in business ethics are the *Business and Professional Ethics Journal*, the *Business Ethics Quarterly*, and the *Journal of Business Ethics*.

 InfoTrac® College Edition: For further information or to conduct research, please go to www.infotrac-college.com.

2

Normative Theories of Ethics

In an award-winning television drama, police captain Frank Furillo firmly believes that the two toughs just brought in by his officers are guilty of the rape-murder of a nun earlier that morning inside the parish church. But the evidence is only circumstantial. As word of the crime spreads, the community is aghast and angry. From all sides—the press, local citizens, city hall, the police commissioner—pressure mounts on Furillo and his department for a speedy resolution of the matter. On the street outside Furillo's office, a mob is growing frenzied, hoping to get their hands on the two young men and administer "street justice" to them. One of the crowd has even taken a shot at the suspects inside the police station!

The police, however, have only enough evidence to arraign the suspects on the relatively minor charge of being in possession of goods stolen from the church. Furillo and his colleagues could demand a high bail, thus keeping the defendants in custody while the police try to turn up evidence that will convict the men of murder. But in a surprise move at the arraignment, the district attorney, acting in conjunction with Furillo, declines to ask the judge for bail. The men are free to go, but they and their outraged public defender, Joyce Davenport, know that their lives will be worthless once they hit the streets: Community members have sworn to avenge the much-loved sister if the police are unable to do their job. To remain in police custody, and thus safe, their only choice is to confess to murder. So the two men confess.

Davenport argues passionately but unsuccessfully against what she considers to be a police-state tactic. Anyone in that circumstance, guilty or innocent, would confess. It is an affront to the very idea of the rule of law, she contends: police coercion by way of mob pressure. No system of justice can permit such conduct from its public officials. Yet the confession allows the police to locate the murder weapon, thus bringing independent confirmation of the culprits' guilt. Furillo's tactic, nevertheless, does not rest easily on his own conscience, and the screenplay closes with him entering the church confessional later that night: "Forgive me, Father, for I have sinned. . . ."

Furillo is understandably worried about whether he did the morally right thing. His action was successful, and it was for a good cause. But does the end always justify the means? Did the police and district attorney behave in a way that accords with due process and the rights of defendants? Should community pressure influence one's professional decisions? Did Furillo act in accordance with some principle that he could defend publicly? In a tough and controversial situation like this, the issue does not concern the moral sincerity of either Furillo or Davenport. Both can be assumed to want to do what is right, but what exactly is the morally justified thing to do? How are we to judge Furillo's tactics?

Chapter 1 noted that a defensible moral judgment must be supportable by a sound moral principle. Moral principles provide the confirmatory standard for moral judgments. The use of these principles, however, is not a mechanical process in which one cranks in data and out pops an automatic moral judgment. Rather, the principles provide a conceptual framework that guides us in making moral decisions. Careful thought and open-minded reflection are always necessary to work from one's moral principles to a considered moral judgment.

But what are the appropriate principles to rely on when making moral judgments? The truth is that there is no consensus among people who have studied ethics and reflected on these matters. Different theories exist as to the proper standard of right and wrong. As the British philosopher Bernard Williams put it, we are heirs to a rich and complex ethical tradition, in which a variety of different moral principles and ethical considerations intertwine and sometimes compete.[1]

This chapter discusses the different normative perspectives and rival ethical principles that are our heritage. After distinguishing between what are called consequentialist and nonconsequentialist normative theories, it looks in detail at several ethical approaches, discussing their pros and cons and their relevance to moral decision making in an organizational context:

1. Egoism, both as an ethical theory and as a psychological theory
2. Utilitarianism, the theory that the morally right action is the one that achieves the greatest total amount of happiness for everyone concerned
3. Kant's ethics, with his categorical imperative and his emphasis on moral motivation and respect for persons
4. Other nonconsequentialist normative themes: duties, moral rights, and prima facie principles

The chapter concludes with an attempt to tie together the major concerns of the different normative theories and suggests a general way of approaching moral decision making.

CONSEQUENTIALIST AND NONCONSEQUENTIALIST THEORIES

In ethics, *normative theories* propose some principle or principles for distinguishing right actions from wrong actions. These theories can, for convenience, be divided into two kinds: consequentialist and nonconsequentialist.

Many philosophers have argued that the moral rightness of an action is determined solely by its results. If its consequences are good, then the act is right; if they are bad, the act is wrong. Moral theorists who adopt this approach are therefore called *conse-quentialists.* They determine what is right by weighing the ratio of good to bad that an action will produce. The right act is the one that produces (or will probably produce) at least as great a ratio of good to evil as any other course of action.

One question that arises here is, Consequences for whom? Should one consider the consequences only for oneself? Or the consequences for everyone affected? The two most important consequentialist theories, *egoism* and *utilitarianism,* are distinguished by their different answers to this question. Egoism advocates individual self-interest as its guiding principle, whereas utilitarianism holds that one must take into account everyone affected by the action. But both theories agree that rightness and wrongness are solely a function of an action's results.

By contrast, *nonconsequentialist* (or *deontological*) theories contend that right and wrong are determined by more than the likely consequences of an action. Nonconsequentialists do not necessarily deny that consequences are morally significant, but they believe that other factors are also relevant to the moral assessment of an action. For example, a nonconsequentialist would hold that for Kevin to break his promise to Cindy is wrong not simply because it has bad results (Cindy's hurt feelings, Kevin's damaged reputation, and so on) but because of the inherent character of the act itself. Even if more good than bad were to come from Kevin's breaking the promise, a nonconsequential-ist might still view it as wrong. What matters is the nature of the act in question, not just its results. This concept will become clearer later in the chapter as we look at some specific nonconsequentialist principles and theories.

EGOISM

In the late summer of 2000, a dismayed American public learned that the Firestone tires on Ford Explorers, one of the country's most popular vehicles, were dangerously prone to split apart on the road, causing the SUVs to roll over and crash. When officials began demanding a recall, the controversy was reminiscent of an earlier one involving Firestone's "500" steel-belted radials, which a House subcommittee had implicated in at least fifteen deaths. When Firestone announced that it was discontinuing the controversial "500," newspapers at the time interpreted this to mean that Firestone would immediately remove the tires from the market. In fact, Firestone intended only a "rolling phaseout" and con-tinued to manufacture the tire. When a Firestone spokesperson was later asked why the company had not corrected the media's misinterpretation of its intent, the spokesperson said that Firestone's policy was to ask for corrections only when it was beneficial to the company to do so—in other words, only when it was in the company's self-interest.

The view that identifies morality with self-interest is referred to as *egoism.* Egoism con-tends that an act is morally right if and only if it best promotes an agent's long-term interests. (Here an "agent" can be a single person or, as in the Firestone example, an organization.) Egoists use their best long-term advantage as the standard for measur-ing an action's rightness. If an action produces or will probably produce for the agent a greater ratio of good to evil in the long run than any other alternative, then that action is the right one to perform, and the agent should take that course to be moral.

Moral philosophers distinguish between two kinds of egoism: personal and imper-sonal. Personal egoists claim they should pursue their own best long-term interests, but they do not say what others should do. Impersonal egoists claim that everyone should follow his or her best long-term interests.

Misconceptions about Egoism

Several misconceptions haunt both versions of egoism. One is that egoists do only what they like, that they believe in "eat, drink, and be merry." Not so. Undergoing unpleasant, even painful experience meshes with egoism, provided such temporary sacrifice is necessary for the advancement of one's long-term interests.

Another misconception is that all egoists endorse *hedonism*, the view that only pleasure (or happiness) is of intrinsic value, the only good in life worth pursuing. Although some egoists are hedonistic—as was the ancient Greek philosopher Epicurus (341–270 B.C.E.)—other egoists have a broader view of what constitutes self-interest. They identify the good with knowledge, power, or what some modern psychologists call self-actualization. Egoists may, in fact, hold any theory of what is good.

A final but very important misconception is that egoists cannot act honestly, be gracious and helpful, or otherwise promote other people's interests. Egoism, however, requires us to do whatever will best further our own interests, and doing this sometimes requires us to advance the interests of others. In particular, egoism tells us to benefit others when we expect that our doing so will be reciprocated or when the act will bring us pleasure or in some way promote our own good. For example, egoism might discourage a shopkeeper from trying to cheat customers because it is likely to hurt business in the long run. Or egoism might recommend to the chair of the board that she hire as a vice president her nephew, who is not the best candidate for the job but of whom she is very fond. Hiring the nephew might bring her more satisfaction than any other course of action, even if the nephew doesn't perform his job as well as someone else might.

Psychological Egoism

So egoism does not preach that we should never assist others but rather that we have no basic moral duty to do so. The only moral obligation we have is to ourselves. Although you and I are not required to act in the interests of others, we should if that is the best way to promote our own self-interest. In short: Always look out for "number one."

Proponents of the ethical theory of egoism generally attempt to derive their basic moral principle from the alleged fact that human beings are by nature selfish creatures. According to this doctrine, termed *psychological egoism*, people are, as a matter of fact, so constructed that they must behave selfishly. Psychological egoism asserts that all actions are in fact selfishly motivated and that truly unselfish actions are therefore impossible. Even such apparently self-sacrificial acts as giving up one's own life to save the lives of one's children or blowing the whistle on one's organization's misdeeds at great personal expense are, according to psychological egoism, done to satisfy the person's own self-interested desires. For example, the parent may seek to perpetuate the family line or to avoid guilt, and the worker may be after fame or revenge.

Problems with Egoism

Although egoism as an ethical doctrine has always had its adherents, the theory is open to very strong objections. It is safe to say that few, if any, philosophers today would advocate it as either a personal or an organizational morality. Consider these objections:

1. *Psychological egoism is not a sound theory.* Of course, self-interest motivates all of us to some extent, and we all know of situations in which someone pretended to be acting

altruistically or morally but was really only motivated by self-interest. The theory of psychological egoism contends, however, that self-interest is the only thing that ever motivates anyone.

Now this claim seems open to many counterexamples. Take the actual case of a man who, while driving a company truck, spotted smoke coming from inside a parked car and a child trying to escape from the vehicle. The man quickly made a U-turn, drove up to the burning vehicle, and found a one-year-old girl trapped in the back seat, restrained by a seat belt. Flames raged in the front seat as heavy smoke billowed from the car. Disregarding his own safety, the man entered the car and removed the infant, who authorities said otherwise would have died from the poisonous fumes and the flames.

Or take a more mundane example. It's Saturday, and you feel like having a beer with a couple of pals and watching the ball game. On the other hand, you believe you ought to take your two children to the zoo, as you had earlier suggested to them you might. Going to the zoo would bring them a lot of pleasure—and besides, you haven't done much with them recently. Of course, you love your children and it will bring you some pleasure to go to the zoo with them, but—let's face it—they've been rather cranky lately and you'd prefer to watch the ball game. Nonetheless, you feel an obligation and so you go to the zoo.

These appear to be cases in which people are acting for reasons that are not self-interested. Of course, the reasons that lead you to take your children to the zoo—a sense of obligation, a desire to promote their happiness—are your reasons, but that by itself does not make them self-interested reasons. Still less does it show that you are self-ish. Anything that you do is a result of your desires, but that fact doesn't establish what the believer in psychological egoism claims—namely, that the only desires you have, or the only desires that ultimately move you, are self-interested desires.

Psychological egoists (that is, advocates of the theory of psychological egoism) will claim that deep down both the heroic man who saved the girl and the unheroic parent who took the children to the zoo were really motivated by self-interest in some way or another. Maybe the hero was hoping to win praise or the parent to advance his or her own pleasure by enhancing the children's affection for the parent. Or maybe some other self-interested consideration motivated them. Psychological egoists can always claim that some yet-to-be-identified subconscious egoistic motivation is the main impulse behind any action.

At this point, though, the psychological egoists' claims sound a little far-fetched, and we may suspect them of trying to make their theory true by definition. Whatever example we come up with, they will simply claim that the person is really motivated by self-interest. One may well wonder how scientific this theory is, or how much con-tent it has, when both the hero and the coward, both the parent who goes to the zoo and the parent who stays home, are equally selfish in their motivations.

A defender of egoism as an ethical doctrine could concede that people are not fully egoistic by nature and yet continue to insist that people ought morally to pursue only their own interests. Yet without the doctrine of psychological egoism, the ethical thesis of egoism becomes less attractive. Other types of ethical principles are possible. We all care about ourselves, but how much sense does it make to see self-interest as the basis of right and wrong? Do we really want to say that someone acting altruistically is behaving immorally?

2. *Ethical egoism is not really a moral theory at all.* Many critics of egoism as an ethical standard contend that it misunderstands the nature and point of morality. As Chapter 1 explained, morality serves to restrain our purely self-interested desires so we can all live together. If our interests never came into conflict—that is, if it were never advantageous for one person to deceive or cheat another—then we would have no need for morality. The moral standards of a society provide the basic guidelines for cooperative social existence and allow us to resolve conflicts by appeal to shared principles of justification.

It is difficult to see how ethical egoism could perform this function. In a society of egoists, people might publicly agree to follow certain rules so their lives would run more smoothly. But it would be a very unstable world, because people would not hesitate to break the rules if they thought they could get away with it. Nor can egoism provide a means for settling conflicts and disputes, because it simply tells each party to do whatever is necessary to promote effectively his or her interests.

Many moral theorists maintain that moral principles apply equally to the conduct of all persons and that their application requires us to be objective and impartial. Moral agents are seen as those who, despite their own involvement in an issue, can be reasonably disinterested and objective—those who try to see all sides of an issue without being committed to the interests of a particular individual or group, including themselves. If we accept this attitude of detachment and impartiality as at least part of what it means to take a moral point of view, then we must look for it in any proposed moral principle.

Those who make egoism their moral standard are anything but objective, for they seek to guide themselves by their own best interests, regardless of the issue or circumstances. They do not even attempt to be impartial, except insofar as impartiality furthers their own interests. And, according to their theory, any third party offering advice should simply represent his or her own interest.

3. *Ethical egoism ignores blatant wrongs.* The most common objection to egoism as an ethical doctrine is that by reducing everything to the standard of best long-term self-interest, egoism takes no stand against seemingly outrageous acts like stealing, murder, racial and sexual discrimination, deliberately false advertising, and wanton pollution. All such actions are morally neutral until the test of self-interest is applied.

Of course, the defender of egoism might argue that this objection begs the question by assuming that such acts are immoral and then repudiating egoism on this basis when, in fact, their morality is the very issue that moral principles such as egoism are meant to resolve. Still, egoism must respond to the widely observed human desire to be fair or just, a desire that at least sometimes seems stronger than competing selfish desires. A moral principle that allows the possibility of murder in the cause of self-interest offends our basic intuitions about right and wrong; it clashes with many of our considered moral beliefs.

UTILITARIANISM

Utilitarianism is the moral doctrine that we should always act to produce the greatest possible balance of good over bad for everyone affected by our actions. By "good," utilitarians understand happiness or pleasure. Thus, the greatest happiness of all constitutes the standard that determines whether an action is right or wrong. Although the basic theme of utilitarianism is present in the writings of many earlier thinkers, Jeremy Bentham (1748–1832) and John Stuart Mill (1806–1873) were the first to develop the theory explicitly and in detail. Both Bentham and Mill were philosophers with a strong interest in legal and social reform. They used the utilitarian standard to evaluate and criticize the social and political institutions of their day—for example, the prison system. As a result, utilitarianism has long been associated with social improvement.

Bentham viewed a community as no more than the individual persons who compose it. The interests of the community are simply the sum of the interests of its members. An action promotes the interests of an individual when it adds to the individual's pleasure or diminishes the person's pain. Correspondingly, an action augments the happiness of a community only insofar as it increases the total amount of individual happiness. In this way, Bentham argued for the utilitarian principle that actions are right if they promote the greatest human welfare, wrong if they do not.

For Bentham, pleasure and pain are merely types of sensations. He offered a "hedonic calculus" of six criteria for evaluating pleasure and pain exclusively by their quantitative differences—in particular, by their intensity and duration. This calculus, he believed, makes possible an objective determination of the morality of anyone's conduct, individual or collective, on any occasion.

Bentham rejected any distinctions based on quality of pleasure except insofar as they might indicate differences in quantity. Thus, whenever equal amounts of pleasure are involved, throwing darts is as good as writing poetry and baking a cake as good as composing a symphony; reading Stephen King is of no less value than reading Shakespeare. Although he himself was an intelligent, cultivated man, Bentham maintained that there is nothing intrinsically better about cultivated and intellectual pleasures than about crude and prosaic ones. The only issue is which yields the greater amount of enjoyment.

John Stuart Mill thought Bentham's concept of pleasure was too simple. He viewed human beings as having elevated faculties that allow them to pursue various kinds of pleasure. The pleasures of the intellect and imagination, in particular, have a higher value than those of mere physical sensation. Thus, for Mill the utility principle allows consideration of the relative quality of pleasure and pain, not just their intensity and duration.

Although Bentham and Mill had different conceptions of pleasure, both men equated pleasure and happiness and considered pleasure the ultimate value. In this sense they are hedonists: Pleasure, in their view, is the one thing that is intrinsically good or worthwhile. Anything that is good is good only because it brings about pleasure (or happiness), directly or indirectly. Take education, for example. The learning process itself might be pleasurable to us; reflecting on or working with what we have learned might bring us satisfaction at some later time; or by making possible a career and life that we could not have had otherwise, education might bring us happiness indirectly. In contrast, critics of Bentham and Mill contend that things other than happiness are also inherently good—for example, knowledge, friendship, and aesthetic satisfaction. The implication is that these things are valuable even if they do not lead to happiness.

Some moral theorists have modified utilitarianism so that it aims at other consequences in addition to happiness. Other utilitarians, wary of trying to compare one person's happiness with another's, have interpreted their theory as requiring us not to maximize happiness but rather to maximize the satisfaction of people's desires or preferences. The focus here will be utilitarianism in its standard form, in which the good to be aimed at is human happiness or welfare, but what will be said about standard or classical utilitarianism applies, with the appropriate modifications, to other versions as well.

Although this chapter will also consider another form of utilitarianism, known as *rule utilitarianism*, utilitarianism in its most basic version, often called *act utilitarianism*, states that we must ask ourselves what the consequences of a particular act in a particular situation will be for all those affected. If its consequences bring more total good than those of any alternative course of action, then this action is the right one and the one we should perform. Thus a utilitarian could defend Frank Furillo's decision not to request bail, thereby coercing a confession from the suspects.

Consider another example: In a famous case, medical researchers initiated a long-range study of viral hepatitis at Willowbrook State Hospital, a New York institution for mentally retarded children. The researchers were interested in understanding the pathogenesis of viral hepatitis and the effectiveness of gamma globulin as an agent for inoculating people against hepatitis. Willowbrook seemed like a good choice for the investigation because the disease was rampant there. To get the kind of precise data they considered most useful, the researchers decided to deliberately infect some of the incoming children with the strain of hepatitis virus epidemic at the institution.

The value of the Willowbrook research is well documented. As a direct result, we increased our scientific understanding of viral hepatitis and how to treat it. But nagging moral questions persist. Should retarded children have been used as subjects in experiments that were not directly therapeutic? Supporters of the research insist that the consent of the children's parents was obtained. But even if the facts warranted another conclusion, some people would still defend the Willowbrook experiments on the grounds that they produced the most good for the whole society. In other words, the suffering of some individuals was justified because it maximized the total happiness produced.

Six Points about Utilitarianism

Before evaluating utilitarianism, one should understand some points that might lead to confusion and misapplication. First, when deciding which action will produce the greatest happiness, we must consider unhappiness or pain as well as happiness. Suppose, for example, that an action produces eight units of happiness and four units of unhappiness. Its net worth is four units of happiness. Suppose also that an opposed action produces ten units of happiness and seven units of unhappiness; its net worth is three units. In this case we should choose the first action over the second. In the event that both lead not to happiness but to unhappiness, and there is no third option, we should choose the one that brings fewer units of unhappiness.

Second, actions affect people to different degrees. Your playing your radio loudly might enhance two persons' pleasure a little, cause significant discomfort to two others, and leave a fifth person indifferent. The utilitarian theory is not that each person votes on the basis of his or her pleasure or pain, with the majority ruling, but rather that we add up the various pleasures and pains, however large or small, and go with the action that brings about the greatest net amount of happiness.

Third, because utilitarians evaluate actions according to their consequences, and actions produce different results in different circumstances, almost anything might, in principle, be morally right in some particular circumstance. For example, whereas breaking a promise generally produces unhappiness, there can be circumstances in which, on balance, more happiness would be produced by breaking a promise than by keeping it. In those circumstances, utilitarianism would require us to break the promise.

Fourth, utilitarians wish to maximize happiness not simply immediately but in the long run as well. All the indirect ramifications of an act have to be taken into account. Lying might seem a good way out of a tough situation, but if and when the people we deceive find out, not only will they be unhappy, but our reputations and our relationships with them will be damaged. This is a serious risk that a utilitarian cannot ignore.

Fifth, utilitarians acknowledge that we often do not know with certainty what the future consequences of our actions will be. Accordingly, we must act so that the expected or likely happiness is as great as possible. If I take my friend's money, unbeknownst to him, and buy lottery tickets with it, there is a chance that we will end up millionaires and that my action will have maximized happiness all around. But the odds are definitely against it; the most likely result is loss of money (and probably of a friendship, too). Therefore, no utilitarian could justify gambling with purloined funds on the grounds that it might maximize happiness.

Sometimes it is difficult to determine the likely results of alternative actions, and no modern utilitarian really believes that we can assign precise units of happiness and unhappiness to people. But as Mill reminds us, we really do have quite a lot of experience as to what typically makes people happy or unhappy. In any case, as utilitarians our duty is to strive to maximize total happiness, even when it may seem difficult to know what action is likely to promote the good effectively.

Finally, when choosing among possible actions, utilitarianism does not require us to disregard our own pleasure. Nor should we give it added weight. Rather, our own pleasure and pain enter into the calculus equally with the pleasures and pains of others. Even if we are sincere in our utilitarianism, we must guard against the possibility of being biased in our calculations when our own interests are at stake. For this reason, and because it would be time-consuming to do a utilitarian calculation before every action, utilitarians encourage us to rely on rules of thumb in ordinary moral circumstances. We can make it a rule of thumb, for example, to tell the truth and keep our promises, rather than to calculate possible pleasures and pains in every routine case, because we know that in general telling the truth and keeping promises result in more happiness than lying and breaking promises.

Utilitarianism in an Organizational Context

Several features about utilitarianism make it appealing as a standard for moral decisions in business and nonbusiness organizations.

First, utilitarianism provides a clear and straightforward basis for formulating and testing policies. By utilitarian standards, an organizational policy, decision, or action is good if it promotes the general welfare more than any other alternative. A policy is considered wrong (or in need of modification) if it does not promote total utility as well as some alternative would. Utilitarians do not ask us to accept rules, policies, or principles blindly. Rather, they require us to test their worth against the standard of utility.

Second, utilitarianism provides an objective and attractive way of resolving conflicts of self-interest. This feature of utilitarianism dramatically contrasts with egoism, which seems incapable of resolving such conflicts. By proposing a standard outside self-interest, utilitarianism greatly minimizes and may actually eliminate such disputes. Thus, individuals within organizations make moral decisions and evaluate their actions by appealing to a uniform standard—the general good.

Third, utilitarianism provides a flexible, result-oriented approach to moral decision making. By recognizing no actions of a general kind as inherently right or wrong, utilitarianism encourages organizations to focus on the results of their actions and policies, and it allows them to tailor their decisions to suit the complexities of their situations. This facet of utilitarianism enables organizations to make realistic and workable moral decisions.

Critical Inquiries of Utilitarianism

1. *Is utilitarianism really workable?* Utilitarianism instructs us to maximize happiness, but in difficult cases we may be very uncertain about the likely results of the alternative courses of action open to us. Furthermore, comparing your level of happiness or unhappiness with mine is at best tricky, at worst impossible—and when many people are involved, the matter may get hopelessly complex. Even if we assume that it is possible to make comparisons and to calculate the various possible results of each course of action that a person might take (and the odds of each happening), is it realistic to expect people to take the time to make those calculations and, if they do, to make them accurately? Some critics of act utilitarianism have contended that teaching people to follow the basic utilitarian principle would not in fact promote happiness because of the difficulties in applying utilitarianism accurately.

2. *Are some actions wrong, even if they produce good?* Like egoism, utilitarianism focuses on the results of an action, not on the character of the action itself. For utilitarians, no action is in itself objectionable. It is objectionable only when it leads to a lesser amount of total good than could otherwise have been brought about. Critics of utilitarianism, by contrast, contend that some actions can be immoral and thus things we must not do, even if doing them would maximize happiness.

Suppose a dying woman has asked you to promise to send the $25,000 under her bed to her nephew in another part of the country. She dies without anyone else's knowing of the money or of the promise that you made. Now suppose, too, that you know the nephew is a spendthrift and a drunkard and, were the money delivered to him, it would be wasted in a week of outrageous partying. On the other hand, a very fine orphanage in your town needs such a sum to improve and expand its recreational facilities, something that would provide happiness to many children for years to come. It seems clear that on utilitarian grounds you should give the money to the orphanage, because this action would result in more total happiness.

Many people would balk at this conclusion, contending that it would be wrong to break your promise, even if doing so would bring about more good than keeping it. Having made a promise, you have an obligation to keep it, and a deathbed promise is particularly serious. Furthermore, the deceased woman had a right to do with her money as she wished; it is not for you to decide how to spend it. Likewise, having been bequeathed the money, the nephew has a right to it, regardless of how wisely or foolishly he might spend it. Defenders of utilitarianism, however, would insist that promoting happiness is all that really matters and warn you not to be blinded by moral prejudice.

Critics of utilitarianism, on the other hand, maintain that utilitarianism is morally blind in not just permitting, but requiring, immoral actions in order to maximize happiness. Philosopher Richard Brandt states the case against act utilitarianism this way:

> Act-utilitarianism . . . implies that if you have employed a boy to mow your lawn and he has finished the job and asks for his pay, you should pay him what you promised only if you cannot find a better use for your money. . . . It implies that if your father is ill and has no prospect of good in his life, and maintaining him is a drain on the energy and enjoyments of others, then, if you can end his life without provoking any public scandal or setting a bad example, it is your positive duty to take matters into your own hands and bring his life to a close.[2]

In the same vein, ethicist A. C. Ewing concludes that "[act] utilitarian principles, logically carried out, would result in far more cheating, lying and unfair action than any good man would tolerate."[3]

Defenders of act utilitarianism would reply that these charges are exaggerated. Although it is theoretically possible, for example, that not paying the boy for his work might maximize happiness, this is extremely unlikely. Utilitarians contend that only in very unusual circumstances will pursuit of the good conflict with our ordinary ideas of right and wrong, and in those cases—like the deathbed promise—we should put aside those ordinary ideas. The anti-utilitarian replies that the theoretical possibility that utilitarianism may require immoral conduct shows it to be an unsatisfactory moral theory.

3. *Is utilitarianism unjust?* Utilitarianism concerns itself with the sum total of happiness produced, not with how that happiness is distributed. If policy X brings two units of happiness to each of five people and policy Y brings nine units of happiness to one person, one unit each to two others, and none to the remaining two, then Y is to be preferred (eleven units of happiness versus ten), even though it distributes that happiness very unequally.

Worse still from the critic's point of view, utilitarianism may even require that some people's happiness be sacrificed in order to achieve the greatest overall amount of happiness. Sometimes the general utility may be served only at the expense of a single individual or group. Under the right of eminent domain, for example, the government may appropriate private property for public use, usually with compensation to the owner. Thus, the government may legally purchase your house from you to widen a highway— even if you don't want to sell the house or want more money than the government is willing to pay. The public interest is served at your private expense. Is this just?

Or consider the Dan River experiment, part of the long-running controversy over the cause of brown lung disease. Claiming that the disease is caused by the inhalation of microscopic fibers in cotton dust, textile unions fought for years for tough regulations to protect their workers. The Occupational Safety and Health Administration (OSHA) responded by proposing cotton dust standards, which would require many firms to install expensive new equipment. A few months before the deadline for installing the equipment, officials at Dan River textile plants in Virginia asked the state to waive the requirements for a time so the company could conduct an experiment to determine the precise cause of brown lung disease. Both the state and the Department of Labor allowed the extension.

In response, the Amalgamated Clothing and Textile Workers Union asked OSHA to stop the proposed project, charging, "It is simply unconscionable to allow hundreds of cotton mill workers to continue to face a high risk of developing brown lung disease."[4]

Suppose that the Dan River project does expose workers to a "high risk" of contracting lung disease. If so, then a small group of individuals—633 textile workers at ten locations in Danville, Virginia—are being compelled to carry the burden of isolating the cause of brown lung disease. Is this just?

Although their critics would say no, utilitarians would respond that it is, if the experiment maximizes the total good of society. Does it? If the project succeeds in identifying the exact cause of the disease, then thousands of textile workers across the country and perhaps around the world will benefit. Researchers might also discover a more economical way to ensure worker safety, which in turn would yield a consumer benefit: more economical textiles than the ones produced if the industry installs expensive new equipment. Certainly, utilitarians would introduce the potential negative impact on workers at Dan River, but merely as one effect among many others. After the interests of all affected parties are equally weighed, if extending the deadline would likely yield the greatest net utility, then doing so is just—despite the fact that workers may be injured. (This discussion is not intended to justify the project or to foreclose a fuller utilitarian analysis of the case but merely to illustrate generally the utilitarian approach.)

The Interplay Between Self-Interest and Utility

Both self-interest and utility play important roles in organizational decisions, and the views of many businesspeople blend these two theories. To the extent that each business pursues its own interests and each businessperson tries to maximize personal success, business practice can be called egoistic. But business practice is also utilitarian in that pursuing self-interest is thought to maximize the total good, and playing by the established rules of the competitive game is seen as advancing the good of society as a whole. The classical capitalist economist Adam Smith (1723–1790) held such a view. He argued that if business is left to pursue its self-interest, the good of society will be served. Indeed, Smith believed that only through egoistic pursuits could the greatest economic good for the whole society be produced. The essence of Smith's position can be seen in the following passage from *The Wealth of Nations* (1776), in which Smith underscores the interplay between self-interest and the social good and between egoism and utilitarianism:

> Every individual is continually exerting himself to find out the most advantageous employment for whatever capital he can command. It is his own advantage, indeed, and not that of the society, which he has in view. But the study of his own advantage, naturally, or rather necessarily, leads him to prefer that employment which is most advantageous to the society. . . .
>
> As every individual, therefore, endeavours as much as he can . . . to employ his capital . . . [so] that its produce may be of the greatest value, every individual necessarily labors to render the annual revenue of the society as great as he can. He generally, indeed, neither intends to promote the public interest, nor knows how much he is promoting it. . . . He intends only his own security; and by directing that industry in such a manner as its product may be of the greatest value, he intends only his own gain, and he is in this, as in many other cases, led by an invisible hand to promote an end which was no part of his intention. Nor is it always the worse

for the society that it was no part of it. By pursuing his own interest he frequently promotes that of the society more effectually than when he really intends to promote it. I have never known much good done by those who affected to trade for the public good. It is an affectation, indeed, not very common among merchants, and very few words need be employed in dissuading them from it.[5]

Many today would agree with Smith,* conceding that business is part of a social system, that cooperation is necessary, and that certain competitive ground rules are needed and should be followed. At the same time, they would argue that the social system is best served by the active pursuit of self-interest within the context of established rules. Thus, the position these individuals recommend has been dubbed the ethics of "restrained egoism." It is egoistic because it recommends the pursuit of self-interest; it is restrained because it permits pursuit of self-interest only within the rules of business practice.[6]

KANT'S ETHICS

Most of us find the ideal of promoting human happiness and well-being an attractive one and, as a result, admire greatly people like Mother Teresa (1910–1997), who devoted her life to working with the poor. Despite the attractiveness of this ideal, many moral philosophers are critical of utilitarianism—particularly because, like egoism, it reduces all morality to a concern with consequences. Although nonconsequentialist normative theories vary significantly, adopting different approaches and stressing different themes, the writings of the preeminent German philosopher Immanuel Kant (1724–1804) provide an excellent example of a thoroughly nonconsequentialist approach to ethics. Perhaps few thinkers today would endorse Kant's theory on every point, but his work has greatly influenced subsequent philosophers and has helped shape our general moral culture.

Kant sought moral principles that do not rest on contingencies and that define actions as inherently right or wrong apart from any particular circumstances. He believed that moral rules can, in principle, be known as a result of reason alone and are not based on observation (as are, for example, scientific judgments). In contrast to utilitarianism and other consequentialist doctrines, Kant's ethical theory holds that we do not have to know anything about the likely results of, say, my telling a lie to my boss in order to know that it is immoral. "The basis of obligation," Kant wrote, "must not be sought in human nature, [nor] in the circumstances of the world." Rather it is *a priori,* by which he meant that moral reasoning is not based on factual knowledge and that reason by itself can reveal the basic principles of morality.

Good Will

Chapter 1 mentioned Good Samaritan laws, which shield from lawsuits those rendering emergency aid. Such laws, in effect, give legal protection to the humanitarian impulse behind emergency interventions. They formally recognize that the interventionist's heart was in the right place, that the person's intention was irreproachable. And because the person acted from right intention, he or she should not be held liable for any inadvertent harm except in cases of extreme negligence. The widely observable

---

*Chapter 4 examines Smith's position in more detail.

human tendency to introduce a person's intentions in assigning blame or praise is a good springboard for engaging Kant's ethics.

Nothing, said Kant, is good in itself except a good will. This does not mean that intelligence, courage, self-control, health, happiness, and other things are not good and desirable. But Kant believed that their goodness depends on the will that makes use of them. Intelligence, for instance, is not good when used by an evil person.

By *will* Kant meant the uniquely human capacity to act from principle. Contained in the notion of good will is the concept of duty: Only when we act from duty does our action have moral worth. When we act only out of feeling, inclination, or self-interest, our actions—although they may be otherwise identical with ones that spring from the sense of duty—have no true moral worth.

Suppose that you're a clerk in a small stop-and-go store. Late one night a customer pays for his five-dollar purchase with a twenty-dollar bill, which you mistake for a ten. It's only after the customer leaves that you realize you short-changed him. You race out the front door and find him lingering by a vending machine. You give him the ten dollars with your apologies, and he thanks you profusely.

Can we say with certainty that you acted from a good will? Not necessarily. You may have acted from a desire to promote business or to avoid legal entanglement. If so, you would have acted in accordance with, but not from, duty. Your apparently virtuous gesture just happened to coincide with duty. According to Kant, if you do not will the action from a sense of your duty to be fair and honest, your action lacks moral worth. Actions have true moral worth only when they spring from a recognition of duty and a choice to discharge it.

But then what determines our duty? How do we know what morality requires of us? Kant answered these questions by formulating what he called the "categorical imperative." This extraordinarily significant moral concept is the linchpin of Kant's ethics.

The Categorical Imperative

We have seen that egoists and utilitarians allow factual circumstances or empirical data to determine moral judgments. In contrast, Kant believed that reason alone can yield a moral law. We need not rely on empirical evidence relating to consequences and to similar situations. Just as we know, seemingly through reason alone, such abstract truths as "Every change must have a cause," so we can arrive at absolute moral truth through nonempirical reasoning, and thereby discover our duty.

For Kant, an absolute moral truth must be logically consistent, free from internal contradiction. For example, it is a contradiction to say that an effect does not have a cause. Kant aimed to ensure that his absolute moral law would avoid such contradictions. If he could formulate such a rule, he maintained, everyone would be obliged to follow it without exception.

Kant believed that there is just one command (imperative) that is categorical—that is necessarily binding on all rational agents, regardless of any other considerations. From this one categorical imperative, this universal command, we can derive all commands of duty. Kant's *categorical imperative* says that we should always act in such a way that we can will the maxim of our action to become a universal law. So Kant's answer to the question "What determines whether an act is right?" is that an act is morally right if and only if we can will it to become a universal law of conduct.

The obvious and crucial question that arises here is, "When are we justified in saying that the maxim of our action can become a universal law of conduct?"

By *maxim*, Kant meant the subjective principle of an action, the principle (or rule) that people in effect formulate in determining their conduct. For example, suppose building contractor Martin promises to install a sprinkler system in a project but is willing to break that promise to suit his purposes. His maxim can be expressed this way: "I'll make promises that I'll break whenever keeping them no longer suits my purposes." This is the subjective principle, the maxim, that directs his action.

Kant insisted that the morality of any maxim depends on whether we can logically will it to become a universal law. Could Martin's maxim be universally acted on? That depends on whether the maxim as law would involve a contradiction. The maxim "I'll make promises that I'll break whenever keeping them no longer suits my purposes" could not be universally acted on because it involves a contradiction of will. On the one hand, Martin is willing that it be possible to make promises and have them honored. On the other, if everyone intended to break promises when they so desired, then promises would not be honored in the first place, because it is in the nature of promises that they be believed. A law that allowed promise breaking would contradict the very nature of a promise. Similarly, a law that allowed lying would contradict the very nature of serious communication, for the activity of serious communication (as opposed to joking) requires that participants intend to speak the truth. I cannot, without contradiction, will both serious conversation and lying. By contrast, there is no problem, Kant thinks, in willing promise keeping or truth telling to be universal laws.

Consider, as another example, Kant's account of a man who, in despair after suffering a series of major setbacks, contemplates suicide. While still rational, the man asks whether it would be contrary to his duty to take his own life. Could the maxim of his action become a universal law of nature? Kant thinks not:

> His maxim is this: From self-love I make it my principle to shorten my life when its continued duration threatens more evil than it promises satisfaction. There only remains the question whether this principle of self-love can become a universal law of nature. One sees at once a contradiction in a system of nature whose law would destroy life by means of the very same feeling that acts so as to stimulate the furtherance of life. . . . Therefore, such a maxim cannot possibly hold as a universal law of nature and is, consequently, wholly inconsistent with the supreme principle of all duty.[7]

When Kant insists that a moral rule be consistently universalizable, he is saying that moral rules prescribe categorically, not hypothetically. A hypothetical prescription tells us what to do if we desire a particular outcome. Thus, "If I want people to like me, I should be nice to them" and "If you want to go to medical school, you must take biology" are hypothetical imperatives. They tell us what we must do on the assumption that we have some particular goal. If that is what we want, then this is what we must do. On the other hand, if we don't want to go to medical school, then the command to take biology does not apply to us. In contrast, Kant's imperative is categorical—it commands unconditionally. That is, it is necessarily binding on everyone, regardless of his or her specific goals or desires, regardless of consequences.

A categorical imperative takes the form of "Do this" or "Don't do that"—no ifs, ands, or buts.

Universal Acceptability   There is another way of looking at the categorical imperative. Each person, through his or her own acts of will, legislates the moral law. The moral rules that we obey are not imposed on us from the outside. They are self-imposed and self-recognized, fully internalized principles. The sense of duty that we obey comes from within; it is an expression of our own higher selves.

Thus, moral beings give themselves the moral law and accept its demands on themselves. But that is not to say we can prescribe anything we want, for we are bound by reason and its demands. Because reason is the same for all rational beings, we all give ourselves the same moral law. In other words, when you answer the question "What should I do?" you must consider what all rational beings should do. If the moral law is valid for you, it must be valid for all other rational beings.

To see whether a rule or principle is a moral law, we can thus ask if what the rule commands would be acceptable to all rational beings acting rationally. In considering lying, theft, or murder, for example, you must consider the act not only from your own viewpoint but from the perspective of the person lied to, robbed, or murdered. Presumably, rational beings do not want to be lied to, robbed, or murdered. The test of the morality of a rule, then, is not whether people in fact accept it but whether all rational beings thinking rationally would accept it regardless of whether they are the doers or the receivers of the actions. This is an important moral insight, and most philosophers see it as implicit in Kant's discussion of the categorical imperative, even though Kant (whose writings are difficult to understand) did not make the point in this form.

The principle of universal acceptability has important applications. Suppose a man advocates a hiring policy that discriminates against women. For this rule to be universally acceptable, the man would have to be willing to accept it if he were a woman, something he would presumably be unwilling to do. Or suppose the manufacturer of a product decides to market it even though the manufacturer knows that the product is unsafe when used in a certain common way and that consumers are ignorant of this fact. Applying the universal acceptability principle, the company's decision makers would have to be willing to advocate marketing the product even if they were themselves in the position of uninformed consumers. Presumably they would be unwilling to do this. So the rule that would allow the product to be marketed would fail the test of universal acceptability.

Humanity as an End, Never as Merely a Means   In addition to the principle of universal acceptability, Kant explicitly offered another very famous way of formulating the core idea of his categorical imperative. According to this formulation, rational creatures should always treat other rational creatures as ends in themselves and never as only means to ends. This formulation underscores Kant's belief that every human being has an inherent worth resulting from the sheer possession of rationality. We must always act in a way that respects this humanity in others and in ourselves.

As rational beings, humans would act inconsistently if they did not treat everyone else the way they themselves would want to be treated. Here we see shades of the Golden Rule. Indeed, Kant's moral philosophy can be viewed as a profound reconsideration of this basic nonconsequentialist principle. Because rational beings recognize their own inner worth, they would never wish to be used as entities possessing worth only as means to an end.

Thus, when brokers at the Dallas office of Prudential Securities encouraged unnecessary buying and selling of stocks in order to reap a commission (a practice called "churning"), they were treating their clients simply as a means and not respecting them as persons, as ends in themselves.[8] Likewise, Kant would object to using patients as subjects in a medical experiment without their consent. Even though great social benefit might result, the researchers would intentionally be using the patients solely as a means to the researchers' own goals and thus would be failing to respect the patients' basic humanity.

Kant maintained, as explained first, that an action is morally right if and only if we can will it to be a universal law. We now have two ways of reformulating his categorical imperative that may be easier to grasp and apply:

First reformulation: An action is only right if the agent would be willing to be so treated were the positions of the parties reversed.

Second reformulation: One must always act so as to treat other people as ends in themselves.

Kant in an Organizational Context

Like utilitarianism, Kant's moral theory has application for organizations.

First, the categorical imperative gives us firm rules to follow in moral decision making, rules that do not depend on circumstances or results and that do not permit individual exceptions. No matter what the consequences may be or who does it, some actions are always wrong. Lying is an example: No matter how much good may come from misrepresenting a product, such deliberate misrepresentation is always wrong. Similarly, one cannot justify exposing uninformed children to the risk of hepatitis on the grounds that it advances medical knowledge.

Second, Kant introduces an important humanistic dimension into business decisions. One of the principal objections to egoism and utilitarianism is that they permit us to treat humans as means to ends. Kant's principles clearly forbid this. Many would say that respect for the inherent worth and dignity of human beings is much needed today in business, in which encroaching technology and computerization tend to dehumanize people under the guise of efficiency. Kant's theory puts the emphasis of organizational decision making where it belongs: on individuals. Organizations, after all, involve human beings working in concert to provide goods and services for other human beings. The primacy Kant gives the individual reflects this essential aspect of business.

Third, Kant stresses the importance of motivation and of acting on principle. According to Kant, it is not enough just to do the right thing; an action has moral worth only if it is done from a sense of duty—that is, from a desire to do the right thing for its own sake. The importance of this point is too often forgotten. Sometimes when individuals and organizations believe that an action promotes the interests of everyone, they are actually rationalizing—doing what is best for themselves and only imagining that somehow it will also benefit others. Worse still, they may defend their actions as morally praiseworthy when, in fact, they are only behaving egoistically. They wouldn't do the morally justifiable thing if they didn't think it would pay off for them. By stressing the importance of motivation, a Kantian approach serves as a corrective to this. Even an action that helps others has moral value for Kant only if the person doing it is morally motivated—that is, acting on principle or out of moral conviction.

Critical Inquiries of Kant's Ethics

1. *What has moral worth?* According to Kant, the clerk who returns the ten dollars to the customer is doing the right thing. But if his action is motivated by self-interest (perhaps he wants to get a reputation for honesty), then it does not have moral worth. That seems plausible. But Kant also held that if the clerk does the right thing out of instinct, habit, or sympathy for the other person, then the act still does not have moral worth. Only if it is done out of a sense of duty does the clerk's action have moral value. Many moral theorists have felt that Kant was too severe on this point. Do we really want to say that giving money to famine relief efforts has no moral worth if one is emotionally moved to do so by pictures of starving children rather than by a sense of duty? We might, to the contrary, find a person with strong human sympathies no less worthy or admirable than the person who gives solely out of an abstract sense of duty.

2. *Is the categorical imperative an adequate test of right?* Kant said that a moral rule must function without exception. Critics wonder why the prohibition against such actions as lying, promise breaking, suicide, and so on must be exceptionless. They say that Kant failed to distinguish between saying that a person should not except himself or herself from a rule and that the rule itself has no exceptions.

If stealing is wrong, it's wrong for me as well as for you. "Stealing is wrong, except if I do it" is not universalizable, for then stealing would be right for all to do, which contradicts the assertion that stealing is wrong. But just because no one may make of oneself an exception to a rule, it does not follow that the rule itself has no exceptions.

Suppose, for example, that we decide that stealing is sometimes right, perhaps in the case of a person who is starving. Thus, the rule becomes "Never steal except when starving." This rule seems just as universalizable as "Never steal." The phrase "except . . ." can be viewed not as justifying a violation of the rule but as building a qualification into it. Critics in effect are asking why a qualified rule is not just as good as an unqualified one. If it is, then we no longer need to state rules in the simple, direct, unqualified manner that Kant did.

In fairness to Kant, it could be argued that his universalization formula can be interpreted flexibly enough to meet commonsense objections. For example, perhaps we could universalize the principle that individuals should steal rather than starve to death or that it is permissible to take one's own life to extinguish unspeakable pain. And yet to qualify the rules against stealing, lying, and taking one's life seems to invite a non-Kantian analysis to justify the exceptions. One could, it seems, universalize more than one moral rule in a given situation: "Do not lie unless a life is at stake" versus "Lying is wrong unless necessary to avoid the suffering of innocent people." If so, then the categorical imperative would supply at best a necessary, but not a sufficient, test of right. But once we start choosing among various alternative rules, then we are adopting an approach to ethics that Kant would have rejected.

3. *What does it mean to treat people as means?* Kant's mandate that individuals must always be considered as ends in themselves and never merely as means expresses our sense of the intrinsic value of the human spirit and has profound moral appeal. Yet it is not always clear when people are being treated as ends and when merely as means. For example, Kant believed that prostitution is immoral because, by selling their sexual services, prostitutes allow themselves to be treated as means. Prostitutes, however, are not the only ones to sell their services. Anyone who works for a wage does so. Does that mean that we are all being treated immorally, because our employers are presumably hiring us as a means to advance their own ends? Presumably not, because we freely agreed to do the work. But then the prostitute might have freely chosen that line of work, too.

OTHER NONCONSEQUENTIALIST PERSPECTIVES

For Kant, the categorical imperative provided the basic test of right and wrong, and he was resolutely nonconsequentialist in his application of it. You know now what he would say about the case of the deathbed promise: The maxim permitting you to break your promise cannot be universalized, and hence it would be immoral of you to give the money to the orphanage, despite the happiness that doing so would bring. But nonconsequentialists are not necessarily Kantians, and several different nonutilitarian moral concerns emerged in the discussion of the deathbed promise example.

Critics of act utilitarianism believe that it is faulty for maintaining that we have one and only one moral duty. A utilitarian might follow various principles as rules of thumb, but they are only calculation substitutes. All that matters morally to utilitarians is the maximization of happiness. Yet this idea, many philosophers think, fails to do justice to the richness and complexity of our moral lives.

Prima Facie Principles

One influential philosopher who argued this way was the British scholar W. D. Ross (1877–1971).[9] Ross rejected utilitarianism as too simple and as untrue to the way we ordinarily think about morality and about our moral obligations. We see ourselves, Ross and like-minded thinkers contend, as being under various moral duties that cannot be reduced to the single obligation to maximize happiness. Often these obligations grow out of special relationships into which we enter or out of determinate roles that we undertake. Our lives are intertwined with other people's in particular ways, and we have, as a result, certain specific moral obligations.

For example, as a professor, Rodriguez is obligated to assist her students in the learning process and to evaluate their work in a fair and educationally productive way—obligations to the specific people in her classroom that she does not have to other people. As a spouse, Rodriguez must maintain a certain emotional and sexual fidelity to her partner. As a parent, she must provide for the individual human beings who are her children. As a friend to Smith, she may have a moral responsibility to help him out in a time of crisis. Having borrowed money from Chang, Rodriguez is morally obligated to pay it back. Thus, different relationships and different circumstances generate a variety of specific moral obligations.

In addition, we have moral duties that do not arise from our unique interactions and relationships with other people. For example, we ought to treat all people fairly, do what we can to remedy injustices, and make an effort to promote human welfare generally. The latter obligation is important, but for a nonconsequentialist like Ross it is only one among various obligations that people have.

At any given time, we are likely to be under more than one obligation, and sometimes these obligations can conflict. That is, we may have an obligation to do *A* and an obligation to do *B,* where it is not possible for us to do both *A* and *B.* For example, I promise to meet a friend on an urgent matter, and now, as I am hurrying there, I pass an injured person who is obviously in need of assistance. Stopping to aid the person will make it impossible for me to fulfill my promise. What should I do? For moral philosophers like Ross, there is no single answer for all cases. What I ought to do will depend on the circumstances and relative importance of the conflicting obligations. I have an obligation to keep my promise, and I have an obligation to assist people in distress. What I must decide is which of these obligations is, in the given circumstance, the more important. I must weigh the moral significance of the promise against the comparative moral urgency of assisting the injured person.

Ross and many contemporary philosophers believe that all (or at least most) of our moral obligations are prima facie ones. A *prima facie obligation* is an obligation that can be overridden by a more important obligation. For instance, we take the keeping of promises seriously, but almost everyone would agree that in some circumstances—for example, when a life is at stake—it would be not only morally permissible, but morally required, to break a promise. Our obligation to keep a promise is a real one, and if there is no conflicting obligation, then we must keep the promise. But that obligation is not absolute or categorical; it could in principle be outweighed by a more stringent moral obligation. The idea that our obligations are prima facie is foreign to Kant's way of looking at things.

Consider an example that Kant himself discussed.[10] Imagine that a murderer comes to your door, wanting to know where your friend is so that he can kill her. Your friend is in fact hiding in your bedroom closet. Most people would probably agree that your obligation to your friend overrides your general obligation to tell the truth and that the right thing to do would be to lie to the murderer to throw him off your friend's trail. Although you have a genuine obligation to tell the truth, it is a prima facie obligation, one that other moral considerations can outweigh. Kant disagreed. He maintained that you must always tell the truth—that is, in all circumstances and without exception. For him, telling the truth is an absolute or categorical obligation, not a prima facie one.

Ross thought that our various prima facie obligations could be divided into seven basic types: duties of fidelity (that is, to respect explicit and implicit promises), duties of reparation (for previous wrongful acts), duties of gratitude, duties of justice, duties of beneficence (that is, to make the condition of others better), duties of self-improvement, and duties not to injure others.[11] Unlike utilitarianism, Ross's ethical perspective is pluralistic in recognizing a variety of genuine obligations. But contrary to Kant, Ross does not see these obligations as absolute and exceptionless. On both points, Ross contended that his view of morality more closely fits with our actual moral experience and the way we view our moral obligations.

Ross also saw himself as siding with commonsense morality in maintaining that our prima facie obligations are obvious. He believed that the basic principles of duty are as self-evident as the simplest rules of arithmetic and that any person who has reached the age of reason can discern that it is wrong to lie, to break promises, and to injure people needlessly. However, what we should do, all things considered, when two or more prima facie obligations conflict is often difficult to judge. In deciding what to do in any concrete situation, Ross thought, we are always "taking a moral risk."[12] Even after the fullest reflection, judgments about which of these self-evident rules should govern our conduct are only "more or less probable opinions which are not logically justified conclusions from the general principles that are recognised as self-evident."[13]

Assisting Others

Nonconsequentialists believe that utilitarianism presents too simple a picture of our moral world. In addition, they worry that utilitarianism risks making us all slaves to the maximization of total happiness. Stop and think about it: Isn't there something that you could be doing—for instance, volunteering at the local hospital or orphanage, collecting money for Third World development, helping the homeless—that would do more for the general good than what you are doing now or are planning to do tonight or tomorrow? Sure, working with the homeless might not bring you quite as much pleasure as what you would otherwise be doing, but if it would nonetheless maximize total happiness, then you are morally required to do it. However, by following this reasoning, you could end up working around the clock, sacrificing yourself for the greater good. This notion seems mistaken.

Most nonutilitarian philosophers, like Ross, believe that we have some obligation to promote the general welfare, but they typically view this obligation as less stringent than, for example, the obligation not to injure people. They see us as having a much stronger obligation to refrain from violating people's rights than to promote their happiness or well-being.

From this perspective, a manufacturing company's obligation not to violate OSHA regulations and thereby endanger the safety of its employees is stronger than its obligation to open up day-care facilities for their children, even though the cost of both is the same. The company, in other words, has a stronger duty to respect its contractual and legal employment-related obligations than to promote its employees' happiness in other ways. Likewise, for a company to violate people's rights by despoiling the environment through the discharge of pollutants would be morally worse than for it to decide not to expand a job training program in the inner city, even if expanding the program would bring about more total good.

Different nonutilitarian philosophers may weight these particular obligations differently, depending on their particular moral theory. But they typically believe that we have a stronger duty not to violate people's rights or in some other way injure them than we do to assist people or otherwise promote their well-being. A utilitarian, concerned solely with what will maximize happiness, is less inclined to draw such a distinction.

Many moral philosophers draw a related distinction between actions that are morally required and charitable or *supererogatory* actions—that is, actions that it would be good to do but not immoral not to do. Act utilitarianism does not make this distinction. While we admire Mother Teresa and Albert Schweitzer for devoting their lives to doing good works among the poor, we see them as acting above and beyond the call of duty; we do not expect so much from ordinary people. Yet people who are not moral heroes or who fall short of sainthood may nonetheless be living morally satisfactory lives.

Nonutilitarian theorists see the distinction between morally obligatory actions and supererogatory actions not so much as a realistic concession to human weakness but as a necessary demarcation if we are to avoid becoming enslaved to the maximization of the general welfare. The idea here is that each of us should have a sphere in which to pursue our own plans and goals, to carve out a distinctive life plan. These plans and goals are limited by various moral obligations, in particular by other people's rights, but the demands of morality are not all-encompassing.

Moral Rights

What, then, are rights, and what rights do people have? Broadly defined, a *right* is an entitlement to act or have others act in a certain way. The connection between rights and duties is that, generally speaking, if you have a right to do something, then someone else has a correlative duty to act in a certain way. For example, if you claim a "right" to drive, you mean that you are entitled to drive or that others should—that is, have a duty to—permit you to drive. Your right to drive under certain conditions is derived from our legal system and is thus considered a *legal right.*

In addition to rights that are derived from some specific legal system, we also have *moral rights.* Some of these moral rights derive from special relationships, roles, or circumstances in which we happen to be. For example, if Tom has an obligation to return Bob's car to him on Saturday morning, then Bob has a right to have Tom return his car. If I have agreed to water your plants while you are on vacation, you have a right to expect me to look after them in your absence. As a student, you have a right to be graded fairly, and so on.

Even more important are rights that do not rest on special relationships, roles, or situations. For example, the rights to life, free speech, and unhampered religious affiliation are widely accepted, not just as the entitlements of some specific political or legal system but as fundamental moral rights. More controversial, but often championed as moral rights, are the rights to medical care, decent housing, education, and work. Moral rights that are not the result of particular roles, special relationships, or specific circumstances are called *human rights.* They have several important characteristics.

First, human rights are universal. For instance, if the right to life is a human right, as most of us believe it is, then everyone, everywhere, and at all times, has that right. By contrast, there is nothing universal about your right that I keep my promise to help you move or about my right to drive 65 miles per hour on certain roads.

Second, and closely related, human rights are equal rights. If the right to free speech is a human right, then everyone has this right equally. No one has a greater right to free speech than anyone else. In contrast, your daughter has a greater right than do the daughters of other people to your emotional and financial support.

Third, human rights are not transferable, nor can they be relinquished. If we have a fundamental human right, we cannot give, lend, or sell it to someone else. We cannot waive it, and no one can take it from us. That is what is meant in the Declaration of Independence when certain rights—namely, life, liberty, and the pursuit of happiness—are described as "unalienable." By comparison, legal rights can be renounced or transferred, as when one party sells another a house or a business.

Fourth, human rights are natural rights, not in the sense that they can be derived from a study of human nature, but in the sense that they do not depend on human institutions the way legal rights do. If people have human rights, they have these rights simply because they are human beings. They do not have them because they live under a certain legal system. Human rights rest on the assumption that people have certain basic moral entitlements merely on the basis of their humanity. No authoritative body assigns them human rights. The law may attempt to protect human rights, to make them explicit and safe through codification, but the law is not their source.

Rights, and in particular human rights, can be divided into two broad categories: negative rights and positive rights. *Negative rights* reflect the vital interests that human beings have in being free from outside interference. The rights guaranteed in the Bill of Rights—freedom of speech, assembly, religion, and so on—fall within this category, as do the rights to freedom from injury and to privacy. Correlating with these are duties that we all have not to interfere with others' pursuit of these interests and activities. *Positive rights* reflect the vital interests that human beings have in receiving certain benefits. They are rights to have others provide us with certain goods, services, or opportunities. Today, positive rights often are taken to include the rights to education, medical care, a decent neighborhood, equal job opportunity, comparable pay, and so on. Correlating with these are positive duties for appropriate parties to assist individuals in their pursuit of these interests.

Thus a child's right to education implies not just that no one should interfere with the child's education but also that the necessary resources for that education ought to be provided. In the case of some positive rights—for example, the right to a decent standard of living, as proclaimed by the United Nations' 1948 Human Rights Charter—who exactly has the duty to provide the goods and services required to fulfill those rights is unclear. Also, interpreting a right as negative or positive is sometimes controversial. For example, is my right to liberty simply the right not to be interfered with as I live my own life, or does it also imply a duty on the part of others to provide me with the means to make the exercise of that liberty meaningful?

The significance of positing moral rights is that they provide grounds for making moral judgments that differ radically from utilitarianism's grounds. Once moral rights are asserted, the locus of moral judgment becomes the individual, not society. For example, if every potential human research subject has a moral right to be fully informed about the nature of a medical experiment and the moral right to decide freely for himself or herself whether to participate, then it is wrong to violate these rights—even if, by so doing, the common good would be served. Again, if workers have a right to compensation equal to what others receive for doing comparable work, then they cannot be paid less on the grounds that this will maximize total well-being. And if everyone has a right to equal consideration for a job regardless of color or sex, then sex and color cannot be introduced merely because so doing will result in greater net utility.

Utilitarianism, in effect, treats all such entitlements as subordinate to the general welfare. Thus, individuals are entitled to act in a certain way and entitled to have others allow or aid them to so act only insofar as acknowledging this right or entitlement achieves the greatest good. The assertion of moral rights, therefore, decisively sets nonconsequentialists apart from utilitarians.

Nonconsequentialism in an Organizational Context

We have already looked at Kant's ethics in an organizational context, but the themes of the other nonconsequentialist approaches also have important implications for moral decision making in business and nonbusiness organizations.

First, in its non-Kantian forms nonconsequentialism stresses that moral decision making involves the weighing of different moral factors and considerations. Unlike utilitarianism, nonconsequentialism does not reduce morality solely to the calculation of consequences; rather, it recognizes that an organization must usually take into account other equally important moral concerns. Theorists like Ross emphasize that, contrary to what Kant believed, there can often be rival and even conflicting obligations on an organization. For example, obligations to employees, stockholders, and consumers may pull the corporation in different directions, and determining the organization's proper moral course may not be easy.

Second, nonconsequentialism acknowledges that the organization has its own legitimate goals to pursue. There are limits to the demands of morality, and an organization that fulfills its moral obligations and respects the relevant rights of individuals is morally free to advance whatever (morally permissible) ends it has—public service, profit, government administration, and so on. Contrary to utilitarianism, organizations and the people in them need not see themselves as under an overarching obligation to seek continually to enhance the general welfare.

Third, nonconsequentialism stresses the importance of moral rights. Moral rights, and in particular human rights, are a crucial factor in most moral deliberations, including those of organizations. Before it acts, any morally responsible business or nonbusiness organization must consider carefully how its actions will impinge on the rights of individuals—not just the rights of its members, such as stockholders and employees, but also the rights of others, such as consumers. Moral rights place distinct and firm constraints on what sorts of things an organization can do to fulfill its own ends.

Critical Inquiries of Nonconsequentialism

1. *How well justified are these nonconsequentialist principles and moral rights?* Ross maintained that we have immediate intuitive knowledge of the basic prima facie moral principles, and indeed it would seem absurd to try to deny that it is wrong to cause needless suffering or that making a promise imposes some obligation to keep it. Only someone the moral equivalent of colorblind could fail to see the truth of these statements; to reject them would seem as preposterous as denying some obvious fact of arithmetic—for example, that $12 + 4 = 16$. Likewise, it appears obvious—indeed, as Thomas Jefferson wrote, "self-evident"—that human beings have certain basic and inalienable rights, unconditional rights that do not depend on the decrees of any particular government.

Yet we must be careful. What seems obvious, even self-evident, to one culture or at one time in human history may turn out to be not only not self-evident but actually false. That the earth is flat and that heavier objects fall faster than lighter ones were two "truths" taken as obvious in former centuries. Likewise, the inferiority of women and of various nonwhite races was long taken for granted; this supposed fact was so obvious that it was hardly even commented on. The idea that people have a right to practice a religion that the majority "knows" to be false—or, indeed, to practice no religion whatsoever—would have seemed morally scandalous to many of our forebears and is still not embraced in all countries today. Today, many vegetarians eschew meat eating on moral grounds and contend that future generations will consider our treatment of animals, factory farming in particular, to be as morally benighted as slavery. So what seems obvious, self-evident, or simple common sense may not be the most reliable guide to morally sound principles.

2. *Can nonconsequentialists satisfactorily handle conflicting rights and principles?* People today disagree among themselves about the correctness of certain moral principles. Claims of right, as we have seen, are often controversial. For example, do employees have a moral right to their jobs—an entitlement to be fired only with just cause? To some of us, it may seem obvious that they do; to others, perhaps not. And how are we to settle various conflicting claims of right? Jones, for instance, claims a right to her property, which she has acquired honestly through her labors; that is, she claims a right to do with it as she wishes. Smith is ill and claims adequate medical care as a human right. Because he cannot afford the care himself, acknowledging his right will probably involve taxing people like Jones and thus limiting their property rights.

To sum up these two points: First, even the deliverances of moral common sense have to be examined critically; and second, nonconsequentialists should not rest content until they find a way of resolving disputes among conflicting prima facie principles or rights. This is not to suggest that nonconsequentialists cannot find deeper and theoretically more satisfactory ways of grounding moral claims and of handling disputes between them. The point to be underscored here is simply the necessity of doing so.

UTILITARIANISM ONCE MORE

Until now, the discussion of utilitarianism has focused on its most classic and straightforward form, called act utilitarianism. According to act utilitarianism, we have one and only one moral obligation, the maximization of happiness for everyone concerned, and every action is to be judged according to how well it lives up to this standard. But a different utilitarian approach, called rule utilitarianism, is relevant to the discussion of the moral concerns characteristic of nonconsequentialism—in particular, relevant to the nonconsequentialist's criticisms of act utilitarianism. The rule utilitarian would, in fact, agree with many of these criticisms. (Rule utilitarianism has been formulated in different ways, but this discussion follows the version defended by Richard Brandt.)

Rule utilitarianism maintains that the utilitarian standard should be applied not to individual actions but to moral codes as a whole. The rule utilitarian asks what moral code (that is, what set of moral rules) a society should adopt to maximize happiness. The principles that make up that code would then be the basis for distinguishing right actions from wrong actions. As Brandt explains:

> A rule-utilitarian thinks that right actions are the kind permitted by the moral code optimal for the society of which the agent is a member. An optimal code is one designed to maximize welfare or what is good (thus, utility). This leaves open the possibility that a particular right act by itself may not maximize benefit. . . . On the rule-utilitarian view, then, to find what is morally right or wrong we need to find which actions would be permitted by a moral system that is "optimal" for the agent's society.[14]

The "optimal" moral code does not refer to the set of rules that would do the most good if everyone conformed to them all the time. The meaning is more complex. The optimal moral code must take into account what rules can reasonably be taught and obeyed, as well as the costs of inculcating those rules in people. Recall from Chapter 1 that if a principle or rule is part of a person's moral code, then it will influence the person's behavior. The person will tend to follow that principle, to feel guilty when he or she does not follow it, and to disapprove of others who fail to conform to it. Rule utilitarians must consider not just the benefits of having people motivated to act in certain ways but also the costs of instilling those motivations in them. As Brandt writes:

> The more intense and widespread an aversion to a certain sort of behavior, the less frequent the behavior is apt to be. But the more intense and widespread, the greater the cost of teaching the rule and keeping it alive, the greater the burden on the individual, and so on.[15]

Thus, the "optimality" of a moral code encompasses both the benefits of reduced objectionable behavior and the long-term costs. Perfect compliance is not a realistic goal. "Like the law," Brandt continues, "the optimal moral code normally will not produce 100 percent compliance with all its rules; that would be too costly."[16]

Elements of the rule-utilitarian approach were clearly suggested by Mill himself, although he did not draw the distinction between act and rule utilitarianism. According to the rule-utilitarian perspective, we should apply the utilitarian standard only to the assessment of alternative moral codes; we should not try to apply it to individual actions. That is, we should seek to determine the specific set of principles that would in fact best promote total happiness for society. Those are the rules we should promulgate, instill in ourselves, and teach to the next generation.

What Will the Optimal Code Look Like?

Rule utilitarians such as Brandt argue strenuously that the ideal or optimal moral code for a society will not be the single act-utilitarian command to maximize happiness. They contend that teaching people that their only obligation is to maximize happiness would not in fact maximize happiness.

First, people will make mistakes if they always try to promote total happiness. Second, if all of us were act utilitarians, such practices as keeping promises and telling the truth would be rather shaky, because we would expect others to keep promises or tell the truth only when they believed that doing so would maximize happiness. Third, the act-utilitarian principle is too demanding, because it seems to imply that each person should continually be striving to promote total well-being.

For these reasons, rule utilitarians believe that more happiness will come from instilling in people a pluralistic moral code, one with a number of different principles. By analogy, imagine a traffic system with just one rule: Drive your car in a way that maximizes happiness. Such a system would be counterproductive; we do much better in terms of total human well-being to have a variety of traffic regulations—for example, obey stop signs, yield to the right, and pass only on the left. In such a pluralistic system we cannot justify cruising through a red light with the argument that doing so maximizes total happiness by getting us home more quickly.

The principles of the optimal code would presumably be prima facie in Ross's sense— that is, capable of being overridden by other principles. Different principles would also have different moral weights. It would make sense, for example, to instill in people an aversion to killing that is stronger than the aversion to telling white lies. In addition, the ideal code would acknowledge moral rights. Teaching people to respect moral rights maximizes human welfare in the long run.

The rules of the optimal code provide the sole basis for determining right and wrong. An action is not necessarily wrong if it fails to maximize happiness; it is wrong only if it conflicts with the ideal moral code. Rule utilitarianism thus gets around many of the problems that plague act utilitarianism. At the same time, it provides a plausible basis for deciding which moral principles and rights we should acknowledge and how much weight we should attach to them. We try to determine those principles and rights that, generally adhered to, would best promote human happiness.

Still, rule utilitarianism has its critics. There are two common objections. First, act utilitarians maintain that a utilitarian who cares about happiness should be willing to violate rules in order to maximize happiness. Why make a fetish out of the rules?

Second, nonconsequentialists, while presumably viewing rule utilitarianism more favorably than act utilitarianism, still balk at seeing moral principles determined by their consequences. They contend, in particular, that rule utilitarians ultimately subordinate rights to utilitarian calculation and therefore fail to treat rights as fundamental and independent moral factors.

MORAL DECISION MAKING: TOWARD A SYNTHESIS

Theoretical controversies permeate the subject of ethics, and as we have seen, philosophers have proposed rival ways of understanding right and wrong. These philosophical differences of perspective, emphasis, and theory are significant and can have profound practical consequences. This chapter has surveyed some of these issues, but obviously it cannot settle all of the questions that divide moral philosophers. Fortunately, however, many problems of business and organizational ethics can be intelligently discussed and even resolved by people whose fundamental moral theories differ (or who have not yet worked out their own moral ideas in some systematic way). This section discusses some important points to keep in mind when analyzing and discussing business ethics and offers, as a kind of model, one possible procedure for making moral decisions.

In the abstract, it might seem impossible for people to reach agreement on controversial ethical issues, given that ethical theories differ so much and that people themselves place moral value on different things. Yet in practice moral problems are rarely so intractable that open-minded and thoughtful people cannot, by discussing matters calmly, rationally, and thoroughly, make significant progress toward resolving them. Chapter 1 stressed that moral judgments should be logical, should be based on facts, and should appeal to sound moral principles. Bearing this in mind can often help, especially when various people are discussing an issue and proposing rival answers.

First, in any moral discussion, make sure participants agree about the relevant facts. Often moral disputes hinge not on matters of moral principle but on differing assessments of what the facts of the situation are, what alternatives are open, and what the probable results of different courses of action will be. For instance, the directors of an international firm might acrimoniously dispute the moral permissibility of a new overseas investment. The conflict might appear to involve some fundamental clash of moral principles and perspectives and yet, in fact, be the result of some underlying disagreement about what effects the proposed investment will have on the lives of the local population. Until this factual disagreement is acknowledged and dealt with, little is apt to be resolved.

Second, once there is general agreement on factual matters, try to spell out the moral principles to which different people are, at least implicitly, appealing. Seeking to determine these principles will often help people clarify their own thinking enough to reach a solution. Sometimes they will agree on what moral principles are relevant and yet disagree over how to balance them; identifying this discrepancy can itself be useful. Bear in mind, too, that skepticism is in order when someone's moral stance on an issue appears to rest simply on a hunch or intuition and cannot be related to some more general moral principle. As moral decision makers, we are seeking not just an answer to a moral issue but an answer that can be publicly defended, and the public defense of a moral judgment usually requires an appeal to general principle. By analogy, judges do not hand down judgments based simply on what strikes them as fair in a particular case. They must relate their decisions to general legal principles or statutes.

A reluctance to defend our moral decisions in public is almost always a warning sign. If we are unwilling to account for our actions publicly, chances are that we are doing something we cannot really justify morally. In addition, Kant's point that we must be willing to universalize our moral judgments is relevant here. We cannot sincerely endorse a principle if we are not willing to see it applied generally. Unfortunately, we occasionally do make judgments—for example, that Alfred's being late to work is a satisfactory reason for firing him—that rest on a principle we would be unwilling to apply to our own situations; hence, the moral relevance of the familiar question: "How would you like it if . . . ?" Looking at an issue from the other person's point of view can cure moral myopia.

Obligations, Ideals, Effects

As a practical basis for discussing moral issues in organizations, it is useful to try to approach those issues in a way that is acceptable to individuals of diverse moral viewpoints. We want to avoid as much as possible presupposing the truth of one particular theoretical perspective. By emphasizing factors that are relevant to various theories, both consequentialist and nonconsequentialist, we can find some common ground on which moral decision making can proceed. Moral dialogue can thus take place in an objective and analytical way, even if the participants do not fully agree on all philosophical issues.

What concerns, then, seem common to most ethical systems? Following Professor V. R. Ruggiero, three common concerns suggest themselves.[17] A first concern is with *obligations.* Every significant human action—personal and professional—arises in the context of human relationships. These relationships can be the source of specific duties and rights. In addition, we are obligated to respect people's human rights. Obligations bind us. In their presence, morality requires us, at least prima facie, to do certain things and to avoid doing others.

A second concern common to most ethical systems is the impact of our actions on important *ideals.* An ideal is some morally important goal, virtue, or notion of excellence worth striving for. Clearly, different cultures impart different ideals and, equally important, different ways of pursuing them. Our culture respects virtues like tolerance, compassion, and loyalty, as well as more abstract ideals like peace, justice, fairness, and respect for persons. In addition to these moral ideals, there are institutional or organizational ideals: efficiency, productivity, quality, customer service, and so forth. Does a particular act serve or violate these ideals? Both consequentialists and nonconsequentialists can agree that this is an important concern in determining the moral quality of actions.

A third common consideration regards the *effects* of actions. When reflecting on a possible course of action, one needs to take into account its likely results. Although nonconsequentialists maintain that things other than consequences or results can affect the rightness or wrongness of actions, few if any of them would ignore consequences entirely. Almost all nonconsequentialist theories place some moral weight on the results of our actions.

Ruggiero isolated, then, three concerns common to almost all ethical systems: obligations, ideals, and effects. In so doing he provided a kind of practical synthesis of consequentialist and nonconsequentialist thought that seems appropriate for our purposes. A useful approach to moral questions in an organizational context will therefore reflect these considerations: the obligations that derive from organizational relationships or are affected by organizational conduct, the ideals at stake, and the effects or consequences of alternative courses of action. Any action that honors obligations while respecting ideals and benefiting people can be presumed to be moral. An action that does not pass scrutiny in these respects will be morally suspect.

This view leads to what is essentially a two-step procedure for evaluating actions and choices. The first step is to identify the important considerations involved: obligations, ideals, and effects. Accordingly, we should ask if any basic obligations are involved. If so, what are they and who has them? What ideals does the action respect or promote? What ideals does it neglect or thwart? Who is affected by the action and how? How do these effects compare with those of the alternatives open to us? The second step is to decide which of these considerations deserves emphasis. Sometimes the issue may be largely a matter of obligations; other times, some ideal may predominate; still other times, consideration of effects may be the overriding concern.

Keep the following rough guidelines in mind when handling cases of conflicting obligations, ideals, and effects:

1. When two or more moral obligations conflict, choose the stronger one.
2. When two or more ideals conflict, or when ideals conflict with obligations, honor the more important one.
3. When rival actions will have different results, choose the action that produces the greater good or the lesser harm.

These guidelines imply that we know (1) which one of the conflicting obligations is greater, (2) which of the competing ideals is higher, and (3) which of the actions will achieve the greater good or the lesser harm. They also suggest that we have some definite way of balancing obligations, ideals, and effects when these considerations pull in different directions.

The fact is that we have no sure procedure for making such comparative determinations, which involve assessing worth and assigning relative priorities to our assessments. In large part, the chapters that follow attempt to sort out the values and principles embedded in the tangled web of frequently subtle, ill-defined problems we meet in business and organizational life. It is hoped that examining these issues will help you (1) identify the obligations, ideals, and effects involved in specific moral issues and (2) decide where the emphasis should lie among the competing considerations.

SUMMARY

1. Consequentialist moral theories see the moral rightness or wrongness of actions as a function of their results. If the consequences are good, the action is right; if they are bad, the action is wrong. Nonconsequentialist theories see other factors as also relevant to the determination of right and wrong.

2. Egoism is the consequentialist theory that an action is right when it promotes the individual's best interests. Proponents of this theory base their view on the alleged fact that human beings are, by nature, selfish (the doctrine of psychological egoism). Critics of egoism argue that (a) psychological egoism is implausible, (b) egoism is not really a moral principle, and (c) egoism ignores blatant wrongs.

3. Utilitarianism, another consequentialist theory, maintains that the morally right action is the one that provides the greatest happiness for all those affected. In an organizational context, utilitarianism provides an objective way to resolve conflicts of self-interest and encourages a realistic and result-oriented approach to moral decision making. But critics contend that (a) utilitarianism is not really workable, (b) some actions are wrong even if they produce good results, and (c) utilitarianism incorrectly overlooks considerations of justice and the distribution of happiness.

4. Kant's theory is an important example of a purely nonconsequentialist approach to ethics. Kant held that only when we act from duty does our action have moral worth. Good will is the only thing that is good in itself.

5. Kant's categorical imperative states that an action is morally right if and only if we can will that the maxim (or principle) represented by the action be a universal law. For example, a person making a promise with no intention of keeping it cannot universalize the maxim governing his action, because if everyone followed this principle, promising would make no sense. Kant believed that the categorical imperative is binding on all rational creatures, regardless of their specific goals or desires and regardless of the consequences.

6. There are two alternative formulations of the categorical imperative. The first is that an act is right only if the actor would be willing to be so treated if the positions of the parties were reversed. The second is that one must always act so as to treat other people as ends, never merely as means.

7. Kant's ethics gives us firm standards that do not depend on results; it injects a humanistic element into moral decision making and stresses the importance of acting on principle and from a sense of duty. Critics, however, worry that (a) Kant's view of moral worth is too restrictive, (b) the categorical imperative is not a sufficient test of right and wrong, and (c) distinguishing between treating people as means and respecting them as ends in themselves may be difficult in practice.

8. Other nonconsequentialist theories stress other moral themes. Philosophers such as Ross argue, against both Kant and consequentialists, that we are under a variety of distinct moral obligations. These are prima facie, meaning that any one of them may be outweighed in some circumstances by other, more important moral considerations. Nonconsequentialists believe that a duty to assist others and to promote total happiness is only one of a number of duties incumbent on us.

9. Nonconsequentialists typically emphasize moral rights—entitlements to act in a certain way or to have others act in a certain way. These rights can rest on special relationships and roles, or they can be general human rights. Rights can be negative, protecting us from outside interference, or they can be positive, requiring others to provide us with certain benefits or opportunities.

10. In an organizational context, nonconsequentialism (in its non-Kantian forms) stresses the plurality of moral considerations to be weighed. While emphasizing the importance of respecting moral rights, it acknowledges that morality has limits and that organizations have legitimate goals to pursue. Critics question whether (a) nonconsequentialist principles are adequately justified and whether (b) nonconsequentialism can satisfactorily handle conflicting rights and principles.

11. Rule utilitarianism is a hybrid theory. It maintains that the proper principles of right and wrong are those that would maximize happiness if society adopted them. Thus, the utilitarian standard does not apply directly to individual actions but rather to the adoption of the moral principles that guide individual action. Rule utilitarianism avoids many of the standard criticisms of act utilitarianism.

12. Despite disagreements on controversial theoretical issues, people can make significant progress in resolving practical moral problems through open-minded and reflective discussion. One useful approach is to identify the (possibly conflicting) obligations, ideals, and effects in a given situation and then to identify where the emphasis should lie among these different considerations.

CASE 2.1

The Ford Pinto

There was a time when the "made in Japan" label brought a predictable smirk of superiority to the face of most Americans. The quality of most Japanese products usually was as low as their price. In fact, few imports could match their domestic counterparts, the proud products of Yankee know-how. But by the late 1960s, an invasion of foreign-made goods chiseled a few worry lines into the countenance of U.S. industry. In Detroit, worry was fast fading to panic as the Japanese, not to mention the Germans, began to gobble up more and more of the subcompact auto market.

Never one to take a back seat to the competition, Ford Motor Company decided to meet the threat from abroad head-on. In 1968, Ford executives decided to produce the Pinto. Known inside the company as "Lee's car," after Ford president Lee Iacocca, the Pinto was to weigh no more than 2,000 pounds and cost no more than $2,000.[18]

Eager to have its subcompact ready for the 1971 model year, Ford decided to compress the normal drafting-board-to-showroom time of about three-and-a-half years into two. The compressed schedule meant that any design changes typically made before production-line tooling would have to be made during it.

Before producing the Pinto, Ford crash-tested various prototypes, in part to learn whether they met a safety standard proposed by the National Highway Traffic Safety Administration (NHTSA) to reduce fires from traffic collisions. This standard would have required that by 1972 all new autos be able to withstand a rear-end impact of 20 mph without fuel loss, and that by 1973 they be able to withstand an impact of 30 mph. The prototypes all failed the 20-mph test. In 1970 Ford crash-tested the Pinto itself, and the result was the same: ruptured gas tanks and dangerous leaks. The only Pintos to pass the test had been modified in some way—for example, with a rubber bladder in the gas tank or a piece of steel between the tank and the rear bumper.

Thus, Ford knew that the Pinto represented a serious fire hazard when struck from the rear, even in low-speed collisions. Ford officials faced a decision. Should they go ahead with the existing design, thereby meeting the production timetable but possibly jeopardizing consumer safety? Or should they delay production of the Pinto by redesigning the gas tank to make it safer and thus concede another year of subcompact dominance to foreign companies? Ford not only pushed ahead with the original design but stuck to it for the next six years.

What explains Ford's decision? The evidence suggests that Ford relied, at least in part, on cost-benefit reasoning, which is an analysis in monetary terms of the expected costs and benefits of doing something. There were various ways of making the Pinto's gas tank safer. Although the estimated price of these safety improvements ranged from only $5 to $8 per vehicle, Ford evidently reasoned that the increased cost outweighed the benefits of a new tank design.

How exactly did Ford reach that conclusion? We don't know for sure, but an internal report, "Fatalities Associated with Crash-Induced Fuel Leakage and Fires," reveals the cost-benefit reasoning that the company used in cases like this. This report was not written with the Pinto in mind; rather, it concerns fuel leakage in rollover accidents (not rear-end collisions), and its computations applied to all Ford vehicles, not just the Pinto. Nevertheless, it illustrates the type of reasoning that was probably used in the Pinto case.

In the "Fatalities" report, Ford engineers estimated the cost of technical improvements that would prevent gas tanks from leaking in rollover accidents to be $11 per vehicle. The authors go on to discuss various estimates of the number of people killed by fires from car rollovers before settling on the relatively low figure of 180 deaths per year. But given that number, how can the value of those individuals' lives be gauged? Can a dollars-and-cents figure be assigned to a human being? NHTSA thought so. In 1972, it estimated that society loses $200,725 every time a person is killed in an auto accident (adjusted for inflation, today's figure would, of course, be considerably higher). It broke down the costs as follows:

Future productivity losses	
Direct	$132,000
Indirect	41,300
Medical costs	
Hospital	700
Other	425
Property damage	1,500
Insurance administration	4,700
Legal and court expenses	3,000
Employer losses	1,000
Victim's pain and suffering	10,000
Funeral	900
Assets (lost consumption)	5,000
Miscellaneous accident costs	200
Total per fatality	$200,725

Putting the NHTSA figures together with other statistical studies, the Ford report arrives at the following overall assessment of costs and benefits:

Benefits

Savings:	180 burn deaths, 180 serious burn injuries, 2,100 burned vehicles
Unit cost:	$200,000 per death, $67,000 per injury, $700 per vehicle
Total benefit:	$(180 \times \$200,000) + (180 \times \$67,000) + (2,100 \times \$700) = \$49.5$ million

Costs

Sales: 11 million cars, 1.5 million light trucks
Unit cost: $11 per car, $11 per truck
Total cost: 12.5 million × $11 = $137.5 million

Thus, the costs of the suggested safety improvements outweigh their benefits, and the "Fatalities" report accordingly recommends against any improvements—a recommendation that Ford followed.

Likewise in the Pinto case, Ford's management, whatever its exact reasoning, decided to stick with the original design and not upgrade the Pinto's fuel tank, despite the test results reported by its engineers. Here is the aftermath of Ford's decision:

- Between 1971 and 1978, the Pinto was responsible for a number of fire-related deaths. Ford puts the figure at 23; its critics say the figure is closer to 500. According to the sworn testimony of Ford engineers, 95 percent of the fatalities would have survived if Ford had located the fuel tank over the axle (as it had done on its Capri automobiles).

- NHTSA finally adopted a 30-mph collision standard in 1976. The Pinto then acquired a rupture-proof fuel tank. In 1978 Ford was obliged to recall all 1971–1976 Pintos for fuel-tank modifications.

- Between 1971 and 1978, approximately fifty lawsuits were brought against Ford in connection with rear-end accidents in the Pinto. In the Richard Grimshaw case, in addition to awarding over $3 million in compensatory damages to the victims of a Pinto crash, the jury awarded a landmark $125 million in punitive damages against Ford. The judge reduced punitive damages to $3.5 million.

- On August 10, 1978, eighteen-year-old Judy Ulrich, her sixteen-year-old sister Lynn, and their eighteen-year-old cousin Donna, in their 1973 Ford Pinto, were struck from the rear by a van near Elkhart, Indiana. The gas tank of the Pinto exploded on impact. In the fire that resulted, the three teenagers were burned to death. Ford was charged with criminal homicide. The judge in the case advised jurors that Ford should be convicted if it had clearly disregarded the harm that might result from its actions, and that disregard represented a substantial deviation from acceptable standards of conduct. On March 13, 1980, the jury found Ford not guilty of criminal homicide.

For its part, Ford has always denied that the Pinto is unsafe compared with other cars of its type and era. The company also points out that in every model year the Pinto met or surpassed the government's own standards. But what the company doesn't say is that successful lobbying by it and its industry associates was responsible for delaying for seven years the adoption of any NHTSA crash standard. Furthermore, Ford's critics claim that there were more than forty European and Japanese models in the Pinto price and weight range with safer gas-tank position. "Ford made an extremely irresponsible decision," concludes auto safety expert Byron Bloch, "when they placed such a weak tank in such a ridiculous location in such a soft rear end."

Has the automobile industry learned a lesson from Ford's experience with the Pinto? Some observers thought not when, in February 1993, an Atlanta jury held the General Motors Corporation responsible for the death of a Georgia teenager in the fiery crash of one of its pickup trucks. At the trial, General Motors contended in its defense that when a drunk driver struck seventeen-year-old Shannon Moseley's truck in the side, it was the impact of the high-speed crash that killed Moseley. However, the jury was persuaded that Moseley survived the collision only to be consumed by a fire caused by his truck's defective fuel-tank design. Finding that the company had known that its "side-saddle" gas tanks, which are mounted outside the rails of the truck's frame, are dangerously prone to rupture, the jury awarded $4.2 million in actual damages and $101 million in punitive damages to Moseley's parents.

What undoubtedly swayed the jury was the testimony of former GM safety engineer Ronald E. Elwell. Although Elwell had testified in more than fifteen previous cases that the pickups were safe, this time he switched sides and told the jury that the company had known for years that the side-saddle design was defective but had intentionally hidden its knowledge and had not attempted to correct the problem. At the trial, company officials attempted to paint Elwell as a disgruntled employee, but his testimony was supported by videotapes of General Motors' own crash tests. After the verdict, General Motors said that it still stood behind the safety of its trucks and contended "that a full examination by the National Highway Traffic Safety Administration of the technical issues in this matter will bear out our contention that the . . . pickup trucks do not have a safety related defect."

Since then, however, the Department of Transportation has determined that GM pickups of the style Shannon Moseley drove do pose a fire hazard and that they are more prone than competitors' pickups to catch fire when struck from the side. Still, GM has rejected requests to recall the pickups and repair them. Meanwhile, the Georgia Court of Appeals threw out the jury's verdict in the Shannon Moseley case on a legal technicality—despite ruling that the evidence submitted in the case showed that GM was aware that the gas tanks were hazardous but did not try to make them safer to save the expense involved.

Discussion Questions

1. What moral issues does the Pinto case raise?

2. Suppose Ford officials were asked to justify their decision. What moral principles do you think they would invoke? Assess Ford's handling of the Pinto from the perspective of each of the moral theories discussed in this chapter.

3. Utilitarians would say that jeopardizing motorists does not by itself make Ford's action morally objectionable. The only morally relevant matter is whether Ford gave equal consideration to the interests of each affected party. Do you think Ford did this?

4. Is cost-benefit analysis a legitimate tool? What role, if any, should it play in moral deliberation? Critically assess the example of cost-benefit analysis given in the case study. Is there anything unsatisfactory about it? Could it have been improved upon in some way?

5. Speculate about Kant's response to the NHTSA's placing a monetary value on a human life.

6. What responsibilities to its customers do you think Ford had? What are the most important moral rights, if any, operating in the Pinto case?

7. Would it have made a moral difference if the savings resulting from not improving the Pinto gas tank had been passed on to Ford's customers? Could a rational customer have chosen to save a few dollars and risk having the more dangerous gas tank? What if Ford had told potential customers about its decision?

8. Is it wrong for business to sell a product that is not as safe as it could be, given current technology? Is it wrong to sell a product that is less safe than competing products on the market?

9. The maxim of Ford's action might be stated: "When it would cost more to make a safety improvement than not, it's all right not to make it." Can this maxim be universalized? Does it treat humans as ends in themselves? Would manufacturers be willing to abide by it if the positions were reversed and they were in the role of consumers?

10. Should Ford have been found guilty of criminal homicide in the Ulrich case?

11. Was GM responsible for Shannon Moseley's death? Compare that case with Ford and the Pinto.

CASE 2.2

Blood for Sale

Sol Levin was a successful stockbroker in Tampa, Florida, when he recognized the potentially profitable market for safe and uncontaminated blood and, with some colleagues, founded Plasma International. Not everybody is willing to make money by selling his or her own blood, and in the beginning Plasma International bought blood from people addicted to drugs and alcohol. Although innovative marketing increased Plasma International's sales dramatically, several cases of hepatitis were reported in recipients. The company then began looking for new sources of blood.[19]

Plasma International searched worldwide and, with the advice of a qualified team of medical consultants, did extensive testing. Eventually they found that the blood profiles of several rural West African tribes made them ideal prospective donors. After negotiations with the local government, Plasma International signed an agreement with several tribal chieftains to purchase blood.

Business went smoothly and profitably for Plasma International until a Tampa paper charged that Plasma was purchasing blood for as little as fifteen cents a pint and then reselling it to hospitals in the United States and South America for $25 per pint. In one recent disaster, the newspaper alleged, Plasma International had sold 10,000 pints, netting nearly a quarter of a million dollars.

The newspaper story stirred up controversy in Tampa, but the existence of commercialized blood marketing systems in the United States is nothing new. Approximately half the blood and plasma obtained in the United States is bought and sold like any other commodity. About 40 percent is given to avoid having to pay for blood received or to build up credit so blood will be available without charge if the donor needs it. By contrast, the National Health Service in Great Britain relies entirely on a voluntary system of blood donation. Blood is neither bought nor sold. It is available to anyone who needs it without charge or obligation, and donors gain no preference over nondonors.

In an important study, economist Richard Titmuss showed that the British system works better than the American one in terms of economic and administrative efficiency, price, and blood quality. The commercialized blood market, Titmuss argued, is wasteful of blood and plagued by shortages. In the United States, bureaucratization, paperwork, and administrative overhead result in a cost per unit of blood that is five to fifteen times higher than in Great Britain. Hemophiliacs, in particular, are disadvantaged by the U.S. system and have enormous bills to pay. In addition, commercial markets are much more likely to distribute contaminated blood.

Titmuss also argued that the existence of a commercialized system discourages voluntary donors. People are less apt to give blood if they know that others are selling it. Philosopher Peter Singer has elaborated on this point:

> If blood is a commodity with a price, to give blood means merely to save someone money. Blood has a cash value of a certain number of dollars, and the importance of the gift will vary with the wealth of the recipient. If blood cannot be bought, however, the gift's value depends upon the need of the recipient. Often, it will be worth life itself. Under these circumstances blood becomes a very special kind of gift, and giving it means providing for strangers, without hope of reward, something they cannot buy and without which they may die. The gift relates strangers in a manner that is not possible when blood is a commodity.
>
> This may sound like a philosopher's abstraction, far removed from the thoughts of ordinary people. On the contrary, it is an idea spontaneously expressed by British donors in response to Titmuss's questionnaire. As one woman, a machine operator, wrote in reply to the question why she first decided to become a blood donor: "You can't get blood from supermarkets and chain stores. People themselves must come forward; sick people can't get out of bed to ask you for a pint to save their life, so I came forward in hopes to help somebody who needs blood."
>
> The implication of this answer, and others like it, is that even if the formal right to give blood can coexist with commercialized blood banks, the respondent's action would have lost much of its significance to her, and the blood would probably not have been given at all. When blood is a commodity, and can be purchased if it is not given, altruism becomes unnecessary, and so loosens the bonds that can otherwise exist between strangers in a community. The existence of a market in blood does not threaten the formal right to give blood, but it does away with the right to give blood which cannot be bought, has no cash value, and must be given freely if it is to be obtained at all. If there is such a right, it is incompatible with the right to sell blood, and we cannot avoid violating one of these rights when we grant the other.[20]

Both Titmuss and Singer believe that the weakening of the spirit of altruism in this sphere has important repercussions. It marks, they think, the increasing commercialization of our lives and makes similar changes in attitude, motive, and relationships more likely in other fields.

Discussion Questions

1. Is Sol Levin running a business "just like any other business," or is his company open to moral criticism? Defend your answer by appeal to moral principle.
2. What are the contrasting ideals of the British and U.S. blood systems? Which system, in your opinion, best promotes human freedom and respect for people?
3. Examine the pros and cons of commercial transactions in blood from the egoistic, the utilitarian, and the Kantian perspectives.
4. Are Titmuss and Singer right to suggest that the buying and selling of blood reduces altruism? Does knowing that you can sell your blood (and that others are selling theirs)

make you less inclined to donate your blood? Do we have a right to give blood that cannot be bought?

5. Many believe that commercialization is increasing in all areas of modern life. If this is so, is it something to be applauded or condemned? Is it wrong to treat certain things—such as human organs—as commodities?

6. Did Plasma International strike a fair bargain with the West Africans who supplied their blood to the company? Or is Plasma guilty of exploiting them in some way? Explain your answer.

7. Do you believe that we have a moral duty to donate blood? If so, why and under what circumstances? If not, why not?

Notes

1. Bernard Williams, *Ethics and the Limits of Philosophy* (Cambridge, Mass.: Harvard University Press, 1985), 16.

2. Richard B. Brandt, "Toward a Credible Form of Utilitarianism," in Hector-Neri Castañeda and George Nakhnikian, eds., *Morality and the Language of Conduct* (Detroit: Wayne State University Press, 1963), 109–110.

3. A. C. Ewing, *Ethics* (New York: Free Press, 1965), 40.

4. Molly Moore, "Did the Experts Really Approve the 'Brown Lung' Experiment?" *Washington Post National Weekly Edition,* June 4, 1984, 31.

5. Adam Smith, *The Wealth of Nations* (New York: Modern Library, 1985), 223–225.

6. Tom L. Beauchamp and Norman E. Bowie, eds., *Ethical Theory and Business,* 6th ed. (Upper Saddle River, N.J.: Prentice Hall, 2001), 16.

7. Immanuel Kant, *Grounding for the Metaphysics of Morals* (Indianapolis: Hackett, 1988), 30–31 (translation modified).

8. Kurt Eichenwald, "Commissions Are Many, Profits Few," *New York Times,* May 24, 1993, C1.

9. See, in particular, W. D. Ross, *The Right and the Good* (London: Oxford University Press, 1930).

10. Immanuel Kant, *Practical Philosophy,* ed. M. J. Gregor (Cambridge: Cambridge University Press, 1996), 611–615.

11. Ross, *The Right and the Good,* 21.

12. Ibid., 30.

13. Ibid., 31.

14. Richard B. Brandt, "The Real and Alleged Problems of Utilitarianism," *Hastings Center Report,* April 1983, 38.

15. Ibid., 42.

16. Ibid., 42.

17. Vincent Ryan Ruggiero, *The Moral Imperative* (Port Washington, N.Y.: Alfred Publishers, 1973).

18. This case study is based on Douglas Birsch and John H. Fielder, eds., *The Ford Pinto Case* (Albany, N.Y.: State University of New York Press, 1994); "G.M. Is Held Liable Over Fuel Tanks in Pickup Trucks," *New York Times,* February 5, 1993, A1; and "Federal Study Finds Danger of Fire in G.M. Pickup Trucks," *New York Times,* October 18, 1994, A1.

19. This and the following three paragraphs are based on a case created by T. W. Zimmerer and P. L. Preston in R. D. Hay, E. R. Gray, and J. E. Gates, eds., *Business and Society* (Cincinnati: South-Western, 1976). The remainder of the case draws on Peter Singer, "Rights and the Market," in John Arthur and William H. Shaw, eds., *Justice and Economic Distribution,* 2nd ed. (Englewood Cliffs, N.J.: Prentice Hall, 1991), and Richard M. Titmuss, *The Gift Relationship* (London: George Allen & Unwin, 1972).

20. Singer, "Rights and the Market." Reprinted by permission of the author. See also "Blood Donation—Altruism or Profit?" *British Medical Journal,* May 4, 1996, 1114.

Further Reading for Chapter 2

Tom L. Beauchamp, *Philosophical Ethics*, 3rd ed. (New York: McGraw-Hill, 2001) is an introductory text with selected readings covering classical ethical theories, rights, and the nature of morality.

William H. Shaw, *Contemporary Ethics: Taking Account of Utilitarianism* (Oxford: Blackwell, 1999) sympathetically examines the utilitarian approach to ethics.

Peter Singer, ed., *A Companion to Ethics* (Oxford: Blackwell, 1991) is a comprehensive reference work with survey essays by many individual authors.

Christina Hoff Sommers, ed., *Right and Wrong* (New York: Harcourt Brace Jovanovich, 1986), **Judith A. Boss**, ed., *Perspectives on Ethics,* 2nd ed. (New York: McGraw-Hill, 2003), and **Mark Timmons**, ed., *Conduct and Character*, 4th ed. (Belmont, Calif.: Wadsworth, 2003) provide good selections of readings on egoism, relativism, utilitarianism, Kantianism, and other normative theories.

(See also the readings suggested at the end of Chapter 1.)

InfoTrac College Edition: For further
information or to conduct research,
please go to www.infotrac-college.com.

3

Justice and Economic Distribution

It seems strange to recall that until the early years of the twentieth century, there was no federal tax on personal income. Only with the passing of the Sixteenth Amendment to the U.S. Constitution in 1913 was Congress granted the right to collect tax on the income of its citizens. Since then, the income tax laws have grown enormously complex. Lawyers study for years to master the intricacies of the system, and most people with middle incomes or better require professional assistance to file their annual tax forms. Because the tax rules do so much to shape the character of our economy and the distribution of income and wealth across the country, their fairness is something that concerns most Americans.

Fairness was a theme when both George Bush and his Democratic opponent, Al Gore, campaigned for president in 2000 by promising tax reductions. And, indeed, one of the first things President Bush did, once in office, was to push a sheaf of income tax cuts through Congress. True, his predecessor, Bill Clinton, had raised the federal income tax, but only on individuals with a taxable income over $115,000. They saw their income tax rate increase from 31 percent to 36 percent. Clinton also slapped a 10 percent surcharge on those with incomes above $240,000. However, until Ronald Reagan lowered it, the tax rate for the wealthiest individuals had been 63 percent (indeed, until 1960 it had been 91 percent). When President Reagan reduced taxes on the wealthy, he also eliminated some important tax loopholes. But the most significant feature of his tax policy was its rejection of the principle of "progressivity"—namely, that the wealthy ought to pay taxes at a higher rate than the poor.

Although recent tax cuts mostly benefit the well-to-do, our wealthier citizens still, of course, pay the bulk of the nation's income taxes—for the simple reason that most of the nation's income goes to them. Indeed, in recent years wealthier Americans have been getting more and more, as the distribution of national income has grown increasingly unequal. Since 1977, after-tax incomes for the bottom 60 percent of Americans have declined 12 percent, while the top 1 percent have seen their incomes double.[1]

The disproportionate gains of the well-to-do mean that they are getting a larger share of the pie than before. According to the U.S. Census Bureau, as Table 3.1 shows, over recent decades the nation's total income has been getting divided in an increasingly unequal way, with those who are already very well off securing a steadily growing share of aggregate family income. The flip side, of course, is that the bottom 60 percent are now receiving a smaller share than before.

Table 3.1 Share of Aggregate Family Income[2]

	1970	1980	1990	2001
Best-off fifth	40.9%	41.1%	44.3%	47.7%
Second fifth	23.8%	24.4%	23.8%	22.9%
Middle fifth	17.6%	17.6%	16.6%	15.4%
Fourth fifth	12.2%	11.6%	10.8%	9.7%
Poorest fifth	5.4%	5.3%	4.6%	4.2%
Top 5%	15.6%	14.6%	17.4%	21.0%

The gap between the wealthiest 10 percent and the poorest 10 percent is greater in the United States than in any industrialized country except Russia.[3] Moreover, for the last three decades, median family income, measured in constant dollars, has gone up only because wives are working more than before. Although real wages for production and nonsupervisory workers grew by 75 percent from 1947 to 1973, since then wages have declined and remain below their 1973 peak.[4]

By contrast, middle-level managers have fared much better, and top executives have done spectacularly well. In 2003 *Business Week*'s annual survey of the two highest-paid executives at America's largest companies showed their average total pay (salary, bonuses, and long-term compensation) to be $7.4 million. Among the highest paid were Orin Smith of Starbucks and Millard Drexler of GAP, who took home $38.8 million and $91 million, respectively. But even their pay appears modest compared to the $194.9 million that Alfred Lerner of MBNA received, not to mention the whopping $705.1 million pocketed the year before by Lawrence Ellison of Oracle, which broke all previous records for CEO compensation.[5]

The United States leads the world in executive pay.[6] Japan's CEOs, for example, earn a salary of only $300,000 to $500,000 a year, with far fewer bonuses and stock options than their American counterparts.[7] As a result of the stock market slump, average pay for American CEOs has declined slightly since 2000. Nevertheless, since 1980 the compensation of CEOs has grown from 40 times that of the average worker to 400 times greater.[8] The median weekly salary for all workers is $610.[9] If the average CEO works 60 hours a week, 52 weeks a year, then he or she earns that much every 15 minutes. Since 1990, CEO pay has gone up 571 percent. In comparison, corporate profits have grown by a relatively modest 114 percent, and the average worker's pay by a mere 37 percent (which is just above inflation at 32 percent).[10] A schoolteacher who made $31,166 in 1990 would now make $177,958 if teachers' salaries had grown at the same rate as CEO pay.

Our well-heeled CEOs symbolize the well-documented increase in income inequality in the United States. This chapter will not speculate on the causes of this income shift, but we can see the evidence of it all around us—for example, in corporate America's two-tiered marketing. Instead of aiming their products and services at a mass middle-class market, companies must now position their offerings as either upscale or down-scale, tailoring them either to affluent professionals or to low-wage earners.[11] Our economy has created millions of new jobs in the last twenty years, but these have been predominantly in low-income sectors of the economy, such as the fast-food industry. Good, well-paying middle-income jobs—especially in industries such as steel, auto-motives, and machine tools—are scarcer than ever. More and more families require two incomes just to get by; those with only one income frequently find themselves unable to sustain a middle-class lifestyle.

Not only is income inequality increasing in our society and the middle class shrink-ing (from 61 percent of families in 1969 to 50 percent today), but also workers at the bottom are less likely to move up in their lifetimes. The United States has always prided itself on being a land of opportunity and upward mobility, but recent evidence suggests that the economy is becoming more rigid and class bound. "You can't take solace any-more in the American dream of working hard and migrating up through society," says William J. McDonough, president of the Federal Reserve Bank of New York. In fact, today there is significantly less upward mobility for low-wage earners in the United States than there is in Europe.[12]

These trends are even more alarming when set against the background of the extremely unequal distribution of wealth in this country. Not only do the top 1 percent receive a disproportionate share of the total income, but they already own nearly 40 per-cent of the nation's total net worth—more than is owned by the entire bottom 90 per-cent of U.S. households. This economic elite own half of all stocks, mutual funds, financial securities, and trusts, two-thirds of all business equity, and 36 percent of non-residential real estate.[13] In contrast, the bottom 60 percent of Americans owns only 5 percent of the nation's wealth, and the lowest 40 percent less than 1 percent.[14]

There is nothing inevitable about such great inequalities in income and wealth. The distribution of income in Japan and Germany is far more equal than in the United States, and both nations are just as thoroughly capitalist as we are. In fact, the United States is the most unequal industrialized nation in the world in terms of income and wealth.[15] Although it has the highest child poverty rate of any industrial country, with more than 21 percent of its children growing up poor, the United States chooses to spend only 0.6 percent of its gross national product on basic income support for children; Canada spends 1.6 percent.[16] Inequality of income is not some brute fact of nature, even in market-oriented societies. Rather, political choices determine how income is ultimately distributed. How much inequality a society is willing to accept reflects both its moral values and the relative strength of its contending social and political forces.

Arguments can be made for and against different degrees of income inequality, for and against progressivity in taxation, and for and against more specific tax regula-tions. But whatever one's position on these issues, it probably relies on some theory of economic justice for evaluating a particular tax regulation, the tax system as a whole, or even the society's economic system. The topic of economic justice deals with that con-stellation of moral issues raised by a society's distribution of wealth, income, status, and power.

Ethical questions arise daily about how wealth and goods should be allocated. Given the relative scarcity of a society's resources, deciding how these resources should be distributed is an important moral task. Should everyone receive roughly the same amount? Or should people be rewarded according to how hard they work or how much they contribute to society? To what extent should economic distribution take need into account? For example, with modern technology at their disposal, today's hospitals are able to perform life-prolonging feats of medicine that were undreamed of only a couple of decades ago, but these services are often extraordinarily costly. Who, then, should have access to them? Those who can afford them? Any who need them? Those who are most likely to benefit?

Chapter 2 discussed several basic moral theories and the general principles of right and wrong associated with them. This chapter focuses on the more specific topic of justice and economic distribution—that is, on the principles that are relevant to the moral assessment of society's distribution of economic goods and services. Although the topic is an abstract one, it is particularly relevant to the study of business ethics, because it concerns the moral standards to be used in evaluating the institutional frameworks within which both business and nonbusiness organizations operate. Specifically, this chapter will examine:

1. The concept of justice, its relation to fairness, equality, rights, and what people deserve, and some rival principles of economic distribution

2. The utilitarian approach to justice in general and economic justice in particular

3. The libertarian theory, which places a moral priority on liberty and free exchange

4. The contractarian and egalitarian theory of John Rawls

THE NATURE OF JUSTICE

Justice is an old concept with a rich history, a concept that is fundamental to any discussion of how society ought to be organized. Philosophical concern with justice goes back at least to ancient Greece. For Plato and some of his contemporaries, justice seems to have been the paramount virtue or, more precisely, the sum of virtue with regard to our relations with others. Philosophers today, however, generally distinguish justice from the whole of morality. The complaint that something is "unjust" is more specific than that it is "bad" or "immoral." What, then, makes an act, policy, or institution unjust? Unfortunately, the terms *just* and *unjust* are vague, and different people use them in different ways. Still, talk of justice or injustice typically focuses on at least one of several related ideas—fairness, equality, desert, or rights.

First, justice is often used to mean *fairness*. Justice frequently concerns the fair treatment of members of groups of people or else looks backwards to the fair compensation of prior injuries. Exactly what fairness requires is difficult to say, and different standards may be pertinent in different cases. If corporate manager Smith commits bribery, he is justly punished under our laws. If other managers commit equally serious crimes but are allowed to escape punishment, then Smith suffers a comparative injustice because he was unfairly singled out. On the other hand, Smith and other white-collar criminals are treated unfairly and thus unjustly, although this time for the opposite reason, if stiffer sentences are meted out to common criminals for less grave offenses.

One way unfairness creates injustice is when like cases are not treated in the same fashion. Following Aristotle, most philosophers believe that we are required, as a formal

priniciple of justice, to treat similar cases alike except where there is some relevant difference. This principle emphasizes the role of impartiality and consistency in justice,
but it is a purely formal principle because it is silent about which differences are relevant
and which are not. Furthermore, satisfying this formal requirement does not guarantee that justice is done. For example, a judge who treats similar cases alike can succeed
in administering fairly and nonarbitrarily a law that is itself unjust (like a statute requiring racial segregation).

Related to Aristotle's fairness requirement is a second idea commonly bound up
with the concept of justice, namely, that of *equality*. Justice is frequently held to require
that our treatment of people reflect their fundamental moral equality. While Aristotle's
formal principle of justice does not say whether we are to assume equality of treatment
until some difference between cases is shown or to assume the opposite until some relevant similarities are demonstrated, a claim of injustice based on equality is meant to
place the burden of proof on those who would endorse unequal treatment. Still, the
premise that all persons are equal does not establish a direct relationship between justice and economic distribution. We all believe that some differences in the treatment of
persons are consistent with equality (punishment, for example), and neither respect for
equality nor a commitment to equal treatment necessarily implies an equal distribution of economic goods.

Despite equality, then, individual circumstances—in particular, what a person has
done—make a difference. We think it is unjust, for example, when a guilty person goes
free or an innocent person hangs, regardless of how others have been treated. This
suggests that justice sometimes involves, as a third aspect, something in addition to
equal or impartial treatment. Justice also requires that people get what they *deserve* or,
as a number of ancient moralists put it, that each receive his or her due.

This is closely related to a fourth and final idea, namely, that one is treated unjustly
when one's moral *rights* are violated. John Stuart Mill, in fact, made this the defining
characteristic of injustice. In his view, what distinguishes injustice from other types of
wrongful behavior is that it involves a violation of the rights of some identifiable
person:

> Whether the injustice consists in depriving a person of a possession, or in break-
> ing faith with him, or in treating him worse than he deserves, or worse than other
> people who have no greater claims—in each case the supposition implies two
> things: a wrong done, and some assignable person who is wronged. . . . It seems
> to me that this feature in the case—a right in some person, correlative to the moral
> obligation—constitutes the specific difference between justice and generosity or
> beneficence. Justice implies something which it is not only right to do, and wrong
> not to do, but which some individual person can claim from us as a moral right.[17]

Rival Principles of Distribution

Justice, then, is an important subclass of morality in general, a subclass that generally involves appeals to the overlapping notions of fairness, equality, desert, and rights.
Turning to the topic of distributive justice—that is, to the proper distribution of social
benefits and burdens (in particular, economic benefits and burdens)—a number of rival
principles have been proposed. Among the principles most frequently recommended
as a basis of distribution are: to each an equal share, to each according to individual need,

to each according to personal effort, to each according to social contribution, and to each according to merit. Every one of these principles has its advocates, and each seems plausible in some circumstances. But only in some. There are problems with each. For example, if equality of income were guaranteed, then the lazy would receive as much as the industrious. On the other hand, effort is hard to measure and compare, and what one is able to contribute to society may depend on one's luck in being at the right place at the right time. And so on. No single principle seems to work in enough circumstances to be defended successfully as the sole principle of justice in distribution.

It often seems that we simply employ different principles of distributive justice in different circumstances. For example, corporations in certain industries may be granted tax breaks because of their social contribution; welfare programs operate on the basis of need; and business firms award promotions for meritorious performance. Moreover, multiple principles may often be relevant to a single situation. Sometimes they may pull in the same direction, as when wealthy professionals such as doctors defend their high incomes simultaneously on grounds of superior effort, merit, social contribution, and even (because of the high cost of malpractice insurance) need. Or the principles may pull in different directions, as when a teacher must balance effort against performance in assigning grades to pupils. Some philosophers are content to leave the situation here. As they see it, there are various equally valid, prima facie principles of just distribution—equality, need, effort, and so on—and one must try to find the principle that best applies in the given circumstances. If several principles seem to apply, then one must simply weigh them the best one can.

In his book *Spheres of Justice*, Michael Walzer pursues a more sophisticated version of this pluralistic approach.[18] Skeptical of the assumption that justice requires us to implement (in different contexts) some basic principle or set of principles, Walzer argues

> that different goods ought to be distributed for different reasons, in accordance with different procedures, by different agents; and that all these differences derive from different understandings of the social goods themselves—the inevitable product of historical and cultural particularism.[19]

Different norms and principles govern different distributive spheres, and these norms and principles are shaped by the implicit social meanings of the goods in question. He continues:

> Every social good or set of goods constitutes, as it were, a distributive sphere within which only certain criteria and arrangements are appropriate. Money is inappropriate in the sphere of ecclesiastical office. . . . There is no single standard [against which all distributions are to be measured]. But there are standards (roughly knowable even when they are also controversial) for every social good and every distributive sphere in every particular society.[20]

As Walzer sees it, distributive criteria are determined by the particular, historically shaped social meanings of the goods in question. The philosophical task is to tease out the inner logic of each type of good, thus revealing the tacit, socially shared values that govern (or should govern) its distribution.

Walzer's historically informed discussion of topics like medical care or dirty and degrading work are rich and intriguing, but his view implies that when it comes to issues of distributive justice, the best philosophers can do is to try to unravel the implicit, socially specific norms that govern the distribution of different goods in a particular society. Many contemporary philosophers disagree. They believe that we should step further back than Walzer does from existing norms and social arrangements and seek some general theory of justice in economic distribution, on the basis of which we can assess current social practices. Three such theories are the utilitarian, the libertarian, and the Rawlsian (egalitarian).

THE UTILITARIAN VIEW

For utilitarians, as Chapter 2 explained, happiness is the overarching value. Whether one assesses the rightness and wrongness of actions in terms of how much happiness they produce, as an act utilitarian does, or uses happiness as the standard for deciding what moral principles a society should accept as the basis for determining right and wrong, as a rule utilitarian does, happiness is the only thing that is good in and of itself. On that utilitarians are agreed.

Earlier we considered John Stuart Mill's idea that injustice involves the violation of the rights of some identifiable person. This is what distinguishes it from other types of immoral behavior. But if injustice involves the violation of moral rights, the question arises of how a utilitarian like Mill understands talk of rights. Mill's position was that saying I have a right to something is saying I have a valid claim on society to protect me in the possession of that thing, either by the force of law or through education and opinion. And I have that valid claim in the first place because society's protection of my possession of that thing is warranted on utilitarian grounds. "To have a right, then, is . . . to have something which society ought to defend me in the possession of. If the objector goes on to ask why it ought, I can give him no other reason than general utility."[21] What utilitarianism identifies as rights are certain moral rules, the observance of which is of the utmost importance for the long-run, overall maximization of happiness.

Accordingly, Mill summed up his view of justice as follows:

> Justice is a name for certain classes of moral rules which concern the essentials of human well-being more nearly, and are therefore of more absolute obligation, than any other rules for the guidance of life; and the notion which we have found to be of the essence of the idea of justice—that of a right residing in an individual—implies and testifies to this more binding obligation.
>
> The moral rules which forbid mankind to hurt one another (in which we must never forget to include wrongful interference with each other's freedom) are more vital to human well-being than any maxims, however important, which only point out the best mode of managing some department of human affairs.[22]

Although justice for Mill was ultimately a matter of promoting social well-being, not every issue of social utility was a matter of justice. The concept of justice identifies certain important social utilities, that is, certain rules or rights, the upholding of which is crucial for social well-being.

For utilitarians, then, justice is not an independent moral standard, distinct from their general principle. Rather, the maximization of happiness ultimately determines what is just and unjust. Critics of utilitarianism contend that knowing what will promote happiness is always difficult. People are bound to estimate consequences differently, thus making the standard of utility an inexact and unreliable principle for determining what is just. Mill, however, did not see much merit in this criticism. For one thing, it presupposes that we all agree about what the principles of justice are and how to apply them. This is far from the case, Mill argued. Indeed, without utilitarianism to provide a determinate standard of justice, one is always left with a plethora of competing principles, all of which seem to have some plausibility but are mutually incompatible.

As an example, Mill pointed to the conflict between two principles of justice that occurs in the realm of economic distribution. Is it just or not, he asked, that more talented workers should receive a greater remuneration? There are two possible answers to this question:

> On the negative side of the question it is argued that whoever does the best he can deserves equally well, and ought not in justice to be put in a position of inferiority for no fault of his own; that superior abilities have already advantages more than enough . . . without adding to these a superior share of the world's goods; and that society is bound in justice rather to make compensation to the less favored for this unmerited inequality of advantages than to aggravate it.[23]

This argument sounds plausible, but then so does the alternative answer:

> On the contrary side it is contended that society receives more from the more efficient laborer; that, his services being more useful, society owes him a larger return for them; that a greater share of the joint result is actually his work, and not to allow his claim to it is a kind of robbery; that, if he is only to receive as much as others, he can only be justly required to produce as much.[24]

Here we have two conflicting principles of justice. How are we to decide between them? The problem, Mill said, is that both principles seem plausible:

> Justice has in this case two sides to it, which it is impossible to bring into harmony, and the two disputants have chosen opposite sides; the one looks to what it is just that the individual should receive, the other to what it is just that the community should give.[25]

Each disputant is, from his or her own point of view, unanswerable. "Any choice between them, on grounds of justice," Mill continued, "must be perfectly arbitrary." What, then, is the solution? For Mill, the utilitarian, it was straightforward: "Social utility alone can decide the preference."[26] The utilitarian standard must be the ultimate court of appeal in such cases. Only the utilitarian standard can provide an intelligent and satisfactory way of handling controversial questions of justice and of resolving conflicts between two competing principles of justice.

Utilitarianism and Economic Distribution

The utilitarian theory of justice ties the question of economic distribution to the promotion of social well-being or happiness. Utilitarians want an economic system that will bring more good to society than any other system. But what system is that? Utilitarianism itself, as a normative theory, provides no answer. The answer depends on the relevant social, economic, and political facts. A utilitarian must understand the various possibilities, determine their consequences, and assess the available options. Obviously, this is not a simple task. Deciding what sort of economic arrangements would best promote human happiness requires the utilitarian to consider many things, including (1) the type of economic ownership (private, public, mixed); (2) the way of organizing production and distribution in general (pure laissez faire, markets with government planning and regulation, fully centralized planning); (3) the type of authority arrangements within the units of production (worker control versus managerial prerogative); (4) the range and character of material incentives; and (5) the nature and extent of social security and welfare provisions.

As a matter of historical fact, utilitarians in the early nineteenth century tended to favor free trade and the laissez-faire view of Adam Smith that unregulated market relations and free competition best promote the total social good.[27] Today it is probably fair to say that few, if any, utilitarians believe happiness would be maximized by a pure nineteenth-century-style capitalism, without any welfare arrangements. However, they are not in agreement on the question of what economic arrangements would in fact maximize happiness. Nonetheless, many utilitarians would favorably view increased worker participation in industrial life and more equal distribution of income.

Worker Participation   In his *Principles of Political Economy*, originally published in 1848, Mill argued for the desirability of breaking down the sharp and hostile division between the producers, or workers, on the one hand, and the capitalists, or owners, on the other. Not only would this be a good thing, it was also something that the advance of civilization was tending naturally to bring about: "The relation of masters and workpeople will be gradually superseded by partnership, in one or two forms: in some cases, association of the labourers with the capitalist; in others, and perhaps finally in all, association of labourers among themselves."[28] These developments would not only enhance productivity but—more importantly—promote the fuller development and well-being of the people involved. The aim, Mill thought, should be to enable people "to work with or for one another in relations not involving dependence."[29]

By the association of labor and capital, Mill had in mind different schemes of profit sharing. For example, "in the American ships trading to China, it has long been the custom for every sailor to have an interest in the profits of the voyage; and to this has been ascribed the general good conduct of those seamen."[30] This sort of association, however, would eventually give way to a more complete system of worker cooperatives:

> The form of association, however, which if mankind continue to improve, must be expected in the end to predominate, is not that which can exist between a capitalist as chief, and workpeople without a voice in the management, but the association of the labourers themselves on terms of equality, collectively owning the capital with which they carry on their operations, and working under managers elected and removable by themselves.[31]

In *Principles* Mill discussed several examples of successful cooperative associations and viewed optimistically the future of the cooperative movement:

> Eventually, and in perhaps a less remote future than may be supposed, we may, through the cooperative principle, see our way to a change in society, which would combine the freedom and independence of the individual, with the moral,

intellectual, and economical advantages of aggregate production; and which . . . would realize, at least in the industrial department, the best aspirations of the democratic spirit.[32]

What that transformation implied for Mill was nothing less than "the nearest approach to social justice, and the most beneficial ordering of industrial affairs for the universal good, which it is possible at present to foresee."[33]

Greater Equality of Income   Utilitarians are likely to be sympathetic to the argument that steps should be taken to reduce the great disparities in income that characterize our society. That is, they are likely to believe that making the distribution of income more equal is a good strategy for maximizing happiness. The reason for this goes back to what economists would call "the declining marginal utility of money." This phrase simply means that successive additions to one's income produce, on average, less happiness or welfare than did earlier additions.

The declining utility of money follows from the fact, as Professor Richard Brandt explains it, that the outcomes we want are preferentially ordered, some being more strongly wanted than others:

> So a person, when deciding how to spend his resources, picks a basket of groceries which is at least as appealing as any other he can purchase with the money he has. The things he does not buy are omitted because other things are wanted more. If we double a person's income, he will spend the extra money on items he wants less (some special cases aside), and which will give less enjoyment than will the original income. The more one's income, the fewer preferred items one buys and the more preferred items one already has. On the whole, then, when the necessities of life have been purchased and the individual is spending on luxury items, he is buying items which will give less enjoyment. . . . This conclusion corresponds well with common-sense reflection and practice.[34]

The obvious implication is that a more egalitarian allocation of income—that is, an allocation that increases the income of those who now earn less—would boost total happiness. Brandt, for one, therefore defends equality of after-tax income on utilitarian grounds, subject to the following exceptions: supplements to meet special needs, supplements necessary for incentives or to allocate resources efficiently, and variations to achieve other socially desirable ends, such as population control.[35] Brandt states that this guiding principle of distribution is of only prima facie force and may have to be balanced against other principles and considerations. Still, it illustrates the point that utilitarians today are likely to advocate increased economic equality.

THE LIBERTARIAN APPROACH

Whereas utilitarians associate justice with social utility, philosophers who endorse what is called *libertarianism* identify justice with an ideal of liberty. For them, liberty is the prime value, and justice consists in permitting each person to live as he or she pleases, free from the interference of others. Accordingly, one libertarian asserts: "We are concerned with the condition of men in which coercion of some by others is reduced as much as possible in society."[36] Another maintains that libertarianism is "a philosophy of personal liberty—the liberty of each person to live according to his own choices, provided he does not attempt to coerce others and thus prevent them from living according to their choices."[37] Such views show clearly the libertarian's association of justice with liberty and of liberty itself with the absence of interference by other persons.

Libertarians firmly reject utilitarianism's concern for total social well-being. Utilitarians are willing to restrict the liberty of some, to interfere with their choices, if doing so will promote greater net happiness than not doing so. Libertarians cannot stomach this approach. As long as you are not doing something that interferes with anyone else's liberty, then no person, group, or government should disturb you in living the life you choose—not even if its doing so would maximize social happiness.

Although individual liberty is something that all of us value, it may not be the only thing we value. For the libertarian, however, liberty takes priority over other moral concerns. In particular, justice consists solely of respect for individual liberty. A libertarian world, with a complete commitment to individual liberty, would be a very different world from the one we now live in. Consider the following: Until 2003, the U.S. Supreme Court upheld laws forbidding sodomy between consenting male homosexuals; the government registers young men for military service and can, if it chooses, draft them; laws prevent adults from ingesting substances that the legislature deems harmful or immoral (such as marijuana and cocaine); and the state imposes taxes on our income to—among many other things—support needy citizens, provide loans to college students, and fund various projects for the common good. From a libertarian perspective, none of these policies is just.

Given the assumption that liberty means noninterference, libertarians generally agree that liberty allows only a minimal or "night-watchman" state. Such a state is limited to the narrow functions of protecting its citizens against force, theft, and fraud; enforcing contracts; and performing other such basic maintenance functions. In this view, a more extensive state—in particular, one that taxes its better-off citizens to support the less fortunate ones—violates the liberty of individuals by forcing them to support projects, policies, or persons they have not freely chosen to support.

Nozick's Theory of Justice

Although libertarians differ in how they formulate their theory, the late Harvard professor Robert Nozick's *Anarchy, State, and Utopia* is a very influential statement of the libertarian case.[38] Nozick's challenging and powerful advocacy of libertarianism has stimulated much debate, obliging philosophers of all political persuasions to take the libertarian theory seriously. His views are thus worth presenting in detail.

Nozick begins from the premise that people have certain basic moral rights, which he calls "Lockean rights." By alluding to the political philosophy of John Locke (1632–1704), Nozick wishes to underscore that these rights are both negative and natural. They are negative because they require only that people forbear from acting in certain ways—in particular, that we refrain from interfering with others. Beyond this, we are not obliged to do anything positive for anyone else, nor is anyone required to do anything positive for us. We have no right, for example, to be provided with satisfying work or with any material goods that we might need. These negative rights, according to Nozick, are natural in the sense that we possess them independently of any social or political institutions.

These individual rights impose firm, virtually absolute restrictions (or, in Nozick's phrase, "side constraints") on how we may act. We cannot morally infringe on someone's rights for any purpose. Not only are we forbidden to interfere with a person's liberty in order to promote the general good, we are prohibited from doing so even if violating that individual's rights would somehow prevent other individuals' rights from being violated. Each individual is autonomous and responsible, and should be left to fashion his or her own life free from the interference of others—as long as doing so is compatible with the rights of others to do the same. Only an acknowledgment of this almost absolute right to be free from coercion, Nozick argues, fully respects the distinctiveness of individuals, each with a unique life to lead.

A belief in these rights shapes Nozick's theory of economic justice, which he calls the "entitlement theory." Essentially, Nozick maintains that people are entitled to their holdings (that is, goods, money, and property) as long as they have acquired them fairly. Stated another way, if you have obtained your possessions without violating other people's Lockean rights, then you are entitled to them and may dispose of them as you choose. No one else has a legitimate claim on them. If you have secured a vast fortune without injuring other people, defrauding them, or otherwise violating their rights, then you are morally permitted to do with your fortune whatever you wish—bequeath it to a relative, endow a university, or squander it in riotous living. Even though other people may be going hungry, justice imposes no obligation on you to help them.

The first principle of Nozick's entitlement theory concerns the original acquisition of holdings—that is, the appropriation of unheld goods or the creation of new goods. If a person acquires a holding in accordance with this principle, then he or she is entitled to it. If, for example, you retrieve minerals from the wilderness or make something out of materials you already legitimately possess, then you have justly acquired this new holding. Nozick does not spell out this principle or specify fully what constitutes a just original acquisition, but the basic idea is clear and reflects the thinking of John Locke.

Property is a moral right, said Locke, because individuals are morally entitled to the products of their labor. When they mix their labor with the natural world, they are entitled to the resulting product. Thus, if a man works the land, then he is entitled to the land and its products because through his labor he has put something of himself into them. This investment of self through labor is the moral basis of ownership, Locke wrote, but there are limits to this right:

> In the beginning . . . men had a right to appropriate, by their labour, each one of himself, as much of the things of nature, as he could use. . . . Whatsoever he tilled and reaped, laid up and made use of, before it spoiled, that was his peculiar right; whatsoever he enclosed, and could feed, and make use of, the cattle and product was also his. But if either the grass of his inclosure rotted on the ground, or the fruit of his planting perished without gathering, and laying up, this part of the earth . . . was still to be looked on as waste, and might be the possession of any other.[39]

In this early "state of nature" prior to the formation of government, property rights were limited not only by the requirement that one not waste what one claimed, but also by the restriction that "enough and as good" be left for others—that is, that one's appropriation not make others worse off. Later, however, with the introduction of money, Locke thought that both these restrictions were overcome. You can pile up money beyond your needs without its spoiling; and if your property is used productively and the proceeds offered for sale, then your appropriation leaves others no worse off than before.

Nozick's second principle concerns transfers of already-owned goods from one person to another: how people may legitimately transfer holdings and how they may legitimately get holdings from others. If a person possesses a holding because of a legitimate transfer, then he or she is entitled to it. Again, Nozick does not work out the details, but it is clear that acquiring something by purchase, as a gift, or through exchange would constitute a legitimate acquisition. Gaining it through theft, force, or fraud would violate the principle of justice in transfer.

Nozick's third and final principle states that one can justly acquire a holding only in accord with the two principles just discussed. If you come by a holding in some other way, you are not entitled to it. Nozick sums up his theory this way:

1. A person who acquires a holding in accordance with the principle of justice in acquisition is entitled to that holding.

2. A person who acquires a holding in accordance with the principle of justice in transfer, from someone else entitled to the holding, is entitled to the holding.

3. No one is entitled to a holding except by (repeated) applications of 1 and 2.

In short, the distribution of goods in a society is just if and only if all are entitled to the holdings they possess. Nozick calls his entitlement theory "historical" because what matters is how people come to have what they have. If people are entitled to their possessions, then the distribution of economic holdings is just, regardless of what the actual distribution happens to look like (for instance, how far people are above or below the average income) or what its consequences are.

The Wilt Chamberlain Example

Nozick argues that respect for liberty inescapably leads one to repudiate other conceptions of economic justice in favor of his entitlement approach. One of his most ingenious examples features Wilt Chamberlain, the late basketball star. Suppose, Nozick says, that things are distributed according to your favorite nonentitlement theory, whatever it is. (He calls this distribution D_1.) Now imagine that Wilt Chamberlain signs a contract with a team that guarantees him $5 from the price of each ticket. Whenever people buy a ticket to a game, they drop $5 into a special box with Chamberlain's name on it. To them it is worth it to see him play. Imagine then that in the course of a season 1 million people attend his games and Chamberlain ends up with far more than the average income—far more, indeed, than anyone else in the society earns. This result (D_2) upsets the initial distributional pattern (D_1).

Can the proponent of D_1 complain? Nozick thinks not:

Is [Chamberlain] entitled to this income? Is this new distribution, D_2, unjust? If so, why? There is *no* question about whether each of the people was entitled to the control over the resources they held in D_1; because that was the distribution (your favorite) that (for the purposes of the argument) we assumed was acceptable. Each of these persons *chose* to give [$5] of their money to Chamberlain. . . . If D_1 was a just distribution, and people voluntarily moved from it to D_2, transferring parts of their shares they were given under D_1 . . . isn't D_2 also just? If the people were entitled to dispose of the resources to which they were entitled (under D_1), didn't this include their being entitled to give it to, or exchange it with, Wilt Chamberlain? Can anyone else complain on grounds of justice?[40]

Having defended the legitimacy of Chamberlain's new wealth, Nozick pushes his case further, arguing that any effort to maintain some initial distributional arrangement like D_1 will interfere with people's liberty to use their resources as they wish. To preserve this original distribution, he writes, society would have to "forbid capitalist acts between consenting adults":

> The general point illustrated by the Wilt Chamberlain example . . . is that no [nonentitlement] principle of justice can be continuously realized without continuous interference with people's lives. Any favored pattern would be transformed into one unfavored by the principle, by people choosing to act in various ways; for example, by people exchanging goods and services with other people, or giving things to other people. . . . To maintain a pattern one must either continually interfere to stop people from transferring resources as they wish to, or continually (or periodically) interfere to take from some persons resources that others for some reason chose to transfer to them.[41]

The Libertarian View of Liberty

Libertarianism clearly involves a commitment to leaving market relations—buying, selling, and other exchanges—totally unrestricted.* Force and fraud are forbidden, of course, but there should be no interference with the uncoerced exchanges of consenting individuals. Not only is the market morally legitimate, but any attempt to interfere with consenting and nonfraudulent transactions between adults will be unacceptable. Thus, libertarians are for economic laissez faire and against any governmental economic activity that interferes with the marketplace, even if the point of the interference is to enhance the performance of the economy.

It is important to emphasize that libertarianism's enthusiasm for the market rests on this commitment to liberty. By contrast, utilitarian defenders of the market defend it on the ground that an unregulated market works better than either a planned, socialist economy or the sort of regulated capitalism with some welfare benefits that we in fact have in the United States. That is, if a utilitarian defends laissez faire, he or she does so because of its consequences. Convince a utilitarian that some other form of economic organization better promotes human well-being, and the utilitarian will advocate that instead. With libertarians this is definitely not the case. As a matter of fact, libertarians typically agree with Adam Smith that unregulated capitalist behavior best promotes everyone's interests. But even if, hypothetically, someone like Nozick were convinced that some sort of socialism or welfare capitalism outperformed laissez-faire capitalism economically—greater productivity, shorter working day, higher standard of living—he or she would still reject this alternative as morally unacceptable. To tinker with the market, however beneficial it might be, would involve violating someone's liberty.

Libertarians say that their commitment to an unrestricted market reflects the priority of liberty over other values. However, libertarians do not value liberty in the mundane

*Chapter 4 examines the nature of market economies in general and capitalism in particular.

sense of people's freedom to do what they want to do. Rather, libertarians understand freedom in terms of their theory of rights, thus building a commitment to private property into their concept of liberty. According to them, being able to do what you want does not automatically represent an increase in your liberty. It does so only if you remain within the boundaries set by the Lockean rights of others. Likewise, one is unfree or coerced only when one's rights are infringed.

Imagine, for example, that having purchased the forest in which I occasionally stroll, the new owner bars my access to it. It would seem that my freedom has been reduced because I can no longer ramble where I wish. But libertarians deny that this is a restriction of my liberty. My liberty is restricted if and only if someone violates my Lockean rights, which no one has done. Suppose that I go for a hike in the forest anyway. If the sheriff's deputies arrest me, they prevent me from doing what I want to do. But according to libertarianism, they do not restrict my liberty, nor do they coerce me. Why not? Because my hiking in the forest violates the landowner's rights.

Here libertarians seem driven to an unusual use of familiar terminology, but they have no choice. They cannot admit that abridging the landowner's freedom to do as he wants with his property would expand my freedom. If they did, then their theory would be in jeopardy. They would have to acknowledge that restricting the liberty or property rights of some could enhance the liberty of others. In other words, if their theory committed them simply to promoting as much as possible the goal of people doing what they want to do, then libertarians would be in the position of balancing the freedom of some against the freedom of others. But this sort of balancing and trading off is just what libertarians dislike about utilitarianism.

If liberty means being free to do what you want, it's not true that libertarians value it above everything else. What they value are Lockean property rights, which then set the parameters of liberty. Libertarians frequently contend (1) that private property is necessary for freedom and (2) that any society that doesn't respect private property rights is coercive. But libertarianism makes 1 true by definition, and 2 is incorrect. Any system of property (whether Lockean, socialist, or something in between) necessarily puts restrictions on people's conduct; its rules are coercive. What one system of property permits, another forbids. Society X prevents me from hiking in your woods, whereas society Y prevents you from stopping me. Both systems of rules are coercive. Both grant some freedoms and withhold others.

Markets and Free Exchange

Libertarians defend market relations, then, as necessary to respect human liberty (as their theory understands liberty). However, in doing so, libertarians do not assert that, morally speaking, people deserve what they receive from others through gift or exchange, only that they are entitled to whatever they receive. The market tends generally, libertarians believe, to reward people for skill, diligence, and successful performance. Yet luck plays a role, too. Jack makes a fortune from having been in the right place at the right time with his beanie babies, while Jill loses her investment because the market for bottled water collapses. The libertarian position is not that Jack deserves to be wealthy and Jill does not; rather, it is that Jack is entitled to his holdings if he has acquired them in accordance with the principles of justice.

The same point comes up with regard to gifts and inheritance. Inheritance strikes many people as patently unfair. How can it be just, they ask, that one child inherits a vast fortune, the best schooling, and social, political, and business connections that will ensure his or her future, while another child inherits indigence, inferior schooling, and connections with crime? At birth neither youngster deserves anything—a fact suggesting, perhaps, that an equal division of holdings and opportunities would be the only fair allocation. For his part, Nozick contends that deserving has no bearing on the justice of inherited wealth; people are simply entitled to it as long as it is not ill gotten. Or looking at it the other way, if one is entitled to one's holdings, then one has a right to do with them as one wishes, including using them to benefit one's children.

According to libertarians, a totally free market is necessary for people to exercise their fundamental rights. Sometimes, however, unregulated market transactions can lead to disastrous results. Unfortunately, this is more than just a theoretical possibility. Amartya Sen, the Nobel Prize–winning economist, has shown how in certain circumstances changing market entitlements have led to mass starvation. Although the average person thinks of famine as caused simply by a shortage of food, Sen and other experts have established that famines are frequently accompanied by no shortfall of food in absolute terms. Indeed, even more food may be available during a famine than in nonfamine years— if one has the money to buy it. Famine occurs because large numbers of people lack the financial wherewithal to obtain the necessary food.[42]

For example, drought may cause food output in one area to decline and the peasants in that area to starve because they lack the means to buy food from elsewhere, even though there is no dearth of food in the country as a whole (Ethiopia in 1973). Or famine may result when the purchasing power of one occupational group shoots up, ruining the chances of other groups, whose nominal incomes have not changed, to buy food (Bengal in 1943). A reduction of food output because of potato blight triggered the great Irish famine of the 1840s, which killed a higher proportion of the population than any other famine in recorded history. But if one looks at the United Kingdom as a whole, there was no shortage of food. Food could certainly have moved from Britain to Ireland if the Irish could have afforded to purchase it. As it was, at the height of the famine, food was exported from Ireland to England because the prosperous English could pay a higher price for it.[43]

Libertarians would find it immoral and unjust to force people to aid the starving or to tax the affluent in order to set up programs to relieve hunger or prevent famines in the first place. Nor does justice require that a wealthy merchant assist the hungry children in his community to stay alive. And it would certainly violate the merchant's property rights for the children to help themselves to his excess food. Nevertheless, although justice does not require that one assist those in need, libertarians would generally acknowledge that we have some humanitarian obligations toward others. Accordingly, they would not only permit but also presumably encourage people to voluntarily assist others. Justice does not require the merchant to donate, and it forbids us from forcing him to do so, but charity on his part would be a good thing. This reflects the libertarian's firm commitment to property rights: What you have legitimately acquired is yours to do with as you will.

Property Rights

Nozick's theory makes property rights virtually sacrosanct. From the perspective of libertarianism, property rights grow out of one's basic moral rights, either reflecting one's initial creation or appropriation of the product, some sort of exchange or transfer between consenting persons, or a combination of these. Property rights exist prior to any social arrangements and are morally antecedent to any legislative decisions that a society might make. However, Nozick's critics argue that it is a mistake to think of property as a simple, pre-social relation between a person and a physical thing.

First, property is not restricted to material objects like cars, watches, or houses. In developed societies, it may include more abstract goods, interests, and claims. For instance, property may include the right to pay debts with the balance in a bank account, the right to dividends from a corporate investment, and the right to collect from a pension plan one has joined. In fact, the courts have counted as property a wide range of items such as new life forms, an original idea, pension payments, the news, or a place on the welfare rolls.[44]

Second, property ownership involves a bundle of different rights—for instance, to possess, use, manage, dispose of, or restrict others' access to something in certain specified ways. The nature of this bundle differs among societies, as do the types of things that can be owned. In any society, property ownership is structured by the various implicit or explicit rules and regulations governing the legitimate acquisition and transfer of various types of goods, interests, and claims. Not only do property rights differ between societies, but the nature of ownership can also change over time in any given society. As a general trend, the social restrictions on property ownership in the United States have increased dramatically during our history (much to the displeasure of libertarians).

For these reasons, most nonlibertarian social and political theorists view property rights as a function of the particular institutions of a given society. This is not to say that a society's property arrangements cannot be criticized. On the contrary, their morality can be assessed just as the morality of any other institution can.

RAWLS'S THEORY OF JUSTICE

A Theory of Justice by Harvard University's John Rawls (1921–2002) is generally thought to be the single most influential work of the post–World War II period in social and political philosophy, at least in the English language.[45] Not only has Rawls's elegant theory touched a responsive chord in many readers, but also his book has helped rejuvenate serious work in normative theory. Even those who are not persuaded by Rawls find themselves obliged to come to terms with his thinking. Although Rawls's basic approach is not difficult to explain (and Rawls himself had sketched out his key concepts in earlier articles), *A Theory of Justice* elaborates his ideas with such painstaking care and philosophical thoroughness that even vigorous critics of the book (such as his colleague Robert Nozick) pay sincere tribute to its many virtues.

By his own account, Rawls presents his theory as a modern alternative to utilitarianism, one that he hopes will be compatible with the belief that justice must be associated with fairness and the moral equality of persons. Rawls firmly wishes to avoid reducing justice to a matter of society utility. At the same time, his approach differs fundamentally from Nozick's. Rawls conceives of society as a cooperative venture among its members, and he elaborates a conception of justice that is thoroughly social. He does not base his theory, as Nozick does, on the postulate that individuals possess certain natural rights prior to any political or social organization.

Two main features of Rawls's theory are particularly important: his hypothetical-contract approach and the principles of justice that he derives with it. Rawls's strategy

is to ask what we would choose as the fundamental principles to govern society if, hypothetically, we were to meet for this purpose in what he calls the "original position." He
then elaborates the nature of this original position, the constraints on the choice facing
us, and the reasoning that he thinks people in the original position would follow. In this
way, Rawls offers a modern variant of social contract theory, in the tradition of Hobbes,
Locke, Rousseau, and other earlier philosophers. Rawls argues that people in the original position would agree on two principles as the basic governing principles of their
society, and that these principles are, accordingly, the principles of justice. These principles are examined at some length in a later section. But briefly, the first is a guarantee of certain familiar and fundamental liberties to each person, and the second—more
controversial—holds in part that social and economic inequalities are justified only if
those inequalities benefit the least advantaged members of society.

The Original Position

Various principles of economic justice have been proposed, but an important question for philosophers is whether, and how, any such principles can be justified. Thinking
of possible principles of economic distribution is not all that difficult, but proving the
soundness of such a principle, or at least showing it to be more plausible than its rivals,
is a challenging task. After all, people seem to differ in their intuitions about what is just
and unjust, and their sentiments are bound to be influenced by their social position.
Nozick's entitlement theory, for example, with its priority on property rights, is bound
to seem more plausible to a corporate executive than to a migrant farm worker. The justice of a world in which some children are born into wealth while other children struggle by on welfare is unlikely to seem as obvious to the poor as it may to the well-to-do.

The strategy Rawls employs to identify and justify some basic principles of justice is
to imagine that people come together for the purpose of deciding on the ground rules
for their society, in particular on the rules governing economic distribution. Although
in the past groups of people have written down constitutions and similar political documents, never have the members of a society decided from scratch on the basic principles of justice that should govern them. Nor is it even remotely likely that people will
do this in the future. What Rawls imagines is a thought experiment: The question is
hypothetical: What principles would people choose in this sort of original position? If
we can identify these principles, Rawls contends, then we will have identified the principles of justice just because they are the principles that we would all have agreed to.

The Nature of the Choice   On what basis are we to choose these principles? The most
obvious answer is that we should select principles that strike us as just. But this won't
work. Even if we are all agreed on what is just and unjust, we would be relying on our
already existing ideas about justice as a basis for choosing the principles to govern our
society. Philosophically, this approach doesn't accomplish anything. We would simply
be going in a circle, using our existing conception of justice to prove the principles of
justice.

Rawls suggests instead that we imagine people in the original position choosing
solely on the basis of self-interest. That is, each individual chooses the set of principles
for governing society that will be best for himself or herself (and loved ones). We don't
have to imagine that people are antagonistic or that outside of the original position they

are selfish; we just imagine that they hope to get the group to choose those principles that will, more than any other possible principles, benefit them. If people in the original position can agree on some governing principles on the basis of mutual self-interest, then these principles will be, Rawls thinks, the principles of justice. Why? Because the principles are agreed to under conditions of equality and free choice. By analogy, if we make up a game and all agree ahead of time, freely and equally, on how the game is to be played, nobody can later complain that the rules are unfair.

The Veil of Ignorance   If people in the original position are supposed to choose principles on the basis of self-interest, agreement seems unlikely. If Carolyn has vast real estate holdings, she will certainly want rules that guarantee her extensive property rights, while her tenants are likely to support rules that permit rent control. Likewise, the wealthy will tend to advocate rules rather like Nozick's entitlement theory, while those without property will, on the basis of their self-interest, desire a redistribution of property. Conflicts of self-interest seem bound to create totally irreconcilable demands. For instance, artists may contend that they should be rewarded more than professional people, men that they should earn more than women, and laborers that they merit more than people with desk jobs.

Agreement seems unlikely, given that some rules would benefit one group while other rules would benefit another. As a way around this problem, Rawls asks us to imagine that people in the original position do not know what social position or status they hold in society. They do not know whether they are rich or poor, and they do not know their personal talents and characteristics—whether, for example, they are athletic or sedentary, artistic or tone deaf, intelligent or not very bright, physically sound or handicapped in some way. They do not know their race or even their sex. Behind what Rawls calls the "veil of ignorance," people in the original position know nothing about themselves personally or about what their individual situation will be once the rules are chosen and the veil is lifted. They do, however, have a general knowledge of history, sociology, and psychology—although no specific information about the society they will be in once the veil is lifted.

Under the veil of ignorance, the people in Rawls's original position have no knowledge about themselves or their situation that would lead them to argue from a partial or biased point of view. No individual is likely to argue that some particular group— such as white men, property owners, star athletes, philosophers—should receive special social and economic privileges when, for all that individual knows, he or she will be nonwhite, propertyless, unathletic, and bored by philosophy when the veil is lifted. Because individuals in the original position are all equally ignorant of their personal predicament and they are all trying to advance their self-interest, agreement is possible. The reasoning of any one person will be the same as the reasoning of each of the others, for each is in identical circumstances and each has the same motivation. As a result, no actual group has to perform Rawls's thought experiment. People who read Rawls's book can imagine that they are in the original position and then decide whether they would choose the principles Rawls thinks they would.

The veil of ignorance, in effect, forces people in the original position to be objective and impartial and makes agreement possible. Also, according to Rawls, the fact that people have no special knowledge that would allow them to argue in a biased way accords with our sense of fairness. The circumstances of the original position are genuinely equal and fair, and because of this, the principles agreed to under these conditions have a good claim to be considered the principles of justice.

Choosing the Principles

Although people in the original position are ignorant of their individual circumstances, they know that whatever their particular goals, interests, and talents turn out to be, they will want more, rather than less, of what Rawls calls the "primary social goods." These include not just income and wealth but also rights, liberties, opportunities, status, and self-respect. Of course, once the veil of ignorance is lifted, people will have more specific ideas about what is good for them—they may choose a life built around religion, one spent in commerce and industry, or one devoted to academic study. But whatever these particular individual goals, interests, and plans turn out to be, they will almost certainly be furthered, and definitely never limited, by the fact that people in the original position secured for themselves more rather than less in the way of primary goods.

How, then, will people in the original position choose their principles? *A Theory of Justice* explores in depth the reasoning that Rawls thinks would guide their choice. At the heart of Rawls's argument is the contention that people in the original position will be conservative, in the sense that they will not wish to gamble with their future. In setting up the ground rules for their society, they are determining their own fate and that of their children. This exercise is not something to be taken lightly, a game to be played and replayed. Rather, with so much at stake, people will reason cautiously.

Consider, for example, the possibility that people in the original position will set up a feudal society: 10 percent of the population will be nobles, living a life of incredible wealth, privilege, and leisure; the other 90 percent will be serfs, toiling away long hours to support the extravagant lifestyles of the aristocracy. Perhaps some people would consider the joy of being a pampered noble so great that they would vote for such an arrangement behind the veil of ignorance, but they would be banking on a long shot. When the veil of ignorance is lifted, the odds are nine to one that they will be poor and miserable serfs, not lords. Rawls thinks that people in the original position will not, in fact, gamble with their futures. They will not agree to rules that make it overwhelmingly likely that they will have to face a grim life of hardship.

Rawls argues that for similar reasons people in the original position will not adopt the utilitarian standard to govern their society, because the utilitarian principle might sacrifice the well-being of some to enhance society's total happiness. People in the original position, Rawls argues, will not be willing to risk sacrificing their own happiness, once the veil of ignorance is lifted, for the greater good.

What people in the original position would actually do, Rawls believes, is follow what game strategists call the *maximin rule* for making decisions. This rule says that you should select the alternative under which the worst that could happen to you is better than the worst that could happen to you under any other alternative; that is, you should try to *maxi*mize the *mini*mum that you will receive. This rule makes sense when you care much more about avoiding an unacceptable or disastrous result (such as being a serf) than about getting the best possible result (being a noble) and when you have no real idea what odds you are facing. It is a conservative decision principle, but Rawls thinks that people in the original position will find it a rational and appropriate guideline for their deliberations.

Rawls's Two Principles

Rawls argues that people in the original position considering various alternatives will eventually endorse two principles as the most basic governing principles of their society. These principles, because they are agreed to in an initial situation of equality and fairness, will be the principles of justice. Once these two principles of justice have been decided, the people in the original position can gradually be given more information about their specific society. They can then go on to design their basic social and political institutions in more detail.

Rawls states the two basic principles of justice as follows:

1. Each person is to have an equal right to the most extensive total system of equal basic liberties compatible with a similar system of liberty for all.[46]

2. Social and economic inequalities are to satisfy two conditions: First, they are to be attached to positions and offices open to all under conditions of fair equality of opportunity; and second, they are to be to the greatest expected benefit of the least advantaged members of society.[47]

According to Rawls, the first principle takes priority over the second, at least for societies that have attained a moderate level of affluence. The liberties Rawls has in mind are the traditional democratic ones of freedom of thought, conscience, and religious worship, as well as freedom of the person and political liberty. Explicitly absent are "the right to own certain kinds of property (e.g., means of production), and freedom of contract as understood by the doctrine of laissez-faire." The first principle guarantees not only equal liberty to individuals but also as much liberty to individuals as possible, compatible with others having the same amount of liberty. There is no reason why people in the original position would settle for anything less.

All regulations could be seen as infringing on personal liberty, because they limit what a person may do. The law that requires you to drive on the right-hand side of the road denies you the freedom to drive on either side whenever you wish. Some would argue that justice requires only an equal liberty. For example, as long as every motorist is required to drive on the right-hand side of the road, justice is being served; or if everyone in a dictatorial society is forbidden to criticize the leader's decisions, then all are equal in their liberty. But Rawls argues that if a more extensive liberty were possible, without inhibiting the liberty of others, then it would be irrational to settle for a lesser degree of liberty. In the case of driving, permitting me to drive on either side of the road would only interfere with the liberty of others to drive efficiently to their various destinations, but introducing right-turn-on-red laws enhances everyone's liberty. In the dictatorship example, free speech could be more extensive without limiting anyone's liberty.

The second principle concerns social and economic inequalities. Regarding inequalities, Rawls writes:

It is best to understand not *any* differences between offices and positions, but differences in the benefits and burdens attached to them either directly or indirectly, such as prestige and wealth, or liability to taxation and compulsory services. Players in a game do not protest against there being different positions, such as batter, pitcher, catcher, and the like, nor to there being various privileges and powers as specified by the rules; nor do the citizens of a country object to there being the different offices of government such as president, senator, governor, judge, and so on, each with their special rights and duties.[48]

Rather, at issue are differences in wealth and power, honors and rewards, privileges and salaries that attach to different roles in society.

Rawls's second principle states that insofar as inequalities are permitted—that is, insofar as it is compatible with justice for some jobs or positions to bring greater rewards than others—these positions must be open to all. In other words, there must be meaningful equality of opportunity in the competition among individuals for those positions in society that bring greater economic and social rewards. This, of course, is a familiar ideal, but what exactly a society must do to achieve not just legal but full and fair equality of opportunity will be a matter of debate.

The other part of the second principle is less familiar and more controversial. Called the *difference principle*, it is the distinctive core of Rawls's theory. It states that inequalities are justified only if they work to the benefit of the least advantaged group in society. By "least advantaged," Rawls simply means those who are least well off. But what does it mean to require that inequalities work to the benefit of this group?

Imagine that we are back in the original position. We wish to make sure that under the principles we choose, the worst that can happen to us once the veil of ignorance is lifted is still better than the worst that might have happened under some other arrangement. We might, therefore, choose strict social and economic equality. With an equal division of goods, there's no risk of doing worse than anyone else, no danger of being sacrificed to increase the total happiness of society. In the case of liberty, people in the original position do insist on full equality, but with social and economic inequality, the matter is a little different.

Suppose, for instance, that as a result of dividing things up equally, people lack an incentive to undertake some of the more difficult work that society needs done. It might then be the case that allowing certain inequalities—for example, paying people more for being particularly productive or for undertaking the necessary training to perform some socially useful task—would work to everyone's benefit, including those who would be earning less. If so, then why not permit those inequalities? Compare the two diagrams:

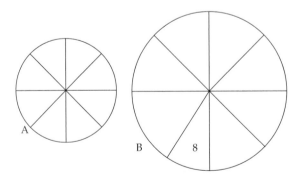

Each pie represents a possible social and economic distribution among eight basic groups (the number eight is arbitrary) in society. In Figure A, things are divided equally; in Figure B, unequally. Imagine that if a society permits inequalities as an incentive to get people to work harder or to do work that they would not have wanted to do otherwise, then the overall amount to be distributed among its members will be greater. That is, the economic pie will increase in size from A to B, and the people with the thinnest slice of B will be better off than they would have been with an equal slice of A.

Which society will people in the original position prefer? Obviously the one represented by Figure B, because the minimum they can attain in B (the slice labeled 8) is bigger than any of the eight equal slices in A. People in the original position do not care about equality of distribution as a value in and of itself; they want the social and economic arrangement that will provide them with the highest minimum.

Rawls is not trying to prove that economic inequalities will always, or even usually, trickle down to the least advantaged (although, of course, some people believe that). Rather, his point is simply that people in the original position would not insist on social and economic equality at all costs. If permitting some people to be better off than the average resulted in the least-well-off segment of society being better off than it would have been under a strictly equal division, then this is what people in the original position will want. Rawls's difference principle is intended to capture this idea. Rawls's principles permit economic inequalities only if they do in fact benefit the least advantaged.

Consider the recurrent proposal to further lower or even eliminate the income tax on capital gains (that is, on personal income from the sale of assets like stocks, bonds, and real estate). Proponents claim that the tax break will spur trading in financial assets, which will in turn lead to growth in tax revenues, and that the cut will trigger more long-term investment, helping revitalize the economy. Critics of the proposal contest both claims. Still, everyone agrees that the tax break would certainly increase the income of the rich because the wealthiest 1.4 percent of households receive 73.2 percent of all capital-gains income.[49] Will lowering taxes on the rich benefit the least advantaged members of society more in the long run than any alternative tax policy?

This question illustrates the application of Rawls's difference principle in a practical context, but we must remember that Rawls intends his principles to be used not as a direct guide to day-to-day policy decisions but rather as the basis for determining what form society's primary social, political, and economic institutions should take in the first place. What will these institutions look like? More specifically, what sort of economic system will best satisfy Rawls's difference principle? Rawls does not answer this question. He sees it as primarily a question for economists and other social scientists, whereas the task of philosophers like himself is the preliminary one of working out a satisfactory conception of justice. Rawls does appear to believe, however, that a liberal form of capitalism, with sufficient welfare provisions, would satisfy his principles, but he does not rule out the possibility that a democratic socialist system could as well.

Fairness and the Basic Structure

Rawls intends his theory as a fundamental alternative to utilitarianism, which he rejects on the grounds that maximizing the total well-being of society could permit an unfair distribution of burdens and benefits. Utilitarianism, in Rawls's view, treats people's pleasures and pains as completely interchangeable: A decrease of happiness here is justified by greater happiness there. Within a person's own life, such trade-offs are sensible. An increase of pain now (as the dentist fills a cavity in my tooth) is justified in terms of greater happiness later (no painful, rotted tooth). But between individuals, as when Jack's happiness is decreased to provide Jill with a more-than-compensating gain, such trade-offs are morally problematic.

Thus Rawls stresses that, in his view,

> each person possesses an inviolability founded on justice that even the welfare of society as a whole cannot override. . . . Therefore . . . the rights secured by justice are not subject to political bargaining or to the calculus of social interests.[50]

And he emphasizes that the difference principle

> excludes, therefore, the justification of inequalities on the grounds that the disadvantages of those in one position are outweighed by the greater advantages of those in another position. This rather simple restriction is the main modification I wish to make in the utilitarian principle as usually understood.[51]

On the other hand, Rawls is equally unsympathetic to the approach adopted by Nozick. Contrary to the entitlement theory, he argues that the primary subject of justice is not, in the first instance, transactions between individuals but rather "the basic structure, the fundamental social institutions and their arrangement into one scheme." Why? As Rawls explains:

> Suppose we begin with the initially attractive idea that the social circumstances and people's relationships to one another should develop over time in accordance with free agreements fairly arrived at and fully honored. Straightaway we need an account of when agreements are free and the social circumstances under which they are reached are fair. In addition, while these conditions may be fair at an earlier time, the accumulated results of many separate and ostensibly fair agreements . . . are likely in the course of time to alter citizens' relationships and opportunities so that the conditions for free and fair agreements no longer hold. The role of the institutions that belong to the basic structure is to secure just background conditions against which the actions of the individuals and associations take place. Unless this structure is appropriately regulated and adjusted, an initially just social process will eventually cease to be just, however free and fair particular transactions may look when viewed by themselves.[52]

Additional considerations support taking the basic structure of society as the primary subject of justice—in particular, the fact that the basic structure shapes the wants, desires, hopes, and ambitions of individuals. Thus, Rawls continues:

> Everyone recognizes that the institutional form of society affects its members and determines in large part the kind of person they want to be as well as the kind of person they are. The social structure also limits people's ambitions and hopes in different ways. . . . So an economic regime, say, is not only an institutional scheme for satisfying existing wants but a way of fashioning desires and aspirations in the future.[53]

Rawls stresses that because the basic structure is the proper focus of a theory of justice, we cannot expect the principles that apply to it to be simply an extension of the principles that govern everyday individual transactions:

> The justice of the basic structure is, then, of predominant importance. The first problem of justice is to determine the principles to regulate inequalities and to adjust the profound and long-lasting effects of social, natural, and historical contingencies, particularly since these contingencies combined with inequalities generate tendencies that, when left to themselves, are sharply at odds with the freedom and equality appropriate for a well-ordered society. In view of the special role of the basic structure, we cannot assume that the principles suitable to it are natural applications, or even extensions, of the familiar principles governing the actions of individuals and associations in everyday life which take place within its framework. Most likely we shall have to loosen ourselves from our ordinary perspective and take a more comprehensive viewpoint.[54]

Benefits and Burdens

The passages quoted here touch on a theme that is central to Rawls's theory. Inevitably, there will be natural differences among human beings—in terms of physical prowess, mental agility, and so on—but there is nothing natural or inevitable about the weight attached by society to those differences. For Rawls, a desirable feature of any account of justice is that it strives to minimize the social consequences of purely arbitrary, natural differences. He stresses that no one deserves his or her particular natural characteristics. We cannot say that Robert Redford deserves to be handsome or that Albert Einstein deserved to be blessed with an excellent mind any more than we can say that Fred merits his shortness or Pamela her nearsightedness. Their attributes are simply the result of a genetic lottery. But Rawls goes beyond this to argue that even personal characteristics like diligence and perseverance reflect the environment in which one was raised:

> We do not deserve our place in the distribution of native endowments, any more than we deserve our initial starting place in society. That we deserve the superior character that enables us to make the effort to cultivate our abilities is also problematic; for such character depends in good part upon fortunate family and social circumstances in early life for which we can claim no credit. The notion of desert does not apply here.[55]

Accordingly, Rawls thinks we cannot really claim moral credit for our special talents or even our virtuous character. In Rawls's view, then, if our personal characteristics are not something that we deserve, we have no strong claim to the economic rewards they might bring. On the contrary, justice requires that the social and economic consequences of these arbitrarily distributed assets be minimized.

> The difference principle represents, in effect, an agreement to regard the distribution of natural talents as in some respects a common asset and to share in the greater social and economic benefits made possible by the complementarities of this distribution. Those who have been favored by nature, whoever they are, may gain from their good fortune only on terms that improve the situation of those who have lost out. The naturally advantaged are not to gain merely because they are more gifted, but only to cover the costs of training and education and for using

their endowments in ways that help the less fortunate as well. No one deserves his greater natural capacity nor merits a more favorable starting place in society. But, of course, this is no reason to ignore, much less to eliminate these distinctions. Instead, the basic structure can be arranged so that these contingencies work for the good of the least fortunate. Thus we are led to the difference principle if we wish to set up the social system so that no one gains or loses from his arbitrary place in the distribution of natural assets or his initial position in society without giving or receiving compensating advantages in return.[56]

This important passage from *A Theory of Justice* reflects well Rawls's vision of society as a cooperative project for mutual benefit.

SUMMARY

1. Justice is one important aspect of morality. Talk of justice and injustice generally involves appeals to the related notions of fairness, equality, desert, and rights. Economic or distributive justice concerns the principles appropriate for assessing society's distribution of social benefits and burdens, particularly wealth, income, status, and power.

2. Economic distribution might be based on pure equality, need, effort, social contribution, or merit. Each of these principles is plausible in some circumstances but not in others. In some situations, the principles pull us in different directions. Dissatisfied with a pluralistic approach, some moral philosophers have sought to develop more general theories of justice.

3. Utilitarianism holds that the maximization of happiness ultimately determines what is just and unjust. Mill contended, more specifically, that the concept of justice identifies certain very important social utilities and that injustice involves the violation of the rights of some specific individual.

4. Utilitarians must examine a number of factual issues in order to determine for themselves which economic system and principles will best promote social well-being or happiness. Many utilitarians favor increased worker participation and a more equal distribution of income.

5. The libertarian theory identifies justice with liberty, which libertarians understand as living according to our own choices, free from the interference of others. They reject utilitarianism's concern for total social well-being.

6. The libertarian philosopher Robert Nozick defends the entitlement theory. His theory holds that the distribution of goods, money, and property is just if people are entitled to what they have—that is, if they have acquired their possessions without violating the rights of anyone else.

7. In the Wilt Chamberlain example, Nozick argues that theories of economic justice not in accord with his inevitably fail to respect people's liberty.

8. Libertarians operate with a distinctive concept of liberty, defend free exchange and laissez-faire markets without regard to results, put a priority on freedom over all other values, and see property rights as existing prior to any social arrangements. Critics contest each of these features of libertarianism.

9. John Rawls's approach lies within the social-contract tradition. He asks us to imagine people meeting in the "original position" to choose the basic principles that are to govern their society. Although in this original position people choose on the basis of self-interest, we are to imagine that they are behind a veil of ignorance, with no personal information about themselves. Rawls contends that any principles agreed to under these circumstances have a strong claim to be considered the principles of justice.

10. Rawls argues that people in the original position would follow the maximin rule for making decisions. They would choose principles guaranteeing that the worst that could happen to them is better than the worst that could happen to them under any rival principles. Rawls argues that they would agree on two principles. The first states that each person has a right to the most extensive scheme of liberties compatible with others having the same amount of liberty. The second principle states that to be justified, any inequalities must be to the greatest expected benefit of the least advantaged and open to all under conditions of fair equality of opportunity.

11. Rawls rejects utilitarianism because it might permit an unfair distribution of burdens and benefits. Contrary to the entitlement theory, he argues that the primary focus of justice should be the basic social structure, not transactions between individuals. He contends that society is a cooperative project for mutual benefit and that justice requires us to reduce the social and economic consequences of arbitrary natural differences among people.

CASE 3.1

Battling over Bottled Water

Water is the lifeblood of the earth, but by 2025, according to the U.N., two-thirds of the world's population could face chronic shortages of water. In fact, some countries are already importing huge supertankers of freshwater from other countries. But one place that's definitely not short of water is the state of Michigan, which has 11,000 lakes and is surrounded by Lakes Michigan, Huron, Superior, and Erie. So it came as a surprise to some that the Nestlé company's new Ice Mountain bottled-water plant in Mecosta County, Michigan, dredged up so much controversy when it began pumping water from a local spring.[57]

Nestlé's willingness to invest $100 million to build a new 410,000-square-foot bottling plant in Mecosta reflects the fact that bottled water is big business, with annual sales of $6 billion (up 35 percent since 1997). Many county residents, in fact, are thrilled about Nestlé's being there. The Ice Mountain plant employs about a hundred people at $12 to $23 per hour, significantly more than many local jobs pay. And the company shells out hundreds of thousands of dollars in local taxes. Township supervisor Maxine McClellan says, "This is probably the best project we've ever brought into Mecosta County." She adds that she wants "a diversified economy where our kids don't have to move away to find jobs."

The problem, as some local residents see it, is that Nestlé has also built a 12-mile stainless steel pipeline from the plant to Sanctuary Spring, which sits on an 850-acre private deer-hunting ranch and is part of the headwaters of the Little Muskegon River, which flows into the Muskegon and then into Lake Michigan. The company now pumps 130 gallons of water every minute from the spring and has plans to pump 400 gallons per minute, or about 262 million gallons a year. But whose water is Nestlé pumping? That's the question being asked by Michigan Citizens for Water Conservation (MCWC), a local Mecosta group that has filed suit contesting Nestlé's right to the spring's waters. Although the company has a ninety-nine-year lease on the land, MCWC contends that the water itself is a public resource. As Jim Olson, MCWC's lawyer, explains it, under the doctrine of "reasonable use" the owners of a stream can use its water for drinking, boating, swimming, or anything else "as long as it's in connection with their land." But, he argues, "this does not include the right to transport water to some distant land for [some other] use. We're arguing that the same is true with groundwater—you can't sever it from the estate."

Michigan State Senator Ken Sikkema, who chaired a task force on Michigan water issues, rejects that argument: "A farmer pumps water out of the ground, waters potatoes, and sends the potatoes to Illinois—there's no real difference. The water in those potatoes is gone." This reasoning hasn't assuaged the fears of three American Indian tribes who have joined the fray. Citing an 1836 treaty that protects their fishing and hunting rights in the Great Lakes region, they have brought a federal lawsuit against Nestlé and Michigan Governor John Engler to stop what they see as a massive water grab. "Our fear," says a spokesperson for the Little Traverse Bay Bands of Odawa Indians, "is that the export could significantly and permanently damage the fishery."

However, David K. Ladd, head of the Office of Great Lakes and an appointee of Governor Engler, argues that bottled water is a special case. Legally, he contends, it's a "food," regulated by the Food and Drug Administration. "There's no difference between Perrier bottling water, Gerber making baby food, or Miller brewing beer. When you incorporate water from the basin into a product, it's no longer water per se." And Brendan O'Rourke, an Ice Mountain plant manager, adds that the 262 million gallons it pumps are less than 1 percent of the annual recharge rate of the local watershed, equivalent to just 14 minutes of evaporation from the surface of Lake Michigan.

For their part, scientists opposed to the project argue that Nestlé's pumping has already lowered the local water table and that northern pike are having trouble spawning in a stream fed by Sanctuary Spring. Jim Olson argues that the Ice Mountain plant should reduce its water consumption to 100 gallons per minute or less, not increase it to 400 gallons. "Every gallon removed is needed for the stream to sustain itself," he states. "The right to withdraw groundwater does not include the right to diminish . . . existing or future uses."

Discussion Questions

1. Should people in Michigan be concerned about how, and by whom, the state's groundwater gets used? In your view, what issues of justice does this case raise?

2. Does Nestlé's pumping 262 million gallons of water per year from Sanctuary Spring constitute "reasonable use"? Is the company treating either local residents or the Native American tribes unfairly, or would it be unfair to restrict Nestlé's use of water from the spring?

3. Is groundwater a public resource, the use of which is appropriate for society to regulate? Or is it the property of those who own the land to use as they see fit? Who has the strongest claim on groundwater—the owners of the land from which it is pumped, the original inhabitants of the area (that is, the local Indian tribes), local residents, citizens of the whole Great Lakes region, or all Americans?

4. Assess this case from the perspective of the utilitarian, libertarian, and Rawlsian theories of justice. How would each address the case? Which theory's approach do you find the most helpful or illuminating?

CASE 3.2

Poverty in America

According to the U.S. Census Bureau, Americans are, in aggregate, doing pretty well. Despite a slight downturn since 2000, for some years now the median income of American households, measured in constant dollars, has been increasing at a fairly steady pace. And the number of families with incomes below the poverty line—defined as $18,392 for a family of four—declined appreciably during the long economic boom of the 1990s, with the poverty rate in 2000 reaching its lowest level since 1973. Since then, however, the poverty rate has inched up to 12.1 percent, and 34.6 million Americans continue to live in poverty, a third of them children. That's more than one out of every nine people.[58] Moreover, the average adult American has a 60 percent chance of living at least one year below the poverty line and a 33 percent chance of experiencing dire poverty.[59]

Most people think that those described as "poor" in the United States are pretty well off by world standards. The truth is, in life expectancy twenty-year-old U.S. males rank thirty-sixth among the world's nations, and twenty-year-old U.S. females rank twenty-first. Our infant mortality rate is worse than that in twenty-one other Western nations. Moreover, millions of Americans endure hunger. According to the U.S. Department of Agriculture, 31 million Americans lack "food security," and in 3 million American households one or more persons go hungry during the year.[60] In addition, one out of every four Americans lives in substandard housing, and in most cities one sees people roaming the streets in tattered clothing, picking their food out of garbage cans. Homeless people—many of them former mental patients released from state hospitals, others jobless individuals and families unable to afford housing—live in abandoned cars and shacks or simply sleep in doorways and on subway grates. Reliable figures are hard to come by, but probably between 700,000 and 800,000 Americans are homeless on any given night and between 2.5 and 3.5 million people homeless sometime during the year.[61]

People in different walks of life and in different circumstances experience poverty. Many others live on the edge of poverty and are in continual danger of falling into it through illness, job loss, or other misfortune. In the United States today, the "working poor"—that is, those who work full time, year around, while earning an income below the poverty line—number 2.8 million. They represent a higher percentage of the workforce than in the 1970s as well-paid unionized manufacturing jobs have been replaced by nonunion service jobs.[62] In 1997, the minimum wage was increased to $5.15 per hour, but it is still less in real terms than it was in 1969. Someone working forty hours a week, every week, for that wage cannot raise his or her family out of poverty. In fact, according to a housing advocacy group, a minimum-wage earner can't afford to rent a two-bedroom home anywhere in the United States.[63]

Many poor people are unable to work and depend on outside assistance. Recent legislative efforts to reform the welfare system rely on certain myths about welfare recipients. Investigation shows, for instance, that most people do not stay on the welfare rolls for years. They move on and off, and less than 1 percent remain on welfare for ten years. Contrary to popular mythology, the majority of those who receive welfare

are young children whose mothers must remain at home. They are not able-bodied adults who are unwilling to work. Nor do welfare mothers differ from nonwelfare mothers in the number of children they have. About 70 percent of welfare families have only one or two children, and there is little financial incentive to have more. Half of the families who receive welfare include an adult who works full or part time, and research consistently demonstrates that poor people have the same strong desire to work that the rest of the population does.[64] Two-thirds of the mothers on welfare did not grow up in families that received welfare—contrary to the stereotype of inter-generational welfare dependency—and only 7.6 percent of them are under eighteen and unmarried.[65]

There has never been a way to live well on welfare. Under the old system of AFDC (Aid to Families with Dependent Children), by 1996 welfare benefits had fallen, in real terms, to 51 percent of what they had been in 1971.[66] With annual cash allowances for a family on AFDC ranging from $1,416 in Mississippi to $6,780 in New York, even in the most generous states stipends were never enough to allow a family to escape from poverty.[67] In 1996 Congress replaced AFDC with TANF (Temporary Assistance to Needy Families). Under the new system, the entitlement of poor people to support has been replaced by block grants to the states to run their own welfare programs. The grants are limited to a certain amount of money; if they run out, the states are not required to make additional expenditures. Welfare recipients are required to work for pay or to enroll in training programs, and financial support is limited to a lifetime maximum of five years. This shift in policy has been controversial. Since the TANF system began, the number of people receiving welfare benefits has declined, but experts disagree about the reasons: Is it a growing economy offering more opportunities, the success of the new approach in encouraging welfare recipients to make themselves employable, or simply people who are not able to take care of themselves being denied support?[68]

One thing that is clear is the large number of women living in poverty. This includes women with inadequate income following divorce, widowhood, or retirement, as well as women raising children alone. Wage discrimination against women is one factor. Women who work full time, year round earn only about two-thirds of what men earn. And millions of women hold full-time jobs that pay wages near or below the poverty line.

Women's responsibilities for child rearing are another important factor. Despite many changes in recent years, women continue to have primary responsibility in this area. When marriages break up, mothers typically take custody and bear the major financial burden. Fewer than half the women raising children alone are awarded child support, and fewer than half of those entitled to it receive the full amount. Of family households headed by women, 48.4 percent have incomes below $25,000 and 26.7 percent have incomes below $15,000.[69]

Most poor people in our nation—about two-thirds of them—are white, but blacks are about three times more likely to be poor. Whereas fewer than one out of every ten white Americans are poor, more than one of every five African Americans and Hispanics live below the poverty line. Many members of the minority communities have succeeded in moving up the economic ladder, but the overall picture is bleak. African-American family income, for instance, is only 64 percent that of white family income.[70]

Discussion Questions

1. Does the existence of poverty imply that our socioeconomic system is unjust? Does the concentration of poverty in certain groups make it more unjust than it would be otherwise?

2. Surveys show that Americans, even poor Americans, favor individualistic explanations of poverty (such as lack of effort or ability, poor morals, poor work skills) over structural explanations (such as inadequate schooling, low wages, lack of jobs), whereas Europeans favor structural explanations of poverty over individualistic explanations.[71] What are the causes of poverty? How is one's answer to this question likely to affect one's view of the justice or injustice of poverty?

3. What moral obligation, if any, do we have individually and as a society to reduce poverty? What steps could be taken? What role should business play?

4. How would a utilitarian view the facts about poverty? What are the implications for our society of the concept of the declining utility of money?

5. How would a libertarian like Nozick view poverty in the United States? How plausible do you find the libertarian's preference for private charity over public welfare?

6. How would our economy be assessed from the point of view of Rawls's difference principle? Can it be plausibly maintained that, despite poverty, our system works to "the greatest expected benefit of the least advantaged"? Is this an appropriate standard?

Notes

1. Laura D'Andrea Tyson, "Tax Cuts for the Rich Are Even More Wrong Today," *Business Week*, July 8, 2002, 26. See also Andrew Hacker, *Money: Who Has How Much and Why* (New York: Simon & Schuster, 1997), 10, and Kevin Phillips, *Wealth and Democracy: A Political History of the American Rich* (New York: Broadway Books, 2002), 127–138.

2. U.S. Bureau of the Census, *Statistical Abstract of the United States 2002* (Washington, D.C.: U.S. Government Printing Office, 2003), Table 659, and "Historical Income Data: Current Population Survey Tables (Families)" at *www.census.gov*.

3. "Would You Like Your Class War Shaken or Stirred, Sir?" *Economist*, September 6, 2003, 28. See also Hacker, *Money*, 54, and John Isbister, *Capitalism and Justice: Envisioning Social and Economic Fairness* (Bloomfield, Conn.: Kumarian Press, 2001), 55.

4. Lester C. Thurow, "The Boom That Wasn't," *New York Times*, January 18, 1999, 17; Edward N. Wolff, "The Stagnating Fortunes of the Middle Class," *Social Philosophy and Policy* 19 (Winter 2002): 55, 58.

5. "Executive Pay," *Business Week*, April 21, 2003, 87; "Executive Pay," *Business Week*, April 15, 2002, 80.

6. "American Pay Rattles Foreign Partners," *New York Times*, January 17, 1999, sec. 4, 1.

7. "Learning How to Talk About Salary in Japan," *New York Times*, April 7, 2002, sec. 3, 12.

8. Albert Hunt, "Greed, Grasso, and A Gilded Age," *Wall Street Journal*, September 18, 2003, A17. See also "Suite Deals," *U.S. News & World Report*, April 29, 2002, 32, and Andrew Tobias, "How Much Is Fair?" *Parade Magazine*, March 2, 2003, 10.

9. Lynn Brenner, "How Did You Do?" *Parade Magazine*, March 2, 2003, 5.

10. "Suite Deals," *U.S. News & World Report*, 33.

11. "Two-Tier Marketing," *Business Week*, March 17, 1997, 82–90.

12. "Is America Becoming More of a Class Society?" *Business Week*, February 26, 1996, 86; see also "Land of Less Opportunity," *Business Week*, June 30, 2003, 28, and "Waking Up from the American Dream," *Business Week*, December 1, 2003, 54.

13. Edward N. Wolff, *Top Heavy: The Increasing Inequality of Wealth in America and What Can Be Done About It*, rev. ed. (New York: New Press, 2002), 8, 27. See also "Would You Like Your Class War?" *Economist*, 28.

14. Ray Boshara, "The $6,000 Solution," *Atlantic Monthly*, January/February 2003, 92.

15. "The $6,000 Solution," *Atlantic Monthly*, 92; "Would You Like Your Class War?" *Economist*, 29; and "Gap in U.S. Called Widest," *New York Times*, April 17, 1995, A1.

16. Leonard Silk, "Rich-Poor Gap Gets Wider in U.S.," *San Francisco Chronicle*, May 12, 1989, C5. See also John Marshall, "Child Poverty Is Abundant," *San Francisco Chronicle*, October 7, 1996, B2, and Catholic Campaign for Human Development, "Poverty Facts," July 2003 (available at *www.usccb.org/cchd/povertyusa*).

17. John Stuart Mill, *Utilitarianism* (Indianapolis: Bobbs-Merrill, 1957), 71.

18. Michael Walzer, *Spheres of Justice* (New York: Basic Books, 1983). See also Jon Elster, *Local Justice: How Institutions Allocate Scarce Goods and Necessary Burdens* (New York: Russell Sage, 1992).

19. Walzer, *Spheres of Justice*, 6.

20. Ibid., 10.

21. Mill, *Utilitarianism*, 66.

22. Ibid., 73.

23. Ibid., 71.

24. Ibid.

25. Ibid.

26. Ibid.

27. Smith's ideas are discussed further in Chapter 4.

28. John Stuart Mill, *Principles of Political Economy*, edited by Donald Winch (Harmondsworth, Middlesex: Penguin, 1970), 129.

29. Ibid., 128.

30. Ibid., 129.

31. Ibid., 133.

32. Ibid., 139–140.

33. Ibid., 140–141.

34. Richard B. Brandt, *A Theory of the Good and the Right* (New York: Oxford University Press, 1979), 312–313.

35. Ibid., 310.

36. F. A. Hayek, *The Constitution of Liberty* (Chicago: University of Chicago Press, 1960), 11.

37. John Hospers, *Libertarianism* (Los Angeles: Nash, 1971), 5.

38. Robert Nozick, *Anarchy, State, and Utopia* (New York: Basic Books, 1974).

39. John Locke, *Second Treatise of Government* (Indianapolis: Hackett Publishing, 1980), 23–24.

40. Nozick, *Anarchy, State, and Utopia*, 161.

41. Ibid., 163.

42. Amartya Sen, *Development as Freedom* (New Delhi: Oxford University Press, 1999), Chapter 7. See also Amartya Sen, *Poverty and Famines* (New York: Oxford University Press, 1981), and Jean Drèze and Amartya Sen, *Hunger and Public Action* (Oxford: Oxford University Press, 1989).

43. Sen, *Development as Freedom*, 167, 170–171.

44. Lawrence C. Becker and Kenneth Kipnis, eds., *Property: Cases, Concepts, Critiques* (Englewood Cliffs, N.J.: Prentice Hall, 1984), 3–5.

45. John Rawls, *A Theory of Justice*, rev. ed. (Cambridge: Harvard University Press, 1999). For subsequent developments in Rawls's thinking, see John Rawls, *Political Liberalism* (New York: Columbia University Press, 1993), and *Justice as Fairness: A Restatement* (Cambridge: Harvard University Press, 2001).

46. Rawls, *A Theory of Justice*, 266; cf. *Political Liberalism*, 291.

47. Rawls, *Political Liberalism*, 6; cf. *A Theory of Justice*, 53, 72, 266.

48. John Rawls, "Justice as Fairness," *Philosophical Review* 67 (April 1958): 167.

49. Arthur MacEwan, "Ask Mr. Dollar," *Dollars & Sense*, November–December 1997, 39; Michelle Cottle, "The Real Class War," *Washington Monthly*, July–August 1997, 12.

50. Rawls, *A Theory of Justice*, 3–4.

51. Rawls, "Justice as Fairness," 168.

52. *Political Liberalism*, 265–266.

53. Ibid., 269.

54. Rawls, "A Kantian Conception of Equality," *Cambridge Review* 96 (February 1975): 95.

55. *A Theory of Justice*, 89.

56. Ibid., 87.

57. This case study is based on "Where They're Boiling over Water," *Business Week*, May 27, 2002, 24E6–24E9, and "Fight over Bottled Water in Court," *Detroit Free Press*, May 5, 2003 (online edition).

58. *Statistical Abstract of the United States 2002*. Tables 653, 662, 665, 669, and "Poverty" at *www.census.com*.

59. Mark R. Rank and Thomas A. Hirschl, "The Likelihood of Poverty Across the American Adult Life Span," *Social Work* 44 (May 1999): 205.

60. Mark Andrews et al., "Household Food Security in the United States 1999" (U.S. Department of Agriculture: Fall 2000).

61. "Gimme a Roof over My Head," *Economist*, August 23, 2003, 19.

62. "Working Full Time Is No Longer Enough," *Wall Street Journal*, June 29, 2000, A2, and "Exploding Myths About the Poor," *Fortune*, September 29, 2003, 54.

63. *Wall Street Journal*, September 19, 2002, A1.

64. See Bob Herbert, "Scapegoat Time," *New York Times*, November 16, 1994, A19, and Ruth Sidel, "The Welfare Scam," *Nation*, December 12, 1994, 712.

65. Ellen L. Bassuk, Angela Browne, and John C. Buckner, "Single Mothers and Welfare," *Scientific American*, October 1996, 66–67.

66. Robert Pear, "Welfare Buying Power Wanes, Report Says," *San Francisco Chronicle*, November 19, 1996, A9.

67. U.S. Bureau of the Census, *Statistical Abstract of the United States* 1998 (Washington, D.C.: U.S. Government Printing Office, 1999), 390.

68. John Isbister, *Capitalism and Justice*. 118; cf. "A Howl from the States," *Economist*, May 25, 2002.

69. *Statistical Abstract of the United States 2002*, Table 660.

70. Ibid., Tables 657, 658, 668.

71. William Julius Wilson, *When Work Disappears* (New York: Random House, 1996), 159–160, 179–181, and "A Nation Apart: A Survey of America," *Economist*, November 8, 2003, 8.

Further Reading for Chapter 3

John Arthur and **William H. Shaw**, eds., *Justice and Economic Distribution*, 2nd ed. (Englewood Cliffs, N.J.: Prentice Hall, 1991) contains substantial extracts from Rawls's *A Theory of Justice* and Nozick's *Anarchy, State, and Utopia*, contemporary presentations of the utilitarian approach, and various recent essays discussing the topic of economic justice.

Joel Feinberg, *Social Philosophy* (Englewood Cliffs, N.J.: Prentice Hall, 1973), Chapter 7, discusses the different types of justice and injustice.

John Isbister, *Capitalism and Justice: Envisioning Social and Economic Fairness* (Bloomfield, Conn.: Kumarian Press, 2001) discusses a number of questions of justice in the real world, such as income distribution, taxation, welfare, and foreign aid, in a readable but thoughtful way.

Will Kymlicka, *Contemporary Political Philosophy*, 2nd ed. (Oxford: Oxford University Press, 2001) covers the major schools of contemporary political thought and their competing views of justice and community.

Robert M. Stewart, ed., *Readings in Social and Political Philosophy*, 2nd ed. (New York: Oxford University Press, 1996), Part III, provides a number of important essays on justice and equality, including contributions from Rawls and Nozick.

Various authors discuss economic inequality in the United States in special issues of *Social Philosophy and Policy* 19 (Winter 2002): "Should Differences in Income and Wealth Matter?" and *Daedalus* (Winter 2002): "On Inequality." See also Kevin Phillips, *Wealth and Democracy* (New York: Broadway Books, 2002).

InfoTrac College Edition: For further information or to conduct research, please go to www.infotrac-college.com.

||

PART TWO

AMERICAN
BUSINESS AND
ITS BASIS

4

The Nature
of Capitalism

In March 1996 the U.S. Department of Labor issued a report that most Americans took to be very good news, indeed: After months of concern about layoffs and declining economic prospects, the economy had added 700,000 jobs the previous month—more jobs than in any month since 1983. Further, the unemployment rate had fallen from 5.8 percent to 5.5 percent. This report wasn't considered good news, however, at the New York Stock Exchange, the heart of American capitalism. The day the report was issued, the Dow Jones industrial average plunged over 171 points, at the time its third largest point decline ever. Why? The reason is complicated. Although economic expansion and increased employment are good for ordinary people, they also raise the specter of inflation. Wall Street traders had been counting on the Federal Reserve Board to lower short-term interest rates and thus add fuel to a bull market, but any hint of inflation, traders feared, would prevent the Fed from doing so.

As it turned out, the sharp drop in the stock market that day was only a minor dip in the upward growth of a long bull market that still had four more years to run. And the brief pain investors felt then was nothing compared to the pain they were to feel in the early years of the present century as the air leaked gradually, but inexorably, out of what, by the end of the 1990s, had clearly become a speculative bubble in the stock market. High-flying dot-com and other technology stocks suffered the most as the laws of capitalist reality—which many pundits thought had been suspended as the United States was supposedly leading the world into a "new economy"—reasserted themselves, reducing the nominal value of American stocks by trillions of dollars. Experts disagree on the exact causes of the long run-up in stock prices (the Dow Jones industrial average had grown from 875 in 1982 to 11,497 in early 2000, and the technology-heavy NASDAQ index from 196 to 4,069). They also disagree on the causes of the stock market's subsequent decline. But they agree that Wall Street's troubles have reverberated around the globe, with stocks suffering in markets as far away as London, Tokyo, Johannesburg, and Hong Kong.

That is not surprising. Capitalism is a worldwide system, multinational firms operate without regard for traditional political boundaries, and the economies of capitalist nations are intricately interconnected. But what exactly is the nature of the economic system called capitalism? What is its underlying economic philosophy? What has it accomplished and what are its prospects for the future? This chapter examines these and related questions.

Looking back in history, one must definitely credit capitalism with helping break the constraints of medieval feudalism, which had severely limited individual possibilities for improvement. In place of a stifling economic system, capitalism offered opportunities for those blessed with imagination, an ability to plan, and a willingness to work. Capitalism must also be credited with enhancing the abundance and diversity of consumer goods beyond Adam Smith's wildest dreams. It has increased our material wealth and our standard of living and has converted our cities from modest bazaars into treasure troves of dazzling merchandise.

In the light of such accomplishments and the acculturation process that tends to glorify them, it is possible to overlook capitalism's theoretical and operational problems, which have serious moral import. This chapter attempts to identify some of these problems and their moral implications. It provides some basic historical and conceptual categories for understanding the socioeconomic framework within which business transactions occur and moral issues arise. In particular, this chapter addresses the following topics:

1. The definition of capitalism and its major historical stages

2. Four of the key features of capitalism: companies, profit motive, competition, and private property

3. Two classical moral justifications of capitalism—the first based on the right to property, the second on Adam Smith's concept of the "invisible hand"

4. Fundamental criticisms of capitalism—in particular, the persistence of inequality and poverty, capitalism's implicit view of human nature, the rise of economic oligarchies, the shortcomings of competition, and the employee's experience of alienation and exploitation on the job

5. The problems facing capitalism in the United States today—in particular, slow growth in productivity, excessive concern with the short term, declining interest in the actual manufacturing of goods, and our changing attitudes toward work

CAPITALISM

Capitalism can be defined ideally as an economic system in which the major portion of production and distribution is in private hands, operating under what is termed a profit or market system. The U.S. economy is the world's leading capitalistic economy. All manufacturing firms are privately owned, including those that produce military hardware for the government. The same applies to banks, insurance companies, and most transportation companies. All businesses—small, medium, and large—are also privately owned, as are power companies. With the exception of government expenditures for such things as health, education, welfare, highways, and military equipment, no central governing body dictates to these private owners what or how much of anything will be produced. For example, officials at Ford, Chrysler, and General Motors design their products and set their own production goals according to anticipated consumer demand.

The private ownership and market aspects of capitalism contrast with its polar opposite, socialism. Ideally, *socialism* is an economic system characterized by public ownership of property and a planned economy. Under socialism, a society's productive equipment is not owned by individuals (capitalists) but by public bodies. Socialism depends primarily on centralized planning rather than on the market system for both its overall allocation of resources and its distribution of income; crucial economic decisions are made not by individuals but by government. In the former Soviet Union, for example, government agencies decided the number of automobiles—including models, styles, and colors—to be produced each year. Top levels of government formulated production and cost objectives, which were then converted to specific production quotas and budgets that individual plant managers had to follow.

A hybrid economic system advocated by some socialists (and once approximated by Yugoslavia) is *worker control socialism.*[1] Individual firms respond to a market in acquiring the necessary factors of production and in deciding what to produce. The workforce of each enterprise controls the enterprise (although it may elect or hire managers to oversee day-to-day operations), and the profits accrue to the workers as a group to divide in whatever manner they agree on. However, although the workers manage their factories, the capital assets of each enterprise are owned by society as a whole and not by private individuals.

Historical Background of Capitalism

What we call capitalism did not fully emerge until the Renaissance in Europe during the fifteenth and sixteenth centuries. Before the Renaissance, business exchanges in medieval Europe were organized through guilds, which were associations of individuals of the same trade.

Today if you want a pair of shoes, you head for a shoe store, where you find an array of shoes. If nothing strikes your fancy, you set out for another shop, and perhaps another, until at last you find what you want. Or, if still disappointed, you might ask the store clerk to order a pair in your size from the manufacturer or its distributor. You certainly wouldn't ask the clerk to have someone make you a pair of shoes. Under the guild organization, shoemakers, who were also shoe sellers, made shoes only to fill orders. If they had no orders, they made no shoes. The shoemaker's sole economic function was to make shoes for people when they wanted them. His labor allowed him to maintain himself, not advance his station in life. When the shoemaker died, his business went with him—unless he had a son to inherit and carry on the enterprise. As for shoe quality and cost, the medieval shopper could generally count on getting a good pair of shoes at a fair price because the cobblers' guild strictly controlled quality and price.

Weaving was another big medieval trade. In fact, in the fourteenth century weaving was the leading industry in the German town of Augsburg. Little wonder, then, that an enterprising young man named Hans Fugger became a weaver when he settled there in 1367. But young Hans had ambitions that stretched far beyond the limits of the weaving trade and the handicraft guild system. And they were grandly realized, for within three short generations a family of simple weavers was transformed into a great German banking dynasty.[2]

Not content with being a weaver, Hans Fugger began collecting and selling the products of other weavers. Soon he was employing lots of weavers, paying them for their labor, and selling their products as his own. His son, Jacob Fugger, continued the business, which was expanded by Jacob Fugger II, the foremost capitalist of the Renaissance. Under his direction, the family's interests expanded into metals and textiles. Jacob Fugger II also lent large sums of money to the Hapsburg emperors to finance their wars, among other things. In return, he obtained monopoly rights on silver and copper ores, which he then traded. When Fugger bought the mines themselves, he had acquired all the components necessary to erect an extraordinary financial dynasty.

Like latter-day titans of American industry, Fugger employed thousands of workers and paid them wages, controlled all his products from raw material to market, set his own quality standards, and charged whatever the traffic would bear. In one brief century, what was once a handicraft inseparable from the craftsperson had become a company that existed outside any family members. What had once motivated Hans Fugger—maintenance of his station in life—had given way to gain for gain's sake, the so-called *profit motive*. Under Jacob Fugger II, the company amassed profits, a novel concept, that well exceeded the needs of the Fuggers. And the profits were measured not in goods or in land but in money.

Capitalism has undergone changes since then.[3] For example, the kind of capitalism that emerged in the Fuggers' time is often termed *mercantile capitalism*, because it was based on mutual dependence between state and commercial interests. Implicit in mercantile capitalism are the beliefs that national wealth and power are best served by increasing exports and collecting precious metals in return, and that the role of government is to provide laws and economic policies designed to encourage production for foreign trade, keep out imports, and promote national supremacy.

In the United States in the period after the Civil War, *industrial capitalism* emerged, which is associated with the development of large-scale industry. The confluence of many postwar factors produced industrial expansion in America, including a sound financial base, the technology for mass production, expanding markets for cheaply manufactured goods, and a large and willing labor force. Exploiting these fortuitous conditions was a group of hard-driving, visionary entrepreneurs called robber barons by their critics and captains of industry by their supporters: Cornelius Vanderbilt, Cyrus McCormick, Andrew Carnegie, John D. Rockefeller, Jay Gould, and others.

As industrialization increased, so did the size and power of business. The private fortunes of a few individuals could no longer underwrite the accelerated growth of business activity. The large sums of capital necessary could be raised only through a corporate form of business, in which risk and potential profit were distributed among numerous investors.

As competition intensified, an industry's survival came to depend on its financial strength to reduce prices and either eliminate or absorb competition. To shore up their assets, industries engaged in *financial capitalism*, characterized by pools, trusts, holding companies, and an interpenetration of banking, insurance, and industrial interests. Hand in hand with this development, the trend continued toward larger and larger corporations, controlling more and more of the country's economic capacity.

The economic and political challenges of the Great Depression of the 1930s helped usher in still another phase of capitalism, often called *state welfare capitalism*, in which government plays an active role in regulating economic activities in an effort to smooth out the boom-and-bust pattern of the business cycle. In addition, government programs like Social Security and unemployment insurance seek to enhance the welfare of the workforce, and legislation legitimizes the existence of trade unions. Today state welfare capitalism prevails. Conservative politicians sometimes advocate less govern- ment control of business, but in reality the governments of all capitalist countries are deeply involved in the management of their economies.

Although the study of capitalism's evolution is best left to economic historians, it is important to keep in mind capitalism's dynamic nature. There is nothing fixed and immutable about this or any other economic system; it is as susceptible to the social forces of change as any other institution. Nevertheless, the capitalism we know does have some prominent features that were evident in the earliest capitalistic businesses.

KEY FEATURES OF CAPITALISM

Complete coverage of capitalism's features has filled many a book. Four features of par- ticular significance—the existence of companies, profit motive, competition, and pri- vate property—will be discussed briefly here.

Companies

Chapter 2 mentioned the Firestone case, in which a media misrepresentation was left uncorrected. When asked why Firestone officials had not corrected the error, a Firestone spokesperson said that Firestone's policy was to ask for corrections only when it was beneficial to the company to do so. Expressions like "Firestone's policy" and "benefi- cial to the company" reflect one key feature of capitalism: the existence of companies or business firms separate from the human beings who work for and within them.

"It's not in the company's interests," "The company thinks that," "From the com- pany's viewpoint," "As far as the company is concerned"—all of us have heard, per- haps even used, expressions that treat a business organization like a person or at least like a separate and distinct entity. Such personifications are not mere lapses into the fig- urative but bespeak a basic characteristic of capitalism: Capitalism permits the cre- ation of companies or business organizations that exist separately from the people associated with them. We take the existence of companies for granted, but some experts believe that it is not church or state, but the company that is "the most important organ- ization in the world."[4]

Today the big companies we're familiar with—General Electric, AT&T, Ford, IBM— are, in fact, incorporated businesses, or corporations. Chapter 5 discusses the nature of the modern corporation, including its historical evolution and its social responsibili- ties. Here it's enough to observe that, in the nineteenth century, Chief Justice John Marshall defined a *corporation* as "an artificial being, invisible, intangible, and existing only in the contemplation of law." Although a corporation is not something that can be seen or touched, it does have prescribed rights and legal obligations within the com- munity. Like you or me, a corporation may enter into contracts and may sue or be sued in courts of law. It may even do things that the corporation's members disapprove of. The corporations that loom large on our economic landscape harken back to a feature of capitalism evident as early as the Fugger dynasty: the existence of the company.

Profit Motive

A second characteristic of capitalism lies in the motive of the company: to make profit. As dollar-directed and gain-motivated as our society is, most of us take for granted that the human being is by nature an acquisitive creature who, left to his or her own devices, will pursue profit with all the instinctual vigor of a cat chasing a mouse. However, as economist Robert Heilbroner points out, the "profit motive, as we understand it, is a very recent phenomenon. It was foreign to the lower and middle classes of Egyptian, Greek, Roman, and medieval cultures, only scattered throughout the Renaissance times, and largely absent in most Eastern civilizations." The medieval church taught that no Christian ought to be a merchant. "Even to our Pilgrim forefathers," Heilbroner writes, "the idea that gain ought to be a tolerable—even a useful—goal in life would have appeared as nothing short of a doctrine of the devil." Heilbroner concludes: "As a ubiquitous characteristic of society, the profit motive is as modern an invention as printing."[5]

Modern or not, profit in the form of money is the lifeblood of the capitalist system. Companies and capitalists alike are motivated by a robust appetite for money profit. Indeed, the profit motive implies and reflects a critical assumption about human nature: that human beings are basically economic creatures, who recognize and are motivated by their own economic self-interests.

Competition

If self-interest and an appetite for money profit drive individuals and companies, then what stops them short of holding up society for exorbitant ransom? What stops capitalists from bleeding society dry?

Adam Smith provided an answer in his monumental treatise on political economy, *An Inquiry into the Nature and Causes of the Wealth of Nations* (1776). Free competition, said Smith, is the regulator that keeps a community activated only by self-interest from degenerating into a mob of ruthless profiteers. When traditional restraints are removed from the sale of goods and from wages and when all individuals have equal access to raw materials and markets (the doctrine of *laissez faire,* from the French meaning "to let [people] do [as they choose]"), we are all free to pursue our own interests. In pursuing our own interests, however, we come smack up against others similarly motivated. If any of us allow blind self-interest to dictate our actions—for example, by price gouging or employee exploitation—we will quickly find ourselves beaten out by a competitor who, let's say, charges less and pays a better wage. Competition thus regulates individual economic activity.

To sample the flavor of Smith's argument, imagine an acquisitive young woman in a faraway place who wants to pile up as much wealth as possible. She looks about her and sees that people need and want strong twilled cotton trousers, so she takes her investment capital and sets up a jeans factory. She charges $45 for a pair of jeans and soon realizes handsome profits. The woman's success is not lost on other business minds, especially manufacturers of formal slacks and dresses, who observe a sharp decline in those markets. Wanting a piece of the jeans action, numerous enterprises start up jeans factories. Many of these start selling jeans for $40 a pair. No longer alone in the market, our hypothetical businesswoman must either check her appetite for profit by lowering her price or risk folding. As the number of jeans on the market increases, their supply eventually overtakes demand, and the price of jeans declines further and further. Inefficient manufacturers start dropping like flies. As the competition thins out, the demand for jeans slowly balances with the supply, and the price regulates itself. Ultimately, an equilibrium is reached between supply and demand, and the price of jeans stabilizes, yielding a normal profit to the efficient producer.

In much this way, Adam Smith tried to explain how economic competition steers individuals pursuing self-interest in a socially beneficial direction. By appealing to their self-interest, society can induce producers to provide it with what it wants—just as manufacturers of formal slacks and dresses were enticed into jeans production. But competition keeps prices for desired goods from escalating; high prices are self-correcting because they call forth an increased supply.

Private Property

In its discussion of the libertarian theory of justice, Chapter 3 emphasized that property should not be identified only with physical objects like houses, cars, and video recorders. Nor should ownership be thought of as a simple relationship between the owner and the thing owned. First, one can have property rights over things that are not simple physical objects, as when one owns stock in a company. Second, property ownership involves a generally complex bundle of rights and rules governing how, under what circumstances, and in what ways both the owner and others can use, possess, dispose of, and have access to the thing in question.

Private property is central to capitalism. To put it another way, capitalism as a socioeconomic system is a specific form of private property. What matters for capitalism is not private property simply in the sense of personal possessions, because a socialist society can certainly permit people to own houses, television sets, and jogging shoes. Rather, capitalism requires private ownership of the major means of production and distribution. The means of production and distribution include factories, warehouses, offices, machines, computer systems, trucking fleets, agricultural land, and whatever else makes up the economic resources of a nation. Under capitalism, private hands control these basic economic assets and productive resources. Thus, the major economic decisions are made by individuals or groups acting on their own in pursuit of profit. These decisions are not directly coordinated with those of other producers, nor are they the result of some overall plan. Any profits (or losses) that result from these decisions about production are those of the owners.

Capital, as an economic concept, is closely related to private property. Putting it simply, capital is money that is invested for the purpose of making more money. Individuals or corporations purchase various means of production or other related assets and use them to produce goods or provide services, which are then sold. They do this not for the purpose of being nice or of helping people out but rather to make money—more money, hopefully, than they spent to make the goods or provide the services in the first place. Using money to make money is at the heart of the definition of capitalism.

MORAL JUSTIFICATIONS OF CAPITALISM

People tend to take for granted the desirability and moral legitimacy of the political and economic system within which they live. Americans are no exception. We are raised in a society that encourages individual competition, praises capitalism, promotes the acquisition of material goods, and worships economic wealth. Newspapers, television, recordings, movies, and other forms of popular culture celebrate these values, and rarely are we presented with fundamental criticisms of or possible alternatives to our socioeconomic order. Small wonder, then, that most of us blithely assume, without ever bothering to question, that our capitalist economic system is a morally justifiable one.

Yet as thinking people and moral agents, it is important that we reflect on the nature and justifiability of our social institutions. The proposition that capitalism is a morally acceptable system is very much open to debate. Whether we decide that capitalism is morally justified will depend, at least in part, on which general theory of justice turns out to be the soundest. Chapter 3 explored in detail the utilitarian approach, the libertarian alternative, and the theory of John Rawls. Now, against that background, this chapter looks at two basic ways defenders of capitalism have sought to justify their system: first, the argument that the moral right to property guarantees the legitimacy of capitalism and, second, the utilitarian-based economic argument of Adam Smith. The chapter then considers some criticisms of capitalism.

The Natural Right to Property

As Americans, we live in a socioeconomic system that guarantees us certain property rights. Although we are no longer permitted to own other people, we are certainly free to own a variety of other things, from livestock to stock certificates, from our own homes to whole blocks of apartment buildings. A common defense of capitalism is the argument that people have a fundamental moral right to property and that our capitalist system is simply the outcome of this natural right.

In Chapter 3, we saw how Locke attempted to base the right to property in human labor. When individuals mix their labor with the natural world, they are entitled to the results. This idea seems plausible in many cases. For example, if Carl diligently harvests coconuts on the island he shares with Adam, while Adam himself idles away his days, then most of us would agree that Carl has an entitlement to those coconuts that Adam lacks. But property ownership as it actually exists in the real world today is a very complex, socially shaped phenomenon. This is especially true in the case of sophisticated forms of corporate and financial property—for example, bonds or stock options.

One could, of course, reject the whole idea of a natural right to property as a fiction, as, for example, utilitarians do. In their view, although various property systems exist, there is no natural right that things be owned privately, collectively, or in any particular way whatsoever. The moral task is to find that property system, that way of organizing production and distribution, with the greatest utility. Yet even if one believes that there is a natural right to property, at least under some circumstances, one need not believe that this right leads to capitalism or that it is a right to have a system of property rules and regulations just like the one we now have in the United States. That is, even if Carl has a natural right to his coconuts, there may still be moral limits on how many coconuts he can rightfully amass and what he can use them for. When he takes his coconuts to the coconut bank and receives further coconuts as interest, his newly acquired coconuts are not the result of any new labor on his part. When we look at capitalistic property—that is, at socioeconomic environments in which people profit from ownership alone—then we have left Locke's world far behind.

A defender of capitalism may reply, "Certainly, there's nothing unfair about Carl's accruing these extra coconuts through his investment; after all, he could have eaten his original coconuts instead." And, indeed, within our system this reasoning seems perfectly correct. It is the way things work in our society. But this fact doesn't prove that Carl has some natural right to use his coconuts to make more coconuts—that is, that it would be unfair or unjust to set up a different economic system (for example, one in which he had a right to consume his coconuts but no right to use them to earn more coconuts).

The argument here is simply that the issue is not an all-or-nothing one. There may be certain fundamental moral rights to property, but those rights need not be unlimited nor guarantee capitalism as we know it.

Adam Smith's Concept of the Invisible Hand

Relying on the idea of a natural right to property is not the only way and probably not the best way to defend capitalism. Another, very important argument defends capitalism in terms of the many economic benefits the system brings, claiming that a free and unrestrained market system, which exists under capitalism, is more efficient and more productive than any other possible system and is thus to be preferred on moral grounds. Essentially, this is a utilitarian argument, but one doesn't have to be a utilitarian to take it seriously. As mentioned in Chapter 2, almost every normative theory puts some moral weight on the consequences of actions. Thus if capitalism does indeed work better than other ways of organizing economic life, then this will be a very relevant moral fact—one that will be important, for instance, for Rawlsians.

This section sketches Adam Smith's economic case for capitalism, as presented in *The Wealth of Nations*. Smith argues that when people are left to pursue their own interests, they will, without intending it, produce the greatest good for all. Each person's individual and private pursuit of wealth results—as if, in Smith's famous phrase, "an invisible hand" were at work—in the most beneficial overall organization and distribution of economic resources. Although the academic study of economics has developed greatly since Smith's times, his classic arguments remain extraordinarily influential.

Smith took it for granted that human beings are acquisitive creatures. Self-interest and personal advantage, specifically in an economic sense, may not be all that motivate people, but they do seem to motivate most people much of the time. At any rate, they are powerful enough forces that any successful economic system must strive to harness them. We are, Smith thought, strongly inclined to act so as to acquire more and more wealth.

In addition, humans have a natural propensity for trading—"to truck, barter, and exchange." Unlike other species, we have an almost constant need for the assistance of others. Yet because people are creatures of self-interest, it is folly for us to expect others to act altruistically toward us. We can secure what we need from others only by offering them something they need from us:

> Whoever offers to another a bargain of any kind, proposes to do this. Give me that which I want, and you shall have this which you want, is the meaning of every such offer; and it is in this manner that we obtain from one another the far greater part of those good offices which we stand in need of. It is not from the benevolence of the butcher, the brewer, or the baker that we expect our dinner, but from their regard to their own interest. We address ourselves, not to their humanity but to their self love, and never talk to them of our own necessities but of their advantages.[6]

This disposition to trade, said Smith, leads to the division of labor—dividing the labor and production process into areas of specialization, which is the prime means of increasing economic productivity.

Thus, Smith reasoned that the greatest utility will result from unfettered pursuit of self-interest. Individuals should be allowed unrestricted access to raw materials, markets, and labor. Government interference in private enterprise should be eliminated, free competition encouraged, and economic self-interest made the rule of the day.

Because human beings are acquisitive creatures, we will, if left free, engage in labor and exchange goods in a way that results in the greatest benefit to society. In our efforts to advance our own economic interests, we inevitably act to promote the economic well-being of society generally:

> Every individual is continually exerting himself to find the most advantageous employment for whatever capital he can command. It is his own advantage, indeed, and not that of the society, which he has in view. . . . [But] by directing that industry in such a manner as its produce may be of the greatest value, he [is] . . . led by an invisible hand to promote an end that was no part of his intention. . . . By pursuing his own interest he frequently promotes that of society more effectually than when he really intends to promote it.[7]

To explain why pursuit of self-interest necessarily leads to the greatest social benefit, Smith invoked the law of supply and demand, which was alluded to in discussing competition. The law of supply and demand tempers the pursuit of self-interest exactly as competition keeps the enterprising capitalist from becoming a ruthless profiteer. The law of supply and demand similarly solves the problems of adequate goods and fair prices.

Some think the law of supply and demand even solves the problem of fair wages, for labor is another commodity up for sale like shoes or jeans. Just as the price of a new product at first is high, like the jeans in our earlier hypothetical example, so, too, are the wages of labor in a new field. But as labor becomes more plentiful, wages decline. Eventually they fall to a point at which inefficient laborers are eliminated and forced to seek other work, just as the inefficient manufacturers of jeans were forced out of that business and into others. And like the price of jeans, the price of labor then stabilizes at a fair level. As for the inefficient laborers, they find work and a living wage elsewhere. In seeking new fields of labor, they help maximize the majority's opportunities to enjoy the necessities, conveniences, and trifles of human life.

Some modern defenders of capitalism claim that it operates as Smith envisioned and can be justified on the same utilitarian grounds. But not everyone agrees.

CRITICISMS OF CAPITALISM

The two major defenses of capitalism have not persuaded critics that it is a morally justifiable system. Their objections to capitalism are both theoretical and operational. Theoretical criticisms challenge capitalism's fundamental values, basic assumptions, or inherent economic tendencies. Operational criticisms focus more on capitalism's alleged deficiencies in actual practice (as opposed to theory)—in particular, on its failure to live up to its own economic ideals.

The following criticisms are a mix of both theoretical and operational concerns. They raise political, economic, and philosophical issues that cannot be fully assessed here. The debate over capitalism is a large and important one; the presentation that follows should be viewed as a stimulus to further discussion and not as the last word on the pros and cons of capitalism.

Inequality

Chapter 3 and Case 3.2 documented the profound economic inequality that exists in our capitalist society. The disparity in personal incomes is enormous; a tiny minority of the population owns the vast majority of the country's productive assets; and at the beginning of the twenty-first century, our society continues to be marred by poverty and homelessness. With divisions of social and economic class comes inequality of opportunity. A child born to a working-class family, let alone to an unwed teenager in an inner-city ghetto, has life prospects and possibilities that pale beside those of children born to wealthy, stock-owning parents. This reality challenges capitalism's claim of fairness, and the persistence of poverty and economic misfortune provides the basis for a utilitarian objection to it.

Few doubt that poverty and inequality are bad things, but defenders of capitalism make several responses to those who criticize it on these grounds:

1. A few extreme supporters of capitalism simply deny that it is responsible for poverty and inequality. Rather, they say, government interference with the market causes these problems. Left to itself, the market would eliminate unemployment and poverty while ultimately lessening inequality. But neither theoretical economics nor the study of history supports this reply. Most economists and social theorists would agree that in the past seventy years or so activist government policies have done much, in all the Western capitalist countries, to reduce poverty and (to a lesser extent) inequality.

2. More moderate defenders of capitalism concede that, in its pure laissez-faire form, capitalism does nothing to prevent and may even foster inequality and poverty. However, they argue that the system can be modified or its inherent tendencies corrected by political action, so that inequality and poverty are reduced or even eliminated. Critics of capitalism reply that the policies necessary to seriously reduce inequality and poverty are either impossible within a basically capitalist economic framework or unlikely to be carried out in any political system based on capitalism.

3. Finally, defenders of capitalism argue that the benefits of the system outweigh this weak point. Inequality is not so important if living standards are rising and even the poor have better lives than they did in previous times. This contention rests on an implicit comparison with what things would be like if society were organized differently and is, accordingly, difficult to assess. Naturally, it seems more plausible to those who are relatively favored by, and content with, the present economic system than it does to those who feel disadvantaged by it.

Some critics of capitalism go on to maintain that, aside from inequalities of income and ownership, the inequality inherent in the worker-capitalist relationship is itself morally undesirable. John Stuart Mill found capitalism inferior in this respect to more cooperative and egalitarian economic arrangements. "To work at the bidding and for the profit of another," he wrote, "is not . . . a satisfactory state to human beings of educated intelligence, who have ceased to think themselves inferior to those whom they serve."[8] The ideal of escaping from a system of "superiors" and "subordinates" was well expressed by the great German playwright and poet Bertolt Brecht when he wrote that "He wants no servants under him / And no boss over his head."[9]

Human Nature and Capitalism

The theory of capitalism rests on a view of human beings as rational economic creatures, individuals who recognize and are motivated largely by their own economic self-interests. Adam Smith's defense of capitalism, for instance, assumes that consumers have full knowledge of the diverse choices available to them in the marketplace. They are supposed to know the price structures of similar products, to be fully aware of product differences, and to be able to make the optimal choice regarding price and quality.

But the key choices facing today's consumers are rarely simple. From foods to drugs, automobiles to appliances, fertilizers to air conditioners, the modern marketplace is a cornucopia of products whose nature and nuances require a high level of consumer literacy. Even with government agencies and public interest groups to aid them, today's consumers are rarely an equal match for powerful industries that can influence prices and create and shape markets. The effectiveness of advertising, in particular, is difficult to reconcile with the picture of consumers as the autonomous, rational, and perfectly informed economic maximizers that economics textbooks presuppose when they attempt to demonstrate the benefits of capitalism. Consumers frequently seem to be pawns of social and economic forces beyond their control.

According to some critics of capitalism, however, what is objectionable about capitalism's view of human beings as essentially economic creatures is not this gap between theory and reality but rather the fact that it presents little in the way of an ideal to which either individuals or societies may aspire. As George Soros puts it, "Humans are capable of transcending the pursuit of narrow self-interest. Indeed, they cannot live without some sense of morality. It is market fundamentalism, which holds that the social good is best served by allowing people to pursue their self-interest without any thought for the social good . . . that is a perversion of human nature."[10] Not only does capitalism rest on the premise that people are basically acquisitive, individualistic, and materialistic, but in practice capitalism strongly reinforces those human tendencies. Capitalism, its critics charge, presents no higher sense of human mission or purpose, whereas other views of society and human nature do.

Christianity, for example, has long aspired to the ideal of a truly religious community united in *agape*, selfless love. And socialism, because it views human nature as malleable, hopes to see people transformed from the "competitive, acquisitive beings that they are (and that they are *encouraged* to be) under all property-dominated, market-oriented systems." In the more "benign environment of a propertyless, non-market social system," socialists believe that more cooperative and less selfish human beings will emerge.[11] Such positive ideals and aspirations are lacking in capitalism—or so its critics charge.

Competition Isn't What It's Cracked Up to Be

As we have seen, one of the key features of capitalism is competition. Unfettered competition supposedly serves the collective interest while offering rich opportunities for the individual. But competition is one of the targets of capitalism's critics. They contend that capitalism breeds oligopolies that eliminate competition and concentrate economic power, that a system of corporate welfare protects many businesses from true marketplace competition, and finally that competition is neither generally beneficial nor desirable in itself.

Capitalism Breeds Oligopolies   As early as the middle of the nineteenth century, the German philosopher and political economist Karl Marx (1818–1883) argued that capitalism leads to a concentration of property and resources, and thus economic power, in the hands of a few. High costs, complex and expensive machinery, intense competition, and the advantages of large-scale production all work against the survival of small firms, said Marx. Many see proof of Marx's argument in today's economy.

Before the Industrial Revolution, capitalism was characterized by comparatively free and open competition among a large number of small firms. Since then the economy has come to be dominated by a relatively small number of enormous companies that can, to a distressing extent, conspire to set prices, eliminate competition, and monopolize an industry. The food industry is a perfect example, with four or fewer firms controlling the vast majority of sales of almost any given product.[12]

Antitrust actions have sometimes fostered competition and broken up monopolies, as in the cases of such corporate behemoths as Standard Oil and AT&T. And recently the government has gone after Microsoft for "exclusionary and predatory" business practices. On the whole, however, such actions have proved ineffectual in halting the concentration of economic power in large oligopolistic firms. Increasingly multinational in character, these giant corporations frequently do business around the globe, disavowing allegiance to any particular nation. Today more than a quarter of the world's economic activity comes from the 200 largest corporations.[13]

Robert Heilbroner suggests that the rise of such giant enterprises has changed the face of capitalism as they attempt to alter the market setting through a system of public and private planning. This planning assumes many guises, from union contracts that eliminate uncertainties in the labor market to sophisticated advertising calculated to foster dependable product markets; from tacit price-fixing within an industry to cozy relationships with government intended to create programs that will ensure continuing high levels of demand. "At its worst," he writes, "we find it in the military-industrial complex— the very epitome of the new symbiotic business-government relations."[14]

Business professor Robert B. Carson concurs that in terms of competition, our present-day economic system differs from the textbook model of capitalism. He writes:

> In surveying the American business system it is obvious that competition still exists; however, it is not a perfect competition. Often it is not price competition at all. With the possible exception of some farm markets where there are still large numbers of producers of similar and undifferentiated products (wheat, for instance), virtually every producer of goods and services has some control over price. The degree of control varies from industry to industry and between firms within an industry. Nevertheless, it does exist and it amounts to an important modification in our model of a free-enterprise economy.[15]

Corporate Welfare Programs Protect Businesses   In March 2002 President Bush slapped tariffs ranging from 8 percent to 30 percent on imported steel, continuing a thirty-year tradition of cosseting the steel industry with various subsidies and protections that has cost users $120 billion. The tariffs were held to be necessary because of a surge of imported steel, even though foreign steel imports had declined 27.5 percent in the preceding four years.[16] Later that year Congress passed a farm bill that dramatically increased subsidies on large staple crops like lentils and peanuts, and reinstated subsidies that had previously been eliminated on crops like honey, wool, and mohair. Overall, the bill increases agricultural subsidies by 80 percent and will cost the government $180 to $190 billion over ten years.[17] Nationally, farm subsidies already total about $20 billion a year—which doesn't include the higher prices that consumers pay. Most of the money goes to the largest and wealthiest farmers, a secret that the

Environment Working Group made public for the first time when, thanks to the Freedom of Information Act, it posted on its Web site a listing of every farm subsidy received by every farmer since 1996.

Subsidies for farmers and tariffs for the steel industry are just the most blatant examples of the way corporate welfare programs assist business and protect it from competition. Thanks to duties, fees, and restrictions on imported products, American consumers pay at least $75 billion a year more for goods than they otherwise would.[18] And this, of course, is in addition to what corporate subsidies cost them as taxpayers.

For example, the Agriculture Department's Market Access Program funds both generic and brand-name advertising abroad for American agricultural products. The program paid $450,000 to Campbell Soup Company to help it entice Japanese, Koreans, and Argentineans to drink V-8 juice, and it also laid out $1 million to M&M Mars to improve consumer recognition of its product; $1.5 million to push sales of mink coats; $6.6 million to promote Sunkist oranges; and $4.9 million to Ernest and Julio Gallo to market its wines internationally.[19] The program's annual price tag is $85 million, which is less than what it costs for the U.S. Forest Service to build roads and subsidize logging in national forests for the benefit of private timber companies.[20] The Foreign Military Financing Program spends around $3.3 billion each year assisting foreign countries to purchase U.S. military products. The Department of Commerce's Advanced Technology Program supports high-tech research. In practice, this has meant payments of $14.5 million to General Electric, $34 million to AT&T, and a whopping $50.9 million to Boeing.[21] Other government-sponsored corporate welfare programs include the Export Enhancement Program, the Export-Import Bank, and the Overseas Private Investment Corporation. In recent years, for example, the latter two agencies have provided $32 billion in loans and financial guarantees for corporate energy projects. Among the beneficiaries are Unocal, which was loaned $350 million to develop an oil and gas field in Indonesia, and ExxonMobil, which received $500 million in financing to build a pipeline in Cameroon.[22]

The list goes on and on.[23] Every year the federal government doles out an estimated $85 billion to private business in direct subsidy programs. In addition, the government spent an estimated $200 billion over a ten-year period bailing out the savings and loan industry. Some put total federal spending for corporate welfare at over $167 billion a year, which is far more than combined state and federal spending on social welfare programs for the poor.[24] And this doesn't begin to take account of corporate subsidies and protectionist restrictions on competition imposed by the individual states. It's impossible to put a price tag on these, but looking at the Internet alone, experts calculate that state impediments to buying and selling cost consumers $15 billion a year. For example, Georgia forbids the sale of contact lenses, and Oklahoma the sale of caskets, on line. And all fifty states shield their car dealers from competition by prohibiting manufacturers from selling directly to consumers over the Internet.[25]

Competition Is Not a Good   Because the profit motive governs capitalism, it should not be surprising that even those companies that preach the doctrine of free competition are willing to shelve it when collusion with other firms, or government tariffs and subsidies, make higher profits possible. How else to explain the fact that the United States forbids foreign companies from owning airlines in America and prevents foreign airlines from picking up passengers at more than one American city?

In these ways, capitalism fails to live up to its own ideal. But some critics of capitalism repudiate the ideal of competition, arguing that competition is neither beneficial in general nor desirable in itself.

The critics point to empirical studies establishing that in business environments there is frequently a negative correlation between performance and individual competitiveness.[26] In other words, it is often cooperation, rather than competitiveness, that best enhances both individual and group achievement. According to Alfie Kohn, the reason is simple: "Trying to do well and trying to beat others are two different things."[27] Competition is an extrinsic motivator; not only does it not produce the kind of results that flow from enjoying the activity itself, but also the use of extrinsic motivators can undermine intrinsic motivation and thus adversely affect performance in the long run. The unpleasantness of competition can also diminish people's performance.

The critics also contend that competition often precludes the more efficient use of resources that cooperation allows. When people work together, coordination of effort and an efficient division of labor are possible. By contrast, competition can inhibit economic coordination, cause needless duplication of services, retard the exchange of information, foster copious litigation, and lead to socially detrimental or counterproductive results such as business failures, mediocre products, unsafe working conditions, and environmental neglect. When presented with examples of the beneficial results of competition, the critics argue that on closer inspection the supposed advantages turn out to be short lived, illusory, or isolated instances.

Exploitation and Alienation

Marx argued that as the means of production become concentrated in the hands of the few, the balance of power between capitalists (bourgeoisie) and laborers (proletariat) tips further in favor of the bourgeoisie. Because workers have nothing to sell but their labor, said Marx, the bourgeoisie is able to exploit them by paying them less than the true value created by their labor. In fact, Marx thought, it is only through such an exploitative arrangement that capitalists make a profit and increase their capital. And the more capital they accumulate, the more they can exploit workers. Marx predicted that eventually workers would revolt. Unwilling to be exploited further, they would rise and overthrow their oppressors and set up an economic system that would truly benefit all.

The development of capitalist systems since Marx's time belies his forecast. Legal, political, and economic changes have tempered many of the greedy, exploitative dispositions of early capitalism. The twentieth century witnessed legislation curbing egregious worker abuse, guaranteeing a minimum wage, and ensuring a safer and more healthful work environment. The emergence of labor unions and their subsequent victories significantly enlarged the worker's share of the economic pie. Indeed, many of the specific measures proposed by Marx and his collaborator Friedrich Engels in the *Communist Manifesto* (1848) have been implemented in capitalist countries: a program of graduated income tax, free education for all children in public schools, investiture of significant economic control in the state, and so on.

Still, many would say that although democratic institutions may have curbed the excesses of capitalism, they can do nothing to prevent the alienation of workers that results from having to do unfulfilling work. Again, because of the unequal positions of capitalist and worker, laborers must work for someone else—they must do work imposed on them as a means of satisfying the needs of others. As a result, they must eventually feel exploited and debased. And this is true, critics of capitalism claim, not just of manual laborers, but also of white-collar workers, many of whom identify with the cubicle dwellers of the cartoon strip *Dilbert*.

But what about workers who are paid handsomely for their efforts? They, too, said Marx, remain alienated, for as the fruits of their labor are enjoyed by someone else, their work ultimately proves meaningless to them. The following selection from Marx's "Economic and Philosophic Manuscripts" (1844) summarizes his notion of alienation as the separation of individuals from the objects they create, which in turn results in one's separation from other people, from oneself, and ultimately from one's human nature:

> The worker is related to the *product of his labor* as to an *alien* object. For it is clear . . . that the more the worker expends himself in work the more powerful becomes the world of objects which he creates in face of himself, the poorer he becomes in his inner life, and the less he belongs to himself. . . . The worker puts his life into the object, and his life then belongs no longer to himself but to the object. . . . What is embodied in the product of his labor is no longer his own. The greater this product is, therefore, the more he is diminished. The *alienation* of the worker in his product means not only that his labor becomes an object, assumes an *external* existence, but that it exists independently, *outside himself,* and alien to him, and that it stands opposed to him as an autonomous power. . . .
>
> What constitutes the alienation of labor? First, that the work is *external* to the worker, that it is not part of his nature; and that, consequently, he does not fulfill himself in his work but denies himself. . . . His work is not voluntary but imposed, *forced labor*. It is not the satisfaction of a need, but only a *means* for satisfying other needs. Its alien character is clearly shown by the fact that as soon as there is no physical or other compulsion it is avoided like the plague. External labor, labor in which man alienates himself, is a labor of self-sacrifice. . . . Finally, the external character of work for the worker is shown by the fact that it is not his own work but work for someone else, that in work he does not belong to himself but to another person. . . .
>
> We have now considered the act of alienation of practical human activity, labor, from two aspects: (1) the relationship of the worker to the *product of labor* as an alien object which dominates him . . . [and] (2) the relationship of labor to the *act of production* within *labor*. This is the relationship of the worker to his own activity as something alien and not belonging to him. . . . This is *self-alienation* as against the above-mentioned alienation of the *thing*.[28]

In Marx's view, when workers are alienated they cannot be truly free. They may have the political and social freedoms of speech, religion, and governance, but even with these rights, individuals still are not fully free. Freedom from government interference and persecution does not necessarily guarantee freedom from economic exploitation and alienation, and it is for this kind of freedom that Marx and Engels felt such passion.

Some would say that one need not wade through Marxist philosophy to get a feel for what he and others mean by worker alienation. Just talk to workers themselves, as writer Studs Terkel did. In different ways the hundreds of workers from diverse occupations that Terkel interviewed speak of the same thing: dehumanization.

Mike Fitzgerald . . . is a laborer in a steel mill. "I feel like the guys who built the pyramids. Somebody built 'em. Somebody built the Empire State Building, too. There's hard work behind it. I would like to see a building, say the Empire State, with a footwide strip from top to bottom and the name of every bricklayer on it, the name of every electrician. So when a guy walked by, he could take his son and say, 'See, that's me over there on the 45th floor. I put that steel beam in.' . . . Everybody should have something to point to."

Sharon Atkins is 24 years old. She's been to college and acidly observes, "The first myth that blew up in my face is that a college education will get you a worthwhile job." For the last two years she's been a receptionist at an advertising agency. "I didn't look at myself as 'just a dumb broad' at the front desk, who took phone calls and messages. I thought I was something else. The office taught me differently."

. . . Harry Stallings, 27, is a spot welder on the assembly line at an auto plant. "They'll give better care to that machine than they will to you. If it breaks down, there's somebody out there to fix it right away. If I break down, I'm just pushed over to the other side till another man takes my place. The only thing the company has in mind is to keep that machine running. A man would be more eager to do a better job if he were given proper respect and the time to do it."[29]

TODAY'S ECONOMIC CHALLENGES

Capitalism faces a number of important critical questions, both theoretical and operational. These criticisms are a powerful challenge, especially to capitalism in its pure laissez-faire form. But, as we have seen, today's capitalism is a long way from the laissez-faire model. Corporate behemoths able to control markets and sway governments have replaced the small-scale entrepreneurs and free-wheeling competition of an earlier day. And governments in all capitalist countries actively intervene in the economic realm; they endeavor to assist or modify the so-called invisible hand; and over the years they have reformed or supplemented capitalism with programs intended to enhance the security of the workforce and increase the welfare of their citizens.

This reality complicates the debate over capitalism. Its defenders may be advocating either the pure laissez-faire ideal or the modified state welfare capitalism that we in fact have. Likewise, those who attack the laissez-faire ideal may do so on behalf of a modified, welfarist capitalism, or they may criticize both forms of capitalism and defend some kind of socialism, in which private property and the pursuit of profit are no longer governing economic principles. We thus have a three-way debate over the respective strengths and weaknesses of laissez-faire capitalism, state welfare capitalism, and socialism.

The rest of this chapter leaves this fundamental debate behind. Instead of looking at criticisms of capitalism in general and at issues relevant to any capitalist society, it examines some of the more specific socioeconomic challenges facing the United States today. These problems include slow growth in productivity, business's obsession with short-term results and its declining interest in production, and our changing attitudes toward work.

Slow Growth in Productivity

At the beginning of Chapter 3, the trend toward an increasingly inequitable distribution of national income was discussed. At the very least, this problem is aggravated by a persistently weak rate of growth in the country's gross domestic product. In the hundred years before 1973, the American economy grew at an annual rate of 3.4 percent; since then it has been growing at an average of only 2.4 percent per year.[30] It might seem that a mere 1 percent drop in the rate of economic growth is nothing to worry about, but, as one economist writes, "the damage done by slow growth accumulates the way interest does in a savings account."[31] The 1 percent yearly reduction in growth has meant a loss of goods and services since 1973 of over $12 trillion, equivalent to a $50,000 loss in earnings for the typical American family. Additional capital would also have been available for investment because of higher individual savings and increased corporate profits.[32]

To most experts, this slowdown in economic growth reflects a declining rate of growth in productivity. From 1973 until the mid-1990s average annual productivity grew by only 1.1 percent a year, far below its 1960–1973 rate of nearly 3 percent a year.[33] In recent years the rate of productivity growth has increased, but whether that growth can sustain itself, now that the '90s economic boom is over, remains to be seen.[34] Wrapped up with the question of productivity growth is the problem of adequate capital formation, that is, with investment in new factories and equipment—an area where America has frequently fallen behind its economic rivals. For instance, plant and equipment investment per U.S. labor force member has typically been half that of Germany, and one-third that of Japan.[35] In turn, their growth in productivity has often been two to three times the U.S. rate.[36] "America's chances of owning the twenty-first century," writes Lester C. Thurow, dean of MIT's Sloan School of Management, "depend upon the answer to a simple question: Can it get its productivity growth rate up to the standards of its chief rivals?"[37]

"Productivity isn't everything," writes Princeton economist Paul Krugman, "but in the long run it is almost everything."[38] If strong, consistent productivity growth is not maintained, our standard of living will stagnate. According to some economic measures, this is already happening. Adjusted for inflation, wages of nonsupervisory workers—some four-fifths of the workforce—have decreased since their peak in 1972.[39] Although median household income has increased in recent years, in real terms it is not that much higher than thirty years ago despite the fact that far more families now have two wage-earners.[40] Although in the past the United States led the world in terms of the standard of living we provide our workers, today we are in thirteenth place—far behind in wages, benefits, health care, pensions, paid vacation days, and educational opportunities.[41]

To make matters worse, for nearly thirty years the United States has been steadily losing its share of both foreign and domestic markets. The nation's huge balance of trade deficit is only the most visible sign of this. After decades and decades of trade surpluses, the United States has posted a trade deficit every year since 1975. This relentlessly growing deficit is now over $400 billion annually, or equivalent to more than 4 percent of GDP. Some economists believe that it is irrelevant that the United States buys more than it sells, but others are worried by the country's consumption-happy ways. For one thing, it has meant an enormous transfer of American assets into foreign hands. The rest of the world now owns $2.5 trillion more of the United States than it owns of other countries, and this gap expands every year as assets, dividends, and interest flow to foreign owners. (To put $2.5 trillion into perspective, it's more than ten percent of the total combined value of the stock market and all residential real estate in the United States.)[42]

Exclusive Focus on Short Term

For a number of years now, observers of the business scene have charged that U.S. companies are preoccupied with short-term performance at the expense of long-term strategies, and that this strategic myopia is an important part of the story behind America's declining rate of productivity. According to the critics, their short-term orientation has made U.S. corporations unimaginative, inflexible, and uncompetitive. The critics take as their classic example the failure of Detroit to respond to increasing foreign competition in the 1960s, with the consequent loss of U.S. dominance of the auto industry. These business strategists have urged U.S. companies to become more visionary, arguing that they must define long-term goals and be willing to stick to them even at the expense of short-term profit. Some businesspeople have accepted this advice, as evidenced by the willingness of Amazon and other dot-com companies to lose money for years as they attempt to build market share.

By a number of measures, U.S. companies have in recent years become more competitive—certainly by comparison with their sluggish performance in the 1970s and 1980s. Today, they are producing better-quality products and doing so more flexibly and innovatively than ever. Yet American companies frequently appear less willing than many foreign rivals to gamble on long-term research and development or to sacrifice current profits for benefits ten or fifteen years into the future. By comparison with countries such as Germany and Japan, established U.S. corporations continue to be obsessed with their stock market performance and to govern themselves far more by short-term indicators such as share price and quarterly profits. As a result, write management consultants Adrian Slywotsky and Richard Wise, "many [American] companies with apparently strong growth records in recent years have achieved them through relatively short-term, unsustainable tactics—acquisitions, international expansion, price increases, or accounting gimmicks."[43]

There's no question that corporate America's obsession with short-term performance—when coupled with what Federal Reserve Chairman Alan Greenspan has called "infectious greed"[44]—has created a high-pressure economic environment conducive to fraudulent behavior. Since the exposure of criminal conduct at Enron in late 2001, a long list of companies—including Adelphia Communications, Computer Associates, Dynegy, Global Crossing, Qwest, Rite Aid, Tyco International, WorldCom, and Xerox, just to name the best-known cases—have been found to have manipulated financial data or committed outright fraud so as to appear to meet their short-term financial goals. These and other revelations of unethical conduct have, in turn, weakened the trust necessary for the efficient functioning of our economic system. This is why President Bush has stated that "at this moment, America's greatest economic need is higher ethical standards." Although it's true, as he has also said, that "in the long run, there's no capitalism without conscience; there is no wealth without character," he may have neglected the extent to which a relentless emphasis on short-term results has pressured some of the nation's most prominent business leaders to do things they wouldn't normally do.[45] As one business ethicist writes:

> Managing a corporation with the single measure of share price is like flying a 747 for maximum speed. You can shake the thing apart in the process. It's like a farmer forcing more and more of a crop to grow, until the soil is depleted and nothing will grow. Or like an athlete using steroids to develop muscle mass, until the body's health is damaged.

Enron's problem was not a lack of focus on shareholder value. The problem was a lack of accountability to anything except share value. This contributed to a mania, a detachment from reality. And it led to a culture of getting the numbers by any means necessary.[46]

Declining Interest in Production

Traditionally, capitalists have made money by producing goods. Manufacturing was the backbone of the American economy and the basis of our prosperity. In industry after industry, however, U.S. companies have conceded manufacturing dominance to foreign competitors. Today, for example, one can't buy a television made in the United States; Wal-Mart employs more people than the Big Three automakers do; and as of 1992, for the first time in our history, more Americans work in government than in manufacturing.

"Hollow Corporations"   Since the 1980s, many U.S. manufacturers have been closing up shop or curtailing their operations and becoming marketing organizations for other producers, usually foreign. The result is the evolution of a new kind of company: manufacturers that do little or no manufacturing. They may perform a host of profit-making functions—from design to distribution—but they lack their own production base. Companies long identified with making goods of all sorts now often produce only the package and the label. In contrast to traditional manufacturers, they have become "hollow" or "weightless."

Many U.S. manufacturers are now pursuing a strategy of "outsourcing"—that is, buying parts or whole products from other producers, both at home and abroad. The manufacturer's traditional vertical structure, in which it makes virtually all crucial parts, is thereby being replaced by a network of small suppliers. Proponents of the new system describe it as flexible and efficient, a logical outcome of the drive to lower the costs of doing business. But critics point to the problems outsourcing can create for the companies that do it.[47] Moreover, they worry about whether the United States can prosper without a strong manufacturing base. As Tsutomu Ohshima, a senior manufacturing director of Toyota Motor Corporation, puts it: "You can't survive with just a service industry."[48] In terms of wages, productivity, and innovation, the service sector fails to compare with basic industry. Moreover, manufacturing jobs generate significantly more goods and services from other industries than do service jobs, and three times as many additional employment opportunities.[49]

As America's manufacturing base dwindles, over 1.3 million manufacturing jobs have moved abroad since 1992.[50] But it's no longer just blue-collar jobs that are disappearing as companies outsource. These days many upscale, non-manufacturing jobs are moving overseas. Engineers, financial analysts, computer technicians, and other white-collar workers living in countries like Russia, India, and the Philippines now handle airline reservations, design chips, draw architectural blueprints, provide accounting services, process loans and insurance claims, and engage in research and development for American corporations.[51] Because these skilled, highly educated employees work for far less than their American counterparts, outsourcing these jobs overseas makes U.S. firms leaner and more profitable. But can America lose these jobs and still prosper? That's the question that is worrying more and more people.[52]

Mergers and Takeovers Also reflective of American business's declining interest in production is the increase in corporate mergers and acquisitions. Takeovers and the extensive corporate restructuring that accompanied them emerged as an important economic trend in the 1980s and have continued to the present day. In fact, since the mid-1990s mergers and acquisition activity has grown sevenfold to around $1.5 trillion annually.[53] Recently, for example, Exxon took over Mobil, Travelers Group acquired Citicorp, and NationsBank merged with BankAmerica, smashing all records for merger and acquisition in a single year. Yet, much of this merger and takeover activity is directed toward making money through the manipulation of existing assets rather than through the production of new or better goods. Many U.S. entrepreneurs and capitalists seem to have found better and easier ways to make profit than the time-honored technique of competing in the production of goods and services. In fact, as one authority remarks, a "table of the world's largest mergers now reads like a Who's Who of corporate scandal."[54]

Changing Attitudes Toward Work

Some commentators believe that the decline in U.S. productivity growth is related not just to takeovers, outsourcing, and a short-term performance mentality, but also to our changing attitudes toward government, social institutions, business, and especially work. Whether or not these pundits are correct, there is little question that people's ideas about the value of work and the role it should play in their lives are continually changing. Coming to grips with these shifting attitudes is one of the challenges facing our socioeconomic system at the beginning of the twenty-first century. In particular, the fabled American work ethic seems to be fading away. Or is it?

The so-called work ethic values work for its own sake, seeing it as something necessary for every person. It also emphasizes the belief that hard work pays off in the end and is thus part and parcel of the American Dream. "If you work hard enough," the expression goes, "you'll make it." Today, however, only one in three people believes this, down from 60 percent in a 1960 survey.[55] In addition, some experts believe that as people become less optimistic about the future and begin to doubt that their efforts will pay off, they become less interested in work than in looking out for themselves. Paul Kostek, a career development expert, contends that "people more so than ever are looking out for themselves and focus on what they want out of their career as the old social contract is broken." "I see more of a 'me-first' attitude," adds management professor Abigail Hubbard.[56]

In addition, with increased education, people are rearranging their ideas about what's important in life and about what they want out of it. The evidence can be seen in the workplace itself. For example, it is not uncommon for operative workers to balk at doing the monotonous tasks their ancestors once accepted, albeit grudgingly. Loyalty to employers seems on the decline, and loyalty to fellow workers seems on the rise. Turnover rates in many industries are enough to make discontinuity an expensive problem. Organizational plans, schedules, and demands no longer carry the authoritative clout they once did; workers today often subordinate them to personal needs, which results in rampant absenteeism. Moreover, employee sabotage and violence, once unheard of, occur frequently enough today to worry management. Adding to industry's woes, employee drug use can lead to theft, absenteeism, and low productivity.

According to an international survey about what matters most to different cultures, Americans place work eighth in importance behind values such as their children's education and a satisfactory love life. (In Japan, by contrast, work ranks second only to good health.)[57] Another survey reveals that more and more Americans—both men and women—are shelving job success to be with their families.[58] Although it is impossible to pin down workers' attitudes toward work today, basically they seem willing to work hard on a job they find interesting and rewarding as long as they have the freedom to influence the nature of their jobs and pursue their own lifestyles. They have a growing expectation that work should provide self-respect, nonmaterial rewards, and substantial opportunities for personal growth. And they have a growing willingness to demand individual rights, justice, and equality on the job.[59]

If industry is to improve productive capacity and be competitive, it must seriously confront these changing social attitudes. As Paul Bernstein argues, it is counterproductive to compare today's worker with an idealized worker of yesteryear. Rather, we must acknowledge that we have a new work ethic, which in Bernstein's words

is part and parcel of the individual desire for meaningful and challenging labor in which some autonomy is an integral feature. An increasingly professionalized work force will not accept a golden embrace unless it is accompanied by fulfilling jobs that have been designed for a labor force that sees work in relation to family, friends, leisure and self-development. Work, for most of us, continues as an important part of our lives, but only in relation to our total experience.[60]

SUMMARY

1. Capitalism is an economic system in which the major portion of production and distribution is in private hands, operating under a profit or market system. Socialism is an economic system characterized by public ownership of property and a planned economy.

2. Capitalism has gone through several stages: mercantile, industrial, financial, and state welfare.

3. Four key features of capitalism are the existence of companies, profit motive, competition, and private property.

4. One basic defense of capitalism rests on a supposed natural moral right to property. Utilitarians deny the existence of such rights; other critics doubt that this right entitles one to have a system of property rules and regulations identical to the one we now have in the United States.

5. Utilitarian defense of capitalism is associated with the classical economic arguments of Adam Smith. Smith believed that human beings are acquisitive and that they have a natural propensity for trading, and he insisted that when people are left free to pursue their own economic interests, they will, without intending it, produce the greatest good for all.

6. Critics question the basic assumptions of capitalism (theoretical challenges) and whether it has delivered on its promises (operational challenges). Specifically, they raise the following issues: Can capitalism eliminate poverty and reduce inequality? Are humans basically economic creatures? Does capitalism breed oligopolies that thwart competition? Is competition valuable? Does capitalism exploit and alienate?

7. As the twenty-first century begins, our capitalist socioeconomic system faces a number of challenges. Among the problems that must be overcome are slow productivity growth, an excessive concern with short-term performance, and a lack of interest in the actual manufacturing of goods. In addition, we must come to grips with our society's changing attitudes toward work.

CASE 4.1

The Downsizing of America

When General Motors decided to close its Willow Run assembly plant in Ypsilanti, Michigan, the company didn't know that Ypsilanti would fight back—which it did by filing suit against GM. In court, Douglas Winters, the attorney for Ypsilanti Township, argued that GM should be required to keep the plant open because it had promised to maintain jobs there in exchange for tax abatements totaling $14 million. Otherwise, Winters contended, GM should return the $14 million and pay damages. To the surprise of GM officials, Michigan Circuit Court Judge Donald Shelton bought Winters's argument, issuing an order preventing GM from closing its Ypsilanti plant and shifting the work elsewhere. Unfortunately for Ypsilanti, though, a higher court later overturned Judge Shelton's ruling, freeing GM to transfer production of large rear-wheel-drive cars from Ypsilanti to Arlington, Texas.[61]

For its part, GM said that closing Willow Run was simply part of a plan to shrink its production facilities to match a smaller market share. In this respect, GM's decision to shut down its Ypsilanti operation reflects a larger trend. Industrial manufacturing is declining in the United States as plants have been closing with alarming frequency in the industrial heartland of America. Old industrial cities, their economies intertwined with the economic health of aging manufacturing plants, are ailing as those plants are being forced to close, cut back, or relocate to remote locales.

Today, sadly, the decline of smokestack America and the pain it has meant for many blue-collar workers and their communities are already old news. The closing of old factories has been pushed out of the headlines by a flood of white-collar layoffs, the result of restructuring and cost cutting in a wide range of industries—not just in manufacturing, but also in banking and finance, communication services, and high technology, among others. In recent years, older, better-educated, and better-paid workers have been more likely to be axed than have blue-collar workers. Take Steven A. Holthausen, for example. For two decades he was a loan officer with a salary of $1,000 a week. He survived three bank mergers only to learn when he returned from a family vacation that he no longer had a job. For a year Holthausen scraped by on commissions earned as a freelance mortgage broker, supplemented by severance pay and unemployment insurance. For a while he pumped gas at a station owned by a former bank customer. His wife left him. Now he earns $1,000 a month—a quarter of his former salary—as a tour guide.

Or meet James E. Sharlow. The same age as Holthausen, Sharlow was laid off by Eastman Kodak after twenty-six years when the company shut down the plant he managed. Over a three-year period, Sharlow sent out over two thousand résumés, but the market for white-collar positions is glutted with job-seekers, and Sharlow landed only ten interviews. He was one of two finalists for a job managing a plant in Southern California, for which 3,000 people had applied. He didn't get the position. Today he works as a consultant in the electronics department of a local college for less than a quarter of the $130,000 he used to make.

Holthausen and Sharlow are among those caught up in a tidal wave of layoffs—layoffs that are no longer concentrated among blue-collar workers in old and uncompetitive manufacturing firms in the industrial heartland. Since 1979 more than 43 million people have been thrown out of work, as companies have sought to modernize their operations, reduce labor costs, and increase their global competitiveness. One-third of all households have seen a family member lose a job, and nearly 40 percent more know a relative, friend, or neighbor who has been laid off. Layoffs affect 3 million people every year, and one is far more likely to be laid off than to be the victim of a violent crime.

The large and established *Fortune* 500 companies have been setting the pace: 50,000 jobs cut at Sears, Roebuck and Company; 16,800 at Eastman Kodak; 18,000 at Delta Airlines; 123,300 at AT&T; and 175,000 at IBM. American firms sacked 677,795 people in 1998 alone,[62] but the layoffs are still going strong. For example, Lucent Technologies cut 29,000 jobs in 2001 and a further 27,000 in 2002; during the same time period DaimlerChrysler cut 26,000, SBC Communications 31,000, Verizon 15,000, Procter & Gamble 9,600, and AT&T a further 23,000.[63] Until the last few years, the American economy was creating enough new jobs to absorb both laid-off workers and new people beginning their careers. However, even when discharged employees do get new jobs, those jobs tend to pay less; only a third of laid-off employees end up in equally remunerative or better-paying jobs. Sometimes, they are even rehired by their original employers at a lower wage or as "independent contractors" without fringe benefits. This disturbing trend has been called the "Downsizing of America," and its human costs are only now beginning to be explored.[64]

Some commentators believe that downsizing is exaggerated, that it barely exceeds the usual turnover in jobs that is characteristic of any capitalist economy.[65] Others challenge the widespread belief that downsizing has meant that U.S. corporations have become less bureaucratic by shedding managerial jobs. Economist David Gordon contends not only that, compared with other nations, U.S. companies are still top-heavy with management and administration, but also that this "bureaucratic burden" has continued to increase.[66]

Nevertheless, employees, including managers, are more fearful than ever of losing their jobs. Job security seems to be a thing of the past. "No one is immune from the job-cutting ax," says James Challenger, a Chicago outplacement authority. "One day you are a member of a team and the next day your entire division is being dismantled."[67] At the workplace, fear of unemployment can easily create suspicion, dampen employee loyalty, and reduce innovation, creativity, and risk taking. Employees complain about managing the orphaned workloads of downsized colleagues and fight for high-profile posts so that if the ax falls, it won't fall on them.[68]

Critics also charge that many companies have downsized blindly, saving money through layoffs that have meant reduced output, poorer-quality products, and frayed relations with customers. For example, after Delta Airlines eliminated more than 10,000 positions, its on-time performance fell to the bottom of the list for major airlines. With airline agents, baggage handlers, and maintenance workers in short supply, customer service deteriorated, and complaints to the Department of Transportation soared. Studies by the American Management Association have found that fewer than half the firms that have cut their workforces since 1990 have succeeded in raising their profits, and only a third increased productivity.[69]

What is even more worrisome to many is that layoffs occur even when companies are doing well. For example, AT&T announced that it was laying off 40,000 employees at a time when it was making record profits and its chairman, Robert E. Allen, was pulling in an annual salary of $14 million. Likewise, BankAmerica decided to lay off 4 percent of its workforce after its stock had risen 50 percent that year and its profits reached an all-time high. Some observers fear that downsizing and widespread fear of unemployment, when coupled with increasing economic inequality, growing poverty, and a stagnating standard of living for the majority, signal the fraying of our social fabric. Princeton University political theorist Alan Ryan writes:

> When we reach a situation in which the bottom 80 percent—not the underclass, but most of the population—sees itself struggling to make ends meet, sees no gains from increased productivity, and sees an elite creaming [off] all the benefits of a transformed economy, trouble looms.[70]

This is a serious concern. History shows that economic fears, class tensions, and social distress can cause social instability. At a time when some business experts are predicting that 90 percent of white-collar jobs in the U.S. will be destroyed beyond recognition in the next ten to fifteen years,[71] one can only hope, then, that downsizing does not become the "capsizing of America."

Update:

In the 1990s, corporate restructuring drove downsizing, as companies reduced middle management positions and laid off white-collar employees in an effort to become leaner, more streamlined, and more efficient. These days, however, globalization is fueling this trend as American companies outsource white-collar jobs to overseas firms, which perform back-office services for a fraction of the cost of hiring American employees. For example, Procter & Gamble is turning to workers in China and the Philippines for tech support and accounting; 20,000 employees in India now do work for General Electric in finance, information technology, and research and development; 6,000 workers in India and the Philippines handle airline reservations and customer service for Delta Air Lines; and Philips has 700 Chinese engineers doing research and development in consumer electronics. By 2005, an estimated 588,000 skilled, white-collar jobs will have moved overseas—jobs in office support, sales, business operations, architecture, management, legal services, computers, life sciences, and art and design. By 2015 the number of U.S. jobs moved offshore will hit an estimated 3.3 million.[72]

Discussion Questions

1. Have you or a family member experienced layoffs, downsizing, or corporate restructuring? Do you know anyone who has?

2. What is causing downsizing? Is it inevitable? Is it economically necessary? What effects are downsizing and the fear of layoffs having on our society?

3. Some would argue that economic change always brings social dislocation and that we should simply accept the current wave of layoffs as one result of automation, international competition, and the workings of a free market. Do you agree?

4. Do corporations have a moral obligation to avoid laying off longtime employees like Steven Holthausen and James Sharlow? Do layoffs ever violate the rights of workers? Should layoffs, plant closures, and outsourcing be regulated in some way?

5. The CEOs who have laid off thousands of workers have often seen their own compensation skyrocket at the same time. Is there anything unjust about this? Does a CEO have an obligation to share the pain? If layoffs increase the company's profits, is the CEO entitled to a boost in pay?

6. What, if anything, does downsizing reveal about the attitudes of corporations toward their employees? Do you find anything in the current plight of America's workers, both blue- and white-collar, that confirms the Marxist view of capitalism?

7. What is your assessment of the future of American manufacturing? What about America's capitalist system in general?

CASE 4.2

Licensing and Laissez Faire

The United States is a capitalist country, and our system of medical care is, to a significant extent, organized for profit. True, many hospitals are nonprofit, but the same cannot be said of doctors, who, judged as a whole, form an extremely affluent and privileged occupational group.

Sometimes physicians themselves seem a little uncomfortable about the business aspect of their professional lives or worry that outsiders will misinterpret their attention to economic matters. For example, the professional journal *Medical Economics,* which discusses such pocketbook issues as malpractice insurance, taxes, fees, and money management (a recent cover story was titled "Are You Overpaying Your Staff?"), works hard at not being available to the general public. When a subscriber left his copy on a commercial airliner, another reader found it and sent the mailing label to the magazine; the magazine's editor sent a cautionary note to the subscriber. The editor advises readers to "do your part by restricting access to your personal copies of the magazine. Don't put them in the waiting room, don't leave them lying about in the examination rooms, and don't abandon them in public places."[73]

Medical Economics probably suspects that even in our capitalist society many people, including probably most doctors, would not like to think of physicians simply as medical entrepreneurs who are in it for the money. And, indeed, many people here and many more in other countries criticize our medical system for being profit oriented. They think medical care should be based on need and that ability to pay should not affect the quality of medical treatment one receives. Interestingly, though, some people criticize medical practice in the United States as being insufficiently market oriented; University of Chicago professor of economics Milton Friedman is one of them.

Friedman has been a longstanding critic of occupational licensure in all fields. His reasoning is straightforward: Licensure—the requirement that one obtain a license from a recognized authority in order to engage in an occupation—restricts entry into the field. Licensure thus permits the occupational or professional group to enjoy a monopoly in the provision of services. In Friedman's view, this contravenes the principles of a free market to the disadvantage of us all.

Friedman has no objection to certification; that is, to public or private agencies certifying that an individual has certain skills. But he rejects the policy of preventing people who do not have such a certificate from practicing the occupation of their choice. Such a policy restricts freedom and keeps the price of the services in question artificially high. When one reads the long lists of occupations for which some states require a license—librarians, tree surgeons, pest controllers, well diggers, barbers, even potato growers, among many others—Friedman's case gains plausibility. But Friedman pushes his argument to include all occupations and professions.

Does this mean we should let incompetent physicians practice? Friedman's answer is yes.[74] In his view the American Medical Association (AMA) is simply a trade union, though probably the strongest one in the United States. It keeps the wages of its members high by restricting the number of those who can practice medicine.

The AMA does this not just through licensure but also, even more effectively, through controlling the number of medical schools and the number of students admitted to them. Today, for instance, over 45,000 applicants vie every year for roughly 16,000 medical school vacancies.[75] The medical profession, Friedman charges, limits entry into the field both by turning down applicants to medical school and by making standards for admission and licensure so difficult as to discourage many young people from ever trying to gain admission.

Viewed as a trade union, the AMA has been singularly effective. As recently as the 1920s, physicians were far down the list of professionals in terms of income; the average doctor made less than the average accountant. Today, physicians constitute the profession that arguably has the highest status and the best pay in the country. Although physicians' incomes vary widely depending on their medical specialty, today the average doctor earns $199,000 a year, more than five times the income of the average full-time worker.[76] Still, the medical establishment remains worried. It believes that there are too many doctors in the United States, and that "this surplus breeds inefficiency and drives up costs."[77]

The economic logic behind this proposition is murky. An increase in the supply of barbers, plumbers, or taxi drivers does not drive up the cost of getting a haircut, having your pipes fixed, or taking a cab. Why should it be different with doctors? Critics of the medical profession believe that its real worry is the prospect of stabilizing or even declining incomes. In any case, the doctors have written two prescriptions.

The first is to reduce the number of medical students by closing down some medical schools; the second is to make it more difficult for foreign doctors to practice here. Although the medical establishment has often expressed concern about the quality of foreign medical training, today the worry is strictly a matter of quantity. "We've got to stop the pipeline of foreign medical graduates," says Dr. Ed O'Neil of the Center for the Health Professions at the University of California, San Francisco. "They are a big chunk of physician oversupply. . . . We're just trying to be rational."[78] As for home-grown doctors, Congress is following medical advice. To stem the supposed glut, it decided to pay hospitals around the country hundreds of millions of dollars to decrease the number of physicians they train. It turns out, however, that the United States has fewer doctors per 1,000 than do Germany, Sweden, France, and many other developed countries.[79] In fact, the United States is now predicted to have a shortage of 200,000 physicians by 2020.[80]

Medical licensure restricts the freedom of people to practice medicine and prevents the public from buying the medical care it wants. Nonetheless, most people would probably defend the principle of licensure on the grounds that it raises the standards of competence and the quality of care. Friedman contests this. By reducing the amount of care available, he contends, licensure also reduces the average quality of care people receive. (By analogy, suppose that automobile manufacturers were forbidden to sell any car that did not have the quality of a Mercedes Benz. As a result, people who owned cars would have cars of higher average quality than they do now. But because fewer people could afford cars and more of them would, therefore, have to walk or ride bicycles, such a regulation would not raise the quality of transportation enjoyed by the average person.) Friedman charges, furthermore, that the monopoly created by the licensing of physicians has reduced the incentive for research, development, and experimentation, both in medicine and in the organization and provision of services.

Since Friedman initially presented his argument forty years ago, some of the alternatives to traditional practice that he proposed have come to pass; prepaid services have emerged, and group and clinic-based practices are on the increase. But what about his main contention that instead of licensure we should allow the marketplace to sort out the competent from the incompetent providers of medical services?

Friedman's critics contend that even if the licensing of professionals "involves violating a moral rule" against restricting individuals' "freedom of opportunity," it is still immoral to allow an unqualified person to engage in potentially harmful activities without having subjected the person to adequate tests of competence.[81] Despite the appeal of Friedman's arguments on behalf of free choice, the danger still remains, they say, that people will be victimized by the incompetent.

Consider, for example, the quack remedies and treatments peddled to AIDS patients here and abroad. Bottles of processed pond scum and concoctions of herbs, injections of hydrogen peroxide or of cells from the glands of unborn calves, the eating of bee pollen and garlic, $800 pills containing substances from mice inoculated with the AIDS virus, and even whacking the thymus gland of patients to stimulate the body's immune system—all these are among the treatments that have been offered to desperate people by the unscrupulous and eccentric.[82] Deregulation of the medical field seems most unlikely to diminish such exploitation.

Discussion Questions

1. What explains the fact that licenses are required for so many occupations? What do you see as the pros and cons of occupational licensure in general? Does it have benefits that Friedman has overlooked?

2. Do you believe that licensure in medicine or any other field is desirable? In which fields and under what circumstances? What standards would you use to determine where licensure is needed?

3. Is occupational licensure consistent with the basic principles and values of capitalism? Is it a violation of the free-market ideal? How would you respond to the argument that licensure illegitimately restricts individual freedom to pursue a career or a trade?

4. Does licensure make the market work more or less effectively? Would you agree that as long as consumers are provided accurate information, then they should be permitted to make their own choices with regard to the services and products they purchase—even when it comes to medical care? Or is licensing necessary to protect them from making incorrect choices?

5. Friedman and others view the AMA as a trade union, and they believe that the high incomes of doctors are due more to artificial restrictions on the free market than to the inherent value of their services. Is this an accurate or fair picture of the medical profession?
6. Is licensing an all-or-nothing issue, or is it possible that although there are certain services that we should permit only licensed practitioners to perform, there are other services now monopolized by the same practitioners that could be performed less expensively but equally competently by paraprofessionals or laypersons?

CASE 4.3

An Internet Parasite

When you're cruising the Web, do those little pop-up ads bother you? If so, one of the companies you have to thank is Gator Corp., an Internet advertising firm. It makes software that monitors what you do online and then displays those ads when you visit certain Web sites. Gator has cut deals with various software makers to have them include its software on their programs. As a result, millions of computer owners have Gator's software on their PCs. Gator also gives away software like "e-wallet," which helps you fill out forms on Web sites, but this free software comes with Gator's "adware" or "spy-ware" built in.[83]

Gator sells those pop-up ads to advertisers, who want to reach people who visit certain Web sites, but without paying the fees that the owners of those Web sites would charge. For example, with Gator adware on their computers people visiting the Hertz Web site may be greeted by pop-up ads for rival car-rental companies. In an ad campaign for an automaker, Gator recently searched its data base and found 1.3 million computers whose users had clicked through automotive Web sites to look at certain types of vehicles. It then sent ads to those computers, varying the message depending on whether the pattern of Web visits suggested the person was close to making a purchase or was looking at competitors' cars.

Gator argues that its ads provide useful information for shoppers who want to compare prices and products. It calls what it does "behavioral marketing." Its critics call the company a "parasite" because it siphons ad money from Web sites that others have constructed. Not only does Gator need other people's Web sites to exist, but also its program threatens the existence of those sites by taking away some of the income they need to keep running. Gator's critics accuse it of unfair competition, and several large American publishing companies with Web sites have filed suit against Gator to protect their online business interests. Ironically, one of the companies joining the lawsuit is the *New York Times*, which once used Gator's services to sell subscriptions to people who visited the Web sites of its competitors.

Although his employer is one of the companies suing Gator, *Wall Street Journal* columnist Lee Gomes worries that the publishers' lawsuit may impinge on your right to control what you do with your computer and to use it to interact with the Internet in the way you choose. "The publishers," he says, "seem to be saying that you should look at their Web sites only the way they say you should. They say you can't have someone else's pop-up ad on top of their sites." If the publishers win, he reasons, this will be another setback for the concept of "fair use"—the idea that people who use copyrighted material have certain rights, too (for example, to record a copyrighted television program for their own use later).

Instead, Gomes thinks the publishers should try persuasion instead of litigation, free speech instead of legal coercion. In particular, the publishers claim that most Gator users don't realize that they have it on their computers or, at least, don't understand how it tracks their Web-surfing habits. Gator denies this, but in any case the publishers could, Gomes says, inform their Web site visitors that there are programs like Ad-aware that allow PC owners to check whether their computers have Gator or other sorts of adware on them and then, if they want, to delete those programs. The publishers could also point out that Microsoft, Yahoo!, and others provide the software that Gator gives away, but without any Gator-like tracking built in. This, Gomes argues, is the right way to respond to the challenge of Gator—by giving computer users more choice, not less.

Discussion Questions

1. Is Gator a threat to the business interests of the publishers and other Web site owners? If so, do they have a legitimate complaint against Gator? Or is this a case of big companies' ganging up to thwart a smaller business rival?

2. Is Gator guilty of unfair competition? Has it violated the implicit rules of a free-market, capitalistic system? Is it a parasite that should be put out of business or a legitimate business operation?

3. What, if anything, should the publishers do about Gator? Is Gomes's "free speech" strategy likely to work? How would you deal with Gator if you owned a popular, expensive-to-run Web site?

4. Does Gator's software violate the right to privacy of PC owners? If the lawsuit succeeds in stopping Gator, would this be a setback for the idea of "fair use"? Would it violate the rights of PC owners?

5. Is your view of this case affected by whether you personally find pop-up ads annoying?

CASE 4.4

One Nation Under Wal-Mart

The huge corporations that produce our cars, appliances, computers and other products—many of them household names like Nike, Coca-Cola, and Johnson & Johnson—are a familiar feature of contemporary capitalism. But Wal-Mart represents something new on the economic landscape. Now the world's largest company, Wal-Mart has achieved its corporate preeminence not in production, but in retail. No other retailer, at any time or in any place, has ever come close to being as large and influential as Wal-Mart has become. After years of non-stop growth, there are now more than 4,750 Wal-Mart stores, visited every week by 138 million shoppers. And the company is opening more stores all the time as it moves beyond its stronghold in the rural South and Midwest and into urban America. In fact, 82 percent of American households purchase at least one item from Wal-Mart every year. As a result, the company's marketplace clout is enormous: It controls about 30 percent of the market in household staples; it sells 15 percent of all magazines and 15–20 percent of all CDs, videos, and DVDs; and it is expected to control soon over 35 percent of U.S. food sales. For most companies selling consumer products, sales from Wal-Mart represent a big hunk of their total business: 28 percent for Dial, 24 percent for Del Monte, and 23 for Revlon. Wal-Mart is also responsible for 10 percent of all goods imported to the U.S. from China.[84]

The good news for consumers is that Wal-Mart has risen to retail supremacy through the bargain prices it offers them. The retail giant can afford its low prices because of the cost efficiencies it has achieved and the pressure it puts on suppliers to lower their prices. And the larger the store gets, the more market clout it has and the further it can push down prices for its customers.

Everyone, of course, loves low prices, but not everyone, it seems, loves Wal-Mart. Why not? Here are some of the charges that critics level against the retail behemoth:

- Wal-Mart's buying power and cost-saving efficiencies force local rivals out of business, thus costing jobs, disrupting local communities, and injuring established business districts. For example, within five years of a Wal-Mart supercenter opening, two other supermarkets close. Further, Wal-Mart often insists on tax breaks when it moves into a community, so its presence does little or nothing to increase local tax revenues.

- Wal-Mart is staunchly anti-union and pays low wages. Its labor costs are 20 percent lower than those of unionized supermarkets; its average sales clerk earns only $8.23 an hour, and most of its 1.4 million employees must survive without company health insurance. Small wonder that employee turnover is 44 percent per year. Moreover, because of its size, Wal-Mart exerts a downward pressure on retail wages and benefits throughout the country. Critics also charge that Wal-Mart's hard line on costs has forced many factories to move overseas.

- As Wal-Mart grows and grows, and as its competitors fall to the wayside, consumer choices narrow, and the retail giant exerts ever greater power as a cultural censor. Wal-Mart, for example, won't carry music or computer games with mature ratings. As a result, the big music companies now supply the chain with sanitized versions of the explicit CDs that they provide to radio stations and that are sold elsewhere. The retailer has removed racy magazines like *Maxim* and *FHM* from its racks, and it obscures the covers of *Glamour, Redbook,* and *Cosmopolitan* with binders. Although most locations offer inexpensive firearms, Wal-Mart won't sell Preven, a morning-after pill—the only one of the top ten drug chains to decline to do so.

As a result, these days Wal-Mart's expansion is frequently meeting determined local resistance, as concerned residents try to preserve their communities and their local stores and downtown shopping areas from disruption by Wal-Mart through petitions, political pressure, and zoning restrictions. As one economist remarks, for Wal-Mart "the biggest barrier to growth" is not competition from rivals like Target or Winn-Dixie stores, but "opposition at the local level." Meanwhile, Professor John E. Hoopes of Babson College takes a long-term view. "The history of the last 150 years in retailing would say that if you don't like Wal-Mart, be patient. There will be new models eventually that will do Wal-Mart in, and Wal-Mart won't see it coming."

Discussion Questions

1. Do you like Wal-Mart? Do you shop there? If so, how frequently? If not, why not?

2. Is there a Wal-Mart store in your area? If so, has it had any impact on your community or on the behavior of local consumers? If there's no store in your area, would you be in favor of Wal-Mart opening one? Explain why or why not.

3. Is Wal-Mart's rapid rise to retail dominance a positive or negative development for our society? What does it tell us about capitalism, globalization, and the plight of workers?

4. Can a retailer ever become too large and too powerful?

5. Is opposition to Wal-Mart's expansion a legitimate part of the political process or is it unfair interference with our market system and a violation of the company's rights? Do opponents of Wal-Mart have any valid concerns?

Notes

1. See David Schweickart, *Against Capitalism* (Boulder, Colo.: Westview, 1996).

2. For a succinct treatment of the rise of the Fugger dynasty, see Ned M. Cross, Robert C. Lamm, and Rudy H. Turk, *The Search for Personal Freedom* (Dubuque, Iowa: William C. Brown Company, 1972), 12.

3. Ibid., 13. See also Robert B. Carson, *Business Issues Today: Alternative Perspectives* (New York: St. Martin's Press, 1982), 3–30.

4. John Micklethwait and Adrian Wooldridge, *The Company: A Short History of a Revolutionary Idea* (New York: Modern Library, 2003), xv.

5. Robert Heilbroner, *The Worldly Philosophers*, 5th ed. (New York: Simon & Schuster, 1980), 22–23.

6. Adam Smith, *The Wealth of Nations* (New York: Modern Library, 1985), 16.

7. Ibid., 223–225.

8. As quoted by G. A. Cohen, *History, Labour, and Freedom* (Oxford: Oxford University Press, 1988), 273.

9. Ibid., 265.

10. Quoted by Joseph E. Stiglitz, "A Fair Deal for the World," *New York Review of Books*, May 23, 2002, 28.

11. Robert Heilbroner, *The Economic Problem* (Englewood Cliffs, N.J.: Prentice-Hall, 1972), 725.

12. Jim Hightower, "Food Monopoly: Who's Who in the Thanksgiving Business?" *Texas Observer*, November 17, 1978. For a study of oligopoly in the breakfast cereal industry, see Deborah Baldwin, "The Cornflake Cartel," *Common Cause Magazine*, Summer 1993.

13. Sarah Anderson and John Cavanagh, "Top 200: The Rise of Corporate Global Power" (Institute for Policy Studies, December 2000), available on line at www.ips-dc.org.

14. Heilbroner, *Worldly Philosophers*, 302.

15. Carson, *Business Issues Today*, 29.

16. For details, see David E. Sanger, "Bush Puts Tariffs of as Much as 30% on Steel Imports," *New York Times*, March 6, 2002, A1; "Rust Never Sleeps," *Economist*, March 9, 2002, 61; and "So Far, Steel Tariffs Do Little," *Wall Street Journal*, September 13, 2002, A1.

17. Laura D'Andrea Tyson, "The Farm Bill Is a $200 Billion Disaster," *Business Week*, June 3, 2002, 26.

18. Keith Bradsher, "As U.S. Urges Free Markets, Its Trade Barriers Are Many," *New York Times*, February 7, 1992, A1.

19. Thomas A. Hemphill, "Confronting Corporate Welfare," *Business Horizons* 40 (Nov.–Dec. 1997): 5.

20. Timothy Taylor, "Corporate 'Welfare' Is Tricky," *San Jose Mercury News,* September 21, 1995, 7F.

21. Stephen Moore, "Corporate Welfare Queens," *National Review,* May 19, 1997, 27–28: see also Ralph Nader, "Investments in Corporate Welfare Pay Off," *San Jose Mercury News,* January 7, 1996, 7C.

22. "Public Money in the Pipeline," *Mother Jones,* January/February 2003, 15–16.

23. See Donald L. Barlett and James B. Steele, "How the Little Guy Gets Crunched," *Time,* February 7, 2000, 34–38; Timothy W. Maier, "Business Fares Well with Welfare," *Insight on the News,* December 29, 1997, 12; Hemphill, "Confronting Corporate Welfare"; Moore, "Corporate Welfare Queens."

24. Paulette Olson and Dell Champlin, "Ending Corporate Welfare As We Know It," *Journal of Economic Issues* 32 (September 1998): 759; Donald L. Barlett and James B. Steele, "Corporate Welfare," *Time,* November 9, 1998, 38; Hemphill, "Confronting Corporate Welfare," 2.

25. W. Michael Cox, "What Would Adam Smith Say?" *Wall Street Journal,* October 21, 2003, A26.

26. Alfie Kohn, *No Contest: The Case Against Competition* (Boston: Houghton Mifflin, 1986), 46–55. This paragraph and the next are based on Chapter 3, "Is Competition More Productive?"

27. Ibid., 55.

28. This extract is from *Karl Marx: Early Writings,* translated by T. B. Bottomore, 1963. Used with permission of McGraw-Hill Book Company.

29. Studs Terkel, "How I Am a Worker," in Leonard Silk, ed., *Capitalism: The Moving Target* (New York: Quadrangle, 1974), 68–69. Reprinted by permission of the *New York Times.*

30. Jeff Madrick, "The End of Affluence," *New York Review of Books,* September 21, 1995, 13, and "Computers: Waiting for the Revolution," *New York Review of Books,* March 26, 1998, 29. See also Simon Head, "The New, Ruthless Economy," *New York Review of Books,* February 29, 1996, and "We Are All Fine-Tuners Now," *Economist,* May 17, 1997, 81.

31. Madrick, "The End of Affluence," 13.

32. Ibid.

33. "A Working Hypothesis," *Economist,* May 11, 1996, 74; Paul Krugman, "How Fast Can the U.S. Economy Grow?" *Harvard Business Review* 75 (July–August 1997): 126; and Robert M. Solow, "Mysteries of Growth," *New York Review of Books,* July 3, 2003, 51.

34. John Cassidy, *Dot.con* (New York: HarperCollins, 2003), 321; David Friedman, "One-Dimensional Growth," *Atlantic Monthly,* January/February, 2003, 109; "Paradox Lost," *Economist,* September 13, 2003, 13.

35. Lester C. Thurow, "Who Owns the Twenty-First Century?" *Sloan Management Review* 33 (Spring 1992): 11.

36. *Economist,* May 11, 1996, 18, 74.

37. Thurow, "Who Owns," 11.

38. Paul Krugman, *The Age of Diminished Expectations,* rev. ed. (Cambridge, Mass.: MIT Press, 1994), 13.

39. David M. Gordon, *Fat and Mean: The Corporate Squeeze of Working Americans and the Myth of Managerial "Downsizing"* (New York: Free Press, 1996), 19–20, and "Working Harder for Less," *Economist,* September 7, 1996, 28.

40. "All Boats Rising," *Economist,* September 30, 2000, 67; U.S. Bureau of the Census, *Statistical Abstract of the United States* 2002 (Washington, D.C.: U.S. Government Printing Office, 2003), Table 653.

41. Bernard Sanders, "Clinton Must Go to the People," *Nation,* June 21, 1993; Gordon, *Fat and Mean,* 27–29; but cf. *Fortune,* April 18, 1994, 54.

42. Warren Buffet, "America's Growing Trade Deficit Is Selling the Nation Out from Under Us," *Fortune,* November 10, 2002, 106–115.

43. Adrian Slywotsky and Richard Wise, "Resist the Urge to Merge," *Wall Street Journal,* July 16, 2002, B2.

44. "Greenspan Issues Hopeful Outlook as Stocks Sink," *Wall Street Journal,* July 17, 2002, A1.

45. "Excerpts from President's Speech," *Wall Street Journal,* July 10, 2002, A8; Bill Straub, "A Matter of Greed," *Rocky Mountain News,* July 5, 2002, 3B.

46. Marjorie Kelly, "Waving Goodbye to the Invisible Hand," *Business Ethics,* March/April 2002, 5.

47. "Has Outsourcing Gone Too Far?" *Business Week,* April 1, 1996; "The Outing of Outsourcing," *Economist,* November 25, 1995.

48. Norman Jonas, "The Hollow Corporation," *Business Week,* March 3, 1986. For a contrasting perspective, see "The Next Society: A Survey of the Near Future," *Economist,* November 3, 2001, 11–13.

49. Friedman, "One-Dimensional Growth," 110, and "Manufacturers Find Themselves Increasingly in the Service Sector," *Wall Street Journal,* February 10, 2003, A2.

50. "Laid-Off Factory Workers Find Jobs Are Drying Up for Good," *Wall Street Journal,* July 21, 2003, A1.

51. "Is Your Job Next?" *Business Week,* February 3, 2003, 50–60, and "Where Your Job Is Going," *Fortune,* November 24, 2003, 84–94.

52. See, for example, "Outsourcing Jobs: Is It Bad?" *Business Week,* August 25, 2003, 36–38, and Geoffrey Colvin, "The U.S. Is Falling Asleep on the Job," *Fortune,* September 1, 2003, 54.

53. Slywotsky and Wise, "Resist the Urge to Merge."

54. *New York Time 2003 Almanac* (New York: Penguin, 2002), 343.

55. A. Alvarez, "Learning from Las Vegas," *New York Review of Books,* January 11, 1996, 16.

56. Sherwood Ross, "Workers Fearful of Being Laid Off," *San Jose Mercury News,* December 17, 1995, 2PC.

57. *New York Times,* May 14, 1989, sec. 3, 1.

58. *Chicago Tribune,* October 29, 1995, sec. 1, 17.

59. Thomas A. Kochan, Harry C. Katz, and Robert B. McKersie, *The Transformation of American Industrial Relations* (New York: Basic Books, 1986), 209; Ian I. Mitcoff and Elizabeth A. Denton, "A Study of Spirituality in the Workplace," *Sloan Management Review* 40 (Summer 1999): 83–92.

60. Paul Bernstein, "The Work Ethic that Never Was," *Wharton Magazine* 4 (Spring 1980): 19–25.

61. See "Waiting for Verdict on GM Plant, Town" and "Court OKs GM Plan to Close Michigan Plant," *Chicago Tribune,* August 3 and 5, 1993.

62. "Overworked and Overpaid," *Economist,* January 30, 1999, 55.

63. "An Alternative to Cocker Spaniels," *Economist,* August 29, 2001, 49; "After the Boom . . . the Bust," *New York Times,* June 26, 2002, B1.

64. See *The Downsizing of America* (New York: Random House, 1996). Except as otherwise noted, this *New York Times* report is the source of the information in this case study. But see also "The Year Downsizing Grew Up," *Economist,* December 21, 1996.

65. John Cassidy, "All Worked Up," *New Yorker,* April 22, 1996.

66. Gordon, *Fat and Mean,* Chapter 2.

67. Ross, "Workers Fearful," 1PC. See also "Despite Humming Economy, Workers Sweat Job Security," *USA Today,* March 2, 1999, 1A.

68. "The Big Squeeze on Workers," *Business Week,* May 13, 2002, 96.

69. Roger E. Alcaly, "Reinventing the Corporation," *New York Review of Books,* April 10, 1997, 38–40. See also "Understaffing Is Becoming a Problem," *USA Today Magazine,* January 1998, 9.

70. Alan Ryan, "Too Nice to Win," *New York Review of Books,* March 21, 1996, 11.

71. Tom Peters, "What Will We Do for Work?" *Time,* May 29, 2000, 50.

72. "Is Your Job Next?" *Business Week,* 56–57; see also "Where Your Job Is Going," *Fortune,* 90.

73. "Memo from the Editor," *Medical Economics,* November 7, 1988.

74. See the chapter entitled "Occupational Licensure" in Milton Friedman, *Capitalism and Freedom* (Chicago: University of Chicago Press, 1962); in particular, 149.

75. "Medical Schools Are Urged to Cut Admissions by 20%," *New York Times,* November 17, 1995, C2.

76. Peter Kilborn, "Doctors' Pay Regains Ground," *New York Times,* April 22, 1998, A20.

77. "Competition and Cutbacks Hurt Foreign Doctors in U.S.," *New York Times,* November 7, 1995, B15.

78. Ibid.

79. U.S. Bureau of the Census, *Statistical Abstract of the United States 2002* (Washington, D.C.: U.S. Government Printing Office, 2003), Table 1311.

80. Jay Greene, "Now Forecast Is for Shortage of Physicians," *amednews.com,* January 21, 2002.

81. Bernard Gert, "Licensing Professions," *Business and Professional Ethics Journal* 1 (Summer 1982): 52; Donald Weinert, "Commentary," *Business and Professional Ethics Journal* 1 (Summer 1982): 62.

82. "Preying on AIDS Patients," *Newsweek,* June 1, 1987; Marian Segal, "Quackery and AIDS" at *www.thebody.com/fda/quackery.html* (June 2002).

83. This case study is based on Lee Gomes's *Boomtown* column, "In Attacking 'Parasite,' Publishers' Lawsuit May Hurt Your Rights," *Wall Street Journal,* July 15, 2002, B1, and "New Battleground Over Web Privacy: Ads That Snoop," *Wall Street Journal,* August 27, 2003, A1.

84. This case study is based on "Is Wal-Mart Too Powerful?" *Business Week,* Oct. 6, 2003, 102–110, which is the source of all quotations. See also "One Nation Under Wal-Mart," *Fortune,* February 18, 2003, 64, and Wal-Mart Watch at *www.walmartwatch.com.*

Further Reading for Chapter 4

Todd G. Buchholz, *New Ideas from Dead Economists,* rev. ed. (New York: Penguin, 1999) is a balanced and readable guide to modern economic thought applied to today's economy.

Robert L. Heilbroner and **Lester C. Thurow**, *Economics Explained,* rev. ed. (New York: Simon & Schuster, 1998) is two respected economists' analysis of how our economy works, what its current difficulties are, and where it is headed.

Tibor R. Machan, ed., *The Main Debate: Communism Versus Capitalism* (New York: Random House, 1986) is a collection of accessible essays that debate the relative merits of capitalism and socialism.

David Schweickart, *After Capitalism* (Lanham, Md.: Rowman & Littlefield, 2002) is an argument for worker control socialism.

"A Survey of Globalisation," *Economist,* September 29, 2001, and "A Survey of Capitalism and Democracy," *Economist,* June 28, 2003, are intelligent, balanced discussions of the capitalist system.

 InfoTrac College Edition: For further information or to conduct research, please go to www.infotrac-college.com.

5

Corporations

Nearly fifty years ago the vice president of Ford Motor Company described the modern business corporation as the dominant institution of American society. Today few observers would disagree. As one of them puts it, "The modern corporation is *the* central institution of contemporary society."[1] As an aggregate, corporations wield awesome economic clout, and the 500 largest U.S. companies constitute at least three-quarters of the American economy. But the dominant role of corporations in our society extends well beyond that. Not only do they produce almost all of the goods and services we buy, but also they and their ethos permeate everything from politics and communications to athletics and religion. And their influence is growing relentlessly around the world—even if the reach of multinational corporations and the negative consequences of globalization are sometimes exaggerated.[2]

By any measure, the biggest corporations are colossi that dominate the earth. Many of them employ tens of thousands of people, and the largest have hundreds of thousands in their ranks. PepsiCo, for example, has about 116,000 employees worldwide, a figure that pales beside General Electric's approximately 340,000 and General Motors's 388,000—not to mention the 1.4 million people who work for Wal-Mart, the world's largest private-sector employer. And their revenues are dazzling. In 2003, for example, General Motors took in more than $186 billion, Wal-Mart $246 billion, Ford $163 billion, and IBM $83 billion. By comparison, the gross domestic product (GDP) of Norway (that is, the total market value of all the goods and services produced there) was around $124 billion; that of New Zealand $68 billion. The state of California, which has far and away the largest annual revenue of any U.S. state, makes about what General Motors makes. But Kansas takes in only around $10.3 billion and Vermont less than a third of that.

And corporations are growing larger and wealthier every year. For example, in 1989 Time Inc. merged with Warner Communications to form Time Warner. Seven years later Time Warner combined with Turner Broadcasting. Then in January 2001, in a move that shook up Wall Street, Time Warner and America Online merged. At a stroke, the new company they created was valued at $350 billion. What does $350 billion mean? It is equivalent to the GDP of India, the fifteenth highest in the world. It is more than the combined GDPs of Hungary, Ukraine, the Czech Republic, New Zealand, Peru, and Pakistan. And it is more than the industrial output of the United Kingdom or the manufacturing output of China.

Like any other modern corporation, in principle AOL Time Warner is a three-part organization, made up of stockholders, who provide the capital, own the corporation, and enjoy liability limited to the amount of their investments; managers, who run the business operations; and employees, who produce the goods and services. However, a corporate giant like AOL Time Warner is less like a single company and more like "a fabulously wealthy investment club with a limited portfolio." Such companies invest in subsidiaries, whose heads, writes business analyst Anthony J. Parisi, "oversee their territories like provincial governors, sovereigns in their own lands but with an authority stemming from the power center. . . . The management committee exacts its tribute (the affiliate's profits from current operations) and issues doles (the money needed to sustain and expand those operations)."[3] In the best-run organizations the management system is highly structured and impersonal. It provides the corporation's overall framework, the formal chain of command, that ensures that the company's profit objectives are pursued.

The emergence of corporate behemoths like AOL Time Warner is one of the more intriguing chapters in the evolution of capitalism. Certainly the political theory of John Locke and the economic theory of Adam Smith admitted no such conglomerates of capital as those that originated in the nineteenth century—as late as 1832 hardly any private firms had ten or more employees[4]—and today dominate America's, even the world's, economic, political, and social life. This book isn't the place to analyze why a people committed to an individualistic social philosophy and a free-competition market economy allowed vast oligopolistic organizations to develop. Rather, the concern here is with the problem of applying moral standards to corporate organizations and with understanding their social responsibilities. After a brief review of the history of the corporation, this chapter looks at the following specific topics:

1. The meaning of *responsibility* and the debate over whether corporations can be meaningfully said to have moral responsibility

2. The controversy between the narrow and the broad views of corporate social responsibility

3. Four key arguments in this debate: the invisible-hand argument, the hand-of-government argument, the inept-custodian argument, and the materialization-of-society argument

4. The importance of institutionalizing ethics within corporations and how this may be done

THE LIMITED-LIABILITY COMPANY

If you ask a lawyer for a definition of *corporation*, you will probably get something like the following: A corporation is a thing that can endure beyond the natural lives of its members and that has incorporators who may sue and be sued as a unit and who are able to consign part of their property to the corporation for ventures of limited liability.[5] *Limited liability* is a key feature of the modern corporation. It means that the members of the corporation are financially liable for corporate debts only up to the extent of their investments.

In addition, limited-liability companies, or corporations, differ from partnerships and other forms of business association in two ways. First, a corporation is not formed simply by an agreement entered into among its first members. It becomes incorporated by being publicly registered or in some other way having its existence officially acknowledged by the law. Second, although a partner is automatically entitled to his or her share of the profits as soon as they are ascertained, the shareholder in a corporation is entitled to a dividend from the company's profits only when it has been "declared." Under U.S. law, dividends are usually declared by the directors of a corporation.

When we think of corporations, we naturally think of giants such as General Motors, ExxonMobil, AT&T, General Electric, and IBM, which exert enormous influence over our economy and society. But the local independently owned convenience store may be a corporation, and historically the concept of a corporation has been broad enough to encompass churches, trade guilds, and local governments. Corporations may be either *for* profit or *non*profit-making. Princeton University, for example, is a nonprofit corporation. Companies like Eastman Kodak, by contrast, aim to make money for shareholders. Corporations may be privately owned or owned (in part or whole) by the government. U.S. corporations are almost entirely privately owned, but Renault of France, for example, was once a publicly owned corporation. A small group of investors may own all the outstanding shares of a privately owned, profit-making corporation (a "privately held" corporation), or its stock may be traded among the general public (a "publicly held" corporation). All companies whose stocks are listed on the New York and other stock exchanges are publicly held corporations.

Several stages mark the evolution of the corporation. The corporate form itself developed during the early Middle Ages, and the first corporations were towns, universities, and ecclesiastical orders. They were chartered by government and regulated by public statute. As corporate bodies, they existed independently of the particular individuals who constituted their membership at any given time. By the fifteenth century, the courts of England had evolved the principle of limited liability—thus setting limits, for example, on how much an alderman of the Liverpool Corporation might be required to pay if the city went bankrupt. During the medieval period, however, the law did not grant corporate status to purely profit-making associations. In those days, something besides economic self-interest had to be seen as uniting the members of the corporation: religion, a trade, shared political responsibilities.

This state of affairs changed during the Elizabethan era, as the actual incorporation of business enterprises began. European entrepreneurs were busy organizing trading voyages to the East and to North America. The East India Company, which epitomizes the great trading companies of this period, was formed in 1600, when Queen Elizabeth I granted to a group of merchants the right to be "one body corporate" and bestowed on it a trading monopoly to the East Indies. In the following decades, numerous other incorporated firms were granted trading monopolies and colonial charters. Much of North America's settlement, in fact, was initially underwritten as a business venture.

Although the earliest corporations typically held special trading rights from the government, their members did not pool capital. Rather, they individually financed voyages using the corporate name and absorbed the loss individually if a vessel sank or was robbed by pirates. But as ships became larger and more expensive, no single buyer could afford to purchase and outfit one, and the loss of a ship would have been ruinous to any one individual. The solution was to pool capital and share liability. Thus emerged the prototype of today's corporations.[6]

The first instance of the corporate organization of a manufacturing enterprise in the United States occurred in 1813, but only after the Civil War did the movement toward the corporate organization of business really begin.[7] The loosening of government restrictions on corporate chartering procedures in the nineteenth century marks this final stage of corporate evolution. Until the mid-1800s, prospective corporations had to apply for charters—in England to the Crown, and in the United States to state governments. Government officials carefully studied applications, rejecting some and burdening others with special conditions (for example, limits on the amount of property that might be owned or restrictions on where it might be held) in order to promote the public good. Critics of the incorporation system charged that it really promoted favoritism, corruption, and unfair monopolies. Gradually, the old system of incorporation was replaced by the system we know today, in which corporate status is granted essentially to any organization that fills out the forms and pays the fees.

Lurking behind this change were two important theoretical shifts. First, underlying the old system was the mercantilist idea that a corporation's activities should advance some specific public purpose. But Adam Smith and, following him, Alexander Hamilton, the first U.S. Secretary of the Treasury, challenged the desirability of a direct tie between business enterprise and public policy. Their idea was that businesspeople should be encouraged to explore their own avenues of enterprise. The "invisible hand" of the market would direct their activities in a socially beneficial direction more effectively than any public official could.

Second, when nineteenth-century reformers argued for changes in incorporation procedures, they talked not only about government favoritism and the advantages of a laissez-faire approach but also about the principle of a corporation's right to exist.[8] Any petitioning body with the minimal qualifications, they asserted, has the right to receive a corporate charter. By contrast, the early Crown-chartered corporations were clearly creations of the state, in accordance with the legal-political doctrine that all corporate status was a privilege bestowed by the state as it saw fit. According to the reformers, however, incorporation is a by-product of the people's right of association, not a gift from the state.

Even though the right of association supports relaxed incorporation procedures, the state must still incorporate companies and guarantee their legal status. Corporations must be recognized by the law as a single agent in order for them to enjoy their rights and privileges. To a large extent, then, the corporation remains, as Chief Justice John Marshall put it in 1819, "an artificial being, invisible, intangible, and existing only in the contemplation of the law."[9]

Corporations are clearly legal agents. But are they also moral agents? And whereas corporations have definite legal responsibilities, what, if any, social and moral responsibilities do they have?

CORPORATE MORAL AGENCY

Some time ago, the citizens of Massachusetts were asked in a referendum whether they wanted to amend the state constitution to allow the legislature to enact a graduated personal income tax. Predictably enough, they said no.

What made an otherwise unremarkable exercise of the initiative process noteworthy was that the First National Bank of Boston and four other businesses in the state wanted to spend money to express opposition to the referendum. The Massachusetts Supreme Judicial Court said they could not, that banks and business corporations are prohibited by law from spending corporate funds to publicize political views that do not materially affect their property, business, or assets. However, the U.S. Supreme Court in a 5 to 4 decision (*First National Bank of Boston v. Bellotti*)[10] struck down the Massachusetts court's decision and thereby defined the free-speech rights of corporations for the first time.

Writing for the majority, Justice Lewis Powell said: "If the speakers here were not corporations, no one would suggest that the state could silence their proposed speech. It is the type of speech indispensable to decision making in a democracy, and this is no less true because the speech comes from a corporation rather than from an individual." In a dissenting opinion, however, Justice Byron R. White said that states should be permitted to distinguish between individuals and corporations. "Ideas which were not a product of individual choice," said White, "are entitled to less First Amendment protection."

Some view the *Bellotti* decision as a blow to consumers and citizens, but the Supreme Court has reaffirmed its position in a number of subsequent cases, most recently in 1999 when it unanimously overturned a federal ban on broadcast advertising of casino gambling. In holding that the First Amendment protects corporations, the Court has blurred the distinction between individuals and corporations. However, in doing so, it has laid a basis for claiming not only that corporations enjoy the same moral and political rights as citizens but also that, because of this, corporations bear the same responsibilities that individual human beings do. In other words, if corporations have the same rights that moral agents have, then, like individuals, they can and should be held morally responsible for their actions.

The problem, of course, is that corporations are not human beings but artificial "persons" created by the law. They are collections of different, changing individuals who set goals and policies and perform specific actions. Given that corporations are not actual persons, in what sense can they be held morally responsible for their actions? Or as Lord Thurlow, an eighteenth-century lawyer, put it, how can you "expect a corporation to have a conscience, when it has no soul to be damned and no body to be kicked?"[11]

At this point, it may help to understand what is meant by "moral responsibility." Often, of course, people are simply said to have a moral responsibility to do whatever it is that morality requires of them. Thus, I may have a moral responsibility to help my neighbor, to keep my promise to Peter, to tell the truth to my colleagues, and to return a misplaced squash racquet to its rightful owner. But reference to an individual's moral responsibility may also have other meanings. Three further senses of "moral responsibility" (or "morally responsible") are relevant here.

Meanings of "Moral Responsibility"

In the first sense, "moral responsibility" refers to holding people morally accountable for some past action. If you leap into a river and rescue a drowning child, you are responsible for the child's being saved and deserve to be praised. If you are playing with your car's radio while you drive and, as a result, cruise through a stop sign, you are responsible for the accident that results; you deserve to be blamed. On the other hand, if the accident resulted from your having suffered a heart attack, you would not be seen as morally responsible (as opposed to legally liable) for it. Morally speaking, the accident was not your fault; we would not criticize you for it. Responsibility in this sense of accountability for actions, therefore, refers to people's meriting blame or praise for particular actions they have performed. Determining responsibility in this sense requires assessing causation and weighing various moral considerations.

In the second sense, "moral responsibility" refers to one's accountability, not for a particular past action, but for the care, welfare, or treatment of other people on things as derived from the specific social role that one plays. Thus, parents are responsible for seeing that their children go to school; teachers are responsible for what occurs in their classrooms; doctors are responsible for the treatment of their hospital patients. These specific role responsibilities are typically set by social or organizational conventions.

The third sense of "moral responsibility" refers to one's capacity for making moral or rational decisions on one's own. When parents hire a babysitter for their young children, they implicitly recognize that their children lack the mental and emotional maturity to make competent, informed decisions. Likewise, when the law grants parents almost complete legal control over their young children, it implicitly asserts that children cannot be trusted to make important decisions regarding their own welfare. They are not yet mature enough to be deemed fully responsible for their actions. On the other hand, the babysitter and the parents presumably are morally responsible agents. They have the capacity to make autonomous, informed, and rational moral decisions.

If a person is not morally responsible in the third sense, he or she cannot be considered morally responsible in either of the other two senses. People who cannot make rational or moral decisions on their own cannot be held accountable for their actions or for the welfare of anyone else. On the other hand, if they can make such decisions, then in theory they can be held accountable for their actions and for fulfilling their obligations to others. The relationship between the third sense of "morally responsible" and the other two, then, is that it is a necessary, although not a sufficient, condition for the others.

The importance of recognizing the logical priority of moral responsibility in the third sense is that once it is established, it is theoretically possible to hold the agent responsible in the other senses. This in turn simplifies the issue of corporate moral responsibility. If corporations, like individuals, can make rational and moral decisions on their own—if they are moral agents—then in theory they can have genuine moral responsibilities to others and can be praised or blamed for their actions.

Although this point seems simple, the task of determining whether corporations can make such decisions remains anything but simple. Immediately, we must ponder whether it makes sense to say that any entity other than individual persons can make decisions in the first place, moral or otherwise.

Can Corporations Make Moral Decisions?

Corporate internal decision (CID) structures amount to established procedures for accomplishing specific goals. For example, consider ExxonMobil's system, as depicted by Anthony J. Parisi:

All through the Exxon system, checks and balances are built in. Each fall, the presidents of the 13 affiliates take their plan for the coming year and beyond to New York for review at a meeting with the management committee and the staff vice presidents. The goal is to get a perfect corporate fit. Some imaginary examples: The committee might decide that Exxon is becoming too concentrated in Australia and recommend that Esso Eastern move more slowly on that continent. Or it might conclude that if the affiliates were to build all the refineries they are proposing, they would create more capacity than the company could profitably use. One of the affiliates would be asked to hold off, even though, from its particular point of view, a new refinery was needed to serve its market.[12]

The implication here is that any decisions coming out of ExxonMobil's annual sessions are formed and shaped to effect corporate goals, "to get a perfect corporate fit." Metaphorically, all data pass through the filter of corporate procedures and objectives. The remaining distillation constitutes the decision. Certainly the participants actively engage in decision making. But in addition to individual persons, the other major component of corporate decision making consists of the framework in which policies and activities are determined.

The CID structure lays out lines of authority and stipulates under what conditions personal actions become official corporate actions. Some philosophers have compared the corporation to a machine or have argued that because of its structure it is bound to pursue its profit goals single-mindedly. As a result, they claim, it is a mistake to see a corporation as being morally responsible or to expect it to display such moral characteristics as honesty, considerateness, and sympathy. Only the individuals within a corporation can act morally or immorally; only they can be held responsible for what it does.[13]

Others have argued the contrary. The CID structure, like an individual person, collects data about the impact of its actions. It monitors work conditions, employee efficiency and productivity, and environmental impacts. Professors Kenneth E. Goodpaster and John B. Matthews argue that, as a result, there is no reason a corporation cannot show the same kind of rationality and respect for persons that individual human beings can. It makes just as much sense, they contend, to speak of corporate moral responsibility as it does to speak of individual moral responsibility.[14] Thomas Donaldson agrees. He argues that a corporation can be a moral agent if moral reasons enter into its decision making and if its decision-making process controls not just the company's actions but also its structure of policies and rules.[15]

Philosopher Peter French arrives at the same conclusion in a slightly different way.[16] The CID structure, says French, in effect absorbs the intentions and acts of individual persons into a "corporate decision." Perhaps no corporate official intended the course or objective charted by the CID structure, but, French contends, the corporation did. And he believes that these corporate intentions are enough to make corporate acts "intentional" and thus make corporations "morally responsible." Professor of philosophy Manuel Velasquez demurs. An act is intentional, says Velasquez, only if the entity that formed the intention brings about the act through its bodily movements.[17] But it is the people who make up the corporation who carry out the acts attributed to it. Velasquez concludes that only corporate members, not the corporation itself, can be held morally responsible.

Vanishing Individual Responsibility

Some might argue that whether or not corporations as artificial entities can properly be held morally responsible, the nature and structure of modern corporate organizations allow virtually everyone to share moral accountability for an action—"moral responsibility" in the first sense. But in practice this diffusion of responsibility can mean that no particular person or persons are held morally responsible. For example, does responsibility for an injury caused by a defective product fall on the shoulders of the worker who last handled the product, the foreman overseeing the running of the assembly line, the factory supervisor, the quality control team, the engineers who designed and tested the equipment, the regional managers who decided to produce the item, or the company's CEO, whose office is in another city? Indeed, each of these individuals may have been only following established procedures and decision-making guidelines. Inside a corporation it may often be difficult, even impossible, to assign responsibility for a particular outcome to any single individual because so many different people, acting within a given CID framework, contributed to it in small ways.

This masking of moral accountability may not seem so surprising: After all, in situations that don't involve corporations, assigning praise and blame can also be problematic. But it raises the troubling possibility that the size and impersonal bureaucratic structure of the corporation may so envelop its members that it becomes vacuous to speak of individual moral agency. This, in turn, raises the specter of actions without actors in any moral sense—of defective products, broken laws, or flouted contracts, without any morally responsible parties.

There are two ways to escape this uncomfortable conclusion. One is to attribute moral agency to corporations just as we do to individual persons. The other, not necessarily incompatible with the first, is to realize that these days too many people are willing, even eager, to duck personal responsibility—"it's not my job," "there's nothing I can do about it," "I was just following procedure"—by submerging it in the protoplasmic CID structures of the modern corporation. Perhaps until CID structures are reconstituted to deal explicitly with noneconomic matters, we can expect more of the same evasion of personal responsibility.

The issue of corporate moral agency undoubtedly will continue to exercise scholars. Meanwhile, the inescapable fact is that corporations are increasingly being accorded the status of biological persons, with all the rights and responsibilities implied by that status. Before it was gobbled up by another corporation, the Continental Oil Company expressed in an in-house booklet the public perception and its implications as follows:

> No one can deny that in the public's mind a corporation can break the law and be guilty of unethical and amoral conduct. Events . . . such as corporate violation of federal laws and failure of full disclosure [have] confirmed that both our government and our citizenry expect *corporations* to act lawfully, ethically, and responsibly.
>
> Perhaps it is then appropriate in today's context to think of Conoco as a *living corporation*; a sentient being whose conduct and personality are the collective effort and responsibility of its employees, officers, directors, and shareholders.[18]

Today, many companies and many of the people inside them accept without hesitation the idea that corporations are moral agents with genuinely moral, not just legal, responsibilities. This point was illustrated recently when Colonial Pipeline of Atlanta published full-page advertisements in several newspapers headlined "We Apologize." The company used the ads to take responsibility for having spilled oil into the Reedy River of South Carolina three years before. True, the ads were part of a plea agreement with the Justice Department for having violated the Clean Water Act (the company also agreed to pay a $7 million fine). Yet the company's words had ethical overtones. As Laura Nash of the Harvard Divinity School comments, they put "moral emotion into what is essentially a legal statement" because "the word 'apologize' . . . admits a sense of shame and humility."[19]

If, then, it makes sense to talk about the social and moral responsibilities of corporations, either in a literal sense or as a shorthand way of referring to the obligations of the individuals that make up the corporation, what are these responsibilities?

CORPORATE RESPONSIBILITY

In 1963 Tennessee Iron & Steel, a subsidiary of United States Steel, was by far the largest employer, purchaser, and taxpayer in Birmingham, Alabama. In the same city at the same time, racial tensions exploded in the bombing of an African-American church, killing four black children. The ugly incident led some to blame U.S. Steel for not doing more to improve race relations, but Roger Blough, chairman of U.S. Steel, defended his company:

> I do not either believe that it would be a wise thing for United States Steel to be other than a good citizen in a community, or to attempt to have its ideas of what is right for the community enforced upon the community by some sort of economic means. . . .
>
>   When we as individuals are citizens in a community we can exercise what small influence we may have as citizens, but for a corporation to attempt to exert any kind of economic compulsion to achieve a particular end in the racial area seems to me quite beyond what a corporation can do.[20]

Not long afterward, Sol M. Linowitz, chairman of the board of Xerox Corporation, declared in an address to the National Industrial Conference Board: "To realize its full promise in the world of tomorrow, American business and industry—or, at least, the vast portion of it—will have to make social goals as central to its decisions as economic goals; and leadership in our corporations will increasingly recognize this responsibility and accept it."[21] Thus, the issue of business's corporate responsibility was joined. Just what responsibilities does a corporation have? Is its responsibility to be construed narrowly as merely profit making? Or more broadly to include refraining from harming society and even contributing actively and directly to the public good?

Narrow View: Profit Maximization

As it happened, the year preceding the Birmingham incident had seen the publication of *Capitalism and Freedom*, in which author Milton Friedman forcefully argued that business has no social responsibilities other than to maximize profits:

> The view has been gaining widespread acceptance that corporate officials and labor leaders have a social responsibility that goes beyond serving the interest of their stockholders or their members. This view shows a fundamental misconception of

the character and nature of a free economy. In such an economy, there is one and only one social responsibility of business—to use its resources and engage in activities designed to increase its profits so long as it stays within the rules of the game, which is to say, engages in open and free competition, without deception or fraud. . . . Few trends could so thoroughly undermine the very foundations of our free society as the acceptance by corporate officials of a social responsibility other than to make as much money for their stockholders as possible.[22]

Although from Friedman's perspective the only responsibility of business is to make money for its owners, obviously a business may not do literally anything whatsoever to increase its profits. Gangsters pursue profit maximization when they ruthlessly rub out their rivals, but such activity falls outside what Friedman referred to as "the rules of the game." Harvard professor Theodore Levitt echoed this point when he wrote, "In the end business has only two responsibilities—to obey the elementary canons of face-to-face civility (honesty, good faith, and so on) and to seek material gain."[23]

What, then, are the rules of the game? Obviously, elementary morality rules out deception, force, and fraud, and the rules of the game are intended to promote open and free competition. The system of rules in which business is to pursue profit is, in Friedman's view, one that is conducive to the laissez-faire operation of Adam Smith's "invisible hand" (which was discussed in Chapter 4). Friedman is a conservative economist who believes that by allowing the market to operate with only the minimal restrictions necessary to prevent fraud and force, society will maximize its overall economic well-being. Pursuit of profit is what makes our system go. Anything that dampens this incentive or inhibits its operation will weaken the ability of Smith's "invisible hand" to deliver the economic goods.

Because the function of a business organization is to make money, the owners of corporations employ executives to accomplish this goal, thereby obligating these managers always to act in the interests of the owners. According to Friedman, to say that executives have social responsibilities means that at least sometimes they must subordinate owner interests to some social objective, such as controlling pollution or fighting inflation. They must then spend stockholder money for general social interests—in effect, taxing the owners and spending these taxes on social causes. But taxation is a function of government, not private enterprise; executives are not public employees but employees of private enterprise. The doctrine of social responsibility thus transforms executives into civil servants and business corporations into government agencies, thereby diverting business from its proper function in the social system.

Friedman is critical of those who would impose on business any duty other than that of making money, and he is particularly harsh with those business leaders who themselves take a broader view of their social responsibilities. They may believe that they are defending the free-enterprise system when they give speeches proclaiming that profit isn't the only goal of business or affirming that business has a social conscience and takes seriously its responsibility to provide employment, refrain from polluting, eliminate discrimination, and so on. But these business leaders are shortsighted; they are helping to undermine capitalism by implicitly reinforcing the view that the pursuit of profit is wicked and must be regulated by external forces.[24]

Friedman acknowledges that often corporate activities are described as an exercise of "social responsibility" when, in fact, they are intended simply to advance the company's self-interest. For example, it might be in the long-term self-interest of a corporation that is a major employer in a small town to spend money to enhance the local community by helping to improve its schools, parks, roads, or social services, thereby attracting good employees to the area, reducing the company's wage bill, or improving worker morale and productivity. By portraying its actions as dictated by a sense of social responsibility, the corporation can generate good will as a by-product of expenditures that are entirely justified by self-interest. Friedman has no problem with a company pursuing its self-interest by these means, but he rues the fact that "the attitudes of the public make it in the self-interest [of corporations] to cloak their actions in this way."[25] Friedman's bottom line is that the bottom line is all that counts, and he firmly rejects any notion of corporate social responsibility that would hinder a corporation's profit maximization.

The Broader View of Corporate Social Responsibility

The rival position to that of Friedman and Levitt is simply that business has other obligations in addition to pursuing profits. The phrase *in addition to* is important. Critics of the narrow view do not as a rule believe there is anything wrong with corporate profit. They maintain, rather, that corporations have other responsibilities as well—to consumers, to employees, to suppliers and contractors, to the surrounding community, and to society at large. This broader view of corporate social responsibility is sometimes called "stakeholder theory" because it maintains that a corporation has obligations, not just to its stockholders, but also to all the other constituencies that affect or are affected by its behavior, that is, to all parties that have a stake in what a corporation does or doesn't do.

If the adherents of the broader view share one belief, it is that corporations have responsibilities beyond simply enhancing their profits because, as a matter of fact, they have such great social and economic power in our society. With that power must come social reponsibility. As professor of business administration Keith Davis puts it:

> One basic proposition is that *social responsibility arises from social power*. Modern business has immense social power in such areas as minority employment and environmental pollution. If business has the power, then a just relationship demands that business also bear responsibility for its actions in these areas. Social responsibility arises from concern about the consequences of business's acts as they affect the interests of others. Business decisions do have social consequences. Businessmen cannot make decisions that are solely economic decisions, because they are interrelated with the whole social system. This situation requires that businessmen's thinking be broadened beyond the company gate to the whole social system. Systems thinking is required.
>
> Social responsibility implies that a business decision maker in the process of serving his own business interests is obliged to take actions that also protect and enhance society's interests. The net effect is to improve the quality of life in the broadest possible way, however quality of life is defined by society. In this manner, harmony is achieved between business's actions and the larger social system. The businessman becomes concerned with social as well as economic outputs and with the total effect of his institutional actions on society.[26]

Adherents of the broader view, such as Davis, stress that modern business is intimately integrated with the rest of society. Business is not some self-enclosed world, like a private poker party. Rather, business activities have profound ramifications throughout society. As a result, although society expects business to pursue its economic interests,

business has other responsibilities as well. Thus, for example, it is wrong for corporations to raid the pension funds of their employees, as many have done,[27] or to evade
taxes through creative accounting, dubious tax shelters, or re-incorporation in tax
havens like Bermuda,[28] even if doing these things is legal and enhances the bottom line.

Melvin Anshen has cast the case for the broader view in a historical perspective.[29] He
maintains that there is always a kind of "social contract" between business and society. This contract is, of course, only implicit, but it represents a tacit understanding
within society about the proper goals and responsibilities of business. In effect, in
Anshen's view, society always structures the guidelines within which business is permitted to operate in order to derive certain benefits from business activity. For instance,
in the nineteenth century society's prime interest was rapid economic growth, which
was viewed as the source of all progress, and the engine of economic growth was identified as the drive for profits by unfettered, competitive, private enterprise. This attitude was reflected in the then-existing social contract.

Today, however, society has concerns and interests other than rapid economic
growth—in particular, a concern for the quality of life and for the preservation of the
environment. Accordingly, the social contract is in the process of being modified. In particular, Anshen writes, "it will no longer be acceptable for corporations to manage their
affairs solely in terms of the traditional internal costs of doing business, while thrust-
ing external costs on the public."

In recent years we have grown more aware of the possible deleterious side effects of
business activity, or what economists call *externalities*. Externalities are the unintended
negative (or in some cases positive) consequences that an economic transaction between
two parties can have on some third party. Industrial pollution provides the clearest illustration. Suppose, for example, that a factory makes widgets and sells them to your firm.
A by-product of this economic transaction is the waste that the rains wash from the factory yard into the local river, waste that damages recreational and commercial fishing
interests downstream. This damage to third parties is an unintended side effect of the
economic transaction between the seller and buyer of widgets.

Defenders of the new social contract, like Anshen, maintain that externalities should
no longer be overlooked. In the jargon of economists, externalities must be "internalized." That is, the factory should be made to absorb the cost, either by disposing of its
waste in an environmentally safe (and presumably more expensive) way or by paying
for the damage the waste does downstream. On one hand, basic fairness requires that
the factory's waste no longer be dumped onto third parties. On the other hand, from
the economic point of view, requiring the factory to internalize the externalities makes
sense, for only when it does so will the price of the widgets it sells reflect their true social
cost. The real production cost of the widgets includes not just labor, raw materials,
machinery, and so on but also the damage done to the fisheries downstream. Unless
the price of widgets is raised sufficiently to reimburse the fisheries for their losses or
to dispose of the waste in some other way, then the buyer of widgets is paying less than
their true cost. Part of the cost is being paid by the fishing interests downstream.

Some advocates of the broader view go beyond requiring business to internalize
its externalities in a narrow economic sense. Keith Davis maintains that in addition
to considering potential profitability, a business must weigh the long-range social
costs of its activities as well. Only if the overall benefit to society is positive should
business act:

For example, a firm that builds row upon row of look-alike houses may be saving $5,000 on each house and passing along $4,000 of the saving to each buyer, thus serving consumer interests. In the long run, however, this kind of construction may encourage the rapid development of a city slum. In this instance, the lack of long-range outlook may result in serious social costs. . . .

In sum, the expectation of the social responsibility model is that a detailed cost/benefit analysis will be made prior to determining whether to proceed with an activity and that social costs will be given significant weight in the decision-making process. Almost any business action will entail some social costs. The basic question is whether the benefits outweigh the costs so that there is a net social benefit. Many questions of judgment arise, and there are no precise mathematical measures in the social field, but rational and wise judgments can be made if the issues are first thoroughly explored.[30]

Corporations, Stockholders, and the Promissory Relationship

When asked, most Americans say that a corporation's top obligation is to its employees; others say it is to the community or nation. Only 17 percent think stockholders deserve the highest priority.[31] The advocates of the narrow view argue that the majority's attitude reflects a widespread misunderstanding of the proper relationship between management and the owners (or stockholders) of a corporation. This relationship is a *promissory* relationship, and it imposes an obligation on management that is inconsistent with any social responsibility other than profit maximization. In effect, management agrees to maximize stockholder wealth in return for specific compensation. It's as if you turned $10,000 over to an investment manager and told her: "Make me as much money with this as you can. In return, I'll give you 10 percent of the earnings." If the consultant agrees to the terms, then you would properly consider any whimsical investment of your capital immoral and probably illegal. Of course, she could refuse your offer, thus precluding any such obligation.

Law professor Christopher D. Stone, however, has argued that the relationship between corporate management and its shareholders is not the same as between you and an investment adviser.[32] For one thing, rarely if ever is the purchase of stock in a corporation couched in such explicitly promissory terms. Would-be investors pick companies that look profitable or are likely to grow or whose policies appeal to them, and they buy shares in those firms. Or they ask their stockbrokers simply to purchase what "looks good." Either way, shares are purchased through a broker from current shareholders, who have acquired their shares the same way. Very few investors put their money directly into a corporation; rather, they buy shares that were initially issued years ago.

Other factors further weaken the analogy between holding stock and entrusting money to a financial manager: (1) Most shareholders aren't even aware who the managers of "their" corporations are; (2) most shareholders never have direct contact with management; (3) the complexity of management systems in most modern corporations makes it impossible to pinpoint a single manager or group of managers directly responsible for keeping the promise; (4) the managers were never given a choice, as your adviser was, of refusing to maximize your profits as a shareholder.

But even if a promissory agreement exists between shareholder and management obligating management to make the most possible money for shareholders, must such a promise always be kept? Promises create obligations, but few people would claim that the existence of a promise automatically settles all the moral issues. For example, if I promise to meet you for lunch, I have an obligation to keep that promise. But that obligation is not absolute. We wouldn't regard the promise to meet at a certain time and place as justification for refusing to give cardiopulmonary resuscitation to a heart attack victim. Better to break the promise and save a life than keep the promise and lose a life. The point is that, even if a promise to maximize profits runs from management to shareholders, it's doubtful that the typical shareholder interprets this promise as a mandate for management to maximize profits at all social costs.

Even if such a promise is so construed, we can still ask: Is such an agreement morally binding? After all, a contract to do evil—for example, to kill someone—is invalid. By the same token, a promise that requires management to subordinate all moral considerations— for example, a healthful environment or safe products—to the end of stockholder profits would be immoral. Management, therefore, would not be obliged to honor it and, in fact, should break it.

But then precisely what is the nature of and the basis for the relationship between share holder and corporate executive? For whom are managers working, and to whom are they responsible: shareholders, society, employees? Friedman argues:

> The whole justification for permitting the corporate executive to be selected by the shareholders is that the executive is an agent serving the interest of his principal. This justification disappears when the corporate executive imposes taxes and spends the proceeds for "social" purposes. He becomes in effect a public employee, a civil servant, even though he remains in name an employee of a private enterprise.[33]

But is it true that stockholders actually select corporate executives? As long ago as 1932 Adolf Berle and Gardiner Means showed that because stock ownership in large corporations is so dispersed, actual control of the corporation has passed to management.[34] Today, as most business observers acknowledge, management handpicks the board of directors, thus controlling the body that is supposed to police it. "The CEO puts up the candidates; no one runs against them, and management counts the votes," says Nell Minow of the Corporate Library, a corporate watchdog Web site. "We wouldn't deign to call this an election in a third-world country."[35] Even in those rare cases when shareholders put up their own candidates, such proxy fights are expensive, and the incumbent management has the corporate coffers at its disposal to fight them.

As a result, the board of directors typically rubber-stamps the policies and recommendations of management. That's why it's not surprising that in 2000 the directors of Enron ignored shareholder interests and approved paying out $750 million in executive compensation—$140 million of it to its chairman—when the company's entire net income was only $975 million. And how else to explain the lavish retirement packages that boards lavish on former CEOs; these often include a million-dollar annual pension, an expensive apartment, a car and driver, and free use of the company aircraft.[36] True, in the past couple of decades, institutional investors like pension funds and large mutual funds have increased their sway over corporate policies, but it's still exceedingly difficult for shareholders to change policies they don't like because the voting rules are rigged in management's favor.[37]

But even if stockholders did select corporate executives, it wouldn't follow that the executives are therefore bound to act solely in the interest of stockholder profits. Some stockholders, for example, might expect executives to act in an environmentally responsible manner, even if that means less profit. And why shouldn't stockholders who want to expand the notion of corporate responsibility fight for just that? Friedman dismisses such cases as "some stockholders trying to get other stockholders . . . to contribute against their will to 'social' causes. . . ." But why couldn't it be a case of the activists trying to open debate about the nature of their corporation's social responsibility? Besides, if activist stockholders wish to make their corporations more socially responsible, why don't they have a right to do that as owners?

Friedman believes that if executives "impose taxes on stockholders and spend the proceeds for 'social' purposes, they then become 'civil servants,' and thus should be selected through a political process." He considers such a proposition absurd, or at best socialistic. And yet others contend that corporations are too focused on profits and fear the damage to society when firms are willing to sacrifice all other values on the altar of the bottom line. They don't think it absurd at all that corporations should take a broader view of their social role and responsibilities. They see nothing in the management-stockholder relationship that would morally forbid corporations from doing so.

Even if Friedman's critics are correct and broadening the notion of corporate social responsibility does not violate a promissory relationship between stockholder and management, the discussion is not over. We must still ask: Should the notion of corporate responsibility be broadened?

SHOULD CORPORATE RESPONSIBILITY BE BROADENED?

Four important arguments against broadening corporate responsibility can be conveniently termed the invisible-hand argument, the hand-of-government argument, the inept-custodian argument, and the materialization-of-society argument.[38] Advocates of broadened corporate responsibility base their case in part on a rejection of these arguments.

The Invisible-Hand Argument

Adam Smith claimed that when each of us acts in a free-market environment to promote our own economic interests we are led by an "invisible hand" to promote the general good. Like-minded contemporary thinkers such as Friedman agree. They point out that corporations, in fact, were chartered by states precisely with utility in mind. If businesses are permitted to seek self-interest, their activities will inevitably yield the greatest good for society as a whole. To encourage corporations to base their policies and activities on anything other than profit making is to politicize business's unique economic function and to hamper its ability to satisfy our material needs. Accordingly, corporations should not be invited to fight racial injustice, poverty, or pollution, to broaden competition, or to help reduce prices or increase accessibility to products, except insofar as these activities enhance corporate profits.

Yet this argument allows that corporations may still be held accountable for their actions. To the degree that they fulfill or fail to fulfill their economic role, they can be praised or blamed. And they can rightly be criticized for breaking the law or violating the rules of the game, for example, by shady accounting practices that mislead investors about company assets. But corporations should not be held morally responsible for noneconomic matters; to do so would distort the economic mission of business in society and undermine the foundations of the free-enterprise system.

Perhaps within a restricted area of economic exchange, when the parties to the exchange are roughly equal, then each pursuing self-interest can result in the greatest net good. But in the real world of large corporations, the concept of an invisible hand orchestrating the common good often stretches credulity. For example, California deregulated its electricity market to promote competition and give the invisible hand room to operate. But the result was a disaster. Instead of cheaper energy, the state got power blackouts and soaring prices as energy companies adroitly and greedily manipulated the market. Each time the state tried to make the market work better, energy sellers devised new ways to exploit the system. The state government only stanched the crisis by a costly intervention that has basically put it in the power business.[39]

Modern corporations bear about as much resemblance to Smith's self-sufficient farmers and craftspersons as today's military complex bears to the Continental militia. Given the sway they have over our economy and society, large corporations are more like public enterprises than private ones. They also have enormous influence over the lives of their millions of employees. As Professor Virginia Held reminds us, today's modern corporation is "an almost feudal structure in its hierarchical structure and lack of democratic organization."[40] And if an invisible hand has been operating, its movements have been decidedly clumsy. Many American workers have seen their standard of living stagnate, and unemployment is as great a threat as ever. Poverty and hunger persist, and the disparity between rich and poor has yet to narrow.

The Hand-of-Government Argument

Others, such as economist and social critic John Kenneth Galbraith, agree that business's social role is purely economic and that corporations should not be considered moral agents.[41] However, these critics reject the assumption that Smith's "invisible hand" will have the effect of moralizing corporate activities. Left to their own self-serving devices, they warn, modern corporations will enrich themselves while impoverishing society. They will pollute, allow racial and sexual inequalities to fester, deceive consumers, and strive to eliminate competition and keep prices high through oligopolistic practices. They will do these things, the argument continues, because as economic institutions they are quite naturally and properly profit motivated. But what is profitable is not necessarily socially useful or desirable; and what is socially useful and desirable is not always profitable.

Then how is the corporation's natural and insatiable appetite for profit to be controlled? Through government regulation. The strong hand of government, through a system of laws and incentives, can and should bring corporations to heel. "I believe in corporations," Teddy Roosevelt once proclaimed. "They are indispensable instruments of our modern civilization; but I believe that they should be so supervised and so regulated that they shall act for the interests of the community as a whole."[42]

"Do not blame corporations and their top executives" for things like layoffs or urge them to acknowledge obligations beyond the bottom line, writes Robert Reich, Secretary of Labor under President Clinton. "They are behaving exactly as they are organized to behave." He pooh-poohs moral appeals and rejects the idea that CEOs should seek to balance the interests of shareholders against those of employees and their communities.

Rather, Reich says, "if we want corporations to take more responsibility" for the economic well-being of Americans, then government "will have to provide the proper incentives."[43]

This advice sounds realistic and is intended to be practical, but it rejects the notion of broadening corporate social responsibility just as firmly as the invisible-hand argument does. That argument puts the focus on the market. Galbraith's and Reich's argument puts it on the visible hand of government. Both positions agree, however, in thinking it misguided to expect or demand that business firms do anything other than pursue profit.

Critics of the hand-of-government view contend that it is a blueprint for big, intrusive government. Moreover, they doubt that government can control any but the most egregious corporate immorality. They fear that many questionable activities will be overlooked, safely hidden within the labyrinth of the corporate structure. Lacking intimate knowledge of the goals and subgoals of specific corporations, as well as of their daily operations, government simply can't anticipate a specific corporation's moral challenges. Rather, it can prescribe behavior only for broad, cross-sectional issues, such as bribery, price-fixing, unfair competition, and the like.

Finally, is government a credible custodian of morality? If recent experience has taught anything, it is that government officials are not always paragons of virtue. Looked at as another organization, government manifests many of the same structural characteristics that test moral behavior inside the corporation. Furthermore, given the awesome clout of corporate lobbyists, one wonders whether, as moral police, government officials will do anything more than impose the values and interests of their most generous financiers. Can we seriously expect politicians to bite the hand that feeds them?

The Inept-Custodian Argument

Some who argue against broadening corporate responsibility say that corporate executives lack the moral and social expertise to make other than economic decisions. To charge them with noneconomic responsibilities would be to put social welfare in the hands of inept custodians. Thus, business analyst Walter Goodman writes: "I don't know of any investment adviser whom I would care to act in my behalf in any matter except turning a profit. . . . The value of these specialists . . . lies in their limitations; they ought not allow themselves to see so much of the world that they become distracted."[44]

It may be true, as Goodman suggests, that corporate members lack the moral or social expertise that a broader view of corporate responsibility would seem to require of them. But more or less the same can be said of most people in organizations: They are not trained moral philosophers or social scientists. And yet we don't ordinarily restrict the activities of these parties, individually or collectively, to carefully circumscribed organizational goals. Physicians, for example, are to provide health care. Is it therefore objectionable for them as physicians to campaign against nuclear arms— indeed, to conceive of their social responsibility in such terms? Is it beyond the role of pediatricians to publicly support legislation requiring the use of seat belts in automobiles? Again, every year the Committee on Public Doublespeak of the National Council of Teachers of English gives a "Doublespeak Award," usually to a business or political leader, for flagrant use of language that pretends to communicate but really does not.

Should the committee's members, all of whom are teachers of English, confine their language instruction to the classroom and avoid trying to attract public attention to good, clear, solid language usage?

Of course, the analogy between physicians and English teachers on the one hand and corporate executives on the other is imperfect. For one thing, English teachers know proper language usage, and physicians are qualified to address the health aspects of nuclear war and the health hazards of driving without restraining devices. Furthermore, the social activism of these professionals does not threaten the earnings of their employers. Nevertheless, such comparisons do make the larger point that responsibility is not always limited to narrow professional or occupational concerns. If we consider physician and teacher activities like the aforementioned defensible, then it seems fair to ask: What, if anything, makes the social role of the corporation unique, so that its responsibility and that of those it employs should be confined solely to profit making?

The Materialization-of-Society Argument

Related to the inept-custodian argument is one expressing the fear that if permitted to stray from strictly economic matters, corporate officials will impose their materialistic values on all of society. Thus, broadening corporate responsibility will "materialize" society instead of "moralizing" corporate activity.

More than forty-five years ago, Harvard professor Theodore Levitt expressed this concern:

> The danger is that all these things [resulting from having business pursue social goals other than profit making] will turn the corporation into a twentieth-century equivalent of the medieval church. . . . For while the corporation also transforms itself in the process, at bottom its outlook will always remain materialistic. What we have then is the frightening spectacle of a powerful economic functional group whose future and perception are shaped in a tight materialistic context of money and things but which imposes its narrow ideas about a broad spectrum of unrelated noneconomic subjects on the mass of man and society. Even if its outlook were the purest kind of good will, that would not recommend the corporation as an arbiter of our lives.[45]

This argument seems to assume that corporations do not already exercise enormous discretionary power over us. But as Keith Davis points out, business already has immense social power. "Society has entrusted to business large amounts of society's resources," says Davis, "and business is expected to manage these resources as a wise trustee for society. In addition to the traditional role of economic entrepreneurship, business now has a new social role of trusteeship. As trustee for society's resources, it serves the interests of all claimants on the organization, rather than only those of owners, or consumers, or labor."[46]

As Paul Camenisch notes, business is already using its privileged position to propagate, consciously or unconsciously, a view of humanity and the good life.[47] Implicit in the barrage of advertisements to which we are subjected daily are assumptions about happiness, success, and human fulfillment. In addition, corporations or industry groups sometimes speak out in unvarnished terms about social and economic issues. For example, ExxonMobil has published editorial-style advertisements in the newspaper criticizing the Clean Air Act Amendments and arguing against using economic sanctions to promote American foreign policy goals; Philip Morris campaigns publicly for the cigarette legislation it favors; and drug companies such as Eli Lilly, Procter & Gamble, and Bristol-Myers Squibb contribute to conservative think tanks that seek to reduce the regulatory powers of the Food and Drug Administration.[48]

The point here is that business already promotes consumerism and materialistic values. It doesn't hesitate to use its resources to express its views and influence our political system on issues that affect its economic interests. If corporations take a broader view of their social responsibilities, are they really likely to have a more materialistic effect on society, as Levitt suggests, than they do now? It's hard to believe they could. Levitt's view implies that there is some threat to society's values when corporations engage in philanthropy or use their economic and political muscle for other than purely self-interested ends. But society's values are not endangered when Sara Lee donates 2 percent of its pretax profits (nearly $13 million) to charitable causes, mostly cultural institutions and organizations serving disadvantaged people,[49] or when General Mills gives away 3 percent of its domestic pretax earnings ($45 million) to community organizations, donates food to people in need, and helps inner-city companies to get up and running.[50] And where is the "materialization of society" if, instead of advertising on a silly situation comedy that reaches a large audience, a corporation spends the same amount underwriting a science program with fewer viewers solely out of a sense of social responsibility?

INSTITUTIONALIZING ETHICS WITHIN CORPORATIONS

The criticisms of these four arguments against broadening corporate responsibility have led many people inside and outside business to adopt the broader view of corporate responsibility—that the obligations of the modern business corporation extend beyond simply making money for itself. Society grants corporations the right to exist, gives them legal status as separate entities, and permits them to use natural resources. It does this not to indulge the profit appetites of owners and managers but, as Camenisch says, because it needs "the available raw materials transformed into needed goods and services, and because business in its contemporary form has been conspicuously successful in doing just that."[51] In return for its sufferance of corporations, society has the right to expect corporations not to cause harm, to take into account the external effects of their activities, and whenever possible to act for the betterment of society.

The list of corporate responsibilities goes beyond such negative injunctions as "Don't pollute," "Don't misrepresent products," and "Don't bribe." Included also are affirmative duties like "See that your product or service makes a positive contribution to society," "Improve the skills of your employees," "Seek to hire the disabled," "Give special consideration to the needs of historically disadvantaged groups," "Contribute to the arts and education," "Locate plants in economically depressed areas," and "Improve working conditions." This class of affirmative responsibilities includes activities that are not intrinsically related to the operations of the corporation—responsibilities that each of us, whether individuals or institutions, has simply by virtue of our being members of society. Precisely how far each of us must go to meet these responsibilities depends largely on our capacity to fulfill them, which, of course, varies from person to person, institution to institution. But given their considerable power and resources, large corporations seem better able to promote the common good than individuals or small businesses.

How corporations are to promote the common good cannot be answered very specifically; methods will depend on the type of firm and its particular circumstances. Proponents of broadening corporate responsibility probably would agree that the first step is to create an ethical atmosphere within the corporation. This means making ethical behavior a high priority. How to do this? At least four actions seem called for:

1. Corporations should acknowledge the importance, even necessity, of conducting business morally. Their commitment to ethical behavior should be unequivocal and highly visible, from top management down.

2. Corporations should make a real effort to encourage their members to take moral responsibilities seriously. This commitment would mean ending all forms of retaliation against those who buck the system and rewarding employees for evaluating corporate decisions in their broader social and moral contexts.

3. Corporations should end their defensiveness in the face of public discussion and criticism. Instead, they should actively solicit the views of all stakeholders—stockholders, employees, suppliers, customers, local communities, and even society as a whole. Corporations should invite outside opinions and conduct a candid ethical audit of their organizational policies, priorities, and practices.

4. Corporations must recognize the pluralistic nature of the social system of which they are a part. Society consists of diverse, interlocked groups, all vying to maintain their autonomy and advance their interests. These groups are so related that the actions of one inevitably affect the standing of another on a variety of levels: economic, political, educational, cultural. As part of society, corporations affect many groups, and these groups affect corporations. Failing to realize this, corporations can lose sight of the social framework that governs their relationship with the external environment.

Undoubtedly, other general directives could be added to this list. Still, if corporate responsibility should be expanded, then something like the preceding approach seems basic.

Limits to What the Law Can Do

Critics of the hand-of-government argument question Galbraith's and Reich's view that society should not expect business to behave morally but rather should simply use government to direct business's pursuit of profit in socially acceptable directions. This issue is worth returning to in the present context. All defenders of the broad view of corporate social responsibility believe that more than laissez faire is necessary to ensure that business behavior is socially and morally acceptable. Yet there is a tendency to believe that law is a fully adequate vehicle for this purpose.

Law professor Christopher Stone has argued, however, that there are limits on what the law can be expected to achieve.[52] Three of his points are particularly important. First, many laws, like controls on the disposal of toxic waste, are passed only after there is general awareness of the problem; in the meantime, damage has already been done. The proverbial barn door has been shut only after the horse has left.

Second, formulating appropriate laws and designing effective regulations are difficult. It is hard to achieve consensus on the relevant facts, to determine what remedies will work, and to decide how to weigh conflicting values. In addition, our political system gives corporations and their lobbyists significant input into the writing of laws. Not only that, but the specific working regulations and day-to-day interpretation of the law require the continual input of industry experts. This is not a conspiracy but a fact of life. Government bureaus generally have limited time, staffing, and expertise, so they must rely on the cooperation and assistance of those they regulate.

Third, enforcing the law is often cumbersome. Legal actions against corporations are expensive and can drag on for years, and the judicial process is often too blunt an instrument to use as a way of managing complex social and business issues. In fact, recourse to the courts can be counterproductive, and Stone argues that sometimes the benefits of doing so may not be worth the costs. Legal action may simply make corporations more furtive, breeding distrust, destruction of documents, and an attitude that "I won't do anything more than I am absolutely required to do."

What conclusion should be drawn? Stone's argument is not intended to show that regulation of business is hopeless. Rather, what he wants to stress is that the law cannot do it alone. We do not want a system in which businesspeople believe that their only obligation is to obey the law and that it is morally permissible for them to do anything not (yet) illegal. With that attitude, disaster is just around the corner. More socially responsible business behavior requires, instead, that corporations and the people within them not just respond to the requirements of the law but hold high moral standards—and that they themselves monitor their own behavior.

Ethical Codes and Economic Efficiency

It is, therefore, important that corporations examine their own implicit and explicit codes of conduct and the moral standards that are being propagated to their employees. Yet ethical behavior in the business world is often assumed to come at the expense of economic efficiency. Defenders of the broader view, like Anshen, as well as defenders of the narrow view, like Friedman, seem to make this assumption. Anshen believes that other values should take priority over economic efficiency, whereas Friedman contends business should concern itself only with profit and, in this way, maximize economic well being. In his important essay "Social Responsibility and Economic Efficiency," Nobel Prize–winning economist Kenneth Arrow has challenged this assumption.[53]

First, any kind of settled economic life requires a certain degree of ethical behavior, some element of trust and confidence. Much business, for instance, is conducted on the basis of oral agreements. In addition, says Arrow, "there are two types of situation in which the simple rule of maximizing profits is socially inefficient: the case in which costs are not paid for, as in pollution, and the case in which the seller has considerably more knowledge about his product than the buyer."

The first type of situation relates to the demand that corporations "internalize their externalities." In the second situation, in which the buyer lacks the expertise and knowledge of the seller, an effective moral code, either requiring full disclosure or setting minimal standards of performance (for example, the braking ability of a new automobile), enhances rather than diminishes economic efficiency. Without such a code, buyers may purchase products or services they don't need. Or because they don't trust the seller, they may refrain from purchasing products and services they do need. Either way, from the economist's point of view the situation is inefficient.

An effective professional or business moral code—as well as the public's awareness of this code—is good for business. Most of us, for example, have little medical knowledge and are thus at the mercy of doctors. Over hundreds of years, however, a firm code of ethical conduct has developed in the medical profession. As a result, people generally presume that their physician will perform with their welfare in mind. They rarely worry that their doctor might be taking advantage of them or exploiting them with unnecessary treatment. By contrast, used-car dealers have historically suffered from a lack of public trust.

For a code to be effective it must be realistic, Arrow argues, in the sense of connecting with the collective self-interest of business. And it must become part of the corporate culture, "accepted by the significant operating institutions and transmitted from one generation of executives to the next through standard operating procedures [and] through education in business schools."

For both Arrow and Stone, then, the development of feasible and effective business and professional codes of ethics must be a central focus of any effort to enhance or expand corporate responsibility. The question is how to create a corporate atmosphere conducive to moral decision making.

Corporate Moral Codes

What can be done to improve the organizational climate so individual members can reasonably be expected to act ethically? If those inside the corporation are to behave morally, they need clearly stated and communicated ethical standards that are equitable and enforced. This development seems possible only if the standards of expected behavior are institutionalized—that is, only if they become a fixture in the corporate organization. To institutionalize ethics within corporations, professor Milton Snoeyenbos suggests that top management should (1) articulate the firm's values and goals, (2) adopt an ethical code applicable to all members of the company, (3) set up a high-ranking ethics committee to oversee, develop, and enforce the code, and (4) incorporate ethics training into all employee-development programs.[54]

The company's code of ethics should not be window dressing or so general as to be useless. It should set reasonable goals and subgoals, with an eye on blunting unethical pressures on subordinates. In formulating the code, the top-level ethics committee should solicit the views of corporate members at all levels regarding goals and subgoals, so that the final product articulates "a fine-grained ethical code that addresses ethical issues likely to arise at the level of subgoals."[55] Moreover, the committee should have full authority and responsibility to communicate the code and decisions based on it to all corporate members, clarify and interpret the code when the need arises, facilitate the code's use, investigate grievances and violations of the code, discipline violators and reward compliance, and review, update, and upgrade the code.

To help employees in ethically difficult situations, a good corporate ethics program must be user-friendly. It should provide a support system with a variety of entry points, one that employees feel confident about using.[56] In addition, part of all employee-training programs should be devoted to ethics. At a minimum, this should include study of the code, review of the company's procedures for handling ethical problems, and discussion of employer and employee responsibilities and expectations. Snoeyenbos and others believe that institutionalizing ethics within the corporation in these ways, when supplemented by the development of industry-wide codes of ethics to address issues beyond a particular firm, will go far toward establishing a corporate climate conducive to individual moral decision making.

Corporate Culture

During the past two decades, organizational theorists and writers on business management have increasingly emphasized "corporate culture" as the factor that makes one company succeed while another languishes. Although intangible in comparison with things like sales revenue and profit margin, corporate culture is often the key to a firm's success. According to one study, 30 percent of the difference in performance between companies can be attributed to differences in culture, but only 5 percent to differences in strategy.[57]

What is corporate culture? One writer describes it as "the shared beliefs top managers have in a company about how they should manage themselves and other employees, and how they should conduct their business(es). These beliefs are often invisible to the top managers but have a major impact on their thoughts and actions."[58] Another writer puts it this way: "Culture is the pattern of shared values and beliefs that gives members of an institution meaning and provides them with rules for behavior in their organization."[59] W. Brooke Tunstall, an assistant vice president of AT&T, provides a fuller definition. He describes corporate culture as "a general constellation of beliefs, mores, customs, value systems and behavioral norms, and ways of doing business that are unique to each corporation, that set a pattern for corporate activities and actions, and that describe the implicit and emergent patterns of behavior and emotions characterizing life in the organization."[60]

Corporate culture may be both explicit and implicit. The formal culture of a corporation, as expressed in idealized statements of values and norms, should also be distinguished from the informal culture that shapes beliefs, values, and behavior. In addition, there may be multiple and overlapping cultures within an organization because employees have different backgrounds, work in different divisions of the organization, and may be subject to different systems of rewards and sanctions.

Organizational theorists emphasize the importance of monitoring and managing corporate culture—beginning with an attempt to understand each corporation's distinctive culture—to prevent dysfunctional behavior and processes. As one consultant puts it, "A corporation's culture is what determines how people behave when they are not being watched."[61] If management does not make explicit the values and behavior it desires, the culture will typically develop its own norms, usually based on the types of behavior that lead to success within the organization. Thus, the desired values must be communicated and transmitted throughout the organization. Conduct congruent with them must be rewarded and conduct inconsistent with them sanctioned. Overlooking behavior that contradicts the desired norms can have the effect of encouraging and even rewarding it.

These points are crucial when it comes to corporate social responsibility. Management needs to understand the real dynamics of its own organization. At Sears, for example, new minimum work quotas and productivity incentives at its auto centers created a high-pressure environment that led employees to mislead customers and sell them unnecessary parts and services, from brake jobs to front-end alignments.[62] Thus, it is necessary for socially responsible executives to ask: How do people get ahead in the company? What conduct is actually rewarded, what values are really being instilled in employees? Andrew C. Sigler, chairman of Champion International, stresses this point: "Sitting up here in Stamford, there's no way I can affect what an employee is doing today in Texas, Montana, or Maine. Making speeches and sending letters just doesn't do it. You need a culture and peer pressure that spells out what is acceptable and isn't and why. It involves training, education, and follow-up."[63]

Internal or external corporate responsibility audits can help close the gap between stated values, goals, and mission, on the one hand, and reality on the other.[64] Another aspect of follow-up is strict enforcement. Chemical Bank, for instance, has fired employees for violations of the company's code of ethics even when nothing illegal was done. Xerox has dismissed people for minor manipulation of records and the padding of expense accounts. (By contrast, some of the nation's most prestigious stock brokerage firms employ salespeople with long records of violating securities laws.[65]) Executives at both Xerox and General Mills also emphasize that civic involvement is a crucial part of corporate ethics. As one General Mills executive puts it: "It's hard to imagine that a person who reads to the blind at night would cheat. . . ."[66]

Johnson & Johnson is widely seen as a model of corporate responsibility, especially because of its decisive handling of the Tylenol crisis of 1982, when seven people in the Chicago area died from cyanide-laced Extra-Strength Tylenol capsules. The company immediately recalled 31 million bottles of Tylenol from store shelves across the nation and notified 500,000 doctors and hospitals about the contaminated capsules. A toll-free consumer hotline was set up the first week of the crisis, and consumers were offered the opportunity to replace Tylenol capsules with a free bottle of Tylenol tablets. Johnson & Johnson was also open with the public instead of being defensive about the deaths. Accurate information was promptly released, and domestic employees and retirees were kept updated on developments. The chairman of the company appeared on the talk show *Donahue* and on *60 Minutes* to answer questions about the crisis, and other executives were interviewed by *Fortune* and *The Wall Street Journal*.

Despite the setback—the recall alone cost Johnson & Johnson $50 million after taxes—Tylenol rebounded within a year, in large part because the public never lost faith in Johnson & Johnson. The company itself credits its sixty-year-old, one-page statement of values, known as the Credo, with enabling it to build the employee trust necessary for maintaining a firm corporate value system. The Credo acknowledges the company's need to make a sound profit while addressing its obligations to provide a quality product, to treat its employees fairly and with respect, and to be a good corporate citizen, supporting the community of which it is a member.

The Credo is "the most important thing we have in this company," says chairman Ralph Larsen. But creating and maintaining a morally sound corporate culture is an ongoing task, and Johnson & Johnson hasn't always been able to live up to its own values. In 1995, for instance, the company agreed to pay $7.5 million in fines and costs after admitting that wayward employees had shredded papers to hinder a federal probe into the marketing of an acne cream. "There was no excuse," admits Larsen. "But it is a huge undertaking to spread our values around the world."[67]

SUMMARY

1. What we know as the modern business corporation has evolved over several centuries, and incorporation is no longer the special privilege it once was.

2. Corporations are legal entities, with legal rights and responsibilities similar but not identical to those enjoyed by individuals. Business corporations are limited-liability companies—that is, their owners or stockholders are liable for corporate debts only up to the extent of their investments.

3. The question of corporate moral agency is whether corporations are the kind of entity that can have moral responsibilities. There are at least three senses of "morally responsible." If corporations can make rational and moral decisions, then they can be held morally blameworthy or praiseworthy for their actions. Philosophers disagree about whether the corporate internal decision (CID) structure makes it reasonable to assign moral responsibility to corporations.

4. This problem is compounded by the difficulty of assigning moral responsibility to individuals inside corporations.

5. Despite these controversies, the courts and the general public find the notion of corporate responsibility useful and intelligible—either in a literal sense or as shorthand for the obligations of individuals in the corporation.

6. The debate over corporate responsibility is whether it should be construed narrowly to cover only profit maximization or more broadly to include refraining from socially undesirable behavior and contributing actively and directly to the public good.

7. Proponents of the narrow view, such as Milton Friedman, contend that diverting corporations from the pursuit of profit makes our economic system less efficient. Business's only social responsibility is to make money within the rules of the game. Private enterprise should not be forced to undertake public responsibilities that properly belong to government.

8. Defenders of the broader view maintain that corporations have additional responsibilities because of their great social and economic power. Business is governed by an implicit social contract that requires it to operate in ways that benefit society. In particular, corporations must take responsibility for the unintended side effects of their business transactions (externalities) and weigh the full social costs of their activities.

9. Advocates of the narrow view stress that management has a promissory relation with the owners (stockholders) of a corporation, which obligates it to focus on profit maximization alone. Critics challenge this argument.

10. Should corporate responsibility be broadened? Four arguments against doing so are the invisible-hand argument, the hand-of-government argument, the inept-custodian argument, and the materialization-of-society argument. Finding flaws with each of these arguments, critics claim there is no solid basis for restricting corporate responsibility to profit making.

11. Those proposing broader corporate responsibilities see the creation of an ethical atmosphere within the corporation as an important first step. Essential to this atmosphere are acknowledgment of the critical importance of ethics, encouragement of morally responsible conduct by all employees, openness to public discussion and review, and recognition of the pluralistic nature of our social system.

12. Corporations and the people who make them up must have high moral standards and monitor their own behavior because there are limits to what the law can do to ensure that business behavior is socially and morally acceptable.

13. All settled economic life requires trust and confidence. The adoption of realistic and workable codes of ethics in the business world can actually enhance business efficiency. This is particularly true when there is an imbalance of knowledge between the buyer and the seller.

14. To improve the organizational climate so individuals can reasonably be expected to act ethically, corporations should adopt an ethical code, set up a high-ranking ethics committee, and include ethics training in their employee-development programs. Attention to corporate culture is also crucial to the successful institutionalization of ethics inside an organization.

CASE 5.1

Selling Infant Formula Abroad

In the mid-1860s Henri Nestlé developed infant formula to save the life of an infant who couldn't be breast fed. According to officials at Nestlé—a Swiss-based corporation that is now the world's largest food company, with annual sales of nearly $60 billion—the Frenchman's concoction has been saving lives ever since, especially in developing countries. They point to relief organizations such as the International Red Cross, which has used the formula to feed thousands of starving infants in refugee camps, for example. Without its infant formula, the Nestlé people say, Third World mothers considering use of a breast-milk substitute would use less nutritious local alternatives. Maybe so. But a hundred years after it was first developed, Henri Nestlé's sweet idea turned sour, threatening the Nestlé Corporation's dominant share of the $5–$6 billion international market for infant formula.[68]

The infant formula controversy began to heat up in 1970 at a United Nations–sponsored meeting on infant feeding in Bogotá, Colombia. Meeting to discuss different aspects of world hunger, the Protein Advisory Group (PAG)—made up of nutritionists, pediatricians, and food-industry representatives—hammered out a broad framework for cooperation among business, health care, and government. They were especially concerned about the worldwide decline in breast feeding, despite the demonstrated superiority of mother's milk over infant formula. But some PAG members bristled at what they thought was PAG's failure to engage a critical issue: the implications of marketing infant formula in Third World countries.

Straightaway the media began reporting some of the common marketing practices of infant-formula companies:

Item—Dressed as health care professionals, representatives of formula companies visited villages to promote the use of infant formula.

Item—While interned in clinics and hospitals, new mothers were given free samples of infant formula.

Item—Free or low-cost supplies of infant formula were given to health institutions, thus routinizing bottle feeding within hospitals and discouraging breast feeding.

Item—Product labels failed to warn of potential dangers from incorrect use of infant formula.

Most damaging from the industry's viewpoint was infant formula's alleged complicity in the death of Third World infants. Dr. Derrick B. Jelliffe, then director of the

Caribbean Food and Nutrition Institute, claimed that millions of infants suffered and died as a result of bottle feeding. A major reason was that Third World mothers could not take sterilization and storage precautions commonplace in homes with modern kitchens.

Outraged by these allegations, the Infant Formula Action Coalition (INFACT) was formed in 1977. It focused its indignation on Nestlé, the largest producer of infant formula worldwide. Chaired by Douglas A. Johnson and joined by a hundred other religious and health organizations, INFACT instituted an international boycott against the Nestlé Company, charging it with aggressive marketing tactics designed to pressure mothers in underdeveloped countries to switch from breast feeding to bottle feeding, thus contributing to high infant-mortality rates.

INFACT's and Jelliffe's bold charges were weakened by a shortage of reliable information—as Nestlé's defenders were quick to point out. Was breast feeding really decreasing in developing nations? Were infant morbidity and mortality in fact increasing? No one really knew. And even if bottle feeding was increasing and even if there was a connection between it and increased infant mortality, no one could claim for certain that Nestlé's promotional practices had much, if anything, to do with it. Also overlooked was the fact that Third World mothers who cannot nurse are also more likely to be subject to the economic factors that make bottle feeding risky.[69]

In May 1981, the World Health Organization (WHO) adopted a "Code of Marketing of Breastmilk Substitutes," which called on governments to prohibit advertising of infant formula that discourages breast feeding. The code would prohibit, for example, sending women dressed as nurses to rural villages or paying local health workers to push infant formula. Of the 119 WHO members who voted, 118 voted for adoption. The sole opposition vote was cast by the United States, which invoked the principles of free trade and free speech. The United States said that WHO had no business telling private business how to sell its products and that it didn't want to make WHO an international Federal Trade Commission.

Speaking in his capacity as president of the International Council of Infant Food Industries, E. W. Saunders, a Nestlé vice president, branded the code unacceptably ambiguous. Nevertheless, Nestlé officials announced that Nestlé would support it. INFACT and others identified four areas for Nestlé to review: educational materials dealing with infant formula, hazard warnings and labels, gifts to health professionals, and free supplies to hospitals. Until Nestlé complied, INFACT threatened to pursue its campaign against the company. However the international boycott against Nestlé was suspended three years later when Nestlé developed procedures for dealing with the four specific points of the code in dispute.

Regarding educational material, Nestlé agreed to include in all materials dealing with the feeding of infants information on (1) the benefits and superiority of breast feeding, (2) maternal nutrition and preparation for maintenance of breast feeding, (3) the negative effect on breast feeding of introducing partial bottle feeding, (4) the difficulty of reversing the decision not to breast-feed, (5) possible health hazards of inappropriate food or feeding methods, and (6) the social and financial consequences of the decision to use infant formula.

Regarding hazard warning labels, Nestlé agreed to test different statements in Third World countries, with the help of specialized consultants recommended by WHO and UNICEF. It specifically promised to ensure that product users fully understood the consequences of inappropriate or incorrect use arising from unclean water, dirty utensils, improper dilution, and storage of prepared foods without refrigeration.

Regarding gifts to health professionals, Nestlé agreed not to give gifts such as chocolate, key rings, and pens to health professionals. It also agreed to avoid product advertising in technical and scientific publications.

Regarding low-cost supplies of infant formula to health institutions, Nestlé recognized that this might inadvertently discourage breast feeding. Accordingly, it agreed to restrict the distribution of supplies to situations in which infants had to be fed on breast-milk substitutes and to help specify the conditions that would warrant such substitutes.

In announcing that a truce had been reached, Nestlé officials and protesters literally broke candy together—Nestlé chocolate, naturally—to celebrate the end of the six-and-a-half-year conflict. Douglas A. Johnson praised Nestlé for moving forward to become a model for the entire industry. The WHO code, said Johnson, has changed from "an urgent moral mandate to the accepted business practice of the largest and singly most important factor in the world." Nestlé officials viewed the settlement as "proof that its efforts" to comply with the WHO code "have finally been recognized." They boasted that Nestlé was the first company to "unilaterally apply the code in developing countries" and to "submit its activities in this area to examination by an independent commission. . . . The time has now come for all interested parties to concentrate their effort on solutions to the fundamental cause of infant mortality and malnutrition in the Third World."[70]

After a verification period of eight months, boycott leaders were satisfied that Nestlé had begun to put into place the agreed-on changes, and the "suspended" boycott was officially ended. Unfortunately, the story of Nestlé and infant formula does not come to a happy end there. Four years later, in October 1988, Douglas A. Johnson and his Minneapolis-based organization Action for Corporate Accountability charged Nestlé with noncompliance. They urged a resumption of the boycott against Nestlé as well as an expansion of the boycott to include American Home Products (AHP), the second-largest distributor of infant formula in developing nations. Nestlé's Taster's Choice Instant Coffee and Carnation Coffeemate became targets of the boycott, along with AHP's Anacin and Advil pain relievers. Action for Corporate Accountability accused both companies of violating at least the spirit—and, according to Johnson, also the letter—of the WHO code.

Specifically, Nestlé and AHP were accused of continuing to dump free supplies of formula on hospitals to induce mothers to bottle-feed their infants. The code permits donations of formula for infants needing breast-milk substitutes, but it prohibits distributing free formula solely for sales promotion. The effectiveness of free samples is well known in the advertising world. Mothers who receive free samples are far more likely to bottle-feed than those who do not. By the time the mother and baby have been discharged from the hospital, the mother's milk will have begun to dry up. She and the baby will have become hooked on the formula, Action for Corporate Accountability argued, just when the companies' donations stop and profit making begins.

Thad Jackson, a Washington spokesperson for Nestlé, insisted that the company was in "total compliance" with national and international codes. He also said that the company never gave the product directly to mothers. "We do not dump supplies in hospitals," he stated. Carol Emerling, an official of AHP, also challenged the boy-cott. "This whole activity is based on allegations that we violate the WHO code—and we flat out deny that."[71]

Monitoring by the United Methodist Church, however, concluded that the indus-try continued to violate restrictions on supplies to hospitals. One study of forty-five hospitals in four Asian countries found that Nestlé was supplying formula to 80 per-cent of them—in enough quantity to feed over 110 percent of their infants. AHP sup-plied formula to 64 percent of the hospitals. Moreover, the companies' own data suggested that the practice was designed to produce sales. In Brazil, for instance, where Nestlé had a monopoly on infant formula, it distributed no free supplies to hos-pitals. When the government of the Ivory Coast conducted a campaign to promote breast feeding, Nestlé stepped up its donations of formula to that nation's hospitals.[72]

Boycotts are difficult to organize and sustain, and Johnson's efforts to mount a second one against Nestlé had little effect. But there was some progress. In March 1992, UNICEF and WHO joined forces to launch a new "Baby-Friendly Hospital Initiative." Nestlé is one of the parties that pledged to coordinate efforts on behalf of this initiative, designed to encourage breast feeding and halt the distribution of free or low-cost samples of infant formula to hospitals in developing nations.

Unfortunately, though, the problem is not limited to the Third World. To secure a contract allowing it to be the only company to provide free formula samples to all mothers giving birth in New York City hospitals, AHP paid $1 million to the New York City Health and Hospital Corporation. New York's plan was to spend the entire sum on promoting breast feeding. Would this counteract the influence of those free samples to mothers? AHP was willing to gamble $1 million that it wouldn't.[73]

Update:

UNICEF estimates that 1.5 million babies die each year because they are not breast fed. And over twenty years after WHO adopted a code of conduct for the market-ing of infant formula, International Baby Food Action Network and affiliated organ-izations like Baby Milk Action continue to campaign against Nestlé and other infant-formula companies, charging that they violate the code by marketing their product aggressively to young mothers and pregnant women in the Third World.[74] These charges gained support from a *British Medical Journal* report published in 2003, which found that the infant formula marketing code was being ignored in the two African countries it studied, with companies failing to include a statement about the health benefits of breastfeeding, instructions for the appropriate preparation and storage of formula, or a warning against the health hazards of inappropriate use. According to the study, 90 percent of health providers had never heard of the code, and two-thirds of mothers using formula had never received any advice on breast-feeding. For its part, Nestlé insists that it has always respected the code and would take "the necessary steps" to remedy any local problems.[75]

Discussion Questions

1. What moral issues are raised by the controversy over infant formula? Do you find anything objectionable in the marketing techniques used to sell infant formula? What moral rights, if any, are at stake in this controversy? How would you respond to the argument that all Nestlé was doing was selling a high-quality product at its normal price to willing buyers?

2. In light of this case, do you think it makes sense to talk of a corporation like Nestlé as a moral agent, or is it only the people in it who can be properly described as having moral responsibility?

3. Identify the views of corporate social responsibility held by the different actors and organizations in this case. In what ways does this case raise questions about the social and moral responsibility of corporations?

4. Appraise Nestlé's actions from the perspective of both the narrow and the broader view of corporate social responsibility.

5. How would you assess Nestlé's conduct throughout the whole controversy? Has Nestlé acted in good faith? Do you think it is sincerely concerned about the drawbacks and dangers of using infant formula?

6. Can boycotts be effective in pressuring corporations to exercise social responsibility? When, if ever, does an individual have a moral obligation to participate in a corporate boycott?

CASE 5.2

Levi Strauss at Home and Abroad

Juvenile Manufacturing of San Antonio, Texas, began making infants' and children's garments in a plant on South Zarzamora Street in 1923; in the 1930s, the company switched to boys' and men's clothing and changed its name to Santone Industries. During the 1970s, Santone manufactured sports jackets for Levi Strauss & Co., which eventually decided to buy out the company. In 1981, Levi Strauss paid $10 million and took over operations on South Zarzamora Street.[76]

Although the garment industry had been struggling in some parts of the country, it had prospered in San Antonio—not least on South Zarzamora Street. One of three Levi's plants in the city, the plant was slowly converted in the late 1980s from making sports jackets to manufacturing the company's popular Dockers trousers, which had surpassed Levi's 501 jeans as the firm's top-selling line. And despite the sweatshop image that the industry brings to people's minds, many of San Antonio's semiskilled workers were happy to be employed at Levi Strauss. They thought that pay at the plant was good. Benefits were respectable, too: paid maternity leave for qualified employees, health insurance, and ten days of paid vacation at Christmas and ten during the summer.

Then in 1990, Levi Strauss decided to close the plant—the largest layoff in San Antonio's history—and move its operations to Costa Rica and the Dominican Republic. This was the course of action that had been recommended the previous year by Bruce Stallworth, the firm's operations controller. Closing the plant would cost $13.5 million, Stallworth calculated, but transferring its production abroad would "achieve significant cost savings," enabling the company to recover its closing costs within two years. In 1989, it cost $6.70 to make a pair of Dockers at the South Zarzamora plant. Plant management had hoped to reduce that to $6.39 per unit in 1990, but even that would be significantly higher than the per unit cost of $5.88 at the Dockers plant in Powell, Tennessee—not to mention the $3.76 per unit cost Levi Strauss could get by using Third World contractors.

Stallworth attributed the San Antonio plant's high costs to workers' compensation expenses, to a less-than-full-capacity plant operation, and to the fact that "conversion from sports coats to Dockers has not been totally successful." Retraining workers who have spent years sewing jackets to sew trousers, it seems, is not that easy. Furthermore, running the San Antonio plant efficiently would mean running it at full capacity, but operating at full capacity on South Zarzamora Street with 1,115 workers—compared with 366 and 746 employees, respectively, at the company's other two U.S. Dockers plants—meant too many pairs of trousers produced by high-priced American labor. Workers at San Antonio averaged six dollars an hour, which is about a day's pay in the Caribbean and Central America for workers with the same level of skill.

Bob Dunn, Levi Strauss vice president of community affairs and corporate communications, denies that the company did anything it shouldn't have done with regard to closing the plant. "We didn't see any way to bring costs in line." And he adds: "As much as people like Dockers, our research shows people are not willing to pay $5 or $10 more for a pair of pants just because the label says 'Made in the U.S.A.'"

Closing plants is nothing new for Levi Strauss. Before closing South Zarzamora Street, it had already closed twenty-five plants and shifted the work overseas, either to its foreign production plants or to overseas contractors. Using overseas contractors saves the firm even more money, because in addition to lower wages the company avoids paying directly for benefits like health insurance and workers' compensation. This time, though, the company's decision to close a domestic plant and move its production abroad prompted local labor activists to fight back. They filed a class-action lawsuit and organized a boycott of Levi's products.

The boycott, however, gained little publicity outside San Antonio, and the lawsuit fizzled out. Neither seems to have dampened sales, but they embarrassed the company, which donated nearly $100,000 to help local agencies retrain its former employees and gave San Antonio an additional $340,000 to provide them with extra job counseling and training services.

Most politicians kept a low profile on the issue, praising Levi Strauss for offering its workers more than was legally required and promising to try to recruit a new company to use the empty factory. U.S. Representative Henry B. Gonzales, however, spoke out harshly: "When a company is so irresponsible—a company that has been making money and then willy-nilly removes a plant to get further profit based on greed and cheaper labor costs in the Caribbean—I say you have a bad citizen for a company."

To this, Bob Dunn responded, "Our sense is we do more than anyone in our industry and more than almost anyone in American industry." He was proud of the way Levi Strauss treated people when it closed plants. "We try to stress the right values," he said. "It's not easy. There isn't always one right answer."

Dunn's emphasis on values reflects the thinking of Levi Strauss's Robert D. Haas, CEO until 1999, now chairman of its board. Ever since he organized a successful leveraged buyout of the company, Haas, great-great-grandnephew of the company founder, Levi Strauss, has tried to create a more values-centered management at Levi Strauss by emphasizing social responsibility and employee rights. A year after the closure on South Zarzamora Street, the company's values-centered management received a second blow when a contractor in the U.S. territory of Saipan was accused of virtually enslaving some of its Chinese workers. When the company learned the contractor was not paying the island's legal minimum wage, it fired him and formed a top-management committee to monitor its overseas contractors. Levi Strauss then went on to become the first multinational to adopt guidelines for its hired factories. The first part of its "Global Sourcing Guidelines" covers the treatment of workers and the environmental impact of production; the second part sets out the company's standards for choosing the countries in which it will do business.

As a result of its guidelines, Levi Strauss stopped all production in China because of human rights abuses and systemic mistreatment of labor. For instance, in a factory in Shenzhen, women sew for twelve hours a day plus overtime and receive only two days off a month. They have no health care and no compensation for injury (although Chinese legislation requires this). Their pay is often below the legal minimum of twelve cents an hour. Back home in San Francisco, the decision to pull out of China caused a fiery debate within the company. Because Chinese labor is so cheap, a committee had recommended that the company stay in China and work to make things better, but Haas decided to withdraw from China altogether. With an annual revenue of $6.5 billion, Levi Strauss is the largest clothing company in the world, and because it has no direct investment in China, it could afford to pull out. But some business analysts worried that in the long run the company could be sacrificing a great deal by leaving China. China is the world's fastest-growing economy, and some predict that it will be the world's largest economy in twenty years.

Many people praised Levi Strauss's decision, but it dumbfounded some companies. At Nike, one executive said, "I can't figure it out. I have no idea what Levi's is doing." Nike was still having trouble figuring it out when the cartoon strip *Doonesbury* began pummeling the athletic footwear company for having its products made in sweatshops in Vietnam. Cheap Asian labor is a high priority for Nike's top executive Philip Knight, and his company has long favored places like Indonesia and China, where pay is poor and labor unions are suppressed. In Indonesia, the women who work at the sweatshops of Nike contractors make $2.20 a day, and it took four years of violent struggle to get the minimum wage raised that high. Now Nike has moved into Vietnam, where labor costs are cheaper yet. At one Nike plant in Vietnam, investigators found that employees worked sixty-five hours a week—more than Vietnamese law allows—for a weekly wage of ten dollars and that 77 percent of them suffered respiratory problems from breathing chemical fumes at work.

By contrast, Levi Strauss believes that a growing number of its customers shun products made in sweatshops. Consumers "don't want to buy a shirt made by children in Bangladesh or forced labor in China," says one industry observer. The firm's top management also believes that Levi Strauss is emblematic of American culture and that its mildly anti-establishment image must be guarded. "Anyone seeking to protect their brand and company reputation will realize these policies make sense," says Bob Dunn, who helped design the company's overseas guidelines. For this reason, some critics do not charge that Levi Strauss was foolish to leave China, but rather that its decision was dictated only by bottom-line profitability—that it was a publicity stunt aimed at attracting more customers.

But the team of inspectors that Levi Strauss has monitoring its contractors is a reality, not a publicity stunt. They regularly visit factories and are prepared to fire violators of the company's guidelines—such as the factory operator who was strip-searching female workers to determine whether they were, as they claimed, menstruating and thus, according to local Muslim law, entitled to a day off with pay. The firm has also pulled out of Myanmar because of human rights abuses in that country. The company is sensitive to local mores, however, and its first goal is not to boycott countries or cancel contracts. In Bangladesh, its inspectors discovered that a contractor was employing children under the age of fourteen—something that is legal there, but contrary to Levi Strauss guidelines. The company didn't want the children discharged, which would hurt the families who are often dependent on their income, but it didn't want the children working, either. So Levi Strauss devised a solution: Younger children would be paid while attending school and would be offered full-time jobs when they turned fourteen.

Update:

Six years after withdrawing from China because of human rights violations, Levi Strauss reported in April 1998 that it would resume manufacturing its clothing there. The company denied, however, that its decision was related to its having just closed several U.S. plants, but the reversal of its China policy provoked an outcry among human rights groups, who accused Levi Strauss of putting profits before its self-proclaimed concern for workers. The company's critics pointed to a National Labor Committee report that found gross labor violations in twenty-one Chinese factories. These include forced overtime (sometimes amounting to a work week of ninety-six hours), wages as low as thirteen cents per hour, and restrictions on workers' freedom to assemble. And the U.S. State Department declared that it had not detected any "appreciable" improvement in China's human rights record during that period. Executives at Levi Strauss responded, however, that it is now possible for the company to operate in China while adhering to its corporate code of conduct. Unlike before, it now has contracting partners who are willing and able to adhere to its code, and improvements in the company's monitoring system enable it to prevent abuses at its own factories.

For its part, Nike has begun to see the light of social responsibility. Bowing to pressure from its critics, the company has now pledged to root out underage workers and to require overseas manufacturers of its wares to meet strict U.S. health and safety standards. It also agreed to allow outsiders from labor and human rights groups to join the auditors who inspect Nike's Asian factories—a demand the company had long resisted. Nike CEO Knight acknowledged the public-relations problem facing his company, which stood accused, he said, of having "singlehandedly lowered the human rights standard for the sole purpose of maximizing profits." Nike had "become synonymous with slave wages, forced overtime and arbitrary abuse." But, Knight continued, "I believe that the American consumer does not want to buy products made in abusive conditions." He did not, however, pledge to increase wages.

Meanwhile, Levi Strauss, which in the early 1980s had fifty U.S. plants, has now abandoned all American production. In 2003, it shut the historic ninety-six year old San Francisco factory that made its 501 jeans, and in 2004 it stopped production at its only remaining North American operations, three manufacturing plants in Canada and two sewing and finishing plants in San Antonio. The company still owns eight manufacturing plants outside the U.S., but it is expected to close these eventually as well. "The closures are an absolutely necessary part of ensuring the long-term competitiveness of our business," said Julie Klee, a Levi Strauss general manager. "Moving away from owned-and-operated manufacturing to a broader sourcing base will strengthen our business by giving us much more flexibility." Levi's Robert Hass added that the closures were inevitable. The company had invested tens of millions of dollars in automated equipment, training, and incentives to keep domestic plants competitive enough to offset the overseas wage differential, but it was not enough, he said. "We've resisted all of the pressures that have been on us to close plants. As you know, we are one of the very last major companies that has any kind of manufacturing presence in North America any more. . . . Belatedly and reluctantly, we're having to follow in the footsteps of other apparel manufacturers" and shift work overseas.

However, to help its displaced workers, Levi Strauss gave them eight months' notice of the layoff, instead of the two months required by law, and is providing them with three week's severance pay per year of service. Levi Strauss has also offered displaced workers up to $6,000 each to help them make the transition into new fields. The money can be used for job training, community college education, English-language lessons, moving expenses, or setting up a small business. "We can't ignore the fact that certain jobs are not . . . sustainable in North America," said Haas. "They're done better in other countries. But companies . . . must be sensitive to [the workers'] circumstances and help move [them] into the next stage of their lives."

Discussion Questions

1. Evaluate the pros and cons of Levi Strauss's decision to close its South Zarzamora Street plant. Was it a sound business decision? Was it a socially responsible decision? Could the company have reasonably been expected to keep the plant running?

2. Having decided to close the plant, was there more that Levi Strauss could and should have done for its laid-off workers?

3. How, if at all, is your assessment of Levi Strauss's responsibilities affected by the fact that the company bought the plant and then closed it nine years later?

4. Should consumers avoid products that are made by sweatshops? Should they shun companies that lay workers off needlessly? Are consumer boycotts ever justified? When are such boycotts likely to be effective? Under what circumstances would you participate in a consumer boycott?

5. How would you feel if you had been an employee at the plant? Bob Dunn said, "My hope is that as time passes and people have a chance to reflect on what we've done, [people who have lost jobs] will judge us to have been responsible and fair." Do you think Levi Strauss's former employees will judge it that way?

6. With regard to Levi Strauss's conduct both at home and abroad, does it make sense to talk about the company as a morally responsible agent whose actions can be critically assessed, or can we assess only the actions and decisions of individual human beings inside the company?

7. Do corporations have a responsibility to monitor the conduct of the companies they do business with—in particular, their contractors and suppliers? Do they have a responsibility to avoid doing business in countries that are undemocratic, violate human rights, or permit exploitative work conditions? Compare and critically assess the conduct of Levi Strauss and Nike in this respect.

8. Should Levi Strauss have resumed its manufacturing operations in China? Should it have pulled out in the first place?

9. Is Levi Strauss sincere in its professed concern for foreign workers? Is Nike?

10. American consumers say that they don't like having their clothes made by exploited workers in foreign sweatshops. Is consumer pressure sufficient to get American companies to improve the pay and working conditions of foreign factory workers?

11. Some pessimists say that because most companies don't make social welfare a priority, competition will ultimately undermine the efforts of companies like Levi Strauss to establish standards. Assess this argument.

CASE 5.3

Free Speech or False Advertising?

With annual sales of over $10.5 billion and annual profits of around $475 million, Nike is one of the giants in the sports apparel business, and its trademark "Swoosh" logo is recognized around the world. However, for a company its size, Nike directly employs surprisingly few workers—only about 22,000. This is because overseas contractors manufacture all of Nike's products. These independent contractors employ approximately 600,000 workers at 910 factories, mostly in China, Indonesia, Vietnam, and Thailand.

Like many other firms, Nike outsources its manufacturing to take advantage of cheap overseas labor. But the price of doing so began getting higher for Nike in the late 1990s, when anti-sweatshop activists started campaigning against the company, charging that the Third World workers making its products were exploited and abused. Activists on many college campuses, for instance, encouraged their peers to boycott Nike shoes and clothing and tried to pressure their universities' athletic departments not to sign deals with Nike for team sports apparel.

Instead of ducking the issue, as other companies might have, Nike responded vigorously to the criticisms. At the University of North Carolina, for example, Nike ran full-page ads in the student newspaper, asserting that it was a good corporate citizen and upheld humane labor standards. It sent representatives to meet with student activists, and the company CEO Philip Knight took the unusual step of showing up at an undergraduate seminar on corporate globalization to defend his company. Nike issued press releases and sent letters to many college presidents and athletic departments, asserting, among other things, that Nike paid "on average, double the minimum wage as defined in countries where its products are produced" and that its workers "are protected from physical and sexual abuse."

Enter Marc Kasky, a 59-year old San Francisco activist. He thought Nike's campaign was misleading the public about working conditions inside its factories, so he sued the company for false advertising under California's consumer protection law. In Kasky's view, the case is simply a matter of protecting consumers from corporate deceit. In response, Nike argues that the statements in question are protected by the

First Amendment because they were made in news releases, letters to the editor, and op-ed essays and because they related to the company's labor practices—which are a matter of public concern—and not the products it sells. Two lower courts agreed with Nike, but then the California Supreme Court overturned their verdict, ruling in a 4-3 decision that the company's campaign was essentially commercial speech (which generally receives less First Amendment protection than political or personal speech) even though Nike was not specifically talking about shoes. In the court's view, Nike's speech was directed at customers and dealt with its business operations; the form in which the information was released was irrelevant. The judges, however, didn't determine whether Nike really did abuse workers or mislead consumers; it left those factual questions for a trial court to decide.

Nike then appealed the case to the U.S. Supreme Court. California Attorney General Bill Lockyer filed a brief in support of Kasky, which 17 other states joined. The brief contends that the case is not about free speech, but rather "Nike's ability to exploit false facts to promote commercial ends." Harvard law professor Laurence Tribe, however, defended the company arguing that treating Nike's letters and press releases as equivalent to advertising would undercut the ability of companies to speak out on political issues. He believes the California decision will have a "chilling effect on freedom of speech." To this, however, the chief author of the California brief, deputy attorney general Roland Reiter responds: "I believe the concerns expressed are really overblown. We have a company talking about itself. It's difficult to see why holding them to the truth would cause any kind of calamity." USC law professor Erwin Chemerinsky agrees. He argues that it doesn't matter whether Nike issued the information in the form of a press release: "If a company makes false statements about its product or practices with the intent of increasing profits, that's commercial speech."

After having heard the case, however, the Supreme Court declined to decide the substantive legal issues at stake. Instead, in June 2003 it dismissed the case on a technicality and sent it back to California for trial. Before the trial began, however, Nike settled out of court with Kasky. As part of the deal, Nike will donate $1.5 million to the Fair Labor Association, a sweatshop monitoring group, and in a joint statement, Kasky and Nike "mutually agreed that investments designed to strengthen workplace monitoring and factory worker programs are more desirable than prolonged litigation." A happy ending? Not in everyone's eyes. Friends of Nike argue that because the Supreme Court did not act forthrightly to protect corporate speech, companies will be reluctant to discuss public issues involving their products. Those on the other side, however, respond that when disclosing information about wages and working conditions, companies should be held to the same standards of truth and accuracy as when they disclose financial data.[77]

Discussion Questions

1. In this case, was Nike engaged in commercial speech, or were its statements political or social speech? What determines whether speech is commercial or not?

2. Was the out-of-court settlement a reasonable resolution of this case? What would have been the good or bad consequences of the Supreme Court's deciding in Nike's favor? Of its deciding in Kasky's favor?

3. Should commercial speech receive less First Amendment protection than other types of speech, or does this violate the rights of corporations? Explain your answer.

4. Do corporations have the same moral rights as individual human beings? Should they have the same political rights? Is it morally permissible to limit the speech of corporations in ways that it would be wrong to limit that of individual citizens? If it is permissible, is it good public policy?

5. Does Nike have a social responsibility to address matters of public concern like the working conditions in its overseas operation? If it chooses to do so, does it have an obligation to make its statements as truthful and accurate as it can? Under what circumstances should corporations be held liable for the truth of their public statements?

CASE 5.4

Charity to Scouts?

"I don't care what BankAmerica does," fumed Lynn Martin at a meeting of the board of directors of Baytown Company, a San Francisco Bay Area firm that runs four different family-oriented restaurants and owns a string of six popular fast-food take-out establishments (called "Tip-Top"). "We took a principled stand at the time," she continued, "and I don't think there's enough evidence to justify changing our minds now."

Like a lot of local companies, Baytown supports various charitable causes in the Bay Area. The company has always figured that it had an obligation to give more back to the community than good food; besides, people in the Bay Area expect local companies to display a sense of social responsibility. Among the groups that Baytown has always helped support is the regional Boy Scouts district. Not only did Baytown think the Scouts worthy of its corporate help but giving to the organization seemed to fit well with Tip-Top's all-American theme and with the family character of Baytown's other restaurants.

A simple thing suddenly got complicated, however, when the San Francisco Bay Area United Way decided to pull $1 million in annual funding for the Scouts because of the group's refusal to admit gays. Soon after that, BankAmerica, Wells Fargo Bank, and Levi Strauss & Co. also decided to stop funding the Boy Scouts. A month later, Baytown's directors resolved to follow suit.

"We were pretty clear at the time," continued Martin, "that we didn't have any business supporting an organization that was perceived as discriminatory."

"Not me," said Tom Boyd. "I always thought that since the Boy Scouts are a private group, they can do whatever they want."

"Well, maybe they have a right to discriminate if they want, but that's not the point," said Ed Framers. "The rest of us agreed with Lynn that as a company we shouldn't be helping a group that discriminates. Of course, that was before everybody around the country started making such a fuss about companies stopping their funding of the Scouts. We all know about those antigay groups demonstrating against the United Way and threatening to boycott the bank."

"Those groups hardly represent thinking in the Bay Area," Lynn Martin shot back.

"That's true," agreed Scott Arming, "but still we run a family-oriented business."

"What's that supposed to mean? Do you think gays and lesbians don't come to our restaurants? Do you think they don't have families? Do you think—"

"O.K., O.K.," Arming interjected.

"Lynn's right about that," Ed Framers said. "In fact, as far as I know, our customers never said much about it, one way or the other."

Executive Director Susan Lee then spoke up: "Well, I got a few phone calls about it, but there weren't really complaints. It was more people wanting to get more information about the situation. Of course, you always get a few cranks. . . ."

"Ain't that the truth," murmured Boyd to Framers.

"Anyway," Lee continued, "things are different now. BankAmerica has reversed its decision and is resuming funding to the Boy Scouts because the Scouts have lifted their ban on gays."

"That's what the bank says," said Lynn Martin. "But the whole thing is pretty murky if you ask me. Here, look at the newspaper story. The article reports company spokesman Peter Magnani as explaining that

> the bank had first interpreted the Scouts membership policy as banning gay members. But after consulting with Boy Scouts national President John Clendenin, the organization clarified its policy and 'made it clear' that membership is open to all boys who subscribe to Scouting oaths and laws.
> 'We take that to mean all boys, regardless of their sexual orientation,' said Magnani.[78]

"But then," Martin continued, "the newspaper goes on to quote a spokesperson for the Boy Scouts of America as saying that there has been 'absolutely no change in our policy. We do not believe that homosexuals provide positive role models.' What are we supposed to make of that? It looks as if the bank is trying to wriggle out of a stand that turned out not to be as popular as it thought it would be."

"That sounds pretty cynical," Ed Framers said. "The bank says here that its decision 'was based solely on the Scouts' clarification of its policy,' and the Scouts' national president is quoted as saying that the organization is 'open to all boys as long as they subscribe to the Boy Scouts Oath and Law.' You weren't a Scout, Lynn, but I was, and the oath and law are only basic stuff about trustworthiness and honesty; there's nothing about sexuality. Besides we're talking about boys, not adults. I think the whole thing has been blown out of proportion."

Martin quickly responded, "Don't you think boys have sexual feelings? Come on, Ed, give me a break. And besides, if there is nothing in the Scout oath or whatever it is about sexuality, why does the organization have to take a stand one way or the other?"

"Maybe the Scouts shouldn't have taken a stand," Susan Lee inserted, "but at this point it looks as if we have to. When we stopped giving to the Scouts, that sent one message; if we reverse our decision now, that sends another. Frankly, I don't like being in the position of having to impose our values, one way or the other."

"Yes, but you yourself said that there's no way to avoid it," Lynn Martin shot back. "So we should at least stand behind the right values."

"And what are those?" asked Lee.

"I don't have the slightest idea myself," Tom Boyd whispered to Scott Arming.

Arming ignored him as he turned to the group: "You know, I think we are and should continue to be a socially responsible company. But maybe we should reconsider whether being socially responsible means giving to charitable causes in the first place. Is that something we are truly obligated to do, or are we just following a fad? I mean, I hate to bring up the bottom line, but every dollar we give to the Boy Scouts or anybody else is one less dollar for the company and its stockholders."

"Come on, Scott, you know it's not as simple as that," responded Susan Lee. "Charitable contributions bring us good will, and it's the kind of thing the community expects an enlightened company to do."

"You may not be persuaded, Scott," Ed Framers added, "but I think what Susan says is right. In any case, we don't need a debate about general principles. We need to figure out what we are going to do about the Boy Scouts."

The meeting continued. . . .

Discussion Questions

1. What do you think Baytown should do? Explain your reasoning. What business factors are relevant to your decision? What moral factors?

2. Are Baytown's directors operating with a broad or a narrow conception of corporate social responsibility?

3. Were Baytown and the other companies right to have withdrawn their support from the Boy Scouts? Is there anything wrong with companies attempting to influence the policies of an organization like the Scouts?

4. What do you think explains BankAmerica's policy reversal? Is Lynn Martin's cynicism warranted?

5. Scott Arming doubts that businesses have an obligation to support charitable organizations. Do they?

Notes

1. John McDermott, *Corporate Society: Class, Property, and Contemporary Capitalism* (Boulder, Colo.: Westview, 1991), 4.

2. "Foreign Friends," *Economist*, January 8, 2000, 87–88.

3. Anthony J. Parisi, "How Exxon Rules Its Great Empire," *San Francisco Chronicle*, August 5, 1980, 27. For an update, see "Inside the Empire of Exxon the Unloved," *Economist*, March 15, 1994.

4. "The Next Society: A Suvey of the Near Future," *Economist*, November 3, 2001, 16.

5. Thomas Donaldson, *Corporations and Morality* (Englewood Cliffs, N.J.: Prentice-Hall, 1982), 2.

6. Ibid., 4.

7. David E. Schrader, "The Oddness of Corporate Ownership," *Journal of Social Philosophy* 27 (Fall 1996): 106.

8. Donaldson, *Corporations and Morality*, 5.

9. Ibid., 3.

10. 435 U.S. 765 (1978).

11. "Prosecutor's Dilemma," *Economist*, June 15, 2002, 76.

12. Parisi, "How Exxon Rules," 38.

13. See John R. Danley, "Corporate Moral Agency: The Case for Anthropological Bigotry," in W. Michael Hoffman and Jennifer M. Moore, eds., *Business Ethics: Readings and Cases in*

Corporate Morality (New York: McGraw-Hill, 1984); and John Ladd, "Morality and the Ideal of Rationality in Formal Organizations," in Thomas Donaldson and Patricia Werhane, eds., *Ethical Issues in Business: A Philosophical Approach,* 2nd ed. (Englewood Cliffs, N.J.: Prentice-Hall, 1983).

14. See Kenneth Goodpaster and John B. Matthews, Jr., "Can a Corporation Have a Conscience?" *Harvard Business Review* 60 (January–February 1982): 132–141.

15. Donaldson, *Corporations and Morality,* 10.

16. See Peter French, "The Corporation as a Moral Person," *American Philosophical Quarterly* 16 (July 1979): 207–215. J. Angelo Corlett, "Corporate Responsibility and Punishment," *Public Affairs Quarterly* 2 (January 1988) criticizes French's theory.

17. Manuel G. Velasquez, "Why Corporations Are Not Morally Responsible for Anything They Do," *Business and Professional Ethics Journal* 2 (Spring 1983): 8. See also Christopher McMahon, "The Political Theory of Organizations and Business Ethics," *Philosophy and Public Affairs* 24 (Fall 1995): 303.

18. "The Conoco Conscience," Continental Oil Company, quoted in Goodpaster and Matthews, "Can a Corporation Have a Conscience?" 141.

19. Jeffrey L. Seglin, "A Safer World for Mea Culpas," *New York Times,* March 21, 1999, sec. 3, 4.

20. Quoted in Clarence C. Walton, *Corporate Social Responsibilities* (Belmont, Calif.: Wadsworth, 1967), 169–170.

21. Quoted in Bernard D. Nossiter, *The Mythmakers: An Essay on Power and Wealth* (Boston: Houghton Mifflin, 1964), 100.

22. Milton Friedman, *Capitalism and Freedom* (Chicago: University of Chicago Press, 1962), 133.

23. Theodore Levitt, "The Dangers of Social Responsibility," *Harvard Business Review* 36 (September–October 1958).

24. Milton Friedman, "The Social Responsibility of Business Is to Increase Its Profits," *New York Times Magazine,* September 13, 1970, 33, 126.

25. Ibid., 124.

26. Reprinted from Keith Davis, "Five Propositions for Social Responsibility," *Business Horizons* 18 (June 1975): 20. Copyright © 1975 by the Foundation for the School of Business at Indiana University. Used with permission.

27. Robert Kuttner, "The Great American Pension-Fund Robbery," *Business Week,* September 8, 2003, 24.

28. "The Corporate Tax Game," *Business Week,* March 31, 2003, 79–83.

29. Melvin Anshen, "Changing the Social Contract: A Role for Business," *Columbia Journal of World Business* 5 (November–December 1970). See also James E. Post, Anne T. Lawrence, and James Weber, *Business and Society: Corporate Strategy, Public Policy, Ethics,* 10th ed. (New York: McGraw-Hill, 2002), 16–17.

30. Davis, "Five Propositions for Social Responsibility," 22 (figures altered).

31. "Work Week," *Wall Street Journal,* May 21, 1996, A1.

32. See Christopher D. Stone, *Where the Law Ends* (New York: Harper & Row, 1975), 80–87.

33. Friedman, "The Social Responsibility of Business," 122.

34. Adolf A. Berle, Jr., and Gardiner C. Means, *The Modern Corporation and Private Property* (New York: Macmillan, 1932).

35. "Design by Committee," *Economist,* June 15, 2002, 71; see also Alan Murray, "Political Capital," *Wall Street Journal,* July 16, 2002, A4.

36. Joann S. Lublin, "How CEOs Retire in Style," *Wall Street Journal,* September 13, 2002, B1. See also Carol Hymowitz, "Directors Should End Extravagant Packages for Departing CEOs," *Wall Street Journal,* April 8, 2003, B1.

37. Louis Lavelle, "How Shareholder Votes Are Legally Rigged," *Business Week,* May 20, 2002, 48.

38. See Goodpaster and Matthews, "Can a Corporation Have a Conscience?" 136.

39. "As California Starved for Energy, U.S. Businesses Had a Feast," *Wall Street Journal,* September 16, 2002, A1, and "How Energy Traders Turned Bonanza into an Epic Bust," *Wall Street Journal,* December 31, 2002, A1.

40. Virginia Held, *Property, Profits, and Economic Justice* (Belmont, Calif.: Wadsworth, 1980), 11.

41. Goodpaster and Matthews, "Can a Corporation Have a Conscience?" 137.

42. As quoted by John Micklethwait and Adrian Wooldridge, *The Company* (New York: Modern Library, 2003), 182.

43. Robert B. Reich, "How to Avoid These Layoffs," *New York Times,* January 4, 1996, A13. See also George F. Will, "A Capable Candidate in Waiting," *San Jose Mercury News,* February 10, 2002, 7P.

44. Walter Goodman, "Stocks Without Sin," *Harper's,* August 1971, 66.

45. Levitt, "The Dangers of Social Responsibility," 44. See also George G. Brenkert, "Private Corporations and Public Welfare," *Public Affairs Quarterly* 6 (April 1992): 155–168.

46. Davis, "Five Propositions for Social Responsibility," 20.

47. Paul F. Camenisch, "Business Ethics: On Getting to the Heart of the Matter," *Business and Professional Ethics Journal* 1 (Fall 1981).

48. See *New York Times,* March 2, 1995, A17; November 28, 1995, C5; and July 30, 1998, A23; *San Jose Mercury News,* May 17, 1996, 13A; and *San Francisco Chronicle,* July 24, 1996.

49. "The Cecil Rhodes of Chocolate-Chip Cookies," *Economist,* May 25, 1996, 74.

50. "Good Citizens of the Community," *Business Ethics,* March/April 2002, 9, and "The Corporate Donors," *Business Week,* December 1, 2003, 92.

51. Camenisch, "Business Ethics."

52. See Stone, *Where the Law Ends,* Chapter 11.

53. Kenneth J. Arrow, "Social Responsibility and Economic Efficiency," *Public Policy* 21 (Summer 1973).

54. Milton Snoeyenbos and Barbara Caley, "Managing Ethics," in Milton Snoeyenbos, Robert Almeder, and James Humber, eds., *Business Ethics,* 3rd ed. (Buffalo, N.Y.: Prometheus, 2001), 143.

55. Snoeyenbos and Caley, "Managing Ethics," 141.

56. Gillian Flynn, "Make Employee Ethics Your Business," *Personnel Journal,* June 1995.

57. "Organisations, Too, Can Be Put on the Couch," *Financial Times,* June 20, 2003, 12.

58. Donald P. Robin and R. Eric Reidenbach, *Business Ethics: Where Profits Meet Value Systems* (Englewood Cliffs, N.J.: Prentice-Hall, 1989), 59.

59. Ibid.

60. Quoted by Robin and Reidenbach, *Business Ethics,* 59.

61. "When Something Is Rotten," *Economist,* July 27, 2002, 53.

62. Lynn Sharp Paine, "Managing for Organizational Integrity," *Harvard Business Review* 72 (March–April 1994): 107–108.

63. "Businesses Are Signing Up for Ethics 101," *Business Week,* February 15, 1988, 56.

64. Sandra Waddock and Neil Smith, "Corporate Responsibility Audits: Doing Well by Doing Good," *Sloan Management Review* 41 (Winter 2000): 75–83.

65. Scot J. Paltrow, "Brokers Who Break the Rules," *Los Angeles Times,* July 1, 1992, A1.

66. "Businesses Are Signing Up," 56.

67. *Economist,* April 8, 1995, 57, and August 19, 1995, 56.

68. For further, more detailed discussions of the marketing of infant formula, see Lisa H. Newton and David P. Schmidt, *Wake-Up Calls: Classic Cases in Business Ethics* (Belmont, Calif.: Wadsworth, 1996), Chapter 3, and Robert F. Hartley, *Business Ethics* (New York: John Wiley, 1993), Chapter 10.

69. Newton and Schmidt, *Wake-Up Calls,* 65–67.

70. "Boycott Against Nestlé over Infant Formula to End Next Month," *Wall Street Journal*, January 27, 1984, 1.

71. "New Boycott Plea in Infant Formula Fight," *San Francisco Chronicle*, October 5, 1988, A9.

72. Carol-Linnea Salmon, "Milking Deadly Dollars from the Third World," *Business and Society* 68 (Winter 1989).

73. Salmon, "Milking Deadly Dollars."

74. See, in particular, *www.babymilkaction.org*.

75. See "Baby Milk Marketing 'Breaks Rules,'" *BBC News*, January 17, 2003 (available on line at *www.bbc.co.uk*) and the *British Medical Journal*, January 18, 2003.

76. The first part of this case study is based on Jeannie Kever, "What Price Layoffs?" *San Francisco Examiner*, November 18, 1990, D1. The second part is based on G. Pascal Zachary, "Exporting Rights," *Wall Street Journal*, July 28, 1994, A1; William Beaver, "Levi's Is Leaving China," *Business Horizon* 38 (March–April 1995), 35–40; Kevin Donaher, "Niketown—Just Don't Do It," *San Francisco Chronicle*, February 20, 1997, A23; Bob Herbert, "Nike's Bad Neighborhood," *New York Times*, June 14, 1996, A29, and "Mr. Young Gets It Wrong," June 27, 1997, A21; and Steven Greenhouse, "Nike Shoe Plant in Vietnam Is Called Unsafe for Workers," *New York Times*, November 8, 1997, A1. The Update is based on reports in the *San Francisco Chronicle*, November 12, 1997, April 9, 1998, February 29, 1999, and September 26, 2003; *New York Times*, April 9 and May 13, 1998; and *San Jose Mercury News*, April 9, 2002, and September 26, 2003.

77. For more on this case, see "Just How Far Does First Amendment Protection Go?" *Wall Street Journal*, January 10, 2003, B1; "Suit Against Nike Raises Free Speech Questions," *San Jose Mercury News*, April 21, 2003, 1A; "Free Speech or False Advertising?" *Business Week*, April 28, 2003, 69; and Robert J. Samuelson, "The Tax on Free Speech," *Newsweek*, July 24, 2003, 41.

78. Fernando Quintero, "B of A Will Now Fund Boy Scouts," *San Jose Mercury News*, August 19, 1992, B3.

Further Reading for Chapter 5

John R. Danley, "Corporate Moral Agency," in Robert E. Frederick, ed., *A Companion to Business Ethics* (Malden, Mass.: Blackwell, 1999) reviews the philosophical literature on this difficult topic with particular attention to the influential views of Peter French.

Thomas Donaldson, *Corporations and Morality* (Englewood Cliffs, N.J.: Prentice-Hall, 1982) discusses the moral status of corporations, arguments for and against corporate social responsibility, and the idea of a social contract for business, among other issues.

Peter A. French, *Collective and Corporate Responsibility* (New York: Columbia University Press, 1984) analyzes the philosophical issues involved in assigning moral responsibility to corporations and other collectivities, whereas his *Corporate Ethics* (Ft. Worth, Tex.: Harcourt Brace, 1996) looks at a wider range of moral issues involving corporations.

Thomas M. Jones, Andrew C. Wicks, and **R. Edward Freeman**, "Stakeholder Theory: The State of the Art," in Norman E. Bowie, ed., *The Blackwell Guide to Business Ethics* (Malden, Mass.: Blackwell, 2002) discusses one influential way of thinking about the obligations of managers to stockholders and other stakeholders.

John Micklethwait and **Adrian Wooldridge**, *The Company: A Short History of a Revolutionary Idea* (New York: Modern Library, 2003) is a readable, well-informed history of the corporation from its earliest beginnings to recent scandals.

John McDermott, *Corporate Society: Class, Property, and Contemporary Capitalism* (Boulder, Colo.: Westview, 1991) analyzes the modern business corporation's impact on society.

David E. Schrader, "The Oddness of Corporate Ownership," *Journal of Social Philosophy* 27 (Fall 1996) argues that stockholders do not own the corporation.

Thomas I. White, ed., *Business Ethics: A Philosophical Reader* (New York: Macmillan, 1993) contains useful essays on corporate personhood and responsibility in Chapter 6 and on the punishing of corporations in Chapter 7.

 InfoTrac College Edition: For further information or to conduct research, please go to www.infotrac-college.com.

III

THE ORGANIZATION AND THE PEOPLE IN IT

6

The Workplace (1):
Basic Issues

Scientists first described acquired immune deficiency syndrome, commonly known as AIDS, in 1981. Apparently the result of a new infection of human beings, AIDS probably stems originally from central or west Africa, where several subspecies of chimpanzees carry a closely related virus. Within three years scientists in the United States and France had isolated human T-lymphotropic virus III, now known as HIV, for "human immunodeficiency virus." HIV is the parent virus of AIDS and a couple of related diseases. To be infected with the virus is not automatically to have AIDS, but most of those infected go on to develop AIDS symptoms and often die from them. After identifying the virus, scientists quickly developed blood tests for its presence, but they have yet to develop a vaccine. The stakes are high. AIDS is the leading cause of death of Americans between the ages of twenty-five and forty-four. Approximately 800,000 people in the United States are infected, and over 450,000 have already died. Researchers estimate that there are 40,000 new infections nationally each year.[1]

No one today can doubt the seriousness of AIDS. Media attention has ensured that the public is aware of its deadliness and the threat it poses, and this is a good thing. But when fear of danger combines with ignorance about a disease's nature and causes, panic is often the result. This has sadly been the case with AIDS—not least in the workplace.

Take what is, unfortunately, a typical case. John L. is a white-collar employee, working in the downtown branch of a firm operating in a middle-sized West Coast city. He had been feeling generally run-down and complained of various small ailments to his physician. When a routine checkup didn't reveal anything specific, John's doctor encouraged him to undergo a blood test for AIDS. He tested positive, which means that the antibodies for HIV are present in his body. Their presence means that he is infected by the virus and that it is probable, given his symptoms, that he has AIDS.

A few of John's friends in the office know of his recent ill health, and gradually word of his test results has circulated. And now problems have begun—not just for John but also for his coworkers and for management. John's colleagues feel uneasy around him; they're not sure what to do or to say, and some of them are very worried about possible contagion. A few coworkers feel strongly that John should not be permitted to go on working there. The boss is concerned not just with the prospect of declining work performance from John but with the effects of his presence on office morale. She may herself also have doubts about the wisdom or even the safety of allowing John to continue to interact with the public, which is part of his job.

The myriad problems, doubts, tensions, possibly even mild hysteria that the mere presence of John L. can create in a business or other organization are easy to imagine, but sorting out the morally relevant factors and deciding how the situation ought to be dealt with is less easy. What are John's rights and interests? How are these to be weighed against the interests and rights of both his coworkers and the organization itself? What responsibilities does an organization have to one of its members who may be facing a terminal illness? Given the size and organizational structure of John's workplace and the type of work in question, how—morally speaking—should management respond?

These are questions that more and more firms must answer. Reliable figures are difficult to come by, but given the nationwide statistics, virtually every large company can be assumed to have had cases of AIDS among its employees or their dependents. Half of all American workers consider AIDS their chief health concern. For the foreseeable future, the problems posed by AIDS in the workplace can only continue to increase. Yet nationwide only a small percentage of firms have or are planning to formulate a policy on AIDS.[2]

Traditionally, the obligations between a business organization and its employees could be boiled down to "A fair wage for an honest day's work." Business's primary, if not sole, obligation to its employees was to pay a decent wage. In return, employees were expected to work efficiently and to be loyal and obedient to their employer. This model of employer-employee relations is obviously too simple and fails to come to terms not just with the dilemmas facing John's office but also with many other major moral issues that arise in today's workplace. This chapter looks at some of these issues, in particular:

1. The state of civil liberties in the workplace

2. The efforts of some successful companies to respect the rights and moral dignity of their employees

3. Moral issues that arise with respect to personnel matters—namely, hiring, promotions, discipline and discharge, and wages

4. The role and history of unions in our economic system, their ideals and achievements, and the moral issues they raise

CIVIL LIBERTIES IN THE WORKPLACE

Employees have all sorts of job-related concerns. Generally speaking, they want to do well at their assignments, to get along with their colleagues, and to have their contributions to the organization recognized. Their job tasks, working conditions, wages, and the possibility of promotion are among the many things that occupy their day-to-day thoughts. Aside from the actual work that they are expected to perform, employees, being human, are naturally concerned about the way their organizations treat them.

Frequently they find that treatment to be morally deficient and complain that the organizations for which they work violate their moral rights and civil liberties.

Consider the case of Louis V. MacIntire, who worked for the DuPont Company in Orange, Texas, for sixteen years. As a chemical engineer he was well paid, and during the course of his career at DuPont he received several promotions. MacIntire also had literary ambitions and wrote a novel, *Scientists and Engineers: The Professionals Who Are Not.* Several characters in the novel inveigh against various management abuses at the novel's fictional Logan Chemical Company and argue for a union for technical employees. Logan Chemical at least superficially resembles MacIntire's real-life employer, DuPont, and some of MacIntire's supervisors were unhappy with his thinly veiled criticisms. He was fired. MacIntire sued DuPont, claiming that his constitutional right of free speech had been violated. A Texas district judge threw that charge out of court.[3]

MacIntire's case illuminates what many see as the widespread absence of civil liberties in the workplace. David W. Ewing, former editor of the *Harvard Business Review,* is one of those writers. He sees the corporate invasion of employees' civil liberties as rampant and attacks it in scathing terms:

> In most . . . [corporate] organizations, during working hours, civil liberties are a will-o'-the-wisp. The Constitutional rights that employees have grown accustomed to in family, school, and church life generally must be left outdoors, like cars in the parking lot. As in totalitarian countries, from time to time a benevolent chief executive or department head may encourage speech, conscience, and privacy, but these scarcely can be called rights, for management can take them away at will. . . . It is fair to say that an enormous corporate archipelago has grown which, in terms of civil liberties, is as different from the rest of America as day is from night. In this archipelago . . . the system comes first, the individual second.[4]

Two historical factors, in Ewing's view, lie behind the absence of civil liberties and the prevalence of authoritarianism in the workplace. One of these factors was the rise of professional management and personnel engineering at the turn of the twentieth century, following the emergence of large corporations. This shaped the attitudes of companies toward their employees in a way hardly conducive to respecting their rights. As Frederick Winslow Taylor, generally identified as the founder of "scientific management," bluntly put it, "In the past, the man has been first. In the future, the system must be first."

The second historical factor is that the law has traditionally given the employer a free hand in hiring and firing employees. A century ago, a Tennessee court expressed this doctrine in memorable form. Employers, the court held, "may dismiss their employees at will . . . for good cause, for no cause, or even for cause morally wrong, without thereby being guilty of legal wrong." Similarly, a California court upheld this traditional rule shortly before World War I, observing that the "arbitrary right of the employer to employ or discharge labor, with or without regard to actuating motives" is a proposition "settled beyond peradventure." And in 1975 a U.S. district court in Missouri upheld the traditional position in ruling against a whistle-blowing engineer at General Motors.[5]

In addition, common law requires that an employee be loyal to an employer, acting solely for the employer's benefit in matters connected to work. The employee is also duty bound "not to act or speak disloyally," except in pursuit of his own interests outside work. It's no wonder, then, that traditional employer-employee law has hardly been supportive of the idea of freedom of speech and expression for employees. Against that background, DuPont's treatment of MacIntire and the court's refusal to see a First Amendment issue in his case are not surprising.

According to common law, then, unless there is an explicit contractual provision to the contrary—and only around 10 percent of American workers have such contracts[6]— every employment is employment "at will," and either side is free to terminate it at any time without advance notice or reason. The common law, however, has been modified in important ways by congressional and state statutory provisions. The Wagner Act of 1935 was, in this respect, a watershed. It prohibited firing workers because of union membership or union activities. The Civil Rights Act of 1964 and subsequent legislation prohibit discrimination on the basis of race, creed, nationality, sex, or age. Equally important, employees in the public sector—that is, in federal, state, and local government—enjoy certain constitutional protections on the job and can be fired only "for cause." And many workers are protected by their union contracts from unjust dismissals.

Thus, today working people have protection against some forms of unjust termination, and many of them enjoy the assurance that they can expect due process and that at least some of their civil liberties and other moral rights will be respected on the job. "But," writes Clyde Summers in the *Harvard Business Review,* "random individuals who are unjustly terminated are isolated and without organizational or political voice. For them the harsh common law rule remains."[7]

Companies That Look Beyond the Bottom Line

The law is not static, however, and some courts have been willing in specific cases to break with tradition to protect employees' rights of speech, privacy, and conscience. The U.S. Supreme Court, for instance, has ruled that a state cannot deny unemployment benefits to employees who are fired because they refuse to work on their Sabbath day, even if they aren't members of an organized religion.[8] And in 1987 Montana became the first and so far the only state in the nation to enact legislation that workers cannot be fired without "good cause." Even without explicit legislation, wrongfully dismissed employees frequently have legal recourse. Thus, for example, a federal jury held that Mobil Chemical Company had wrongfully dismissed one of its top environmental officials after he refused to perform acts that would have violated federal and state environmental laws. The jury ordered Mobil to pay $375,000 in compensatory damages and $1 million in punitive damages. On the other hand, when Daniel Foley, district manager for Interactive Data Corporation, accurately reported to his employer that his new boss was under investigation by the FBI for embezzling funds on a former job, he was dismissed for "inadequate performance" three months later, despite a seven-year record of positive work reviews and a recent $6,700 bonus. He sued Interactive Data for wrongful termination, but the California Supreme Court decided that his dismissal did not violate the "public interest" and rejected his suit.

Thus, although the law seems to be gradually changing, leaving the common-law heritage of employer-employee doctrine behind, recent legal developments are complicated and not entirely consistent. The results not only depend on the details of each case but also vary from jurisdiction to jurisdiction and from court to court. As argued in Chapter 1, however, our moral obligations extend beyond merely keeping within the law. Thus, it is particularly significant that more corporations are coming to acknowledge, and to design institutional procedures that respect, the rights of their employees. Moreover, the firms taking the lead in this regard are often among the most successful companies in the country.

This fact cuts against the old argument that corporate efficiency requires employees to sacrifice their civil liberties and other rights between 9 and 5. Without strict discipline and the firm maintenance of management prerogatives, it has been claimed, our economic system would come apart at the seams. An increasing body of evidence, however, suggests just the opposite. As Ewing writes:

> Civil liberties are far less of a threat to the requirements of effective management than are collective bargaining, labor-management committees, job enrichment, work participation, and a number of other schemes that industry takes for granted. Moreover, the companies that lead in encouraging rights—organizations such as Polaroid, IBM, Donnelly Mirrors, and Delta Airlines—have healthier-looking bottom lines than the average corporation does.[9]

Although under no legal compulsion to do so, a small but growing number of companies encourage employee questions and criticisms about company policies affecting the welfare of employees and the community. Some companies foster open communication through regular, informal exchanges between management and other employees. Others, such as Delta Air Lines, have top officials answer questions submitted anonymously by employees—in the absence of supervisors. Still others, such as General Electric and New England Telephone, have a hotline for questions, worries, and reports of wrongdoing. Finally, some, like Dow Chemical, open the pages of company publications to employee questions and criticisms.

Union contracts frequently require companies to set up grievance procedures and otherwise attempt to see that their members are guaranteed due process on the job. Some enlightened nonunionized companies have done the same. Polaroid, for instance, has a well-institutionalized committee whose job it is to represent an employee with a grievance. The committee members are elected from the ranks, and reportedly a fair number of management decisions are overruled in the hearings. If the decision goes against the aggrieved employee, he or she is entitled by company rules to submit the case to an outside arbitrator.

Some companies—including Johnson Wax, Donnelly, Procter & Gamble, and Aetna Life and Casualty—go further. These companies have long followed no-layoff policies.[10] So do Lincoln Electric and Russell Corporation, the sweatshirt and athletic-wear manufacturer. Another example is Hewlett-Packard. A recession once reduced orders so much that HP management was considering a 10 percent cut in the workforce. Because laying off people was anathema, HP went a different route. It set up a working schedule of nine days out of ten for everybody in the company, from the CEO on down. The program stayed in place for six months, when orders picked up, and the full ten-day schedule returned. "The net result of this program," said William Hewlett, "was that effectively all shared the burden of the recession, good people were not turned out on a very tough job market, and, I might observe, the company benefited by having in place a highly qualified work force when business returned."[11]

Not only, then, is it a moral duty of companies to respect the rights and dignity of their employees, in particular by acknowledging their civil liberties and guaranteeing them due process, but doing so can also work to the company's benefit by enhancing employee morale and, thus, the company's competitive performance. Hence, there is little basis for the widespread belief that efficient management is incompatible with a fair workplace environment.

"What I absolutely believe is that honoring the people who do the work can produce stunning results for the company," says Sidney Harmon, CEO of Harmon International Industries. "If the people in the factory believe there's a real effort to help improve their skills, provide opportunities for advancement and job security, they can do things that will blow your mind."[12] Some business writers push this point even further. For example, Robert Levering and Milton Moskowitz argue that:

> The authoritarian work style—long the standard operating procedure in business—has failed. That failure is at the root of the poor performance of U.S. companies and massive layoffs in the '80s and '90s. When management is disconnected from the people who work in the company, it becomes easy to fire those people. And when workers are disconnected from what they do, it becomes easy not to care about the product or service.[13]

Of course, a company that does not sincerely consider employee rights of inherent moral importance is not likely to reap the benefits of enhanced business performance. Trust, as more and more management theorists are saying,[14] is the key here, and employees can tell the difference between a company that has a genuine regard for their welfare and a company that only pretends to have moral concern.[15]

An example is Pacific Bell, which has won high marks for its humane response to the AIDS problem. With its strong emphasis on two-way commitment and loyalty, Pacific Bell has never considered revoking the medical coverage of employees with AIDS, as some companies have done. (The lifetime cost of medical treatment for an AIDS patient can easily run to six digits.) Pacific Bell has committed itself to keeping employees with AIDS on the job. "They need to keep working," says Pacific Bell's Tim O'Hara. "It gives them a reason to stay alive." The company's executive director of human resources, Jim Henderson, says bluntly, "People with AIDS are sick. We don't fire sick people." The company has also been visible in various AIDS initiatives and innovative in its AIDS education efforts.[16]

So far this chapter has affirmed that the workplace should provide an environment in which employees are treated fairly and their inherent dignity respected, and it has argued that doing so can be perfectly compatible with a firm's business goals. Although important, these points are generalities. They do not provide much guidance for dealing with the specific moral issues and dilemmas that arise day in and day out on the job. The remainder of this chapter and the chapter that follows take a closer look at some of these issues.

PERSONNEL POLICIES AND PROCEDURES

People make up organizations, and how an organization impinges on the lives of its own members is a morally important matter. One obvious and very important way organizational conduct affects the welfare and rights of employees and potential employees is through personnel policies and procedures—that is, how the organization handles the hiring, firing, paying, and promoting of the people who work for it. These procedures and policies structure an organization's basic relationship with its employees.

This section looks at some of the morally relevant concerns to which any organization must be sensitive.

Hiring

A basic task of the employer or personnel manager is hiring. Employers generally seek to hire people who will enable the organization to produce the products or services it seeks to provide or to promote its other goals. Furthermore, the courts have used the principle of negligent hiring to broaden the liability of an employer for damage or injury caused by its employees—even after regular hours and away from the job site. For instance, Avis Rent-A-Car was required to pay $800,000 after a male employee raped a female employee; the jury found that the company had been negligent in hiring the man without thoroughly investigating his background.[17] In making hiring decisions, though, employers must be careful to treat job applicants fairly. As one might imagine, determining the fair thing to do is not always easy. One useful way to approach some of the moral aspects of hiring is to examine the principal steps involved in the process: screening, testing, and interviewing.

Screening   When firms recruit employees, they attempt to screen them—that is, to attract applicants who have a good chance of qualifying for the job and to weed out applicants or potential applicants who are unlikely to succeed at the job. When done properly, screening ensures a pool of competent candidates and guarantees that everyone has been dealt with fairly; when done improperly, it undermines effective recruitment and invites injustices into the hiring process.

Screening begins with a job description and specification. A *job description* lists all pertinent details about a job, including its duties, responsibilities, working conditions, and physical requirements. A *job specification* describes the qualifications an employee needs, such as skills, educational experience, appearance, and physical attributes. Job descriptions and specifications must be complete and accurate. Otherwise, job candidates lack the necessary information for making informed decisions and can waste time and money pursuing jobs they are not suited for. In addition, disappointment and unfairness can result if a position is inaccurately described or wrongly classified.

This sounds simple enough. But in an effort to attract strong job candidates, hiring officers can easily, perhaps even unintentionally, begin to exaggerate what the job offers in terms of opportunities, travel, the ability to work from home, the budget one will control, and so on. And exaggeration can grow into blatant distortion. One recruiter offers this sample lexicon: "Character building" means that the job stinks, "mentoring" translates into babysitting your staff, "expense account" signifies a bagged lunch at your desk, and "work team environment" denotes noisy cubicles.[18] Exaggerations like these may start innocently, but some businesses clearly and intentionally cross the line—for example, by deliberately misclassifying hourly workers as salaried employees in order to avoid paying them overtime. Taco Bell, U-Haul, Farmer's Insurance, and General Dynamics are among the companies that have been accused of this.[19]

Since Congress passed the Americans with Disabilities Act (ADA), which became effective for all firms with fifteen or more employees in July 1994, employers must be careful not to screen out disabled applicants who have the capacity to carry out the job. The ADA is intended, among other things, to protect the rights of people with disabilities to obtain gainful employment, and it forbids employers from discriminating against employees or job applicants with disabilities when making employment decisions.

Employers must also make "reasonable accommodations" for an employee or job applicant with a disability as long as this doesn't inflict "undue hardship" on the business. But there are gray areas. The ADA doesn't protect employees or job applicants who are addicted to drugs, but is it discrimination for a company to refuse to hire someone it had forced to resign two years earlier because of substance abuse, but who is now rehabilitated?

In addition to the ADA, for several decades the law has forbidden discrimination against individuals on the basis of age, race, national origin, religion, or sex, and these are items that generally should never appear in job specifications or recruitment advertisements, nor should they figure in hiring. Consideration of such factors typically excludes job candidates on non-job-related grounds. Firms must be careful about job specifications that discriminate subtly—for example, "young person preferred" or "excellent opportunity for college student." Employers should eliminate such specifications from advertisements, not only because they are probably illegal, but also because they discourage qualified applicants from applying. Most organizations these days try to avoid gender-linked job terminology as well. The terms "salesperson," "mail carrier," and "bartender" are more inclusive than "salesman," "mailman," and "barman." An alternative is to use terms denoting both sexes ("waiter/waitress").

Bona fide occupational qualifications, or BFOQs, are job specifications to which the civil rights law does not apply. But BFOQs are very limited in scope. There are no BFOQs for race or color, and in the case of sex, BFOQs exist only to allow for authenticity (a male model) and modesty (a woman for a women's locker room attendant). In line with this, the Equal Employment Opportunity Commission (EEOC) filed a sex discrimination lawsuit against the restaurant chain Hooters, well known for its buxom "Hooter Girl" waitresses, for hiring only women as servers. Hooters resisted the decision, claiming that the job position is legitimately defined as one that makes sex relevant. After some unfavorable publicity (for one thing, no men had complained of discrimination), the EEOC quietly dropped the suit.

In validating job specifications, firms are not permitted to rely on the preferences of their customers as a reason for discriminatory employment practices. For example, the fact that for decades airline passengers were accustomed to being attended to by young female flight attendants and may even have preferred them could not legally justify excluding men from this occupation. Similarly, a court has ruled that the fact that 20 percent of Domino's customers have a negative reaction to pizza deliverymen with beards does not constitute a substantial business justification for the company's no-beards rule. The EEOC holds that such rules discriminate against black men, who sometimes suffer from a genetic skin disorder that makes shaving difficult and painful.

Bilingual ability (English-Spanish, English-Vietnamese) may be a justifiable job specification in some areas of the country where such skills can be essential for successful job performance. But employers need to be aware of the danger of creating unnecessary specifications for a position, especially if they unfairly discriminate on the basis of national origin. The ability to communicate effectively in English is a common workplace requirement, but it can seriously impede the employment prospects of some workers— Hispanics, in particular. As a result, the EEOC closely scrutinizes employers' language requirements to see if there is a nondiscriminatory business reason for them.

In addition, the EEOC has ruled in several cases that disqualifying a job applicant because the applicant has a pronounced foreign accent is unlawful national origin bias unless it can be proved that the accent would hinder the job-seeker's ability to perform the job.[19] On the other hand, the U.S. Court of Appeals in San Francisco determined that a heavy Filipino accent was a legitimate basis for rejecting an applicant for a job at a state department of motor vehicles office that required dealing with the public, even though the plaintiff had scored higher than all other candidates on a written examination. And in a Texas case, a Vietnamese immigrant was lawfully rejected for the position of energy conservation inspector because of an inadequate oral command of English. The job involved explaining local law to building owners, evaluating their use of light, air, and water, and helping them devise an acceptable conservation plan. The position required constant dialogue with various people, many of whom, in the court's words, were "unaccustomed to the peculiarities of the plaintiff's speech."[20]

In a handful of American cities local ordinances prohibit discrimination against those who are short or overweight. On this basis, Jennifer Portnick brought a case against a San Francisco franchise of Jazzercise, a dance-fitness company. Portnick, who is 5 feet 8 inches tall and weighs 240 pounds, had applied for a job as an aerobics instructor, but Jazzercise rejected her application because it required instructors to have a "fit appearance." After the city of San Francisco sided with Portnick in 2002, Jazzercise revised its job criteria and now agrees that "it may be possible for people of varying weights to be fit."[21]

Some employers wade into morally troubling waters by screening job applicants on the basis of lifestyle. For example, Multi-Developers Inc., a Georgia-based real estate company, won't hire anyone who engages in recreational activities that are "high risk"—like motorcycling, sky diving, motor racing, mountain climbing, or flying one's own plane. In Indianapolis, Best Lock Corporation won't employ anyone who admits to taking even an occasional alcoholic drink. Other companies, such as Turner Broadcasting System, flatly refuse to hire smokers.[22]

Ill-considered educational requirements are also potentially objectionable. Requiring more formal education than a job demands is not fair to candidates or the firm. If the education requirement exceeds job demands, candidates who don't meet it are denied equal consideration. Moreover, one of them may be the best person for the job. Thus, the firm, as well as the less-educated applicant, stands to lose. The other side of the coin is to deny an applicant job consideration because he or she is overqualified in terms of education or experience. To avoid the personal and organizational frustrations that can result from hiring overqualified people, companies are justified in raising the issue. But raising the issue is different from assuming that because on paper an applicant appears overqualified the applicant necessarily spells trouble for the company. The fact is that the employment ranks are filled with people successfully doing jobs for which they are technically overqualified.

One additional matter. As traditional gender roles change, more and more men are leaving the work world for personal reasons, such as to help raise children while their wives complete professional training. These men often face obstacles when they return to work. Employers assume that, because the man once quit work for personal reasons, he may very well do so again. Thus, discontinuity of employment is cutting some men off from job consideration, as it traditionally has for women.

"The hurdles men face returning to the job market are about three times greater" than those faced by women, says Charles Arons, president and chief executive officer for Casco Industries, a Los Angeles–based employment and recruiting firm. "There isn't a male I know of in an executive position who would accept raising kids as a legitimate excuse for not working for three years."

Thomas Schumann, director of selection and placement for Dayton-based Mead Corporation, agrees. "If other qualified candidates are available," he says, "my guess is that a personnel manager would go with somebody who doesn't raise that question."[23]

Certainly, employers in highly technical, rapidly changing fields are warranted in suspecting that an individual's career interruption may have left him (or her) out of touch. But to automatically disqualify a candidate because of this raises a question of fairness.

Tests Testing is an integral part of the hiring process, especially with large firms. Tests are generally designed to measure the applicant's verbal, quantitative, and logical skills. Aptitude tests help determine an applicant's suitability for a job; skill tests measure the applicant's proficiency in specific areas, such as typing, shorthand, or arithmetic; personality tests help determine the applicant's maturity and sociability. In addition, some firms engaged in the design and assembly of precision equipment administer dexterity tests to determine how nimbly applicants can use their hands and fingers.

To be successful, a test must be valid. *Validity* refers to whether test scores correlate with performance in some other activity—that is, whether the test measures the skill or ability it is intended to measure. Just as important, tests must also be reliable. *Reliability* means that a subject's scores will remain relatively consistent from test to test (so that a test-taker won't score high one day and low the next). Clearly, not all tests are both valid and reliable. Many tests are not able to measure desired qualities, and others exhibit a woefully low level of forecast accuracy. Some companies use tests that haven't been designed for the company's particular situation. Legitimizing tests can be an expensive and time-consuming project, but if tests are used, the companies using them are obliged to ensure their validity and reliability. Otherwise, companies risk injuring applicants, stockholders, and even the general public. At the same time, companies must be cautious about the importance they place on such tests, because a test is only one measure in an overall evaluative process.

Even when tests are valid and reliable, they can be unfair—for example, if the tests are culturally biased or are irrelevant to job performance. The U.S. Supreme Court took a stand on this issue in the famous case of *Griggs v. Duke Power Company*.[24] The case involved thirteen African-American laborers who were denied promotions because they scored low on a company-sponsored intelligence test involving verbal and mathematical puzzles. In its decision, the Court found that the Civil Rights Act prohibits employers from requiring a high school education or the passing of a general intelligence test as a prerequisite for employment or promotion without demonstrating that the associated skills relate directly to job performance. The *Griggs* decision makes it clear that, if an employment practice like testing has an adverse impact (or unequal effect) on minority groups, then the burden of proof is on the employer to show the job-relatedness or business necessity of the test or other procedure. Duke Power Company couldn't do this.

In the aftermath of *Griggs* and other cases, many U.S. firms retreated from administering preemployment tests because of doubts about their legal validity. In recent years, though, testing has made a comeback in both the public and private sectors. Today, millions of job applicants are putting pencil to paper on skills tests, leadership tests, personality tests, loyalty tests, and tests to determine accident proneness—even tests to predict what an applicant's coworkers will think of him or her after a year on the job.[25] Management, of course, is seeking through testing to gain a potentially more productive group of workers whose skills match more closely the requirements of their jobs. In addition, many applicants prefer the objectivity of tests to the subjectivity of job interviews. Still, most experts believe that even the best tests cannot be a substitute for face-to-face interviews.

Interviews   When moral issues arise in interviewing, they almost always relate to the manner in which the interview was conducted. Human-resource experts rightly caution against rudeness, coarseness, hostility, and condescension in interviewing job applicants. In guarding against these qualities, personnel managers would do well to focus on the humanity of the individuals who sit across the desk from them, mindful of the very human need that has brought those people into the office. This is especially true when the interviewer might not otherwise identify closely with the person being interviewed because of cultural or other differences. Interviewers must exercise care to avoid thoughtless comments that may hurt or insult the person being interviewed—for instance, a passing remark about a person's physical disability or personal situation (a single parent, for instance). A comment that an unthinking interviewer might consider innocent or even friendly could be distressing to the person sitting across the table.

Roland Wall, a job placement counselor for individuals with disabilities, describes taking a developmentally disabled client, with an I.Q. of about 70, for a job interview. The personnel manager emerged from the room in which Wall's client was taking an initial test along with several other job applicants. The personnel manager asked Wall where his client was and was amazed to learn that she had gone in along with the others for testing. "Really?" he said. "I didn't see one in there." This personnel manager is probably more sensitive about people with disabilities than many employers, given his willingness to interview Wall's client, yet he assumed that because she was mentally retarded, the applicant would look a certain way—would look like "one."[26]

Even though everyone suffers from conscious and unconscious biases and stereotypes, interviewers should strive to free themselves as much as possible from these "idols of the mind," as the English philosopher Francis Bacon (1561–1626) called them. As Bacon put it: "The human understanding is like a false mirror, which, receiving rays irregularly, distorts and discolors the nature of things by mingling its own nature with it."[27] In short, we view things, people included, through the lens of our own preconceptions. Interviewers need to keep this fact in mind. Panel interviews with a uniform list of questions for all applicants can also help increase objectivity.

Proponents of the new but increasingly popular "situational interview" claim that it predicts future job performance more accurately than a standard interview does and also more accurately than résumé analysis, personality assessments, or pen-and-paper tests.[28] In situational interviews, job candidates have to engage in role playing in a mock office scenario. For example, they might have to face a company manager pretending to be a disgruntled customer. Meanwhile the company's interviewers watch and assess the candidates' performance: how they process the information given by "the customer," how they decide to handle the situation, the words they choose, even their body language. Proponents of the technique believe that job candidates have a harder time putting on a false front than in a standard interview, but there's no escaping the fact that bias and preconceptions can still affect the interviewers' assessment of the likely job performance of different candidates based on their role playing skills.

Promotions

It's no secret that factors besides job qualifications often determine promotions. How long you've been with a firm, how well you're liked, whom you know, even when you were last promoted—all these influence promotions in the real business world. As with hiring, the key moral ideal here is fairness. Nobody would seriously argue that promoting the unqualified is fair or justifiable. It's a breach of duty to owners, employees, and ultimately the general public. But many reasonable people debate whether promoting by job qualification alone is the fairest thing to do. Are other criteria admissible? If so, when, and how much weight should those criteria carry? These are tough questions with no easy answers. To highlight the problem we consider seniority, inbreeding, and nepotism, three factors that sometimes serve as bases for promotions.

Seniority   *Seniority* refers to longevity on a job or with a firm. Frequently job transfers or promotions are made strictly on the basis of seniority, but problems can occur with this promotion method. Imagine that personnel manager Manuel Rodriguez needs to fill the job of quality-control supervisor. Carol Martin seems slightly better qualified for the job than Jim Turner, except in one respect: Turner has been on the job for three years longer than Martin. Whom should Rodriguez promote to quality-control supervisor?

The answer isn't easy. Those who'd argue for Carol Martin—opponents of seniority— would undoubtedly claim that the firm has an obligation to fill the job with the most qualified person. In this way, the firm is best served and the most qualified are rewarded. Those advancing Turner's promotion—proponents of seniority—would contend that the company should be loyal to its senior employees, that it should reward them for faithful service. In this way, employees have an incentive to work hard and to remain with the firm.

When company policies indicate what part seniority should play in promotions and job transfers, the problem abates but does not vanish. We can still wonder about the morality of the policy itself. In cases in which no clear policy exists, the problem begs for an answer.

The difficulty of the question is compounded by the fact that seniority in itself does not necessarily indicate competence or loyalty. Just because Jim Turner has been on the job three years longer than Carol Martin does not necessarily mean he is more competent or more loyal. Of course, in some instances seniority may be a real indicator of job qualifications. A pilot who has logged hundreds of hours of flying time with an airline is more qualified for captaincy than one who hasn't.

Then there's the question of employee expectations. If employees expect seniority to count substantially, management can injure morale and productivity by overlooking it. True, worker morale might suffer equally should seniority alone determine promotions. Ambitious and competent workers might see little point in refining skills and developing talents when positions are doled out strictly on the basis of longevity.

It seems impossible, then, to say precisely what part, if any, seniority ought to play in promotions—all the more reason, therefore, for management to consider carefully its seniority policies. Of paramount importance in any decision is that management remember its twin responsibilities of promoting on the basis of qualifications and of recognizing prolonged and constructive contributions to the firm. A policy that provides for promotions strictly on the basis of qualifications seems heartless, whereas one that promotes by seniority alone seems mindless. The challenge for management is how to merge these dual responsibilities in a way that is beneficial to the firm and fair to all concerned.

Inbreeding   All the cautions about seniority apply with equal force to *inbreeding*, the practice of promoting exclusively from within the firm. In theory, whenever managers must fill positions they should look only to competence. The most competent, whether within or outside the firm, should receive the position. In this way responsibilities to owners are best served.

In practice, however, managers must seriously consider the impact of outside recruitment on in-house morale. Years of loyal service, often at great personal expense, invariably create a unique relationship between employer and employee and, with it, unique obligations of gratitude. The eighteen years that Becky Thompson has worked for National Textile create a relationship between her and the firm that does not exist between the firm and an outsider it may wish to hire for the job Thompson seeks. Some would argue that management has a moral obligation to remember this loyalty when determining promotions, especially when outside recruitment departs from established policy.

Nepotism   *Nepotism* is the practice of showing favoritism to relatives and close friends. Suppose a manager promoted a relative strictly because of the relationship between them. Such an action would raise a number of moral concerns, chief among them disregard of managerial responsibilities to the organization and of fairness to other employees.

Not all instances of nepotism raise serious moral concerns. For example, when a firm is strictly a family operation and has as its purpose providing work for family members, nepotistic practices are generally justified. Many people believe that it is unfair to exclude a person from consideration for a job just because he or she is a relative or friend of someone in the company. In fact, Advest Group, a brokerage firm, traditionally brings sons and daughters into the organization. "Good work ethics seem to run throughout families," says senior vice president Robert Rulevich.[29] But that is probably a minority view. Today, it is more common for companies to prohibit the employment of relatives, or at least to restrict such employment to avoid situations in which one relative is supervising another.

Even when a relative of someone in management is qualified for a position or deserving of promotion, one must consider the impact of the decision within the company. Will the selection breed resentment and jealousy among other employees? Will it discourage qualified outsiders from seeking employment with the firm? Will it create problems in future placement, scheduling, or dismissal of the relative? Will it make the person an object of distrust and hostility within the organization?

Discipline and Discharge

For an organization to function in an orderly, efficient, and productive way, managers and personnel departments establish guidelines for behavior based on such factors as appearance, punctuality, dependability, efficiency, and cooperation. This is not the place to examine the morality of specific rules and regulations, only the organization's treatment of employees when infractions occur.

For example, it's one thing to speak with a person privately about some infraction and quite another to chastise or punish the person publicly. Also, trying to correct someone's behavior on a graduated basis, from verbal warning to dismissal, is different from firing someone for a first infraction. The point is that discipline, although desirable and necessary, raises concerns about fairness, noninjury, and respect for persons in the way it's administered. To create an atmosphere of fairness, one in which rules and standards are equally applied, the principles of just cause and due process must operate.

Just cause requires that reasons for discipline or discharge deal directly with job performance. AIC Securities in Chicago, for example, lacked just cause for terminating with one day's notice an experienced employee with a good record because he had been diagnosed as having brain cancer.[30] And it's difficult to see why smoking in your car on company property is just cause for dismissal, even though you can be fired for it at two Motorola plants in Illinois.[31] Of course, distinguishing between a job-related and nonrelated issue is not always easy and can be controversial.

In addition, how a person behaves outside work is often incompatible with the image a company wishes to project. Does the organization have a right to discipline its employees for off-the-job conduct—for example, the doctor who was fired by his HMO for criticizing it on a talk show and at an industry conference?[32] The answer depends largely on the legitimate extent of organizational influence over individual lives—that is, on where precisely the company's legitimate interests stop and one's private life begins. Such concerns raise complex questions about privacy that are explored further in Chapter 7.

The second principle related to fair worker discipline and discharge is *due process*, which refers to the fairness of the procedures an organization uses to impose sanctions on employees. Of particular importance is that the rules be clear and specific, that they be administered consistently and without discrimination or favoritism, and that workers who have violated them be given a fair and impartial hearing. Due process requires both the hearing of grievances and the setting up of a step-by-step procedure by which an employee can appeal a managerial decision.

It is useful to distinguish among four types of discharge. *Firing* is for-cause dismissal—the result of employee theft, gross insubordination, release of proprietary information, and so on. *Termination* results from an employee's poor performance—that is, from his or her failure to fulfill expectations. *Layoff* usually refers to hourly employees and implies that they are "subject to recall," whereas *position elimination* designates the permanent elimination of a job as a result of workforce reduction, plant closing, or departmental consolidation.

Before dismissing an employee, it is important that management analyze carefully the reasons leading to this decision. The frequent success of wrongful termination lawsuits highlights the need for a rational and unbiased decision-making process. The organization must ask itself if its treatment of the employee follows the appropriate procedures for that type of discharge, as those procedures are outlined in the employee handbook, collective bargaining agreement, or corporate policy statement. In addition, the company must guard against preferential treatment. Have there been employees who behaved in the same way but were not let go?

Even-handedness and strict compliance with established procedures may not guarantee fairness. For example, unless it is stated in the contract or employees have union representation, a company may not (depending on the type of case and where it occurs) be legally obligated to give reasons for firing an employee, and it may not be legally obligated to give advance notice. When employers terminate someone without notice or cause, they may have been strictly faithful to contractual agreement or established practice, but have they been just? Have they acted morally?

In answering this question, it's helpful to distinguish between two employer responsibilities. Employers bear the responsibility of terminating the employment of workers who fail to fulfill their contractual obligations, but they are also obliged to terminate these workers as painlessly as possible. In other words, although employers have the right to fire, this does not mean they have the right to fire an employee in whatever way they choose. Because firing can be so materially and psychologically destructive to employees, management should take steps to ease its effects. Moreover, crass firings hurt a company's reputation and impair its ability to attract top-notch employees.[33]

The literature on personnel management provides many suggestions for handling the discharge of employees more compassionately and humanely, ranging from the recommendation not to notify employees of termination on Fridays, birthdays, wedding anniversaries, or the day before a holiday, to various steps to respect the terminated employee's privacy and dignity.[34] A company should not notify employees of their dismissal via e-mail,[35] nor should it give a longtime employee a pink slip, as General Dynamics did, on the day he returns to work after burying his six-year-old son.[36] And, certainly, no employer should do what John Patterson, former head of NCR, a computer company, once did. He fired an underperforming executive by taking his desk and chair outside, dousing it with kerosene and setting it on fire in front of the poor man.[37] Even when an employee is fired for misconduct, the company must be careful not to defame the person—or risk paying the legal price.[38]

One obvious thing employers can do to ease the trauma of firing is to provide sufficient notice. Although federal law requires companies to give sixty days' advance notice of plant closings, many companies ignore this legal obligation.[39] Morally speaking, what constitutes sufficient notice of termination or discharge depends primarily on the nature of the job, the type of skill involved, the availability of similar jobs, and the employee's length of service. Whenever employers have reason to suspect that employees will react to notice of their terminations in a hostile, destructive way, sufficient notice might merely take the form of severance pay. Ideally, the length of notice should be spelled out in a work contract.

For most people who have to do it, firing a worker is painfully difficult, at times impossible. In part to help managers perform the dirty job of terminating, enlightened organizations sometimes enlist the services of displacement companies. For a fee, the displacement company sends in a counselor who assists the displaced employee to assess personal strengths and weaknesses, analyze the causes of the dismissal, and start planning a job search. This makes the distasteful task of firing a little more palatable than it would otherwise be. And to be sure, it protects the company from being sued by the seasoned, middle-aged executive who may feel trifled with. Self-serving interests notwithstanding, companies using displacement experts deserve recognition for their attempt to ease the anguish of those who must fire and to help those terminated salvage both their interrupted careers and their self-respect.

Today—with frequent plant shutdowns and relocations, sizable layoffs and downsizing, and increased automation—moral management requires careful study of responsibilities to workers in times of job elimination. It's debatable whether Valiant Networks, a consulting company, did this. After laying off nearly 100 workers, it asked them to return half of the bonuses they'd received six months earlier. Those bonuses were contingent on the employees staying with the company for a year—which the axed employees hadn't done.[40] When weighing their responsibilities to terminated employees, companies need to remember that termination of employment affects not only workers but their families and the larger community as well. It is impossible here to specify further what measures can or should be taken to ease the effects of displacement. Different circumstances suggest different approaches. In some instances, job retraining might be appropriate, together with adequate notice and sufficient severance pay. When mergers are involved, firms probably should notify workers well in advance and provide them with alternatives. Whatever the approach, the point remains that when firms terminate workers, serious moral questions regarding fair treatment arise.

Wages

Every employer faces the problem of setting wage rates and establishing salaries. From the moral point of view, it is very easy to say that firms should pay a fair and just wage, but what constitutes such a wage? So many variables are involved that no one can say with mathematical precision what a person should be paid for a job. The contribution to the firm, the market for labor and products, the competitive position of the company, the bargaining power of the firm and unions, seasonal labor fluctuations, and individual needs all conspire to make a simple answer impossible. The issue is further complicated by the fact that remuneration can also include health care, retirement programs, perquisites like tips or a company car, and bonuses, commissions, and other incentive awards.

Although some writers believe that a fair wage is whatever an employee is willing to accept,[41] the moral issues are more complex than this. In an ethical organization the basis of remuneration should be distributive justice, with a wage and salary system that centers on the employee's value to the business—his or her contribution to the organization—and not on extrinsic, non-job-related considerations like being a single parent or a relative of the CEO.[42] In addition, salary judgments should be made on criteria that are clear and publicly available and that are impersonally or objectively applied. Consideration of the following more specific factors can provide the well-intentioned business manager with some ethical guidelines and help minimize the chances of setting unfair wages and salaries:

1. *What is the law?* Federal law requires that businesses pay at least the minimum wage, and many cities or counties have enacted "living wage" ordinances that raise this minimum by up to several dollars an hour.[43] Although this is a clear legal and moral mandate, the Department of Labor estimates that half of the nation's garment sewing shops violate the federal minimum-wage law.[44] An organization can, of course, satisfy the minimum requirements of the law and still not act morally. When setting pay scales, employers must consider all factors involved, not just legislative guidelines.

2. *What is the prevailing wage in the industry?* Although this factor is not foolproof, or even a moral barometer, the salaries given for similar positions in the industry can provide some direction for arriving at a fair wage.

3. *What is the community wage level?* This point recognizes that some communities have a higher cost of living than others. For example, it is more expensive to live

in New York City than in Little Rock. The cost of living relates to basic maintenance needs and must be considered very seriously in establishing a wage. To
ignore the cost of living would be to jeopardize worker welfare.

4. *What is the nature of the job itself?* Some jobs require more training, experience, and
   education than others. Some are physically or emotionally more demanding.
   Some jobs are downright dangerous, others socially undesirable. Risky or
   unskilled jobs often attract the least educated and the most desperate for work,
   thus leading to possible worker exploitation. Although it is impossible to draw
   a precise correlation between the nature of the job and what someone should be
   paid, a relationship exists that must be taken into account.

5. *Is the job secure? What are its prospects?* Employment that promises little or no security fails to fufill a basic need of employees. In such cases employers should seek
   to compensate workers for this deprivation through higher pay, better fringe benefits, or both. On the other hand, a secure job with a guarantee of regular work and
   excellent retirement benefits (such as a civil service position) may justify a more
   moderate wage. In addition, a relatively low salary may be acceptable for a job that
   is understood to be a stepping stone to better positions inside the organization.

6. *What are the employer's financial capabilities?* What can the organization afford to
   pay? A start-up company with minimal cash flow and a narrow profit margin may
   be unable to pay more than a minimum wage. A mature company with a secure
   market position might easily afford to pay better wages.

7. *What are other employees inside the organization earning for comparable work?* To avoid
   discrimination and unfairness in setting wage rates, it is important to look at
   what the organization is already paying its present employees for work of a similar nature. Gross salary disparities that are not warranted by the nature of the
   work, the experience required, or other objective considerations can also hurt
   employee morale.

Guidelines 6 and 7 have recently come to the fore as both employees and stockholders have begun scrutinizing the benefits and perks paid to top management. Studies
have found that huge salary imbalances between those at the top and their employees
create resentment: The greater the differential grows, the more employee loyalty declines
and the more turnover increases.[45] That information will come as no surprise to employees of ITT, who saw the company lavish $10.4 million on Chairman Rand Araskog and
$5.3 million on President Bob Rowman the very same year that it fired 125 of the 200
workers at company headquarters in order to save $20 million.[46] At the same time, many
stockholders are getting tired of seeing company profits going to its executives and not
to them; hence, the uproar when the Walt Disney Company awarded CEO Michael
Eisner a ten-year pay package that could yield him around $771 million. Eisner's hand-
some reward came only two months after the company had granted Michael Ovitz a
severance package of $38.9 million in cash plus options on 3 million shares worth $54
million—for having served as Disney's president for fourteen months.[47]

Two final factors are of equal importance with Guidelines 1 through 7. The first is job
performance. Some people work harder or are more talented, and thus accomplish more
for the organization. Most businesses rightly seek to recognize and award achievement.
As with an employee's base salary, however, bonuses and other awards must relate to

business performance and be a function of criteria that are measurable and objectively applied. The second factor is how the wage agreement was arrived at. A fair wage pre-supposes a fair work contract, and the fairness of a work contract requires free nego-tiation and the informed and mutual consent of both employer and employee.

Employees are motivated by many things. One of the most important of these is the desire to be treated fairly. Feeling that they have been reasonably rewarded for their efforts is crucial to people's self-esteem. Beside helping management discharge one of its prime responsibilities to employees, establishing fair wages can thus enhance the work environment and remove a potential source of job dissatisfaction. This may explain why economists have found that, year in and year out, firms paying the high-est wages are the most profitable.[48]

UNIONS

This chapter and Chapter 7 are concerned with a number of moral issues that arise in the workplace between employer and employees, but no discussion of the workplace should overlook one of the basic institutions structuring employer-employee relations, determining the terms and conditions of employment, and shaping the environment in which people work—namely, labor unions. Accordingly, this section briefly exam-ines the history and economic role of unions, the ideals that motivate them, and some of the moral dilemmas they raise.

History of the Union Movement

In a famous remark, Franklin D. Roosevelt said that free and independent labor unions are characteristic of a free and democratic modern nation. Many economists and students of the union movement go on to give it primary credit for raising the standard of living and increasing the security of working people in the United States. They argue that almost all the benefits enjoyed by employees today, whether they happen to be in unions or not, can be traced to union victories or to union-backed legislation. At the same time, the higher wages, paid vacations, health benefits, retirement pensions, and increased job security that unions have brought have, in turn, contributed to social sta-bility in the country and, through enhanced demand, to economic growth itself. Yet as the history of the labor movement reveals, employers have opposed unionization and union demands at almost every step of the way—often with violence.

Just as the roots of capitalism can be traced to the handicraft guilds, so the earliest efforts of American unionism can be found in the craft unions of the eighteenth century.[49] At that time, groups of skilled artisans—carpenters, shoemakers, tailors, and the like— formed secret societies for two basic reasons: to equalize their relationship with their employers and to professionalize their crafts. They agreed on acceptable wages and working hours and pledged not to work for any employer who didn't provide them, and they set minimal admission standards for their crafts. They also agreed to keep their allegiance secret—and for good reason. If found out they would be fired, and if dis-covered trying to cause a strike they could be jailed.

Labor historians generally consider the Knights of Labor (K of L), established in 1869, the first truly national trade union. What distinguished the K of L from previous craft unions was that it assembled in one labor organization both skilled and unskilled workers from an industry. Although this arrangement gave the organization the strength of numbers, it also created resentment among the skilled workers, who viewed the unskilled as inferior and therefore unworthy of their association. Friction and destructive rivalries also broke out between the organization's more radical national leadership and its more conservative local directors. Public sentiment, although never wildly supportive, turned sharply against unions in the wake of the Chicago Haymarket Riot in 1886, in which a bomb was lobbed into a group of police trying to halt a labor rally. Compounding the fledgling union's problems was a sour national economy that left workers fearing for their jobs and avoiding any entanglements that might land them among the growing ranks of the unemployed. In any event, between 1885 and 1890 K of L membership plummeted from 700,000 to 100,000.

But while the K of L was tottering, a new union was being born. In 1886 the American Federation of Labor (AFL) was founded. Within seven years, under the astute and temperate leadership of Samuel Gompers, it built a membership of 500,000, which increased to about 2 million by 1917. Curiously, the survival and prosperity of the AFL must be attributed in no small measure to business itself. Fearing the radical and revolutionary tendencies of the Industrial Workers of the World (the "Wobblies"), business embraced the AFL as the lesser of the evils.

The cause of unionism was significantly advanced in 1935 with the passage of the National Labor Relations Act (also called the Wagner Act). This legislation prohibited employers from interfering with employees trying to organize unions, from attempting to gain control over labor unions, from treating union workers differently from nonunion workers, and from refusing to bargain with union representatives. The act helped increase union membership to almost 12 million by the end of World War II in 1945. Most of these members belonged to the Congress of Industrial Organizations (CIO), an offshoot of the AFL that brought together various workers—auto, sheet metal, steel, and so on—into industrywide unions. The distinct advantage of the CIO over the AFL was that its unions could call a firm's entire workforce out on strike, rather than just its skilled workers.

But increasing union strength also brought public suspicions and fears of union power. Many businesspeople and political critics encouraged these worries and quickly pointed to the wave of strikes after World War II as evidence of union abuse of power. In 1947 a newly elected Republican Congress passed the Taft-Hartley Act, which amended the National Labor Relations Act. The new act outlawed the closed shop (in which a person must be a member of the union before being hired); Section 14(b) permitted individual states to outlaw union shops (in which a person must join the union within a specified time after being hired). Today, twenty-two states, mostly in the South and West, are so-called right-to-work states, with *open shop* laws on their books. These laws prohibit union contracts requiring all employees on a job site to pay union dues or their equivalent, once hired. The Taft-Hartley Act also prohibits various labor practices designated as unfair, such as sympathy strikes and secondary boycotts.

Since the merging of the AFL and CIO in 1955, unions have attempted to increase membership by recruiting outside basic industry—for example, in education, government, white-collar professions, and service jobs. But they have been only moderately successful. For the past twenty years, union membership has been falling, both absolutely and as a percentage of the workforce. Whereas in the 1950s unions represented 36 percent of the private-sector workforce, today union members constitute only 9 percent (or approximately 9.1 million workers plus an additional 7 million government workers).[50] Union membership as a percentage of the workforce is sub-stantially lower in the United States than it is in most Western nations—for instance, Australia, Belgium, France, Germany, Japan, the Netherlands, and the United Kingdom. This fact may explain why hourly compensation for production workers in manufacturing is less in the United States than in those countries; in fact, American workers make only 90 percent of what their Japanese counterparts earn and only 82.6 percent of what German workers make.[51]

In recent years, unions have been more and more on the defensive, as the indus-tries in which they have been traditionally based have declined. The number of days lost to strikes, for instance, has been at a record low, and in the past two decades many unions have been forced to go along with decreases in wages and benefits. Many corporate managements have become increasingly and aggressively anti-union. They try to break existing unions or prevent their formation by harassing and even firing pro-union workers and by waging vigorous, often illegal antiunion cam-paigns.[52] As a result, although half of all nonunion workers say they would vote yes if a union election were held at their company today, many are too intimidated to take a pro-union stance.[53]

The general political and legal climate has been unfavorable to labor for the past two decades. President Reagan set the antiunion tone of the 1980s when he fired nearly 12,000 striking air traffic controllers and broke their union. The union had been con-sidered powerful, but it was soundly defeated. President Reagan prevailed because the controllers are federal employees and are forbidden by law from striking. More recently, the U.S. Supreme Court has allowed private employers to "replace permanently" work-ers who strike, despite the fact that the 1935 Wagner Act makes it illegal for employers to punish workers who go on strike by "firing" them.

Whatever the terminology, if workers risk losing their jobs because of a strike, then the balance of power in collective bargaining is dramatically altered. Instead of nego-tiating in good faith, a company can now provoke a strike, hire new workers to replace the pickets, and cut costs. And management has done exactly this in strikes at Phelps Dodge, International Paper, Greyhound, and the *New York Daily News*. In the latter case, the Tribune Company, which then owned the *Daily News* and had earlier broken three unions in a strike at the *Chicago Tribune*, spent a year preparing for a strike in New York. The company retained a Nashville law firm renowned for its union-busting activ-ities, recruited and trained nonunion workers to produce a strike-breaking newspaper, and then forced the unions at the *Daily News* into calling a strike by locking out the paper's unionized delivery truck drivers.[54]

In the 1980s, Richard Edwards and Michael Podgursky described labor's situation in words that still hold true today:

> Bargaining structures built up over many years are crumbling and collapsing. . . . Rising product market competition, deregulation, and technological changes; adverse labor force dynamics; worsening public policy; and the legacy of the long stagnation have thrust the labor movement into a qualitatively new stage. This new period is characterized . . . by: (a) greater corporate mobility, power, and militancy; (b) ineffective labor law and a growing indifference, and in some cases, outright opposition of the government towards organized labor and collective bargaining; and (c) a waning belief in unions as the agents of working class interests. In these hostile circumstances, American unions face a difficult and troubling future.[55]

Union Ideals

From the beginning, unions have been driven by an attempt to protect workers from abuses of power at the hands of employers. This effort is based on the indisputable premise that employers have tremendous power over individual workers. They can hire and fire, relocate and reassign, set work hours and wages, create rules and control working conditions. Acting individually, a worker rarely is an employer's equal in negotiating any of these items. The position of most workers acting independently is further weakened by their lack of capital, occupational limitations, and personal and family needs. Furthermore, whereas employers obviously need workers, they rarely need any particular worker. They can, generally speaking, select whomever they want, for whatever reasons they choose.

Interestingly, Adam Smith himself recognized this fundamental imbalance in his classic *The Wealth of Nations*. Regarding the respective bargaining power of workers and their "masters," or employers, he wrote that "upon all ordinary occasions" employers "have the advantage in the dispute, and force the other into a compliance with their terms."

> The masters, being fewer in number, can combine much more easily. . . . We have no acts of parliament against combining to lower the price of work; but many against combining to raise it. In all such disputes the masters can hold out much longer. . . . Though they did not employ a single workman [employers] could generally live a year or two upon the stocks which they have already acquired. Many workmen could not subsist a week, few could subsist a month, and scarce any a year without employment. In the long run the workman may be as necessary to his master as his master is to him, but the necessity is not so immediate.[56]

In an attempt, then, to redress the balance of power in their dealings with employers, workers band together. In acting as a single body, a union, workers in effect make employers dependent on them in a way that no individual worker can. The result is a rough equality or mutual dependence, which serves as the basis for collective bargaining—negotiations between the representatives of organized workers and their employers over things such as wages, hours, rules, work conditions, and, increasingly, participation in decisions affecting the workplace. As the World Bank and others have recognized, by giving workers a collective voice, unions do not just push up wages. They can also improve productivity and efficiency, promote stability in the workforce, and make government less likely to meddle in the labor market.[57]

Certainly no one can object to unionism's initial and overriding impulse: to protect workers from abuse and give them a voice in matters that affect their lives. Indeed, these goals reflect two lofty moral ideals: noninjury and autonomy. Ironically, it is out of respect for these ideals that some individuals criticize modern unions.

The critics argue that union shops infringe on the autonomy and right of association of individual workers. Even if workers are not required to join the union but only to pay some equivalent to union dues, the critics contend that this still infringes on their freedom. In addition, evidence suggests that companies in alliance with unions sometimes treat nonunion personnel less favorably than union members. Some workers have gone to court to argue that favoritism to union members is discriminatory and unlawful (see Case 6.5). Whether or not it is, it certainly raises a moral question about the right to determine for oneself organizational membership and participation.

Taking the union's viewpoint reveals competing ideals and other consequences that must be considered. First, there is organized labor's ideal of solidarity, which is vital to collective bargaining and to winning worker equality. Union proponents point to the fact that unionized workers earn more than other workers and that per capita personal income is higher in states with free collective bargaining than in right-to-work states. For instance, of the twenty-two right-to-work states, only Nevada and Virginia have personal incomes above the national average. Practically speaking, if workers receive union benefits without having to belong or pay dues, then they lack an incentive to join the union, which greatly weakens the union's ability to improve wages and strengthen workers' rights.

Second, there is a question of fairness. Is it fair for a nonunion worker to enjoy the benefits won by union members—often at great personal and organizational expense? This question arises most forcefully when unions are attempting to establish an *agency shop,* in which all employees must pay union dues but are not required to join the union. The agency shop is designed to eliminate free riders while respecting the individual worker's freedom of choice. Opponents claim that an agency shop does not so much eliminate free riders as create forced passengers.

Union Tactics

The tactics unions use to try to get management to accept their demands also raise moral issues.

Direct Strikes   The legal right to strike is labor's most potent tool in labor-management negotiations. A strike occurs when an organized body of workers withholds its labor to force the employer to comply with its demands. Because strikes can cause financial injuries to both employer and employee, inconvenience and perhaps worse to consumers, and economic dislocations in society, they always raise serious moral questions. On the other hand, sometimes workers cannot obtain justice and fair play in the workplace in any other way. Austin Fagothey and Milton A. Gonsalves suggest the following conditions of a justified strike:[58]

1. *Just cause.* "Just cause" refers to job-related matters. Certainly, inadequate pay, excessive hours, and dangerous and unhealthful working conditions are legitimate worker grievances and provide just cause for a strike. Revenge, personal ambition, petty jealousies, and the like do not constitute just cause and thus cannot justify a strike.

2. *Proper authorization.* For a strike to be legitimate it must be duly authorized. This means, first, that workers themselves must freely reach the decision without coercion and intimidation. Second, if the workers are organized, then the proposed strike must receive union backing (although this condition becomes difficult to apply when the local union chapter and the national organization don't see eye-to-eye).

3. *Last resort.* To be justified a strike must come as a last resort. This condition acknowledges the serious potential harm of strikes. A basic moral principle is that we should always use the least injurious means available to accomplish the good we desire. Since there is an array of less drastic collective-bargaining tactics that can and usually do achieve worker objectives, all these should be exhausted before a strike is called.

Even when a strike is warranted, however, not every means of implementing it is morally justified. Peaceful picketing and an attempt by striking workers to publicize their cause and peacefully persuade others not to cross the picket line are typically considered moral means of striking. Physical violence, threats, intimidation, and sabotage are not. More controversially, Fagothey and Gonsalves argue that if workers have the right to withhold their labor and strike, then employers have a right to fill their jobs with other workers but not with professional strikebreakers, whose presence incites violence and whose function extends beyond doing work to denying strikers justice and the right to organize.

The preceding discussion deals with direct strikes—that is, cessation of work by employees with the same industrial grievance. There is, however, another kind of strike, far more controversial than the direct strike: the sympathetic strike.

Sympathetic Strikes   A sympathetic strike occurs when workers who have no particular grievance of their own and who may or may not have the same employer decide to strike in support of others. The bigger unions become and the more diverse the workers they count among their members, the more likely are sympathetic strikes aimed at different employers. Indeed, the sympathetic strike can take on global proportions, as when American dockside workers refused to unload freighters from the Soviet Union to show support of the Solidarity movement in Poland.

Sometimes the sympathetic strike involves several groups of workers belonging to different unions but employed by the same company. Acting on a grievance, one group strikes. But because it is so small, it enlists the aid of the other groups; it asks them to engage in a sympathetic strike. Cases like these do not seem to differ in any morally significant way from direct strikes. Indeed, it could be argued that the affiliated groups have obligations of loyalty and beneficence to join the strike. It is true, of course, that the sympathetic strikers do not have personal grievances, but they do have the same unjust employer, and they are in a unique position to help remedy that injustice by withholding their labor.[59]

Sympathetic strikes involving groups of employees working for different employers differ significantly from direct strikes or sympathetic strikes against the same employer. For one thing, the employers being struck out of sympathy may be perfectly innocent victims whose treatment of workers is beyond reproach. They have lived up to their end of the work contract, only to have their workers break it.

On the other hand, such sympathetic strikes can be very effective. J. P. Stevens & Co., the second-largest company in the U.S. textile industry, fought unionization for decades. The company engaged in a variety of flagrantly unfair labor practices and refused to recognize or bargain collectively with the union, despite various court orders to do so.[60] During the boycott of J. P. Stevens products, United Auto Workers members at a General Motors plant in Canada refused to install J. P. Stevens carpeting in the cars they were producing, thus shutting down the assembly line. In less than half a day, J. P. Stevens carpeting was gone from the plant. Had U.S. workers done something similar, both they and the textile workers union would have been subject to legal action, but J. P. Stevens would not have been able to refuse to bargain as long as it did.

Boycotts and Corporate Campaigns   Besides strikes, unions also use boycotts to support their demands. A primary boycott occurs when union members and their supporters refuse to buy products from a company being struck. A secondary boycott occurs when people refuse to patronize companies that handle products of struck companies. Although the Taft-Hartley Act prohibits secondary boycotts, they still occur when unions urge shoppers not to buy from stores that purchase products from companies being struck.

The express purpose of any boycott is the same as a strike: to hurt the employer or company financially and thus strengthen the union's bargaining position. In general, a boycott is justifiable when it meets the same conditions as a strike. In the case of the secondary boycott, which is like a sympathetic strike, the damage is extended to those whose only offense may be that they are handling the products of the unjust employer— and perhaps they are handling them out of financial necessity. In such cases, Fagothey and Gonsalves reject secondary boycotts. But this assessment seems too automatic and doesn't allow us to weigh the likely harms and benefits in particular cases.[61]

A relatively new pressure tactic is the so-called corporate campaign, in which unions enlist the cooperation of a company's creditors to pressure the company to unionize or comply with union demands. The tactic first gained national recognition after it was successfully used to help the Amalgamated Clothing & Textile Workers Union win contracts with Farah Manufacturing Company, a Texas-based men's garment maker. Union representatives persuaded retailers in Birmingham, Alabama, to stop selling Farah slacks by threatening them with a consumer boycott and then persuaded Farah's major creditors to help mediate the dispute.

In another labor conflict, several unions united to mount a corporate campaign to force Washington Gas Company to settle a dispute with the International Union of Gasworkers. The Teamsters, the Service Employees International Union, the Laborers' International Union, and the Communications Workers of America joined forces with several local unions to pressure Crestar Bank—where Washington Gas had a line of credit—to intervene on the union side. To lean on Crestar, the unions had at their disposal pension funds, payroll accounts, normal operating capital for their organizations, and even the mortgages on their buildings. Crestar complained that it was only caught in the middle. "We are not a party to the dispute," said spokesman Barry Koling. "We are neutral with respect to the issues between them." But union spokesman Jorge Rivera responded, "We judge our business partners by their actions concerning workers."[62]

At the heart of the corporate campaign is the issue of corporate governance. In pressuring financial institutions with mass withdrawals and cancellations of policies, unions and administrators of public-employee pension funds are trying to influence those institutions' policies and business relationships. And when the financial institutions accede to union demands, they in turn pressure the recalcitrant company to change its business policies. The harshest critics of the corporate campaign call it corporate blackmail. Its champions view it as an effective way to get financial institutions and companies to become good corporate citizens. Such tactics, they say, are necessary at a time when union wages are stagnating and when management has been so successful at exploiting labor laws and regulations to undermine unions and thwart their recruitment efforts.

SUMMARY

1. Writers like David Ewing believe that too many corporations routinely violate the civil liberties of their employees. Historically, this authoritarianism stems from (a) the rise of professional management and personnel engineering and (b) the common-law doctrine that employees can be discharged without cause.

2. Some very successful companies have taken the lead in respecting employees' rights and human dignity. Corporate profits and efficient management are compatible with a fair workplace environment.

3. Fairness in personnel matters requires, at least, that policies, standards, and decisions affecting workers be directly job-related, based on clear and available criteria, and applied equally.

4. Incomplete or nonspecific job descriptions can injure applicants by denying them information they need to reach informed occupational decisions.

5. Ordinarily, questions of sex, age, race, national origin, and religion are non-job-related and thus should not enter into personnel decisions. Lifestyle and ill-considered educational requirements may also be unfair. Discrimination against the disabled is now expressly forbidden by law.

6. A test is valid if it measures precisely what it is designed to determine and reliable when it provides reasonably consistent results. Tests that lack validity or reliability are unfair. Tests may also be unfair if they are culturally biased or if the performance they measure does not relate directly to job performance.

7. Most moral concerns in interviewing relate to how the interview is conducted. Interviewers should focus on the humanity of the candidate and avoid allowing their personal biases to color their evaluations.

8. A key issue in promotions is whether job qualification alone should determine who gets promoted. Seniority, or longevity on the job, is not necessarily a measure of either competency or loyalty. The challenge for management is to accommodate its twin responsibilities of promoting on the basis of qualifications and recognizing long-term contributions to the company.

9. Inbreeding, or promoting exclusively within the organization, presents challenges similar to those presented by seniority. Nepotism—showing favoritism to relatives or close friends—is not always objectionable, but it may overlook managerial responsibilities to the organization and may result in unfair treatment of other employees.

10. Most moral issues in employee discipline and discharge concern how management carries out these unpleasant tasks. Just cause and due process are necessary for fair treatment. Due process requires that there be procedures for workers to appeal discipline and discharge. To ease the trauma associated with discharge, employers should provide sufficient warning, severance pay, and perhaps displacement counseling.

11. The factors that bear on the fairness of wages include the law, the prevailing wage in the industry, the community wage level, the nature of the job, the security of the job, the company's financial capabilities, and the wages it is paying other employees for comparable work. Also important are job performance and the manner in which the wage is established. Fairness requires a legitimate work contract, one arrived at through free negotiation and informed and mutual consent.

12. Unions attempt to protect workers from abuse and give them a voice in matters that affect their lives. Critics charge that forcing workers to join unions infringes on autonomy and the right of association. They allege that union workers receive discriminatory and unlawful favoritism.

13. A direct strike is justified, argue some moral theorists, when there is just cause and proper authorization and when it is called as a last resort.

14. Sympathetic strikes involve the cessation of work in support of other workers with a grievance. When the companies involved are different, questions arise concerning possible injury and injustice to innocent employers, consumers, and workers.

15. Primary boycotts—refusing to patronize companies being struck—seem morally comparable to direct strikes. Secondary boycotts—refusing to patronize companies handling products of struck companies—are morally analogous to sympathetic strikes. In corporate campaigns, unions enlist the cooperation of a company's creditors to pressure the company to permit unionization or to comply with union demands.

CASE 6.1

AIDS in the Workplace

Carla Lombard always worked well with people. So when she opened her bagel shop Better Bagels seven years ago, she anticipated that managing her employees would be the easy part. She had worked for enough different bosses herself, she thought, to know what it took to be a good employer. Whether she was up to the financial side of running a business was her worry. As it turned out, however, Better Bagels flourished. Not only had Carla gone on to open three smaller branches of Better Bagels, but her bakery also made daily wholesale deliveries to dozens of coffee shops and restaurants around the city. No, the business was prospering. It was just that the personnel issues were more difficult than she had ever expected. Take this week, for example.

On Tuesday, Carla was in the main bagel shop when around noon Tom Walters's ex-wife, Frances, came in. Tom oversaw a lot of the early morning baking at that shop, and like most of Carla's employees put in his share of time working the sales counter. He was a good worker, and Carla had been considering promoting him next month to manager of one of the branch shops. After ordering a bagel, Frances took Carla aside. She beat around the bush for a few minutes before she got to her point, because she was there to tell Carla that Tom had AIDS. Frances said she was telling Carla because she "always liked her and thought she was entitled to know because she was Tom's employer." Carla barely knew Frances, and she was so taken aback that she was at a loss for words. She was shocked and embarrassed and didn't know whether she should even discuss Tom with Frances. While Carla was still trying to recover herself, Frances took her bagel and left.

Carla was still concerned and upset when she saw Tom the next day. Perhaps he had been thinner and looked tired more often the last few months, Carla thought to herself. But she couldn't be sure, and Tom seemed to be his usual upbeat self. Carla wanted to discuss Frances's visit with Tom, but she couldn't bring herself to mention it. She had always liked Tom, but—face it, she thought—he's my employee, not my friend. And it's his business. If I were an employee, I wouldn't want my boss asking me about my health.

Later, however, she began to wonder if it wasn't her business after all. She overheard some customers saying that people were staying away from the local Denny's franchise because one of its cooks was reported to have AIDS. The rumor was that some of his fellow employees had even circulated a petition saying that the cook should go, but a local AIDS support group had intervened, threatening legal action. So the cook was staying, but the customers weren't. Carla knew something about AIDS and thought some of what her customers were saying was bigoted and ill informed. She was pretty sure that you couldn't transmit HIV through food—including bagel—preparation, but she thought that maybe she should double-check her information. But what was really beginning to worry her were the business implications. She didn't want a Denny's-like situation at Better Bagels, but in her customers' comments she could see the possibility of something like that happening once the word got out about Tom, especially if she made him a manager.

Carla was running a business, and even if her customers' fears might be irrational or exaggerated, she couldn't force them to visit her shops or eat her bagels.

Carla knew it was illegal to fire Tom for having AIDS, and in any case that's not the kind of person she was. But she couldn't afford to skirt the whole problem, she realized, as some large companies do, by simply sending the employee home at full pay. To be sure, doing that deprives the employee of meaningful work, but it removes any difficulties in the workplace, and the employee has no legal grounds for complaint if he or she is left on the payroll. And then, of course, there was always the question of Tom's future work performance. Putting the question of promotion aside, if he really was ill, as Frances had said, his work performance would probably decline, she thought. Shouldn't she begin developing some plan for dealing with that?

Discussion Questions

1. What are the moral issues in this case? What ideals, obligations, and consequences must Carla Lombard consider? What rights, if any, are at stake? Will it make a difference whether Carla adopts a Kantian approach or a utilitarian approach to this situation?

2. Would it be wrong of Carla to ask Tom Walters about his health? Why or why not? Defend your answer by appeal to moral principle.

3. Suppose Tom has AIDS; what should Carla do? Is an employee's HIV status a job-related issue? In particular, is it a factor Carla should consider in deciding whether to promote Tom? What part, if any, should the attitudes of Tom's coworkers play in Carla's decision?

4. How should companies address the problem of public fear and prejudice when employees with AIDS have direct contact with customers?

5. Should companies develop programs or policies that deal specifically with AIDS? If so, what characteristics should they have? Or should they deal with the problem only on a case-by-case basis? Should large corporations develop AIDS-awareness programs? Or should AIDS be treated no differently than any other disease?

CASE 6.2

Speaking Out About Malt

When Mary Davis, associate vice president for plant management at Whitewater Brewing Company, wrote an article for a large metropolitan newspaper in her state, she hadn't realized where it would lead. At first she was thrilled to see her words published. Then she was just worried about keeping her job.

It all started when her husband, Bob, who was working on his MBA, talked her into taking an evening class with him. She did, and to her surprise really got into the course, spending most of her weekends that semester working on her term project—a study of wine and beer marketing. Among other things her essay discussed those respectable wine companies like E. & J. Gallo (the nation's largest) that market cheap, fortified wines such as Thunderbird and Night Train Express. With an alcohol content 50 percent greater than regular wine and selling for around $1.75 a pint, these screw-top wines are seldom advertised and rarely seen outside poor neighborhoods, but they represent a $125-million-a-year industry. Skid-row winos are their major consumers, a fact that evidently embarrasses Gallo, because it doesn't even put its company name on the label.[63]

Mary's essay went on to raise some moral questions about the marketing of malt liquor, a beer brewed with sugar for an extra punch of alcohol. It has been around for about thirty years; what is relatively new is the larger size of the container. A few years ago, the industry introduced malt liquor in 40-ounce bottles that sell for about two dollars. Packing an alcohol content roughly equivalent to six 12-ounce beers or five cocktails, 40s quickly became the favorite high of many inner-city teenagers. Ads for competing brands stress potency—"It's got more" or "The Real Power"—and often use gang slang. Get "your girl in the mood quicker and get your jimmy thicker," raps Ice Cube in a commercial for St. Ides malt liquor. Like baggy pants and baseball caps turned backward, 40s soon moved from the inner city to the suburbs. Teenage drinkers like the quick drunk, and this worries drug counselors. They call 40s "liquid crack" and "date rape brew."[64]

Mary's instructor liked her article and encouraged her to rewrite it for the newspaper. The problem was that Whitewater also brews a malt liquor, called Rafter, that it had recently started offering in a 40-ounce bottle. True, Mary's article mentioned Whitewater's brand only in passing, but top management was distressed by her criticisms of the whole industry, which, they thought, damaged its image and increased the likelihood of further state and federal regulation. The board of directors thought Mary had acted irresponsibly, and Ralph Jenkins, the CEO, had written her a memo on the board's behalf instructing her not to comment publicly about malt liquor without first clearing her remarks with him. Mary was hurt and angry.

"I admit that the way the newspaper edited my essay and played up the malt liquor aspect made it more sensationalistic," Mary explained to her colleague Susan Watts, "but everything I said was true."

"I'm sure it was factual," replied Susan, "but the company thought the slant was negative. I mean, lots of ordinary people drink Rafter."

"I know that. Bob even drinks it sometimes. I don't know why they are so upset about my article. I barely mentioned Rafter. Anyway, it's not like Rafter is a big money-maker. Most of our other beers outsell it."

"Well," continued Susan, "the company is really touchy about the whole issue. They think the product is under political attack these days and that you were disloyal."

"That's not true," Mary replied. "I'm no troublemaker, and I have always worked hard for Whitewater. But I do think they and the other companies are wrong to market malt liquor the way they do. It only makes a bad situation worse."

The next day Mary met with Ralph Jenkins and told him that she felt Whitewater was "invading," as she put it, her rights as a citizen. In fact, she had been invited to speak about wine and beer marketing at a local high school as part of its antidrug campaign. She intended to keep her speaking engagement and would not subject her remarks to company censorship.

Jenkins listened but didn't say much, simply repeating what he had already written in his memo. But two days later Mary received what was, in effect, an ultimatum. She must either conform with his original order or submit her resignation.

Discussion Questions

1. Do you think Mary Davis acted irresponsibly or disloyally? Does Whitewater have a legitimate concern about her speaking out on this issue? Does the company have a right to abridge her freedom of expression?

2. Is your answer to Question 1 affected by whether you agree or disagree with the views Mary Davis expressed?

3. Should there be any limits on an employee's freedom of expression? If not, why not? If so, under what circumstances is a company justified in restricting an employee's right to speak out? Does it make a difference what position the employee holds? What policy would you recommend that companies follow?

4. What do you think Mary Davis ought to do? What obligations, ideals, and consequences need to be weighed?

5. Assume that a CEO like Ralph Jenkins is legitimately worried that an employee is making damaging statements about the company. How should the CEO handle the situation? Is discharge or some sort of discipline called for?

CASE 6.3

Old Smoke

The last thing Darlene Lambert felt like doing the first thing Monday morning was inhaling the stench of old cigarette smoke. Darlene wasn't crazy about the smell of cigarettes under the best of circumstances, but today she felt under the weather and the very thought of cigarette fumes made her feel slightly nauseated.

Darlene worked with one other person, a nonsmoker, in a small office of the personnel department at Redwood Associates, but her job sometimes required her to spend extended periods in the main files room, where Frank and Alice worked and smoked. They didn't smoke when Darlene or another nonsmoker had to use their room, and they were always careful to open the windows and air it out ahead of time. But the smell of cigarettes still permeated the room, Darlene thought. Alice and Frank were nice people and sympathetic to her feelings. But Alice had hinted that she thought Darlene was oversensitive to smoke, and Frank sometimes joked about smokers being persecuted these days for their habit.

At 9:05 A.M., Darlene marched into the office of her supervisor, Charles Renford, and told him that she couldn't work in the files room that day because of the odor of smoke. Renford was caught off guard and more than a little put out by Darlene's announcement because top management was suddenly requesting a report—"due yesterday"—and he needed Darlene to begin assembling the data in the files room. He reminded her that Redwood Associates made an effort to accommodate nonsmokers by guaranteeing that certain areas of the building be smoke free, but it wasn't prepared to ban smoking altogether. Not only do smokers have rights, Charles said, it would hurt productivity and morale to make employees leave the building to smoke. "They should quit smoking," Darlene rejoined. "It would be for their own good." "Maybe it would," said Charles, "but the company shouldn't force them to quit. Besides, it is easy for you, who's never smoked, to talk about quitting. I know, I used to smoke myself."

Renford brought the conversation back around to the required report and its importance. Darlene simply said, "I'm sorry, Charles, but if it means going into that room—and it does—then I'm simply not going to do it." And then she got up and returned to her office, leaving Charles Renford trying to figure out what he was going to do.

Discussion Questions

1. Would Charles Renford be within his rights to discipline Darlene Lambert for insubordination? Should he order Frank and Alice to stop smoking in their office altogether, or is Darlene oversensitive? How would you handle this situation if you were Charles? Is it possible for employers to find some compromise between smokers and nonsmokers?
2. Do Frank and Alice have a right to smoke in their office if no one is there? Should companies make an effort to accommodate the needs of smokers? What policy on smoking would you recommend to Redwood Associates? Is it appropriate for employers to ban smoking altogether inside their facilities? What about smoking outside but on company grounds?
3. Do employees have a right to a smoke-free workplace? If so, does this right justify Darlene's refusing to do the report? Does it make a difference how important the report is, or how much her refusal inconveniences her employer?
4. In 1914 Thomas Edison had a policy of employing "no person who smoked cigarettes." Is such a policy discriminatory? Is it reasonable?

CASE 6.4

Web Porn at Work

Al Smetana is the founding president of a medium-sized, Midwestern manufacturing firm, Rayburn Unlimited. He's proud of the way his company has grown, and done so on the basis of an organizational culture committed to honesty, integrity, and the intrinsic value of each individual. But now those values are being put to the test.

It began when Al learned that an employee had tapped into the company's computer system and figured out how to read people's e-mail and to learn what Web sites they visited. Determining who the culprit was wasn't difficult. When confronted about it, the employee admitted what he had done. Al immediately terminated his employment. But as he left, the employee said angrily, "Just ask Lindley about his computer usage," referring to Craig Lindley, associate vice president for human resources and an old friend of Al's. Although Al didn't trust the discharged employee, he was disturbed by his comment and reluctant to let it go. So he called Craig Lindley into his office and asked him about it.

After a few minutes of gentle questioning, Craig started weeping. When he recovered himself, he explained that for the past year or so he had become hooked on pornography on the Web, and at the office sometimes spent an hour or so a day looking at it. Al asked him whether his wife knew. Craig said she didn't. He was too ashamed of his habit to talk to her or anybody about it. Al then told him to take the rest of the day off, to think the matter over, and to return to Al's office the next morning. When Craig left, Al stood and looked out the window, silently asking himself what he should do.[65]

Discussion Questions

1. Is Craig Lindley's behavior a sign of some psychological problem that Rayburn Unlimited should help him overcome, perhaps with psychological counseling? Or is dismissal called for? Should Al Smetana fire Craig to send a message to other employees not to misuse company time and resources?

2. Does Al have just cause for dismissing Craig? Does it matter whether or not Rayburn Unlimited has an explicit policy regarding computer use? Suppose it has such a policy and Craig violated it. Does that settle the matter? Would it affect your judgment of the case if Craig had helped draw up that policy?

3. Does the fact that Craig is a valued member of the company with a long record of service make a difference? Or that he is a personal friend of Al's?

4. Was it right for Al to have asked Craig about his computer usage in the first place? Did he violate Craig's privacy or civil liberties?

5. Because he fired the employee who violated the company's computer system, would it be inconsistent or unfair of Al to treat Craig any differently?

6. Al Smetana and Rayburn Unlimited are committed to honesty and integrity (the upholding of which seems to support dismissal) and the intrinsic worth of each individual (which might argue for more lenient treatment). Are these values in conflict? What would you do if you were Al?

CASE 6.5

Union Discrimination?

The National Right to Work Legal Defense Foundation is one of several anti-union organizations that have been active in recent years. The "right to work," in this context, means the alleged right of an individual to work without being obliged to join a union. To put it the other way around, it means that companies cannot sign contracts with unions agreeing to hire only workers who are willing to join the union.

What follows is one of the Foundation's advertisements, titled "Job Discrimination . . . It Still Exists":[66]

Paul Robertson is not a member of a persecuted minority. But he has experienced blatant discrimination all the same because he has chosen not to join a union.

Paul Robertson is a working man, a skilled licensed electrician with more than 20 years experience. He found out the hard way how a big company and a big union can discriminate on the job.

Paul was hired by the Bechtel Power Corporation to work on their Jim Bridger Power Plant project in the Rock Springs, Wyoming, area. Only three months later, he was fired, supposedly because of a reduction in force.

But during the week preceding his discharge, Bechtel hired at least 19 union electricians referred by the local union and retained at least 65 unlicensed electricians.

A determined Paul Robertson filed unfair labor practice charges against the company and the union.

An administrative law judge ruled and was upheld by the full National Labor Relations Board that the union and the employer had indeed discriminated. The judge ordered that

Robertson and seven other electricians be given the back pay they would have earned if they had been treated fairly.

The NLRB later reversed part of its decision, but Paul Robertson did not give up. With the help of the National Right to Work Legal Defense Foundation, he appealed the Board's decision to the U.S. Court of Appeals, arguing that hiring hall favoritism is discriminatory and unlawful.

Paul Robertson was fortunate. He found experienced legal help—all important because the case dragged on for nearly four years in the courts and the union still refused to obey the NLRB's backpay order.

The National Right to Work Legal Defense Foundation is helping everyone it can—currently in more than 75 cases involving academic and political freedom, protection from union violence, and other fundamental rights. But it would like to do even more.

If you'd like to help workers like Paul Robertson write: The National Right to Work Legal Defense Foundation. . . .

Discussion Questions

1. Assuming the Foundation's description of the case is accurate, was Paul Robertson treated unfairly? Was this a case of discrimination? If Robertson was an "at-will" employee, does he have any legitimate grounds for complaint?

2. Does it make a difference to your assessment of the case whether someone like Robertson knows, when he accepts a job, that he must join the union or that nonunion employees will be the first to be laid off?

3. If union employees negotiate a contract with management, part of which specifies that management will not hire nonunion employees, does this violate anyone's rights? Would a libertarian agree that the resulting union shop was perfectly acceptable?

4. Presumably Paul Robertson could have joined the union, but he chose not to. What principle, if any, do you think he was fighting for? Assess the union charge that people like Paul Robertson are "free riders" who want the benefits and wages that unionization has brought but try to avoid paying the dues that make those benefits and wages possible.

5. What do you see as the likely motivations of Bechtel Power and the union? How would they justify their conduct?

6. Why did the Foundation run this ad? Is the ad antiunion propaganda? Do you think the Foundation is sincerely interested in the rights of individual workers? Or is it simply interested in weakening unions vis-à-vis management?

7. Assess union shops and agency shops from the moral point of view. What conflicting rights, interests, and ideals are at stake? What are the positive and negative consequences of permitting union shops?

Notes

1. "U.S. Rise in HIV Catches the Least Aware," *Wall Street Journal,* July 8, 2002, A17, and the Centers for Disease Control and Prevention at *www.cdc.gov/hiv.stats.htm.*

2. Al Gini and Michael Davis, "AIDS in the Workplace: Options and Responsibilities," in Thomas Donaldson and Al Gini, eds., *Case Studies in Business Ethics,* 4th ed. (Upper Saddle River, N.J.: Prentice-Hall, 1996), 121; Alan Miller, Thomas E. Backer, and Everett M. Rogers, "Business Education and the AIDS Epidemic: Responding in the Workplace," *Business Horizons* 40 (July–August 1997): 78.

3. See David W. Ewing, "Civil Liberties in the Corporation," in Tom L. Beauchamp and Norman E. Bowie, eds., *Ethical Theory and Business,* 2nd ed. (Englewood Cliffs, N.J.: Prentice-Hall, 1983), 141.

4. Ibid., 139–140.

5. Ibid., 140–141.

6. "Women in Suits," *Economist,* March 2, 2002, 61.

7. Clyde W. Summers, "Protecting All Employees Against Unjust Dismissal," *Harvard Business Review* 58 (January–February 1980); but see also "Business for Lawyers," *Economist,* January 23, 1988.

8. Stephen Wermiel, "High Court Backs Refusal to Work on Sabbath Day," *Wall Street Journal,* March 30, 1989, B8.

9. Ewing, "Civil Liberties," 148.

10. See Tad Tuleja, *Beyond the Bottom Line* (New York: Penguin, 1987), Chapter 5, and Jeffrey Pfeffer, "Practices of Successful Organizations: Employment Security," in Joseph R. DesJardins and John J. McCall, eds., *Contemporary Issues in Business Ethics,* 4th ed. (Belmont, Calif.: Wadsworth, 2000).

11. Tuleja, *Beyond the Bottom Line.*

12. Richard W. Stevenson, "Do People and Profits Go Hand in Hand?" *New York Times,* May 9, 1996, C1.

13. "The Work Place 100," *USA Weekend,* January 22–24, 1993, 4.

14. See "Trust in Me," *Economist,* December 16, 1995, 61.

15. Sue Shellenbarger, "Workers Leave If Firms Don't Stick to Values," *San Francisco Sunday Examiner & Chronicle,* June 27, 1999, CL31.

16. David L. Kirp, "Uncommon Decency: Pacific Bell Responds to AIDS," *Harvard Business Review* 67 (May–June 1989): 142.

17. See Marian M. Extejt and William N. Bockanic, "Issues Surrounding the Theories of Negligent Hiring and Failure to Fire," *Business and Professional Ethics Journal* 8 (Winter 1989).

18. "Short Hours, Big Pay and Other Little Lies," *Wall Street Journal,* October 22, 2003, B1.

19. "The Big Squeeze on Workers," *Business Week,* May 13, 2002, 96–97.

20. Eric Matusewitch, "Language Rules Can Violate Title VII," *Personnel Journal,* October 1990, 100. See also "Firms Can Insist on English," *San Jose Mercury News,* July 17, 1993, 9D.

21. "Instructor Wins Weight-Bias Case," *San Jose Mercury News,* May 7, 2002, 1B.

22. "If You Light Up on Sunday, Don't Come in on Monday," *Business Week,* August 26, 1991, 68–70; "Fight over Hiring Bans Reaches Law Makers," *San Jose Mercury News,* April 28, 1994, 1E; "One Whiff of Smoke and You're Out," *San Francisco Chronicle,* January 25, 1997, D2; and "At Risk from Smoking: Your Job," *Business Week,* April 15, 2002, 12.

23. Dean Rotbart, "Father Quit His Job for the Family's Sake; Now Hirers Shun Him," *Wall Street Journal,* April 13, 1981, 1. See also Martha Groves, "Letting Down Their Corporate Shields," *Los Angeles Times,* August 12, 1996, Business Part II, 7.

24. 401 U.S. 424 (1971).

25. "Employers Score New Hires," *USA Today,* July 9, 1997, 1B; "Put Applicants' Skills to the Test," *HR Magazine,* January 2000, 75–80.

26. Roland Wall, "Discovering Prejudice Against the Disabled," *ETC* 44 (Fall 1987): 236.

27. Francis Bacon, *The New Organon* (New York: Bobbs-Merrill, 1960), 48.

28. "Improv at the Interview," *Business Week,* February 3, 2003, 63.

29. "Work Week," *Wall Street Journal,* May 21, 1996, A1. See also Adam Bellow, *In Praise of Nepotism* (New York: Doubleday, 2003), 12.

30. "Disability Act's First Lawsuit," *San Jose Mercury News,* November 8, 1992, 3C.

31. *San Francisco Chronicle,* July 3, 1996, B5.

32. *Santa Cruz Sentinel,* December 27, 1995, B5.

33. "An Alternative to Cocker Spaniels," *Economist,* August 25, 2001, 49.

34. See, for example, "Termination with Dignity," *Business Horizons* 43 (September–October 2000): 4–10, and Jathan W. Janove, "Don't Add Insult to Injury," *HR Magazine,* May 2002, 113–120.

35. John Challenger, "Downsize with Dignity," *Executive Excellence,* March 2002, 17.

36. "Waging War in the Workplace," *Newsweek,* July 19, 1993.

37. "Special Report: Corporate Governance," *Economist,* June 15, 2002, 70.

38. Gabriella Stern, "Companies Discover That Some Firings Backfire into Costly Defamation Suits," *Wall Street Journal,* May 5, 1993, B1. See also "Executions Corporate Style," *HR Magazine,* January 2000, 118–127.

39. "Proper Warning of Layoffs Often Lacking," *San Jose Mercury News,* February 22, 1993, 8A, and "It's Legal, but . . . ," *San Jose Mercury News,* November 15, 1993, 1D.

40. "Axed Workers Asked to Return Bonuses," *San Jose Mercury News,* November 6, 2001, 1C.

41. Tibor R. Machan and James E. Chester, *A Primer on Business Ethics* (Lanham, Md.: Rowman & Littlefield, 2002), 88.

42. Elizabeth Vallance, *Business Ethics at Work* (Cambridge: Cambridge University Press, 1995), 71.

43. See "The Case for Living Wage Laws," *Business Week,* April 22, 2002, 26.

44. "Garment Industry Turns to Self-Policing," *San Jose Mercury News,* May 6, 1996, 8E. See also "Dress Code," *Economist,* April 19, 1997, 28.

45. "High CEO Pay Can Damage Workers' Morale, Report Says," *San Francisco Examiner,* May 4, 1997, CL11.

46. "Zapping the Little Folks," *Newsweek,* May 26, 1997.

47. "Eisner's Pay Package Incites Protest by Disney Stockholders," *San Francisco Chronicle,* February 24, 1997, D6. See also "Who Profits If the Boss Is Overfed?" *New York Times,* June 20, 1999, sec. 3, 9.

48. Robert H. Frank, "Why Is Cost-Benefit Analysis So Controversial?" *Journal of Legal Studies* 29 (June 2000): 920.

49. The historical sketch that follows is based on Robert B. Carson, *Business Issues Today: Alternative Perspectives* (New York: St. Martin's Press, 1984), 139–142.

50. U.S. Bureau of the Census, *Statistical Abstract of the United States* 2002 (Washington, D.C.: U.S. Government Printing Office, 2003), Table 628.

51. Ibid., Table 1354.

52. Robert Kuttner, "Labor and Management—Will They Ever Wise Up?" *Business Week,* May 9, 1994, 16.

53. "How Wal-Mart Keeps Unions at Bay," *Business Week,* October 28, 2002, 96. See also Karen Olsson, "Up Against Wal-Mart," *Mother Jones,* March/April 2003, 54–59.

54. *San Francisco Chronicle,* March 2, 1991, A5; *Economist,* November 3, 1990, 35; "Union-Busting Owners Force Strike on Daily News Workers," *Guardian* (New York), November 7, 1990.

55. "Labor Unions: Context and Crisis" in R. C. Edwards, M. Reich, and T. E. Weisskopf, eds., *The Capitalist System,* 3rd ed. (Englewood Cliffs, N.J.: Prentice-Hall, 1986), 165.

56. Adam Smith, *An Inquiry into the Nature and Causes of the Wealth of Nations* (New York: Modern Library, 1985), 68.

57. See "The Future of Unions" and "Unions for the Poor," *Economist,* July 1, 1995, 16, 56.

58. Austin Fagothey and Milton A. Gonsalves, *Right and Reason: Ethics in Theory and Practice* (St. Louis: Mosby, 1981), 428–429.

59. Ibid., 429.

60. See Chapter 4 of Mary Gibson, *Workers' Rights* (Totowa, N.J.: Rowman & Allanheld, 1983). The film *Norma Rae* portrays the dogged resistance of a company like J.P. Stevens to unionization.

61. Fagothey and Gonsalves, *Right and Reason,* 428–429.

62. "Unions Threaten Huge Bank Withdrawal," *San Jose Mercury News,* April 10, 1996, 1C.

63. David Dietz, "The Bottom of the Barrel," *San Francisco Chronicle,* July 7, 1996, in "Sunday," 1.

64. "The Drink of Choice," *Santa Cruz Sentinel,* May 26, 1996, D1.

65. This case is based on Willard P. Green, "Pornography at Work," *Business Ethics,* Summer 2003, 19

66. Reprinted by permission of the National Right to Work Legal Defense Foundation, Inc., 8001 Braddock Road, Suite 600, Springfield, VA 22160.

Further Reading for Chapter 6

Ronald Duska, "Employee Rights," in Robert E. Frederick, ed., *A Companion to Business Ethics* (Malden, Mass.: Blackwell, 1999) discusses the nature of rights in general and the specific rights claimed for employees in recent times.

Thomas Geoghegan, *Which Side Are You On? Trying to Be for Labor When It's Flat on Its Back* (New York: Penguin, 1992) is the insightful and entertaining memoir of a labor lawyer.

Mary Gibson, *Workers' Rights* (Totowa, N.J.: Rowman & Allanheld, 1983) is rich in factual background and actual cases.

Reed Larson and **William L. Clay** debate right-to-work laws in "Does America Need a National Right-to-Work Law?" *Insight on the News* 14 (August 17, 1998).

Richard L. Lippke, *Radical Business Ethics* (Lanham, Md.: Rowman & Littlefield, 1995), Chapter 6, discusses the right to freedom of speech and conscience in the workplace.

Patricia Werhane, "Individual Rights in Business," in Tom Regan, ed., *Just Business: New Introductory Essays in Business Ethics* (New York: Random House, 1984), provides a useful overview of many basic moral issues in the workplace.

Michael T. Zugelder and **Steven D. Mauer**, "Small Business and the Americans with Disabilities Act," *Business Horizons* 41 (July–August 1998) discusses the rights and responsibilities of employers under the ADA.

 InfoTrac College Edition: For further information or to conduct research, please go to www.infotrac-college.com.

7

The Workplace (2): Today's Challenges

It was a routine business day for Eastern Airlines—until it received an anonymous tip that some of its baggage handlers at Miami International Airport were using drugs. Eastern quickly sprang into action, ordering security guards to round up the ten employees then at work in the airport's plane-loading area. The employees were marched between two rows of guards and into waiting vans—"like terrorists," a lawsuit later claimed—all in full view of other employees and passengers. After questioning the workers, suspicious supervisors put them on board a bus, once again in front of onlookers, and took them to a hospital. There the employees were given an ultimatum: Either take a urine test or be fired on the spot.[1]

The baggage handlers were union members, but they caved in and took the test. All ten of them tested negative (that is, free of drugs), but they weren't happy about what they'd been through. Not long afterward, they filed suit against the airline in federal court, seeking damages of $30,000 each on charges of invasion of privacy, defamation, and intentional infliction of emotional distress. Eastern has since gone out of business, but the case represents in dramatic form one of the major issues dividing employers and employees today—privacy. Companies are delving further into employees' personal lives than ever before, claiming the need to monitor their behavior and probe into their health and habits. Workers are resisting ever more adamantly, fighting back for the right to be left alone.

In 1928, U.S. Supreme Court Justice Louis D. Brandeis described the right to privacy, or "the right to be let alone," as "the right most valued by civilized men." He was referring to the Fourth Amendment's guarantee that citizens are protected against illegal searches and seizures by government. Today many Americans are resisting invasions of their privacy not just by government agencies or pesky telemarketers, but also by intrusive employers. And not without reason: One survey shows that American bosses tend to be less respectful of employees' rights to privacy than their counterparts are in Europe and Canada.[2]

Businesses and other organizations frequently argue that they have a compelling need to know about the personal lives and conduct of their employees, while those employees firmly assert their right to a personal sphere not subject to the needs, interests, or curiosity of their employers. "I don't think politicians and corporate executives realize how strongly Americans feel about it," says a San Francisco lawyer who specializes in employee lawsuits. "It's not a liberal or a conservative issue, and the fear of abuse doesn't emanate from personnel policies. It's coming out of the larger, impersonal notion that workers are fungible, expendable items."[3]

Chapter 6 examined personnel policies and procedures, trade unions, the state of civil liberties on the job, and the efforts of some successful companies to respect the rights, dignity, and moral integrity of their workers. This chapter also focuses on moral issues that emerge in the workplace. It looks in detail at one crucial civil liberty—the right to privacy—and at the ethical choices it poses inside the organization. The remainder of the chapter examines several other topics that are stirring up controversy in today's workplace. More specifically, this chapter explores the following:

1. The nature of privacy and the problems of organizational influence over private decisions

2. The moral issues raised by the use of polygraph and personality tests, employee monitoring, and drug testing in the workplace

3. Working conditions—in particular, health and safety, styles of management, and provision of day-care facilities and maternity leave

4. Job satisfaction and dissatisfaction and the prospects for enhancing the quality of work life

ORGANIZATIONAL INFLUENCE IN PRIVATE LIVES

Privacy is widely acknowledged today to be a fundamental right, yet corporate behavior and policies often threaten privacy, especially in the case of employees. One way this happens is through the release of personal information about employees. The data banks and personnel files of business and nonbusiness organizations contain an immense amount of private information, the disclosure of which can seriously violate employees' rights. Most firms guard their files closely and restrict the type of material that they can contain in the first place, but the potential for abuse is still great. Although a complicated set of laws and court rulings limits access to such information, a wide range of snoops still manage, legitimately or illegitimately, to get their hands on it.

As a related matter, more employees are successfully suing their former bosses for passing on damaging information to prospective employers. The courts have traditionally considered this sort of information exchange between employers to be "privileged," but companies can lose this protection by giving information to too many people or by making false reports. Through fear of defamation suits, in fact, many organizations now refuse to reveal anything about former employees except their dates of employment. Such reticence obviously makes it more difficult for companies to screen job applicants.[4]

More significant are the threats to privacy that can arise on the job itself. For example, some bosses unhesitatingly rummage through the files of their workers, even when they are marked "private." Some companies routinely eavesdrop on their employees' phone calls, and a majority of them read their employees' email and monitor their use of the Internet.[5] Voice mail isn't safe, either, as Michael Huttcut, a manager of a McDonald's outlet in St. Louis, learned the hard way. He was having an affair with a coworker, and the romantic voice-mail messages he sent her were retrieved and played by his boss. When Huttcut complained, he was fired.[6] Other companies secretly quiz managers—or even call in private investigators—to gain knowledge about the personal habits and behavior of workers who call in sick.[7]

Equally important is the way organizations attempt to influence behavior that ought properly to be left to the discretion of their employees—in particular, efforts to impose their own values on their workers. For example, Wal-Mart fired Lauren Allen, who was married but separated from her husband, for dating a coworker, who was single. Wal-Mart says that it "strongly believes in and supports the 'family unit'" and that the conduct of Allen and her coworker violated the company's rules.[8] Or consider those corporations who hit up their employees for political contributions. By bundling these individual contributions together as one gift, companies circumvent the ban on corporate campaign giving. Some people think IBM crossed the line in 1994 by urging its employees to work to defeat the health care bill then before Congress.[9]

There is, however, no consensus among philosophers or lawyers about how to define privacy, how far the right to privacy extends, or how to balance a concern for privacy against other moral considerations. All of us would agree, nonetheless, that we have a clear right to keep private certain areas of our lives and that we need to have our privacy respected if we are to function as complete, self-governing agents. Particularly important is our right to make personal decisions autonomously, free from the illegitimate influence of our employers.

Even when a genuine privacy right is identified, the strength of that right depends on circumstances—in particular, on competing rights and interests. Privacy is not an absolute value. Corporations and other organizations often have legitimate interests that may conflict with the privacy concerns of employees. Determining when organizational infringement on a person's private sphere is morally justifiable is, of course, precisely the question at issue.

Consider the case of Virginia Rulon-Miller, a marketing manager in IBM's office products division. She made the mistake of falling in love. A week after receiving a 13.3 percent pay raise, she was called on the carpet for dating Matt Blum, a former IBM account manager who had gone to a competitor. She and Blum had begun dating when Blum was at IBM, and he still played on the IBM softball team. IBM told Rulon-Miller to give up Blum or be demoted. "I was so steeped in IBM culture," she says, "that I was going to break up with Matt." But the next day, before she had a chance to do anything, she was dismissed. Even though IBM's decision was based on written policy governing conflicts of interest, a California jury decided that Rulon-Miller's privacy had been invaded. It awarded her $300,000.

On the other hand, a year later the Oregon Supreme Court upheld J. C. Penney's firing of a merchandising manager for dating another employee. He claimed that his right to privacy had been violated. Although it may seem harsh to fire an employee on the basis of personal lifestyle, the court said, private firms aren't barred from discriminating against workers for their choice of mates. And a federal district court permitted the firing of a New Mexico employee with an excellent work record because she was married to a worker at a competing supermarket.[10]

As a general rule, whenever an organization infringes on what would normally be considered the personal sphere of an individual, it bears the burden of establishing the legitimacy of that infringement. The fact that a firm thinks an action or policy is justifiable does not, of course, prove that it is. The firm must establish both that it has some legitimate interest at stake and that the steps it is taking to protect that interest are reasonable and morally permissible. But what are the areas of legitimate organizational influence over the individual?

Legitimate and Illegitimate Influence

The work contract; the firm's responsibilities to owners, consumers, and society at large; and the purpose of the firm itself all support the proposition that the firm is legitimately interested in whatever significantly influences work performance. What constitutes a significant influence on work performance, however, eludes precise definition because the connection between an act or policy and the job is often fuzzy. Take, for example, the area of dress. A roofing company has a legitimate interest in the type and quality of shoes its workers wear because footwear affects safety and job performance. And arguably specialty-clothing stores like Gap, Polo Ralph Lauren, and Abercrombie & Fitch have legitimate grounds for requiring their employees to dress in the store's latest styles. Enterprise Rent-A-Car also puts a high priority on employee grooming and appearance. It lays down 30 dress code guidelines for female employees (no denim or skirts more than 2 inches above the knee) and 26 rules for male employees (no beards; dress shirts with coordinated ties). More debatable is the company's requiring employee Angela Garrett to remove the red tints from her hair because they weren't appropriate for her ethnic group (she's African American).[11] Likewise, it's questionable whether American Airlines was legitimately pursuing a genuine corporate interest when it forbade a black employee from wearing her hair in corn rows because the style clashed with the company's corporate image. Or consider the ticket agent who was fired by another airline for refusing to wear makeup. Perhaps this was a legitimate demand in the name of good public relations, but maybe it was arbitrary and narrow minded.[12]

An employer's concern with dress can interfere with an employee's personal choices in other ways. Consider the case of Margaret Hasselman, who worked as a lobby attendant in a New York City high rise. Wearing the new uniform provided by her employer— a poncho with large openings under the arms, dancer's underpants, and white pumps—she repeatedly encountered sexual harassment. She complained about the outfit to her boss, but to no avail. When she eventually refused to wear it, she was fired. Issues of morality, of course, differ from questions of legality. But it is interesting that when Hasselman filed suit, the court ruled that no employer has the right to force workers to wear revealing or sexually provocative clothing. In contrast, in a subsequent case the Equal Employment Opportunity Commission (EEOC) upheld an employer's firing of several female employees who refused to wear swimsuits as part of a swimsuit promotion. The EEOC agreed that the swimsuits were revealing but found no reason to expect that the women would encounter sexual harassment.[13]

The general proposition that a firm has a legitimate interest only in employee behavior that significantly influences work performance applies equally to off-the-job conduct. BankAmerica probably fell afoul of this guideline when it fired Michael Thomasson, a legal secretary, for working as a gay stripper during his off-hours. After a coworker read a personal letter Thomasson had written on a company computer that mentioned his job as an exotic dancer, a group of bank employees, including several of Thomasson's supervisors, went to see him perform. Two weeks later he was dismissed—despite a record of positive job evaluations and a recent merit raise.[14]

Determining when conduct is significantly related to job performance can be difficult. For example, how would you decide the following case? In an off-the-job fight, a plant guard drew his gun on his antagonist. Although no one was injured, the guard's employer viewed the incident as grounds for dismissal. The employer reasoned that such an action indicated a lack of judgment on the part of the guard. Do you think the employer had a right to fire the guard under these circumstances? The courts did. By contrast, consider the employee who sold a small amount of marijuana to an undercover agent, or the employee who made obscene phone calls to the teenage daughter of a client. Their employers fired them, but the employees were reinstated by an arbitrator or the court.

Then there's the amorphous area of company image and the question of whether it can be affected by off-the-job conduct. The political activities of a corporate executive, for example, could significantly affect the image a firm wishes to project, whereas what an obscure worker on the firm's assembly line does politically might have a comparatively insignificant impact on the company's image. Companies and other organizations have an interest in protecting their good names. The off-duty conduct of employees might damage an organization's reputation, but in practice damage is often difficult to establish. For example, two IRS agents were suspended for "mooning" a group of women after leaving a bar. Would you agree with their suspension? An arbitrator didn't and revoked it. He couldn't see that their conduct damaged the IRS's reputation.[15]

Obviously we can't spell out exactly when off-duty conduct affects company image in some material way, any more than we can say precisely what constitutes a significant influence on job performance. But that doesn't prevent us from being able to judge that in many cases organizations step beyond legitimate boundaries and interfere with what should properly be personal decisions by their employees. This interference can take many forms, but three—one traditional, the other two modern—are worth discussing.

Involvement in Civic Activities   To enhance their image in the community, businesses and other organizations have long prodded employees to donate to charitable causes during company-led fund-raising drives, or encouraged them to participate in public-spirited activities off the job—for example, by running for the local school board or joining civic service organizations, such as Kiwanis, Lions, or Rotary. Moreover, since the 1990s there has been a boom in corporate-sponsored employee volunteer programs, with more and more firms encouraging employees to spend off-duty hours helping out at designated charities or donning a company T-shirt and pitching in on Saturdays at some company-run charitable project.[16]

There's no question that the trend toward corporate volunteer programs has been good for society. One in four adults does at least some volunteer work, and corporate programs have probably drawn many of them into doing so. But such programs can collide with accelerating job demands, forcing employees to spend valued off-duty time away from their families and fueling employee resentment and burnout. Moreover, such programs can raise moral questions, especially as the pressure to participate increases. Some employers have "unwritten rules" requiring volunteer work; other companies award employees points for approved volunteer work on their performance evaluations. And employees have been downgraded, disciplined, or even fired for not contributing the "suggested" amount of money to the United Way or other charitable cause sponsored by the firm.

By striving too hard for a do-gooder image, a company can thus be guilty of attempting to influence the personal choices and off-the-job behavior of employees in ways that constitute an invasion of privacy. By explicitly or implicitly requiring employees to associate themselves with a particular activity, group, or cause, firms are telling workers what to believe, what values to support, and what goals to promote outside work.

Health Programs   Sometimes organizations pressure employees in certain directions for "their own good." Recently, for example, a group of employers led by Ford, Pepsi-Co, and General Mills have launched a campaign to get overweight employees to slim down.[17] Consider also the aggressive "wellness" programs that some companies are mounting to push employees toward healthier lifestyles. These paternalistic programs are aimed at helping employees live longer and improve their health and productivity. The programs teach employees about nutrition, exercise, stress, and heart disease and encourage them to give up smoking, eat more healthfully, moderate their drinking, and work out in the company gym or join a company sports team after work.[18]

Wellness programs try to make fitness part of the corporate culture, and that seems innocent enough. But some companies are making employees pay more for their health care benefits if they are overweight, have high blood pressure, or don't exercise.[19] And employees have been fired for smoking or taking a drink at home.[20] "I think employers are going to get deeper and deeper into the wellness business," says Professor Alan F. Westin of Columbia University. "This is going to throw up a series of profound ethical and legal dilemmas about how they should do it and what we don't want them to do."[21]

Intensive Group Experience   In recent years company interference has taken a more subtle form. Modern psychology has made us aware that most people never realize their potential for perceiving, thinking, feeling, creating, and experiencing. Attempts to enlarge the potential for personal growth have resulted in the human potential movement. The focus of this movement is on developing ways to help people lower their defenses, remove their masks, become more aware and open to experience, feel more deeply, express themselves more effectively, be more creative, and become everything they can be.

Intensive group experience goes by various names, such as sensitivity training groups, encounter groups, T-groups, awareness groups, creativity groups, and workshops. Industry frequently uses a form of intensive group experience called team-building groups to facilitate the attainment of production and related goals as well as to provide opportunities for improved human relations and personal growth. In a work context, the intensive group experience brings employees together and through various exercises attempts to enable them to realize their abilities, clarify and strengthen their motivations, and improve their capacity to work with others.

The potential benefits of such experiences in the workplace are exciting, for they can not only boost productivity but also help people meet their higher-level needs. Nevertheless, such group encounters can pose a threat to psychic privacy, especially when groups lay bare a participant's innermost feelings. Although this doesn't always occur, it can. When it does, privacy can be violated.

As with health programs and civic activities, the issue of voluntary participation is crucial. When employees are genuinely free to participate or not, then such group sessions are (optional) opportunities for job enrichment and function as legitimate vehicles for increasing employees' work performance and satisfaction. But when coercion infringes on personal decision making—even in a subtle form, as when participation in such groups becomes an unwritten prerequisite for job promotion—this raises moral concerns.

OBTAINING INFORMATION

It's no secret that firms frequently seek, store, and communicate information about employees without their consent. A firm may bug employee lounges, hoping to discover who's responsible for pilfering. Another firm may use a managerial grapevine, with supervisors meeting once a month to exchange anecdotal material about employees, some of it obtained in confidence, all of it gathered with the hope of anticipating potential troublemakers. Still another company may keep detailed files on the personal lives of its employees to ensure compatibility with organizational image and reputation.

Of special interest here are two common practices organizations engage in: subjecting employees to various tests and monitoring employees on the job to discover sundry information. Before beginning the discussion, however, we need to take a brief look at the concept of informed consent and how it connects with these topics.

Informed Consent

Certainly no employee is ever compelled to take a lie-detector, personality, or genetic screening test in the sense that someone puts a loaded revolver to the person's head and says, "Take the test or else." But compulsion, like freedom, comes in degrees. Although an employee may not be compelled to take a test in the same way that a prisoner of war, for example, is compelled to cooperate with a captor, enough coercion may be present to significantly diminish the worker's capacity to consent freely to privacy-invading procedures.

Obviously if workers submit to an honesty exam or to a test for genetic disorders, they agree to do so. But was their consent valid and legitimate? Was it informed consent? That's the issue, and it is an altogether reasonable issue to raise, because information collected on workers is often intimately personal and private and, when used carelessly, can injure them.

Informed consent implies deliberation and free choice. Workers must understand what they are agreeing to, including its full ramifications, and must voluntarily choose it. Deliberation requires not only the availability of facts but also a full understanding of them. Workers must be allowed to deliberate on the basis of enough usable information, information that they can understand. But usable information is not of itself enough to guarantee informed consent. Free choice is also important—the *consent* part is as significant as the informed part of informed consent.

Everyone agrees that for consent to be legitimate, it must be voluntary. Workers must willingly agree to the privacy-invading procedure. They must also be in a position to act voluntarily. One big factor that affects the voluntariness of consent is the pressures, expressed and implied, exerted on employees to conform to organizational policy.

Especially when these pressures to conform are reinforced with implicit reprisals, they can effectively undercut the voluntariness of consent. Thus, employers who ignore organizational pressures on workers to comply with privacy-invading procedures can misinterpret consent to a test as voluntary when it is not.

Polygraph Tests

When an individual is disturbed by a question, certain detectable physiological changes occur. The person's heart may begin to race, blood pressure may rise, respiration may increase. The polygraph simultaneously records changes in these physiological processes and, thus, is often used in lie detection.

Businesses cite several reasons for using polygraph tests. First, the polygraph is a fast and economical way to verify information provided by a job applicant and to screen candidates for employment. So used, it can help reveal personal philosophy, behavioral patterns, and character traits incompatible with the organization's purpose, function, and image.

Second, the polygraph allows employers to identify dishonest employees or job candidates, at a time when many companies are suffering staggering annual losses through in-house theft. Third, companies argue that the use of polygraphs permits business to abolish audits and oppressive controls. They say the use of polygraphs actually increases workers' freedom.

Those who defend the use of polygraphs rely on three assumptions that are open to question.[22] The first assumption is that lying triggers an involuntary, distinctive response that truth telling does not. But this is not necessarily the case. What the polygraph can do is record that the respondent was more disturbed by one question than by another, but it cannot determine why the person was disturbed. Perhaps the question made the person feel guilty or angry or frightened, but deception does not necessarily lurk behind the emotional response.

A classic case that makes the point involved Floyd Fay of Toledo, Ohio, who was sentenced to life imprisonment for murder, in part on the basis of having failed two polygraph tests. The tests included control questions, such as "Before the age of twenty-five, did you ever think of hurting someone for revenge?" Because Fay's heart beat faster and his palms perspired more when he was asked about the crime than when asked about the control questions, he was regarded as deceptive. Fay spent two years in jail before the real killers confessed.

Second, it is assumed that polygraphs are extraordinarily accurate. Lynn March, president of the American Polygraph Association, says that "when administered correctly by qualified operators, the tests are accurate more than 90 percent of the time."[23] But David T. Lykken, a psychiatry professor, claims that these boasts are not borne out by three scientifically credible studies of the accuracy of polygraphs used on actual criminal suspects. The accuracies obtained by qualified operators in these experiments were 63 percent, 39 percent, and 55 percent.[24] Whether the polygraph is accurate 90 percent of the time or less, the conclusion is the same: It cannot reveal with certainty that a person is or is not telling the truth.

The third major assumption about polygraphs is that they cannot be beaten. Lykken, for one, suggests otherwise. The easiest way to beat the polygraph, the psychiatrist claims, is by augmenting your response to the control question by some form of covert self-stimulation, like biting your tongue. He claims that Fay taught some augmenting techniques to twenty-seven fellow inmates who were charged with smuggling drugs and that twenty-three of them subsequently beat the lie detector. Not everybody believes this. Defenders of the polygraph contend that liars can't fool skilled operators of the machine. But even if the polygraph generally catches the guilty, it will also generate a disturbing number of "false positives"—that is, it will falsely identify as liars people who are telling the truth.

To see this, imagine that the polygraph is 95 percent accurate and suppose, for the sake of illustration, that at a large corporation with an in-house theft problem one out of every fifty employees is stealing from the employer. If the corporation has a thousand employees, then twenty will be crooks and 980 will be honest. If every employee is tested, then the test, being only 95 percent accurate, will identify nineteen of the twenty crooks; one will escape detection. But the test will also identify as liars 5 percent of the company's 980 innocent employees; that is, forty-nine people will be falsely accused. By firing all those who fail the polygraph, a company might well succeed in weeding out the guilty, but it would also seriously harm many innocent employees.

In addition to these considerations, polygraphs infringe on privacy. As professor of politics Christopher Pyle says, they violate "the privacy of beliefs and associations, the freedom from unreasonable searches, the privilege against self-accusation, and the presumption of innocence."[25] That is not to say employers never have the right to abridge privacy or employees never have an obligation to reveal themselves. In important cases of in-house theft, employers may be justified in using a polygraph as a last resort. But the threat to privacy remains.

The moral concerns embedded in the use of polygraphs suggest three points—in addition to the question of informed consent—to consider in evaluating their use in the workplace:

1. The information the organization seeks should be clearly and significantly related to the job. This caveat harks back to a determination of the legitimate areas of organizational influence over the individual.

2. Because the polygraph intrudes on psychic freedom, those administering it should consider whether they have compelling job-related reasons for doing so. Some persons contend that among the reasons must be the fact that the polygraph is the only way the organization can get information about a significant job-related matter. They believe that a firm should not subject employees to polygraph tests without having first exhausted all other means of preventing pilferage.

3. We must be concerned with how the polygraph is being used, what information it's gathering, who has access to this information, and how it will be disposed of.

Responding to moral concerns about polygraphs as well as to their practical and statistical limitations, Congress has passed the Employee Polygraph Protection Act. It prohibits most private employers from using lie detectors in "preemployment testing." Private security firms are exempted from the law, along with drug companies, contractors with certain government agencies, and selected others. The law permits the use of polygraphs in "ongoing investigations of economic loss or injury," but it provides a number of procedural safeguards. For instance, the employer must explain the test's purpose to the employee and the reason why he or she was selected to take it. The worker also has a right to consult with someone who will explain the workings and limitations of the machine. Ultimately, the worker retains the option not to submit to the test, and no one can be fired on the basis of a lie-detector test "without other supporting evidence."

Personality Tests

Companies often wish to determine whether prospective employees are emotionally mature, get along well with others, and have a good work ethic, and whether they would fit in with the organization, so they sometimes administer personality tests. These tests can reveal highly personal information, and they often intrude into areas of our lives and thoughts that we normally consider private. Consent is usually less than fully voluntary because personality tests are generally part of a battery of tests that job applicants must take if they wish to be considered for a position.

Used properly, personality tests serve two purposes in the workplace. First, they help screen applicants for jobs by indicating areas of adequacy and inadequacy. Second, in theory they simplify the complexities of business life by reducing the amount of decision making involved in determining whether an individual has the personal characteristics appropriate for a given job. For example, if a firm knows that Wendy Constantine is an introvert, it would hardly place her in public relations.

But one key premise underlying such tests is questionable. That premise is that all individuals can usefully and validly be placed into a relatively small number of categories in terms of personality types and character traits. In fact, test designers typically believe that one's overall personality is shaped by only three to five factors and that these factors, which they seek to measure, account for "99 percent of the differences in human behavior."[26] However, people rarely represent pure personality types, such as the classic introvert or extrovert. Nor is the possession of a character trait an all-or-nothing thing. Most of us possess a variety of personality traits in various degrees, and social circumstances often influence the characteristics we display and the talents we develop. When organizations attempt to categorize employees, they oversimplify both human nature and their employees' potential and force people into artificial arrangements that may do justice neither to employees nor to the firms they work for.

Personality tests also screen for organizational compatibility, sometimes functioning to eliminate prospective employees whose individuality or creativity may be exactly what the firm needs. Some companies, for example, seek employees who are extremely submissive to authority. Thus, when writer Barbara Ehrenreich submitted to a personality test for a job at Wal-Mart, she was reprimanded for getting the "wrong" answer when she agreed only "strongly" with the proposition, "All rules have to be followed to the letter at all times." The correct answer was "totally agree."[27] When used this way, personality tests raise a pressing moral issue in the employer-employee relationship: conformity of the individual to organizational ideals. Organizations by nature represent a danger to individual freedom and independence. When personality tests are used to screen for conformity to organizational values, goals, and philosophy, they can catalyze this natural tendency into a full-blown assault.

Then, of course, there's the intrusive nature of the questions. Questions like "Does driving give you a sense of power?" "Do you like a lot of excitement in your life?" or "If you could, would you work as an entertainer in Las Vegas?" may seem innocuous, but what about a personality test that delves into your love life or that asks men, "Was there ever a time in your life when you liked to play with dolls?" One disgruntled test-taker complains about "questions you wouldn't even answer for your own mother, if she asked you."[28] Worse, many of the tests asking these questions have little or no research to back them up or have not been validated for use in preemployment situations. Even those who favor testing admit as much. John Kamp, an industrial psychologist, points out that even intelligent businesspeople can be swayed by a good marketing pitch from the companies that peddle invalid or unreliable tests. "That's the unfortunate thing," he says. "A person with a slick pitch and no real research behind their tests can have a good business."[29]

Monitoring Employees on the Job

In the past decade, most major employers have gained the technical ability to monitor the performance of their employees through the computers and telephones they use. In businesses with phone-in customers, the practice is especially prevalent as a way of ensuring better and more efficient service. The Electronic Communications Privacy Act of 1986 restricts the government from eavesdropping on your cellular car phone, email, computer-to-computer transmissions, or private video conferences, but it permits employers to intercept employee communications. Workers don't necessarily resent this monitoring, if it is in the open. "I don't think people mind having their work checked," says Morton Bahr, president of the Communications Workers of America. "It's the secretiveness of it" that bothers employees.[30]

According to the American Management Association, three-quarters of employers record employees' voice mail, email, or phone calls; review their computer files; or even videotape them—often without their knowledge.[31] Overseeing customer service is not the only reason companies monitor their employees. Some companies, for example, check employees' computers to see whether they exceed the allotted time for lunch or work breaks; others listen in on phone conversations and examine email messages to catch employees conducting personal business on company time. "What are they going to think up to do to us next?" wonders one employee. "It's scary. I'll bet no one monitors the phones or email of CEOs or other top executives."[32]

When in-house theft, sabotage, or other threatening conduct occurs, organizations frequently install monitoring devices—mirrors, cameras, and electronic recorders—to apprehend the employees who are responsible. But monitoring suspected trouble spots or private acts can create moral problems. Consider the two male employees of Boston Sheraton Hotel who were secretly videotaped changing clothes in the locker room during a hunt for a drug dealer. They weren't suspects, just bystanders.[33]

As with personality and polygraph tests, monitoring can gather information about employees without their informed consent. Organizations frequently confuse notification of such practices with employee consent, but notification does not constitute consent. When employee restrooms, dressing rooms, locker rooms, and other private places are bugged, an obvious and serious threat to privacy exists—posted notices notwithstanding. It's true that in some cases surveillance devices may be the only way to apprehend the guilty. Nevertheless, they can often do more harm than good by violating the privacy of the vast majority of innocent employees. Obviously, even more serious moral questions arise when monitoring devices are not used exclusively for the purposes intended but also for cajoling, harassing, or snooping on employees.

Drug Testing

Drug testing first became a live issue for some sports fans when the National Collegiate Athletic Association (NCAA) began banning college football players from postseason bowl competition based on the results of steroid testing. But for some years now, political and legal battles have been raging in all states over the drug testing of employees. Many companies have warmly embraced testing. Commonwealth Edison, for example, now routinely screens prospective employees for drug use. Its policy won support from a study published in the *Journal of the American Medical Association*, which showed that postal workers who tested positive for drug use in a preemployment urine test were at least 50 percent more likely to be fired, injured, disciplined, or absent than those who tested negative. Other companies, however, such as BankAmerica and AT&T, remain skeptical of the benefits of testing either current employees or job applicants.[34]

In principle, testing employees to determine whether they are using illegal drugs raises the same questions that other tests raise: Is there informed consent? How reliable are the tests? Is testing really pertinent to the job in question? Are the interests of the firm significant enough to justify encroaching on the privacy of the individual? But rather than reiterate these issues, all of which are important and relevant, this section limits itself to four additional remarks:

1. The issue of drug testing by corporations and other organizations arises in the broader context of the drug-abuse problem in America today (which includes the abuse not just of illegal street drugs but of alcohol and prescription medicines as well). To discuss this problem intelligently, one needs good information, reliable statistics, and sociological insight, yet these are difficult to come by. Popular newsmagazines run frequent and alarming cover stories on drugs, and hours of television news are given over to sensationalistic drug-related stories. Likewise, many politicians find it advantageous to portray themselves as battling courageously against a rising flood of drugs. Yet most of this media coverage and political hoopla is at best superficial, at worst misleading and even hysterical. This is not to minimize the problems that alcohol and drug abuse can pose for businesses and other oganizations. Such problems are real and serious even though the use of illegal drugs, at least, appears to have dropped significantly among workers since the mid-1980s. Rather, the point is that excessive media attention and political posturing can create a false sense of crisis, leading people perhaps to advocate extreme or unnecessary measures.

2. Drugs differ, so one must carefully consider both what drugs one is testing for and why. Steroids, for instance, are a problem for the NCAA but not for IBM. And it is difficult to believe that Ford Meter Box was warranted in urine testing employees for nicotine in order to root out smokers.[35] To be defensible, drug testing must be pertinent to employee performance and there must be a lot at stake. Testing airline pilots for alcohol consumption is one thing; testing the baggage handlers is something else. To go on a fishing trip in search of possible employee drug abuse, when there is no evidence of a problem or of significant danger, seems unreasonable.

3. Drug abuse by an individual is a serious problem, generally calling for medical and psychological assistance rather than punitive action. The moral assessment

of any program of drug testing must rest in part on the potential consequences for those taking the test: Will they face immediate dismissal and potential criminal proceedings, or therapy and a chance to retain their positions? To put the issue another way, when an organization initiates a testing program, does it approach this as a kind of police function? Or is it responsive to the needs and problems of individual employees? Some business writers argue that voluntary, nonpunitive drug-assistance programs are far more cost effective for companies, in any case, than testing initiatives.[36]

4. Any drug-testing program, assuming it is warranted, must be careful to respect the dignity and rights of the persons to be tested. Some alternatives to body fluid testing are less invasive of employee privacy. Due process must also be followed, including advance notification of testing as well as procedures for retesting and appealing test results. All possible steps should be taken to ensure individual privacy.

WORKING CONDITIONS

In a broad sense, the conditions under which people work include personnel policies and procedures, as well as the extent to which an organization is committed to respecting the rights and privacy of its employees. This section, however, examines three other aspects of working conditions: health and safety on the job, styles of management, and the organization's maternity and day-care arrangements.

Health and Safety

A Galveston grain elevator explodes, maiming a dozen workers; a southern poultry plant fire kills twenty-five workers; a methane explosion at a Kentucky mine leaves ten dead. These are dramatic episodes, and they gained national media coverage. And, of course, no American will forget the seven crew members who died when the space shuttle *Columbia* flew apart. By contrast, relatively little news coverage was given to the gasoline barge that exploded in New York harbor later that same month, killing two workers and maiming another, and the national media ignored altogether the deaths of twenty-one-year-old Dennis Claypool and eighteen-year-old Mark DeMoss, who suffocated to death working inside a tanker trailer at a trucking company outside Chicago. The two didn't know that the tanker had recently been cleaned with nitrogen, which removes oxygen from the air. A freak accident? Experts say some 300 workers a year die in such "confined space" incidents.[37]

Industrial accidents don't just happen. They are caused—by inadequate worker training, lack of understanding of the job, improper tools and equipment, hazardous work environments, poor equipment maintenance, and overly tight scheduling.[38] Many experts believe that workplace injuries are related to behavior, not to shortcomings in technology. The key to a safer workplace, says one risk management consultant, is not engineering, but changing the company's "hidden culture"—the "unspoken rules that are adhered to"—to one that is proactively oriented toward safety.[39]

Employees in fact have a legal right to refuse work when it exposes them to imminent danger, and their employers are forbidden to reprimand or otherwise retaliate against them for doing so. The U.S. Supreme Court made this clear when it upheld a lower court ruling in favor of two employees of the Whirlpool Corporation who had refused to follow their foreman's order to undertake maintenance activities they considered unsafe.[40] Although a number of states require companies to inform workers in writing of any life-threatening hazards, employees are often unaware of the dangers they face, many of which may be long-term, rather than imminent, hazards. Take the electronics industry, for example. It may look safe in comparison with many other occupations, but behind its clean, high-tech image lurk health hazards for workers—in particular, the chemical toxins that are indispensable to the manufacture of computer chips.[41]

Despite legislation, the scope of occupational hazards remains awesome and generally unrecognized. According to the Census Bureau, in a given year more than 5,000 workers are killed on the job.[42] The director of the Occupational Safety and Health Administration (OSHA) puts the figure higher. He says an average of thirty-two workers are killed on the job each day of the year in the United States.[43] Deaths are just part of the problem. Census Bureau statistics reveal that although the rate of industrial injury has been declining since 1960, the absolute number of workers disabled at work every year—approximately 3.9 million men and women—is greater than ever. Job-related injuries and illnesses cost the nation $65 billion a year—$171 billion when indirect costs such as lost wages are included.[44] And when we take into account health problems that stem not from specific, identifiable events on the job but rather from years of labor or from long-term exposure to hazardous substances, then the problem escapes reliable measurement.

OSHA With the 1970 Occupational Safety and Health Act the prime responsibility for regulating working conditions passed from the states to the federal government. The thrust of the act is "to ensure so far as possible every working man and woman in the nation safe and healthful working conditions," and it places a duty on employers to provide a workplace "free from recognized hazards that are causing or are likely to cause death or serious injury." In its early years, OSHA, created by the act, added to its own troubles by promulgating some rules that seemed trivial and nitpicking—for example, detailed guidelines regulating toilet seats and the belts to be worn by telephone line workers.[45] Fortunately, most of these rules have been repealed, but controversies have raged over how far OSHA should go in the cause of safety. The organization seeks to require only safeguards that are feasible; it has, for example, never attempted to entirely eliminate toxins in the workplace. But is "feasibility" to be understood in a broad economic and technological sense, or must the gains in safety outweigh the costs that particular companies must bear? And how are those costs and gains to be measured?

In any case, with limited resources and only a few thousand inspectors to monitor millions of workplaces, OSHA has always faced a daunting task, and its performance has been spotty. Worse, the relationship between OSHA and the businesses and industries it regulates has often been too cozy. Consider the case of Stephen Golab, a fifty-nine-year-old immigrant from Poland who worked for a year stirring tanks of sodium cyanide at the Film Recovery Services plant in Elk Grove, Illinois. One day he became dizzy from the cyanide fumes, went into convulsions, and died. OSHA then inspected the plant and fined Film Recovery Services $4,855 for twenty safety violations. OSHA subsequently cut the fine in half. In contrast, the state attorney general for Cook County filed criminal charges. Three company officials were convicted of murder and fourteen counts of reckless conduct. The company itself was also convicted of manslaughter and reckless conduct and was fined $24,000.

Since the Golab case, budget cuts have shrunk OSHA's staff further, and inspections and citations have dropped. At the same time Congress has pushed the agency from rule-making and enforcement to helping businesses comply with federal requirements. Critics call OSHA a "toothless tiger," which has moved from "beat cop to social worker."[46]

New Health Challenges   One problem that both OSHA and business will have to address in the future is the epidemic of occupational injury and illness known as musculoskeletal disorders. In offices and factories across the country, millions of workers suffer from aching backs, crippled fingers, sore wrists, and other problems caused or aggravated by their jobs. Carpal tunnel syndrome, low back pain, sciatica, tendinitis, and other musculoskeletal disorders account for one-third of all serious workplace injuries and cause more than 640,000 workers a year to miss time on the job.[47]

Telephone operators, court stenographers, and supermarket checkout clerks are just a few of the workers who must live with numb fingers, swollen knuckles, and aching wrists from the constant repetition of awkward hand and arm movements. The ailments in question may sound like minor complaints, but they are anything but trivial to those who suffer from them. Ask Janie Jue of San Francisco. For seventeen years she keyed in up to 48,000 strokes a day on an automatic letter-sorting machine for the post office. Today, just picking up a book or coffee pot sends bolts of pain tearing up her hand and arm. "I wish I could work," she says, "but it hurts from my elbow to my fingertips."[48] "For many years," remarks one expert, "it was just considered a cost of doing business. If you did certain jobs, you would end up with hands crippled at the end of your career. That's not acceptable in this country any more."[49]

The breaking up of jobs into smaller and smaller units, with each worker performing fewer tasks but repeating them thousands of times a day, has contributed to the problem in manufacturing industries. Garment workers, meat packers, and others in hand-intensive jobs used to be able to recover at night from the cumulative stress on their bodies, but increased assembly-line speed and piecework rates now make it more difficult for their bodies to bounce back the next day. Moreover, musculoskeletal disorders are rampant among white-collar office workers, who are supposedly in safe office jobs. Those who spend all day at the video display terminal risk developing tendinitis, carpal tunnel syndrome, and other hand, neck, or back ailments.

The redesign of jobs, adjustable chairs, training in the proper use of video display terminals, and other preventive measures can often reduce the problem. In the meantime, it is not only the employees who are suffering. Musculoskeletal disorders decrease productivity and dampen morale, and having a skilled worker go out on long-term disability and vocational rehabilitation can cost a company a small fortune.[50] Nevertheless, various employer groups and business lobbies continue to fight vigorously any step toward ergonomic regulation, even thwarting a 13-year effort by the National Safety Council to draft voluntary guidelines for preventing repetitive-motion injuries.[51]

One aspect of work life over which OSHA exercises little direct control is the shifts people work. Yet a team of scientists from Harvard and Stanford universities believes that the health and productivity of 25 million Americans whose work hours change regularly can be measurably improved if employers schedule shift changes to conform with the body's natural and adjustable sleep cycles. This is particularly important given that sleep deprivation and fatigue are prime causes of industrial accidents.[52] According to one expert, they cost Americans $100 billion a year in lost production, illnesses, absences, accidents, and death.[53] This fact makes worrisome the current trend in factory work toward shorter work weeks with longer weekdays (for example, four twelve-hour workdays, followed by three days off, then three twelve-hour workdays on followed by four days off), with employees alternating from day shifts one month to night shifts the next.[54]

Related to fatigue is an aspect of work life we have only recently begun to appreciate fully—the health implications of stress. Three-quarters of Americans say their jobs cause them stress.[55] One reason may be that the average American worker is logging more overtime and working more hours per week than at any time since the 1950s.[56] In fact, Americans put in longer hours on the job than do the workers of any other major industrialized nation.[57] And many of us complain about the pressure of excessive workloads.[58] Stressful job conditions diminish mental health and damage physical functioning as much as smoking does.[59] Revamping work environments that produce stress and helping employees learn to cope with stress are among the major health challenges facing American business now and in the years to come.

Management Styles

How managers conduct themselves on the job can do more to enhance or diminish the work environment than any other single facet of employer-employee relations. In survey after survey, employees rank honest company communications, personal recognition, and respectful treatment as more important than good pay. Unfortunately, according to a Columbia University psychologist, millions of workers suffer from bosses who are abusive, dictatorial, devious, dishonest, manipulative, and inhumane.[60]

This workplace reality runs contrary to the teachings of almost all management theorists. For example, in his classic work *The Human Side of Enterprise*, Douglas McGregor formulated Theory X to describe the management style premised on the belief that workers dislike work and will do everything they can to avoid it.[61] These managers insist that the average person wishes to avoid responsibility, lacks ambition, and values security over everything else. Accordingly, he or she must be coerced and bullied into conformity with organizational objectives. McGregor advocated Theory Y, which assumes that employees basically like work and view it as something natural and potentially enjoyable. Workers are seen as motivated as much by pride and a desire for self-fulfillment as by money and job security. They don't dodge responsibility but accept it and even seek it out.

Since McGregor's book, other management writers have pursued this line of thought and recommended countless other management styles—including Theory Z, which touts Japanese-style respect for workers. More recently, some theorists have advocated an alternative management style that eschews a masculine, hierarchical, aggressive, analytic, winner-take-all approach in favor of a more personal, empathetic, and collaborative style, thought to be characteristic of, and more congenial to, women. This is not the place to discuss different theories of management, but clearly the management styles recommended by different writers, as well as the management styles actually adopted by different bosses, rest on implicit or explicit assumptions about human nature.

However, no set of assumptions about human nature is absolutely correct or incorrect, nor is there one perfectly right way to manage. But that's precisely the point.

Problems inevitably arise when managers routinize their leadership style, regardless of the needs, abilities, and predilections of their particular employees. When managers ignore individual differences, they risk creating a work atmosphere that's distressing to workers and less productive than it might be. Moreover, implicit assumptions about human nature can easily become self-reinforcing because people tend to behave as they are treated. Thus, managers who treat employees as if they were incapable of taking initiative will probably end up with employees who don't take initiative. As a result managers must carefully examine their preconceptions when determining the most appropriate leadership style to adopt in their workplace.

Critics frequently charge that U.S. corporations are too bureaucratic—the United States has more managers per employee than any other industrial nation[62]—and that their managerial style is too conservative, traditional, and inflexible. Too many managers, it is alleged, put their personal ambition ahead of everything else. One such critic is H. Ross Perot. Perot became the largest shareholder in General Motors and a member of its corporate board when he sold his computer services company, Electronic Data Systems Corporation, to GM for $2.5 billion. Two years later GM ousted Perot from the board, buying back his GM stock for $700 million.

Why the buyback? Observers agree that the fiery Perot was more than GM could handle. Perot dared to question longstanding management practices; he talked to workers on the factory floor about new ideas; he shopped anonymously at GM dealerships, trying to evaluate customer service. All that was too much for GM. Under the buyback agreement, Perot isn't supposed to make negative comments about GM, but he does say the corporation is beset by power-hungry executives who spend all their time trying to move up the corporate ladder and care little about their product. "Corporate infighting," "management power struggles," "maneuvering and politics and power-grabbing," and "Machiavellian intrigues" are his phrases to describe the reality of corporate life today.[63]

We must be careful about generalizing from the experiences of one person in one company, but Perot's reports tally with too many others' to ignore what he says. Managers who devote their energies to corporate infighting and personal advancement and corporations that are too tradition-bound to handle strong criticism, even inside the boardroom itself, are real problems. Dealing with them is part of the economic challenge facing America today, as discussed in Chapter 4. But problems of management style also unfavorably affect employees' working conditions.

Day Care and Maternity Leave

One often overlooked area in discussions of working conditions is the provision of maternity/paternity leave and child-care services for workers with children. The need for both these things is steadily growing, as more and more women enter the paid labor force. Women's participation in the labor force has nearly doubled since 1960; today they constitute nearly half of it. In 1960 only 18.6 percent of married women with children under the age of six were in the paid labor force; today nearly two-thirds are.[64] And the number of families with a stay-at-home parent has slumped from 71 percent in 1960 to 28 percent today.[65] Despite these statistics, the United States lags behind many other industrialized nations in the provision of child care. These countries, unlike the United States, view child care as a national responsibility and publicly subsidize it. The situation is even more striking with respect to maternity leave. Approximately 120 other countries provide paid maternity leave whereas only unpaid leave is mandated in the U.S.—except in California, which began requiring paid family leave in 2004.

Given that women in our society continue to bear the primary responsibility for child rearing, their increasing participation in the paid workforce represents a growing demand for reasonable maternity-leave policies and affordable child-care services. Nor is this demand likely to diminish. Many families are unable to make satisfactory child-care arrangements, either because the services are unavailable or for the simple reason that the parents cannot afford them. An estimated 5 million children are thus left alone without any supervision while their parents work. The need for child-care services is particularly acute among single-parent families, 91 percent of which are headed by women. Single mothers have a higher rate of participation in the labor force than do married mothers. Nevertheless, many of them are too poor to pay for satisfactory child-care services.

Some companies try hard to help with employee child care.[66] Campbell Soup Co., for example, offers on-site day care, spending over $200,000 annually to subsidize 50 percent of tuition costs at the child-care center for the children of employees at corporate headquarters. Procter & Gamble holds priority rights for 75 percent of the spaces in two off-site centers near its Cincinnati headquarters. It also provides a day-care resource and referral service for the entire community. IBM provides a free nationwide referral system for its 267,000 employees and has helped develop child-care services where they have been deficient or lacking. Polaroid Corporation provides assistance with child-care costs for permanent employees earning less than $30,000. Because its employees work at all hours, America West Airlines provides 24-hour child care with a sliding scale subsidy to make it affordable. Goldman, Sachs, and Company, Time Warner, and Chase Manhattan Bank have opened child-care centers for employees whose regular child-care arrangements are temporarily disrupted. Despite these examples, the overall corporate record on child care is not all that impressive.

Employers are in a good position to assist in the provision of child-care services, especially in light of cutbacks in federal funding. Few if any employers, however, currently feel obligated to offer child-care services, primarily because initiating and maintaining such programs cost money. Yet viewed from a broader perspective, day-care arrangements set up by companies themselves or by several companies together in the same area are socially cost-effective. With in-house day-care arrangements, parents need not make special trips to pick up and drop off their children. Because the parents are not far away, they can have more interaction with their children. Depending on the specific organization of work and the firm's flexibility, parents could share in the actual running of the child-care facility at assigned intervals during the course of their working day. Hewlett-Packard took an innovative step in this regard when, in conjunction with the local school district, it set up kindergarten and first-grade classes on company grounds for the children of employees. Other companies are now doing the same thing.[67]

Some business writers have argued, moreover, that offering child care as a fringe benefit and dealing as flexibly as possible with employees' family needs can prove advantageous for most employers. Such policies can be cost-effective in the narrower sense by decreasing absenteeism, boosting morale and loyalty to the firm, and enhancing productivity. This is an important consideration.

Even more important are the underlying moral issues. First, women have a right to compete on an equal terrain with men. The legal requirement that firms with fifty or more workers provide at least unpaid maternity leave and reinstatement respects this right. Whether firms should also provide paid maternity leave is more controversial, although one might argue that paid leave is necessary to give substance to this right. Or one might defend such a policy on the utilitarian ground that it would enhance total social welfare. In fact, many organizations find it in their self-interest to provide paid leave so they can attract better and more talented employees. On the other hand, the trend toward tough performance standards and no-fault absence policies can penalize workers for missing work regardless of the reason. A person's performance appraisal, year-end raise, or bonus can be affected by his or her taking a legally protected, unpaid family leave.[68]

Second, from various ethical perspectives, the development of our potential capacities is a moral ideal—perhaps even a human right. For this reason, or from the point of view of promoting human well-being, many theorists would contend that women should not be forced to choose between childbearing and the successful pursuit of their careers. Nor should they be forced to reduce the quality of their commitment either to their children or to their careers. If employment circumstances force them to do so, and if those circumstances could reasonably be changed, then we have not lived up to the ideal of treating those women as persons whose goals are worthy of respect.

Third, although the past two or so decades have seen many criticisms of, and attempts to move beyond, the traditional male-female division of labor within the family, there can be little doubt that the world of work tends to reproduce those patterns. For instance, as mentioned in Chapter 6, men who leave work to help raise children often face enormous hurdles when returning to the job market. It seems clear that many fathers today feel hampered by work arrangements that pit meaningful career advancement against a fully developed family life. Enhanced opportunities for part-time employment and job sharing, along with generous parental leave arrangements and flexible, affordable, and accessible firm-sponsored child-care facilities, could enable both fathers and mothers to achieve a more personally desirable balance between paid work and family relations.

The moral value here is not to promote any single vision of the good life but rather to permit individuals, couples, and families as much autonomy as possible, given other social goals. They should be able to define the good life for themselves and to seek the arrangement of work and personal relations that makes that life possible. Firm-affiliated child-care services and other institutional arrangements that accommodate parental needs can clearly play a key role in the overall redesigning of work to enhance workers' well-being.

REDESIGNING WORK

Chapter 4 looked at alienation under capitalism and changing attitudes toward work in America. It remains true that many, perhaps even most, employees are dissatisfied with their jobs to some extent. Any investigation of the moral issues arising around the workplace and any discussion of the challenges facing business today must confront this basic problem and consider ways of improving the quality of work life.

Dissatisfaction on the Job

In the early 1970s the federal government conducted a major study of work in America, the basic findings of which are still relevant today.[69] The study identified three chief sources of worker dissatisfaction. The first concerned industry's preoccupation with quantity, not quality; the rigidity of rules and regulations; and the fracturing of work into the smallest possible tasks, together with the monotonous repetition of these tasks. The second source of dissatisfaction concerned the lack of opportunities to be one's own boss. The third source of dissatisfaction concerned "bigness": More people work for large corporations now than ever before. Other studies since then have cited workers' feelings of powerlessness, meaninglessness, isolation, and self-estrangement or depersonalization.

The *Work in America* survey reported similar feelings in the managerial ranks. One out of three middle managers at that time was willing to join a union. Moreover, just as industrial workers voiced general complaints about work, so did middle managers. Some objected to the little influence they had in their organizations, and others objected to the organization's goals, policies, and ways of operating. Still other managers complained about tension, frustration, and infighting that intraorganizational competition can breed. Beyond these complaints, the *Work in America* survey reported that many managers felt like cogs in a machine, like parts that could and would be replaced when a better part came along.

Other studies confirm that workers at all occupational levels express dissatisfaction with employer policies and practices and with the behavior of top management.[70] If industry is to improve productive capacity and be more competitive, it must seriously confront these attitudes and the sources of employee dissatisfaction. It must devise ways to make work more satisfying and to improve the quality of work life.

As early as the 1920s, researchers began to realize that workers would be more productive if management met those needs that money cannot buy. Managers at the Hawthorne factory of Western Electric Company were conducting experiments to determine the effect of the work environment on worker productivity. In the literature of work motivation, these studies have become known as the Hawthorne studies. What they discovered has been termed the "Hawthorne effect."

Researchers in the Hawthorne studies chose a few employees to work in an experimental area, apart from the thousands of employees in the rest of the factory. Every effort was made to improve working conditions, from painting walls a cheerful color to making lights brighter. Worker productivity increased with each improvement. Then the experimenters decided to reverse the process. For example, lights were made dimmer. To everyone's surprise, productivity continued to increase.

The conclusion the researchers drew was that workers were producing more because they were receiving attention. Instead of feeling that they were spokes in an organizational wheel, they felt important and recognized. The attention had the effect of heightening their sense of personal identity and feeling of control over their work environment. Recognition of this effect can help management increase worker motivation and job satisfaction and also increase the organization's productivity.

Subsequent research corroborates and deepens the Hawthorne results.[71] In studying the problem of poor worker motivation, the influential management theorist Frederick Herzberg discovered that factors producing job satisfaction differed from those producing job dissatisfaction. Herzberg found that although job dissatisfaction frequently arises from extrinsic problems (such as pay, supervision, working conditions, and leadership styles), resolving those extrinsic problems does not necessarily produce satisfied workers. They can still express little or no job satisfaction. The reason, Herzberg contends, is that worker satisfaction depends on such factors as a sense of accomplishment, responsibility, recognition, self-development, and self-expression.[72] Recent surveys add support to Herzberg's findings. When employees at all occupational levels are asked to rank what is important to them, they list interesting work; sufficient help, support, and information to accomplish the job; enough authority to carry out the work; good pay; the opportunity to develop special skills; job security; and a chance to see the results of their work.

Numerous mental health problems stem from a lack of job satisfaction—low self-esteem, anxiety, impaired interpersonal relations, and psychosomatic ailments such as ulcers and hypertension—especially in low-status, boring, unchallenging jobs that offer little autonomy. Furthermore, such jobs tend to inhibit intellectual growth and the pursuit of richer, more fulfilling activities outside work.[73] Even worse, researchers have found that workers in boring, passive jobs are 33 to 35 percent more likely to die prematurely than workers in active jobs. Stressful work that offers little decision-making opportunity (like assembly-line work) makes an untimely demise even more likely.[74] These findings are of particular relevance to today's workforce, in which many persons of relatively high educational achievement occupy comparatively low-status jobs.

One of the most intriguing studies not only suggests a correlation between longevity and job satisfaction but also contends that job satisfaction is the strongest predictor of longevity.[75] The second major factor for longevity is happiness. Both of these factors predict longevity better than either the physical health or genetic inheritance of individuals.

Because the design of work materially affects the total well-being of workers, work content and job satisfaction are paramount moral concerns. But if we also assume that a happier, more contented worker is generally a more productive one, then it follows that business has an economic reason as well as a moral obligation to devise ways, in concert with labor and perhaps even government, to improve the quality of work life (QWL).

Quality of Work Life (QWL)

This book isn't the place for determining precisely what QWL measures firms should take. For some firms QWL may mean providing workers with less supervision and more autonomy. For others it may mean providing work opportunities to develop and refine skills. Still other firms might try to provide workers with greater participation in the conception, design, and execution of their work—that is, with greater responsibility and a deeper sense of achievement. Perhaps all companies ought to examine the impact of technology on job satisfaction. While typically increasing the efficiency of operations and eliminating the physical drudgery that plagued yesterday's workers, today's technology sometimes results in repetitive and boring tasks that, in the long run, may destroy job satisfaction and diminish productivity.

QWL programs can thaw the antagonistic worker-boss climate that exists in many plants, but the only way management can implement such programs is with the full cooperation of workers and their representatives, and some union members are a little wary. "The largest loss is the union's autonomy," says one.[76] "We become one with the corporate agenda. It's an unnatural place for the union to be." Investigators believe that the success of QWL programs and other workplace reform efforts depends on the ability of the organization to reinforce high levels of trust. To the extent that it does so, organizational performance can improve. But, warns William Cooke, professor at Wayne State University and author of a book on workplace reform, "if [workers] perceive management as doing this without due consideration for the welfare of employees . . . it will have the potential of destroying the efforts altogether."[77]

Granting workers new responsibilities and respect can benefit the entire organization. Randy Pennington, vice president of Performance Systems Corporation, tells of a friend who showed an ad for a new American car to a Japanese businessperson. The ad said that the car "set a new standard for quality because it was examined by 34 different quality inspectors." "Now, *this*," he said to his Japanese colleague, "is what we need to compete with you. Imagine: 34 quality inspectors!" The Japanese looked at the ad, smiled, and said, "You don't need 34 inspectors to get quality. You just need everyone who works on the car to be proud of the work. Then you'll need only one inspector."[78]

Today, closer union-management relations characterize many GM plants. Mike Spitzley, manager of GM's 5,300-worker car-truck plant in Janesville, Wisconsin, for example, says "most of the things we talk about, it's 'we.' It's not us versus them. We've pretty much realized that our goals are the same" as the union's. Mike O'Brien, president of the local chapter of the United Auto Workers, agrees. "There's something different going on," he says. "Years ago, it wasn't any of our business what went on in the business." The most striking example is GM's Saturn Corporation, where union and management share all big decisions, from choosing suppliers to picking the company's advertising agency.[79]

At GM, the ideals of improved job atmosphere, employee participation, and worker job security have meshed nicely with the goal of increased productivity. Studies provide evidence of this compatibility in many other cases, too. Not only is productivity 5 to 10 percent higher in companies with profit sharing, but productivity is also consistently higher in enterprises with an organized program of worker participation.[80] In the car industry, the key to success has been shown to be people, not robots or high-tech automation.[81] At United Airlines, cooperation, efficiency, and market share increased when employees bought 55 percent of the company.[82] In fact, compensation for top executives at the airline is now tied to worker satisfaction as measured by an outside survey firm.[83] This is in line with the views of many experts, who insist that worker-friendly companies outperform traditional command-and-control employers. They argue that new organizational structures and work practices that put a premium on collaboration and cooperation are fundamental to the nation's future economic success.[84]

Although a range of social and economic research supports this conclusion, there is no water-tight guarantee that worker participation and an improved quality of work life will always boost productivity; sometimes an apparent QWL improvement can lead to a decrease in productivity. For example, although diversifying tasks may make work more satisfying, it might hurt productivity or quality. Japanese carmakers, to cite one case, have effectively reduced the number of rejects on their assembly line, not by diversifying, but by standardizing the cars produced. Again, Volkswagen has found that its productivity and quality were higher when production consisted solely of the standard Rabbit than when other models were introduced. Job-enlargement programs, by definition, add to the variety of tasks the worker is assigned; job-enrichment programs add some planning, designing, and scheduling to the operative worker's tasks. Both programs can tax the abilities of workers and in some cases may slow output and bruise quality. Worker involvement in production management may not fit well, some argue, with the two other ingredients that managers and management consultants see as essential for manufacturing efficiency: a just-in-time approach to eliminating waste and rigorous statistical process control to improve quality.

On the other hand, employee involvement is essential to work elimination programs—programs that eliminate wasteful and unnecessary tasks, thus enhancing job satisfaction while making the organization leaner and more productive.[85] This is particularly important as competition pressures manufacturers in the car industry and elsewhere to move to smaller, more flexible factories.[86] Still, the possibility of a conflict between the obligation to make work more satisfying and the goal of increasing productivity will likely be at the heart of moral decisions in this area for years to come. To resolve them will require a cooperative effort by labor and management, rooted in the recognition that trade-offs are inevitable.

SUMMARY

1. Individuals have a right to privacy, in particular a right to make personal decisions autonomously, free from illegitimate influence. Whenever an organization infringes on an individual's personal sphere, it must justify that infringement.

2. A firm is legitimately interested in whatever significantly influences job performance, but there is no precise definition of "significant influence." Organizations may be invading privacy when they coerce employees to contribute to charities, do volunteer work, or participate in wellness programs or in so-called intensive group experiences.

3. Information-gathering on employees can be highly personal and subject to abuse. The critical issue here is *informed consent*, which implies deliberation and free choice. Deliberation requires that employees be provided all significant facts concerning the information-gathering procedure and understand their consequences. Free choice means that the decision to participate must be voluntary and uncoerced.

4. Polygraph tests, personality tests, drug tests, and the monitoring of employees on the job can intrude into employee privacy. The exact character of these devices, the rationale for using them to gather information in specific circumstances, and the moral costs of doing so must always be carefully evaluated.

5. Health and safety remain of foremost moral concern in the workplace. The scope of occupational hazards, including shift work and stress, and the number of employees harmed by work-related injuries and diseases are greater than many people think. Enforcement of existing regulations has too often been lax.

6. Management style greatly affects the work environment. Managers who operate with rigid assumptions about human nature or who devote themselves to infighting and political maneuvering damage employees' interests.

7. Day-care services and reasonable parental-leave policies also affect working conditions. Despite the genuine need for and the ethical importance of both day care and flexible work arrangements for parents, only a handful of companies makes serious efforts to provide them.

8. Studies report extensive job dissatisfaction at all levels. Various factors influence satisfaction and dissatisfaction on the job. Redesigning the work process can enhance the quality of work life, the well-being of workers, and even productivity.

CASE 7.1

Testing for Honesty

"Charity begins at home." If you don't think so, ask the Salvation Army. Some years ago, one of the Army's local branches discovered that it had a problem with theft among its kettle workers, the people who collect money for the Army during the Christmas season. Some of the Army's kettlers were helping themselves to the Army's loot before the organization had a chance to dole it out. To put a stop to the problem, Army officials sought the assistance of Dr. John Jones, director of research for London House Management Consultants.

London House is one of several companies that market honesty tests for prospective employees. Some of these tests, such as London House's Personnel Selection Inventory (PSI), also measure the applicant's tendency toward drug use and violence. All three categories—honesty, drugs, and violence—play a major part in company losses, according to the makers of these tests.

The company losses in question are astronomical. The U.S. Chamber of Commerce estimates that employee theft costs U.S. companies $40 billion annually; some unofficial estimates run three times as high. Moreover, 20 percent of the businesses that fail do so because of employee crime.[87] Compounding the problem is the cost of employee drug use in terms of absenteeism, lost initiative, inattentiveness, accidents, and diminished productivity. Employee violence also costs companies millions of dollars in damage, lost productivity, and lawsuits.

Honesty-test makers say that the only way to deal with these problems is before workers are hired, not after—by subjecting them to a preemployment psychological test that will identify those prospective employees who will be likely to steal, who have a history of violence or emotional instability, or who have used illegal drugs on a regular basis.

James Walls, one of the founders of Stanton Corporation, which has offered written honesty tests for twenty-five years, says that dishonest job applicants are clever at hoodwinking potential employers in a job interview. "They have a way of conducting themselves that is probably superior to the low-risk person. They have learned what it takes to be accepted and how to overcome the normal interview strategy," he says. "The high-risk person will get hired unless there is a way to screen him." For this reason, Walls maintains, written, objective tests are needed to weed out the crooks.[88]

Millions of written honesty tests are given annually. Since 1988 demand has been booming as a result of congressional restrictions on polygraph testing, which prohibit about 85 percent of applicant and employee polygraph testing in the United States. As a result, purveyors of written tests have also been in high demand: The British Maxwell Communication Corporation, for instance, spent $17.4 million to acquire London House; Business Risk International took over the Stanton Corporation; and Wackenhut Corporation of Coral Gables, Florida, acquired marketing rights to the Phase II Profile, a widely used honesty test.[89]

In addition to being legal, honesty tests are also more economical than polygraph tests. They cost between $7 and $14 per test, compared with $90 or so for a polygraph. Furthermore, the tests are easily administered at the workplace by a staff member to any category of worker, are easily and quickly evaluated by the test maker, and assess the applicant's overall answers rather than a few isolated responses. The tests are also nondiscriminatory. The Equal Employment Opportunity Commission's "Uniform Guidelines on Employee Selection Procedures" (1978) permits tests that measure psychological traits because the race, gender, or ethnicity of applicants has no significant impact on scores.[90]

A typical test begins with some cautionary remarks. Test-takers are told to be truthful because dishonesty can be detected, and they are warned that incomplete answers will be considered incorrect, as will any unanswered questions. Then applicants ordinarily sign a waiver permitting the results to be known to their prospective employer and authorizing the testing agency to check out their answers. Sometimes, however, prospective employees are not told that they are being tested for honesty, only that they are being asked questions about their background. James Walls justifies this less-than-frank explanation by saying that within a few questions it is obvious that the test deals with attitudes toward honesty. "The test is very transparent, it's not subtle."[91]

Some questions do indeed seem transparent—for example, "If you found $100 that was lost by a bank truck on the street yesterday, would you turn the money over to the bank, even though you knew for sure there was no reward?" But other questions are more controversial: "Have you ever had an argument with someone and later wished you had said something else?" If you were to answer no, you would be on your way to failing. Other questions that may face the test-taker are: "How strong is your conscience?" "How often do you feel guilty?" "Do you always tell the truth?" "Do you occasionally have thoughts you wouldn't want made public?" "Does everyone steal a little?" "Do you enjoy stories of successful crimes?" "Have you ever been so intrigued by the cleverness of a thief that you hoped the person would escape detection?" Or consider questions like "Is an employee who takes it easy at work cheating his employer?" or "Do you think a person should be fired by a company if it is found that he helped employees cheat the company out of overtime once in a while?" These ask you for your reaction to hypothetical dishonest situations. "If you are a particularly kind-hearted person who isn't sufficiently punitive, you fail," says Lewis Maltby, director of the workplace rights office at the American Civil Liberties Union. "Mother Teresa would never pass some of these tests."[92]

A big part of some tests is a behavioral history of the applicant. Applicants are asked to reveal the nature, frequency, and quantity of specific drug use, if any. They also must indicate if they have ever engaged in drunk driving, illegal gambling, traffic violations, forgery, vandalism, and a host of other unseemly behaviors. They must also state their opinions about the social acceptability of drinking alcohol and using other drugs.

Some testing companies go further in this direction. Instead of honesty exams, they offer tests designed to draw a general psychological profile of the applicant, claiming that this sort of analysis can predict more accurately than either the polygraph or the typical honesty test how the person will perform on the job. Keith M. Halperin, a psychologist with Personnel Decision, Inc. (PDI), a company that offers such tests, complains that most paper-and-pencil honesty tests are simply written equivalents of the polygraph. They ask applicants whether they have stolen from their employers, how much they have taken, and other questions directly related to honesty. But why, asks Halperin, "would an applicant who is dishonest enough to steal from an employer be honest enough to admit it on a written test?" It is more difficult for applicants to fake their responses to PDI's tests, Halperin contends.[93]

Not everyone is persuaded. Phyllis Bassett, vice-president of James Bassett Company of Cincinnati, believes tests developed by psychologists that do not ask directly about the applicant's past honesty are poor predictors of future trustworthiness.[94] This may be because, as some psychologists report, "it is very difficult for dishonest people to fake honesty." One reason is that thieves tend to believe that "everybody does it" and that therefore it would be implausible for them to deny stealing.[95] In general, those who market honesty exams boast of their validity and reliability, as established by field studies. They insist that the tests do make a difference, that they enable employers to ferret out potential troublemakers—as in the Salvation Army case.

Dr. Jones administered London House's PSI to eighty kettler applicants, which happened to be the number that the particular theft-ridden center needed. The PSIs were not scored, and the eighty applicants were hired with no screening. Throughout the fund-raising month between Thanksgiving and Christmas, the center kept a record of each kettler's daily receipts. After the Christmas season, the tests were scored and divided into "recommended" and "not recommended" for employment. After accounting for the peculiarities of each collection neighborhood, Jones discovered that those kettlers the PSI had not recommended turned in on the average $17 per day less than those the PSI had recommended. Based on this analysis, he estimated the center's loss to employee theft during the fund drive at $20,000.

The list of psychological-test enthusiasts is growing by leaps and bounds, but the tests have plenty of detractors. Many psychologists have voiced concern over the lack of standards governing the tests; the American Psychological Association favors the establishment of federal standards for written honesty exams. But the chief critics of honesty and other psychological exams are the people who have to take them. They complain about having to reveal some of the most intimate details of their lives and opinions.

For example, until an employee filed suit, Rent-A-Center, a Texas corporation, asked both job applicants and employees being considered for promotion true-false questions like these: "I have never indulged in any unusual sex practices," "I am very strongly attracted by members of my own sex," "I go to church almost every week," and "I have difficulty in starting or holding my bowel movements." A manager who was fired for complaining about the test says, "It was ridiculous. The test asked if I loved tall women. How was I supposed to answer that? My wife is 5 feet 3 inches." A spokesman for Rent-A-Center argues that its questionnaire is not unusual and that many other firms use it.[96]

Firms who use tests like Rent-A-Center's believe that no one's privacy is being invaded because employees and job applicants can always refuse to take the test. Critics disagree. "Given the unequal bargaining power," says former ACLU official Kathleen Bailey, "the ability to refuse to take a test is one of theory rather than choice—if one really wants the job."[97]

Discussion Questions

1. Describe how you'd feel having to take a psychological test or an honesty test either as an employee or as a precondition for employment. Under what conditions, if any, would you take such a test?

2. How useful do you think such tests are? Assuming that tests like those described are valid and reliable, are they fair? Explain.

3. Do you think tests like these invade privacy? Explain why or why not.

4. What ideals, obligations, and effects must be considered in using psychological tests as preemployment screens? In your view, which is the most important consideration?

5. If you were an employer, would you require either employees or job applicants to pass an honesty exam? Explain the moral principles that support your position.

6. What do you think a business's reaction would be if the government required its executive officers to submit to a personality test as a precondition for the company's getting a government contract? The tests would probe attitudes about questionable business practices, such as bribery, product misrepresentation, unfair competition, and so forth. If, in your opinion, the business would object, does it have any moral grounds for subjecting workers to comparable tests?

7. Utilitarians would not find anything inherently objectionable about psychological tests as long as the interests of all parties are taken into account and given equal consideration before such tests are made a preemployment screen. Do you think this is generally the case?

8. Should there be a law prohibiting or regulating psychological tests as a preemployment screen? Should a decision to use these tests be made jointly by management and labor, or is testing for employment an exclusive employer right?

CASE 7.2

She Snoops to Conquer

Jean Fanuchi, manager of a moderately large department store, was worried. Shrinkage in the costume jewelry department had continued to rise for the third consecutive month. In fact, this time it had nearly wiped out the department's net profit in sales. Worse, it couldn't be attributed to damage or improper handling of markdowns or even to shoplifting. The only other possibility was in-house theft.

Fanuchi ordered chief of security Matt Katwalski to instruct his security people to keep a special eye on jewelry department employees as they went about their business. She also instructed that packages, purses, and other containers employees carried with them be searched when workers left the store. When these measures failed to turn up any leads, Katwalski suggested they hire a couple of plainclothes officers to observe the store's guards. Fanuchi agreed. But still nothing turned up.

"We're going to have to install a hidden camera at the checkout station in the jewelry department," Katwalski informed the manager.

"I don't know," Fanuchi replied.

"Of course," said Katwalski, "it won't be cheap. But you don't want this problem spreading to other departments, do you?" Fanuchi didn't.

"One other thing," Katwalski said. "I think we should install some microphones in the restroom, stockroom, and employee lounge."

"You mean snoop on our own employees?" Fanuchi asked, surprised.

"We could pick up something that could crack this thing wide open," Katwalski explained.

"But what if our employees found out? How would they feel, being spied on? And then there's the public to consider. Who knows how they'd react? Why, they'd probably think that if we are spying on our own workers, we were surely spying on them. No, Matt," Fanuchi decided. "Frankly, this whole approach troubles me."

"Okay, Ms. Fanuchi, but if it was my store . . ."

Fanuchi cut in, "No."

"You're the boss," said Katwalski.

When the shrinkage continued, Fanuchi finally gave in. She ordered Katwalski to have the camera and microphones installed. Within ten days the camera had nabbed the culprit.

The microphones contributed nothing to the apprehension of the thief. But because of them Fanuchi and Katwalski learned that at least one store employee was selling marijuana and perhaps hard drugs, that one was planning to quit without notice, that three were taking food stamps fraudulently, and that one buyer was out to discredit Fanuchi. In solving their shrinkage problem, the pair had unwittingly raised another: What should they do with the information they had gathered while catching the thief?[98]

Discussion Questions

1. If you were Jean Fanuchi, how would you feel about your decision to order the installation of the viewing and listening devices? What other options did she have? Did she overlook any moral considerations or possible consequences?

2. Do employees have a right not to be spied on? If you were an employee at Fanuchi's store, would you think your privacy had been wrongly invaded?

3. How would you assess Fanuchi's actions if you were the owner of the store? Whose interests are more important in this case—the employer's or the employees'?

4. Do you think Fanuchi acted immorally? Why or why not? Evaluate her action by appeal to ethical principles.

5. How should Fanuchi and Katwalski handle the information they've gathered about their employees? Explain by appealing to relevant ideals, obligations, and effects.

CASE 7.3

Protecting the Unborn at Work

The unobtrusive factory sits behind a hillside shopping center in the small college town of Bennington, Vermont. The workers there make lead automobile batteries for Sears, Goodyear, and other companies. Of the 280 workers employed there a decade or so ago, only twelve were women, none of whom was able to have children. The company, Johnson Controls, Inc., refused to hire any who could.[99]

Why? Because tiny toxic particles of lead and lead oxide fill the air inside the plant. According to the company, the levels of lead are low enough for adults, but too high for children and fetuses. Numerous scientific studies have shown that lead can damage the brain and central nervous system of a fetus; moreover, lead lingers in the bloodstream, which means that fetuses can be affected by it even if a woman limits her exposure to lead once she learns she is pregnant. Because of this, Johnson Controls decided that it would exclude women at all fourteen of its factories from jobs that entail high exposure to lead—unless they could prove that they couldn't become pregnant.

The company made no exceptions for celibate women or women who used contraceptives. The company's position was simple: "The issue is protecting the health of unborn children."

Johnson Controls's stance was in line with the National Centers for Disease Control's recommendation that women of childbearing age be excluded from jobs involving significant lead exposure. Because by law its standards must be "feasible," Occupational Safety and Health Administration (OSHA) regulations permit chemicals in the workplace that are known to cause harm both to fetuses and to some adult employees. But OSHA holds that employers have a general duty to reduce the hazards of the workplace as far as possible. On this basis, employers such as Olin Corporation, American Cyanamid, General Motors, Monsanto, Allied Chemical, Gulf Oil, and B. F. Goodrich also adopted policies excluding women from chemical plant jobs judged to be hazardous to their potential offspring.

Scientific studies of the effect of exposure to toxic manufacturing chemicals on workers' reproductive health are, unfortunately, few. Only a small percentage of the workplace chemicals with a potential for damaging reproduction have been evaluated, and each year many new chemicals are introduced into factories. Although employers are obviously dealing with many unknowns, no one doubts that they have a moral and legal obligation to control and limit these risks as best they can. Lawsuits and even criminal sanctions have battered companies that have managed hazardous chemicals irresponsibly. Monsanto Chemical Company, for example, agreed to pay $1.5 million to six employees because exposure to a chemical additive used for rubber production allegedly gave them bladder cancer. Fetal protection policies aren't just dictated by management, though. "Women who become pregnant," the *New York Times* reports, "are beginning to demand the right to transfer out of jobs they believe to be hazardous, even when there is only sketchy scientific evidence of any hazard."

But many women were unhappy about the decision of Johnson Controls. They worried that fetal protection policies would be used to exclude women from more and more workplaces on the grounds that different chemical substances or certain tasks such as heavy lifting might be potential causes of miscarriage and fetal injury. In line with this, the United Automobile Workers, which represents many of the Johnson employees, sought to overturn the U.S. Court of Appeals decision that judged Johnson's policy to be "reasonably necessary to the industrial safety-based concern of protecting the unborn child from lead exposure." The union contends, to the contrary, that the policy discriminates against women, jeopardizing their hard-won gains in male-dominated industries.

Many women's advocates see the issue in slightly different terms. They believe policies like that of Johnson Controls challenge a woman's right not only to control her fetus, but to control her unfertilized eggs as well. In addition, such policies infringe on privacy: By taking a job at Johnson, a woman was in effect telling the world that she was sterile. And there is also the fundamental question of who knows what is best for a woman.

After bearing two children, Cheryl Chalifoux had a doctor block her fallopian tubes so that she couldn't become pregnant again. Although career advancement wasn't the reason she made her decision, it did enable her to switch from a factory job paying $6.34 an hour to one at Johnson's Bennington plant paying $15 an hour.

Still, she says that the policy was unfair and degrading. "It's your body," she complains. "They're implying they're doing it for your own good." Cheryl Cook, also a mother of two who had surgery for the same reason, joined Chalifoux in leaving the other company to work for Johnson Controls. She says, "I work right in the lead. I make the oxide. But you should choose for yourself. Myself, I wouldn't go in there if I could get pregnant. But they don't trust you."

Isabelle Katz Pizler, director of women's rights at the American Civil Liberties Union, agrees. "Since time immemorial," she says, "the excuse for keeping women in their place has been because of their role in producing the next generation. The attitude of Johnson Controls is: 'We know better than you. We can't allow women to make this decision. We have to make it for them.'" And the ACLU has argued in court that "since no activity is risk-free, deference to an employer's analysis of fetal risk could limit women's participation in nearly every area of economic life."

To this the company responded that it has a moral obligation to the parties that cannot participate in the woman's decisions—namely, the unfertilized ovum and the fetus. In addition, the company has an obligation to stockholders, who would bear the brunt of lawsuits brought by employees' children born with retardation, nervous system disorders, or other disorders that lead can cause.

Joseph A. Kinney, executive director of the National Safe Workplace Institute in Chicago, sides with Johnson Controls, but only because he believes that letting women assume the burden of their safety undermines OSHA's responsibility to mandate workplace safety rules. "The discrimination side of the issue needs to be resolved," Kinney says. "But the ideal thing is to regulate lead out of the workplace and any other toxin that poses fetal damage."

However, the U.S. Supreme Court has ruled unanimously that the fetal protection policy at Johnson Controls violated the Civil Rights Act of 1964, which prohibits sex discrimination in employment.[100] Pointing to evidence that lead affects sperm and can thus harm the offspring of men exposed to it at the time of conception, the Court stated:

> Respondent does not seek to protect the unconceived children of all its employees. Despite evidence in the record about the debilitating effect of lead exposure on the male reproductive system, Johnson Controls is concerned only with the harms that may befall the unborn offspring of its female employees. . . . [The company's policy is] discriminatory because it requires only a female employee to produce proof that she is not capable of reproducing.

On the other hand, the Court was divided over whether fetal protection policies could ever be legally justified. Justice Harry A. Blackmun, writing for a majority of the Court, declared that they could not, that the Civil Rights Act prohibited all such policies:

> Decisions about the welfare of future children must be left to the parents who conceive, bear, support and raise them rather than to the employers who hire those parents. Women as capable of doing their jobs as their male counterparts may not be forced to choose between having a child and having a job.

Referring to the Pregnancy Discrimination Act of 1978, which amended the 1964 Civil Rights Act and prohibits employment discrimination on the basis of pregnancy or potential pregnancy, Blackmun added:

Employment late in pregnancy often imposes risks on the unborn child, but Congress indicated that the employer may take into account only the woman's ability to get her job done.

A minority of the justices, however, were unwilling to go so far, and in a concurring opinion, Justice Byron R. White wrote that "common sense tells us that it is part of the normal operation of business concerns to avoid causing injury to third parties as well as to employees." But he added that, in his view, a fetal protection policy would not be defensible unless an employer also addressed other known occupational health risks.

Discussion Questions

1. Do you agree that Johnson Controls's fetal protection policy discriminated against women? Do pregnant women have a moral—not just a legal—right to work with lead?

2. Suppose exposure to lead did not affect sperm or the male reproductive system. Would Johnson's policy still have been discriminatory? Would it hamper women's efforts to win equality in the workplace?

3. Can there be a nondiscriminatory fetal protection policy? Is Justice White correct in arguing that companies have an obligation to avoid causing injury to fetuses just as they do other "third parties"?

4. Suppose a company forbids any employee capable of reproducing from working with lead. Would such a policy wrongly interfere with employees' freedom of choice? Would it be an invasion of their privacy? Would it be fair to employees who are fertile but plan to have no children?

5. Evaluate fetal protection policies from the egoistic, utilitarian, and Kantian perspectives. What rights are involved? What are the likely benefits and harms of such policies?

6. Assuming they are fully informed, do employees with a certain medical condition have a right to work at jobs that can be hazardous to the health of people in their condition? Or can company policy or OSHA regulations justifiably prevent them from doing so for their own good?

7. Would you agree with Joseph Kinney that the real issue is to remove toxins from the workplace? Is this a realistic goal?

CASE 7.4

The Mommy Track

"The cost of employing women in management is greater than the cost of employing men. This is a jarring statement, partly because it is true, but mostly because it is something people are reluctant to talk about." So begins a provocative article by Felice N. Schwartz.[101] Schwartz goes on to contend that the rate of turnover in management positions is two-and-a-half times higher among top-performing women than it is among men. Moreover, one-half of the women who take maternity leave return to their jobs late or not at all. "We know that women also have a greater tendency to plateau or to interrupt their careers," she writes. "But we have become so sensitive to charges of sexism and so afraid of confrontation, even litigation, that we rarely say what we know to be true."

Schwartz's article exploded like a bombshell. What really upset her critics was the distinction Schwartz drew between two types of women: the career-primary woman and the career-and-family woman.[102] Those in the first category put their careers first. They remain single or childless, or if they do have children, they are satisfied to have others raise them. The automatic association of all women with babies is unfair to these women, according to Schwartz—after all, some 90 percent of executive men but only 35 percent of executive women have children by age forty. "The secret to dealing with such women," Schwartz writes, "is to recognize them early, accept them, and clear artificial barriers from their path to the top."

The majority of women fall into Schwartz's second category. They want to pursue genuine careers while participating actively in the rearing of their children. Most of them, Schwartz contends, are willing to trade some career growth and compensation for freedom from the constant pressure to work long hours and weekends. By forcing these women to choose between family and career, companies lose a valuable resource and a competitive advantage. Instead, firms must plan for and manage maternity, they must provide the flexibility to help career-and-family women be maximally productive, and they must take an active role in providing family support and in making high-quality, affordable child care available to all women.

Schwartz's various suggestions of ways for organizations to serve the needs of working mothers and benefit from their expertise seem humane and practical. But her feminist critics see her as distinguishing between the strivers and the breeders, between women who should be treated as honorary males and those who should be shunted onto a special lower-paid, low-pressure career track—the now-notorious "mommy track." Former congresswoman Patricia Schroeder of Colorado says that Schwartz actually "reinforces the idea that you can either have a family or a career, but not both, if you're a woman."[103] And other women worry that Schwartz's article will encourage corporations to reduce pay and withhold promotions in exchange for the parental leave, flextime, and child care that they will sooner or later have to provide as they become more and more dependent on female talent.[104]

Barbara Ehrenreich and Deirdre English challenge Schwartz's data and call her article "a tortured muddle of feminist perceptions and sexist assumptions, good intentions and dangerous suggestions—unsupported by any acceptable evidence at all." What they resent is that Schwartz makes no mention of fathers or of shared parental responsibility for child raising. Schwartz is also accused of assuming that mothers don't need top-flight careers and of taking for granted the existing values, structures, and biases of a corporate world that is still male-dominated. "Bumping women—or just fertile women, or married women, or whomever—off the fast track may sound smart to cost-conscious CEOs," they write. "But eventually it is the corporate culture itself that needs to slow down to a human pace . . . [and end] work loads that are incompatible with family life."[105]

"What's so disturbing about Felice Schwartz's article," adds Fran Rodgers, president of Work-Family Directions, a Massachusetts research and referral group, "is that it is devoted to fitting women into the existing culture, instead of finding ways to change that culture." And Rodgers rejects the idea of "dividing women into two groups, but completely ignoring the diversity among men."[106]

Other observers fear that men will simply leave the mommy trackers in the dust. "In most organizations, the mommy track is a millstone around your neck," says Richard Belous, an economist at the National Planning Association. "CEOs and rain-makers don't come out of the mommy track," he warns. "If you go part-time, you're signaling to your employer you're on the B-team."[107] Traditionally, men who make it to the upper ranks have relied on their wives to raise the kids and to take full responsibility at home. A fast-track woman who wants children, however, gets caught in a time and energy squeeze, even if her husband is an equal partner at home. And even though more men today are willing to share child-raising responsibilities, most still seem hesitant about making significant career sacrifices for spouse and family. There's no analogous "daddy track," it seems.

In fact, the evidence points to what's been called a "daddy penalty"—at least for dads in dual-career families. Two recent studies have shown that male man-agers whose wives stay home to care for their children earn more than their coun-terparts with working wives. Even when differences in the numbers of hours worked, years of experience, field of employment, and career interruptions are taken into account, men who are the sole breadwinners for their families enjoy incomes that are 20 to 25 percent higher than married men with children whose wives have careers.[108] Why? No one knows for sure. Some observers suggest that men who are the sole income earners work more, produce more, and push harder for raises and promotions. Others suggest that having a wife at home is a signifi-cant career resource, allowing the man to perform more effectively in his job. Yet others speculate that men who are strongly career oriented choose wives who support that choice in the first place, whereas men who want more balance between work and family are more likely to marry women who want to work. And, finally, there are those who believe that the data reflect a corporate prejudice in favor of traditional families.

Discussion Questions

1. Do you think Schwartz is correct to assert that the cost of employing women in management is greater than that of employing men? If you agree, what are the implications for corporate policy?

2. Can working women accurately be divided into Schwartz's two categories? Is it desirable for companies to distinguish the different types of career paths followed by female employees?

3. Do you think there already is such a thing as a mommy track? Is the idea of a mommy track a good one? Is it somehow discriminatory against women? Against men?

4. Should special organizational arrangements be made for workers who wish to combine career and child raising? Identify the steps that companies can take to accommodate parental needs more effectively.

5. Does a firm have an obligation to give employees the flexibility to work out the particular balance of career and family that is right for them? Or does this go beyond the social responsibilities of business?

Notes

1. The facts reported here are from "Privacy," *Newsweek*, March 28, 1988, 61–68.
2. "Don't Pry," *Economist*, October 6, 1990, 18.

3. Quoted in "Privacy."

4. See Jeffrey L. Seglin, "Too Much Ado about Giving References," *New York Times,* February 21, 1999, sec. 3, 4. See also David W. Arnesen, C. Patrick Fleenor, and Martin Blizinsky, "Name, Rank, and Serial Number? The Dilemma of Reference Checks," *Business Horizons* 41 (July–August 1998): 71–78.

5. Eilene Zimmerman, "HR Must Know When Employee Surveillance Crosses the Line," *Workforce,* February 2002, 38.

6. "Is Office Voice Mail Private?" *Wall Street Journal,* February 28, 1995, B1.

7. "As Abuse of Sick Leave Increases, Crackdown Raises Issues of Privacy," *New York Times,* November 30, 1992, A1.

8. Charles Reich, "The Corporate Control of Big Government," *Business and Society Review* 95 (1996): 61.

9. "How Would You Have Reacted to IBM's E-mail Health Care Plea?" *San Jose Mercury News,* August 27, 1994, 10D.

10. "Firms Find It Tougher to Dismiss Employees for Off-Duty Conduct," *Wall Street Journal,* March 29, 1988, 31.

11. "Enterprise Takes Idea of Dressed for Success to a New Extreme," *Wall Street Journal,* November 20, 2002, B1.

12. *Dollars and Sense,* April 1989, 4; *San Francisco Examiner,* May 12, 1994, A14.

13. *Dollars and Sense,* 4.

14. "Legal Secretary Fired over Gay Stripper Job," *Santa Cruz Sentinel,* June 7, 1992, A10.

15. Terry L. Leap, "When Can You Fire for Off-Duty Conduct?" *Harvard Business Review* 66 (January–February 1988): 36.

16. See Sue Shellenbarger, "Unpaid Overtime: Coping with Pressure to Volunteer for Company Causes," *Wall Street Journal,* November 20, 2003, D1, which is also the source of the next paragraph.

17. "Firms Aim to Trim Fat, Literally," *International Herald Tribune,* June 19, 2003, 12.

18. See Scott Campbell, "Better Than the Company Gym," *HR Magazine,* June 1995, and "Wellness Becomes an Issue in the Workplace," *Santa Cruz Sentinel,* April 28, 2002, D-1.

19. Greg Jaffe, "Weighty Matters," *San Francisco Examiner,* February 22, 1998, J1.

20. "Shape Up—Or Else," *Newsweek,* July 1, 1991, 42; "If You Light Up on Sunday, Don't Come In on Monday," *Business Week,* August 26, 1991, 68–70.

21. "Privacy," 68.

22. See David T. Lykken, "Three Big Lies about the Polygraph," *USA Today,* February 17, 1983, 10A. See also William A. Nowlin and Robert Barbato, "The Truth about Lie Detectors," *Business and Society Review* 66 (Summer 1988), and "Scientists Say Lie Detector Doesn't Always Tell Truth," *Wall Street Journal,* October 9, 2002, B1.

23. Lynn March, "Lie Detectors Are Accurate and Useful," *USA Today,* February 17, 1983, 10A.

24. Lykken, "Three Big Lies."

25. Christopher H. Pyle, "These Tests Are Meant to Scare People," *USA Today,* February 17, 1983, 10A.

26. "Personality Counts," *HR Magazine,* February 2, 2002, 30–31. See also "Psychometric Testing Stays Forever Jung," *Financial Times,* June 20, 2003, 12, and "Getting to Know You Is as Easy as A, B, C, or D," *New York Times,* November 30, 2003, sec. 3, 8.

27. Barbara Ehrenreich, "Two-Tiered Morality," *New York Times,* June 30, 2002, sec. 4, 15.

28. "Trying to Get a Job? Check Yes or No," *New York Times,* November 28, 1997, B1.

29. Ibid.

30. "Privacy," 68.

31. See "2001 AMA Survey: Workplace Monitoring and Surveillance" at *www.amanet.org.*

32. Kleiman, "The Boss May Be Listening," *San Jose Mercury News,* February 25, 1996, 1PC.

33. "What the Boss Knows about You," *Fortune,* August 9, 1993.

34. "Study May Spur Job-Applicant Drug Screening," *Wall Street Journal*, November 28, 1990, B1. See also *New York Times*, November 29, 1990, A17.

35. "If You Light Up on Sunday," 68.

36. James T. Wrich, "Beyond Testing: Coping with Drugs at Work," *Harvard Business Review* 66 (January–February 1988).

37. William Serrin, "The Wages of Work," *Nation*, January 28, 1991, 80–82.

38. Myron I. Peskin and Francis J. McGrath, "Industrial Safety: Who Is Responsible and Who Benefits?" *Business Horizons* 35 (May–June 1992).

39. Beth Rogers, "Creating a Culture of Safety," *HR Magazine* (February 1995), 85. See also James Reason, "Achieving a Safe Culture: Theory and Practice," *Work & Stress* 12 (July–September 1998): 293–306.

40. *Whirlpool Corporation v. Marshall*, 445 U.S. 1 (1980).

41. See Joseph LaDoc, "The Not-So-Clean Business of Making Chips," *Technological Review* 87 (May–June 1984), and "Chip Makers Promise Action on Toxics," *San Jose Mercury News*, December 4, 1992, 1A.

42. U.S. Bureau of the Census, *Statistical Abstract of the United States 2002* (Washington, D.C.: U.S. Government Printing Office, 2003), Table 621.

43. "OSHA Vows to Make Workplace Safer," *San Jose Mercury News*, April 3, 1994, 1PC.

44. "Job Injuries, Illnesses Cost the U.S. as Much as Heart Disease, Study Says," *San Francisco Chronicle*, July 28, 1997, A5.

45. Archie B. Carroll, *Business and Society*, 2nd ed. (Cincinnati: SouthWestern, 1993), 453–454.

46. Dana Wilkie, "The Uphill Struggle for Workplace Health," *State Legislatures* 23 (June 2, 1997): 27–32. See also "A Dangerous Business," *Frontline*, January 9, 2003, interview with Charles Jeffress (available at www.pbs.org).

47. "U.S. Acts to Cut Aches on the Job," *New York Times*, February 20, 1999, A1; Jennifer Powell, "A New Pain in the Neck," *PC/Computing*, April 2000, 44; and "New Ballgame for Repetitive-Stress Ailments," *Wall Street Journal*, April 28, 2002, D-6.

48. David Tuller, "The '90s 'Occupational Epidemic,'" *San Francisco Chronicle*, June 12, 1989, C1.

49. "U.S. Acts to Cut Aches," A8.

50. "Make Ergonomics," *HR Magazine*, April 2000, 37–42.

51. "Employers Win Ergonomics Duel by Achieving Delay in Guidelines," *Wall Street Journal*, November 3, 2003, A3.

52. See "Fatigue: The Hidden Culprit," *USA Weekend*, January 29–31, 1993, and "Worker Fatigue Can Be Deadly," *San Jose Mercury News*, March 3, 1996.

53. Dorothy Foltz-Gray, "Sheepless Nights," *American Way*, May 1, 1999, 72.

54. "In Their Quest for Efficiency, Factories Scrap the 5-Day Week," *New York Times*, June 4, 1996, A1.

55. "Stress on the Job," *Newsweek*, April 25, 1988; see also "Is Job Stress Taking Its Toll in Your Facility?" *Safety Management*, February 2003, 3.

56. "If Workplace Is Stressful, There's a Way to Calm Down," *San Jose Mercury News*, April 4, 1993, 2PC; "Workaholics Anonymous," *Economist*, October 22, 1994, 20.

57. "Yes, American Workers Are Putting in Longer Hours," *San Francisco Examiner*, March 28, 1999, J-5.

58. Sue Shellenbarger, "Work and Family," *San Francisco Examiner*, March 21, 1999, CL 29.

59. Yawen Cheng et al., "Association Between Psychosocial Work Characteristics and Health Functioning in American Women," *British Medical Journal* 30 (May 27, 2000): 1432–1436.

60. Harvey Hornstein, *Brutal Bosses and Their Prey* (New York: Putnam, 1996).

61. Douglas McGregor, *The Human Side of Enterprise* (New York: McGraw-Hill, 1960).

62. David M. Gordon, *Fat and Mean: The Corporate Squeeze of Working Americans and the Myth of Managerial "Downsizing"* (New York: Free Press, 1996), 43; "The Glut of Managers," *Business Week*, March 25, 2002, 26.

63. "For Ross Perot, GM Ouster Still Rankles," *International Herald Tribune,* November 19, 1987.

64. *Statistical Abstract of the United States 2002,* Table 568.

65. Karen Korubluh, "The Parent Trap," *Atlantic Monthly*, January/February 2003, 111, 114.

66. See Bonnie Harris, "Child Care Comes to Work," *Los Angeles Times,* November 19, 2000, W1.

67. "Kids Go to School at H-P Work Site," *San Jose Mercury News,* February 10, 1993, 1A; "Companies Providing Schools for Workers' Children," *San Jose Mercury News,* July 28, 1996, 1PC.

68. Sue Shellenbarger, "A Downside of Taking Family Leave: Getting Fired While You're Gone," *Wall Street Journal,* January 23, 2003, D1.

69. *Work in America: Report of a Special Task Force to the Secretary of Health, Education, and Welfare* (Cambridge: MIT Press, 1972).

70. See "Work Week," *Wall Street Journal,* August 21, 2002, B2; "Poll Gives Workers Morale Boost," *Wall Street Journal,* January 29, 2003, D2; and "Hate Your Job? Join the Club," *Business Week,* October 6, 2003, 40.

71. But for a criticism of the original study, see "Scientific Myths That Are Too Good to Die," *New York Times,* December 9, 1998, sec. 4, 2.

72. For a discussion of Herzberg's ideas, see J. Michael Syptak, David M. Marsland, and Deborah Ulmer, "Job Satisfaction: Putting Theory into Practice," *Family Practice Management,* October 1999, 26.

73. A. R. Gini and T. J. Sullivan, *It Comes with the Territory* (New York: Random House, 1989), 27–29.

74. "Bored to Death at Work—Literally," *Business Week,* July 1, 2002, 16.

75. E. Palmore, "Predicting Longevity: A Follow-Up Controlling for Age," *Gerontologist* 9 (1969): 247–250.

76. Sharon Cohen, "Management, Unions Join Forces," *San Francisco Examiner,* December 9, 1990, D3.

77. Cohen, "Management, Unions."

78. Randy Pennington, "Collaborative Labor Relations: The First Line Is the Bottom Line," *Personnel,* March 1989, 78.

79. Cohen, "Management, Unions." See also "Japanese Plants in the U.S. Lose Edge to the Big Three," *International Herald Tribune,* June 17–18, 2000, 14, and "The NUMMI Road to Japan," *San Jose Mercury News,* May 18, 2002, 1C.

80. Alan S. Blinder, "Want to Boost Productivity? Try Giving Workers a Say," *Business Week,* April 17, 1989, 10; "A Firm of Their Own," *Economist,* June 11, 1994, 59. See also Joseph Blasi, Douglas Kruse, and Aaron Bernstein, *In the Company of Owners: The Truth About Stock Options (and Why Every Employee Should Have Them)* (New York: Basic Books, 2003).

81. "When GM's Robots Ran Amok," *Economist,* August 10, 1991, 64–65.

82. "United We Own," *Business Week,* March 18, 1996, 96.

83. "UAL: Labor Is My Co-Pilot," *Business Week,* March 1, 1999, 38.

84. See Roger E. Alcaly, "Reinventing the Corporation," *New York Review of Books,* April 10, 1997.

85. D. Keith Denton, "!*#@#! I Hate This Job," *Business Horizons* 37 (January–February 1994).

86. "Special Report: Car Manufacturing," *Economist,* February 23, 2002, 72.

87. Samuel Greengard, "Theft Control Starts with HR Strategies," *Personnel Journal,* April 1993, 81–88; "The Thief on the Payroll," *San Jose Mercury News,* April 14, 1996, 1PC. See also "Taking at the Office Reaches New Heights," *New York Times,* July 12, 2000, C8, and "Amid the Recession, More Employees Are Stealing from Work," *Santa Cruz Sentinel,* March 24, 2002, D1.

88. Judith Crossen, "Job Applicants Would Disappoint Diogenes," *San Francisco Examiner,* December 18, 1988, D15.

89. "Honest Answers—Postpolygraph," *Personnel,* April 1988, 8.

90. Susan Tempor, "More Employers Attempt to Catch a Thief by Giving Job Applicants 'Honesty' Exams," *Wall Street Journal,* August 3, 1981.

91. Crossen, "Job Applicants."

92. "Trying to Get a Job? Check Yes or No," *New York Times,* November 28, 1997, B1.

93. "Honest Answers," 10.

94. Ibid.

95. "Searching for Integrity," *Fortune,* March 8, 1993, 140.

96. "Texas Company Settles over Nosy Questions to Employees," *San Francisco Chronicle,* July 8, 2000, A3.

97. Tempor, "More Employers Attempt to Catch a Thief," 15.

98. This case study is based on a case reported in Thomas Garrett et al., *Cases in Business Ethics* (Englewood Cliffs, N.J.: Prentice Hall, 1968), 9–10.

99. Peter T. Kilborn, "Who Decides Who Works at Jobs Imperiling Fetuses?" *New York Times,* September 2, 1990, 1, is the main source for this case study.

100. *New York Times,* March 21, 1991, A1. Excerpts from *Automobile Workers v. Johnson Controls* quoted in the following paragraphs are from page A14.

101. Felice N. Schwartz, "Management Women and the New Facts of Life," *Harvard Business Review* 67 (January–February 1989): 65.

102. Ibid., 69.

103. Tamar Lewin, "New Look at Working Moms," *San Francisco Chronicle,* March 8, 1989, A1.

104. Barbara Ehrenreich and Deirdre English, "Blowing the Whistle on the 'Mommy Track,'" *Ms.,* July–August 1989, 56.

105. Ibid., 58.

106. Lewin, "New Look at Working Moms."

107. "The Mommy Track," *Newsweek,* March 20, 1989, 132.

108. "Men Whose Wives Work Earn Less, Studies Show," *New York Times,* October 11, 1994, A1; see also "Marriage's 'Unique Effect,'" *Business Week,* May 13, 2002, 32.

Further Reading for Chapter 7

David Barstow and **Lowell Bergman**, "Dangerous Business," *New York Times,* January 8, 9, and 10, 2003, is a disturbing, detailed investigative report on the company with the worst safety record in the U.S.

Douglas Birsch, "The Universal Drug Testing of Employees," *Business and Professional Ethics Journal* 14 (Fall 1995).

Michael Cranford, "Drug Testing and the Right to Privacy," *Journal of Business Ethics* 17 (November 1998), and **John R. Rowan**, "Limitations on the Moral Permissibility of Employee Drug Testing," *Business and Professional Ethics Journal* 19 (Summer 2000) examine the ethics of drug testing employees.

Gertude Ezorsky, ed., *Moral Rights in the Workplace* (Albany: State University of New York Press, 1987) is a good collection of articles on the right to meaningful work, occupational health and safety, employee privacy, unions, industrial flight, and related topics.

Ben Hamper, *Rivethead* (New York: Warner Books, 1992) is a riotous look at life on a GM assembly line.

Sylvia Ann Hewlett, "Executive Women and the Myth of Having It All," *Harvard Business Review* 80 (April 2002) discusses the factors that prevent successful career women from having children.

John Kaler, "Understanding Participation," *Journal of Business Ethics* 21 (September 2000) discusses different types of employee participation while **John J. McCall**, "Employee Voice in Corporate Governance," *Business Ethics Quarterly* 11 (January 2001) argues for a strong employee right to co-determine corporate policy.

Scott O. Lilienfeld, "Do 'Honesty' Tests Really Measure Honesty?" *Skeptical Inquirer* 18 (Fall 1993) is a critique of honesty exams.

Robert Mayer, "Is There a Right to Workplace Democracy?" *Social Theory and Practice* 26 (Summer 2000) argues on nonlibertarian grounds against such a right.

Adam D. Moore, "Employee Monitoring and Computer Technology," *Business Ethics Quarterly* 10 (July 2000) discusses the tension between privacy and evaluative surveillance.

Ira Sprotzer and **Ilene V. Goldberg**, "Fetal Protection: Law, Ethics, and Corporate Policy," *Journal of Business Ethics* 11 (October 1992) analyzes fetal protection policies and suggests some practical guidelines.

(Consult also the readings suggested at the end of Chapter 6.)

 InfoTrac College Edition: For further information or to conduct research, please go to www.infotrac-college.com.

8

Moral Choices
Facing Employees

When his eldest daughter asked him, "Why don't you just do what they want?" George Betancourt wasn't sure how he should answer. Betancourt was a senior engineer at Northeast Utilities, which operates five nuclear plants in New England, and all he had done was to speak up and express his professional judgment. Now Northeast wanted him to shut up. First, Northeast's human-resources officer had called him in. After complaining that Betancourt wasn't being a "team player," she described to him the company's termination policies. Three weeks later, Betancourt was informed he was being reassigned. "We'd like to help you, George," Eric DeBarba, vice president of technical services, told him. "But you've got to start thinking company."[1]

George Galatis was the Northeast engineer on whose behalf George Betancourt had spoken up. Galatis had discovered what he considered to be a glaring safety problem at Northeast's Millstone No. 1 nuclear power plant. In an effort to save downtime (and hence money) during the refueling process, the plant's procedures routinely violated federal guidelines and pushed its spent-fuel pool well beyond its design capacity. For eighteen months, Galatis's supervisors denied the problem existed and refused to report it to the Nuclear Regulatory Commission (NRC). Northeast brought in a series of outside experts to prove Galatis wrong, but the consultants ended up agreeing with him. Within the company, Betancourt backed up Galatis's safety concerns. When Northeast finally began to acknowledge a possible problem, it didn't move fast enough to satisfy Galatis. Two years after having initially raised his safety concerns, he finally took the case directly to the NRC, only to learn that it had known about the unsafe procedures for years. He also discovered evidence that suggested collusion between Northeast and NRC officials to subordinate safety to profitability.

As a result of going to the NRC, Galatis says he experienced "subtle forms of harassment, retaliation, and intimidation." He wasn't just being paranoid. Two dozen Millstone No. 1 employees claimed they were fired or demoted for raising safety concerns. Some of his colleagues sided with the company, however, accusing Galatis of aiding antinuclear activists and trying to take away their livelihood. But Galatis didn't stop. He hired a lawyer who specializes in representing whistle-blowers and kept after the NRC. With the lawyer's help, the public spotlight was focused on Millstone No. 1. Local politicians began asking questions. Even though the NRC ignored Galatis, it ended up validating his concerns, and Millstone No. 1 was shut down. Citing chronic safety concerns, employee harassment, and a "historic emphasis on cost savings vs. performance," the NRC also put Northeast's other two Millstone plants on its high-scrutiny "watch list." And a new NRC head vowed to shake up the regulatory body itself.

Galatis and Betancourt managed to hang on to their jobs, but their careers are at a standstill. "The two Georges had better watch their backs," says one engineer. "Up at Northeast, they've got long memories." A disillusioned Galatis says, "If I had it to do over again, I wouldn't."

For someone in the shoes of George Galatis or George Betancourt, two general issues come up. First is a question of where an employee's overall moral duty lies. For a professional engineer to go public with documented safety concerns may seem to be a more straightforward moral decision than that faced by an employee who suspects irregularities, unsafe procedures, or wrongdoing in an area unrelated to his or her own job. In that case, the employee may possibly have conflicting moral obligations. Furthermore, if an employee reports irregularities to the appropriate authority, the employee must then decide whether he or she is morally obligated to pursue the matter further. Again other moral considerations come into play.

Second, once they have decided that they ought to blow the whistle, employees must face the possible negative consequences. Galatis and Betancourt are skilled, mature, and respected professionals, with established records and good credentials; in terms of employment options, they may have less to risk than do potential whistle-blowers who are just starting their careers or who have restricted job options or heavy financial obligations. Nor is this simply a tug of war between moral duty and self-interest. Most moral theorists would agree that depending on the circumstances, certain personal sacrifices might be so great that we cannot reasonably be morally obliged to make them.

These two themes—determining one's moral responsibility amid a welter of conflicting demands and paying the personal costs that can be involved in living up to one's obligations—recur throughout this chapter. In particular, this chapter looks at the following topics:

1. The obligations employees have to the firm, company loyalty, and the problem of conflicts of interest

2. Illegitimate use of one's official position for private gain, through insider trading or access to proprietary data

3. Domestic and foreign bribery and the factors to consider in determining the morality of giving and receiving gifts in a business context

4. The obligations employees have to third parties and the considerations they should weigh in cases of conflicting moral duties or divided loyalties

5. What whistle-blowing is and the factors relevant to evaluating its morality

6. The problem of how considerations of self-interest are to be weighed by an employee facing a tough moral choice

OBLIGATIONS TO THE FIRM

When you accept employment, you generally agree to perform certain tasks, usually during certain specified hours, in exchange for financial remuneration. Whether it is oral or written, implicit or explicit, a contract governs your employment relationship and provides the basic framework for understanding the reciprocal obligations between you and your employer. Your employment contract determines what you are supposed to do or accomplish for your employer, and it may cover a variety of other matters from parking privileges to your dress and deportment while carrying out your responsibilities. The terms of your employment contract may be specific and detailed or vague and open-ended.

Loyalty to the Company

Because you are hired to work for your employer, you have an obligation, when acting on behalf of the organization, to promote your employer's interests. Insofar as you are acting as an agent of your employer, the traditional law of agency places you under a legal obligation to act loyally and in good faith and to carry out all lawful instructions. But it would be morally benighted to view employees simply as agents of their employers or to expect them to subordinate entirely their autonomy and private lives to the organization. Morality requires neither blind loyalty nor total submission to the organization.

Some writers, however, have gone to the opposite extreme, denying that employees have any obligation of loyalty to the company, even a prima facie obligation, "because companies are not the kind of things that are properly objects of loyalty." Why not? Because a business firm functions to make money, the argument goes, self-interest is all that binds it together. But "loyalty depends on ties that demand self-sacrifice with no expectation of reward."[2] From this perspective, then, one can owe loyalty to family, friends, or country, but not to a corporation. Employees simply work to get paid, and they are misguided if they see themselves as owing loyalty to the company.

However, the notion of company loyalty is commonplace, and most people find it a coherent and legitimate concept. For the many employees who willingly make sacrifices for the organization above and beyond their job descriptions, loyalty is a real and important value. Loyalty, though, is a two-way street, and most employees believe it's up to the company to earn and retain their loyalty to it. Indeed, it is not clear how well any business or organization could function without winning employee loyalty, and certainly most companies want more than minimal time and effort from their employees.

Arguably, some obligations of loyalty simply come with the job—for example, the obligation to warn the organization of danger, the obligation to act in a way that protects its legitimate interests, and the obligation to cooperate actively in the furtherance of legitimate corporate goals.[3] To be sure, many businesses demand more than this in the name of loyalty. They may expect employees to defend the company if it is maligned, to work overtime when the company needs it, to accept a transfer if necessary for the good of the organization, or to demonstrate their loyalty in countless other ways. Displaying loyalty in these ways certainly seems morally permissible, even if it is not morally required.[4] In addition, employees, like other individuals, can come to identify with the groups they are part of, accepting group goals and norms as their own. Some moral theorists believe not only that loyalty to the group can become an important value for the individual

employee, but also that in the appropriate circumstances the process of group identifi-
cation can create an additional obligation of loyalty that the employee would not otherwise have.[5]

Conflicts of Interest

Of course, even the most loyal employees can find that their interests collide with
those of the organization. You want to dress one way, the organization requires you to
dress another way; you'd prefer to show up for work at noon, the company expects you
to be present at 8 A.M.; you'd like to receive $75,000 for your services, the organization
pays you a fraction of that figure. The reward, autonomy, and self-fulfillment that
workers seek aren't always compatible with the worker productivity that the organization desires. Whatever the matter in question, the perspectives of employee and
employer can differ.

Sometimes this clash of goals and desires can take the serious form of a *conflict of
interest*. In an organization, a conflict of interest arises when employees at any level have
private interests that are substantial enough to interfere with their job duties; that is,
when their private interests lead them, or might reasonably be expected to lead them,
to make decisions or act in ways that are detrimental to their employer's interests. This
was certainly the case when Enron's chief financial officer, Andrew Fallon, represented
the company in negotiations with firms he was a managing partner of (and as such eventually earned millions of dollars from the deals).

As we have seen, the work contract is the primary source of an organization's right
to expect employees to act on its behalf in a way that is unprejudiced by their personal
interests. In general, if the contents of the work agreement are legal and if the employee
freely consents to them, then he or she is under an obligation to fulfill the terms of the
agreement. Implicit in any work contract is the assumption that employees will not sacrifice the interests of the organization for personal advantage. Of course, individuals
may seek to benefit from being employed with a certain business or organization, but
in discharging their contractual employment duties, employees should not subordinate
the welfare of the organization for their own gain.

When the situation is such that the employee's private interests run counter to the
interests of his or her employer, a conflict of interest exists. Sometimes these private interests may lead an employee to sacrifice the interests of his or her employer. For example, Bart Williams, sales manager for Leisure Sports World, gives all his firm's
promotional work to Impact Advertising because its chief officer is Bart's brother-in-
law. As a result, Leisure Sports World pays about 15 percent more in advertising costs
than it would if its work went to another agency. Here Bart has allowed his decisions
as an employee to be influenced by his personal interests, to the detriment of Leisure
Sports World. Note that Williams's interest is not financial; a conflict of interest can take
various forms.

Suppose that Bart Williams does not throw all of his company's promotional work
to his brother-in-law; rather, he gives the firm's business to his brother-in-law only
when he sincerely believes that doing so is best for Leisure Sports World. Nevertheless,
a conflict of interest can still be said to exist. Because of his brother-in-law, Bart Williams
still has a private interest in his business dealings for Leisure Sports World that could
possibly lead him to act against the interests of the company. In other words, there is
a danger that Bart's judgment may not be as objective as it should be.

Conflicts of interest are morally worrisome not only when an employee acts to the detriment of the organization but also when the employee's private interests are significant enough that they could tempt the employee to do so. That's why alarm bells went off when *Business Week* disclosed that two members of the audit committee at Qwest Communications, which was already under fire for its dubious accounting practices, directed companies with million-dollar contracts with Qwest, thus raising questions about their ability to exercise independent judgment.[6] By definition, to have a conflict of interest is to be in a morally risky situation; that is why employees should avoid such situations. But deciding when the employee's private interests in a business transaction are substantial enough for the situation to constitute a conflict of interest can be difficult. Equally difficult can be deciding what employees should do when they find themselves with a conflict of interest. The answers to these questions probably need to be determined on a case-by-case basis.

Financial Investments   Conflicts of interest may exist when employees have financial investments in suppliers, customers, or distributors with whom their organizations do business. For example, Monica Walters, purchasing agent for Trans-Con Trucking, owns a substantial amount of stock with Timberline Office Works. When ordering office supplies, Walters buys exclusively from Timberline, even though she could get equivalent supplies cheaper from another supplier. In this case, Walters has acted against Trans-Con's interests. But even if Walters never advantages herself this way, a conflict of interest still exists.

During the dot-com boom, executives at high tech firms often owned stock in other young companies in the same or closely related fields. These tangled financial relationships sometimes produced conflicts of interest. For example, eight executives at EMC were heavily invested in the startup StorageNetworks. They recommended it to their clients, and these referrals quickly grew to 40 percent of the younger company's business. But as StorageNetworks got larger and as EMC expanded its own services division, the two companies found themselves competing, leading some at EMC to complain that the other firm was poaching its employees and interfering with its customer relationships. Today EMC says the impact on business was negligible. But a former board member maintains that the eight executives were recommending Storage-Networks when they should have been pushing EMC equipment: "No question, it had an impact on their day-to-day decisions. It was a tremendous financial incentive."[7]

How much of a financial investment does it take to create a conflict of interest? There's no simple answer. Certainly it is acceptable to hold a small percentage of stock in a publicly held corporation that is listed on the stock exchange. Sometimes companies state what percentage of outstanding stock their employees may own in a potential supplier, customer, distributor, or competitor (usually up to 10 percent). But neither of these rules of thumb helps with the previous case. The EMC executives owned shares of StorageNetworks before the company went public, and with the latter's stock rocketing from 50 cents a share over $90, adhering to the 10 percent rule wouldn't have prevented the problem. Frequently companies require key officials to make a full disclosure of all outside interests that could cloud their judgment or adversely affect their ability to promote the organization's interests. That's important, but full disclosure alone doesn't make the conflict disappear; steps must still be taken. Organizations need a detailed policy, customized to reflect their needs and interests, that spells out the limits of permissible outside financial investments and what employees should do when they have possible conflicts of interests. Because such a policy can affect the financial well-being of those who fall under it, however, it should be open to negotiation just as employee compensation is.

ABUSE OF OFFICIAL POSITION

The use of one's official position for personal gain always raises moral concerns and questions because of the risk that one will thereby violate one's obligations to the firm or organization. Examples range from using subordinates for non-organization-related work to abusing a position of trust within an organization to enhance one's own financial leverage and holdings. Executives who use corporate funds for private purposes like health club memberships, extravagant parties, vacation travel, or remodeling their homes are guilty of this, as are CEOs like Bernard J. Ebbers of WorldCom, John Legere of Global Crossing, or L. Dennis Kozlowski of Tyco International, who used their high positions to borrow huge amounts of money at below market rates—in Ebbers's case over $400 million—from the companies they worked for.[8]

Insider Trading

One common way of abusing one's official position is through insider trading. *Insider trading* refers to the buying or selling of stocks (or other financial securities) by business "insiders" on the basis of information that has not yet been made public and is likely to affect the price of the stock. For example, as soon as he learned that the Food and Drug Administration was not going to approve his company's highly touted cancer drug Erbitux, Dr. Sam Waksal, the CEO of ImClone Systems, knew its stock would plummet. Before the FDA's decision was made public, however, Waksal quickly but quietly sold his stock in the company and told his father and one of his daughters to do so as well. He is also alleged to have passed the word on to his friend Martha Stewart, who dumped her ImClone stock the day before the FDA announced its decision.[9] One doesn't have to profit personally to cross the line, however. For example, the wife of the president and chief executive of Genentech was charged with insider trading for providing confidential information to her brother. Before the biotechnology firm was partly acquired by another company, she told her brother that "some good things were about to happen" to the company and suggested that he buy a few thousand dollars' worth of stock, even if he had to borrow the funds. She also advised him to keep the purchase secret and make it in the name of a "trustworthy" friend.[10]

Inside traders ordinarily defend their actions by claiming that they don't injure anyone. It's true that trading by insiders on the basis of nonpublic information seldom directly injures anyone. But moral concerns arise from indirect injury, as well as from direct. As one author puts it, "What causes injury or loss to outsiders is not what the insiders knew or did; rather it is what [the outsiders] themselves did not know. It is their own lack of knowledge which exposes them to risk of loss or denies then an opportunity to make a profit."[11] Case in point: the famous Texas Gulf Sulphur stock case.

When test drilling by Texas Gulf indicated a rich ore body near Timmins, Ontario, some officials at Texas Gulf attempted to play down the potential worth of the Timmins property in a press release by describing it as only a prospect. But four days later a second press release termed the Timmins property a major discovery. In the interim, inside investors made a handsome personal profit through stock purchases. At the same time, stockholders who unloaded stock after the first press release or who sold the stock short, anticipating its price would fall, lost money.

The Securities and Exchange Commission (SEC), which is charged with policing the stock market, subsequently charged that a group of insiders—including Texas Gulf directors, officers, and employees—had violated the disclosure section of the Securities Exchange Act of 1934 by purchasing stock in the company while withholding information about the rich ore strike the company had made. The courts upheld the charge, finding that the first press release was "misleading to the reasonable investor using due care."[12] As a result, the courts not only ordered the insiders to pay into a special court-administered account all profits they made but also directed them to repay profits made by outsiders whom they had tipped. The courts then used this account to compensate persons who had lost money by selling their Texas Gulf Sulphur stock on the basis of the first press release.

Insider dealings raise intriguing questions. When can employees buy and sell securities in their own companies? How much information must they disclose to stockholders about the firm's plans and prospects? When must this information be disclosed? There's also the question, Who is considered an insider? Corporate executives, directors, officers, and other key employees are certainly insiders. But what about outsiders whom a company temporarily employs, such as accountants, lawyers, and contractors? Or what about those who just happen upon inside information?

In its effort to police the marketplace, the SEC has interpreted "insider" in a broad sense to mean anyone who buys or sells stock based on nonpublic information—whether or not the person is a corporate officer or otherwise linked to the company whose stock is being bought or sold. However, in 1980 the U.S. Supreme Court challenged the SEC's broad conception of insider trading in the case of Vincent Chiarella, a financial printer who traded on information he culled from documents passing through his shop. The Court ruled that Chiarella was not an insider with fiduciary responsibilities and thus had not violated the Securities Exchange Act. The Court reinforced its decision three years later when it reversed the conviction of securities analyst Raymond Dirks, who advised several of his clients to dump their shares in a company that he was about to blow the whistle on for fraud. In so ruling, the Court held that there is nothing improper about an outsider's using information, as long as the information is not obtained from an insider who breaches a legal duty to the corporation's shareholders for personal gain or to show favor to friends.

Since then the SEC has developed a new tactic, arguing that people who trade on confidential information but are not traditional company insiders are guilty of insider trading if they have "misappropriated" sensitive information. Although some appellate courts had rejected the SEC's approach, in 1997 the Supreme Court endorsed the misappropriation theory of insider trading in *U.S. v. O'Hagan,* thus upholding one of the SEC's main legal weapons against insider trading. In this case, James O'Hagan, a lawyer, had reaped a $4.3 million profit after learning that a company represented by his law firm was planning a hostile takeover of another company. O'Hagan had not worked on the case himself, but he had—the Court ruled—misappropriated confidential information belonging to his firm and its client. Writing for the majority, Justice Ruth Bader Ginsburg stressed that the Court's decision reflected the "animating purpose" of the Securities Exchange Act, namely, "to insure honest securities markets and thereby promote investor confidence."[13]

Arthur Levitt, Jr., chairman of the Securities and Exchange Commission at the time, applauds the Court's decision, stating that it "reaffirms the SEC's effort to make the stock market fair to all people, whether you're a Wall Street veteran or a Main Street newcomer."[14] Law professor Henry Manne, however, sees nothing inherently wrong with insider trading and thinks the SEC should stay totally out of the insider-trading field. "The use of insider information should be governed by private contractual relationships," he believes, such as those between corporations and their personnel or between a law firm and its members.[15]

At the core of this disagreement are two opposed perspectives on what makes the market work. Levitt and like-minded analysts contend that the marketplace can work only if it is perceived as being honest and offering equal investment opportunity. Insider trading, they argue, makes that impossible. Those who think like Manne believe that permitting insiders to trade is good for the market because it accelerates the flow of positive or negative information about the stock to other shareholders and investors. As a result, this information is more quickly reflected in the stock's price, which is healthy for the market. They also believe that permitting insider trading can benefit a company by providing employees an incentive to invent new products, put together deals, or otherwise create new information that will increase the value of a company's stock.

Philosophy professor Jennifer Mills Moore agrees with Manne that it is difficult to prove that insider trading harms ordinary investors or to show that there is something unfair about it. However, she argues that insider trading is wrong because it undermines the fiduciary relationship that is central to business management. Employees have a duty to act in the interests of the firm and its shareholders, but many ways of profiting from insider information do not benefit the company at all—indeed, they may seriously damage its interests.[16]

The information that employees garner within the company is not always the kind that affects stock prices. Sometimes the information concerns highly sensitive data related to company research, technology, product development, and so on. How employees treat such secret or classified data can also raise important moral issues.

Proprietary Data

Companies guard information that can affect their competitive standing with all the zealousness of a bulldog guarding a ham bone. Take Procter & Gamble, for example. Having patented the baking technique of its Duncan Hines brand of homemade-style chocolate chip cookies a few years ago, it then sued three rival food chains, charging them with using the patented process to make "infringing cookies." P&G further claimed that these companies had spied at a sales presentation and at cookie plants. One company allegedly even flew a spy plane over a P&G plant under construction. One of the defendants, Frito-Lay, admitted to sending a worker to photograph the outside of a Duncan Hines bakery. But it denied telling the man's college-age son to walk into the plant and ask for some unbaked cookie dough—which the enterprising youth did, and got. Frito-Lay insisted that it destroyed both the pictures and the dough without scrutinizing either and formally apologized to P&G. It also countersued P&G for trying to eliminate competition.[17]

When novel information is patented or copyrighted, it is legally protected but not secret. Others may have access to the information, but they are forbidden to use it (without permission) for the life of the patent or copyright. When a company patents a process, as Kleenex did with pop-up tissues, for example, the company has a monopoly on that process. Until the patent expires, no other firm may compete in the production of pop-up facial tissues. Although on the face of it this rule violates the ideal of a free market and would appear to slow the spread of new processes and technology, patents and copyrights are generally defended on the ground that without them technological innovation would be hampered. Individuals and companies would not be willing to invest in the development of a new process if other firms could then immediately exploit any new invention without having themselves invested in developing it.

Although patent law is complicated and patents are not easy to acquire, what it means for something to be patented is well defined legally. By contrast, the concept of a *trade secret* is broad and imprecise. The standard legal definition says that a trade secret is "any formula, pattern, device, or compilation of information which is used in one's business and which gives him an opportunity to obtain an advantage over competitors who do not know or use it."[18] Virtually any information that is not generally known (or whose utility is not recognized) is eligible for classification as a trade secret, as long as such information is valuable to its possessor and is treated confidentially. Most states have laws against the theft of trade secrets, and the Economic Espionage Act of 1996 makes it a federal crime. Nevertheless, trade secrets do not enjoy the same protection as patented information. The formula for Coca-Cola, for instance, is secret but not patented. No competitor has yet succeeded in figuring it out by "reverse engineering," but if your company managed to do so, then it would be entitled to use the formula itself.

There are at least three arguments for legally protecting trade secrets: (1) trade secrets are the intellectual property of the company; (2) the theft of trade secrets is unfair competition; and (3) employees who disclose trade secrets violate the confidentiality owed to their employers.[19] In individual cases, what constitutes intellectual property, unfair competition, or a violation of confidentiality can often be controversial. But clearly one of the biggest challenges facing an organization can be to prevent its trade secrets and proprietary data from being misused by its own employees.

This is an especially troublesome problem in high-tech firms, in which employees who are privy to sensitive information are especially prone to job hopping. (For example, the average job tenure of an executive in the software industry is a scant twenty-two months.[20]) Two factors conspire to make this a morally complicated problem: (1) the individual's right to seek new employment and (2) the difficulty of separating trade secrets from the technical knowledge, experience, and skill that are part of the employee's own intellect and talents.

A classic case involved Donald Wohlgemuth, who worked in the spacesuit department of B. F. Goodrich in Akron, Ohio.[21] Eventually Wohlgemuth became general manager of the spacesuit division and learned Goodrich's highly classified spacesuit technology for the Apollo flights. Shortly thereafter, Wohlgemuth, desiring a higher salary, joined Goodrich's competitor, International Latex Corporation in Dover, Delaware, as manager of engineering for the industrial area that included making spacesuits in competition with Goodrich. Goodrich protested by seeking an order restraining Wohlgemuth from working for Latex or for any other company in the space field. The Court of Appeals of Ohio denied Goodrich's request for an injunction, respecting Wohlgemuth's right to choose his employer, but it did provide an injunction restraining Wohlgemuth from revealing Goodrich's trade secrets.

Cases like Wohlgemuth's are fundamentally different from those involving insider trading, for they pit a firm's right to protect its secrets against an employee's right to seek employment wherever he or she chooses. As a result, the moral dilemmas that arise in proprietary-data cases are not easily resolved. For one thing, the trade secrets that companies seek to protect have often become an integral part of the departing employee's job skills and capabilities. These may manifest themselves simply in a subconscious or intuitive sense of what will or will not work in the laboratory. Wohlgemuth's total intellectual capacity included the information, experience, and technical skills acquired at his former workplace. Goodrich might be justified in claiming much of Wohlgemuth's intellectual capacity as its corporate property, but it is difficult to see how he could divest himself of it.

One can also ask whether Wohlgemuth acted morally in leaving Goodrich for a competitor, the legality of his action notwithstanding. Wohlgemuth certainly thought so. When asked by Goodrich management whether he considered his action moral, he replied, "Loyalty and ethics have their price, and International Latex has paid the price."

BRIBES AND KICKBACKS

A *bribe* is a remuneration for the performance of an act that's inconsistent with the work contract or the nature of the work one has been hired to perform. The remuneration can be money, gifts, entertainment, or preferential treatment.

A typical but blatant case was that of Norman Rothberg, an accountant working at ZZZZ Best Carpet Cleaning Company in the Los Angeles area. When he learned that ZZZZ Best had falsified accounts on insurance restoration jobs, he gave the information to the accounting firm of Ernst & Whinney, which was overseeing ZZZZ Best's planned multimillion-dollar acquisition of another carpet-cleaning chain. When an investigation began, Rothberg accepted $17,000 from ZZZZ Best officials to back off from his initial reports.[22]

Rothberg's conduct was wrong because he accepted money in exchange for violating his responsibilities as an accountant. By contrast, a server who accepts a gratuity for providing good service to a restaurant customer is not accepting a bribe, for she is not violating her duties. However, the situation would be different if she took money in exchange for not charging the customer for the drinks he ordered. Of course, bribery can occur in more subtle forms than in the Rothberg case. For instance, in exchange for a "sympathetic reading of the books," a company gives a state auditor a trip to Hawaii. Or a sporting goods company provides the child of one of its retailers with free summer camp in exchange for preferred display space for its products. In both instances, individuals have received payments inconsistent with their job contract or the nature of the work they are expected to perform.

Bribery sometimes takes the form of *kickbacks,* a practice that involves a percentage payment to a person able to influence or control a source of income. Thus, Alice Farnsworth, sales representative for Sisyphus Books, offers a book-selection committee member a percentage of the handsome commission she stands to make if a Sisyphus civics text is adopted. The money the committee member receives for the preferred consideration is a kickback. A flagrant case of kickbacks involved American executives of the Honda Motor Company. For years they pocketed millions in bribes and kickbacks from local car dealers; in return, the dealers received permission to open lucrative dealerships and had no trouble obtaining models (such as the Acura) that were in scarce supply and could be sold at a large profit.[23]

The Foreign Corrupt Practices Act

Bribery is generally illegal in the United States, but U.S. companies have a history of paying off foreign officials for business favors. Such acts were declared illegal in the Foreign Corrupt Practices Act (FCPA) of 1977, which was passed in the wake of the discovery that nearly 400 U.S. companies had made such payments over several years amounting to about $300 million. Egregious within this sordid pattern of international bribery was Lockheed Aircraft Corporation's $22 million in secret payoffs to foreign politicians to get aircraft contracts. Lest one understate the effects of such bribery, it is worth noting that revelations of Lockheed bribes in Japan caused a government crisis there and that in Holland Prince Bernhard was forced to resign his government duties after admitting that he took a $1 million payoff from Lockheed. Gulf Oil also admitted to making secret payments to foreign politicians—specifically, $4 million to the ruling political party in South Korea to firm up its investments there. Exxon confirmed that it paid $59 million to Italian politicians to promote its business objectives in that country. And only after the suicide of United Brands chairman Eli Black did an SEC investigation reveal that the company had paid a $1.25 million bribe to a Honduran official to win a reduction in that country's business export tax.

The FCPA provides stiff fines and prison sentences for corporate officials engaging in bribery overseas and requires corporations to establish strict accounting and auditing controls to guard against the creation of slush funds from which bribes can be paid. The FCPA does not, however, prohibit "grease payments" to the employees of foreign governments who have primarily clerical or ministerial responsibilities. These payments are sometimes necessary to ensure that the recipients carry out their normal job duties. On the other hand, the FCPA makes no distinction between bribery and extortion. A company is extorted by a foreign official if, for instance, the official threatens to violate the company's rights, perhaps by closing down a plant on some legal pretext, unless the official is paid off.

One company caught violating the FCPA was Ashland Oil. Under its then-CEO Orin Atkins, Ashland had agreed to pay an entity controlled by an Omani government official approximately $29 million for a majority interest in Midlands Chrome, Inc., a price far higher than it was worth, for the purpose of obtaining crude oil at a highly favorable price. When Atkins proposed the acquisition of Midlands Chrome to his board of directors, he said that although the acquisition was a high-risk project, it "had the potential for being more than offset by a potential crude oil contract." Midlands Chrome did not in fact prove particularly profitable, but the Omani government awarded Ashland a contract for 20,000 barrels a day for one year at a three-dollar-per-barrel discount from the regular selling price—a discount worth $21.9 million.[24]

The Case Against Overseas Bribery

The FCPA has been weakened by amendments that expand the exemption for grease payments and offer corporations more defenses against prosecution. In 1998, however, the law was extended to include bribery by foreign firms on American territory, and, thanks to the Federal Sentencing Guidelines, penalties are now stiffer than those originally specified by the FCPA. Few companies, though, are charged with violating the law—the Justice Department brings an average of only 1.5 cases per year, the SEC even fewer.[25] Nevertheless, critics of the FCPA insist that it puts American corporations at a competitive disadvantage in relation to foreign firms whose governments permit them to bribe. They assert that the law has resulted in lost exports for the United States.

However, competition is not always a factor in foreign bribes, as the United Brands case illustrates. In addition, studies show that before passage of the FCPA, when U.S. companies used bribery to beat out competitors, their competitors were usually other U.S. companies. As former Commerce Secretary Elliot Richardson reported to Congress, "in a multitude of cases—especially those involving the sale of military and commercial aircraft—payments have been made not to outcompete foreign competitors, but rather to gain a competitive edge over other U.S. manufacturers."[26] Furthermore, studies show that the FCPA has been at most a minor disincentive to export expansion. Even in nations where the FCPA is alleged to have hurt American business, there has been no statistically discernible effect on U.S. market share. In fact, since passage of the FCPA, U.S. trade with bribe-prone countries has outpaced its trade with other countries.[27]

In 1997 the world's industrialized nations—the twenty-nine members of the Organization for Economic Cooperation and Development—formally agreed for the first time to a treaty that outlaws the bribing of foreign officials. This agreement makes it less likely that the FCPA will put American companies at a competitive disadvantage in the future. But even if the FCPA does handicap U.S. firms and cause them to lose exports, this fact would have to be carefully weighed against the ample documentary evidence of the serious harm done to individuals, companies, and governments as a result of systematic bribery overseas.

A frequently heard argument against the FCPA is that the law imposes U.S. standards on foreign countries and that bribery and payoffs are common business practices in other nations. But this argument is too glib, especially when it comes from those who don't really have a working knowledge of another culture. In some other nations, to be sure, bribery does seem more widespread than it is here, but that doesn't imply that bribery is considered morally acceptable even in those nations. (Drug dealing is not morally acceptable here, even though it is, unfortunately, widespread.) If other countries really did consider bribery and related practices to be morally acceptable, then presumably the people engaging in them would not mind having this fact publicized. But it is difficult to find a real-life example of foreign officials willing to let the public know they accept bribes.

Certainly the FCPA reflects our own moral standards, but those standards are not simply matters of taste (like clothing styles) or completely arbitrary (like our decision to drive on the right, whereas the British drive on the left). Good, objective arguments can be given against bribery and related corrupt practices because they are intended to induce people inside a business or other organization to make a decision that would not be justifiable according to normal business or other criteria. For example, by encouraging on nonmarket grounds the purchase of inferior goods or the payment of an exorbitant price, bribery can clearly injure a variety of legitimate interests—from stockholders to consumers, from taxpayers to other businesses. It subverts market competition by giving advantage in a way that is not directly or indirectly product related.

There is nothing "relative" about the damage that such corruption can do to a society. Studies show that the more corrupt a nation is, the less it invests and the slower its economic growth.[28] If we were to permit U.S. companies to engage in bribery overseas, we would be encouraging in other countries practices that we consider too harmful to tolerate at home. Moreover, even an occasional corporate bribe overseas can foster bribery and kickbacks at home and lead employees to subordinate the interest of the organization to their own private gain. Corruption is difficult to cordon off; once a company engages in it, corruption can easily spread throughout the organization.

The multiple impacts of bribery can be succinctly drawn out in one final case, which involved Bethlehem Steel Corporation, the nation's second-largest steel company. Bethlehem was fined $325,000 by a federal judge for bribery and other corrupt practices stretching over four years. Bethlehem admitted paying bribes to shipowners' representatives, including officers of the Colombian Navy. The bribes were paid to ensure that ships needing repairs would be steered into Bethlehem's eight shipyards. Thus, competitive bidding for the contracts was effectively eliminated, various members of the Colombian Navy were corrupted, and the Colombian government presumably ended up paying more for the repair work than it had to. Beyond this, Bethlehem generated more than $1.7 million for the payoffs by padding bills and skimming profits from legitimate shipyard repair work. Thus, unsuspecting clients of Bethlehem were made to pay the bill for Bethlehem's bribery.

GIFTS AND ENTERTAINMENT

Business gifts and entertainment of clients and business associates are a familiar part of the business world. Still, both practices can raise conflict-of-interest problems and even border on bribery, but knowing where to draw the line is not always easy. One thing is clear: Those who cross that line, wittingly or not, can end up in big trouble. Ask the former General Services Administration (GSA) official who pleaded guilty to a criminal charge of accepting free lunches from a subsidiary of the BellSouth Corporation, which was seeking a telephone contract with the GSA.[29]

The federal government, in fact, now provides its procurement officers with two days' worth of lectures and case-study discussions on the ethics of government contracting. Procurement officers, for example, are taught that they may accept an invitation to speak before a trade association consisting of the contractors they buy from, but they must decline the fifty-dollar honorarium, whatever the topic of their talk. They must also refuse a ticket for their transportation to the meeting, although they may be permitted to accept lunch as a guest seated at the head of the table, if this is compatible with the policy of their particular agency.[30]

For people in the business world, the rules are not so cut-and-dried. In fact, some of them manage to ignore altogether the conflict-of-interest issues that gifts create. Consider Colin Dalzell, an executive at MCI Systemhouse. Just before it went public, the e-biz software maker, Commerce One, offered Dalzell, who had done business with it, a chance to buy its shares. He did, and in one day made a profit of $40,000, which he used to buy a 1965 Cobra racing-car kit. Dalzell says that he had a long, established relationship with Commerce One and that the payment wasn't enough to influence his future dealings with it.[31] But most companies and most business people view behavior like his as morally problematic, to say the least.

Determining the morality of giving and receiving gifts in a business situation is not always easy. But there are several factors a conscientious businessperson should take into account:

1. *What is the value of the gift?* Is the gift of nominal value, or is it substantial enough to influence a business decision? Undoubtedly, definitions of "nominal" and "substantial" are open to interpretation and are often influenced by situational and cultural variables. Nevertheless, many organizations consider a gift worth twenty-five dollars or less given infrequently—perhaps once a year—only nominal, but anything larger or more frequent would constitute a substantial gift. Although this standard won't fit all cases, it does indicate that accepting even a rather inexpensive gift might be deemed inappropriate.

2. *What is the purpose of the gift?* Dick Randall, a department store manager, accepts small gifts such as pocket calculators from an electronics firm. He insists that the transactions are harmless and that he doesn't intend to give the firm any preferential treatment in terms of advertising displays in the store. As long as the gift is not intended or received as a bribe and remains nominal, there doesn't appear to be any serious problem. But it would be important to ascertain the electronics firm's intention in giving the gift. Is it to influence how Randall lays out displays? Does Randall himself expect it as a palm-greasing device before he'll ensure that the firm receives equal promotional treatment? If so, extortion may be involved. Important to this question of purpose is a consideration of whether the gift is directly tied to an accepted business practice. For example, appointment books, calendars, or pens and pencils with the donor's name clearly imprinted on them serve to advertise a firm. Trips to Hawaii rarely serve this purpose.

3. *What are the circumstances under which the gift was given or received?* A gift given during the holiday season, for a store opening, or to signal other special events is circumstantially different from one unattached to any special event. Whether the gift was given openly or secretly should also be considered. An open gift, say, with the donor's name embossed on it, raises fewer questions than a gift known only to the donor and recipient.

4. *What is the position and sensitivity to influence of the person receiving the gift?* Is the person in a position to affect materially a business decision on behalf of the gift giver? In other words, could the recipient's opinion, influence, or decision result in preferential treatment for the donor? Another important point is whether the recipients have made it abundantly clear to the donors that they don't intend to allow the gift to influence their action one way or the other.

5. *What is the accepted business practice in the industry?* Is this the customary way of conducting this kind of business? Monetary gifts and tips are standard practice in numerous service industries. Their purpose is not only to reward good service but to ensure it again. But it's not customary to tip the head of the produce department in a supermarket so the person will put aside the best tomatoes for you. When gratuities are an integral part of customary business practice they are far less likely to pose moral questions.

6. *What is the company's policy?* Many firms explicitly forbid the practice of giving and receiving gifts to minimize even the suspicion that a conflict may exist. Kmart, for example, adopted such a policy, which it requires not only its managers, but also its vendors, suppliers, and real estate associates to sign, after one of its corporate directors was indicted for accepting kickbacks.[32] When such a policy exists, the giving or receiving of a gift would normally be wrong.

7. *What is the law?* Certain federal, state, or local government employees, for example, may be forbidden by law from receiving any gifts from firms with which they do business. When gift transactions violate the law, they are clearly unacceptable.

Related to gift giving is the practice of entertaining. Some companies distinguish entertainment from gifts as follows: If you can eat or drink it on the spot, it's entertainment. In general, entertainment should be interpreted more sympathetically than gifts because it usually occurs within the context of doing business in a social situation. Still, the morality of entertainment should be evaluated along the same lines as gifts— that is, with respect to value, purpose, circumstances, position and sensitivity to influence of the recipient, accepted business practice, company policy, and the law. In each case the ultimate moral judgment hinges largely on whether an objective party could reasonably suspect that the gift or entertainment might lead the recipient to sacrifice the interest of the firm for his or her personal gain.

OBLIGATIONS TO THIRD PARTIES

Consider the following situations:

An employee knows that a coworker occasionally sips whiskey on the job. Should she inform the boss?

A dishwasher knows that the restaurant's chef typically reheats three- or four-day-old food and serves it as fresh. When he informs the manager, he is told to forget it. What should the dishwasher do?

A consulting engineer discovers a defect in a structure that is about to be sold. If the owner will not disclose the defect to the potential purchaser, should the engineer do so?

A clerical worker learns that the personnel department has authorized hirings that violate the firm's anti-nepotism rules and neglect its affirmative action commitments. What should she do about it?

On a regular basis, a secretary is asked by her boss to lie to his wife about his whereabouts. "If my wife telephones," he tells her, "don't forget that 'I'm calling on a client.'" In fact, as the secretary well knows, the boss is having an affair with another woman. What should the secretary do?

Such cases are not unusual, but they are different from the ones previously considered in this chapter because they involve workers caught in the crossfire of competing ethical concerns and moral responsibilities. Should the employee ensure the welfare of the organization by reporting the fellow worker who drinks, or should she be loyal to her coworker and say nothing? Should the dishwasher go public with what he knows or should he simply forget the matter? Should the secretary carry out her boss's instructions, or should she tell his wife the truth? In each case the employee may experience conflicting obligations, diverging ideals, and divided loyalties.

Many of the difficult moral decisions that employees sometimes face involve such conflicts. How are they to be resolved? According to the procedure recommended in Chapter 2, our moral decisions should take into account our specific obligations, any important ideals that our actions would support or undermine, and, finally, the effects or consequences of the different options open to us. To begin with the latter consideration, remember that even staunch nonconsequentialists acknowledge that the likely results of our actions are relevant to their moral assessment and that we have some duty to promote human well-being. In general, the fuller our understanding of the possible results of the different actions we might take in the specific situation before us—that is, the better we understand the exact ramifications of the alternatives—the more likely we are to make a sound moral decision. Reflecting on the effects of these different courses of action can help us understand what ideals are at stake and determine the exact strength of the more specific obligations we have.

The impact of our actions on significant moral ideals is the second consideration to be weighed. Any serious moral decision should take into account the various ideals advanced or respected, ignored or hindered, by the alternative courses of conduct open to us. In addition, our moral choices are often strongly influenced by the personal weight we place on the different values at stake in a specific situation. Sometimes these values can point in different directions, as when our simultaneous commitment to professional excellence, personal integrity, and loyalty to friends pulls us in different ways.

Finally, any responsible moral decision must, of course, take into account the more specific obligations we have—in particular, those obligations that are a function of the particular relationships, roles, or circumstances we happen to be in. This chapter has already discussed the obligations employees have to the organization based on a freely negotiated work contract, and it is easy to see that employees have moral obligations arising from the business, professional, or organizational roles they have assumed. For example, teachers have an obligation to grade fairly, bartenders to refrain from over-serving intoxicated customers, engineers to guarantee the safety of their projects, and accountants to certify that financial statements present data fairly and according to generally accepted accounting principles. Because of his or her role responsibilities, an auditor who suspects some irregularity has an obligation to get to the bottom of the matter, whereas an ordinary employee who has a hunch that something is not in order in another department probably would not have that responsibility.

Thus, employees have certain general duties to their employers, and because of the specific business, professional, or organizational responsibilities they have assumed, they may have other more precise role-based obligations. In addition, employees are human beings with moral responsibilities to friends, family, and coworkers—to those flesh-and-blood people with whom their lives are intertwined, both inside and outside the workplace. These ongoing relationships are the source of important moral obligations.

What about the obligations of employees to other parties or to society in general? In particular, what obligations do employees have to people with whom they have no relationship and for whom they have no specific professional, organizational, or other role responsibility? Here different moral theories may steer us in slightly different directions, but simply as a matter of ordinary commonsense morality it is clear that employees—like everyone else—have certain elementary duties to other people. Of particular significance are the obligations to avoid injuring others and to be truthful and fair.

When faced with a moral decision, then, employees should follow the two-step procedure set forth in Chapter 2: identify the relevant obligations, ideals, and effects and then try to decide where the emphasis should lie among these considerations. There is nothing mechanical about this process, but when we as employees weigh moral decisions, two simple things can help keep our deliberations free from the various rationalizations to which we are all prone. First, we can ask ourselves whether we would be willing to read an account of our actions in the newspaper. That is, when we have made our decisions, are the contemplated actions ones that we would be willing to defend publicly? Second, discussing a moral dilemma or ethical problem with a friend can often help us avoid bias and gain a better perspective. People by themselves, and especially when emotionally involved in a situation, sometimes focus unduly on one or two points, ignoring other relevant factors. Input from others can keep us from overlooking pertinent considerations, thus helping us make a better, more objective moral judgment.

As the preceding discussion mentioned, employees sometimes learn about the illegal or immoral actions of a supervisor or firm. When an employee tries to correct the situation within institutional channels and is thwarted, a central moral question emerges: Should the employee go public with the information? Should a worker who is ordered to do something illegal or immoral, or who knows of the illegal or immoral behavior of a supervisor or organization, inform the public?

WHISTLE-BLOWING

Morris H. Baslow, a forty-seven-year-old biologist and father of three, won't forget the day he dropped an envelope in the mail to Thomas B. Yost, an administrative law judge with the Environmental Protection Agency (EPA). For later that day, Baslow was fired from his job with Lawler, Matusky & Skelly, an engineering consulting firm that had been hired by Consolidated Edison of New York to help it blunt EPA demands. The EPA was insisting that the power company's generating plants on the Hudson River had to have cooling towers to protect fish from excessively warm water that it was discharging into the river.

Baslow claimed that the documents he sent showed that Con Ed and Lawler, Matusky & Skelly had knowingly submitted to the EPA invalid and misleading data, giving the false impression that the long-term effects of the utility's effluent on fish were negligible. On the basis of his own research, Baslow believed that the fish could be significantly harmed by the warm-water discharge. He said that for two years he tried to get his employers to listen, but they wouldn't.

Shortly after being fired, Baslow sent seventy-one company documents supporting his allegation to the EPA, the federal Energy Regulatory Commission, and the Justice Department. In the month following these disclosures, Baslow's employers accused him of stealing the documents and sued him for defamation. Baslow countersued, citing the Clean Water Act, which protects consultants from reprisals for reporting findings prejudicial to their employers and clients.

A year later, Lawler, Matusky & Skelly dropped all legal action against Baslow and gave him a cash settlement, reportedly of around $100,000. In return, Baslow wrote to the EPA and other government agencies, withdrawing his charges of wrongdoing and perjury but not recanting his own scientific conclusions. Asked why he finally accepted the cash payment, the unemployed Baslow said, "I've had to bear the brunt of this financially by myself. . . . I just wish somebody had listened to me six months ago."[33]

The Baslow case and scores more like it illustrate the ethical problem and personal risks facing employees who blow the whistle on what they perceive as organizational misconduct.

Whistle-blowing refers to an employee's informing the public about the illegal or immoral behavior of an employer or organization. One expert more fully defines whistle-blowing as:

> A practice in which employees who know that their company is engaged in activities that (a) cause unnecessary harm, (b) are in violation of human rights, (c) are illegal, (d) run counter to the defined purpose of the institution, or (e) are otherwise immoral inform the public or some governmental agency of those activities.[34]

Another business ethicist spells out the concept this way:

> Whistle-blowing is the voluntary release of nonpublic information, as a moral protest, by a member or former member of an organization outside the normal channels of communication to an appropriate audience about illegal and/or immoral conduct in the organization or conduct in the organization that is opposed in some significant way to the public interest.[35]

These definitions limit the scope of what constitutes whistle-blowing. Whistle-blowing is something that can be done only by a (past or present) member of an organization. An investigative reporter, for example, who exposes corporate malfeasance is not a whistle-blower. Nor is an employee who spreads gossip about in-house gaffes and indiscretions, thus abusing confidentiality and acting disloyally to colleagues and to the organization. By contrast, whistle-blowing refers to exposing activities that are harmful, immoral, or contrary to the public interest or to the legitimate goals and purposes of the organization. It does not encompass sabotage or taking retaliatory action against the employer or firm, but it does require going outside normal channels. (This doesn't imply, however, that whistle-blowing must be external. Most writers on the subject hold that there can also be internal whistle-blowing, where disclosure of inappropriate conduct is made to someone inside the organization.)

When Is Whistle-Blowing Justified?

Professor of philosophy Norman Bowie correctly points out that today's discussion of whistle-blowing parallels the discussion of civil disobedience in the 1960s.[36] Just as civil disobedients of that time felt their duty to obey the law was overridden by other moral obligations, so the whistle-blower overrides loyalty to colleagues and to the organization in order to serve the public interest. Coleen Rowley, for example, was a veteran FBI agent with twenty-one years of experience who had never worked for anyone else—indeed, she had wanted to be an agent ever since she was in fifth grade. When she decided to go public with evidence that her bosses had failed to follow up on information that might have thwarted the terrorist attacks of September 11, 2001, and were now misleading the public about what the FBI had known, her desire to do what was right took precedence over her lifelong love of the Bureau. Although whistle-blowers like Rowley are often stigmatized as "disloyal," many of them see themselves as acting in the best interests of the organization.

What motivates whistle-blowers? Often, it's simply a sense of professional responsibility. Take F. Barron Stone for example. He warned his bosses at Duke Power that they were overcharging ratepayers in the Carolinas. When they wouldn't listen, he told state regulators. This triggered an investigation, which led to Duke Power's agreeing to change its accounting procedures and reimburse customers. "I was just doing my job" is all Stone says.[37] Or consider Cynthia Cooper. An internal auditor at WorldCom, she got wind that some of the company's divisions were engaged in crooked accounting practices. She raised the matter with the firm's external auditor, Arthur Andersen, but it assured her there was no problem. When she didn't drop the issue, WorldCom's chief financial officer, Scott Sullivan, told her that everything was fine and she should back off. Troubled and suspicious about what was going on, Cooper ignored Sullivan's order. She and her team began doing what the external auditor was supposed to do. For weeks and weeks they pored over company books, working late at night to avoid detection by management, before eventually exposing the accounting scams Sullivan and others were involved in. "I'm not a hero," she told friends and colleagues. "I'm just doing my job."[38]

Whistle-blowing does, however, present dangers, as Professor Sissela Bok reminds us.[39] The whistle can be blown in error or malice, privacy invaded, and trust undermined. Not least, publicly accusing others of wrongdoing can be very destructive and brings with it an obligation to be fair to the persons accused. In addition, internal prying and mutual suspicion make it difficult for any organization to function. And, finally, one must bear in mind that whistle-blowers are only human beings, not saints, and they can sometimes have their own self-serving agenda.[40]

In developing his analogy with civil disobedience, Professor Bowie proposes several conditions that must be met for an act of whistle-blowing to be morally justified. These conditions may not be the last word on this controversial subject, but they do provide a good starting point for further debate over the morality of whistle-blowing. According to Bowie, whistle-blowing is morally justified if and only if:

1. *It is done from an appropriate moral motive.* For an act of whistle-blowing to be justified, it must be motivated by a desire to expose unnecessary harm, illegal or immoral actions, or conduct counter to the public good or the defined purpose of the organization. Desire for attention or profit or the exercise of one's general tendency toward stirring up trouble is not a justification for whistle-blowing.

   Although, as Chapter 2 explained, the question of motive is an important one in Kantian ethics, not all moral theorists would agree with Bowie's first condition. Might not an employee be justified in blowing the whistle on serious wrongdoing by the employer, even if the employee's real motivation was the desire for revenge? Granted that the motivation was ignoble, the action itself might nonetheless have been the morally right one. An action can still be morally justified, say some theorists, even when it is done for the wrong reason. Still, many people were troubled to learn that the whistle-blowing paralegal who provided anti-tobacco lawyers with crucial documents about a tobacco company's secret studies on the health dangers of cigarettes was paid more than $100,000 by the lawyers.[41]

2. *The whistle-blower, except in special circumstances, has exhausted all internal channels for dissent before going public.* The duty of loyalty to the firm obligates workers to seek an internal remedy before informing the public of a misdeed. This is an important consideration, but in some cases the attempt to exhaust internal channels may result in dangerous delays or expose the would-be whistle-blower to retaliation.

3. *The whistle-blower has compelling evidence that wrongful actions have been ordered or have occurred.* Spelling out what constitutes "compelling evidence" is difficult, but employees can ask themselves whether the evidence is strong enough that any reasonable person in a similar situation would be convinced that the activity is illegal or immoral. Although this may not be a decisive guideline, the standard of what a reasonable person would believe is commonly invoked in other cases, such as deceptive advertising and negligence lawsuits.

4. *The whistle-blower has acted after careful analysis of the danger: How serious is the moral violation? How immediate is the problem? Can the whistle-blower point to specific misconduct?* These criteria focus on the nature of the wrongdoing. Owing loyalty to employers, employees should blow the whistle only for grave legal or moral matters. The greater the harm or the more serious the wrongdoing, the more likely is the whistle-blowing to be justified. Indeed, in some circumstances, whistle-blowing may not only be morally justified; it may be morally required. Additionally, employees should consider the time factor. The greater the time before the violation is to occur, the more likely the firm's own internal mechanisms will prevent it; and the more immediate a violation, the more justified the whistle-blowing. Finally, the whistle-blower must be specific. General allegations, such as that a company is "not operating in the best interests of the public" or is "systematically sabotaging the competition," won't do. Concrete examples are needed that can pass the other justificatory tests.

5. *The whistle-blowing has some chance of success.* This criterion recognizes that the chances of remedying an immoral or illegal action are an important consideration. Sometimes the chances are good; other times they're slim. Probably most cases fall somewhere between these extremes. In general, given the potential harmful effects, whistle-blowing that stands no chance of success is less justified than that with some chance of success. Even so, sometimes merely drawing attention to an objectionable practice, although it may fail to improve the specific situation, encourages government and society to be more watchful of certain behavior.

THE QUESTION OF SELF-INTEREST
So far the discussion of obligations to third parties and the special problem of whistle-blowing has paid scant attention to the worker's own interests. And yet for many employees, protecting themselves or safeguarding their jobs is the primary factor in deciding whether to put third-party interests above those of the firm.

Concern with self-interest in cases that pit loyalty to the firm against obligations to third parties is altogether understandable and even warranted. After all, workers who subordinate the organization's interests to an outside party's expose themselves to charges of disloyalty, disciplinary action, freezes in job status, forced relocations, and even dismissal. Furthermore, even when an employee successfully blows the whistle, he or she can be blacklisted in an industry. Given the potential harm to self and family that employees risk in honoring third-party obligations, it is perfectly legitimate to inquire about the weight considerations of self-interest should be given in resolving cases of conflicting obligations.

Sadly, there is no clear, unequivocal answer to this question. Moral theorists and society as a whole do distinguish between prudential reasons and moral reasons. "Prudential" (from the word *prudence*) refers here to considerations of self-interest; "moral" refers here to considerations of the interests of others and the demands of morality. Chapter 1 explained that it is possible for prudential and moral considerations to pull us in different directions. One way of looking at their relationship is this: If prudential concerns outweigh moral ones, then employees may do what is in their own best interest. If moral reasons override prudential ones, then workers should honor their obligations to others.

Consider the case of a cashier at a truck stop who is asked to write up phony chits so truckers can get a larger expense reimbursement from their employers than they really deserve. The cashier doesn't think this is right, so she complains to the manager. The manager explains that the restaurant is largely dependent on trucker business and that this is a good way to ensure it. The cashier is ordered to do the truckers' bidding and is thus being told to violate at least three duties owed to any outside party (in this case, the trucking firms): truth, noninjury, and fairness. Given these moral considerations, the cashier ought to refuse, and perhaps she should even report the conduct to the trucking companies.

But let's suppose that the cashier happens to be a recent divorcée with no formal education. She lacks occupational skills and stands little chance of getting another job in an economy that happens to be depressed—for months she was unemployed before landing her present position. With no other means of support, the consequences of job loss for her would be serious indeed. Now, given this scenario and given that the wrongdoing at issue is relatively minor, prudential concerns would probably take legitimate precedence over moral ones. In other words, the cashier would be justified in "going along," at least on a temporary basis.

Some moral theorists would agree with this conclusion but analyze the case somewhat differently. They think it is incorrect to say that in some circumstances we may permit prudential considerations to outweigh moral considerations. There is no neutral perspective outside both morality and self-interest from which one can make such a judgment. Furthermore, they would say that, by definition, nothing can outweigh the demands of morality.

Does that mean the cashier should refuse to do what her manager wants and, thus, lose her job? Not necessarily. Morality does not, these theorists contend, require us to make large sacrifices to right small wrongs. Writing up phony chits does violate some basic moral principles, and the cashier has some moral obligation not to go along with it. But morality does not, all things considered, require her—under the present circumstances—to take a course of action that would spell job loss. She should, however, take less drastic steps to end the practice (like continuing to talk to her boss and the truckers about it) and perhaps eventually find other work. Thus, according to this way of thinking, the cashier is not sacrificing morality to self-interest in "going along" for a while. The idea is that morality does not impose obligations on us without regard to their cost; it does not, under the present circumstances, demand an immediate resignation by the cashier.

Whichever way one looks at it, the question of balancing our moral obligations to others and our own self-interest is particularly relevant to whistle-blowing. In situations in which whistle-blowing threatens one's livelihood and career, prudential concerns may properly be taken into account in deciding what one should do, all things considered. This doesn't mean that if the worker blows the whistle despite compelling prudential reasons not to, he or she is not moral. On the contrary, such an action could be highly moral. (As Chapter 2 explained, ethical theorists term such actions "supererogatory," meaning that they are, so to speak, above and beyond the call of duty.) On the other hand, when the moral concerns are great (for example, when the lives of others are at stake), elementary morality and personal integrity can require people to make substantial sacrifices.

A couple of further remarks are in order here. First, an evaluation of prudential reasons obviously is colored by one's temperament and perceptions of self-interest. Each of us has a tendency to magnify potential threats to our livelihood or career. Exaggerating the costs to ourselves of acting otherwise makes it easier to rationalize away the damage we are doing to others. In the business world, for instance, people talk about the survival of the firm as if it were literally a matter of life and death. Going out of business is the worst thing that can happen to a firm, but the people who make it up will live on and get other jobs. Keeping the company alive (let alone competitive or profitable) cannot justify seriously injuring innocent people.

Not only do we tend to exaggerate the importance of self-interested considerations, but also most of us have been socialized to heed authority. As a result, we are disinclined to question the orders of someone above us, especially when the authority is an employer or supervisor with power to influence our lives for better or worse. It's easy for us to assume that any boat rocking will be very harmful, even self-destructive.

It follows, then, that each of us has an obligation to perform a kind of character or personality audit. Do we follow authority blindly? Do we suffer from moral tunnel vision on the job? Do we mindlessly do what is demanded of us, oblivious to the impact of our cooperation and actions on outside parties? Have we given enough attention to our possible roles as accomplices in the immoral undoing of other individuals, businesses, and social institutions? Do we have a balanced view of our own interests versus those of others? Do we have substantial evidence for believing that our livelihoods are really threatened, or is that belief based more on an exaggeration of the facts? Have we been imaginative in trying to balance prudential and moral concerns? Have we sought to find some middle ground, or have we set up a false self-other dilemma in which our own interests and those of others are erroneously viewed as incompatible? These are just some of the questions that a personal inventory should include if we are to combat the all-too-human tendency to stack the deck in favor of prudential reasons whenever they are pitted against moral ones.

A second observation about the relationship between prudential and moral considerations concerns the welfare of society. In some cases, as we have seen, considerations of self-interest may mean one does not have an overriding moral obligation to blow the whistle; when that occurs, how can society be protected from wrongdoing? Is the welfare of society to be left to those few heroic souls willing to perform supererogatory actions? Perhaps the only reasonable solution is to restructure business and social institutions so such acts no longer carry such severe penalties.

Although a hodgepodge of legal precedents and state and federal legislation already affords some assistance to employees who blow the whistle, the Sarbanes-Oxley Act of 2002 marks an important advance. The act provides sweeping new legal protection for employees who report possible securities fraud, making it unlawful for companies to "discharge, demote, suspend, threaten, harass, or in any other manner discriminate against" them. Fired workers can sue, and they are guaranteed the right to a jury trial instead of having to endure months or years of administrative hearings. In addition, the Labor Department can order companies to rehire terminated whistle-blowers with no court hearings whatsoever. Moreover, executives who retaliate against employees who report possible violations of *any* federal law now face imprisonment for up to ten years.

Unfortunately, Sarbanes-Oxley came too late to help Christine Casey. After a few years working at Mattel, Casey was assigned by the toy maker to develop a system to allocate production among its factories. But she soon discovered that Mattel's official sales forecasts were so high that managers routinely ignored the numbers. "It was a joke around the office," she says. Managers kept two sets of figures and would telephone around to find out what they should really tell their factories to produce. Casey went to a company director with a proposal to fix the numbers and help the company forecast profits more accurately. She then began experiencing hostility from company executives, received her first negative performance review, and was shunted off to a tiny cubicle, stripped of most of her work responsibilities. When Mattel's chief financial officer ignored her concerns, and its human resources department turned a blind eye to her mistreatment, she telephoned the SEC. Although Mattel later had to pay $122 million to shareholders who sued it for deliberately inflating its sales forecasts, Casey lost her wrongful termination suit against the company for having harassed her into resigning. She has little chance for getting another job like it because big companies routinely check job applicants' litigation history.[42]

It is not enough, however, merely to change the law. Corporate attitudes need to change as well. In America, the *Economist* magazine writes, "it is almost always thought cheaper to fire whistle-blowers than to listen to them, despite years of legislation designed to achieve the opposite."[43] Kris Kolesnik, director of the National Whistleblower Center, is equally pessimistic. "No matter how many protections whistleblower laws have created over the years," he says, "the system always seems to defeat them."[44] In the long run, however, organizations benefit more from encouraging employees to come forward with their ethical concerns than they do from ignoring possible wrongdoing and retaliating against those who raise awkward queries. Openness and a receptive attitude toward moral questioning by employees give the organization a chance to take corrective action. This can save it money (by rooting out embezzlement, say, or forestalling litigation) or at least—as recent scandals make clear—help it to head off worse trouble when the problems bothering employees eventually leak out to the public.

To discharge their moral responsibilities and safeguard their own interests, companies need to develop explicit, proactive whistle-blowing policies. As a minimum, these policies should state that employees aware of possible wrongdoing have a responsibility to disclose that information; specific individuals or groups outside the chain of command should be designated to hear those concerns; employees who in good faith disclose perceived wrongdoing should be protected from adverse employment consequences; and there should be a fair and impartial investigative process.[45] In these ways, management can create organizational procedures and a corporate culture that make it less likely that employees will be forced to blow the whistle externally.

SUMMARY

1. The employment contract creates various obligations to one's employer. In addition, employees often feel loyalty to the organization. Conflicts of interest arise when employees have a personal interest in a transaction substantial enough that it does, or might reasonably be expected to, lead them to act against the interests of the organization.

2. When employees have financial investments in suppliers, customers, or distributors with whom the organization does business, conflicts of interest can arise. Company policy usually determines the permissible limits of such financial interests.

3. *Insider trading* refers to buying or selling stocks based on nonpublic information likely to affect stock prices. Insider trading seems unfair and can injure other investors. In practice, determining what counts as insider trading is not always easy, but it typically involves misappropriating sensitive information. Some writers defend insider trading as performing a necessary and desirable economic function.

4. *Proprietary data* refers to an organization's classified or secret information. Increasingly, problems arise as employees in high-tech occupations with access to sensitive information and trade secrets quit and take jobs with competitors. Proprietary-data issues pose a conflict between two legitimate rights: the right of employers to keep certain information secret and the right of individuals to work where they choose.

5. A *bribe* is payment in some form for an act that runs counter to the work contract or the nature of the work one has been hired to perform. The Foreign Corrupt Practices Act prohibits corporations from engaging in bribery overseas. Bribery generally involves injury to individuals, competitors, or political institutions and damage to the free-market system.

6. The following considerations are relevant in determining the moral acceptability of gift giving and receiving: the value of the gift, its purpose, the circumstances under which it is given, the position and sensitivity to influence of the person receiving the gift, accepted business practice, company policy, and what the law says.

7. Employees have duties to their employers, and they may also have more specific obligations based on the business or professional roles and responsibilities they have assumed. In addition, they have the same elementary moral obligations that all human beings have—including the obligation not to injure others and to be truthful and fair.

8. Balancing our obligations to employer or organization, to friends and coworkers, and to third parties outside the organization can create conflicts and divided loyalties. In resolving such moral conflicts, we must identify the relevant obligations, ideals, and effects and decide where the emphasis among them should lie.

9. *Whistle-blowing* refers to an employee's informing the public about the illegal or immoral behavior of an employer or organization.

10. An act of whistle-blowing can be presumed to be morally justified if it is done from the appropriate moral motive; if the whistle-blower, except in special circumstances, has exhausted internal channels before going public; if the whistle-blower has compelling evidence; if the whistle-blower has carefully analyzed the dangers; and if the whistle-blowing has some chance of success.

11. Prudential considerations based on self-interest can conflict with moral considerations, which take into account the interests of others. Some sacrifices of self-interest would be so great that moral considerations must give way to prudential ones. But employees must avoid the temptation to exaggerate prudential concerns, thereby rationalizing away any individual moral responsibility to third parties. Legislation and changes in corporate culture are necessary so that whistle-blowing involves less personal sacrifice.

CASE 8.1

Changing Jobs and Changing Loyalties

Cynthia Martinez was thrilled when she first received the job offer from David Newhoff at Crytex Systems. She had long admired Crytex, both as an industry leader and as an ideal employer, and the position the company was offering her was perfect. "It's just what I've always wanted," she told her husband, Tom, as they uncorked a bottle of champagne. But as she and Tom talked, he raised a few questions that began to trouble her.

"What about the big project you're working on at Altrue right now? It'll take three months to see that through," Tom had reminded her. "The company has a lot riding on it, and you've always said that you're the driving force behind the project. If you bolt, Altrue is going to be in a real jam."

Cynthia explained that she had mentioned the project to David Newhoff. "He said he could understand I'd like to see it through, but Crytex needs someone right now. He gave me a couple of days to think it over, but it's my big chance."

Tom looked at her thoughtfully and responded, "But Newhoff doesn't quite get it. It's not just that you'd like to see it through. It's that you'd be letting your whole project team down. They probably couldn't do it without you, at least not the way it needs to be done. Besides, Cyn, remember what you said about that guy who quit the Altrue branch in Baltimore."

"That was different," Cynthia responded. "He took an existing account with him when he went to another firm. It was like ripping Altrue off. I'm not going to rip them off, but I don't figure I owe them anything extra. It's just business. You know perfectly well that if Altrue could save some money by laying me off, the company wouldn't hesitate."

"I think you're rationalizing," Tom said. "You've done well at Altrue, and the company has always treated you fairly. Anyway, the issue is what's right for you to do, not what the company would or wouldn't do. Crytex is Altrue's big competitor. It's like you're switching sides. Besides, it's not just a matter of loyalty to the company, but to the people you work with. I know we could use the extra money, and it would be a great step for you, but still . . ."

They continued to mull things over together, but the champagne no longer tasted quite as good. Fortunately, she and Tom never really argued about things they didn't see eye to eye on, and Tom wasn't the kind of guy who would try to tell her what she should or shouldn't do. But their conversation had started her wondering whether she really should accept that Crytex job she wanted so much.

Discussion Questions

1. What should Cynthia do? What ideals, obligations, and effects should she take into account when making her decision?
2. Would it be unprofessional of Cynthia to drop everything and move to Crytex? Would it show a lack of integrity? Could moving abruptly to Crytex have negative career consequences for her?

3. Is it morally wrong, morally permissible, or morally required for Cynthia to take the new job? Examine Cynthia's choice from a utilitarian point of view. How would Kant and Ross look at her situation?

4. What does loyalty to the company mean, and how important is it, morally? Under what circumstances, if any, do employees owe loyalty to their employers? When, if ever, do they owe loyalty to their coworkers?

CASE 8.2

Two Who Made
Waves for the Navy

Zeke Storms, a fifty-two-year-old retired Navy chief, began his career as a whistle-blower when he wrote Congressman Charles Pashayan to protest proposed cuts in the federal budget.[46] Storms had been employed as a civilian repairing flight simulators at the Lemoore Naval Air Base station near Fresno, California, since his retirement ten years before. Now he was suggesting that instead of supporting reductions in the Civil Service pay scale, Pashayan ought to take a closer look at Navy procurement practices. Enclosed in the letter was a list of spare parts showing that defense contractors were charging $435 for ordinary claw hammers and $100 or more for such electronic spare parts as diodes, transistors, and semiconductors, which cost less than $1 each. He also charged that the Navy purchased transistors at $100 each, which it could have obtained through the federal supply system for five cents apiece.

Storms's letter prompted Pashayan to query the Defense Department, which in turn kicked off an interservice investigation of military procurement practices. The Defense Department inspector general's office reported that the Navy had indeed failed to determine the most economical manner to acquire the spare parts Zeke Storms had listed. It also suggested that the spare-parts-overcharge problem was more widespread than at first thought. The investigative body left no doubt that the Navy was wasting millions of dollars annually.

In the wake of this report, the Secretary of Defense ordered a tightening of procurement procedures to ensure the lowest price for spare parts. Meanwhile, Navy Secretary John Lehman ordered contractors at Lemoore to refund $160,000 in overcharges. He also gave Storms a $4,000 award.

But Storms wasn't about to lay down his muckrake. He suggested that Defense Department auditors review overpayment for jet-aircraft support equipment in the base shops. The auditors did and discovered overpayment of $482,000, most of it spent on four spectrum analyzers. Had the items been bought through the federal supply system, they would have cost $47,500.

Storms then discovered that the Navy had engaged private contractors to operate its flight simulators for a new aircraft. "I got mad," he says. "[The Navy] had spent $1 million training their own people to do the work, then they just scrapped that and turned the maintenance over to the contractor." The contractor in question apparently was demanding $785,000 to maintain the simulators, which worked out to about

$100,000 per person per year. "I showed them that we [a team of Navy and Civil Service technicians] could do it for one-fourth that cost, so the contract was dropped to $411,000," says Storms.

That $411,000 was still higher than Storms believed the Navy had to pay, especially since the Navy had been maintaining its own simulators for two decades. So he took his case directly to Lehman, arguing that Office of Management and Budget (OMB) regulations required the Navy to do comparative cost studies to ensure the most cost-effective means. Lehman balked at Storms's proposal, saying that such studies would cost $45,000 each. That was too high a price to pay "to indulge Mr. Storms's eccentricities," the Secretary said in a letter to Congressman Pashayan.

Evidently deciding it was time to quiet the querulous Storms, Lehman then sent nine Navy brass to Lemoore. In the two-hour session that ensued, Storms did most of the talking. In the end, a commodore, four captains, two commanders, and two lieutenant commanders could do nothing to divert Storms from his course.

It was shortly thereafter that the ex-Navy chief did the "unpardonable." He accused Secretary Lehman and "his admirals" of lying. He said he had turned over to OMB officials Navy documents showing that Navy admirals willfully ignored requirements to do cost studies for private maintenance work. One of the documents included a message from Vice Admiral Robert F. Schoultz, the commander of naval forces in the Pacific. Addressing Admiral James D. Watkins, then commander of the Pacific Fleet, Schoultz wrote: "It is our intention to contract out all major training device maintenance. . . . [However] under the [contract] program our objective is hindered with cost studies that would yield inappropriate results." Schoultz's "inappropriate results" apparently was an allusion to the report by the fleet's top training officer, who estimated that the Navy's own people could do for $7 million the same work for which private contractors would charge $28 million.

In response to Storms, N. R. Lessard, officer in charge of the flight training groups for whom the ten-year Lemoore veteran was working, informed him that "your recent comments concerning senior Navy officials . . . constitute unacceptable employee conduct." To which Storms replied in a way most befitting a tobacco-chewing old salt: "[The Navy is] covering up, goddammit. I've got the facts, and they know it."

By contrast, Aaron Ahearn isn't an old salt, and he doesn't chew tobacco. But when the environmentally conscious, twenty-year-old sailor blew the whistle on the Navy's practice of dumping trash at sea, he made waves as big as Storms's.[47] Ahearn was a fireman's apprentice assigned to the scullery aboard the USS *Abraham Lincoln*, the world's largest nuclear-powered aircraft carrier. As part of his duties, Ahearn was supposed to dispose of the ship's garbage by tossing overboard up to 200 bags of plastic and other trash—some of it alleged to be toxic waste—every day. As a surfer who loves the ocean, Ahearn says that his conscience was troubled by what he had to do. He also reports seeing sailors dump broken desks, chairs, and computers into the ocean. When Ahearn's request for a change of assignment was denied, he jumped ship.

Environmentalists contend that plastic trash kills thousands of marine turtles, birds, and mammals annually and that it litters the beaches and wrecks boat propellers. Although private vessels can be fined up to $500,000 for dumping plastic debris, federal law specifically exempts the Navy. For its part, the Navy has always claimed that it can't avoid dumping plastic garbage because its ships house up to 5,500 sailors and spend months at sea.

Meanwhile, Ahearn, who had left the *Abraham Lincoln* on a weekend pass, went into hiding for two months, spending the time living with his girlfriend and surfing in the beach town of Santa Cruz, California. Eventually he decided to turn himself in. Before doing so, he received counseling from the Resource Center for Nonviolence and went to the media, saying his conscience would not allow him to pollute the ocean as ordered. He also announced that he wanted conscientious objector status on environmental grounds. Ahearn's story gained national coverage and focused pressure on the Navy to conform with international law governing plastic and trash disposal at sea. "What he did was commendable and brave," says Jil Zilligen of the Center for Marine Conservation in San Francisco. "I don't think many people realized this was going on at all."

Instead of battening down the hatches in response to the storm that Ahearn's allegations stirred up, the Navy announced that it would stop dumping plastic from all its surface ships and proposed a timetable for full compliance with the relevant international laws. What about Ahearn? Although environmental groups called him a hero, the Navy court-martialed him as a deserter who used his pollution allegations to cover up his unauthorized absence and as an excuse to leave the Navy. The ship's skipper, Navy Captain Ray Archer, contended that Ahearn told friends that he was going to jump ship to visit his girlfriend and would use his environmental concerns to justify it. And the Navy prosecutor, Lieutenant Tony Viera, said that Ahearn simply did not like his duty and needed to "grow up." The scullery is hot and sweaty, Viera remarked, and everybody hates working in it. But instead of sticking it out, Ahearn ran away and went surfing.

Ahearn and his attorney, Robert Rivkin, denied these charges, but the issue was never officially settled. In fact, at the court-martial, there was no mention at all of the environmental issues Ahearn had raised—except for the slogan "Pack Your Trash" tattooed across the back of his neck above the collar of his dress white Navy uniform. Instead, as part of a plea bargain, Ahearn pleaded guilty to unauthorized absence and to missing a ship's movement and was fined five hundred dollars and sentenced to thirty-five days in the brig. "Overall," commented his attorney, "it was a pretty good deal. It is a fair and reasonable sentence for what he did." Vicki Nichols, executive director of Save Our Shores, a marine conservation group, added, "I can't imagine that the Navy would ever admit a sailor who went AWOL has had any positive impact. But he did."

Discussion Questions

1. Do you think Storms and Ahearn qualify as whistle-blowers? What do you think their motives were?

2. Examine Storms's and Ahearn's actions from the perspective of Bowie's criteria for justified whistle-blowing. Are those criteria satisfied in both cases? Are Bowie's criteria themselves satisfactory?

3. What specific obligations, ideals, and effects should have been considered before either man became a whistle-blower?

4. Based on the details provided, would you consider Storms morally justified in having gone public with his information? Was Ahearn's conduct justified? Explain.

5. If you believe Storms's whistle-blowing was permissible, do you also believe that it was morally required of him? What about Ahearn's? Would someone in Storms's position have been justified in subordinating moral reasons to prudential concerns and thus in remaining silent? Explain.

6. What are the advantages and disadvantages of laws protecting whistle-blowers? Are they likely to work? Will they have good results, or will they encourage irresponsible whistle-blowing? If you favor such laws, what should they say?

7. How should corporations address the question of whistle-blowing? How should they deal with whistle-blowers or potential whistle-blowers? How should they handle disgruntled employees who make inaccurate or unfounded allegations? Should companies try to develop explicit policies and procedures or deal with each situation on a case-by-case basis? If the former, what policies and procedures should they put in place?

CASE 8.3

The Housing Allowance

Wilson Mutambara grew up in the slums outside Stanley, capital of the sub-Saharan African country of Rambia.[48] Through talent, hard work, and luck he made it through secondary school and won a scholarship to study in the United States. He eventually received an MBA and went to work for NewCom, a cellular telephone service. After three years in the company's Atlanta office, Wilson was given an opportunity to return to Rambia, where NewCom was setting up a local cellular service. Eager to be home, Wilson Mutambara couldn't say yes fast enough.

NewCom provides its employees in Rambia with a monthly allowance of up to $2,000 for rent, utilities, and servants. By Western standards, most of the housing in Stanley is poor quality, and many of its neighborhoods are unsafe. By providing the allowance, NewCom's intention is to see that its employees live in areas that are safe and convenient and that they live in a style that is appropriate to the company's image.

To claim their housing allowance, NewCom's employees in Rambia are supposed to turn in receipts, and every month Wilson Mutambara turned in an itemized statement for $2,000 from his landlord. Nobody at NewCom thought it was unusual that Wilson never entertained his coworkers at home. After all, he worked long hours and traveled frequently on business. However, after Wilson had been in Rambia for about fifteen months, one of his coworkers, Dale Garman, was chatting with a Rambian customer, who referred in passing to Wilson as a person living in Old Town. Garman knew Old Town was one of the slums outside Stanley, but he kept his surprise to himself and decided not to mention this information to anyone else until he could independently confirm it. This wasn't difficult for him to do. Wilson was indeed living in Old Town in the home of some relatives. The house itself couldn't have rented for more than $300, even if Wilson had the whole place to himself, which he clearly didn't. Dale reported what he had learned to Wilson's supervisor, Barbara Weston.

When Weston confronted him about the matter, Wilson admitted that the place did rent for a "little less" than $2,000, but he vigorously defended his action this way: "Every other NewCom employee in Rambia receives $2,000 a month. If I live economically, why should I be penalized? I should receive the same as everyone else." In response, Weston pointed out that NewCom wanted to guarantee that its employees had safe, high-quality housing that was in keeping with the image that the company wanted to project. Wilson's housing arrangements were "unseemly," she said, and not in keeping with his professional standing. Moreover, they reflected poorly on the company. To this, Wilson Mutambara retorted: "I'm not just a NewCom employee; I'm also a Rambian. It's not unsafe for me to live in this neighborhood, and it's insulting to be told that the area I grew up in is 'unseemly' or inappropriate for a company employee."

Barbara Weston pointed out that the monthly receipts he submitted had been falsified. "Yes," he admitted, "but that's common practice in Rambia. Nobody thinks twice about it." However, she pressed the point, arguing that he had a duty to NewCom, which he had violated. As the discussion continued, Mutambara became less confident and more and more distraught. Finally, on the verge of tears, he pleaded, "Barbara, you just don't understand what's expected of me as a Rambian or the pressure I'm under. I save every penny I have to pay school fees for eight nieces and nephews. I owe it to my family to try to give those children the same chance I had. My relatives would never understand my living in a big house instead of helping them. I'm just doing what I have to do."

Discussion Questions

1. Did Wilson Mutambara act wrongly? Explain why or why not. Assess each of the arguments he gives in his own defense. What other courses of action were open to him? What would you have done in his place?

2. Was Dale Garman right to confirm the information he had received and to report the matter? Was it morally required of him to do so?

3. What should Barbara Weston and NewCom do? Should Wilson be ordered to move out of Old Town and into more appropriate housing? Should he be terminated for having falsified his housing receipts? If not, should he be punished in some other way?

4. Is NewCom unfairly imposing its own ethnocentric values on Wilson Mutambara? Is the company's housing policy fair and reasonable? Is it culturally biased?

CASE 8.4

Ethically Dubious Conduct

Brenda Franklin has worked at Allied Tech for nearly eight years. It's a large company, but she likes it and enjoys the friendly work environment. When she tacked her list onto the bulletin board outside her office, she didn't intend to make things less friendly. In fact, she didn't expect her list to attract much attention at all.

It had all started the week before when she joined a group of coworkers for their weekly lunch get-together, where they always talked about all sorts of things. This time they had gotten into a long political discussion, with several people at the table going on at great length about dishonesty, conflicts of interest, and shady dealings among politicians and corporate leaders. "If this country is going to get on the right track, we need people whose integrity is above reproach," Harry Benton had said to nods of approval around the table, followed by a further round of complaints about corruption and corner-cutting by the powerful.

Brenda hadn't said much at the time, but she thought she sniffed a whiff of hypocrisy. Later that night, after pondering the group's discussion, she typed up her list of "Ethically Dubious Employee Conduct." The next day she posted it outside her door.

Harry Benton was the first one to stick his head in the office. "My, my, aren't we smug?" was all he said before he disappeared. Later that morning, her friend Karen dropped by. "You don't really think it's immoral to take a pad of paper home, do you?" she asked. Brenda said no, but she didn't think one could just take it for granted that it was okay to take company property. She and Karen chatted more about the list. On and off that week, almost everyone she spoke with alluded to the list or commented on some of its items. They didn't object to her posting it, although they seemed to think it was a little strange. One day outside the building, however, an employee she knew only by sight asked Brenda sarcastically whether she was planning on turning people in for "moral violations." Brenda ignored him.

Now she was anticipating her group's weekly lunch. She had little doubt about what the topic of discussion would be, as she again glanced over her list:

Ethically Dubious Employee Conduct

1. Taking office supplies home for your personal use.
2. Using the telephone for personal, long-distance phone calls.
3. Making personal copies on the office machine.
4. Charging the postage on your personal mail to the company.
5. Making nonbusiness trips in a company car.
6. On a company business trip: staying in the most expensive hotel, taking taxis when you could walk, including wine as food on your expense tab, taking your spouse along at company expense.
7. Using your office computer to shop online, trade stocks, view pornography, or e-mail friends on company time.
8. Calling in sick when you need personal time.
9. Taking half the afternoon off, when you're supposedly on business outside the office.
10. Directing company business to vendors who are friends or relatives.
11. Providing preferential service to corporate customers who have taken you out to lunch.

Discussion Questions

1. Review each item on Brenda's list and assess the conduct in question. Do you find it morally acceptable, morally unacceptable, or somewhere in between? Explain.

2. Examine Brenda's list from both the utilitarian and Kantian perspectives. What arguments can be given for and against the conduct on her list? Is the rightness or wrongness of some items a matter of degree? Can an action (such as taking a pad of paper) be both trivial and wrong?

3. Someone might argue that some of the things listed as ethically dubious are really employee entitlements. Assess this contention.

4. How would you respond to the argument that if the company doesn't do anything to stop the conduct on Brenda's list, then it has only itself to blame? What about the argument that none of the things on the list is wrong unless the company has an explicit rule against it?

5. What obligations do employees have to their employers? Do companies have moral rights that employees can violate? What moral difference, if any, is there between taking something that belongs to an individual and taking something that belongs to a company?

6. What, if anything, can we learn about an employee's character based on whether he or she does or does not do the things on Brenda's list? Would you admire someone who scrupulously avoids doing any of these ethically dubious things?

7. What should Brenda do when she finds a fellow employee engaging in what she considers ethically dubious conduct?

Notes

1. See "Nuclear Warriors," *Time*, March 4, 1996, 47–54, from which the details that follow are taken.

2. Ronald Duska, "Whistleblowing and Employee Loyalty," in Tom L. Beauchamp and Norman E. Bowie, eds., *Ethical Theory and Business*, 6th ed. (Upper Saddle River, N.J.: Prentice Hall, 2001), 328.

3. John H. Fielder, "Organizational Loyalty," *Business and Professional Ethics Journal* 11 (Spring 1992): 87.

4. Richard T. De George, *Business Ethics*, 5th ed. (Upper Saddle River, N.J.: Prentice Hall, 1999), 413.

5. Fielder, "Organizational Loyalty," 80–84.

6. "A Case of Conflicts at Qwest," *Business Week*, April 22, 2002, 37.

7. "Tech's Kickback Culture," *Business Week*, February 10, 2003, 76.

8. "Loans to Corporate Officers Unlikely to Cease Soon," *Wall Street Journal*, July 2, 2002, A8.

9. "Insider Trading Alleged," *San Jose Mercury News*, June 13, 2002, 3C.

10. Douglas Frantz, "Genentech Chief's Wife Settles SEC's Insider Trading Charges," *Los Angeles Times*, November 21, 1990, D1.

11. John A. C. Hetherington, "Corporate Social Responsibility, Stockholders, and the Law," *Journal of Contemporary Business* (Winter 1973): 51.

12. "Texas Gulf Ruled to Lack Diligence in Minerals Case," *Wall Street Journal* (Midwest Edition), February 9, 1970, 1.

13. "Supreme Court Upholds S.E.C.'s Theory of Insider Trading," *New York Times*, June 26, 1997, C1.

14. Ibid.

15. "SEC, Professor Split on Insider Trades," *Wall Street Journal*, March 2, 1984, 8. See also Henry G. Manne, "The Case for Insider Trading," *Wall Street Journal*, March 17, 2003, A14.

16. Jennifer Moore, "What Is Really Unethical About Insider Trading?" *Journal of Business Ethics* 9 (March 1990).

17. "Cookie Cloak and Dagger," *Time*, September 10, 1984, 44; see also "The Harm of Patents," *Economist*, August 22, 1992, 17.

18. Sissela Bok, *Secrets* (New York: Vintage, 1983), 136.

19. John R. Boatright, *Ethics and the Conduct of Business*, 4th ed. (Upper Saddle River, N.J.: Prentice Hall, 2003), 128–136.

20. Rory J. O'Connor, "Trade-Secrets Case Casts Chill," *San Jose Mercury News*, March 7, 1993, 1A.

21. See Michael S. Baram, "Trade Secrets: What Price Loyalty?" *Harvard Business Review* 46 (November–December 1968).

22. Kim Murphy, "Accountant for ZZZZ Best Convicted of Fraud," *Los Angeles Times*, December 20, 1988, II-1.

23. "Prosecutors Link Honda Fraud Cases to U.S. Executives," *New York Times*, March 15, 1994, A1.

24. Bill Shaw, "Foreign Corrupt Practices Act: A Legal and Moral Analysis," *Journal of Business Ethics* 7 (October 1988): 789–790.

25. "Special Report: Bribery and Business," *Economist*, March 2, 2002, 64.

26. Norman C. Miller, "U.S. Business Overseas: Back to Bribery?" *Wall Street Journal*, April 30, 1981, 22.

27. Bartley A. Brennan, "The Foreign Corrupt Practices Act Amendments of 1988: 'Death' of a Law," *North Carolina Journal of International Law and Commerce Regulation* 15 (1990): 229–247; Wesley Cragg and William Woof, "The U.S. Foreign Corrupt Practices Act: A Study of Its Effectiveness," *Business and Society Review* 107 (Spring 2002): 99.

28. "A Global War Against Bribery," *Economist*, January 16, 1999, 22–23; "The Worm That Never Dies," *Economist*, March 2, 2002, 12.

29. Calvin Sims, "Ex-U.S. Official Admits Guilt on Phone Contract," *New York Times*, May 24, 1989, C2.

30. David Johnston, "Boning Up on New Ethics of Procurement," *New York Times*, May 24, 1989, A16.

31. "Tech's Kickback Culture," *Business Week*, 75, 77.

32. "New Kmart Code Bans Gifts, Bribes," *San Jose Mercury News*, April 12, 1996, 6C.

33. "Speaking Up Gets Biologist into Big Fight," *Wall Street Journal*, November 26, 1980, sec. 2, 25.

34. Ronald F. Duska, "Whistleblowing," in R. Edward Freeman and Patricia H. Werhane, eds., *The Blackwell Encyclopedic Dictionary of Business Ethics* (Oxford: Blackwell, 1998), 654.

35. Boatright, *Ethics and the Conduct of Business*, 106.

36. Norman Bowie, *Business Ethics* (Englewood Cliffs, N.J.: Prentice Hall, 1982), 142.

37. "The Whistle-Blowers," *Business Week*, January 13, 2003, 90.

38. "The Night Detective," *Time*, December 30, 2002–January 6, 2003, 45–50. See also "How Three Unlikely Sleuths Discovered Fraud at WorldCom," *Wall Street Journal*, October 30, 2002, A1.

39. Bok, *Secrets*, Chapter 14.

40. Dan Seligman, "Blowing Whistles, Blowing Smoke," *Forbes*, September 6, 1999.

41. "Tobacco Whistle-Blower Acknowledges He's Paid," *New York Times*, May 1, 1996, A12.

42. "Christine Casey: Whistleblower," *Economist*, January 18, 2003, 66.

43. "Peep and Weep," *Economist*, January 12, 2002, 56.

44. Ibid.

45. Tim Barnett, "Why *Your* Company Should Have a Whistleblowing Policy," *SAM Advanced Management Journal* 57 (Autumn 1992); cf. Boatright, *Ethics and the Conduct of Business*, 118–119.

46. The facts and quotations about Storms come from Ronald B. Taylor, "Making Waves: Whistle-Blower Keeps Heat on Navy in Revealing Waste of Millions of Dollars," *Los Angeles Times*, June 26, 1984.

47. The discussion that follows is based on news stories in the *Santa Cruz Sentinel*, August 14 and 17, 1993, and the *San Jose Mercury News*, August 17, 1993.

48. This case study was inspired by one in *Across the Board* 36 (January 1999).

Further Reading for Chapter 8

Sissela Bok, *Secrets* (New York: Vintage, 1983) includes insightful writing on trade secrets and patents in Chapter 10 and on whistle-blowing in Chapter 14.

Thomas L. Carson, "Conflicts of Interest," *Journal of Business Ethics* (May 1994) analyzes the concept and discusses the wrongness of conflicts of interest. Also useful is **Michael Davis,** "Conflict of Interest Revisited," *Business and Professional Ethics Journal* 12 (Winter 1993).

Natalie Dandekar, "Can Whistleblowing Be Fully Legitimated? A Theoretical Discussion," *Business and Professional Ethics Journal* 10 (Fall 1990), **Mike W. Martin,** "Whistleblowing: Professionalism, Personal Life, and Shared Responsibility for Safety in Engineering," *Business and Professional Ethics Journal* 11 (Summer 1992), and **C. Fred Alford,** "Whistleblowers and the Narrative of Ethics," *Journal of Social Philosophy* 32 (Fall 2001) are good studies of the moral complexity of whistle-blowing.

Tibor Machan, "What Is Morally Right with Insider Trading," *Public Affairs Quarterly* 10 (April 1996) is a succinct libertarian defense of insider trading.

Brian Schrag, "The Moral Significance of Employee Loyalty," *Business Ethics Quarterly* 11 (January 2001) discusses the meaning of loyalty and whether it is good for either the employee or employer.

Martin Snoeyenbos, Robert Almeder, and **James Humber,** eds., *Business Ethics,* 3rd ed. (Buffalo: Prometheus, 2001), Part 3, provides essays and cases on conflict of interest, gifts and pay-offs, patents, and trade secrets.

InfoTrac College Edition: For further information or to conduct research, please go to www.infotrac-college.com.

9

Job
Discrimination

When Notre Dame opened its 2002 football season, its team was led by a new coach, Tyrone Willingham. Nothing surprising about that, one might think; after all, colleges are always hiring and firing coaches. But Coach Willingham's arrival was newsworthy simply because he's African American. That makes him Notre Dame's first black coach in any sport, and it makes the Fighting Irish the only top-flight football team in the nation with a black coach. Indeed, looking at all Division 1-A schools, one finds only four black head football coaches. That's less than 3 percent of the total, even though half of all 1-A players are black.[1]

What explains this imbalance? Experts suggest several answers. At many universities, football is the biggest moneymaking sport, and search committees may fear that boosters and alumni will donate less if the team has a black coach. Another reason is that black men are often passed over for decision-making positions early in their athletic careers. Relatively few blacks play quarterback, for instance, and black assistant coaches may be relegated to recruiting or smoothing out race relations rather than calling plays. In addition, young black athletes may pursue careers in which they have seen their role models succeed—going on to the pros, in particular, instead of becoming a coach.

Finally, most commentators agree that the "old boys' network" among athletic directors and coaches is part of the problem. "I don't see the problem as being the same as it was 30 or 40 years ago, when people said they didn't want a 'Negro' around," says Allen L. Sach, director of sports management at the University of New Haven. "It's more systematic than it is overt." Athletic directors, naturally enough, tend to look to people they know to fill coaching positions, and only 4 percent of the former are ethnic minorities, according to the Center for the Study of Sport in Society at Northeastern University. "Athletic directors, to the extent that they're white, generally have contacts who are also white, and they use those contacts as they engage in searches at the informal level," says sociologist Jay Oakley of the University of Colorado at Colorado Springs.

It's no secret that Willingham wasn't Notre Dame's first choice. It had initially hired George O'Leary, who resigned five days later when it became known that he had lied on his résumé about his academic and athletic background. In discussing the appointment, Notre Dame Athletic Director Kevin White explained that he had been charmed by O'Leary's Irish-American background and his rah-rah style. O'Leary was like "something out of central casting," White said. In other words, the flamboyant O'Leary fit White's stereotype about what a Notre Dame coach should look like. Sports columnist Mark Purdy writes that White's remark "basically confirms that athletic directors—at Notre Dame and too many other places—really do look for middle-aged white guys as the top choices for the top jobs. And that's depressing." It's to Notre Dame's credit, however, that after the O'Leary debacle, it took a second look at Willingham and, putting aside racial preconceptions and "central casting" stereotypes, went for a coach with a proven track record, one whose integrity, drive, and quiet competence more than make up for any lack of flamboyance.

Most people oppose racial or sexual bias and reject job discrimination as immoral. But, as the paucity of minority coaches reveals, explicit prejudice and overt discrimination are just part of the problem. Even open-minded people may operate on implicit assumptions that work to the disadvantage of women and minorities, and many who believe themselves to be unprejudiced harbor unconscious racist or sexist attitudes.

Stanford law professor Charles R. Lawrence III, for instance, recalls his college days as a token black presence in a white world. Companions would say to him, "I don't think of you as a Negro." Their conscious intent was benign and complimentary. The speaker was saying, "I think of you as a normal human being, just like me."

> But he was not conscious of the underlying implications of his words. What did this mean about most Negroes? Were they not normal human beings?. . . To say that one does not think of a Negro as a Negro is to say that one thinks of him as something else. The statement is made in the context of the real world, and implicit in it is a comparison to some norm. In this case the norm is whiteness. The white liberal's unconscious thought . . . is, "I think of you as different from other Negroes, as more like white people."[2]

In other cases unconscious racist stereotypes, which are normally repressed, slip out, as when sportscaster Howard Cosell, carried away by the excitement of the game, referred to an African-American football player as a "little monkey" or when Nancy Reagan told a public gathering that she wished her husband could be there to "see all these beautiful white people."[3]

Slavery in our country resulted in a long legacy of legally institutionalized racism and socioeconomic subordination of African Americans and other minorities. That history, and centuries of discrimination against women, lie behind the racially and sexually prejudiced attitudes so prevalent in the United States. We must bear that history and those attitudes in mind as we explore the area of job discrimination. In particular, this chapter examines the following topics:

1. The meaning of job discrimination and its different forms
2. The statistical and attitudinal evidence of discrimination
3. The historical and legal context of affirmative action
4. The moral arguments for and against affirmative action

5. The doctrine of comparable worth and the controversy over it

6. The problem of sexual harassment in employment—what it is, what forms it takes, what the law says about it, and why it's wrong

THE MEANING OF JOB DISCRIMINATION

According to Professor Manuel G. Velasquez, to discriminate in employment is to make an adverse decision against employees or job applicants based on their membership in a certain group.[4] Determining whether discrimination occurs in employment depends on three basic facts: (1) whether the decision is a function of an employee's or job applicant's membership in a certain group, rather than individual merit; (2) whether the decision is based on prejudice, false stereotypes, or the assumption that the group is in some way inferior and thus deserving of unequal treatment; and (3) whether the decision in some way harms those it's aimed at. Because historically most discrimination in the American workplace has been aimed at women and at minorities such as African Americans and Hispanics, the following discussion focuses on these groups.

Job discrimination can take different forms.[5] Individuals can intentionally discriminate out of personal prejudice or on the basis of stereotypes. An example is the executive at Rent-A-Center, the nation's largest rent-to-own furniture and home appliance company, who purposely disregarded job applications from women because he believed that they "should be home taking care of their husbands and children."[6] On the other hand, individuals may discriminate because they unthinkingly or unconsciously accept traditional practices or biased stereotypes. For example, suppose the merit pay recommendations that a manager at Wal-Mart makes are influenced by an implicit assumption that his male employees are career-oriented and have families to support, whereas his female employees are just there to make a little extra money.[7] If the manager is unaware that this bias affects his decisions, his actions would fall into this category.

Institutions can also discriminate. Sometimes they do so explicitly and intentionally—for example, employment agencies that screen out African Americans, Latinos, older workers, and others at the request of their corporate clients[8] or the Shoney's restaurants that color-coded job applications to separate blacks from whites and that directed blacks, if hired, into kitchen jobs so they would not be seen from the dining room.[9] On the other hand, the routine operating procedures of a company may reflect stereotypes and prejudiced practices that it is not fully aware of. For example, for years the FBI routinely transferred its Hispanic agents around the country on temporary, low-level assignments where a knowledge of Spanish was needed; the agents functioned as little more than assistants to non-Hispanic colleagues. Hispanic agents dubbed this the "taco circuit" and claimed that it adversely affected their opportunities for promotion. A federal court agreed with them that the practice is indeed discriminatory.[10]

In addition, institutional practices that appear neutral and nondiscriminatory may harm members of groups that are traditionally discriminated against. When membership in an all-white craft union, for instance, requires nomination by those who are already members, racial exclusion is likely to result even if the motivation of those who do the nominating is purely nepotistic and results from no racially motivated ill will or stereotyping. Similarly, when USAir had a special backdoor hiring channel for pilots recommended by employees or friends of the company, only white pilots were ever hired this way.[11] Although the policy may look racially neutral, its outcome was biased. Institutional procedures like these may not involve job discrimination in the narrow sense, but they clearly work to the disadvantage of women and minority groups, denying them full equality of opportunity.

From a variety of moral perspectives there are compelling moral arguments against job discrimination on racial or sexual grounds. Since discrimination involves false assumptions about the inferiority of a certain group and harms individual members of that group, utilitarians would reject it because of its ill effects on total human welfare. Kantians would clearly repudiate it as failing to respect people as ends in themselves. Universalizing the maxim underlying discriminatory practices is virtually impossible. No people who now discriminate would be willing to accept such treatment themselves. Discrimination on grounds of sex or race also violates people's basic moral rights and mocks the ideal of human moral equality. Furthermore, such discrimination is unjust. To use Rawls's theory as an illustration, parties in the original position would clearly choose for themselves the principle of equal opportunity.

On the other hand, there are no respectable arguments in favor of racial and sexual discrimination. Whatever racist or sexist attitudes people might actually have, no one today is prepared to defend job discrimination publicly, any more than someone would publicly defend slavery or the repeal of the Nineteenth Amendment (which gave women the right to vote). This attitude toward job discrimination is reflected in legal and political efforts to develop programs to root out job discrimination and ameliorate the results of past discrimination.

Before looking at the relevant legal history and the controversies surrounding various anti-discrimination measures, this chapter examines the relative positions of whites and minorities and of males and females in the American workplace to see what they reveal about ongoing discrimination.

EVIDENCE OF DISCRIMINATION

When investigators sent equally qualified young white and black men—all of them articulate and conventionally dressed—to apply for entry-level jobs in Chicago and Washington, D.C., the results clearly showed racial discrimination against young African-American men.[12] Similarly, blacks and Hispanics are more likely to be turned down for home mortgages than are whites at the same income level. And a study has shown that if you work for the federal government, you're more likely to be fired if you're black—regardless of your job status, experience, or education. In fact, race is more important in predicting who gets fired than job-performance ratings or even prior disciplinary history.[13] Job discrimination certainly exists, but determining how widespread it is isn't easy. However, when (1) statistics indicate that women and minorities play an unequal role in the work world and (2) endemic attitudes, practices, and policies are biased in ways that seem to account for the skewed statistics, then there is good reason to believe that job discrimination is a pervasive problem.

Statistical Evidence

According to government data, the median wealth of white households is seven times that of black households—$ 120,900 versus $ 17,100.[14] And 29 percent of African-American households, but only 9 percent of all white households, are reported as having no wealth at all, meaning that they own no assets or that their liabilities exceed their assets.[15] Racial minorities bear the brunt of poverty in our nation. African Americans are about three times more likely to be poor than whites. Whereas one out of every ten white Americans is poor, one out of every four or five African Americans and Hispanics is poor. Today a black child has nearly one chance in three of being born into poverty.[16]

Thus, it is not too surprising that whereas white Americans have, according to U.N. figures, the highest standard of living in the world, African Americans come in thirty-first and Hispanics thirty-fifth.[17] The median income of African-American families is only two-thirds that of white households; Hispanic family income is about 75 percent.[18]

Unemployment hits racial minorities hard, because they are often last hired and first fired. Unemployment among African Americans is in general twice as high as that of whites. Of every three minority workers, one is employed irregularly or has given up looking for work, and one in three is engaged primarily in a job that pays less than a living wage. Official unemployment figures for inner-city African-American youths exceed 40 percent, but the actual figures are thought to be much higher.

About 40 percent of working African Americans hold white-collar jobs, up from 11 percent in 1960. But black workers with an advanced degree earn 25 percent less than whites with the same education.[19] Moreover, black and other minority workers still tend to be clustered in low-paying, low-prestige, dead-end work. U.S. government statistics reveal clearly the extent to which the most desirable occupations (in management and administration, professional and technical jobs, sales, and crafts) are dominated by whites; blacks, Hispanics, and other ethnic minorities are relegated to less desirable jobs (in manual labor, service, and farmwork). African Americans make up 11 percent of the workforce, but 28 percent of parking lot attendants, 29 percent of bus drivers, 31 percent of garbage collectors, 32 percent of guards, and 33 percent of nursing aids. In contrast, only 3.1 percent of the architects, 0.6 percent of the commercial pilots, and 1.9 percent of the geologists are black.[20]

Women, too, are clustered in poorer-paying jobs—the so-called pink-collar occupations. They tend to work as librarians, nurses, elementary schoolteachers, salesclerks, secretaries, bank tellers, and waitresses, jobs that generally pay less than traditionally male occupations such as electrician, plumber, auto mechanic, shipping clerk, or truck driver. It's not surprising, then, that 80 percent of working women earn less than $25,000 per year, although two-fifths of them are the sole head of a household.[21] In the real world of work, the top-paying occupations have been, and to a large extent continue to be, almost exclusively male preserves. For example, 96.8 percent of dental hygienists, but only 19.9 percent of dentists, are women.[22] Although women hold 43 percent of executive, administrative, and managerial positions, they account for less than 5 percent of the top executive positions nationwide.[23]

Even when women do the same work as men, they make less money. In fact, according to a General Accounting Office report, since 1995 the pay difference between full-time female managers and their male counterparts has increased in seven of the ten industries that collectively employ 71 percent of all female workers.[24] For example, in entertainment and recreation female managers now earn only 62 cents for each dollar earned by males; in finance, insurance, and real estate, it's 68 cents, and in retail trade, 65 cents. In education and in hospital and medical services, women managers have done better. Their earnings have increased to 91 and 85 percent, respectively, of what men make. The across-the-board wage gap between men and women shrank during the 1980s, but has since leveled off, with women who work full time continuing to take home, on average, less than 75 percent of what men make.[25] And one-third of the women polled in a recent survey complained that they do not receive equal pay at their current jobs.[26]

To be sure, in recent decades both women and minorities have made inroads into white-collar and professional ranks, but few have made it to the very top of their professions—as a glance at the companies that make up the *Fortune* 500 confirms. Only five of those companies have a female CEO. And when he took charge of Fannie Mae in 1999, Franklin Raines became the first African American to lead a *Fortune* 500 company. Now there are two more.

Attitudinal Evidence

Although some would disagree, statistics alone do not conclusively establish discrimination because one can always argue that other things account for the disparities in income and positions between men and women and between whites and other races. The U.S. Supreme Court, in fact, has stated that "no matter how stark the numerical disparity of the employer's work force," statistical evidence by itself does not prove discrimination.[27] But when widespread attitudes and institutional practices and policies are taken into account, they point to discrimination as the cause of the statistical disparities.

Take the case of Bari-Ellen Roberts. She left an $80,000-a-year job at Chase Manhattan Bank to join Texaco's finance department after a white friend, whose husband worked for the company, assured her that "Texaco's changing" and that the company was "looking for blacks." Her new job was closer to home and held the promise of overseas assignments, but her friend was mistaken about Texaco's having changed. Soon after she arrived, Roberts found herself subjected to demeaning racial comments from colleagues and superiors (for example, one referred to her as a "little colored girl"). They couldn't understand why Roberts found such remarks offensive. A report on diversity that she and some other black employees were asked to prepare was summarily dismissed with the comment "the next thing you know we'll have Black Panthers running down the halls." And a supervisor downgraded her performance record because he thought she was "uppity."[28]

Fed up with a "plague of racial insults" and "egregious acts of bigotry," she and several other black employees filed a discrimination suit citing "the poisonous racial atmosphere" at Texaco. Texaco settled the suit for $141 million in retroactive raises after the news media got a hold of a tape recording of an executive strategy session at Texaco. In the meeting, one official referred to black employees as "black jelly beans," saying, "This diversity thing, you know how all the black jelly beans stick together." To which another responded, "That's funny. All the black jelly beans seem to be stuck at the bottom of the bag." One of Roberts's supervisors said, "I can't punch her [Roberts] in the face, so I play mind games with her." The executives were also heard agreeing to shred incriminating personnel records.

Consider also the case of Elizabeth Hishon, who went to work for King & Spaulding, a big Atlanta law firm. Customarily, associates like Hishon are given a period of time to either make partner or seek another job. So when Hishon had not attained partner status after seven years, she was terminated. Hishon, however, claimed that her failure to become a partner was due to the law firm's sexism, and she filed a suit seeking monetary damages under Title VII of the Civil Rights Act of 1964, which prohibits sexual and racial discrimination at work. A federal district court held that the rights guaranteed by Title VII do not apply to the selection of partners in a law firm, but the Supreme Court overturned that ruling in a unanimous decision that held that women can bring sex-discrimination suits against law firms that unfairly deny them promotions to partner. In the meantime, however, Elizabeth Hishon had settled out of court with King & Spaulding, and the case never went to trial.

In November 1990, Nancy O'Mara Ezold became the first woman to win a sex-discrimination trial against a law firm in a partnership decision. A few days later, in a case in which the Supreme Court had already found sex discrimination, a federal appeals judge ruled that Price Waterhouse, the accounting firm, must give a partnership and back pay to Ann Hopkins, against whom it had discriminated. And in 2002 the Equal Employment Opportunity Commission filed its first sex-discrimination lawsuit against a major Wall Street firm, alleging that Morgan Stanley fired Allison Schieffelin, one of its top bond dealers, for complaining about pay discrimination. These cases have had a significant impact on partnerships and professional firms nationwide, causing pay and promotional practices to be reevaluated, not only in law and accounting firms, but also in advertising agencies, brokerage houses, architectural concerns, and engineering firms.

Of particular interest here are the discriminatory attitudes and policies revealed by these cases. In the Ezold case, the judge found that the prominent Philadelphia law firm for which she had worked had applied tougher standards to women seeking partnerships than to men. Ezold said, "It wasn't just that similarly situated men were treated better than me, which is the double-standard idea. Another thing that came out of the trial was that in the year preceding the partnership decision, [the firm] assigned me to less complex cases and to fewer partners than it did men, so that I was denied the exposure that was critical to the partnership decision."[29]

In Ann Hopkins's case, sex stereotyping was at the root of the discrimination. Though she was considered an outstanding worker, Price Waterhouse denied her the position because she was allegedly an abrasive and overbearing manager. Coworkers referred to her as "macho," advised her to go to charm school, and intimated that she was overcompensating for being a woman. One partner in the firm even told her that she should "walk more femininely, talk more femininely, dress more femininely, wear makeup, have her hair styled, and wear jewelry." Hopkins argued, and the Court agreed, that comments like these revealed an underlying sexism at the firm and that her strident manner and occasional cursing would have been overlooked if she had been a man.[30] The same issue comes up in the Schieffelin case, who was viewed by her firm as insubordinate, verbally abusive, and "physically threatening."

As for the Hishon decision, the case is noteworthy because the defendants expressed no specific complaints about Hishon's work. They apparently denied her a partnership based on a general feeling that "she just didn't fit in." In the words of another woman who had been an associate at King & Spaulding, "If you can't discuss the Virginia–North Carolina basketball game, you're an outcast."[31] Her pithy comment speaks volumes about how deep-seated attitudes operate against women and minorities in the workplace.

A woman entering males' turf can find herself uncomfortably measured according to the predominant male value system. Here's how Florence Blair, a twenty-five-year-old African American, described working as a civil engineer at Corning Glass Works:

> As a minority woman, you are just so different from everyone else you encounter. . . . I went through a long period of isolation. . . . When I came here, I didn't have a lot in common with the white males I was working with. I didn't play golf, I didn't drink beer, I didn't hunt. All these things I had no frame of reference to.
>
> You need to do your job on a certain technical level, but a lot of things you do on the job come down to socializing and how well you mesh with people. Sometimes I look at my role as making people feel comfortable with me.
>
> Sometimes it's disheartening. You think why do I have to spend all of my time and my energy making them feel comfortable with me when they're not reciprocating?[32]

Surveys support the evidence of these cases. Over the years, they have indicated that sex stereotyping and sexist assumptions are widespread in business.[33] Male managers frequently assume that women place family demands above work considerations; that they lack the necessary drive to succeed in business; that they take negative feedback personally rather than professionally; and that they are too emotional to be good managers. Myths, stereotypes, false preconceptions, and hostile attitudes victimize both women and minorities in the world of work, leading to decisions that disadvantage them in the areas of employee selection, promotion, and career development.

For example, a survey shows that three out of four whites believe that African Americans and Hispanics are more likely than whites to prefer living on welfare, and a majority of whites also believe that African Americans and Hispanics are more likely to be lazy, unpatriotic, and prone to violence.[34] Another survey, this time of Ivy League graduates, class of 1957, also illustrates the prevalence of racial stereotypes and assumptions.[35] For these men, "dumb" came to mind when they thought of African Americans. Only 36 percent of the Princeton class, 47 percent of the Yale class, and 55 percent of the Harvard men agreed with the statement "Blacks are as intelligent as whites." These are graduates of three leading universities who are now at an age typical of those holding senior corporate positions. In discussing this survey, Edward W. Jones, Jr., writes:

> All people possess stereotypes, which act like shorthand to avoid mental overload. . . . Most of the time stereotypes are mere shadow images rooted in one's history and deep in the subconscious. But they are very powerful. For example, in controlled experiments the mere insertion of the word black into a sentence has resulted in people changing their responses to a statement.
>
> One reason for the power of stereotypes is their circularity. People seek to confirm their expectations and resist contradictory evidence, so we cling to beliefs and stereotypes that become self-fulfilling. If, for example, a white administrator makes a mistake, his boss is likely to tell him, "That's OK. Everybody's entitled to one goof." If, however, a black counterpart commits the same error, the boss thinks, "I knew he couldn't do it. The guy is incompetent." The stereotype reinforces itself.[36]

Taken together, the statistics and the personal and institutional attitudes, assumptions and practices provide powerful evidence of intractable discrimination against women and minorities in the American workplace. Recognizing the existence of such discrimination and believing for a variety of reasons that it is wrong, we have as a nation passed laws to provide equality of opportunity to women and minorities. Such laws expressly forbid discrimination in recruitment, screening, promotion, compensation, and firing. But anti-discrimination laws do not address the present-day effects of past discrimination. To remedy the effects of past discrimination and counteract visceral racism and sexism, some companies and institutions have adopted stronger and more controversial affirmative action measures.

AFFIRMATIVE ACTION: THE LEGAL CONTEXT

In 1954 the Supreme Court decided in the case of *Brown v. Board of Education* that racially segregated schooling is unconstitutional. In doing so, the Court conclusively rejected the older doctrine that "separate but equal" facilities are legally permissible. Not only were segregated facilities in the South unequal, the Court found, but the very idea of separation of the races, based as it was on a belief in black racial inferiority, inherently led to unequal treatment. That famous decision helped launch the civil rights movement in this country. One fruit of that movement was a series of federal laws and orders that attempt to implement the right of each person to equal treatment in employment.

The changes began in 1961, when President John F. Kennedy signed Executive Order 10925, which decreed that federal contractors should "take affirmative action to ensure that applicants are employed without regard to their race, creed, color, or national origin." In 1963, the Equal Pay Act was passed by Congress. Aimed especially at wage discrimination against women, it guaranteed the right to equal pay for equal work. That was followed by the Civil Rights Act of 1964 (which was later amended by the Equal Employment Opportunity Act of 1972). It prohibits all forms of discrimination based on race, color, sex, religion, or national origin. Title VII, the most important section of the act, prohibits discrimination in employment. It says:

> It shall be an unlawful employment practice for an employer (1) to fail or refuse to hire or to discharge any individual, or otherwise discriminate against any individual with respect to his compensation, terms, conditions, or privileges of employment, because of such individual's race, color, religion, sex, or national origin; or (2) to limit, segregate, or classify his employees or applicants for employment in any way that would deprive or tend to deprive any individual of employment opportunities or otherwise adversely affect his status as an employee, because of such individual's race, color, religion, sex, or national origin.

The Civil Rights Act of 1964 applies to all employers, both public and private, with fifteen or more employees. In 1967 the Age Discrimination in Employment Act was passed (amended in 1978), and in 1990 the Americans with Disabilities Act extended to people with disabilities the same rights to equal employment opportunities that the Civil Rights Act of 1964 guarantees to women and minorities. In addition, several acts and executive orders regulate government contractors and subcontractors and require equal opportunities for veterans. All of these acts are enforced through the Equal Employment Opportunity Commission (EEOC).

By the late 1960s and early 1970s, companies contracting with the federal government (first in construction and then generally) were required to develop *affirmative action programs,* designed to correct imbalances in employment that exist directly as a result of past discrimination. These programs corresponded with the courts' recognition that job discrimination can exist even in the absence of conscious intent to discriminate.[37] Affirmative action riders were added, with various degrees of specificity, into a large number of federal programs. Many state and local bodies adopted comparable requirements.

What do affirmative action programs involve? The EEOC lists general guidelines as steps to affirmative action. Under these steps, firms must issue a written equal-employment policy and an affirmative action commitment. They must appoint a top official with responsibility and authority to direct and implement their program and to publicize their policy and affirmative action commitment. In addition, firms must survey current female and minority employment by department and job classification. Whenever underrepresentation of these groups is evident, firms must develop goals and timetables to improve in each area of underrepresentation. They then must develop specific programs to achieve these goals, establish an internal audit system to monitor them, and evaluate progress in each aspect of the program. Finally, companies must develop supportive in-house and community programs to combat discrimination.

We saw earlier that Texaco was forced to pay its black employees $141 million, the largest race-discrimination settlement in history, because the company had discriminated against qualified African Americans by refusing to promote them or pay them comparable salaries. It had also retaliated against those who asserted their civil rights. Other firms are guilty of ignoring the spirit of equal employment opportunity even if they don't violate the letter of the law. For example, some companies forbid their employees from speaking Spanish among themselves even when their jobs do not require English proficiency or dealing with the public;[38] others, such as the Florida-based Publix grocery chain, have not tried to expand employment opportunities for women or minorities.[39] Yet today most large corporations not only accept the necessity of affirmative action but also find that the bottom line benefits when they make themselves more diverse. Because four-fifths of those entering the workforce today are minorities or immigrants,[40] affirmative action expands the pool of talent from which corporations can recruit. It also allows them to reach out to a demographically wider customer base—between now and 2020 most new customers will be minorities[41]—and makes them better able to compete both in the global marketplace and in an increasingly multicultural environment at home. United Parcel Service, for example, credits its commitment to diversity for its high customer-satisfaction ratings, and Nicole Barde, a network manager at Intel Corporation, says, "We view diversity as one of our major competitive advantages. It allows us to understand global markets and the needs of our customers."[42] As Christine A. Edwards, chief legal officer at Bank One, puts it, "Diversity is good business."[43]

However, in recent years political opposition to affirmative action, especially to government affirmative action programs, has grown greater than ever. Critics of affirmative action charge that it means, in practice, illegal quotas, preferential treatment of African Americans and women, and even reverse discrimination against white men. In the 1960s and early 1970s, federal courts dismissed legal challenges to affirmative action, and in 1972 Congress gave it increased legislative validity by passing the Equal Employment Opportunity Act. Eventually, however, the Supreme Court had to address the question. Although its decisions determine the law of the land with regard to affirmative action, the Court's rulings have not always been as simple and straightforward as one might wish.

The Supreme Court's Position

The U.S. Supreme Court's first major ruling on affirmative action was in 1978, in the case of *Bakke v. Regents of the University of California*. Allan Bakke, a white man, applied for admission to the medical school at the University of California at Davis. Only a tiny percentage of doctors are not white. To help remedy this situation, Davis's affirmative action program set aside for minority students 16 out of its 100 entrance places. If qualified minority students could not be found, those places were not to be filled. In addition to the special admissions process, minority students were free to compete through the regular admissions process for the unrestricted 84 positions. When Bakke was refused admission, he sued the University of California, contending that it had discriminated against him in violation of both the 1964 Civil Rights Act and the Constitution. He argued that he would have won admission if those 16 places had not been withdrawn from open competition and reserved for minority students. Bakke's grades, placement-test scores, and so on were higher than those of several minority students who were admitted. The university did not deny this but defended its program as legally permissible and socially necessary affirmative action.

Bakke won his case, although it was a close, 5 to 4 decision. Four justices sided with the University of California at Davis; four found that Davis's program was illegal in light of the 1964 Civil Rights Act; and one justice (Lewis Powell) held that even though the program did not violate that act, it was invalid on constitutional grounds. In announcing the judgment of the Court, Powell's opinion rejected explicit racial criteria setting rigid quotas and excluding nonpreferred groups from competition. At the same time he held that the selection process can take race and ethnic origin into account as one factor and pointed to Harvard's admission program as a model. In such a program, "race or ethnic background may be deemed a 'plus' in a particular applicant's file, yet it does not insulate the individual from comparison with all other candidates for the available seats." Powell also granted that numerical goals may be permissible when the institution in question has illegally discriminated in the past.

A year later, in *United Steelworkers of America v. Weber,* the Supreme Court took up the issue again—but in a different situation and with a different verdict. At Kaiser Aluminum's Gramercy, Louisiana, plant, only 5 out of 273 skilled craft workers were black, although the local workforce was 39 percent black. Kaiser therefore entered into a collective bargaining agreement with the United Steelworkers that contained a plan "to eliminate conspicuous racial imbalances" in Kaiser's skilled craft positions. Kaiser agreed to set up a training program to qualify its own workers for craft positions and to choose trainees from the existing workforce on the basis of seniority, except that 50 percent of the positions would be reserved for African Americans until their percentage in these jobs approximated the percentage of African Americans in the local workforce.

Brian Weber, a young semiskilled worker at Kaiser, was one of several whites who had failed to gain admission to the training program for skilled craft positions, despite having more seniority than the most senior African-American trainee. Weber sued, arguing that he had been discriminated against on the basis of his race. This time the Supreme Court upheld the affirmative action program in a 5 to 2 decision. In delivering the Court's opinion, Justice William Brennan made clear that legal prohibition of racial discrimination does not prevent "private, voluntary, race-conscious affirmative action plans." He wrote:

> We need not today define in detail the line of demarcation between permissible and impermissible affirmative action plans. It suffices to hold that the challenged Kaiser-USWA affirmative action plan falls on the permissible side of the line. The purposes of the plan mirror those of the [Civil Rights] statute. Both were designed to break

down old patterns of racial segregation and hierarchy. Both were structured to "open employment opportunities for Negroes in occupations which have been traditionally closed to them.". . .

At the same time, the plan does not unnecessarily trammel the interest of the white employees. . . . Moreover, the plan is a temporary measure . . . simply to elim- inate a manifest racial imbalance.

In 1984, however, the Supreme Court upheld seniority over affirmative action in *Memphis Firefighters v. Stotts.* The city of Memphis, Tennessee, began hiring African Americans as firefighters only in 1955. Between 1950 and 1976, the fire department hired 1,683 whites but only 94 blacks. A class-action suit was filed in 1977, charging the city with racial discrimination in hiring and promoting firefighters, and in 1980 the city signed a consent decree with the Justice Department. While not admitting it had engaged in racial discrimination, the city agreed to attempt to give 50 percent of new jobs and 20 percent of promotions to African Americans. Under the plan, the percent- age of black firefighters rose from 4.0 to 11.5 percent.

When financial difficulties forced the city to lay off firefighters, it followed the seniority rules negotiated with the union. Last hired were to be let go first. Fearing that the progress black firefighters had made would be quickly lost, Carl Stotts, who had brought the original suit, asked a federal district court to protect blacks from layoffs. It did, and seventy-two whites, but only eight African Americans, were laid off or demoted.

The Supreme Court reversed the district court's ruling, holding that seniority systems are racially neutral and that the city may not lay off white workers to save the jobs of black workers with less seniority. Speaking for the majority, Justice Byron White wrote, "It is inappropriate to deny an innocent employee the benefits of his seniority . . . to provide a remedy in a [case] such as this." A court can award competitive seniority to an individual African American only when he or she has been the actual victim of ille- gal discrimination.

The principle of affirmative action was, however, upheld again in 1987, this time in a case concerning women. In *Johnson v. Transportation Agency,* the Supreme Court affirmed that considerations of sex were permissible as one factor in promoting Diane Joyce, a female county employee, to the position of road dispatcher over an equally qualified male employee, Paul Johnson. In summing up the Court's position, Justice Brennan stated that the promotion of Joyce "was made pursuant to an affirmative action plan that represents a moderate, flexible, case-by-case approach to effecting a gradual improvement in the representation of minorities and women in the Agency's work force."

As these cases show, the Supreme Court has approached affirmative action cau- tiously, basing its position on the relatively specific details of each case. Nevertheless, until 1989 a solid majority of the Court upheld the general principle of affirmative action. Since then, however, the Court has handed down a series of legal rulings gen- erally considered antagonistic to affirmative action, with the result that in recent years the overall legal status of affirmative action has become less clear.

In *City of Richmond v. Croson,* the Court invalidated a Richmond, Virginia, law that channeled 30 percent of public-works funds to minority-owned construction compa- nies (see Case 9.1). In another case, it reversed an eighteen-year-old precedent and removed from employers the burden of proving that job requirements that tend to screen out minorities or women are a business necessity; rather, plaintiffs must prove that such requirements are not necessities. And the Court has made it easier for white men to challenge court-approved consent decrees in which employers undertake programs to hire and promote African Americans, even when the plan was approved years earlier.[44]

In 1995 in *Adarand Constructors v. Pena,* the Supreme Court examined a federal program that provided financial incentives for contractors to hire "socially or economically disadvantaged" subcontractors. In her majority opinion in the 5 to 4 decision, Justice Sandra Day O'Connor affirmed the principle that "federal racial classification, like those of a State, must serve a compelling government interest, and must be narrowly tailored to further that interest." Accordingly, all government action based on race should be subjected to "the strictest judicial scrutiny" to ensure that no individual's right to equal protection has been violated. The Court then sent the case back to a lower court for rehearing.[45]

In addition to O'Connor's majority opinion, however, five other justices wrote opinions in the *Adarand* case, and these reveal a range of perspectives on affirmative action. For instance, Justice David Souter criticized the Court for departing from past practice, reminding his colleagues that it is well established "that constitutional authority to remedy past discrimination is not limited to the power to forbid its continuation, but extends to eliminating those effects that would otherwise persist and skew the operation of public systems even in the absence of current intent to practice any discrimination."

In his dissenting opinion, Justice John Paul Stevens also defended the general principle of affirmative action:

> There is no moral or constitutional equivalence between a policy that is designed to perpetuate a caste system and one that seeks to eradicate racial subordination. . . .
>
> A decision by representatives of the majority to discriminate against the members of a minority race is fundamentally different from those same representatives' decision to impose incidental costs on the majority of their constituents in order to provide a benefit to a disadvantaged minority. Indeed, as I have previously argued, the former is virtually always repugnant to the principles of a free and democratic society, whereas the latter is, in some circumstances, entirely consistent with the ideal of equality.

However, Justice Clarence Thomas explicitly challenged Stevens's position. In an opinion concurring with the majority's judgment, he asserted that

> there is a "moral and constitutional equivalence" between laws designed to subjugate a race and those that distribute benefits on the basis of race in order to foster some current notion of equality. Government cannot make us equal; it can only recognize, respect, and protect us as equal before the law. . . .
>
> In my mind, government-sponsored racial discrimination based on benign prejudice is just as noxious as discrimination inspired by malicious prejudice. In each instance, it is racial discrimination, plain and simple.

The upshot of recent judicial developments relative to affirmative action is not clear, tangled up as the rulings are in details, legal technicalities, and split opinions. Furthermore, Congress has intervened, passing the Civil Rights Act of 1991. Initially intended to overturn several of the Court's decisions hostile to affirmative action, the language of the act ended up so watered down and poorly written that it is subject to very different interpretations. The legal future is difficult to predict. Clearly, the Court is increasingly antagonistic to job-discrimination suits and more attuned than ever to what it perceives to be excesses in the cause of affirmative action. Nevertheless, when in 2003 the Supreme Court revisited affirmative action in higher education for the first time in twenty-five years, it reaffirmed the principles it had enunciated in *Bakke*.

In *Grutter v. Bollinger* the Court upheld, by a 5 to 4 majority, the affirmative action program at the University of Michigan's law school. Citing testimony from various business and military leaders, who urged that diversity is essential to the country's economy and security, the Court ruled that the state has a "compelling interest" in promoting educational diversity and that the law school's method of doing so was "narrowly tailored" to meet that interest. Under the law school's "highly individualized" and "holistic" approach, minority race is a "plus factor" in evaluating potential students, but it's also possible for a white student likely to make a particularly interesting contribution to the law school's academic climate to beat out a minority student with better grades and test scores. On the other hand, in *Gratz v. Bollinger*, a companion case, a different majority of justices ruled, 6 to 3, that Michigan's undergraduate affirmative action program was unconstitutionally rigid and mechanistic because it gave members of underrepresented groups an automatic 20-point bonus on the 150-point scale used to rank applicants.

Despite a division of opinion among the justices, in light of the Michigan cases it appears unlikely that the Supreme Court will reverse itself directly and outlaw moderate and flexible affirmative action programs. However, the Court is clearly impatient. In her majority opinion in *Grutter*, Justice O'Connor stated that "race-conscious admissions policies must be limited in time" and that the Court "expect[s] that 25 years from now, the use of racial preferences will no longer be necessary." That's a hope undoubtedly shared by those on both side of the debate over affirmative action.

AFFIRMATIVE ACTION: THE MORAL ISSUES

Understanding the Supreme Court's evolving position on affirmative action is important, because the Court sets the legal context in which business operates and lets employers know what they are and are not legally permitted to do. But legal decisions by themselves do not exhaust the relevant moral issues. Employers—as well as women, minorities, and white men—want to know whether affirmative action programs are morally right. Indeed, it is a safe bet that the Supreme Court's own decisions are influenced not just by technical legal questions but also by how the justices answer this moral question.

Before evaluating arguments for and against affirmative action, one needs to know what is being debated. "Affirmative action" here means programs taking the race or sex of employees or job candidates into account as part of an effort to correct imbalances in employment that exist as a result of past discrimination, either in the company itself or in the larger society. To keep the discussion relevant, it is limited to affirmative action programs that might reasonably be expected to be upheld by the Supreme Court. Excluded are programs that establish rigid, permanent quotas or that hire and promote unqualified persons. Included are programs that hire or promote a woman or African American who might not otherwise, according to established but fair criteria, be the best-qualified candidate.

A word about terminology: Critics of affirmative action often label it "reverse discrimination," but this term is misleading. According to the definition offered earlier, job discrimination involves prejudice, inaccurate stereotypes, or the assumption that a certain group is inferior and deserves unequal treatment. No such forces are at work in the affirmative action cases already discussed. Those who designed the programs that worked to the disadvantage of Allan Bakke, Brian Weber, and Paul Johnson did not do so because they were biased against white men and believed them inferior and deserving of less respect than other human beings. Those who designed the programs in question were themselves white men.

Arguments for Affirmative Action

1. *Compensatory justice demands affirmative action programs.*

POINT: "As groups, women and minorities have historically been discriminated against, often viciously. As individuals and as a nation, we can't ignore the sins of our fathers and mothers. In fact, we have an obligation to do something to help repair the wrongs of the past. Affirmative action in employment is one sound way to do this."

COUNTERPOINT: "People today can't be expected to atone for the sins of the past. We're not responsible for them, and in any case, we wouldn't be compensating those who rightly deserve it. Young African Americans and women coming for their first job have never suffered employment discrimination. Their parents and grandparents may deserve compensation, but why should today's candidates receive any special consideration? No one should discriminate against them, of course, but they should have to compete openly and on their merits, just like everybody else."

2. *Affirmative action is necessary to permit fairer competition.*

POINT: "Even if young blacks and young women today have not themselves suffered job discrimination, blacks in particular have suffered all the disadvantages of growing up in families that have been affected by discrimination. In our racist society, they have suffered from inferior schools and poor environment. In addition, as victims of society's prejudiced attitudes, young blacks and young women have been hampered by a lack of self-confidence and self-respect. Taking race and sex into account makes job competition fairer by keeping white men from having a competitive edge that they don't really deserve."

COUNTERPOINT: "Your point is better when applied to blacks than to women, it seems to me, but I'm still not persuaded. You overlook the fact that there are a lot of disadvantaged whites out there, too. Is an employer going to have to investigate everyone's life history to see who had to overcome the most obstacles? I think an employer has a right to seek the best-qualified candidate without trying to make life fair for everybody. And isn't the best-qualified person entitled to get the job or the promotion?"

3. *Affirmative action is necessary to break the cycle that keeps minorities and women locked into low-paying, low-prestige jobs.*

POINT: "You advocate neutral, nondiscriminatory employment practices, as if we could just ignore our whole history of racial and sexual discrimination. Statistics show that African Americans in particular have been trapped in a socioeconomically subordinate position. If we want to break that pattern and eventually heal the racial rifts in our country, we've got to adopt vigorous affirmative action programs that push more African Americans into middle-class jobs. Even assuming racism were dead in our society, with mere nondiscrimination alone it would take a hundred years or more for blacks to equalize their position."

COUNTERPOINT: "You ignore the fact that affirmative action has its costs, too. You talk about healing the racial rifts in our country, but affirmative action programs make everybody more racially conscious. They also cause resentment and frustration among white men. Many African Americans and women also resent being advanced on grounds other than merit. Finally, if you hire and promote people faster and further than they merit, you're only asking for problems."

Arguments Against Affirmative Action

1. *Affirmative action injures white men and violates their rights.*

POINT: "Even moderate affirmative action programs injure the white men who are made to bear their brunt. Other people design the programs, but it is Allan Bakke, Brian Weber, Paul Johnson, and others like them, who find their career opportunities hampered. Moreover, such programs violate the right of white men to be treated as individuals and to have racial or sexual considerations not affect employment decisions."

COUNTERPOINT: "I'm not sure Bakke, Weber, and Johnson have the rights you are talking about. Racial and sexual considerations are often relevant to employment decisions. Jobs and medical school slots are scarce resources, and society may distribute these in a way that furthers its legitimate ends—like breaking the cycle of poverty for minorities. I admit that with affirmative action programs white men do not have as many advantages as they did before, and I'm against extreme programs that disregard their interests altogether. But their interests have to be balanced against society's interest in promoting these programs."

2. *Affirmative action itself violates the principle of equality.*

POINT: "Affirmative action programs are intended to enhance racial and sexual equality, but you can't do that by treating people unequally. If equality is the goal, it must be the means, too. With affirmative action programs, you use racial and sexual considerations— but that is the very thing that has caused so much harm in the past and that affirmative action itself is hoping to get rid of."

COUNTERPOINT: "I admit that it is distasteful to have to take racial and sexual considerations into account when dealing with individuals in employment situations. I wish we didn't have to. But the unfortunate reality is that in the real world racial and sexual factors go a long way toward determining what life prospects an individual has. We can't wish that reality away by pretending the world is colorblind when it is not. Formal, colorblind equality has to be infringed now if we are ever to achieve real, meaningful racial and sexual equality."

3. *Nondiscrimination will achieve our social goals; stronger affirmative action is unnecessary.*

POINT: "The 1964 Civil Rights Act unequivocally outlaws job discrimination, and numerous employees and job candidates have won discrimination cases before the EEOC or in court. We need to insist on rigorous enforcement of the law. Also, employers should continue to recruit in a way that attracts minority applicants and to make sure that their screening and review practices do not involve any implicit racist or sexist assumptions. And they should monitor their internal procedures and the behavior of their white male employees to root out any discriminatory behavior. Stronger affirmative action measures, in particular taking race or sex into account in employment matters, are unnecessary. They only bring undesirable results."

COUNTERPOINT: "Without affirmative action, progress often stops. The percentage of minorities and women employed by those subject to federal affirmative action requirements has risen much higher than it has elsewhere. Take the example of Alabama. In the late 1960s, a federal court found that only 27 out of the state's 3,000 clerical and managerial employees were African American. Federal Judge Frank Johnson ordered extensive recruiting of blacks, as well as the hiring of the few specifically identified blacks who could prove they were victims of discrimination. Nothing happened. Another suit was filed, this time just against the state police, and this time a 50 percent hiring quota was imposed, until blacks reached 25 percent of the force. Today Alabama has the most thoroughly integrated state police force in the country."[46]

The debate over affirmative action is not the only controversy connected with job discrimination. Two other issues, both primarily concerning women, have been the topic of recent moral, legal, and political discussion: the issue of comparable worth and the problem of sexual harassment on the job.

COMPARABLE WORTH

Louise Peterson was a licensed practical nurse at Western State Hospital in Tacoma, Washington. For supervising the daily care of sixty men convicted of sex crimes, she was paid $192 a month less than the hospital's groundskeepers and $700 a month less than men doing work similar to hers at Washington State prisons. Convinced of the inequity of the state's pay scale, Peterson filed a suit claiming that she and other women were being discriminated against because men of similar skills and training and with similar responsibilities were being paid significantly more. A federal judge found Washington guilty of sex discrimination and ordered the state to reimburse its female employees a whopping $838 million in back pay.

Prodded by this and by its biggest public employee union, the state of Washington began a program intended to raise the pay for government jobs typically considered "women's work." Even though the program had flaws,[47] it helped raise to national prominence the doctrine of comparable worth and signaled a dramatic escalation in women's fight for equal employment rights.

In essence, the doctrine of *comparable worth* holds that women and men should be paid on the same scale, not just for doing the same or equivalent jobs, but for doing different jobs of equal skill, effort, and responsibility. One legal-affairs expert says, "The issue pits against each other two cherished American values: the ethic of nondiscrimination versus the free enterprise system."[48]

Advocates of comparable worth point to the substantial statistical evidence demonstrating that women are in more low-paying jobs than men. They also note the consistent relationship between the percentage of women in an occupation and the salary of that occupation: The more women dominate an occupation, the less it pays. Comparable-worth advocates contend that women have been shunted into a small number of pink-collar occupations and that a biased and discriminatory wage system has kept their pay below that of male occupations requiring a comparable degree of skill, education, responsibility, and so on. For example, studies have shown that legal secretaries and instrument-repair technicians hold jobs with the same relative value for a company in terms of accountability, know-how, and problem-solving skill. Yet legal secretaries, who are almost all women, earn an average of $9,432 less than instrument-repair technicians, who are generally men.[49]

As comparable-worth advocates see it, justice demands that women receive equal pay for doing work of comparable value. Jobs should be objectively evaluated in terms of the education, skills, and experience required and in terms of responsibilities, working conditions, and other relevant factors. Equivalent jobs should receive equivalent salaries, even if discriminatory job markets would otherwise put them on different pay scales. Some comparable-worth advocates further argue that when women have not received equivalent pay for jobs of comparable worth, justice requires that employers pay them reparation damages for the money they have lost. That would be expensive. But whether pay adjustments are retroactive or not, all comparable-worth programs envision adjusting the salary schedules of women upward rather than the pay of men downward.

Opponents of comparable worth insist that women, desiring flexible schedules and less taxing jobs, have freely chosen lower-paying occupations and thus are not entitled to any readjustment in pay scales. Phyllis Schlafly, for one, calls comparable worth "basically a conspiracy theory of jobs. . . . It asserts that, first, a massive societal male conspiracy has segregated or ghetto-ized women into particular occupations by excluding them from others; and then, second, devalued the women's job by paying them lower wages than other occupations held primarily by men." She adds: "Not a shred of evidence has been produced to prove those assumptions. For two decades at least women have been free to go into any occupation. . . . But most women continue to choose traditional, rather than non-traditional, jobs. This is their own free choice. Nobody makes them do it."[50]

Others who are sympathetic to the concept of comparable worth worry about its implementation. How are different jobs to be evaluated and compared, they wonder. "How do you determine the intrinsic value of one job and then compare it to another?" asks Linda Chavez, former staff director of the Commission on Civil Rights. She points out that "for 200 years, this has been done by the free marketplace. It's as good an alternative as those being suggested by comparable-worth advocates. I'm not sure the legislative bodies or courts can do any better."[51] Even if judgments of comparability are possible, opponents worry about the cost: Revising salaries could cost a medium-sized company millions of dollars in annual pay increases and increased pension benefits.

Advocates of comparable worth respond to these criticisms by pointing not only to statistical evidence demonstrating the inequity of pay scales but also to massive research documenting the reality of visceral sexism in the workplace and to the hundreds of legal cases involving workplace discrimination against women. They argue that it is not by accident or free choice that women find themselves in jobs paying less than men doing similar work. They have been victimized by a combination of institutional discrimination and a socialization process that has directed them to "female jobs." Moreover, proponents of comparable worth reject the argument that implementing comparable worth would be prohibitively expensive. They point to Minnesota, for example, which phased in a comparable-worth program over several years so the state incurred an expense of only about 1 percent a year. But the core of their argument remains an appeal to fairness and equity, which, they insist, cannot be sacrificed on the altar of economy.

The comparable-worth issue continues to engender legal controversy. The federal courts have not explicitly accepted the doctrine of comparable worth, even when they've rendered legal decisions that seem to support it. One form of job discrimination against women that the courts agree about, however, is sexual harassment.

SEXUAL HARASSMENT

Many men find the term *sexual harassment* amusing and have a difficult time taking it seriously. "It wouldn't bother me," they feel certain. "In fact," they chuckle, "I wouldn't mind being harassed a little more often." Others shrug it off, saying, "What's the big deal? You know what the world is like. Men and women, love and sex, they make it go 'round. Only uptight women are going to complain about sexual advances." But for millions of working women, the reality of sexual harassment is not something to be shrugged off. For them it is no laughing matter.

The courts agree. Sexual-harassment claims have emerged in the past two decades as a potent force in the effort to eliminate sex discrimination. These claims fall primarily under Title VII of the Civil Rights Act, which in certain circumstances imposes liability on employers for the discriminatory acts of their employees—including sexual harassment. The Supreme Court has joined a number of federal district and appeals courts in holding that sexual harassment violates the Civil Rights Act because it is based on the sex of the individual.[52] In short, sexual harassment is illegal.

It is also expensive and—unfortunately—widespread. A survey by *Working Woman* magazine revealed that 90 percent of the companies that make up the *Fortune* 500 have received complaints of sexual harassment.[53] One expert has estimated that the average cost to these firms of each sexual harassment complaint is $200,000—even if it doesn't go to court.[54] And this figure doesn't include the costs incurred when employees quit their jobs because of harassment, take leaves of absence, or stay at their jobs but become less productive. Since the early 1990s, the number of complaints of sexual harassment in the workplace filed annually with the EEOC or state and local authorities has increased by 50 percent—to around 15,000 a year.[55]

According to the Supreme Court, men, as well as women, can be victims of sexual harassment.[56] The focus here is on women, however, because they are the ones who suffer most from it. The U.S. Merit Systems Protection Board found that 42 percent of all female employees of the federal government had been sexually harassed; a study of private employers found that 62 percent of the women surveyed had been harassed in the office. And nine-tenths of the 9,000 women who responded to a questionnaire in *Redbook* magazine reported sexual harassment on the job.[57]

We are all familiar with the stereotype of construction workers who whistle and make lewd comments about women who walk by. But the truth is that all types of men in all sorts of occupations have been reported as harassers. Survey after survey, for example, reveals that high percentages of female professors and female students have encountered some form of sexual harassment from a person in authority at least once while they were in the university.

Critics may find it odd that sexual harassment is viewed by the courts as a kind of sex discrimination. If an infatuated supervisor harasses only the female employee who is the object of his desire, is his misconduct really best understood as discrimination against women? He does not bother women in general, just this particular individual. In viewing sexual harassment as a violation of the 1964 Civil Rights Act, however, the courts are rightly acknowledging that such behavior, and the larger social patterns that reinforce it, rest on male attitudes and assumptions that work against women.

Accepting this viewpoint still leaves puzzles, however. Assume that the infatuated supervisor is a woman and the employee a man. Are we to interpret this situation as sex discrimination, considering that it does not take place against a social backdrop of exploitation and discrimination against men? Or imagine a bisexual employer who sexually harasses both male and female employees. Because he discriminates against neither sex, is there no sexual harassment?

These conceptual puzzles have to do with the law's interpretation of sexual harassment as a kind of sex discrimination. Practically speaking, this interpretation has benefited women and brought them better and fairer treatment on the job, but it clearly has its limits. Legally speaking, the most important aspect of sexual harassment may be that it represents discrimination, but it is doubtful that discrimination is morally the worst aspect of sexual harassment. Morally, there is much more to be said about the wrongness of sexual harassment.*

What exactly is sexual harassment? The Equal Employment Opportunity Commission says that it is "unwelcome sexual advances, requests for sexual favors, and other verbal or physical conduct of a sexual nature." Catherine A. MacKinnon, author of *Sexual Harassment of Working Women,* describes sexual harassment as "sexual attention imposed on someone who is not in a position to refuse it." Alan K. Campbell, director of the Federal Office of Personnel Management, defines it as "deliberate or repeated unsolicited verbal comments, gestures, or physical contact of a sexual nature which are unwelcome."[58] Here is one useful legal definition of sexual harassment, which reflects the way most courts understand it:

> Unwelcome sexual advances, requests for sexual favors, and other verbal or physical conduct of a sexual nature constitute sexual harassment when (1) submission to such conduct is made either explicitly or implicitly a term or condition of an individual's employment, (2) submission to or rejection of such conduct by an individual is used as the basis for employment decisions affecting such individual, or (3) such conduct has the purpose or effect of substantially interfering with an individual's work performance or creating an intimidating, hostile, or offensive working environment.[59]

This definition helps us distinguish three different types of sexual harassment. Sexual threats are the first type—in its crudest form, "You'd better agree to sleep with me if you want to keep your job." The immorality of such threats seems clear. In threatening harm, they are coercive and violate the rights of the person threatened, certainly depriving him or her of equal treatment on the job. Obviously such threats can be seriously psychologically damaging and are hence wrong.

Sexual offers are the second type: "If you sleep with me, I'm sure I can help you advance more quickly in the firm." Often such offers harbor an implied threat, and unlike with genuine offers, the employee may risk something by turning them down. Larry May and John Hughes have argued that such offers by a male employer to a female employee put her in a worse position than she was before and, hence, are coercive. Even sexual offers without hint of retaliation, they suggest, change the female employee's working environment in an undesirable way.[60] In the case of both threats and offers, the employer is attempting to exploit the power imbalance between him and the employee.

The third category—hostile work environment—is the broadest, but it may be the most important because it is so pervasive. Sexual harassment includes behavior of a

---

* By analogy, compare the fact that often the only grounds on which the federal government can put a murderer on trial is on the charge of having violated the civil rights of his or her victim. The charge of violating the victim's civil rights doesn't get to the heart of the murderer's wrongdoing, even if it is the only legally relevant issue.

sexual nature that is distressing to women and interferes with their ability to perform on the job, even when the behavior is not an attempt to pressure the woman for sexual favors. Sexual innuendos; leering or ogling at a woman; sexist remarks about women's bodies, clothing, or sexual activities; the posting of pictures of nude women; and unnecessary touching, patting, or other physical conduct can all constitute sexual harassment. Such behavior is humiliating and degrading to its victim. It interferes with her peace of mind and undermines her work performance.

Neither the wrongness nor the illegality of sexual harassment requires that the harassing conduct be by the employee's supervisor. This is particularly relevant in the third category, in which the harassment a woman endures may come from coworkers. Firms, however, are responsible for providing a work environment in which an employee is free from harassment, and they can be sued for damages if they fail to do so. Different courts have reached different decisions on the question of whether supervisory personnel must be notified or made aware of sexual harassment by employees before the firm can be found legally liable. One can nevertheless safely say that, morally speaking, a company needs to be alert to the possibility of sexual harassment by its employees and take reasonable steps to guard against it.

Legally, a woman is not required to prove that she was psychologically damaged or unable to work in order to establish sexual harassment. On the other hand, an isolated or occasional sexist remark or innuendo does not constitute harassment. Harassment of the third type requires that the objectionable behavior be persistent. The same holds for racial slurs and epithets. An ethnic joke by itself does not constitute discriminatory harassment, but a concerted pattern of "excessive and opprobrious" racially derogatory remarks and related abuse does violate the law.[61]

Human beings are sexual creatures, and when men and women work together, there may be sexual undertones to their interactions. Women as well as men can appreciate, with the right persons and at the appropriate times, sexual references, sex-related humor, and physical contact with members of the opposite sex. Flirting, too, is often appreciated by both parties. It is not necessary that a serious and professional work environment be entirely free from sexuality, nor is this an achievable goal.

When, then, is behavior objectionable or offensive enough to constitute harassment? What one person views as innocent fun or a friendly overture may be seen as objectionable and degrading by another. Comments that one woman appreciates or enjoys may be distressing to another. Who can decide what is right? In the case of sexual harassment, who determines what is objectionable or offensive?

To answer this question, the courts ask what the hypothetical "reasonable woman" would find offensive. What matters morally, however, is to respect each person's choices and wishes. Even if the other women in the office like it when the boss gives them a little hug, it would still be wrong to hug the one woman who is made uncomfortable. If the behavior is unwanted—that is, if the woman doesn't like it—then persisting in it is wrong. The fact that objectionable behavior must be persistent and repeated to be sexual harassment allows for the possibility that people can honestly misread coworkers' signals or misjudge their likely response to a sexual innuendo, a joke, or a friendly pat. That may be excusable; what is not excusable is persisting in the behavior once you know it is unwelcome.

Practically speaking, what should a female employee do if she encounters sexual harassment? First, she must make it clear that the behavior is unwanted. This may be more difficult to do than it sounds, because most of us like to please others and do not want to be thought to be prudes or to lack a sense of humor. The employee may wish to be tactful and even pleasant in rejecting behavior she finds inappropriate, especially if she thinks the offending party is well intentioned. But in any case, she has to make her feelings known clearly and unequivocally. Second, if the behavior persists, she should try to document it by keeping a record of what has occurred, who was involved, and when it happened. If others have witnessed some of the incidents, then that will help her document her case.

The third thing the female employee must do when faced with sexual harassment is to complain to the appropriate supervisor, sticking to the facts and presenting her allegations as objectively as possible. She should do this immediately in the case of sexual threats or offers by supervisors; in the case of inappropriate behavior by coworkers, she should generally wait to see if it persists despite her having told the offending party that she objects. If complaining to her immediate supervisor does not bring quick action, then she must try whatever other channel is available to her in the organization—the grievance committee, for example, or the chief executive's office.

Fourth, if internal complaints do not bring results, then the employee should seriously consider seeing a lawyer and learning in detail what legal options are available. Many women try to ignore sexual harassment, but the evidence suggests that in most cases it continues or grows worse. When sexual threats or offers are involved, a significant number of victims are subject to unwarranted reprimands, increased work loads, or other reprisals. The employee must remember, too, that she has both a moral and a legal right to work in an environment free from sexual harassment.

SUMMARY

1. Discrimination in employment involves adverse decisions against employees or job applicants based on their membership in a group that is an object of prejudice or viewed as inferior or deserving of unequal treatment. Discrimination can be intentional or unintentional, institutional or individual.

2. Statistics, together with evidence of deep-seated attitudes and institutional practices and policies, point to racial and sexual discrimination in the workplace.

3. The Civil Rights Act of 1964 forbids discrimination in employment on the basis of race, color, sex, religion, and national origin. In the late 1960s and early 1970s, many companies developed affirmative action programs to correct racial imbalances existing as a result of past discrimination. Critics charge that in practice affirmative action has often meant preferential treatment of women and minorities and even reverse discrimination against white men.

4. The Supreme Court has adopted a case-by-case approach to affirmative action. Although the legal situation is complex, in a series of rulings over the years a majority of the Court has upheld the general principle of affirmative action, as long as such programs are moderate and flexible. Race can legitimately be taken into account in employment-related decisions, but only as one among several factors. Affirmative action programs that rely on rigid and unreasonable quotas or that impose excessive hardship on present employees are illegal.

5. The moral issues surrounding affirmative action are controversial. Its defenders argue that compensatory justice demands affirmative action programs; that affirmative action is necessary to permit fairer competition; and that affirmative action is necessary to break the cycle that keeps minorities and women locked into poor-paying, low-prestige jobs.

6. Critics of affirmative action argue that affirmative action injures white men and violates their rights; that affirmative action itself violates the principle of equality; and that non-discrimination (without affirmative action) will suffice to achieve our social goals.

7. The doctrine of comparable worth holds that women and men should be paid on the same scale for doing different jobs of equal skill, effort, and responsibility.

8. Advocates of comparable worth say that women have been forced into low-paying jobs and justice requires that women receive equal pay for doing jobs of equal worth. Some contend further that monetary reparations are due to women who in the past have not received equal pay for doing jobs of equal value.

9. Opponents of comparable worth claim that women have freely chosen their occupations and are not entitled to compensation. They contend that only the market can and should determine the value of different jobs. Revising pay scales would also be expensive.

10. Sexual harassment is widespread. It includes unwelcome sexual advances and other conduct of a sexual nature in which submission to such conduct is a basis for employment decisions or such conduct substantially interferes with an individual's work performance. Sexual harassment is a kind of discrimination and is illegal.

11. Employees encountering sexually harassing behavior from coworkers should make it clear that the behavior is unwanted. If it persists, harassed employees should document the behavior and report it to the appropriate person or office in the organization. In the case of sexual threats or offers from supervisors, they should do this immediately. If internal channels are ineffective, employees should seek legal advice.

CASE 9.1

Minority Set-Asides

Richmond, Virginia, is the former capital of the Confederacy. It's not the sort of place one would normally associate with controversial efforts at affirmative action. But aware of its legacy of racial discrimination and wanting to do something about it, the Richmond City Council adopted what it called the Minority Business Utilization Plan—a plan that eventually brought it before the Supreme Court.

The plan, which the council adopted by a 5 to 2 vote after a public hearing, required contractors to whom the city awarded construction contracts to subcontract at least 30 percent of the dollar amount of their contracts to Minority Business Enterprises (MBEs). A business was defined as an MBE if minority group members controlled at least 51 percent of it. There was no geographical limit, however; a minority-owned business from anywhere in the United States could qualify as an MBE subcontractor. (The 30 percent set-aside did not apply to construction contracts that were awarded to minority contractors in the first place.)

Proponents of the set-aside provision relied on a study that indicated that whereas the general population of Richmond was 50 percent African American, only 0.67 percent of the city's construction contracts had been awarded to minority businesses. Councilperson Marsh, a proponent of the ordinance, made the following statement:

> I have been practicing law in this community since 1961, and I am familiar with the practices in the construction industry in this area, in the state, and around the nation. And I can say without equivocation, that the general conduct of the construction industry. . . is one in which race discrimination and exclusion on the basis of race is widespread.

Opponents, on the other hand, questioned both the wisdom and the legality of the ordinance. They argued that the disparity between minorities in the population of Richmond and the low number of contracts awarded to MBEs did not prove racial discrimination in the construction industry. They also questioned whether there were enough MBEs in the Richmond area to satisfy the 30 percent requirement.

The city's plan was in effect for five years. During that time, though, the plan was challenged in the courts. A federal district court upheld the set-aside ordinance, stating that the city council's "findings [were] sufficient to ensure that, in adopting the Plan, it was remedying the present effects of past discrimination in the construction industry." However, the case was appealed to the Supreme Court, which ruled in *City of Richmond v. Croson* that the Richmond plan was in violation of the equal protection clause of the Fourteenth Amendment.[62] In delivering the opinion of the majority of the Court, Justice O'Connor argued that Richmond had not supported its plan with sufficient evidence of past discrimination in the city's construction industry:

> A generalized assertion that there has been past discrimination in an entire industry provides no guidance for a legislative body to determine the precise scope of the injury it seeks to remedy. It "has no logical stopping point.". . . "Relief" for such an ill-defined wrong could extend until the percentage of public contracts awarded to MBEs in Richmond mirrored the percentage of minorities in the population as a whole.
>
> [The City of Richmond] argues that it is attempting to remedy various forms of past discrimination that are alleged to be responsible for the small number of minority businesses in the local contracting industry. . . While there is no doubt that the sorry history of both private and public discrimination in this country has contributed to a lack of opportunities for black entrepreneurs, this observation, standing alone, cannot justify a rigid quota in the awarding of public contracts in Richmond, Virginia. Like the claim that discrimination in primary and secondary schooling justifies a rigid racial preference in medical school admissions, an amorphous claim that there has been past discrimination cannot justify the use of an unyielding racial quota.
>
> It is sheer speculation how many minority firms there would be in Richmond absent past societal discrimination, just as it was sheer speculation how many minority medical students would have been admitted to the medical school at Davis absent past discrimination in educational opportunities. Defining these sorts of injuries as "identified discrimination" would give local governments license to create a patchwork of racial preferences based on statistical generalizations about any particular field of endeavor.
>
> These defects are readily apparent in this case. The 30% quota cannot in any realistic sense be tied to any injury suffered by anyone. . . .
>
> In sum, none of the evidence presented by the city points to any identified discrimination in the Richmond construction industry. We, therefore, hold that the city has failed to demonstrate a compelling interest in apportioning public contracting opportunities on the basis of race. To accept Richmond's claim that past societal discrimination alone can serve as the basis for rigid racial preference would be to open the door to competing claims for "remedial relief" for every disadvantaged group. The dream of a Nation of equal citizens in a society where race is irrelevant to personal opportunity and achievement would be lost in a mosaic of shifting preferences based on inherently unmeasurable claims of past wrongs. . . . We think such a result would be contrary to both the letter and spirit of a constitutional provision whose central command is equality.

But the Court's decision was not unanimous, and Justice Thurgood Marshall was joined by Justices Brennan and Harry Blackmun in dissenting vigorously to the opinion of the majority. Justice Marshall wrote:

> The essence of the majority's position is that Richmond has failed to . . . prove that past discrimination has impeded minorities from joining or participating fully in Richmond's construction contracting industry. I find deep irony in second-guessing Richmond's judgment on this point. As much as any municipality in the United States, Richmond knows what racial discrimination is; a century of decisions by this and other federal courts has richly documented the city's disgraceful history of public and private racial discrimination. In any event, the Richmond City Council *has* supported its determination that minorities have been wrongly excluded from local construction contracting. Its proof includes statistics showing that minority-owned businesses have received virtually no city contracting dollars; . . . testimony by municipal officials that discrimination has been widespread in the local construction industry; and . . . federal studies . . . which showed that pervasive discrimination in the Nation's tight-knit construction industry had operated to exclude minorities from public contracting. These are precisely the types of statistical and testimonial evidence which, until today, this Court has credited in cases approving of race-conscious measures designed to remedy past discrimination.

Discussion Questions

1. What was the Richmond City Council trying to accomplish with its Minority Business Utilization Plan? If you had been a member of the council, would you have voted for the plan?

2. What are the pros and cons of a minority set-aside plan like Richmond's? Will it have good consequences? Does it infringe on anyone's rights? What conflicting moral principles, ideals, and values are at stake?

3. Do you believe that there was sufficient evidence of racial discrimination to justify the city's plan? Who is right about this—Justice O'Connor or Justice Marshall?

4. Justice O'Connor and the majority of the Court seem to believe that there must be some specific, identifiable individuals who have been discriminated against before race-conscious measures can be adopted to remedy past discrimination. Do you agree that affirmative action measures must meet this standard?

5. In light of the fact that no federal statute specifically bars racial discrimination in private domestic commercial transactions between two business firms, and given the evidence that racism is an obstacle to African-American business success,[63] what obligation, if any, does state, local, or federal government have to assist minority-owned companies?

6. What measures could Richmond have taken that would have increased opportunities for minority business but would not have involved racial quotas? Would such measures be as effective as the original plan?

CASE 9.2

Hoop Dreams

In basketball, talent plus hard work equals success. That's an equation that holds true for women as well as men, and in recent years, dedicated female athletes have raised women's basketball to new heights and won the allegiance of many new fans.[64]

But what about their coaches? Do any obstacles stand between them and their dreams? Marianne Stanley didn't think so when she began coaching women's basketball for the University of Southern California, where she earned $64,000 a year—a fair sum, one might think, but less than half that of her counterpart, George Raveling, who coached the men's team. True, Raveling had been coaching for thirty-one years, had been an assistant on the U.S. Olympic team, and was twice named coach of the year. But Stanley was no slouch. She had been a head coach for sixteen years and won three national championships. In her last two years at USC, she had win-loss records of 23–8 and 22–7, which compared favorably with Raveling's 19–10 and 24–6.

So when her initial four-year contract expired, Marianne Stanley sought pay parity with Raveling. Stanley knew that Raveling was also earning tens of thousands of dollars in perks, but she was willing to overlook that and settle for an equal base salary of $135,000. Instead, USC offered Stanley a three-year contract starting at $88,000 and increasing to $100,000. When she rejected that offer, USC countered with a one-year contract for $96,000. Stanley declined the offer and left USC, her hoop dreams diminished, although she later began coaching at UC Berkeley, where her salary was equivalent to that of the men's coach.

For his part, George Raveling didn't mind Stanley's making as much money as he did. But he understood why USC paid him more. He was, after all, a hot property, and if USC was going to prevent his being lured away by some other university trying to boost its basketball program, then it had to pay him a high salary. By contrast, Marianne Stanley didn't have any other job offers.

Too bad, one might say, but that's how the market works in a capitalist society. But what if the market itself is discriminatory? Defenders of comparable worth argue that it is and that coaches like Stanley can't negotiate for comparable salaries because women's basketball isn't valued as highly as men's. And it's college administrators, they argue, who are to blame for that. As one feminist puts it:

> The women didn't get the advertising and marketing dollars. They didn't get the PR. Then when fans weren't showing up, the TV stations weren't carrying the games and other universities weren't fighting over the best coaches, administrators told the women that, because they and their sport didn't draw as much attention as men, they shouldn't be paid as much.

In response, defenders of USC deny that it or any other university is responsible for the fact that men's sports are big revenue earners and women's are not. The higher pay for those who coach men simply reflects that social and cultural reality, which is something college administrators have no control over. If someone like Marianne Stanley wants to enter the big leagues, then she should coach men.

Update:
Sadly, sometimes even those who have fought against discrimination can discriminate against others. In 2002 Sharrona Alexander, formerly an assistant women's basketball coach at UC Berkeley, filed suit against the university, alleging that head coach Marianne Stanley told her to get an abortion or lose her job. Stanley denies the abortion allegation, but admits that she did ask Alexander to resign because of her pregnancy. Either way, a champion of women's rights was guilty of trampling on someone else's hoop dreams. Ironically, Stanley herself played college basketball

when she was pregnant (returning to practice eleven days after her daughter was born) and went on, single and with a toddler, to coach Old Dominion University to three national championships. Moreover, some sports commentators believe that, far from beinga handicap, motherhood can give a coach an edge in recruiting because the parents of prospective recruits prefer their daughters to be coached by women who, when they say that they treat their teams as family, know what they are talking about. In addition, Arizona State coach Charli Turner Thorne says, because "you're taking young ladies at a very formative time, you have to play the parent role." She adds, "There's absolutely no doubt [motherhood] makes me a better coach."

Discussion Questions

1. The doctrine of comparable worth holds that men and women should be paid the same wage for doing jobs of equal skill, effort, and responsibility. Were Marianne Stanley and George Raveling doing work of comparable value?
2. Was Stanley treated unfairly or in some way discriminated against? Should USC have offered to pay her more?
3. Why do sports played by men tend to be more popular and generate more revenue than sports played by women? Are female athletes—and their coaches—disadvantaged? Are they discriminated against? If so, who is responsible for this discrimination, and do colleges and universities have an obligation to do something about it?
4. Should universities like USC base their coaching salaries entirely on market considerations? Or should they pay the coaches of men's and women's sports comparable salaries based on experience, skill, and performance?
5. Respond to the argument that because men are free to coach women's teams and women to coach men's teams, there is nothing discriminatory in the fact that one job pays more than the other.
6. Was Sharrona Alexander's pregnancy likely to have adversely affected her coaching performance? If so, was Marianne Stanley wrong to ask her to resign? How should Stanley have handled the situation?

CASE 9.3

Consenting to Sexual Harassment

In the case of *Vinson v. Taylor*, heard before the federal district court for the District of Columbia, Mechelle Vinson alleged that Sidney Taylor, her supervisor at Capital City Federal Savings and Loan, had sexually harassed her.[65] But the facts of the case were contested. In court Vinson testified that about a year after she began working at the bank, Taylor asked her to have sexual relations with him. She claimed that Taylor said she "owed" him because he had obtained the job for her.

Although she turned down Taylor at first, she eventually became involved with him. She and Taylor engaged in sexual relations, both during and after business hours, in the remaining three years she worked at the bank. The encounters included intercourse in a bank vault and in a storage area in the bank basement. Vinson also testified that Taylor often actually "assaulted or raped" her. She contended that she was forced to submit to Taylor or jeopardize her employment.

Taylor, for his part, denied the allegations. He testified that he had never had sex with Vinson. On the contrary, he alleged that Vinson had made advances toward him and that he had declined them. He contended that Vinson had brought the charges against him to "get even" because of a work-related dispute.

In its ruling on the case, the court held that if Vinson and Taylor had engaged in a sexual relationship, that relationship was voluntary on the part of Vinson and was not employment related. The court also held that Capital City Federal Savings and Loan did not have "notice" of the alleged harassment and was therefore not liable. Although Taylor was Vinson's supervisor, the court reasoned that notice to him was not notice to the bank.

Vinson appealed the case, and the Court of Appeals held that the district court had erred in three ways. First, the district court had overlooked the fact that there are two possible kinds of sexual harassment. Writing for the majority, Chief Judge Spottswood Robinson distinguished cases in which the victim's continued employment or promotion is conditioned on giving in to sexual demands and those cases in which the victim must tolerate a "substantially discriminatory work environment." The lower court had failed to consider Vinson's case as possible harassment of the second kind.

Second, the higher court also overruled the district court's finding that because Vinson voluntarily engaged in a sexual relationship with Taylor, she was not a victim of sexual harassment. Voluntariness on Vinson's part had "no bearing," the judge wrote, on "whether Taylor made Vinson's toleration of sexual harassment a condition of her employment." Third, the Court of Appeals held that any discriminatory activity by a supervisor is attributable to the employer, regardless of whether the employer had specific notice.

In his dissent to the decision by the Court of Appeals, Judge Robert Bork rejected the majority's claim that "voluntariness" did not automatically rule out harassment. He argued that this position would have the result of depriving the accused person of any defense, because he could no longer establish that the supposed victim was really "a willing participant." Judge Bork contended further that an employer should not be held vicariously liable for a supervisor's acts that it didn't know about.

Eventually the case arrived at the Supreme Court, which upheld the majority verdict of the Court of Appeals, stating that:

> [T]he fact that sex-related conduct was "voluntary," in the sense that the complainant was not forced to participate against her will, is not a defense to a sexual harassment suit brought under Title VII. The gravamen of any sexual harassment claim is that the alleged sexual advances were "unwelcome.". . . The correct inquiry is whether respondent by her conduct indicated that the alleged sexual advances were unwelcome, not whether her actual participation in sexual intercourse was voluntary.

The Court, however, declined to provide a definite ruling on employer liability for sexual harassment. It did, however, reject the Court of Appeals's position that employers are strictly liable for the acts of their supervisors, regardless of the particular circumstances.[66]

Discussion Questions

1. According to her own testimony, Vinson acquiesced to Taylor's sexual demands. In this sense her behavior was "voluntary." Does the voluntariness of her behavior mean that she had "consented" to Taylor's advances? Does it mean that they were "welcome"? Do you agree that Vinson's acquiescence shows there was no sexual harassment? Which court was right about this? Defend your position.

2. In your opinion, under what circumstances would acquiescence be a defense to charges of sexual harassment? When would it not be a defense? Can you formulate a general rule for deciding such cases?

3. Assuming the truth of Vinson's version of the case, should her employer, Capital City Federal Savings and Loan, be held liable for sexual harassment it was not aware of? Should the employer have been aware of it? Does the fact that Taylor was a supervisor make a difference? In general, when should an employer be liable for harassment?

4. What steps do you think Vinson should have taken when Taylor first pressed her for sex? Should she be blamed for having given in to him? Assuming that there was sexual harassment despite her acquiescence, does her going along with Taylor make her partly responsible or mitigate Taylor's wrongdoing?

5. In court, Vinson's allegations were countered by Taylor's version of the facts. Will there always be a "your word against mine" problem in sexual harassment cases? What could Vinson have done to strengthen her case?

CASE 9.4

Facial Discrimination

Scene: A conference room of a branch office of Allied Products, Inc., where Tom, Frank, and Alice have been interviewing college students for summer internships.

Tom: Did you see that last candidate? Jeez, was he sorry looking.

Frank: Too ugly to work here, that's for sure. And those thick glasses didn't help. Still, he wasn't as ugly as that young woman you hired last summer. What was her name … Allison? Boy, she was enormous, and remember that hair of hers. It wasn't surprising we had to let her go.

Alice: Come on, Frank. Don't be so hung up on looks. That last guy seemed to know his stuff, and he certainly was enthusiastic about working for Allied.

Frank: Hey, don't get me wrong, Alice. I know you don't have to be beautiful to work for Allied—after all, look at Tom here. Still, with a face like that guy's, you got to wonder.

Tom: Wisecracks aside, Alice, Frank's got a point. Studies show that it's natural for people to discriminate on the basis of looks. I've read that even babies will look at a pretty face longer than an ugly face.

Alice: I know that. Studies also show that people attribute positive characteristics to people they find attractive and that they treat unattractive people worse than other people in lots of ways. Strangers are less likely to do small favors for unattractive people than they are for attractive people, and even parents and teachers have lower expectations for ugly, fat, or odd-looking children. But what this really boils down to is implicit discrimination.

Tom: That's what I'm saying. It's natural. Besides, it's not illegal to discriminate on the basis of appearance.

Frank: That's right. You wouldn't want us to hire somebody with green hair and rings in his nose and put him out at the front desk, would you? This is a business, not a freak show.

Alice: Hey, slow down, guys. First, it may be natural and it may even be legal to favor good-looking people, but that doesn't make it right. And second, I'm not talking about grooming or dress. It's your choice to dye your hair and decorate your face, and if you don't fit in because of that, that's your fault. But the guy we talked to today didn't choose to be ugly, so why hold it against him?

Frank: I suppose next you'll be telling us that we should have kept Allison on last summer just because she was fat.

Alice: No, I'm not saying you have to give preferential treatment to overweight people. But I think that nobody in the office cut her any slack. If she'd been normal size, things would have worked out okay, but people took one look at her and prejudged her to be a loser. You know, Frank, some courts have held that discrimination against the obese violates the Americans with Disabilities Act.

Tom: That's only if it's a medical condition.

Frank: Yeah, Allison's only problem was that she liked to eat.

Alice: You don't know that. You don't know anything about her.

Frank: I suppose her hair was a medical condition, too.

Tom: Okay, you two, take it easy. Seriously, though, Alice, a number of our interns have to interact with the public, and people can be put off by having to deal with ugly people, fat people, or even very short people. So why aren't an employee's looks a job-relevant issue?

Alice: No, I think that as long as the person is clean and well groomed, then the public shouldn't be put off by having to deal with someone who is unattractive or unusual looking. It's unreasonable.

Tom: That's what you say. But what if the public is "unreasonable"? What if they prefer companies with attractive or at least normal-looking employees?

Alice: It's still irrelevant. It's the same as if a company had customers who didn't like dealing with blacks. That's no reason for it not to hire blacks.

Tom: Yeah, I can see that.

Frank: Okay, but what about this ugly guy? Do we have to offer him an internship?

Discussion Questions

1. How frequently are people discriminated against on the basis of their looks? Is it a serious problem in job situations?

2. Assess the argument that there is nothing wrong with "facial discrimination"—that it simply reflects the fact that human beings are naturally attracted to, or repelled by, other human beings on the basis of their physical characteristics.

3. Under what circumstances is physical attractiveness a job-related employment criterion? Is it relevant to being a salesperson, a flight attendant, or a receptionist?

4. What arguments can be given for and against a law preventing job discrimination on the basis of immutable aspects of one's appearance?

5. Assess the argument that because fat, ugly, or strange-looking people have it tougher throughout their lives than do attractive people, we should give them preferential treatment whenever we can—for example, in job situations—to make up for the disadvantages they've suffered and to help level the playing field.

6. Are businesses morally obligated to try to prevent or reduce appearance discrimination in the workplace? What steps can they take?

Notes

1. This and the following three paragraphs are based on Edward Wong, "The Mystery of the Missing Minority Coaches," *New York Times*, January 6, 2002, sec. 4, 5; Mark Purdy, "Riley Seems Right for Stanford, and That's Just the Problem," *San Jose Mercury News*, January 6, 2002, 1D; and Ann Killion, "Willingham Kept Dreams Quiet, Then Played His Hand Wisely," *San Jose Mercury News*, January 3, 2002, 1D.

2. Charles R. Lawrence III, "The Id, the Ego, and Equal Protection: Reckoning with Unconscious Racism," *Stanford Law Review* 39 (January 1987): 318, 340.

3. Ibid., 339–340.

4. Manuel G. Velasquez, *Business Ethics*, 5th ed. (Upper Saddle River, N.J.: Prentice Hall, 2002), 389.

5. Ibid., 390.

6. "A Texas-Size Case of Discrimination?" *Business Week*, March 18, 2002, 14.

7. "Wal-Mart Facing Possibly Huge Suit," *San Jose Mercury News*, September 24, 2003, 3C.

8. "Screening Out Minority Workers," *San Francisco Chronicle*, December 5, 1990, A1.

9. "Restaurant Chain Must Pay $105 Million for Racial Bias," *San Jose Mercury News*, February 5, 1993, 14A.

10. Philip Shenon, "Judge Finds F.B.I. Is Discriminatory," *New York Times*, October 1, 1988, 1.

11. Tom L. Beauchamp and Norman E. Bowie, *Ethical Theory and Business*, 4th ed. (Englewood Cliffs, N.J.: Prentice Hall, 1993), 437.

12. Gertrude Ezorsky, *Racism and Justice: The Case for Affirmative Action* (Ithaca, N.Y.: Cornell University Press, 1991), 27. See also Velasquez, *Business Ethics*, 388–389.

13. "Black Staff Fired More, Study Finds," *San Jose Mercury News*, October 20, 1994, C1.

14. "Boom, Bust Felt Mainly by the Rich," *Wall Street Journal*, January 23, 2003, D2.

15. Robert Pear "Rich Got Richer in 80s; Others Held Even," *New York Times*, January 11, 1991, A1.

16. U.S. Bureau of the Census, *Statistical Abstract of the United States 2002* (Washington, D.C.: U.S. Government Printing Office, 2003), Tables 668, 669.

17. "90% of World Lacks Full Rights, U.N. Says," *San Jose Mercury News*, May 16, 1993, 14A.

18. *Statistical Abstract*, Table 653.

19. "Progress Without Parity," *Business Week*, July 14, 2003, 102.

20. *Statistical Abstract*, Table 588, and *New York Times 2003 Almanac* (New York: Penguin, 2002), 332.

21. "Equal Pay Top Issue for Women," *San Francisco Chronicle*, September 5, 1997, A8; Julianne Malveaux, "On the Economy," *San Francisco Examiner*, April 13, 1997, B2.

22. *Statistical Abstract*, Table 588.

23. Susan J. Wells, "A Female Executive Is Hard to Find," *HR Magazine*, June 2001, 42.

24. "Women Losing Ground on Pay," *San Jose Mercury News*, January 24, 2002, 1C, and Toddi Gutner, "How to Shrink the Pay Gap," *Business Week*, June 24, 2002, 151.

25. Lisa Girion, "Wage Gap Continues to Vex Women," *Los Angeles Times*, February 11, 2001, W1.

26. "Equal Pay Top Issue for Women."

27. *Wards Cove Packing Co., Inc. v. Atonio,* 109 S. Ct. 2115 (1989).

28. This paragraph and the next are based on Andrew Hacker, "Grand Illusion," *New York Review of Books,* June 11, 1998, 28–29.

29. Tamar Lewin, "Sex Bias Found in Awarding of Partnerships at Law Firm," *New York Times,* November 30, 1990, B14.

30. "Judge Orders Partnership in a Bias Case," *Wall Street Journal,* December 5, 1990, B6; *Price Waterhouse v. Hopkins,* 109 S. Ct. 1775 (1989).

31. Ellen Goodman, "Women Gain a Better Shot at the Top Rungs," *Los Angeles Times,* May 29, 1984, II-45.

32. Lee Dembart, "Science: Still Few Chances for Women," *Los Angeles Times,* March 7, 1984, 1. See also "An Outsider's View of the Corporate World," *San Francisco Chronicle,* October 27, 1997, B2.

33. Benson Roxen and Thomas H. Jerdee, "Sex Stereotyping in the Executive Suite," *Harvard Business Review* 52 (May–June 1974); Crystal L. Owen and William D. Todor, "Attitudes Toward Women as Managers: Still the Same," *Business Horizons* 36 (March–April 1993).

34. "Racial Stereotypes Still Persist Among Whites, Survey Finds," *San Francisco Chronicle,* January 9, 1991, A10.

35. Edward W. Jones, Jr., "Black Managers: The Dream Deferred," *Harvard Business Review* 64 (May–June 1986): 84.

36. Jones, "Black Managers," 88.

37. See *Griggs v. Duke Power Co.,* 401 U.S. 424 (1971), and *Wards Cove Packing Co., Inc. v. Atonio,* 109 S. Ct. 2115 (1989) at 2115, in which the Court reiterates that Title VII can be violated by "not only overt discrimination but also practices that are fair in form but discriminatory in practice."

38. "Language Rights," *ACLU News* (San Francisco), March–April 1994, 7; "But Some Entry-Level Workers Still Face Difficulties," *San Francisco Chronicle,* April 7, 1997, B1.

39. "Revolt at the Deli Counter," *Business Week,* April 1, 1996, 32.

40. "Diversity Is About to Get More Elusive, Not Less," *Business Week,* July 7, 2003, 31.

41. Ibid.

42. "Business Affirmative on Diversity," *San Jose Mercury News,* August 24, 1995, 3B.

43. "Memo to the Supreme Court: 'Diversity Is Good Business,'" *Business Week,* January 27, 2003, 96.

44. *Wards Cove Packing Co., Inc. v. Atonio* (1989) and *Martin v. Wilks* (1989).

45. *Adarand Constructors, Inc. v. Pena,* 115 S. Ct. 2097 (1995).

46. Herman Schwartz, "Affirmative Action," in Gertrude Ezorsky, ed., *Moral Rights in the Workplace* (Albany: State University of New York Press, 1987), 276.

47. Peter Kilborn, "Comparable-Worth Pay Plan Creates Unseen Woe for State," *Denver Post,* June 3, 1990, 3A.

48. Nina Totenberg, "Why Women Earn Less," *Parade Magazine,* June 10, 1984, 5.

49. Velasquez, *Business Ethics,* 427.

50. Caroline E. Mayer, "The Comparable Pay Debate," *Washington Post National Weekly Edition,* August 6, 1984, 9.

51. Ibid.

52. *Meritor Savings Bank v. Vinson* (1986); *Harris v. Forklift Systems* (1993).

53. Ronnia Sandroff, "Sexual Harassment in the *Fortune* 500," *Working Woman,* December 1988, 69.

54. Anne B. Fisher, "Sexual Harassment: What to Do?" *Fortune,* August 1993, 85.

55. *www.eeoc.gov/stats/harass.html* (February 6, 2003); cf. "Women in Suits," *Economist,* March 2, 2002, 60–61.

56. *Oncale v. Sundowner Offshore Service* (1998).

57. Mary Jo Shaney, "Perceptions of Harm: The Consent Defense in Sexual Harassment Cases," *Iowa Law Review* 71 (May 1986): 1112n; and "Is Sexual Harassment Still on the Job?" *Business and Society Review* 67 (Fall 1988): 5, 8.

58. Shaney, "Perceptions of Harm," 1109.

59. Ibid.

60. Larry May and John C. Hughes, "Sexual Harassment," in Ezorsky, ed., *Moral Rights*.

61. Terry L. Leap and Larry R. Smeltzer, "Racial Remarks in the Workplace: Humor or Harassment?" *Harvard Business Review* 62 (November–December 1984).

62. *City of Richmond v. J. A. Croson Co.*, 109 S. Ct. 706 (1989).

63. Robert E. Suggs, "Rethinking Minority Business Development Strategies," *Harvard Civil Rights–Civil Liberties Law Review* 25 (Winter 1990); and Brent Bowers, "Black Owners Fight Obstacles to Get Orders," *Wall Street Journal,* November 16, 1990, B1.

64. This case study is based on Joan Ryan, "Playing Field Is Still Not Level," *San Francisco Chronicle,* June 13, 1999, "Sunday," 1, and Ann Killion, "Belief That Coach Can't Be Pregnant Outdated," *San Jose Mercury News,* September 17, 2002, 1A.

65. See Shaney, "Perceptions of Harm," for the relevant legal citations and a presentation of the facts of this case.

66. *Meritor Savings Bank v. Vinson*, 106 S. Ct. 2399 (1986).

Further Reading for Chapter 9

Affirmative Action

Steven M. Cahn, ed., *The Affirmative Action Debate*, 2nd ed. (New York: Routledge, 2002); **Francis Beckwith** and **Todd E. Jones**, eds., *Affirmative Action: Social Justice or Reverse Discrimination?* (Buffalo, N.Y.: Prometheus, 1997); and **George E. Curry,** ed., *The Affirmative Action Debate* (Reading, Mass.: Addition-Wesley, 1996) are good sources of essays both for and against affirmative action. Philosophers **Carl Cohen** and **James P. Sterba** debate the issue in their valuable book *Affirmative Action, and Racial Preferences* (New York: Oxford University Press, 2003).

Gertrude Ezorksy, *Racism and Justice: The Case for Affirmative Action* (Ithaca, N.Y.: Cornell University Press, 1991), provides a succinet, well-informed defense. **Louis P. Pojman**, "The Case Against Affirmative Action," in William H. Shaw, ed., *Social and Personal Ethics*, 5th ed. (Belmont, Calif.: Wadsworth, 2005) is a robust critique.

How Race Is Lived in America (New York: Henry Holt, 2001) is a collection of personal narratives and conversations, produced by the *New York Times*, that probes race relations today from various individual perspectives.

Comparable Worth

Laura Pincus and **Bill Shaw**, "Comparable Worth: An Economic and Ethical Analysis," *Journal of Business Ethics* 17 (April 1998) presents opposing views on adopting comparable worth as a public policy.

Helen Remick and **Ronnie J. Steinberg**, "Comparable Worth and Wage Discrimination," and **Robert L. Simon**, "Comparable Pay for Comparable Work?" in Tom L. Beauchamp and Norman E. Bowie, eds., *Ethical Theory and Business*, 4th ed. (Eaglewood Cliffs, N.J.: Prentice Hall, 1993) provide a clear and thorough introduction to the comparable worth debate.

Sexual Harassment

Karen A. Crain and **Kenneth A. Heischmidt**, "Implementing Business Ethics: Sexual Harassment," *Journal of Business Ethics* 14 (April 1995) is a useful essay that discusses what actions companies should take.

Linda LeMoncheck and **Mane Hajdin**, *Sexual Harassment: A Debate* (Totowa, N.J.: Rowman & Littlefield, 1997) probes the philosophical and ethical issues. Also relevant are **M. J. Booker**, "Can Sexual Harassment Be Salvaged?" *Journal of Business Ethics* 17 (August 1998); **Vrinda Dalmiya**, "Why Is Sexual Harassment Wrong?" *Journal of Social Philosophy* 30 (Spring 1999);

and **Linda L. Peterson**, "The Reasonableness of the Reasonable Woman Standard," *Public Affairs Quarterly* 13 (April 1999).

Workplace Discrimination

John Chandler, "Mandatory Retirement and Justice," *Social Theory and Practice* 22 (Spring 1996) argues against viewing mandatory retirement as unjust age discrimination.

D. W. Haslett, "Workplace Discrimination, Good Cause, and Color Blindness," *Journal of Value Inquiry* 36 (March 2002) provides a helpful theory of what constitutes unethical discrimination in the workplace.

Elizabeth Kristen, "Addressing the Problem of Weight Discrimination in Employment," *California Law Review* 90 (January 2002) argues that job discrimination against the overweight is a serious problem that the law should address.

 InfoTrac College Edition: For further information or to conduct research, please go to www.infotrac-college.com.

BUSINESS AND SOCIETY

10

Consumers

The "Marlboro man" has long mesmerized people around the world, and few can deny the glamour of the ruggedly good-looking Marlboro cowboy, with boots, hat, chaps—and, of course, a cigarette in his mouth. Product of one of the most successful advertising campaigns in history, the Marlboro man revolutionized the image of Marlboro cigarettes, making it the best-selling brand in the United States. Few people remember, however, that the actor who originally portrayed the Marlboro man died of lung cancer as a result of smoking.

Everybody, of course, knows that smoking is hazardous to one's health—everyone, that is, but the tobacco industry. It continues, publicly at least, to deny any cause-and-effect relationship between smoking and disease, even though a smoker has ten times the chance of getting lung cancer and twice the chance of developing heart disease that a nonsmoker has. According to the Centers for Disease Control and Prevention (CDC), smoking remains the leading cause of preventable deaths in the United States and is responsible for 16 percent of all deaths nationwide. Although the percentage of Americans who smoke is dropping, the absolute number of smokers—and smoking's death toll—remains as high as ever. More than 440,000 Americans die each year of tobacco-related causes, at an annual price tag of $75 billion in medical expenditures and another $80 billion in indirect costs.[1]

In the mid-1990s forty-six state governments came together to sue the big tobacco companies, demanding compensation for the money that the states have had to spend on health problems caused by smoking. The suit was settled in 1998 for $206 billion. Among other things, the agreement requires tobacco firms to accept a tax hike on their products, to finance anti-smoking commercials, to cease tobacco-product placement in films and television shows, and to end outdoor tobacco advertisements. As a result, cigarette billboards came down across the country, including a famous 64-foot-high Marlboro man that loomed for years over Sunset Strip in Los Angeles.

Virtually no other consumer good compares to cigarettes in terms of individual injury and social cost. Because of this, during the Clinton administration the Food and Drug Administration (FDA) began laying plans to regulate the sale of cigarettes more closely. Because 90 percent of all smokers get hooked before age twenty-one, the FDA's prime interest was to discourage young people from taking up cigarettes in the first place. In 2000, however, the Supreme Court ruled that the FDA lacks jurisdiction over tobacco. This victory for cigarette manufacturers hasn't, of course, prevented smokers from suing them for injuries allegedly caused by their deadly habit. Despite the warnings that have been required on cigarette packs and ads since 1966, many smokers— or their estates—contend that they were addicted and couldn't stop. Many of these lawsuits are large class-action suits involving dozens of law firms with the collective resources to take on the big tobacco companies. As a result, the smokers have been winning. In cases around the country, juries have been penalizing the tobacco companies with compensatory and punitive damage verdicts for millions, even billions, of dollars (although the companies often succeed in getting the largest of these judgments, like that of a Miami jury for $144.8 billion, reduced or overturned on appeal).

These lawsuits have produced evidence that the tobacco companies suppressed research results establishing that cigarette smoke contains carcinogens and that nicotine is addictive. Industry documents have come to light that also show that the companies view cigarettes as nicotine dispensers and carefully manipulate the dose provided by their different brands. Even so-called low-tar and low-nicotine cigarettes, marketed as "light" or "ultra-light," have been designed so that addicted smokers can inhale just as much nicotine as they always have.[2]

Cigarettes are an especially dangerous product, and their manufacture, marketing, advertising, and sale raise a number of acute questions relevant to the consumer issues discussed in this chapter. For instance, what are the responsibilities to consumers of companies that sell potentially or (in the case of cigarettes) inherently harmful products? To what extent do manufacturers abuse advertising? When is advertising deceptive? Can advertisers create or at least stimulate desires for products that consumers would not otherwise want or would not otherwise want as much? How, if at all, should advertising be restricted?

Are consumers sufficiently well informed about the products they buy? Are they misled by deceptive labeling and packaging? In general, how far should society go in controlling the claims of advertisers, in regulating product packaging and labels, in monitoring product quality and price, and in upholding explicit standards of reliability and safety? What are the moral responsibilities of businesses in these matters? In a market-oriented economic system, how do we balance the interests of business with the rights of consumers? How do we promote social well-being while still respecting the choices of individuals?

These are among the issues probed in this chapter—in particular:

1. Product safety—the legal and moral responsibilities of manufacturers and the pros and cons of government regulations designed to protect consumers

2. The responsibilities of business to consumers concerning product quality, prices, labeling, and packaging

3. Deceptive and morally questionable techniques used in advertising

4. The choice between the "reasonable" consumer and "ignorant" consumer standards as the basis for identifying deceptive advertisements

5. Advertising and children

6. The social desirability of advertising in general—is it a positive feature of our economic system? Does it manipulate, or merely respond to, consumer needs?

PRODUCT SAFETY

Business's responsibility for understanding and providing for consumer needs derives from the fact that citizen-consumers depend on business to satisfy their needs. This dependence is particularly true in our highly technological society, characterized as it is by a complex economy, intense specialization, and urban concentration. These conditions contrast with those prevailing in the United States when the country was primarily agrarian, composed of people who could satisfy most of their own needs. Today, however, we rely on others to provide the wherewithal for our survival and prosperity. We rarely make our own clothing, supply our own fuel, manufacture our own tools, or construct our own homes, and our food is more likely to come from thousands of miles away than from our own gardens.

The increasing complexity of today's economy and the growing dependence of consumers on business for their survival and enrichment have heightened business's responsibilities to consumers—particularly in the area of product safety. From toys to tools, consumers use products believing that they won't be harmed or injured by them. Because consumers lack the technical expertise to judge many of the sophisticated products that are necessary for contemporary life, they must rely primarily on the conscientious efforts of business to ensure consumer safety.

Unfortunately, statistics indicate that the faith consumers place in manufacturers is often misplaced. Every year millions of Americans require medical treatment from product-related accidents. For example, in a typical year yard and garden equipment sends 70,000 consumers to hospital emergency rooms while personal use items cause 160,000 people to seek emergency care, toys 191,000 people, and packaging and containers for household products 271,000 people.[3] Consumer products also electrocute approximately 200 people annually.[4]

The Legal Liability of Manufacturers

If any of us is injured by a defective product, we can sue the manufacturer of that product. We take this legal fact for granted, but it wasn't always true. Before the landmark case of *MacPherson v. Buick Motor Car* in 1916, injured consumers could recover damages only from the retailer of the defective product—that is, from the party with whom they had actually done business. That made sense in a bygone day of small-scale, local capitalism. If the shoes you bought from the local shoemaker were defective, then your complaint was against him. By contrast, when a wheel fell off Donald MacPherson's Buick, the firm he had bought the Buick from hadn't actually made it.

Legal policy before *MacPherson* based a manufacturer's liability for damage caused by a defective product on the contractual relationship between it and the purchaser. Their contractual relationship is simply the sale—that is, the exchange of money for a commodity of a certain description. But that contractual relationship is an important source of moral and legal responsibilities for the producer. It obligates business firms to provide customers with a product that lives up to the claims the firm makes about the product. Those claims shape customers' expectations about what they are buying and lead them to enter into the contract in the first place. The question in *MacPherson*, however, was whether a manufacturer's liability for defective products was limited to those with whom it had a direct contractual relationship.

The New York Court of Appeals's *MacPherson* decision recognized the twentieth-century economic reality of large manufacturing concerns and national systems of product distribution. Among other things, local retailers are not as likely as large manufacturers to be able to bear financial responsibility for defective products that injure others. One can also see the court moving in *MacPherson* to a "due-care" theory of the manufacturer's duties to consumers. *Due care* is the idea that consumers and sellers do not meet as equals and that the consumer's interests are particularly vulnerable to being harmed by the manufacturer, who has knowledge and expertise the consumer does not have.[5] MacPherson, for instance, was in no position to have discovered the defective wheel before the Buick was purchased. According to the due-care view, then, manufacturers have an obligation, above and beyond any contract, to exercise due care to prevent the consumer from being injured by defective products.

As the concept of due care spread, legal policy moved decisively beyond the old doctrine of *caveat emptor,* which was seldom the guiding principle by the time of *MacPherson* anyway. *Caveat emptor* means "let the buyer beware," and today we associate it with an era of patent medicines and outrageously false product claims. Although legally the doctrine of "let the buyer beware" was never upheld across the board, it still symbolizes a period in which consumers themselves had a greater legal responsibility to accept the consequences of their product choices.

Consumers at that time were held to the ideal of being knowledgeable, shrewd, and skeptical. It was their free choice whether to buy a certain product. Accordingly, they were expected to take the claims of manufacturers and salespeople with a grain of salt, to inspect any potential purchase carefully, to rely on their own judgment, and to accept any ill results of their decision to use a given product. In the first part of the twentieth century, however, the courts repudiated this doctrine, largely on grounds of its unrealistic assumptions about consumer knowledge, competence, and behavior.

Despite *MacPherson*'s support for the due-care theory and for a broader view of manufacturer's liability, the case still left the injured consumer with the burden of proving that the manufacturer had been negligent. Not only might such an assertion be difficult to prove, but also a product might be dangerously defective despite the manufacturer's having taken reasonable steps to avoid such a defect.

Two important cases changed this situation. In the 1960 New Jersey case *Henningsen v. Bloomfield Motors* and in the 1963 California case *Greenman v. Yuba Power Products,* injured consumers were awarded damages without having to prove that the manufacturers of the defective products were negligent. Consumers, the courts ruled, have a right to expect that the products they purchase are reasonably safe when used in the intended way. On the basis of these and hundreds of subsequent cases, the "strict liability" approach to product safety has come to dominate legal thinking.

The doctrine of *strict product liability* holds that the manufacturer of a product has legal responsibilities to compensate the user of that product for injuries suffered because the product's defective condition made it unreasonably dangerous, even though the manufacturer has not been negligent in permitting that defect to occur. Under this doctrine a judgment for the recovery of damages could conceivably be won even if the manufacturer adhered to strict quality-control procedures. Strict liability, however, is not absolute liability. The manufacturer is not responsible for any injury whatsoever that might befall the consumer. The product must be defective, and the consumer always has the responsibility to exercise care.

Strict product liability is not without its critics, however. They contend that the doctrine is unfair. If a firm has exercised due care and taken reasonable precautions to avoid or eliminate foreseeable dangerous defects, they argue, then it should not be held liable for defects that are not its fault—that is, for defects that happen despite its best efforts to guard against them. To hold the firm liable anyway seems unjust.

The argument for strict liability is basically utilitarian. Its advocates contend, first, that only such a policy leads firms to bend over backward to guarantee product safety. Because they know that they will be held liable for injurious defects no matter what, they make every effort to enhance safety. Second, proponents of strict liability contend that the manufacturer is best able to bear the cost of injuries due to defects. Naturally, firms raise the price of their products to cover their legal costs (or pay for liability insurance). Defenders of strict liability do not disapprove of this. They see it as a perfectly reasonable way of spreading the cost of injuries among all consumers of the product, rather than letting it fall on a single individual—a kind of insurance scheme.

Protecting the Public

These developments in product liability law set the general framework within which manufacturers must operate today. In addition, a number of government agencies have become involved in regulating product safety. Congress created one of the most important of these agencies in 1972 when it passed the Consumer Product Safety Act. This act empowers the Consumer Product Safety Commission to protect the public "against unreasonable risks of injury associated with consumer products." The three-member commission sets standards for products, bans products presenting undue risk of injury, and in general polices the entire consumer-product marketing process from manufacture to final sale.

In undertaking its policing function, the commission aids consumers in evaluating product safety, develops uniform standards, gathers data, conducts research, and coordinates local, state, and federal product safety laws and enforcement. The commission's jurisdiction extends to more than 15,000 products, and it has the power to require recalls, public warnings, and refunds. Exceptionally risky products can be seized and condemned by court order. Rather than stressing punitive action, however, the commission emphasizes developing new standards and redesigning products to accommodate possible consumer misuse. It is less concerned with assigning liability than with avoiding injuries in the first place.

Despite the obvious public benefits of safety regulations, critics worry about the economic costs. New safety standards add millions of dollars to the cumulative price tag of various goods. Often economists can estimate how many lives a regulation saves and then compare that with the cost of implementing the rule. For example, the cost of requiring labels showing the trans-fat content of foods is only $3,000 per life saved, whereas the cost of insulation to protect against fire in airplane cabins is $300,000. For other regulations the cost to save one life is considerably higher: stronger automobile doors $500,000; flame-retardant children's sleepwear $2.2 million; and reducing the asbestos exposure of factory workers $5.5 million.[6] Is the expense always worth it? And what about recalls? They, too, can be expensive. BMW's 2002 recall of 17,000 7 Series sedans to check problematic electronic fuel pumps set the company back $3 million—a large sum, one might think, but only a tiny fraction of the $200–$300 million Ford spent six years earlier to recall 8.7 million vehicles with fire-prone ignition switches. And the estimated cost of Firestone's 2000 recall of 6.5 million tires it had made for Ford

Explorers—the largest product recall in the United States since the Tylenol scare of 1982—surpasses that.

In addition, consumers sometimes reject mandated safety technology. In 1974, for example, Congress legislated an interlock system that would require drivers to fasten their seat belts before their cars could move. A public outcry forced lawmakers to rescind the law.

Safety regulations may also prevent individuals from choosing to purchase a riskier, though less expensive, product. Take the notorious Ford Pinto with its unsafe gas tank, for example. In 1978, after all the negative publicity, scores of lawsuits, and the trial of Ford Motor Company for reckless homicide, the sale of Pintos fell dramatically. Consumers evidently preferred a safer car for comparable money. However, when the state of Oregon took all the Pintos out of its fleet and sold them, at least one dealer reported brisk sales of the turned-in Pintos at their low, secondhand price.[7] Some consumers were willing to accept the risks of a Pinto if the price was right.

Economists worry about the inefficiencies of preventing individuals from balancing safety against price. Philosophers worry about interfering with people's freedom of choice. Take automobile safety again. Because smaller cars provide less protection than larger ones, people in small cars are less likely to survive accidents. Bigger, safer cars are more expensive, however, and many would prefer to spend less on their cars despite the increased risk. If only those cars that were as safe as, say, a Mercedes-Benz were allowed on the market, then there would be fewer deaths on the highways. But then fewer people could afford cars.

This example touches on the larger controversy over *legal paternalism,* which is the doctrine that the law may justifiably be used to restrict the freedom of individuals for their own good. No one doubts that laws justifiably restrict people from harming other people, but a sizable number of moral theorists deny that laws should attempt to prevent people from running risks that affect only themselves. Requiring your car to have brakes protects others; without brakes, you are more likely to run over a pedestrian. On the other hand, requiring you to wear a seat belt when you drive affects only you. Anti-paternalists would protest that your being forced to wear a seat belt despite your wishes fails to respect your moral autonomy. Nonetheless, in the past hundred years a growing number of paternalistic laws have been enacted.

Paternalism is a large issue that can't be done justice here, but in regard to safety regulations, three comments are in order. First, the safety of some products or some features of products (such as a car's brakes) affects not just the consumer who purchases the product but third parties as well. Regulating these products or product features can be defended on nonpaternalistic grounds. Second, anti-paternalism gains plausibility from the view that individuals know their own interests better than anyone else and that they are fully informed and able to advance those interests. But in the increasingly complex consumer world, this assumption is often doubtful. Whenever citizens lack knowledge and are unable to make intelligent comparisons and safety judgments, they may find it in their collective self-interest to set minimal safety standards. Such standards are particularly justifiable when few, if any, reasonable persons would want a product that did not satisfy those standards.

Finally, the controversy over legal paternalism pits the values of individual freedom and autonomy against social welfare. Requiring people to wear seat belts may infringe the former but saves thousands of lives each year. We may simply have to acknowledge that clash of values and be willing to make trade-offs. This doesn't imply a defense of paternalism across the board. Arguably, some paternalistic regulations infringe autonomy more than laws about seat belts do but bring less gain in social welfare. In the end, one may have to examine paternalistic product safety legislation case by case and weigh the conflicting values and likely results.

How Effective Is Regulation?

Consumers usually assume that if a product is on the market, especially if it is something they ingest, then it has been certified as safe. But this assumption can be mistaken. Unapproved drugs, for instance, can linger on the market for years while the Food and Drug Administration (FDA) studies them. For example, since it became available in 1964, millions and millions of women have taken the hormone replacement Estratest, but the drug is still under FDA review and has yet to be approved.[8] Herbal remedies and dietary supplements are another source of concern because they are exempt from the regulatory scrutiny the FDA applies to drugs. There are few studies of the effectiveness of folk medicines like kava, gingseng, and ginko biloba. For example, ephedra is supposed to help people lose weight, but it contains a potent chemical that can mimic the effects of amphetamines, causing heart attack, stroke, and arrhythmia. When Baltimore Orioles pitcher Steve Bechler died while taking it in 2003, the FDA proposed rules to give consumers more information about what's in herbal supplements and to standardize their manufacture to ensure purity and uniformity. But merely informing consumers what's in the bottle doesn't tell them what risks they run in taking it.

In some other cases regulation may interfere with rather than safeguard consumer interests. For example, in the late 1960s the FDA, with considerable fanfare, banned the sweetener cyclamate. Several years later, scientific bodies around the world determined that cyclamate was safe, and Abbott Laboratories, makers of cyclamate, asked the FDA to rescind the ban. The FDA refused, so Abbott took it to court. In doing so, it uncovered compelling evidence of the FDA's abuse of both regulatory process and scientific method, as well as a massive attempt at a cover-up. In particular, Abbott put into the record damning affidavits from a meeting between the FDA commissioner and corporate executives: The commissioner conceded that cyclamate was safe but would remain banned for political reasons. Abbott also forced the agency to turn over internal memos and other documents in which qualified FDA staffers admitted without reservation that cyclamate was safe and that superiors merely saw no point in permitting it back on the market.

In this instance, the interests of the consuming public do not seem to have been served. But regulations often prod business to recognize and act on its responsibilities to consumers. Sometimes even without applying the force of law, agencies can effectively safeguard the health and safety of consumers. A good example concerns the connection between certain kinds of tampons and the sometimes fatal disease called toxic shock syndrome.

In 1980 the CDC discovered a correlation between toxic shock and tampon use but deemed the rate of incidence too low to recommend that women stop using tampons. A couple of months later it found that women with toxic shock were more than twice as likely as a similar group of healthy women to have used Procter & Gamble's Rely, which had garnered about one-quarter of the tampon market. From the moment that the CDC's second report became public, Procter & Gamble repeatedly denied its product's complicity in toxic shock. Knowing that Procter & Gamble was sensitive to bad publicity and aware of its own mandate to protect the public health, the FDA, the regulatory agency charged with acting on CDC findings, deliberately used the media as a weapon to drive Rely off the market. In the words of Wayne L. Pines, an associate FDA commissioner at the time: "Throughout the series of events, we made sure the press was notified so as to keep the story alive. We wanted to saturate the market with information on Rely. We deliberately delayed issuing press releases for a day to maximize the media impact. There was quite a concerted and deliberate effort to keep a steady flow of information before the public."[9]

As a result Procter & Gamble later that year voluntarily agreed to withdraw Rely from the market. Because Procter & Gamble remained convinced that Rely was a safe product, it's fair to surmise that it would not have withdrawn the product without agency pressure. After all, there was no incontrovertible clinical evidence implicating its tampons in the incidence of toxic shock until over a year later. Had the FDA not acted as it did and had Procter & Gamble continued to sell the product, many women undoubtedly would have suffered and even died in the interval.

Do regulations, then, help business meet its responsibility to consumers? Judging from these cases, the answer is generally yes but sometimes no. Nonetheless, the prevailing view today among businesspeople favors self-regulation. Such a view certainly is in keeping with the tenets of classical capitalism and is arguably an attractive ideal. However, self-regulation can easily become an instrument for subordinating consumer interests to profit making when the two goals clash. Under the guise of self-regulation, businesses may end up ignoring or minimizing responsibility to consumers.

Consider the auto industry, which has a long history of fighting against safety regulations. For example, it successfully lobbied the federal government to delay the requirement that new cars be equipped with air bags or automatic seat belts. Each year of the delay saved the industry millions of dollars. But the price paid by consumers was high: According to the National Highway Traffic Safety Administration, driving with your seat belt on in a car with air bags cuts in half your chance of dying in a crash.

When the law finally required passive restraint systems in new vehicles, Chrysler Motors became (in 1989) the first U.S. auto manufacturer to install driver-side air bags in all its new models. Only five years earlier, Chrysler chairman Lee Iacocca had boasted in his autobiography of fighting against air bags since their invention in the mid-1960s. In 1971, he and Henry Ford II (then the top executives at Ford) met secretly with President Richard Nixon to persuade him to kill a pending Department of Transportation regulation requiring air bags in every new car sold in the United States.[10] Had air bags been made standard equipment in 1974, more than 70,000 deaths and many times that number of severe injuries would have been avoided.

As car buyers have become better informed, automobile manufacturers are rethinking Iacocca's old bromide, "Safety doesn't sell." But even if safety does sometimes sell, for an industry to wait for marketplace demand before increasing safety standards can be irresponsible. Antilock brakes, for instance, save lives because they greatly improve a car's ability to stop short without skidding. Although the technology has been around for years, antilock brakes are still not required on new vehicles. Hardly any cars built in the United States have electronic stability control (ESC), to take another example, although a majority of new vehicles in Germany and northern Europe come with it. ESC prevents the kind of skids that often lead to rollovers, but it will remain a rare and expensive option until regulation requires it, thus bringing down the cost through manufacturing economies of scale. If society always waited for marketplace demand before insisting on public health and safety regulations, then pasteurization of milk and sprinkler systems to suppress fires in public places would still be "options."

The Responsibilities of Business

Simply obeying laws and regulations does not exhaust the moral responsibilities of business in the area of consumer safety. The Consumer Product Safety Commission, for example, has long required toy manufacturers to analyze their products for choking hazards, and it has banned toys that small children can easily choke on. By contrast, until 2003 no agency conducted safety testing of, or otherwise regulated or monitored, candy for its potential to choke children—even though in recent years many more children have choked to death on candy, particular little gel candies, than on toys.[11] However, this regulatory asymmetry between toy manufacturers and candy manufacturers marked no significant difference in their moral obligations. Regardless of what the law does or doesn't require, candy manufacturers have as great a responsibility as toy manufacturers do to minimize choking deaths.

When it comes to product safety, the exact nature of business's moral responsibilities is difficult to specify in general, because much depends on the particular product or service being provided. But abiding by the following steps would do much to help business behave morally with respect to consumer safety:

1. *Business should give safety the priority warranted by the product.* This injunction is important because businesses often base safety considerations strictly on cost. If the margin of safety can be increased without significantly insulting budgetary considerations, fine; if not, then safety questions are shelved.

   Cost cannot be ignored, of course, but neither can two other factors. One is the seriousness of the injury the product can cause. For example, because lawn mowers can cause serious injury, their safety is of the utmost importance. The second factor to consider is the frequency of occurrence. How often is a particular product involved in an accident? Car crashes, for instance, are the leading killer of Americans under age thirty-five. When a product scores high on both the seriousness and frequency tests, it warrants the highest priority as a potential safety hazard.

2. *Business should abandon the misconception that accidents occur exclusively as a result of product misuse and that it is thereby absolved of all responsibility.* At one time such a belief may have been valid, but in using today's highly sophisticated products, even people who follow product instructions explicitly sometimes still suffer injuries. In any case, the point is that the company shares responsibility for product safety with the consumer. Rather than insisting that consumers' abuse of product leads to most accidents and injuries, firms would probably accomplish more by carefully pointing out how their products can be used safely.

   A Pennsylvania court has endorsed this perspective. It awarded $11.3 million in damages to a twenty-year-old Philadelphia woman who was accidentally shot in the head when a handgun owned by her neighbor went off. The court decided the shop that had sold the weapon should pay 30 percent of the damages, because it had provided the buyer with no demonstration or written instructions for safe use of the gun.[12]

Both manufacturers and retailers have an obligation to try to anticipate and minimize the ways their products can cause harm, whether or not those products are misused. For example, a four-year-old girl was seriously injured when she stood on an oven door to peek into a pot on top of the stove and her weight caused the stove to tip over. A manufacturer can reasonably foresee that a cook might place a heavy roasting pan on the oven door. If doing so caused the stove to tip over, a court would almost certainly find the stove's design defective. But should the manufacturer have foreseen the use of the door not as a shelf but as a stepstool? The courts ruled that it should have. In the case of guns, manufacturers could make their product safer with trigger locks or internal safety locks, and they could work with wholesalers to crack down on dealers who repeatedly sell weapons that end up in hands of criminals (the police give gun makers the serial numbers of any of their guns used in crimes).

If a product poses a serious potential threat, a company may need to take extraordinary measures to ensure continued safe use of it. Determining the extent to which the company must go, however, isn't an easy task. Sometimes a firm's moral responsibility for ensuring safety doesn't reach much beyond the sale of the product. Other times it may extend further. Consider, for example, a company that produces heavy machinery. Workers using its products could easily fall into bad habits. Some would argue, therefore, that the company has an obligation to follow up the sale of such a product, perhaps by visiting firms using its machinery to see if they've adopted dangerous shortcuts.

3. *Business must monitor the manufacturing process itself.* Frequently firms fail to control key variables during the manufacturing process, resulting in product defects. Companies should periodically review working conditions and the competence of key personnel. At the design stage of the process, they need to predict ways the product might fail and the consequences of such failure. For production, companies ordinarily can select materials that have been pretested or certified as flawless. If a company fails to do this, then we must question its commitment to safety. Similar questions arise when companies do not make use of available research about product safety. To answer some questions a company may have to generate its own research. However, independent research groups ensure impartial and disinterested analysis and are usually more reliable than in-house studies.

Testing should be rigorous and simulate the toughest conditions. Tests shouldn't assume that the product will be used in just the way the manufacturer intends it to be used. Even established products should be tested. The courts have repeatedly held that a trouble-free history does not justify the assumption that the product is free of defects.[13]

When a product moves into production, it is often changed in various ways. These changes should be documented and referred to some appropriate party, such as a safety engineer, for analysis. The firm must be scrupulous about coordinating department activities so manufacturing specifications are not changed without determining any potential dangers related to these changes.

4. *When a product is ready to be marketed, companies should have their product safety staff review their market strategy and advertising for potential safety problems.* This step is necessary because both product positioning and advertising influence how a product is used, which in turn affects the likelihood of safety problems. For example, the low-cost, appealing Suzuki Samurai was marketed to young adults. Because young drivers have comparatively little driving experience and a propensity to take risks behind the wheel, they are more likely to encounter those handling situations in which the Samurai was dangerously prone to roll over. Another example is a feeder auger manufacturer whose promotional brochure states that "even a child can do your feeding." The brochure had a photograph of the auger with its safety cover removed to show the auger's inner workings. When a young boy was injured while using the feeder auger with the safety cover removed, a jury found the promotional brochure misleading with respect to operating conditions and product safety.[14]

5. *When a product reaches the marketplace, firms should make available to consumers written information about the product's performance.* This information should include operating instructions, the product's safety features, conditions that will cause it to fail, a complete list of the ways the product can be used, and a cautionary list of the ways it should not be used. Warnings must be specific.

    But no matter how specific they are, warnings are of little value if a consumer cannot read them. St. Joseph Aspirin for Children is marketed in Spanish-speaking areas and is advertised in the Spanish-language media. But you have to know English to read the crucial warning: "Children and teenagers should not use this medicine for chicken pox or flu symptoms before a doctor is consulted about Reye's Syndrome, a rare but serious illness reported to be associated with aspirin." Because his mother spoke only Spanish and couldn't read the label on the St. Joseph's box, little Jorge Ramirez of Modesto, California, contracted Reye's Syndrome. Today, he is blind, quadriplegic, and mentally impaired.[15]

6. *Companies should investigate consumer complaints.* This process encourages firms to deal fairly with consumers and to use the most effective source of product improvement: the opinions of those who use it.

Even if firms seriously attended to these safety considerations, they couldn't guarantee an absolutely safe product. Some hazards invariably attach to certain products, heroic efforts notwithstanding. But business must acknowledge and discharge its responsibilities in this area. Morally speaking, no one's asking for an accident- and injury-proof product, only that a manufacturer do everything reasonable to approach that ideal.

Cigarette fires illustrate the shortcomings of the tobacco industry in this respect. According to government estimates, about 1,500 Americans are killed each year in cigarette fires, making cigarettes the country's leading cause of fatal fires. Cigarette fires are responsible for 7,000 serious injuries per year and for property damage of $400 million annually. For years, however, research has shown that small design changes in cigarettes would make them less likely to ignite furniture and bedding, and lawmakers in a number of states have called for legislation to set a fire-resistance standard for cigarettes. But only in January 2000 did a tobacco company announce that it would introduce a cigarette designed to stop burning if the smoker forgets to puff.[16]

The tire industry offers another example. On a Montana road, the tread on the left rear tire of Joseph Cartus's classic sports car separated, causing it to flip and leaving his girlfriend disfigured and with brain damage. The tire had only 4,000 miles on it, but it was eleven years old, and as the NHTSA has now documented, even pristine tires deteriorate with age and become prone to sudden failure. "The age issue is the tire industry's dirty little secret," says one safety expert. Tire makers are reluctant to address the age problem because it would create havoc with their distribution systems. New tires often sit around for two years or more before being sold, and if they had "use by" dates on them, then consumers would do what they do when buying milk or meat, namely, refuse to buy anything other than the freshest item.[17]

Unfortunately, there are numerous other examples of companies and entire industries that play fast and loose with safety, resisting product improvements and dodging responsibility for consumer injury. But many companies do respond quickly to perceived or suspected hazards. Consider two examples of successful companies that place a premium on product safety.[18]

J.C. Penney and Burning Radios   Back in the early 1960s, a few of the radios sold by J.C. Penney were reported to have caught fire in customers' homes. J.C. Penney tested the radios and discovered a defective resistor in a few of them—less than 1 percent. Nonetheless, J.C. Penney informed the manufacturer, withdrew the entire line of radios, ran national ads informing the public of the danger, and offered immediate refunds. "This was before the Consumer Product Safety Commission even existed," said J.C. Penney vice chairman Robert Gill. "I guess some people might have thought we were crazy, and said that liability insurance was specifically designed to take care of such problems. But we felt we just could not sell that kind of product."

Johnson Wax and Fluorocarbons   In the mid-1970s, environmentalists became seriously alarmed at the possibility that fluorocarbons released from aerosol cans were depleting the earth's thin and fragile ozone layer. The media rapidly picked up the story, but virtually all manufacturers of aerosol cans denounced the scientific findings and stood by their products. The exception was Johnson Wax. The company acknowledged that the scientific questions were difficult to resolve, but it took seriously consumer concern about ozone depletion. Years before the FDA ban, Johnson Wax withdrew all its fluorocarbon products worldwide. "We picked up a lot of flak from other manufacturers," recalled company chairman Samuel Johnson, "and we lost business in some areas, but I don't have any question we were right. . . . Our belief is that as long as you can make do without a potentially hazardous material, why not do without it?"

OTHER AREAS OF BUSINESS RESPONSIBILITY

Product safety is naturally a dominant concern of consumers. No one wants to be injured by the products he or she uses. But safety is far from the only interest of consumers. The past forty years have seen a general increase in consumer awareness and an ever stronger consumer advocacy movement. One chief consumer issue has been advertising and its possible abuse, which will be discussed in subsequent sections. Three other areas of business responsibility—product quality, pricing, and packaging and labeling—are equally important and are taken equally seriously by the consumer movement.

Product Quality

The demand for high-quality products is closely related to a number of themes mentioned in the discussion of safety. Most people would agree that business bears a general responsibility to ensure that the quality of a product measures up to the claims made about it and to reasonable consumer expectations. They would undoubtedly see this responsibility as deriving primarily from the consumer's basic right to get what he or she pays for.

Although high product quality can also be in a company's interest, sometimes business shirks this responsibility. For example, in 1973 new car bumpers had to withstand a 5-mile-per-hour collision with no damage. Ten years later, the auto industry succeeded in getting this quality standard lowered: The speed was cut in half, and damage to the bumpers themselves was no longer taken into account. Or consider the bottled water industry. Most people who buy bottled water do so because they believe that it is purer and safer than tap water. Not so, reports the Natural Resources Defense Council, which recently tested 103 brands and found that one-third of them, including some of the best-known brands, contained contaminants that exceeded state or federal standards. These results do not mean that bottled water is dangerous, but they do suggest that consumers are not getting the product quality they're paying for.[19]

One way that business assumes responsibilities to consumers for product quality and reliability is through *warranties*, which are obligations to purchasers that sellers assume. People generally speak of two kinds of warranties, express and implied. *Express warranties* are the claims that sellers explicitly state—for example, that a product is "shrinkproof" or will require no maintenance for two years. The moral concern, of course, is whether a product lives up to its billing. Express warranties include assertions about the product's character, assurances of product durability, and other statements on warranty cards, labels, wrappers, and packages or in the advertising of the product. Many companies offer detailed warranties that are very specific about what defects they cover. Few go as far as L. L. Bean does with its "100% guarantee," which allows customers to return any purchase at any time for a full refund if it proves unsatisfactory.

Implied warranties include the claim, implicit in any sale, that a product is fit for its ordinary, intended use. The law calls this the implied warranty of *merchantability*. It's not a promise that the product will be perfect; rather, it's a guarantee that it will be of passable quality or suitable for the ordinary purpose for which it is used. Implied warranties can also be more specific—for example, when the seller knows that a buyer has a particular purpose in mind and is relying on the seller's superior skill or judgment to furnish goods adequate for that purpose.

The concept of an implied warranty is relevant to the case of Kodak's instant cameras. When Polaroid won a patent violation judgment against Kodak, Kodak was forced not only to stop selling its instant cameras but also to compensate previous purchasers, who could no longer obtain film for their cameras. These purchasers had relied on the implicit claim that Kodak would not suddenly make its products obsolete.[20]

With or without warranties, however, consumers today are more militant than ever in their insistence on product quality and on getting exactly what they paid for. For example, when Ira Gore learned that his new $40,000 car had been damaged and repainted before he took delivery, he sued BMW for having reduced his car's value by $4,000 and sought punitive damages based on the fact that BMW had sold 983 such "refinished" cars over a ten-year period. An Alabama jury agreed with Gore. It viewed the practice as consumer fraud and awarded him $4 million in punitive damages—not bad recompense for an injury to his car that it had cost BMW only $601.78 to fix. The Alabama Supreme Court subsequently cut the award in half, and in 1996 the U.S. Supreme Court ordered Alabama to lower it still further, holding that $2 million is "grossly excessive" punishment for the minor economic injury Gore had suffered.[21] Although the Court's precedent-setting ruling cheered many corporations, it left no doubt that punitive damages are appropriate in product-quality cases like this. The only question is whether they are excessive.

Prices

Have you ever wondered why a product sells at three for a dollar or is priced at $2.99 rather than simply $3.00? Or why a product that retails for $3.80 on Monday is selling for $4.10 on Friday? The answer may have little to do with the conventional determinants of product price such as overhead, operating expenses, and the costs of materials and labor. More and more frequently, purely psychological factors enter into the price-setting equation.

For example, why would a retailer price T-shirts at $9.88 instead of $9.99? "When people see $9.99, they say, 'That's $10,'" explains the general sales manager of one company. "But $9.88 isn't $10. It's just psychological."[22] Similar psychological considerations are at work when airlines advertise one-way fares that are available only with the purchase of a round-trip ticket for twice the price.

For many consumers, higher prices mean better products, so manufacturers arbitrarily raise the price of a product to give the impression of superior quality or exclusivity. But as often as not, the price is higher than the product's extra quality. For example, a few years ago Proctor-Silex's most expensive fabric iron sold for $54.95, a price $5 higher than the company's next most expensive. Its wholesale price was $26.98 against $24.20, a difference of only $2.78. Moreover, the extra cost of producing the top model was less than $1 for a light that signaled when the iron was ready.[23]

Manufacturers trade on human psychology when they sell substantially identical products at different prices. For example, Heublein raised the price of its Popov brand vodka from about $3.80 to $4.10 a fifth without altering the vodka that went into the fifth. Why the price increase? Heublein sales representatives believed that consumers wanted a variety of vodka prices to choose from. Apparently they were right: Even though Popov lost 1 percent of its market share, it increased its profits by 30 percent. Applying its theory further, Heublein offers vodka drinkers an even more expensive vodka: Smirnoff. Analysts insist that there is no qualitative difference among vodkas made in the United States.[24] In this case, the use of psychological pricing is closely related to the problem of pricing branded products higher than generic products that are otherwise indistinguishable. Consumers pay more assuming that the brand name or the higher price implies a better product.

Sometimes consumers are misled by prices that conceal a product's true cost. Hidden charges, surcharges, and other stealth fees can boost the consumer's actual cost significantly above announced price: for example, charges for mounting and balancing when you buy tires; multiple taxes and services fees on cellphone plans; "visitor" taxes and collision insurance on rental cars; "convenience" charges, processing fees, and shipping charges on concert tickets. In addition, manufacturers often disguise price increases by reducing the quality or quantity of the product—downsizing a pound of coffee to 13 ounces, for example, or shrinking a candy bar but not its price. Another ethically dubious practice is printing on packages a suggested retail price that is substantially higher than what retailers are known to charge. When retailers mark a new, lower price over the "suggested price," customers receive the false impression that the item is selling below its usual price. Retailers themselves are on questionable ethical ground when they use special pricing codes or fail to post a price on or near products, thus hindering consumers from easily comparing prices. And too many electronic scanners these days ring up prices incorrectly. One study found an error rate of 9 percent, with most mistakes favoring the stores; other studies place the error rate at 2 to 15 percent depending on the store and the type of merchandise. Whether store managers are deliberately padding their profits or whether sloppy practices are the problem, overcharging is costing consumers more than $1 billion a year.[25]

Promotional pricing can also be manipulative. Discount cards and "card specials" lure consumers into grocery stores like Dominick's, Kroger, and Safeway, where customers typically pay more for their food overall than they would at rival stores.[26] Department stores today sell more products at "sale" prices—over 60 percent of their volume—and are marking them down more than ever before. But their initial markup has also increased.[27] A survey of San Francisco area furniture stores illustrates how misleading sale prices can be. While one retailer was advertising a Henredon sofa, model no. 8670, at an "original price" of $2,320, on sale for $2,170, and another small retailer had it on sale for $2,476, or 20 percent off an original price of $3,095, a major department store was offering the same sofa, with the same "E-grade" upholstery, for $2,500, "35 percent off" the "original price" of $4,000.[28]

Many practical consumers think of these pricing practices and gimmicks as a nuisance or irritant that they must live with, not as something morally objectionable. But tricky or manipulative pricing does raise moral questions—not least about business's view of itself and its role in the community—that businesspeople and ethical theorists are now beginning to take seriously.

Price Fixing   Much more attention has been devoted to price fixing, which despite its prevalence is widely recognized as a violation of the rules of the game in a market system whose ideal is open and fair price competition. For example, in 1997 a federal judge found Toys "R" Us guilty of conspiring to keep prices for Barbie, Mr. Potato Head, and other popular toys artificially high. The retail giant used its market clout to force Mattel, Hasbro, and other major toymakers not to sell their toys to warehouse clubs like Sam's Club and Costco. Toys "R" Us threatened not to buy any toy that a manufacturer sold to a cost-cutting competitor, and it would use the acquiescence of one toymaker to force other manufacturers to go along.[29]

Often, of course, it is the manufacturer, not the retailer, that engages in price fixing. For example, Panasonic was found guilty of pressuring retailers such as Circuit City, Kmart, and Montgomery Ward into selling its products at the company's suggested retail price and not at a discount. Although manufacturers often suggest prices to their retailers, the retailers are supposed to be free to set their own prices, depending on the profit they foresee in the market. Any agreement between a manufacturer and a retailer to fix a price is illegal. Panasonic sales executives, however, badgered stores that did not honor the manufacturer's minimum prices and threatened to stop doing business with retailers that didn't comply. Until one large New York retailer finally complained to the New York State Attorney General's office, not only did the stores and chains go along, but they also reported uncooperative competitors to Panasonic.[30]

When a few companies gain control of a market, they are often in a position to force consumers to pay artificially high prices. To take a notorious example, in 1960 General Electric, Westinghouse, and twenty-seven other companies producing electrical equipment were found guilty of fixing prices in that billion-dollar industry. The companies were made to pay about $2 million in fines and many more millions to their corporate victims.[31] Given the oligopolistic nature of the electrical equipment market, consumers could not reasonably be said to have had the option to take their business elsewhere and thus drive down prices. (In fact, until it was exposed, they had no reason to believe they were being victimized by price fixing.) More recently, federal and state investigators have established that executives at the nation's largest national and regional dairy companies have conspired—sometimes for decades—to rig bids on milk products sold to schools and military bases. Forty-three companies, among them Borden, Pet, Dean, and Flav-O-Rich, have been convicted of price fixing and bid rigging.[32]

Of course, controlling prices need not be done so blatantly. Firms in an oligopoly can tacitly agree to remain uncompetitive with one another, thereby avoiding losses that might result from price-cutting competition. They can then play "follow the leader": Let the lead firm in the market raise its prices, and then the rest follow suit. The result is a laundered form of price fixing.

Even without tacit price fixing, the firms that dominate a field often implicitly agree not to compete in terms of price. Nobody, they say to themselves, wants a price war, as if price competition were a threat to our market system rather than its lifeblood. Familiar rivals such as Pepsi and Coca-Cola or McDonald's and Burger King usually prefer to compete in terms of image and jingles rather than price.

Price Gouging   From the moral point of view, prices, like wages, should be just or fair. Merchants cannot morally charge whatever they want or whatever the market will bear any more than employers can pay workers whatever they (the employers) wish or can get away with. In particular, price gouging is widely viewed as unethical, although what exactly constitutes price gouging is often debated. Some define it as charging what the market will bear regardless of production costs. But this definition doesn't take into account supply and demand. Because they are in short supply, tickets for the World Series or houses in a popular neighborhood may command an extremely high price relative to their production costs, and yet this does not constitute price gouging. Price gouging is better understood as a seller's exploiting a short-term situation in which buyers have few purchase options for a much needed product by raising prices substantially. New York hotels that doubled or tripled their prices in the aftermath of the September 11, 2001, attacks were guilty of this, and indeed some jurisdictions do make it illegal for retailers to raise their prices during a natural or other disaster. However, the morality or immorality of some instances of possible gouging seems open to debate. Is it unethical for a hardware store to boost the price of snow shovels from $15 to $20 after a large snowstorm or for a car dealer to mark up the price of a popular car model that is temporarily in short supply?

When a gas station raises the price of its current stock of gasoline because the wholesale price is scheduled to go up or when the big oil companies set the wholesale price of

gasoline 10 to 19 cents a gallon higher in San Francisco than in Los Angeles because average household income is greater there,[33] this may not fit the definition of price gouging,
but it strikes many people as unfair. So does the fact that Americans have to pay substantially more for medicines than do Canadians or Europeans. This is not a matter of
cheap generics or illegal knockoffs. Brand-name drugs like Lipitor, Zoloft, Vioxx, and
Nexium cost 30 to 100 percent more in the United States than in Canada or Europe.[34]

In the end, however, the question "What is a fair price?" probably defies a precise
answer. Still, one can approach an answer by assessing the factors on which the price
is based and the process used to determine it. Certainly factors such as the costs of material and production, operating and marketing expenses, and profit margin are relevant
to price setting. One can also ask whether a seller's pricing practices treat buyers as ends
in themselves or try to exploit them by taking advantage of a lack of competition or some
other buyer vulnerability. Also relevant is whether it would be good for our socioeconomic system as a whole if a particular pricing practice were widespread or generally
followed.

In a market-oriented society, of course, consumer choice is a key variable affecting
price. Product price, in other words, reflects in part the consuming public's judgment
of the relative value of the article. This judgment is formed in the open market in a free
interplay between sellers and buyers. However, for this process to function satisfactorily,
buyers must be in a position to exercise informed consent. As discussed in Chapter 7,
informed consent calls for deliberation and free choice, which require in turn that
buyers understand all significant relevant facts about the goods and services they are
purchasing. But consumers are at least sometimes, perhaps often, denied informed
consent. They do not always receive the clear, accurate, and complete information
about product quality and price that they need to make prudent choices.

Labeling and Packaging

Business's general responsibility to provide clear, accurate, and adequate information undoubtedly applies to product labeling and packaging. The reason is that, despite
the billions of dollars spent annually on advertising, a product's label and package
remain the consumer's primary source of product information. Often, however, labels
and packages do not tell consumers what they need to know, or even what exactly they
are getting. For example, only recently did the Liggett tobacco company introduce cartons that list the ingredients in its L&M cigarettes—a first among tobacco companies.*
Yet even when product labels provide pertinent information, they are often difficult to
understand or even misleading, and what they omit may be more important than what
they say. For example, nothing is more misleading than environmental labeling.
Manufacturers label products "biodegradable," "environmentally safe," or "recyclable"
without defining these terms or providing any scientific evidence to back them up.

Consumers have long been equally baffled by food labels such as "light" or "97 percent fat-free," but the Food and Drug Administration has recently come to their aid. The
FDA's labeling requirements now oblige manufacturers of packaged food to provide
standardized nutritional information that is clearer, more specific, and of greater benefit to health-conscious consumers. Although the FDA relaxed many of its rules in the

---

*In addition to tobacco, L&M cigarettes contain molasses, patchouli oil, high fructose corn syrup, sugar, natural and
artificial licorice flavor, artificial milk chocolate and natural chocolate flavor, phenylacetic acid, glycerol, propylene glycol,
isovaleric acid, hexanoic acid, 3-methylpentanoic acid, valerian root extract, vanilla extract, and cedarwood oil.

1980s and required only voluntary compliance, recently it has been getting tougher. For example, it has cracked down on grain and vegetable cooking oils that label themselves "cholesterol-free." Although it is true that only animal products or by-products contain cholesterol, cooking oils are often replete with saturated vegetable fats and hydrogenated oils, which the body converts into cholesterol. The FDA has also gone after Procter & Gamble for changing the name of its orange juice from "Citrus Hill Select" to "Citrus Hill Fresh Choice" in violation of the FDA's 1963 ban on using the word *fresh* to describe processed orange juice. Although labeled "pure, squeezed, 100% orange juice," Citrus Hill is in fact made by adding water to concentrated orange juice, pulp, and "orange essence."

A particularly blatant example of label abuse is Sebastiani Vineyards' wine product, Domaine Chardonnay. "Chardonnay" has a high level of name recognition and a positive reputation among wine consumers. Unfortunately for them, however, there isn't a drop of chardonnay in Domaine Chardonnay, which is a blend of chenin blanc, sauvignon blanc, French colombard, riesling, and other grapes. After a public outcry when the wine was introduced, the Bureau of Alcohol, Tobacco, and Firearms required the company to redesign its label, which now has a large "DC" and a small "Domaine Chardonnay" at the bottom. Many people, however, continue to feel that letting Sebastiani use the name of a grape varietal as a brand name is a travesty of labeling law—even if Sebastiani decides in the future to include a little chardonnay in the wine mixture.

The question of misleading labels takes an interesting twist in the case of companies that choose to omit their corporate logo from products. For example, a brand called Cascadian Farm sells organic breakfast cereal, but from looking at the box you can't tell that it's actually made by General Mills. That's because General Mills is aiming the cereal at buyers who tend to eschew the brands of the big conglomerates. Similarly, you can't guess from reading the label of Blue Moon beer that it comes from Adolph Coors Company, and the label of Red Dog beer identifies its maker as Plank Road Brewery although it is really produced by Miller Brewing Company. This practice is spreading as big food and drink makers buy up the little brands that populate organic food stores or create their own "natural" products and boutique brands.[35]

In addition to misleading labels, package shape can trick consumers by exploiting certain optical illusions. Tall and narrow cereal boxes look larger than short, squat ones that actually contain more cereal; shampoo bottles often have pinched waists to give the illusion of quantity; fruits are packed in large quantities of syrup; and dry foods often come in tins or cartons stuffed with cardboard. Package terms such as *large, extra large, jumbo, economy size,* and *value pack* frequently confuse or mislead shoppers about what they are buying and how good a deal they are getting. Although in theory unit pricing helps shoppers to compare the relative prices of items, in practice the spread of bar codes thwarts their ability to do so. By eliminating price tags from packages, bar codes make it harder for time-pressed buyers to recall specific prices for individual items.

This is part of the explanation of why many retailers are able to sell "economy size" items for a higher per unit price than their smaller counterparts. These "quantity surcharges" are a much wider spread phenomenon than most people realize. For example, at 3.7 ounces the candy bar that Snickers calls "The Big One" is nearly twice the size of the familiar 2.07-ounce bar, which runs about 50 cents. But when priced at 99 cents—which it was at a store visited by the *Wall Street Journal*—The Big One costs 11 percent more. At another store the gallon jug of Ocean Spray cranberry juice—so big it had a special handle on it—cost 41 cents more than two half-gallon bottles. Although consumers frequently compare prices between brands, they generally neglect to make intra-brand comparisons because they take it for granted that the larger the volume, the better the deal. "You assume 'bigger' is a better deal," says Tom Pirko, president of a beverage and food consulting company, "and that gives marketers an open door to take advantage of people."[36] Because quantity surcharges exploit a common consumer error, the practice raises at least two moral questions: Can it be justified as a conscious pricing policy, and can retailers ethically remain silent about its existence?[37]

In general, the moral issues involved in packaging and labeling, as in marketing as a whole, relate primarily to truth telling and consumer exploitation. Sound moral conduct in this matter must rest on a strong desire to provide consumers with clear and usable information about the price, quality, and quantity of a product so they can make intelligent comparisons and choices. When marketers are interested primarily in selling a product and only secondarily in providing relevant information, then morally questionable practices are bound to follow. Those responsible for labeling and packaging would be well advised to consider at least the following questions, a negative answer to any of which could signal a moral problem: Is there anything about the packaging that is likely to mislead consumers? Have we clearly and specifically identified the exact nature of the product in an appropriate part of the label? Is the net quantity prominently displayed? Is it readily understandable to those wishing to compare prices? Are ingredients listed so they can be readily recognized and understood? Have we indicated and represented the percentage of the contents that is filler, such as the bone in a piece of meat?

These questions represent only some that a morally responsible businessperson might ask. In addition, we must not forget people whose health necessitates certain dietary restrictions. They often have great difficulty determining what products they can safely purchase.

DECEPTION AND UNFAIRNESS IN ADVERTISING

We tend to take advertising for granted, yet sociologically and economically it is enormously important. Ads dominate our environment. Famous ones become part of our culture; their jingles dance in our heads, and their images haunt our dreams and shape our tastes. Advertising is also big business. Sprint, for example, shells out $1.2 billion a year on advertising, Philip Morris spends $1.8 billion, Ford $2.4 billion, Procter & Gamble $2.5 billion, and General Motors a whopping $3.4 billion.[38] As a whole, advertisers in the United States spend annually nearly $250 billion on all forms of media advertising.[39] That works out to about $800 for every person in the country.

When people are asked what advertising does, their first thought is often that it provides consumers with information about goods and services. In fact, advertising conveys very little information. Nor are most ads intended to do so. Except for classified ads (by amateurs!) and newspaper ads reporting supermarket prices, very few advertisements offer any information of genuine use to the consumer. (Those wanting useful product information must go to a magazine like *Consumer Reports,* which publishes objective and comparative studies of various products.) Instead, advertisements offer us jingles, rhymes, and attractive images.

The goal of advertising, of course, is to persuade us to buy the products that are being touted. Providing objective and comparative product information may be one way to do this. But it is not the only way, and judging from ads these days—which frequently say nothing at all about the product's qualities—it is not a very common way. The similarity among many competing products may be the explanation. One writer identifies the effort to distinguish among basically identical products as the "ethical, as well as economic, crux of the [advertising] industry"; another refers to it as the "persistent, underlying bad faith" of much American advertising.[40]

Deceptive Techniques

Because advertisers are trying to persuade people to buy their products and because straight product information is not necessarily the best way to do this, there is a natural temptation to obfuscate, misrepresent, or even lie. In an attempt to persuade, advertisers are prone to exploit ambiguity, conceal facts, exaggerate, and use psychological appeals.

Ambiguity   When ads are ambiguous, they can be deceiving. For example, the Continental Baking Company was charged with such ambiguity by the Federal Trade Commission (FTC). In advertising its Profile bread, Continental implied that eating the bread would lead to weight loss. The fact was that Profile had about the same number of calories per ounce as other breads; each slice contained seven fewer calories but only because it was sliced thinner than most breads. Continental issued a corrective advertisement.

Ambiguous ads can mislead the consumer. The Profile ad is a good example. A large number of people interpreted that ad to mean that eating Profile bread would lead to weight loss.[41] Likewise, for years consumers inferred from its advertisements that Listerine mouthwash effectively fought bacteria and sore throats. Not so; accordingly, the FTC ordered Listerine to run a multimillion-dollar disclaimer. And when Sara Lee began promoting its Light Classics desserts, the implicit implication was that "light" meant the products contained fewer calories than other Sara Lee desserts. When pressed by investigators to support this implied claim, Sara Lee contended that "light" referred only to the texture of the product.[42] In cases like these, advertisers and manufacturers invariably deny that they intended consumers to draw false inferences, but sometimes the ambiguity is such that a reasonable person wouldn't infer anything else.

Aiding and abetting ambiguity is the use of "weasel" words, words used to evade or retreat from a direct or forthright statement. Consider the weasel word *help*. "Help" means "aid" or "assist" and nothing else. Yet as one author has observed, "'help' is the one single word which, in all the annals of advertising, has done the most to say something that couldn't be said."[43] Because the word *help* is used to qualify, almost anything can be said after it. Thus we're exposed to ads for products that "help us keep young," "help prevent cavities," "help keep our houses germ-free." Consider for a moment how many times a day you hear or read phrases like these: helps stop, helps prevent, helps fight, helps overcome, helps you feel, helps you look. And, of course, *help* is hardly the only weasel word. *Like, virtual* or *virtually, can be, up to* (as in "provides relief up to eight hours"), *as much as* (as in "saves as much as one gallon of gas"), and numerous other weasel words are used to imply what can't be said. Sometimes weasel words deprive the message of any meaning whatsoever, as when *up to* and *more* come together in "save up to 40 to 50 percent and more."

The fact that ads are open to interpretation doesn't exonerate advertisers from the obligation to provide clear information. Indeed, this fact intensifies their responsibility, because the danger of misleading through ambiguity increases as the ad is subject to interpretation. At stake are not only people's money but also their health, loyalties, and expectations. The potential harm a misleading ad can cause is great, not to mention its cavalier treatment of the truth. For these reasons ambiguity in ads is of serious moral concern.

Concealed Facts   When advertisers conceal facts, they suppress information that is unflattering to their products. That is, they neglect to mention or distract consumers' attention away from information, knowledge of which would probably make their products less desirable.

Shell, for example, used to advertise that its gasoline had "platformate" but neglected to mention that all other brands did too. Similarly, subway ads for the Bowery Bank in New York touted the fact that it is "federally insured," but then so is almost every bank in the country. And Kraft advertised its Philadelphia Cream Cheese as having "half the calories of butter," but didn't tell consumers that it is also high in fat. When peanut butter makers advertise their products as cholesterol free, they omit the fact that only animal products contain cholesterol and that peanut butter is rich in fat. Weight Watchers tells consumers that its frozen meals are without butter, chicken fat, or tropical oils but not that they are high in salt. Caverject promotes itself as an alternative to Viagra as a treatment for male impotence. Its ads say that "Caverject can help you and your partner enjoy renewed spontaneity and sexual satisfaction." But they don't say that Caverject is a prescription medicine that must be injected with a needle inserted directly into the penis.

Ads that promise savings for dialing long distance with a 10-10 number rarely mention the hidden costs that often make these services more expensive than the discount plan offered by one's regular long-distance carrier. Indeed, many of the most popular dial-around numbers are subsidiaries of the large carriers. For example, AT&T owns Lucky Dog (10-10-343), although you won't find that information on any Lucky Dog ads. As a result, some customers who dial a 10-10 number end up using their own long-distance carrier—and paying a higher rate to boot.

Likewise, advertisements for painkillers routinely conceal relevant information. For years, Bayer aspirin advertised that it contained "the ingredient that doctors recommend most." What is that ingredient? Aspirin. The advertising claim that "last year hospitals dispensed ten times as much Tylenol as the next four brands combined" does not disclose the fact that Johnson & Johnson supplies hospitals with Tylenol at a cost well below what consumers pay. Interestingly, American Home Products sued Johnson & Johnson on the grounds that the Tylenol ad falsely implies that it is more effective than competing products. But at the same time, American Home Products was advertising its Anacin-3 by claiming that "hospitals recommended acetaminophen, the aspirin-free pain reliever in Anacin-3, more than any other pain reliever"—without telling consumers that the acetaminophen hospitals recommend is, in fact, Tylenol.

Concealment of relevant facts and information can exploit people by misleading them; it also undermines truth telling. Unfortunately, truth rarely seems foremost in the minds of advertisers. For example, Coors continued to advertise its beer as brewed from "Rocky Mountain spring water" even after it opened plants outside Colorado that use local water. And Perrier advertised its bottled water as having bubbled up from underground springs decades after it had begun pumping the water up from the ground through a pipe and combining it with processed gas.

As one advertising-industry insider writes: "Inside the agency the basic approach is hardly conducive to truth telling. The usual thinking in forming a campaign is first what can we say, true or not, that will sell the product best? The second consideration is, how can we say it effectively and get away with it so that (1) people who buy won't feel let down by too big a promise that doesn't come true, and (2) the ads will avoid quick and certain censure by the FTC."[44] This observation shows the common tendency to equate what's legal with what's moral. It's precisely this outlook that leads to advertising behavior of dubious morality.

Examples of ads that conceal important facts are legion. An old Colgate-Palmolive ad for its Rapid Shave Cream used sandpaper to demonstrate the cream's effect on tough beards. Colgate concealed the fact that the "sandpaper" in the ad was actually Plexiglas and that actual sandpaper had to be soaked in Rapid Shave for about eighty minutes before it came off in a stroke. A few years ago, Campbell vegetable soup ads showed pictures of a thick, rich brew calculated to whet even a gourmet's appetite. What the ads didn't show were clear glass marbles deposited in that bowl to give the soup the appearance of solidity. Similarly, a television ad for Volvo showed a row of cars being crushed by a bigwheel truck, with only a Volvo remaining intact. What the ad neglected to say was that the Volvo had been reinforced and the other cars weakened. More recently, the ads the Bermuda government runs in travel magazines to encourage Americans to vacation there have pictured people swimming or diving or on the beach—in Hawaii.

If business has an obligation to provide clear, accurate, and adequate information, we must wonder if it meets this charge when it hides facts relevant to the consumer's purchase of a product. Concealing information raises serious moral concerns relative to truth telling and consumer exploitation. When consumers are deprived of comprehensive knowledge about a product, their choices are constricted and distorted.

If pushed further, the moral demand for full information challenges almost all advertising. Even the best advertisements never point out the negative features of their products or that there is no substantive difference between the product being advertised and its competitors, as is often the case. In this sense, they could be accused of concealing relevant information. Most advertisers would be shocked at the suggestion that honesty requires an objective presentation of the pros and cons of their products, and in fact consumers don't expect advertisers or salespeople to be impartial. Nevertheless, it is not clear why this moral value should not be relevant to assessing advertising. And it can be noted that retail salespeople, despite a sometimes negative reputation, often do approach this level of candor—at least when they are fortunate enough to sell a genuinely good and competitive product or when they do not work on commission.

Exaggeration   Advertisers can mislead through exaggeration—that is, by making claims unsupported by evidence. For example, claims that a pain reliever provides "extra pain relief" or is "50 percent stronger than aspirin" or is "superior to any other nonprescription painkiller on the market" contradict evidence that all analgesics are effective to the same degree.[45] Manufacturers of vitamins and other dietary supplements are notorious for exaggerating the possible benefits of their products. Some drug companies do the same. Ads for Propecia tell men, "Starting today, you need not face the fear of more hair loss." But while Propecia can slow hair loss, it doesn't necessarily stop it.

Nabisco's advertising of its 100 percent bran cereal as being "flavored with two naturally sweet fruit juices" is typical of exaggerated product claims. Although fig juice and prune juice have indeed been added to the product, they are its least significant ingredients in terms of weight; the primary sweetener is sugar. As in this case, exaggeration often goes hand in hand with concealed information. Until stopped by legal action, General Electric advertised its 90-watt Energy Choice bulb as an energy-saving replacement for a conventional 100-watt bulb. But there is nothing special about the GE bulb; it simply produces fewer lumens than a 100-watt bulb. Trident chewing gum, to take another example, has long advertised that it helps fight cavities, but its ads (which describe Trident as a "dental instrument") clearly exaggerate the benefits of chewing Trident. Chewing gum can indeed help dislodge debris on dental enamel, but so can eating an apple or rinsing one's mouth with water. And the sugar substitute used by Trident (sorbitol) can indirectly promote tooth decay: It nurtures the normally harmless bacteria that sugar activates into decay-producing microorganisms.

"Anti-aging" skin-care products are one of the fastest-growing segments of the cosmetic industry, partly because the baby boom generation is getting older. Some companies misleadingly portray their products as "repairing cells" or skin layers below the surface rather than having only an external effect. Part of the labeling for Avon's Bioadvance Beauty Recovery System, for example, claimed that it "actually helps reverse many signs of facial aging in six weeks . . . helps revitalize and invigorate your skin's regenerative system," while Alfin Fragrances asserted that its anti-aging skin cream makes skin "function as if it were young again."[46]

The line between deliberate deception and so-called *puffery* is not always clear. Puffery is the supposedly harmless use of superlatives and subjective praise in advertisements. Thus advertisers frequently boast of the merits of their products by using words such as *best, finest,* or *most,* or phrases and slogans like *king of beers, breakfast of champions,* or *the ultimate driving machine.* In most instances, puffery appears innocuous, but sometimes it's downright misleading, as in the Dial soap ad that claimed Dial was "the most effective deodorant soap you can buy." When asked to substantiate that claim, the Armour-Dial company insisted that it was not claiming product superiority; all it meant was that Dial soap was as effective as any other soap.

The law permits puffery on the grounds that it doesn't deceive people. University of Wisconsin professor Ivan L. Preston, however, argues that puffery shouldn't be immune from regulation. Why? Because the public is often taken in by it. Consider the following pieces of puffery: "State Farm is all you need to know about life insurance," "Ford has a better idea," and "It's the real thing [Coca-Cola]." Although these statements may seem like meaningless verbal posturing, in one survey 22 percent of those sampled thought the first claim was "completely true" while 36 percent considered it "partly true." The second claim was judged "completely true" by 26 percent and "partly true" by 42 percent while 35 percent believed the third claim was "completely true" and 29 percent "partly true."[47] Moreover, argues Preston, if puffery didn't work, salespeople and advertisers wouldn't use it.[48]

Psychological Appeals   A psychological appeal is one that aims to persuade by appealing primarily to human emotional needs and not to reason. This is potentially the area of greatest moral concern in advertising. An automobile ad that presents the product surrounded by people who look wealthy and successful appeals to our need and desire for status. A life insurance ad that portrays a destitute family woefully struggling in the aftermath of a provider's death tries to persuade through pity and fear. Reliance on such devices, although not unethical per se, raises moral concerns because rarely do such products fully deliver what the ads promise.

Ads that rely extensively on pitches to power, prestige, sex, masculinity, femininity, acceptance, approval, and the like aim to sell more than a product. They are peddling psychological satisfaction. Perhaps the best example is the increasingly explicit and pervasive use of sexual pitches in ads:

Scene:	An artist's skylit studio. A young man lies nude, the bedsheets in disarray. He awakens to find a tender note on his pillow. The phone rings and he gets up to answer it.
Woman's Voice:	You snore.
Artist (smiling):	And you always steal the covers.

More cozy patter between the two. Then a husky-voiced announcer intones: "Paco Rabanne. A cologne for men. What is remembered is up to you."[49]

Although sex has always been used to sell products, it has never before been used as explicitly in advertising as it is today—as the nudes in the ads for Calvin Klein products demonstrate. And the sexual pitches are by no means confined to products like cologne or clothes. The California Avocado Commission supplemented its "Love Food from California" recipe ads with a campaign featuring a leggy actress sprawled across two pages of some eighteen national magazines to promote the avocado's nutritional value. The copy line reads: "Would this body lie to you?" Similarly, Dannon yogurt ran ads featuring a bikini-clad beauty and this message: "More nonsense is written on dieting than any other subject—except possibly sex."

Some students of marketing claim that ads like these appeal to the subconscious mind of both marketer and consumer. Purdue University psychologist and marketing consultant Jacob Jacoby contends that marketers, like everyone else, carry around sexual symbols in their subconscious that, intentionally or not, they use in ads. A case in point: the Newport cigarette "Alive with Pleasure" campaign. One campaign ad featured a woman riding the handlebars of a bicycle driven by a man. The main strut of the bike wheel stands vertically beneath her body. In Jacoby's view, such symbolism needs no interpretation.

Author Wilson Bryan Key, who has extensively researched the topic of subconscious marketing appeals, claims that many ads take a subliminal form. *Subliminal advertising* is advertising that communicates at a level beneath our conscious awareness, where, some psychologists claim, the vast reservoir of human motivation primarily resides. Most marketing people would deny that such advertising occurs. Key disagrees. Indeed, he goes so far as to claim: "It is virtually impossible to pick up a newspaper or magazine, turn on a radio or television set, read a promotional pamphlet or the telephone book, or shop through a supermarket without having your subconscious purposely massaged by some monstrously clever artist, photographer, writer, or technician."[50]

Concern with the serious nature of psychological appeals appears to have motivated the California Wine Institute to adopt an advertising code of standards. The following restrictions are included:

No wine ad shall present persons engaged in activities with appeal particularly to minors. Among those excluded: amateur or professional sports figures, celebrities, or cowboys; rock stars, race car drivers.

No wine ad shall exploit the human form or "feature provocative or enticing poses or be demeaning to any individual."

No wine ad shall portray wine in a setting where food is not presented.

No wine ad shall present wine in "quantities inappropriate to the situation."

No wine ad shall portray wine as similar to another type of beverage or product such as milk, soda, or candy.

No wine ad shall associate wine with personal performance, social attainment, achievement, wealth, or the attainment of adulthood.

No wine ad shall show automobiles in a way that one could construe their conjunction.

In adopting such a rigorous code of advertising ethics, the California Wine Institute rightly acknowledged the subtle implications and psychological nuances that affect the message that an ad communicates.

The Federal Trade Commission's Role

The Federal Trade Commission was originally created in 1914 as an antitrust weapon, but its mandate was expanded to include protecting consumers against deceptive advertising and fraudulent commercial practices. Although the FTC is not the only regulatory body monitoring advertisements, it is mainly thanks to the FTC that today we are spared the most blatant abuses of advertising.

One important question running through the FTC's history is relevant to all efforts to prohibit deceptive advertising: whether the FTC (or any other regulatory body) is obligated to protect only reasonable, intelligent consumers who conduct themselves sensibly in the marketplace, or whether it should also protect ignorant consumers who are careless or gullible in their purchases?[51] If the FTC uses the reasonable-consumer standard, then it should prohibit only advertising claims that would deceive reasonable people. People who are more gullible or less bright than average and are taken in as a result would be unprotected. On the other hand, if the FTC uses the ignorant-consumer standard and prohibits an advertisement that misleads anyone, no matter how ill informed and naive, then it will handle a lot more cases and restrict advertising much more. But in spending its time and resources on such cases, it is not clear that the FTC will be proceeding in response to a substantial public interest, as it is legally charged with doing.

The reasonable-person standard was traditional in a variety of areas of the law long before the FTC was established. If you are sued for negligence, you can successfully defend yourself if you can establish that you behaved as a hypothetical reasonable person would have behaved under like circumstances. On the other hand, in the law of misrepresentation, when you as a deceived consumer sue a seller on grounds that you were misled, then—assuming the deception is not proved to be intentional—you must establish that you were acting reasonably in relying on the false representation. If a reasonable person would not have been misled in like circumstances, then you will not win your case. Ads that make physically impossible or obviously exaggerated claims would thus escape legal liability under the reasonable-person standard.

One decisive case in the legal transition away from the reasonable-person standard in matters of advertising, sales, and marketing was *FTC v. Standard Education* in 1937.[52] In this case an encyclopedia company was charged by the FTC with a number of deceptive and misleading practices. The company's agents told potential customers that their names had been specially selected and that the encyclopedia they were being offered was being given away free as part of an advertising plan in return for use of their name for advertising purposes and in testimonials. The customer was only required to pay $69.50 for a series of looseleaf update volumes. Potential buyers were not told that both books and supplements regularly sold for $69.50.

In deciding the case, the U.S. Supreme Court considered the view of the appellate court, which had earlier dismissed the FTC's case. Writing for the appellate court, Judge Learned Hand had declared that the FTC was occupying itself with "trivial niceties" that only "divert attention from substantial evils." "We cannot take seriously the suggestion," he wrote, "that a man who is buying a set of books and a ten years' 'extension service,' will be fatuous enough to be misled by the mere statement that the first are given away, and that he is paying only for the second." The Supreme Court itself, however, looked at the matter in a different light and held for the FTC and against Standard Education.

First, it noted that the practice had successfully deceived numerous victims, apparently including teachers, doctors, and college professors. But instead of resting its decision on the claim that a reasonable person might have been deceived, it advocated a change of standard to something like the ignorant-consumer standard:

> The fact that a false statement may be obviously false to those who are trained and experienced does not change its character, nor take away its power to deceive others less experienced. There is no duty resting upon a citizen to suspect the honesty of those with whom he transacts business. Laws are made to protect the trusting as well as the suspicious. The best element of business has long since decided that honesty should govern competitive enterprises, and that the rule of *caveat emptor* should not be relied upon to reward fraud and deception.

The decision in *FTC v. Standard Education,* as Ivan L. Preston notes, led the FTC to apply the ignorant-person standard liberally, even in cases in which there was no intent to deceive. In the 1940s the FTC challenged ads in some cases in which it is difficult to believe that anyone could possibly have been deceived. For example, it issued a complaint against Bristol-Myers's Ipana toothpaste on the grounds that its "smile of beauty" slogan would lead some to believe that Ipana toothpaste would straighten their teeth. Eventually, however, the FTC abandoned the ignorant-consumer standard in its extreme form and stopped trying to protect everybody from everything that might possibly deceive them. It now follows the "modified" ignorant-consumer standard and protects consumers from ads that mislead significant numbers of people, whether those people acted reasonably or not.[53]

Still, deciding what is likely to be misleading to a significant number of consumers is not necessarily easy. Consider these advertising claims, which are contested by some as deceptive: that Kraft Cheez Whiz is real cheese; that Chicken McNuggets are made from "whole breasts and thighs" (when they allegedly contain processed chicken skin as well and are fried in highly saturated beef fat); that ibuprofen causes stomach irritation (as Tylenol's ads seem to imply). Is Sprint's "dime-a-minute" ad campaign deceptive when a minute-and-a-half telephone call is rounded up to twenty cents? Was it deceptive of Diet Coke to proclaim that it was sweetened "now with NutraSweet," even though the product also contained saccharin? Under legal pressure, Diet Coke changed its ads to read "NutraSweet blend." Is that free of any misleading implications?

Ads Directed at Children

The FTC has always looked after one special group of consumers without regard to how reasonable they are: children. Still, several consumer groups think the FTC has not done enough, and they advocate even stricter controls over advertisements that reach children.

Advertising to children is big business. Every year children under twelve spend $33 billion and teenagers a whopping $155 billion.[54] And this figure doesn't begin to take into account the billions of adult purchases for gifts, clothes, and groceries that are influenced by children. In recent years advertising aimed specifically at children has grown exponentially. Advertisers now spend more than $1.5 billion a year on ads for children, and there are more and more venues for such ads—with new magazines, Web sites, and entire television channels aimed at children.[55]

Furthermore, it's no longer just cereal, candy, and toys that are being advertised. Advertisers of other products are wooing children in an effort to create customers for the future. As Jackie Pate of Delta Air Lines puts it, "By building brand loyalty in children today, they'll be the adult passengers of the future." Ann Moore, Chairman and CEO of Time Inc., which publishes *Sports Illustrated for Kids*, adds, "We believe children make brand decisions that will carry into their adult lives."[56] Although the magazine attracts mostly eight- to fourteen-year-old boys as readers, a recent issue featured a two-page spread for the Chevy Venture minivan.

Of course, advertisers admit that it's not just future consumers they want. "We're relying on the kid to pester the mom to buy the product, rather than going straight to the mom," says Barbara A. Martino of Grey Advertising. And Karen Francis, brand manager for the Chevy Venture, reports that even she was surprised how often parents tell her that their kids played a tie-breaking role in deciding which car to buy. Naturally, advertisers argue that parents still have ultimate control over what gets purchased and what doesn't. But is the strategy of selling to parents by convincing the children a fair one? As one parent complains, "Brand awareness has been an incredibly abusive experience—the relentless requests to go to McDonald's [or] to see movies that are inappropriate for six-year-olds [but] that are advertised on kids' shows."

Television and advertising play a large role in most children's lives. At age seven a typical child sees 20,000 television commercials a year, and children remember what they see. For example, in the 1990s researchers found that the frogs in the Budweiser beer commercials were more widely recognized among children then any cartoon characters other than Bugs Bunny. The problem is that children, particularly young children, are naïve and gullible and thus particularly vulnerable to advertisers' enticements. Consider, for example, ads in which children are shown, after eating a certain cereal, to have enough power to lift large playhouses. No adult would be misled by that ad, but children lack experience and independent judgment. This provides at least a prima facie case for protecting them.

"Kids are the most pure consumers you could have," says one advertising expert. "They tend to interpret your ad literally. They are infinitely open." This problem is growing greater because the line between children's shows and the commercials that come with them is fading away. Children's entertainment features characters whose licensed images are stamped on toys, sheets, clothes, and food. Moreover, at the same time that movies and television shows are ever more tightly linked to the selling of toys and other items, commercials are becoming more like entertainment. Is it any wonder that many children perceive little difference between ads and television shows? As one nine-year-old sees it, the only distinction is that "commercials are shorter."

Advertising to children obviously raises the question of children's special suscepti-bilities and how far we need to go to protect them from possible manipulation. It also leads to the larger question of the nature and desirability of advertising's role in today's media-dominated society, which is our next topic.

THE DEBATE OVER ADVERTISING

The controversy over advertising does not end with the issue of deceptive techniques and unfair advertising practices. Advertising provides little usable information to con-sumers. Advertisements almost always conceal relevant negative facts about their products, and they are frequently based on subtle appeals to psychological needs, which the products they peddle are unlikely to satisfy. These realities are the basis for some critics' wholesale repudiation of advertising on moral grounds. They also desire a less commercially polluted environment, one that does not continually reinforce materialistic values.

Consumer Needs

Some defenders of advertising take these points in stride. They concede that images of glamour, sex, or adventure sell products, but they argue that these images are what we, the consumers, want. We don't want just blue jeans; we want romance or sophis-tication or status with our blue jeans. By connecting products with important emotions and feelings, advertisements can also satisfy our deeper needs and wants. As one advertising executive puts it:

> Advertising can show a consumer how a baby powder helps affirm her role as a nurturing mother—Johnson & Johnson's "The Language of Love." Or it can show a teenager how a soft drink helps assert his or her emerging independence—Pepsi's "The Choice of a New Generation."[57]

Harvard business professor Theodore Levitt has drawn an analogy between adver-tising and art. Both take liberties with reality, both deal in symbolic communication, and neither is interested in literal truth or in pure functionality. Rather, both art and advertising help us repackage the otherwise crude, drab, and generally oppressive reality that surrounds us. They create "illusions, symbols, and implications that prom-ise more." They help us modify, transform, embellish, enrich, and reconstruct the world around us. "Without distortion, embellishment, and elaboration," Levitt writes, "life would be drab, dull, anguished, and at its existential worst." Advertising helps satisfy this legitimate human need. Its handsome packages and imaginative promises produce that "elevation of the spirit" that we want and need. Embellishment and distortion are therefore among advertising's socially desirable purposes. To criticize advertising on these counts, Levitt argues, is to overlook the real needs and values of human beings.[58]

Levitt's critics contend that even if advertising appeals to the same deep needs that art does, advertising promises satisfaction of those needs in the products it sells, and that promise is rarely kept. At the end of the day, blue jeans are still just blue jeans, and your love life will be unaffected by which soap you shower with. The imaginative, symbolic, and artistic content of advertising, which Levitt sees as answering real human needs, is viewed by critics as manipulating, distorting, and even creating those needs.

In his influential books *The Affluent Society* and *The New Industrial State*, John Kenneth Galbraith has criticized advertising on just this point. Galbraith argues that the process of production today, with its expensive marketing campaigns, subtle advertising techniques, and sophisticated sales strategies, creates the very wants it then satisfies. Producers, that is, create both the goods and the demand for those goods. If a new breakfast cereal or detergent were so much wanted, Galbraith reasons, why must so much money be spent trying to get the consumer to buy it? He thinks it is obvious that "wants can be synthesized by advertising, catalyzed by salesmanship, and shaped by" discreet manipulations.

Accordingly, Galbraith rejects the economist's traditional faith in "consumer sovereignty": the idea that consumers should and do control the market through their purchases. Rather than independent consumer demand shaping production, as classical economic theory says it does, nowadays it is the other way around. Galbraith dubs this the "dependence effect": "As a society becomes increasingly affluent, wants are increasingly created by the process by which they are satisfied."[59]

One consequence, Galbraith thinks, is that our system of production cannot be defended on the ground that it is satisfying urgent or important wants. We can't defend production as satisfying wants if the production process itself creates those wants. "In the absence of the massive and artful persuasion that accompanies the management of demand," Galbraith argues,

> increasing abundance might well have reduced the interest of people in acquiring more goods. They would not have felt the need for multiplying the artifacts—autos, appliances, detergents, cosmetics—by which they were surrounded.[60]

Another consequence is our general preoccupation with material consumption. In particular, Galbraith claims, our pursuit of private goods, continually reinforced by advertising, leads us to neglect public goods and services. We need better schools, parks, artistic and recreational facilities; safer and cleaner cities and air; more efficient, less crowded transportation systems. We are rich in the private production and use of goods, Galbraith thinks, and starved in public services. Our preoccupation with private consumption leads us to overlook opportunities for enjoyment that could be provided more efficiently by public production.

Galbraith's critics have concentrated their fire on a couple of points. First, Galbraith never shows that advertising has the power he attributes to it. Despite heavy advertising, most new products fail to win a permanent place in the hearts of consumers. Advertising campaigns like that for Listerine in the 1920s, which successfully created the problem of "halitosis" in order to sell the new idea of "mouthwash," are rare.* Although it is true that we are inundated with ads, experiments suggest we no longer care much about them. Each of us sees an average of 1,600 advertisements a day, notices around 1,200 of them, and responds favorably or unfavorably to only about 12. We also appear to pay more attention to ads for products that we already have.[61]

---

*Given that the saliva in one's mouth is completely replenished every fifteen minutes or so anyway, no mouthwash can have an effect longer than that.

Second, critics have attacked Galbraith's assumption that the needs supposedly created by advertisers and producers are, as a result, "false" or "artificial" needs and therefore less worthy of satisfaction. Human needs, they stress, are always socially influenced and are never static. How are we to distinguish between "genuine" and "artificial" wants, and why should the latter be thought less important? Ads might produce a want that we would not otherwise have had without that want being in any way objectionable.

Although conclusive evidence is unavailable, critics of advertising continue to worry about its power to influence our lives and shape our culture and civilization. Even if producers cannot create wants out of whole cloth, many worry that advertising can manipulate our existing desires—that it can stimulate certain desires, both at the expense of other, nonconsumer-oriented desires and out of proportion to the likely satisfaction that fulfillment of those desires will bring.

Market Economics

Defenders of advertising are largely untroubled by these worries. They see advertising as an aspect of free competition in a competitive market, which ultimately works to the benefit of all. But this simple free-market defense of advertising has weaknesses. First, advertising doesn't fit too well into the economist's model of the free market. Economists can prove, if we grant them enough assumptions, that free-market buying and selling lead to optimal results.* One of these assumptions is that everyone has full and complete information, on the basis of which they then buy and sell. But if this were so, advertising would be pointless.

One might argue that advertising moves us closer to the ideal of full information, but there is good reason to doubt this. Even if we put aside the question of whether ads can create, shape, or manipulate wants, they do seem to enhance brand loyalty, which generally works to thwart price competition. A true brand-name consumer is willing to pay more for a product that is otherwise indistinguishable from its competitors. He or she buys a certain beer despite being unable to taste the difference between it and other beers.

More generally, critics of advertising stand the invisible-hand argument on its head. The goal of advertisers is to sell you products and to make money, not to maximize your well-being. Rational demonstration of how a product will in fact enhance your well-being is not the only way advertisers can successfully persuade you to buy their products. Indeed, it is far from the most common technique. Critics charge, accordingly, that there is no reason to think that advertising even tends to maximize the well-being of consumers.

Defenders of advertising may claim that, nonetheless, advertising is necessary for economic growth, which benefits us all. The truth of this claim, however, is open to debate. Critics maintain that advertising is a waste of resources and serves only to raise the price of advertised goods. Like Galbraith, they may also contend that advertising in general reinforces mindless consumerism. It corrupts our civilization and misdirects our society's economic effort toward private consumption and away from the public realm. The never-ending pursuit of material goods may also divert us as a society from the pursuit of a substantially shorter workday.[62]

---

* *Technically, they lead to *Pareto optimality,* which means that no one person can be made better off without making someone else worse off.

Free Speech and the Media

Two final issues should be briefly noted. Defenders of advertising claim that, despite criticisms, advertising enjoys protection under the First Amendment as a form of speech. Legally this claim probably requires qualification, especially in regard to radio and television, for which one must have a license to broadcast. Banning cigarette advertisements from television, for instance, did not run contrary to the Constitution. More important, even if we concede advertisers the legal right to free speech, not every exercise of that legal right is morally justifiable. If advertisements in general or of a certain type or for certain products were shown to have undesirable social consequences, or if certain sorts of ads relied on objectionable or nonrational persuasive techniques, then there would be a strong moral argument against such advertisements regardless of their legal status.

Advertising subsidizes the media, and that is a positive but far from conclusive consideration in its favor. This is not the place to launch a discussion of the defects of American television. But the very fact that it is free results in far more consumption than would otherwise be the case and probably, as many think, far more than is good for us. Although satellite and cable television have improved things, the mediocrity of much American television fare is hardly accidental. The networks need large audiences. Obviously they can't run everyone's favorite type of program, because people's tastes differ, so they seek to reach a common denominator. If viewers instead of advertisers paid for each show they watched, things would be different.

SUMMARY

1. The complexity of today's economy and the dependence of consumers on business increase business's responsibility for product safety.

2. The legal liability of manufacturers for injuries caused by defective products has evolved over the years. Today the courts have moved to the doctrine of *strict liability,* which holds the manufacturer of a product responsible for injuries suffered as a result of defects in the product, regardless of whether the manufacturer was negligent.

3. Government agencies such as the Consumer Product Safety Commission have broad powers to regulate product safety. Critics contend that these regulations are costly and that they prevent individuals from choosing to purchase a riskier but less expensive product. This argument touches on the controversy over *legal paternalism,* the doctrine that the law may justifiably be used to restrict the freedom of individuals for their own good.

4. Although there are exceptions, regulations generally help ensure that business meets its responsibilities to consumers. Businesspeople, however, tend to favor selfregulation and government deregulation.

5. To increase safety, companies need to give safety the priority necessitated by the product, abandon the misconception that accidents are solely the result of consumer misuse, monitor closely the manufacturing process, review the safety implications of their marketing and advertising strategies, provide consumers with full information about product performance, and investigate consumer complaints. Some successful companies already put a premium on safety.

6. Business also has other obligations to consumers: Product quality must live up to express and implied warranties; prices should be fair, and business should refrain from price fixing, price gouging, and manipulative pricing, and product labeling and packaging should provide clear, accurate, and adequate information.

7. Advertising tries to persuade people to buy products. Ambiguity, the concealment of relevant facts, exaggeration, and psychological appeals are among the morally dubious techniques that advertisers use.

8. The Federal Trade Commission protects us from blatantly deceptive advertising. But it is debatable whether the FTC should ban only advertising that is likely to deceive reasonable people or whether it should protect careless or gullible consumers as well. The FTC now seeks to prohibit advertising that misleads a significant number of consumers, regardless of whether it was reasonable for them to have been misled.

9. Advertising to children is big business, but children are particularly susceptible to the blandishments of advertising. Advertisers contend that parents still control what gets purchased and what doesn't. However, critics doubt the fairness of selling to parents by appealing to children.

10. Defenders of advertising view its imaginative, symbolic, and artistic content as answering real human needs. Critics maintain that advertising manipulates those needs or even creates artificial ones. John Kenneth Galbraith contends that today the same process that produces products also produces the demand for those products (the dependence effect). Galbraith argues, controversially, that advertising encourages a preoccupation with material goods and leads us to favor private consumption at the expense of public goods.

11. Defenders of advertising see it as a necessary and desirable aspect of competition in a free-market system, a protected form of free speech, and a useful sponsor of the media, in particular television. Critics challenge all three claims.

CASE 10.1

Breast Implants

In the last few decades, silicone has become a crucial industrial product, playing a role in the manufacture of thousands of products, from lubricants to adhesive labels to Silly Putty. One of its medical uses, however, has been controversial—namely, as the gel used for breast implants. Dow Corning, which was founded in 1943 to produce silicones for commercial purposes, invented mammary prostheses in the 1960s. Since then a million American women have had bags of silicone gel implanted in their breasts. For many of them, silicone implants are part of reconstructive surgery after breast cancer or other operations. However, by 1990 four out of five implants were for the cosmetic augmentation of normal, healthy breasts—a procedure that became increasingly popular in the 1980s as celebrities such as Cher and Jenny Jones spoke openly of their surgically enhanced breasts.

Today, however, what used to be a common elective operation is rarely performed.[63] The reason dates from the 1980s, when women with silicone breast implants first began reporting certain patterns of illness. There were stories of ruptured or leaky bags, although the estimates of the proportion of women affected ranged from 1–5 percent to 32 percent. And there were allegations that the silicone implants were responsible for various autoimmune disorders—such as rheumatoid arthritis, lupus erythematosus, and scleroderma—in which the body's immune system attacks its own connective tissue. Then, in 1991, a jury heard the case of Mariann Hopkins, who claimed that her implants had ruptured and released silicone gel, causing severe joint and muscle pain, weight loss, and fatigue. On the basis of documents suggesting that Dow Corning knew of the dangers of leaky bags, a San Francisco jury found the company guilty of negligence and fraud and awarded Hopkins $7.3 million.

When Dow Corning first sold breast implants in 1965, they were subject to no specific government regulations. In 1978 the Food and Drug Administration classified them as "Class II" devices, meaning that they did not need testing to remain on the market. In 1989, however, as worries about the dangers of silicone implants increased, the FDA reclassified them as "Class III" devices and in 1991 required all manufacturers to submit safety and effectiveness data. Although some FDA staff members were scathingly critical of the poor and inconclusive documentation submitted by the manufacturers, the FDA's advisory panel ruled that the implants were not a major threat to health. Based on public need, it voted to keep them on the market.

After the Hopkins case, however, David A. Kessler, the FDA's new chairman, called for a moratorium on breast implants. He asked doctors to stop performing the operation, but told women who had already had the operation not to have the bags removed. Still, the moratorium terrified the women who had had breast implants, a few of whom tried in desperation to carve them out themselves, and it galvanized a political movement led by women who were upset about having been used, yet again, as guinea pigs for an unsafe medical procedure. For them, it was just one more episode in a long history of the mistreatment of women by a medical, scientific, and industrial establishment that refused to treat them as persons and take their needs seriously. The FDA moratorium also galvanized the legal forces marshaled against the manufacturers of silicone bags. By 1994, some 20,000 lawsuits had been filed against Dow Corning alone. Entrepreneurial lawyers organized most of these actions into a few large class-action suits so that their pooled legal resources would be more than a match for the manufacturers.

Meanwhile, Kessler instructed the FDA's advisory panel to restudy the breast implant question. Presented with a series of anecdotal reports about diseases that are not rare, the panel complained about the lack of hard scientific data. From the scientific point of view, the problem was how to distinguish coincidence from causation. For example, if connective-tissue disease strikes 1 percent of all women and if 1 million women have implants, then statistically one should expect that 10,000 women will have both implants and connective-tissue disease. So if a woman develops the disease, can it correctly be said that it was caused by her breast implants? Moreover, not only does silicone appear to be chemically inert, but silicone from a ruptured breast implant will remain trapped inside a fibrous capsule of scar tissue. Nevertheless, the panel recommended that silicone be used only for reconstruction and that cosmetic breast augmentation be done only with saline packs.

At this point the gulf between science, on the one hand, and the FDA and public opinion, on the other, began to widen further. A Mayo Clinic study published in the prestigious *New England Journal of Medicine* in June 1994 showed that there was no difference between women with breast implants and other women with respect to incidence of connective-tissue disease; by the summer of 1995 two larger studies had confirmed the Mayo Clinic's report. On top of this, the FBI and other investigators exposed several labs that were selling to lawyers and victims fraudulent test results purporting to show the presence of silicone in the blood of women with breast implants.

Lawyers and other advocates for the women with implants repudiate these studies, contending that the women have a new disease. To this contention scientists respond that the description of the symptoms of this supposed disease keeps changing. Some say it looks like fibromyalgia, which is included in their studies. Many feminist activist groups distrust science; they believe that we should pay less attention to statistics and medical studies and greater attention to the women who have suffered. These women know what their bodies have been through, and they are convinced that their implants are responsible. This reasoning, and the skepticism toward science and statistics that it represents, has swayed jurors. After Dow Corning filed bankruptcy in 1995, which brought to a halt the lawsuits against it, new lawsuits were filed against its parent company, Dow Chemical. The first of these resulted in a $14.1 million verdict against the company, despite the lack of scientific evidence. Disregarding the studies in the *New England Journal of Medicine,* the jurors were convinced that this particular plaintiff's suffering somehow stemmed from her Dow-manufactured breast implant.

Although the FDA admits that there is no evidence that breast implants are dangerous, it has not permitted the manufacturers to reenter the market, arguing that the companies that manufacture the implants have not adequately proved their safety. If the companies want to sell silicone implants in the future, they must resubmit applications to the FDA and demonstrate the safety of their products to the FDA's satisfaction. Given the legal situation, none of the companies intends to do so.

Update:

In June 1999, women who said their silicone breast implants made them ill agreed to settle their claims against Dow Corning for $3.2 billion. The settlement is part of its bankruptcy reorganization plan and is similar to a settlement entered into earlier by 3M, Bristol-Myers Squibb, and other manufacturers of breast implants. By now, however, more than twenty reputable scientific studies have been conducted on implant safety. Three European governments have convened scientific panels. The American College of Rheumatology, the American Academy of Neurology, the Institute of Medicine, and the American Medical Association have all published reviews of the evidence, as has an independent scientific panel appointed by a federal court. The conclusion is unanimous and unequivocal: There is no evidence that breast implants cause disease of any kind.[64]

In light of these scientific findings, a FDA committee of outside experts recommended that the agency permit the general use of silicone implants for breast enchancements. But the committee was split 9 to 6, and the FDA has rejected its recommendation. Mary McGrath, a surgeon at the University of California, was one of those voting to recommend approval. "I came looking for hard evidence, hard data," she said, "and there was an accumulated amount to show" that silicone implants are safe. However, Michael Coti of Johns Hopkins disagreed: "There just isn't enough information to provide reasonable assurance of long-term safety."[65]

Discussion Questions

1. What does the breast implant controversy reveal about society's attitudes toward product safety, about the legal liability of manufacturers, and about the role of regulatory agencies like the FDA in protecting consumers? Is our society too cautious about product safety or not cautious enough?

2. Was the FDA justified in placing a moratorium on breast implants? Is the agency right to have effectively halted cosmetic breast implants by requiring manufacturers to resubmit their silicone prostheses for approval? Is the agency too concerned with public opinion? Should it pay greater attention to scientific evidence or to the individual women who have suffered?

3. Was it irresponsible of the manufacturers of breast implants to have marketed them without first conclusively proving they were safe? If you were on the jury, would you have found Dow Corning or its parent company liable for the illnesses suffered by women who have had breast implants?

4. On safety matters, should the FDA or any regulatory agency err on the side of overprotection or underprotection? Is the FDA's stance on breast implants fair to the women who would like breast augmentation but cannot now get it? Some people disapprove of cosmetic augmentation or believe it to be a frivolous operation. Do you think that attitudes like this played a role in the controversy over the safety of breast implants?

5. Some argue that in the case of new drugs or medical procedures in which the dangers are uncertain, consumers should be free to decide for themselves whether they wish to run the health risks associated with these products or services. Assess this argument.

CASE 10.2

Hot Coffee at McDonald's

To aficionados of the bean, there's nothing like a piping-hot cup of java to get the day off to a good start, and nothing more insipid than lukewarm coffee. That's what McDonald's thought, anyway—until it learned differently, the hard and expensive way, when seventy-nine-year-old Stella Liebeck successfully sued the company after she was burned by a spilled cup of hot coffee that she'd bought at the drive-through window of her local McDonald's. The jury awarded her $160,000 in compensatory damages and a whopping $2.7 million in punitive damages. After the trial judge reduced the punitive damages to $480,000, she and McDonald's settled out of court for an undisclosed sum.[66]

Unlike most other lawsuits, news of the hot-coffee verdict received nationwide attention, most of it unfavorable. To many ordinary people, the case epitomized the excesses of a legal system out of control. If hot coffee is dangerous, what's next: soft drinks that are too cold? To conservatives, the case represented the all-too-familiar failure of consumers to take responsibility for their own conduct, to blame business rather than themselves for their injuries. More policy-oriented pundits used the case as an occasion to call for reform of product liability law—in particular, to make winning frivolous suits more difficult and to restrict the punitive awards that juries can hand down.

However, those who examined the facts more closely learned that the Liebeck case was more complicated than it first appeared. For one thing, Liebeck suffered third-degree burns on her thighs and buttocks that were serious enough to require skin grafting and leave permanent scars. After her injury, she initially requested $10,000 for medical expenses and an additional amount for pain and suffering. When McDonald's refused, she went to court, asking for $300,000. Lawyers for the company argued in response that McDonald's coffee was not unreasonably hot and that Liebeck was responsible for her own injuries.

The jury saw it differently, however. First, McDonald's served its coffee at 185 degrees Fahrenheit, significantly hotter than home-brewed coffee. The jury was persuaded that coffee at that temperature is both undrinkable and more dangerous than a reasonable consumer would expect. Second, before Liebeck's accident, the company had received over 700 complaints about burns from its coffee. In response to the complaints, McDonald's had in fact put a warning label on its cups and designed a tighter-fitting lid for them. Ironically, the new lid was part of the problem in the Liebeck case because she had held the coffee cup between her legs in an effort to pry it open.

Although the jury found that Liebeck was 20 percent responsible for her injuries, it also concluded that McDonald's had not done enough to warn consumers. The jury's $2.7 million punitive-damage award was intended, jurors later said, to send a message to fast-food chains. Although the judge reduced the award—equivalent to only about two days' worth of coffee sales for McDonald's—he called McDonald's conduct "willful, wanton, reckless, and callous."

Discussion Questions

1. Is hot coffee so dangerous, as the jury thought? Should a reasonable consumer be expected to know that coffee can burn and to have assumed this risk? Is a warning label sufficient? Is our society too protective of consumers these days, or not protective enough?

2. In serving hot coffee, did McDonald's act in a morally responsible way? What ideals, obligations, and effects should it have taken into consideration?

3. McDonald's claims that most consumers would prefer to have their coffee too hot than not hot enough. After all, if it's too hot, they can always wait a minute before drinking it. Suppose this is true; how does it affect McDonald's responsibilities? Given that McDonald's serves millions of cups of coffee every week, how important are a few hundred complaints about its coffee being too hot?

4. Was Liebeck only 20 percent responsible for her injuries? Do you agree with the amount of compensatory and punitive damages that the jury awarded her? If not, what would have been a fairer monetary award?

5. Should juries be permitted to award punitive damages in product liability cases? If so, should there be a limit to what they can award? Is it right for a jury to award punitive damages against one company in order to send a message to a whole industry?

CASE 10.3

Sniffing Glue
Could Snuff Profits

Harvey Benjamin Fuller founded the H. B. Fuller Company in 1887. Originally a one-man wallpaper-paste shop, H. B. Fuller is now a leading manufacturer of industrial glues, coatings, and paints, with operations worldwide. The company's 10,000 different varieties of glue hold together everything from cars to cigarettes to disposable diapers. However, some of its customers don't use Fuller's glues in the way they are intended to be used.

That's particularly the case in Central America, where Fuller derives 27 percent of its profits and where tens of thousands of homeless children sniff some sort of glue. Addicted to glue's intoxicating but dangerous fumes, these unfortunate children are called *resistoleros* after Fuller's Resistol brand. Child-welfare advocates have urged the company to add a noxious oil to its glue to discourage abusers, but the company has resisted, either because it might reduce the glue's effectiveness or because it will irritate legitimate users.[67]

Either way, the issue is irritating H. B. Fuller, which has been recognized by various awards, honors, and socially conscious mutual funds as a company with a conscience. Fuller's mission statement says that it "will conduct business legally and ethically, support the activities of its employees in their communities and be a responsible corporate citizen." The St. Paul–based company gives 5 percent of its profits to charity; it has committed itself to safe environmental practices worldwide (practices that are "often more stringent than local government standards," the company says); and it has even endowed a chair in business ethics at the University of Minnesota. Now Fuller must contend with dissident stockholders inside, and demonstrators outside, its annual meetings.

The glue-sniffing issue is not a new one. In 1969 the Testor Corporation added a noxious ingredient to its hobby glue to discourage abuse, and in 1994 Henkel, a German chemical company that competes with Fuller, stopped making certain toxic glues in Central America. However, Fuller seems to have been singled out for criticism not only because its brand dominates Central America but also because—in the eyes of its critics, anyway—the company has not lived up to its own good-citizen image. Timothy Smith, executive director of the Interfaith Center for Corporate Responsibility, believes that companies with a reputation as good corporate citizens are more vulnerable to attack. "But as I see it," he says, "the hazard is not in acting in a socially responsible way. The hazard is in over-marketing yourself as a saint."

Saintly or not, the company has made matters worse for itself by its handling of the issue. In 1992 H. B. Fuller's board of directors acknowledged that "illegal distribution was continuing" and that "a suitable replacement product would not be available in the near future." Accordingly, it voted to stop selling Resistol adhesives in Central America. "We simply don't believe it is the right decision to keep our solvent product on the market," a company spokesman said.

The Coalition on Resistoleros and other corporate gadflies were ecstatic, but their jubilation turned to anger when they learned a few months later that Fuller had not in fact stopped selling Resistol in Central America, and did not intend to. True, Fuller no longer sold glue to retailers and small-scale users in Honduras and Guatemala, but it continued to sell large tubs and barrels of it to industrial customers in those countries and to a broader list of commercial and industrial users in neighboring countries.

The company says that it has not only restricted distribution but also taken other steps to stop the abuse of its product. It has altered Resistol's formula, replacing the sweet-smelling but highly toxic solvent toluene with the slightly less toxic chemical cyclohexane. In addition, the company has tried—without success, it says—to develop a nonintoxicating water-based glue, and it contributes to community programs for homeless children in Central America. But the company's critics disparage these actions as mere image polishing. Bruce Harris, director of Latin American programs for Covenant House, a nonprofit child-welfare advocate, asserts that Resistol is still readily available to children in Nicaragua and El Salvador and, to a lesser extent, in Costa Rica. "If they are genuinely concerned about the children," he asks, "why haven't they pulled out of all the countries—as their board mandated?"

Discussion Questions

1. What are H. B. Fuller's moral obligations in this case? What ideas, effects, and consequences are at stake? Have any moral rights been violated? What would a utilitarian recommend? A Kantian?

2. What specifically should H. B. Fuller do about Resistol? Are the critics right that the steps the company has taken so far are mere image polishing? Is the company's only moral option to withdraw from the Central American market altogether?

3. When, if ever, is a company morally responsible for harm done by the blatant misuse of a perfectly legitimate and socially useful product? Does it make a difference whether the abusers are adults or children? Is it relevant that other companies market similar products?

4. Tobacco companies have a strong financial interest in cultivating future smokers, and although they deny doing so, they consciously market their product to make it attractive to young people. Contrast their conduct with that of H. B. Fuller.

5. Given H. B. Fuller's conduct in other matters, would you judge it to be a morally responsible company, all things considered? Are companies that pride themselves on being morally responsible likely to be held to a higher standard than other companies? If so, is this fair?

CASE 10.4

Closing the Deal

Now that she had to, Jean McGuire wasn't sure she could. Not that she didn't understand what to do. Wright Boazman, sales director for Sunrise Land Developers, had made the step clear enough when he described a variety of effective "deal-closing techniques."

As Wright explained it, very often people actually want to buy a lot but suffer at the last minute from self-doubt and uncertainty. The inexperienced salesperson can misinterpret this hesitation as a lack of interest in a property. "But," as Wright pointed out, "in most cases it's just an expression of the normal reservations we all show when the time comes to sign our names on the dotted line."

In Wright's view, the job of a land salesperson was "to help the prospect make the decision to buy." He didn't mean to suggest that salespeople should misrepresent a piece of property or in any way mislead people about what they were purchasing. "Law prohibits this," he pointed out, "and personally I find such behavior repugnant. What I'm talking about is helping them buy a lot that they genuinely want and that you're convinced will be compatible with their needs and interests." For Wright Boazman, salespeople should serve as motivators, people who can provide whatever impulse was needed for prospects to close the deal.

In Wright's experience, one of the most effective closing techniques was what he termed "the other party." It goes something like this.

Suppose someone like Jean McGuire had a hot prospect, someone who was exhibiting real interest in a lot but who was having trouble deciding. To motivate the prospect into buying, Jean ought to tell the person that she wasn't even sure the lot was still available because a number of other salespeople were showing the same lot, and they could already have closed a deal on it. As Wright put it, "This first ploy generally has the effect of increasing the prospect's interest in the property, and more important to us, in closing the deal pronto."

Next Jean should say something like, "Why don't we go back to the office, and I'll call headquarters to find out the status of the lot?" Wright indicated that such a suggestion ordinarily "whets their appetite" even more. In addition, it turns prospects away from wondering whether they should purchase the land and toward hoping that it's still available.

When they return to the office, Jean should make a call in the presence of the prospect. The call, of course, would not be to "headquarters" but to a private office only yards from where she and the prospect sit. Wright or someone else would receive the call, and Jean should fake a conversation about the property's availability, punctuating her comments with contagious excitement about its desirability. When she hangs up, she should breathe a sigh of relief that the lot's still available— but barely. At any minute, Jean should explain anxiously, the lot could be "green-tagged," meaning that headquarters is expecting a call from another salesperson who's about to close a deal and will remove the lot from open stock. (An effective variation of this, Wright pointed out, would have Jean abruptly excuse herself on hanging up and dart over to another sales representative with whom she'd engage in a heated, although staged, debate about the availability of the property—loud enough, of course, for the prospect to hear. The intended effect, according to Wright, would be to place the prospect in a "now or never" frame of mind.)

When Jean first heard about this and other closing techniques, she felt uneasy. Even though the property was everything it was represented to be and the law allowed purchasers ten days to change their minds after closing a deal, she instinctively objected to the use of psychological manipulation. Nevertheless, Jean never expressed her reservations to anyone, primarily because she didn't want to endanger her job. She desperately needed it owing to the recent death of her husband, which had left her as the sole supporter of herself and three young children. Besides, Jean had convinced herself that she could deal with closures more respectably than Wright and other salespeople might. But the truth was that, after six months of selling land for Sunrise, Jean's sales lagged far behind those of the other sales representatives. Whether she liked it or not, Jean had to admit she was losing a considerable number of sales because she couldn't close. And she couldn't close because, in Wright Boazman's words, she lacked technique. She wasn't using the psychological closing devices that he and others had found so successful.

Now as she drove back to the office with two hot prospects in hand, she wondered what to do.

Discussion Questions

1. Do you disapprove of this sales tactic, or is it a legitimate business technique? How might it be morally defended?

2. Suppose you knew either that the prospect would eventually decide to buy the property anyway or that it would genuinely be in the prospect's interest to buy it. Would that affect your moral assessment of this closing technique? Do customers have any grounds for complaining about this closing technique if the law allows them ten days to change their minds?

3. What ideals, obligations, and effects must Jean consider? What interests and rights of the customer are at stake?

4. What weight should Jean give to self-interest in her deliberations? What do you think she should do? What would you do?

5. What rule, if any, would a rule utilitarian encourage realtors in this situation to follow? What should the realtors' professional code of ethics say about closing techniques?

Notes to Chapter 10

1. See the CDC's Web site, *www.cdc.gov/tobacco/issue.htm* (September 23, 2003).

2. "Low-Tar Duplicity," *New York Times,* December 3, 2001, A22.

3. U.S. Bureau of the Census, *Statistical Abstract of the United States 2002* (Washington, D.C.: U.S. Government Printing Office, 2003), Table 172. See the Consumer Product Safety Commission's regular reports on toy-related deaths and injuries at *www.cpsc.gov.*

4. The Consumer Product Safety Commission reports regularly on electrocutions associated with consumer products. See *www.cpsc.gov.*

5. Manuel G. Velasquez, *Business Ethics,* 5th ed. (Upper Saddle River, N.J.: Prentice Hall, 2002), 348–350.

6. Ira Sager, "Upfront," *Business Week,* September 15, 2003, 12.

7. Richard T. De George, "Ethical Responsibilities of Engineers in Large Organizations," *Business and Professional Ethics Journal* 1 (Fall 1981).

8. "Unapproved Drugs Linger on the Market," *Wall Street Journal,* March 20, 2003, A4.

9. Dean Rothbart and John A. Prestbo, "Taking Rely Off Market Costs Procter & Gamble a Week of Agonizing," *Wall Street Journal,* November 3, 1980, 1.

10. Dan Oldenburg, "Chrysler's Reversal in Airbag Debate," *San Francisco Chronicle,* August 23, 1989, in "Business Briefing," 9.

11. "Dangerous Candies," *San Jose Mercury News,* June 13, 2002, 1A.

12. Milo Geyelin, "Gun Dealer Is Held Liable in Accident for Not Teaching Customer Safe Use," *Wall Street Journal,* June 6, 1989, B10.

13. Marisa Manley, "Products Liability: You're More Exposed Than You Think," *Harvard Business Review* 65 (September–October 1987): 28–29.

14. Melvyn A. J. Menezes, "Ethical Issues in Product Policy," in N. Craig Smith and John A. Quelch, eds., *Ethics in Marketing* (Homewood, Ill.: Irwin, 1993), 286.

15. "Child Contracts Reye's Syndrome," *ACLU News* (San Francisco), July–August 1993, 1.

16. Terry Ann Halbert, "The Fire-Safe Cigarette: The Other Tobacco War," *Business and Society Review* 102–103 (1998): 25–36, and J. Jennings Moss, "Smoke, But No Fire" (January 11, 2000), available at *www.abcnews.go.com*

17. "Expiration Dates Sought for Tires," *Wall Street Journal,* September 22, 2003, A8.

18. These are taken from Tad Tuleja, *Beyond the Bottom Line* (New York: Penguin, 1987), 77–78.

19. *New York Times,* March 31, 1999, A16, and *San Francisco Chronicle,* March 31, 1999, A1.

20. Smith and Quelch, *Ethics in Marketing,* 337–339.

21. "For First Time, Justices Reject Punitive Awards," *New York Times,* May 21, 1996, C1.

22. Jeffrey H. Birnbaum, "Pricing of Product Is Still an Art, Often Having Little Link to Costs," *Wall Street Journal,* November 25, 1981, sec. 2, 29.

23. Ibid.

24. Ibid.

25. "Scanners That Err at Checkout Counter," *International Herald Tribune,* June 13, 1994, 3, and "Store Scanners in the Crosshairs," *San Francisco Chronicle,* April 5, 1997, A15.

26. "The Discount Cards That Don't Save You Money," *Wall Street Journal,* January 21, 2003, D1.

27. Smith and Quelch, *Ethics in Marketing,* 405–406.

28. Ibid., 407.

29. *San Francisco Chronicle,* October 1, 1997, A3.

30. Constance L. Hays, "Panasonic to Return $16 Million to Consumers," *New York Times,* January 19, 1989, A1.

31. For a thorough look at this case, see M. David Ermann and Richard J. Lundman, *Corporate Deviance* (New York: Holt, Rinehart & Winston, 1982), Chapter 5.

32. "Price-Fixing Probe Nets Dairy Giants," *San Jose Mercury News,* May 23, 1993, 8A.

33. *San Francisco Chronicle,* May 9, 1997, A1.

34. "Why Do We Pay More?" *Business Week,* August 11, 2003, 26–27.

35. Kevin Helliker, "In Natural Foods, a Big Name's No Big Help," *Wall Street Journal,* June 6, 2002, B1.

36. Michael J. McCarthy, "Taking the Value Out of Value-Sized," *Wall Street Journal,* August 14, 2002, D1. See also Omprakash K. Gupta and Anna S. Rominger, "Blind Man's Bluff: The Ethics of Quantity Surcharges," *Journal of Business Ethics* 15 (1996): 1299–1312.

37. Gupta and Rominger, "Blind Man's Bluff."

38. *New York Times 2003 Almanac* (New York: Penguin, 2002), 351.

39. "The Top 5 Rules of the Ad Game," *Business Week,* January 20, 2003, 72.

40. Roger Draper, "The Faithless Shepherd," *New York Review of Books,* June 26, 1986, 17.

41. See "Mea Culpa, Sort Of," *Newsweek,* September 27, 1971, 98.

42. *Business and Society Review* 67 (Fall 1988): 27.

43. Paul Stevens, "Weasel Words: God's Little Helpers," in Paul A. Eschhol, Alfred A. Rosa, and Virginia P. Clark, eds., *Language Awareness* (New York: St. Martin's Press, 1974), 156.

44. Samm Sinclair Baker, *The Permissible Lie* (New York: World Publishing, 1968), 16.

45. See the *Washington Post*'s health supplement, January 8, 1994.

46. Ann Hagedorn, "FDA Cracks Down on Cosmetic Firms' Age-Treatment Drugs," *Wall Street Journal,* April 27, 1987.

47. Ivan L. Preston, *The Great American Blow-Up: Puffery in Advertising and Selling,* rev. ed. (Madison, Wis.: University of Wisconsin Press, 1996), 181.

48. Preston, *Great American Blow-Up,* 24.

49. Gail Bronson, "Sexual Pitches in Ads Become More Explicit and Pervasive," *Wall Street Journal,* November 18, 1980, 1.

50. Wilson Bryan Key, *Subliminal Seduction* (New York: New American Library, 1973), 11.

51. Preston, *Great American Blow-Up,* 113–123.

52. 302 U.S. 112 (1937).

53. Preston, *Great American Blow-Up,* 122–123.

54. "Reclaiming Childhood," *San Francisco Chronicle,* March 11, 2003, D4.

55. "Hey Kid, Buy This," *Business Week,* June 30, 1997, 63. Except as otherwise noted, the following four paragraphs are based on this article.

56. Lisa J. Moore, "The Littlest Consumers," *San Francisco Chronicle,* January 13, 1991, in "This World," 8.

57. Randall Rothenberg, "Executives Defending Their Craft," *New York Times,* May 22, 1989, C7.

58. Theodore Levitt, "The Morality (?) of Advertising," *Harvard Business Review* 48 (July–August 1970): 84–92.

59. John Kenneth Galbraith, *The Affluent Society,* 3rd ed. (New York: Houghton Mifflin, 1976), 131.

60. John Kenneth Galbraith, *The New Industrial State* (New York: Signet, 1967), 219.

61. Draper, "The Faithless Shepherd," 16.

62. See Al Gini, "Work, Identity, and Self: How We Are Formed by the Work We Do," *Journal of Business Ethics* 17 (May 1998): 711.

63. This case study is based on the *Frontline* program "Breast Implants on Trial," aired on PBS, February 27, 1996. For background details, see Anne T. Lawrence, "Dow Corning and the

Silicone Breast Implant Controversy," in John R. Boatright, ed., *Cases in Ethics and the Conduct of Business* (Englewood Cliffs, N.J.: Prentice Hall, 1995).

64. See "Talk of the Town," *New Yorker,* January 11, 1999, 23–24, and *New York Times,* July 11 and November 10, 1998, and June 2, June 29, and December 2, 1999.

65. "Panel Urges End to Implant Ban," *San Jose Mercury News,* October 16, 2003, 3A.

66. This case study is based on one in Joseph R. DesJardins and John J. McCall, eds., *Contemporary Issues in Business Ethics,* 4th ed. (Belmont, Calif.: Wadsworth, 2000), 345–346.

67. This case study is based on Diana B. Henriques, "Black Mark for a 'Good Citizen,'" *New York Times,* November 26, 1995, sec. 3, 1.

Further Reading for Chapter 10

Robert L. Arrington, "Advertising and Behavior Control," *Journal of Business Ethics* 1 (February 1982); **John Waide,** "The Making of Self and World in Advertising," *Journal of Business Ethics* 6 (February 1987); **Roger Crisp,** "Persuasive Advertising, Autonomy, and the Creation of Desire, "*Journal of Business Ethics* 6 (July 1987); **Richard L. Lippke,** "Advertising and the Social Conditions of Autonomy," *Business and Professional Ethics Journal* 8 (Winter 1989); and **Andrew Gustafson,** "Advertising's Impact on Morality in Society: Influencing Habits and Desires of Consumers," *Business and Society Review* 106 (Fall 2001) are valuable, philosophical discussions of advertising.

Joseph R. DesJardins and **John J. McCall,** eds., *Contemporary Issues in Business Ethics,* 4th ed. (Belmont, Calif.: Wadsworth, 2000) contains important and useful essays on product liability, consumer regulation, advertising and free speech, subliminal advertising, and advertising to children, among other issues.

David M. Holley, "A Moral Evaluation of Sales Practices," *Business and Professional Ethics Journal* 5 (Fall 1987) is a seminal discussion of the ethics of sales. Holley revisits the subject in "Information Disclosure in Sales," *Journal of Business Ethics* 17 (April 1998). **Thomas Carson** offers a rival perspective in "The Ethics of Sales," in William H. Shaw, ed., *Ethics at Work* (New York: Oxford University Press, 2003).

Gene R. Laczniak and **Patrick E. Murphy,** *Ethical Marketing Decisions* (Boston: Allyn and Bacon, 1993) is an informative survey of a wide range of issues in marketing ethics.

Juliet Schor, *Do Americans Shop Too Much?* (Boston: Beacon Press, 2000) is a provocative essay on contemporary consumerism, followed by nine responses to Schor by other writers.

N. Craig Smith and **John A. Quelch,** *Ethics in Marketing* (Homewood, Ill.: Irvin, 1993) contains informative essays and case studies on all aspects of marketing ethics.

Manuel G. Velasquez, *Business Ethics,* 5th ed. (Upper Saddle River, N.J.: Prentice Hall, 2002), and **John R. Boatright,** *Ethics and the Conduct of Business,* 4th ed. (Upper Saddle River, N.J.: Prentice Hall, 2003) provide good discussions of consumer issues.

 InfoTrac College Edition: For further information or to conduct research, please go to www.infotrac-college.com.

11

The Environment

In feeding, clothing, and sheltering ourselves and in manufacturing and consuming countless different kinds of products, human beings have scarred the globe, contaminated the natural environment, and gobbled up the earth's resources. The effects of this environmental recklessness are now coming home to roost. Our rivers and lakes are dirty, and our air is unclean. The planet is warming, its protective ozone fraying. Lush forests are disappearing, and with them countless species of plants and animals. As our numbers have multiplied, half the world's wetlands have disappeared. Eighty percent of its grasslands now suffer from soil degradation; 20 percent of its drylands are in danger of turning into deserts, and groundwater is seriously depleted. As a result, the earth is losing its capacity to continue to provide the goods we need, threatening our economic well-being and ultimately our survival—so concludes a mammoth United Nations Assessment of global ecosystems.[1]

The environment is a huge topic, but as one expert remarks, "the concerns of environmental ethics might begin with the food on our plate."[2] With fertilizers, herbicides, and pesticides, agriculture uses hundreds of chemicals in crop production. Although chemically intensive agriculture has yielded many benefits, it is hard on the environment—both in terms of what it consumes and in its impact on the surrounding ecosystem. In addition to the ecological price we pay for what we eat, there is the risk of chemical residues left in food.

In the United States pesticide use has doubled in the past thirty years and poses a greater danger than most people realize.[3] Because of exposure to pesticides, many fish and birds in the Great Lakes region have lost their ability to reproduce. After a pesticide spilled into Florida's Lake Apopka, alligators were born with half-sized penises. When laboratory rats were fed DDT, they developed genital abnormalities. Now researchers believe that by mimicking estrogen and testosterone, the chemicals in pesticides may threaten human reproduction by disrupting the endocrine system that regulates it. These "endocrine disrupters" may explain certain disturbing reproductive problems now being seen in human beings: a rise in breast cancer rates, a drop in sperm count, and an increase in the incidence of testicular cancer.[4] The pesticide problem is even more alarming when we consider children. Because they have smaller bodies and different eating patterns than adults, children's exposure to carcinogens and neurotoxins can be hundreds of times what is safe for them.[5] Yet until recently, the Environmental Protection Agency (EPA) set the legal limits on the amount of pesticide residues allowed to remain on food with adults in mind.

The contaminants that infiltrate the food chain can also spread into our water. Toxic chemicals used in farming can and do run off into underground reservoirs, a major source of drinking water. In 1972, Congress passed the Clean Water Act, which proclaimed the goal of eliminating all water pollution by 1985. Since Congress acted, billions have been spent on pollution control. Some streams and lakes have improved; others have gotten worse. On average, though, according to government figures, water quality hasn't changed much.

Pollutants also contaminate the air we breathe, despoiling vegetation and crops, corroding construction materials, and threatening our lives and health. Although precise figures are impossible to obtain, there is little doubt that air pollution is responsible for thousands of deaths and millions of sick days every year because of air-related ailments such as asthma, emphysema, and lung cancer. Moreover, pregnant women living in regions with high levels of air pollution are up to three times more likely to give birth to children with serious heart defects.[6] According to a congressional survey of toxic air pollution, 2.4 billion pounds of hazardous pollutants are emitted into the air each year, including tons of toxic chemicals that can cause cancer and damage the nervous system.[7] These figures don't include emissions of nontoxic substances such as sulfur and nitrogen oxides that are a major source of acid rain and of the smog that blankets so many U.S. cities. And the figures also omit fine-particle pollution—dust, soot, smoke, and tiny droplets of acid—a form of air pollution that the EPA began to regulate only in 1997. Yet recent studies conclude that fine-particle pollution causes 15,000 premature deaths every year.[8]

Thanks to the groundbreaking Clean Air Act of 1970, our air is better than it would otherwise have been, and by some measures it is better than it was thirty years ago. In particular, by banning lead as a fuel additive in gasoline, the act has reduced its presence in the air by nearly 90 percent. And the Clean Air Act Amendments of 1990 require new measures to be taken to fight smog, acid rain, and toxic emissions. But the fact remains: More than three decades after Congress first set a strict deadline for reducing air pollution to safe levels, the air in more than fifty U.S. cities remains a health risk.

Related to the problem of atmospheric pollution is the issue of global warming. After years of study and debate, there is now a scientific consensus that human activity is indeed heating up the planet.[9] As we burn coal, oil, and gasoline for heat, electricity, and transportation, carbon dioxide (CO_2) is released into the atmosphere, trapping excess energy from the sun and warming the globe—the so-called greenhouse effect. The evidence of global warming is all around us. The past decade has been the hottest on record; in the Northern Hemisphere, spring now comes, on average, a week earlier than it used to. Storms have become more intense and weather patterns more erratic. Only by drastically reducing the consumption of fossil fuels can we hope to slow down this trend and stabilize the climate at current levels of disruption.

Surprisingly, one of the largest sources of pollution is not all that exotic—namely, the animals we raise for food. In fact, the ecological costs of producing beef, poultry, and pork are second only to the manufacture and use of cars and light trucks. In addition to the electrical energy, fuel, fertilizer, and pesticides consumed by the meat industry is the manure problem. Mega-farms with tens or hundreds of thousands of animals have replaced factories as the biggest polluters of America's waterways. The United States generates 1.4 billion tons of animal manure every year—130 times more than the annual production of human waste. This waste wasn't a problem when small farms criss-crossed the nation, and farmers used the manure as fertilizer. But giant farms with 100,000 hogs or a million chickens all defecating in the same place seriously damage the environment.[10] Heretofore runoff and water pollution have been the major concern, but now scientists are also worried about air pollution and the emission of noxious fumes from the disposal of animal waste.[11]

Nuclear wastes, of course, are in a class by themselves. Significant danger arises from even the small amounts that are released into the atmosphere during normal operation of a nuclear power plant or in mining, processing, or transporting nuclear fuels. A nuclear-plant accident would, of course, have frightening consequences, as the 1986 dis-aster at Chernobyl, Ukraine, brought vividly home to the world. Illnesses caused by the fallout from Chernobyl are still emerging, nearly twenty years later.[12] In addition, the disposal of nuclear wastes has to worry anyone who is sensitive to the legacy we leave future generations. Will the nuclear wastes we bury today return to haunt us tomorrow?

It is little wonder, then, that considerable attention has focused on business's and indus-try's responsibility for preserving the integrity of our natural environment. This chapter explores some of the moral dilemmas posed for business by our environmental relation-ships—not just the problem of pollution but also the ethical issues posed by the depletion of natural resources and by our treatment of animals. The chapter's purpose is not to argue that the environmental problems facing us are serious and that industry has greatly contributed to them. Few people today doubt this. Rather, this chapter is largely con-cerned with a more practical question: Given the problems of environmental degradation, of resource depletion, and of the abuse of animals for commercial purposes, what are business's responsibilities? Specifically, this chapter examines the following topics:

1. The meaning and significance of *ecology*

2. The traditional business attitudes toward the environment that have encouraged environmental degradation and resource depletion

3. The moral problems underlying business's abuse of the environment—in par-ticular, the question of externalities, the problem of free riders, and the right to a livable environment

4. The costs of environmental protection and the question of who should pay them

5. Three methods—regulations, incentives, and pricing mechanisms—for allocating the costs of environmental protection

6. Some of the deeper and not fully resolved questions of environmental ethics: What obligations do we have to future generations? Does nature have value in itself? Is our commercial exploitation of animals immoral?

BUSINESS AND ECOLOGY

To deal intelligently with the question of business's responsibilities for the environment, one must realize that as business uses energy and materials, discharges waste, and produces products and services, it is functioning within an ecological system. *Ecology* refers to the science of the interrelationships among organisms and their environments.

The operative term is "interrelationships," implying that an interdependence exists among all entities in the environment. In particular, we must not forget that human beings are part of nature and thus intricately connected with and interrelated to the natural environment.

In speaking about ecological matters, ecologists frequently use the term *ecosystem*, which refers to a total ecological community, both living and nonliving. Webs of interdependency structure ecosystems. Predators and prey, producers and consumers, hosts and parasites are linked together, creating interlocking mechanisms—checks and balances—that stabilize the system.

An ordinary example of an ecosystem is a pond. It consists of a complex web of animal and vegetable life. Suppose that the area where the pond is located experiences a prolonged period of drought, or that someone begins to fish in the pond regularly, or that during a period of excessive rainfall, plant pesticides begin to spill into it. Under any of these circumstances, changes will occur in the relationships among the pond's constituent components. Damage to a particular form of plant life may mean that fewer fish can live in the pond; a particular species might even disappear. A change in the pond's ecosystem may also affect other ecosystems. Because of water contamination, for example, a herd of deer that live nearby may have to go elsewhere for water; their presence there may reduce the berry crop which had previously supported other animals. The point is that in considering any ecosystem, one must remember its complex and interrelated nature and the intricate network of interdependencies that bind it to other ecosystems.

Every living organism affects its environment, yet *Homo sapiens* possesses the power to upset dramatically the stability of natural ecosystems. In particular, many human commercial activities (for example, using pesticides and establishing oil fields) have unpredictable and disruptive consequences for ecosystems. For example, farmers in the Midwest use nitrogen fertilizer liberally. Excess nitrogen runs off their fields and finds its way into the Mississippi River and eventually into the Gulf of Mexico. There, in what has historically been the nation's best shrimping grounds, it has created what is known as the dead zone, where the water is devoid of life to about 10 feet below the surface. This dead zone has now grown to about 8,500 square miles, an area the size of New Jersey.[13]

On the other hand, tampering with ecosystems does not always have injurious effects. Sometimes unforeseen benefits result, as was true years ago when oil and gas drilling expanded into the Gulf. Much to everyone's surprise, the operational docks, pipes, and platforms provided a better place for lower forms of life to attach themselves than the silt-laden sea ever did. This in turn increased the fish catch in the area. But even in fortuitous instances like this, environmental intrusions affect the integrity of ecosystems. And that's the point. Because an ecosystem represents a delicate balance of interrelated entities and because ecosystems are interlocked, an intrusion into one will affect its integrity and the integrity of others. And we are not usually so lucky in the results. Dr. Paul Ehrlich, one of the best-known exponents of ecological awareness, has put the matter succinctly. "There are a number of ecological rules it would be wise for people to remember," Ehrlich has written. "One of them is that there is no such thing as a free lunch. Another is that when we change something into something else, the new thing is usually more dangerous than what we had originally."[14]

In its role as the major instrument of production in our society, business must intrude into ecosystems. Yet not all intrusions or all kinds of intrusions are justifiable. In fact, precisely because of the interrelated nature of ecosystems and because intrusions generally produce serious unfavorable effects, business must scrupulously avoid actions, practices, and policies that have an undue impact on the environment. There's ample documentation to show that business traditionally has been remiss in both recognizing and adequately discharging its obligations in this regard. We needn't spend time retelling the sorry tale, but it does seem worthwhile to isolate some business attitudes that have been responsible for this indifference.

Business's Traditional Attitudes Toward the Environment

Several related attitudes prevalent in our society in general and in business in particular have led to or increased our environmental problems. One of these is the tendency to view the natural world as a "free and unlimited good"—that is, as something we can exploit, even squander, without regard to the future. Writer John Steinbeck once reflected on this attitude:

> I have often wondered at the savagery and thoughtlessness with which our early settlers approached this rich continent. They came at it as though it were an enemy, which of course it was. They burned the forests and changed the rainfall; they swept the buffalo from the plains, blasted the streams, set fire to the grass, and ran a reckless scythe through the virgin and noble timber. Perhaps they felt that it was limitless and could never be exhausted and that a man could move on to new wonders endlessly. Certainly there are many examples to the contrary, but to a large extent the early people pillaged the country as though they hated it, as though they held it temporarily and might be driven off at any time.
>
> This tendency toward irresponsibility persists in very many of us today; our rivers are poisoned by reckless dumping of sewage and toxic industrial wastes, the air of our cities is filthy and dangerous to breathe from the belching of uncontrolled products from combustion of coal, coke, oil, and gasoline. Our towns are girdled with wreckage and debris of our toys—our automobiles and our packaged pleasures. Through uninhibited spraying against one enemy we have destroyed the natural balances our survival requires. All these evils can and must be overcome if America and Americans are to survive; but many of us conduct ourselves as our ancestors did, stealing from the future for our clear and present profit.[15]

Traditionally, business has considered the environment to be a free, virtually limitless good. In other words, air, water, land, and other natural resources from coal to beavers (trapped almost to extinction for their pelts in the nineteenth century) were seen as available for business to use as it saw fit. In this context, pollution and the depletion of natural resources are two aspects of the same problem: Both involve using up natural resources that are limited. Pollution uses up clean air and water, just as extraction uses up the minerals or oil in the ground. The belief that both sorts of resources are unlimited and free promotes wasteful consumption of them.

Garrett Hardin describes the consequences of this attitude in his modern parable, "The Tragedy of the Commons." Hardin asks us to imagine villagers who allow their animals to graze in the commons, the collectively shared village pasture. Even though it is in the interest of each to permit his or her animals to graze without limit on the public land, the result of doing so is that the commons is soon overgrazed, making it of no further grazing value to anyone.[16]

Today the international fishing industry exemplifies Hardin's point: Overfishing by ships armed with advanced technology is dramatically reducing the world's stock of fish, threatening to undermine the whole industry.[17] But the moral of Hardin's story is perfectly general: When it comes to "the commons"—that is, to public or communal goods like air, water, and wilderness—problems arise as the result of individuals' and companies' following their own self-interest. Each believes that his or her own use of the commons has only a negligible effect, but the cumulative result can be the gradual destruction of the public domain, which makes everyone worse off. In the tragedy of the commons we have the reverse of Adam Smith's invisible hand: Each person's pursuit of self-interest makes everyone worse off.

The tragedy of the commons also illustrates the more general point that there can be a difference between the private costs and the social costs of a business activity. Chapter 5 discussed this issue when it described what economists call "externalities," but it is worth reviewing the point in the present context.

Suppose a paper mill only partially treats the chemical wastes it releases into a lake that's used for fishing and recreational activities, thus saving on production costs. If the amount of effluent is great enough to reduce the fishing productivity of the lake, then while the mill's customers pay a lower price for its paper than they otherwise would, other people end up paying a higher price for fish. Moreover, the pollution may make the lake unfit for recreational activities such as swimming or for use as a source of potable water. The result is that other people and the public generally pay the cost of the mill's inadequate water-treatment system. Economists term this disparity between private industrial costs and public social costs a *spillover* or *externality.* In viewing things strictly in terms of private industrial costs, business overlooks spillover. This is an economic problem because the price of the paper does not reflect the true cost of producing it. Paper is underpriced and overproduced, thus leading to a misallocation of resources. This is also a moral problem because the purchasers of paper are not paying its full cost. Instead, part of the cost of producing paper is being unfairly imposed on other people.

In sum, then, spillovers or externalities, pursuit of private interest at the expense of the commons, and a view of the environment as a free good that can be consumed without limit have combined with an ignorance of ecology and of the often fragile interconnections and interdependencies of the natural world to create the serious environmental problems facing us today.

THE ETHICS OF ENVIRONMENTAL PROTECTION

Much of what we do to reduce, eliminate, or avoid pollution and the depletion of scarce natural resources is in our collective self-interest. Many measures that we take—for example, recycling our cans or installing catalytic converters in our cars—are steps that benefit all of us, collectively and individually: Our air is more breathable and our landscapes less cluttered with garbage. But even if such measures benefit each and every one of us, there will still be a temptation to shirk individual responsibilities and be a "free rider." The individual person or company may rationalize that the little bit it adds to the total pollution problem doesn't make any difference. The firm benefits from the efforts of others to prevent pollution but "rides for free" by not making the same effort itself.

The unfairness here is obvious. Likewise, as explained in the previous section, the failure of companies to "internalize" their environmental "externalities" spells unfairness.

Others are forced to pick up the tab when companies do not pay all the environmental costs involved in producing their own products. As mentioned in Chapter 5, those who adopt the broader view of corporate social responsibility emphasize that business and the rest of society have an implicit social contract. This contract reflects what society hopes to achieve by allowing business to operate; it sets the "rules of the game" governing business activity. Companies that try to be free riders in environmental matters or who refuse to address the spillover or external costs of their business activity violate this contract.

So far this chapter has emphasized that we need to view the environment differently if we are to improve our quality of life and even to continue to exist. And it has just stressed how the failure of an individual or business to play its part is unfair. Some moral theorists, like William T. Blackstone, have gone further to argue that each of us has a human right to a livable environment. "Each person," Blackstone argues, "has this right *qua* being human and because a livable environment is essential for one to fulfill his human capacities."[18] This right has emerged, he contends, as a result of changing environmental conditions, which affect the very possibility of human life as well as the possibility of realizing other human rights.

Recognition of a right to a livable environment would strengthen further the ethical reasons for business to respect the integrity of the natural world. In addition, recognition of this moral right could, Blackstone suggests, form a sound basis for establishing a legal right to a livable environment through legislation and even, perhaps, through a constitutional amendment or an environmental bill of rights. An official recognition of such rights would enhance our ability to go after polluters and other abusers of the natural environment.

Acknowledging a human right to a livable environment, however, does not solve many of the difficult problems facing us. In the effort to conserve irreplaceable resources, to protect the environment from further degradation, and to restore it to its former quality, we are still faced with difficult choices, each with its economic and moral costs. The next section focuses on pollution control, but most of the points apply equally to other problems of environmental protection, as well as to the conservation of scarce resources.

The Costs of Pollution Control

It is easy to say that we should do whatever it takes to improve the environment. Before this answer has any operational worth, however, we must consider a number of things. One is the quality of environment that we want. This can vary from an environment restored to its pristine state to one minimally improved over its current condition. Then there's the question of precisely what is necessary to bring about the kind of environment we want. In some cases we may lack the technological capacity to restore the environment. Finally, an important concern in any determination of what should be done to improve the environment is a calculation of what it will cost.

To draw out this point, we must consider a major technique for determining the total costs of environmental improvement. *Cost-benefit analysis* is a device used to determine whether it's worthwhile to incur a particular cost—for instance, the cost of employing a particular pollution-control device. The general approach is to evaluate a project's direct and indirect costs and benefits, the difference being the net result for society. Suppose that the estimated environmental damage of operating a particular plant is $1 million per year, that closing the plant would have dire economic consequences for the community, and that the only technique that would permit the plant to operate in an environmentally nondamaging way would cost $6 million per year. In this case, cost-benefit analysis would rule against requiring the plant to introduce the new technique.* If the cost of the technique had been only $800,000, however, cost-benefit analysis would have favored it.

Cost-benefit analysis can quickly get very complicated. For example, in determining whether it would be worthwhile to initiate more stringent air-pollution standards for a particular industry, a multitude of factors must be considered. Possible costs might include lower corporate profits, higher prices for consumers, unfavorable effects on employment, and adverse consequences for the nation's balance of payments. On the side of anticipated benefits, a reduction in airborne particulates over urban areas would reduce illness and premature death from bronchitis, lung cancer, and other respiratory diseases by some determinate percentage. The increase in life expectancy would have to be estimated along with projected savings in medical costs and increases in pro-ductivity. In addition, diminished industrial discharges would mean reduced property and crop damage from air pollution, and that would save more money.

This example suggests the extreme difficulty of making reliable estimates of actual costs and benefits, of putting price tags on the different effects of the policy being considered. Any empirical prediction in a case like this is bound to be controversial. This problem is compounded by the fact that decision makers are unlikely to know for certain all future results of the policy being studied. Not only is estimating the likelihood of its various possible effects difficult, but some future effects may be entirely unanticipated.

The new discipline of ecological economics is attempting to expand further the boundaries of environmental cost-benefit analysis by calculating the value of an ecosys-tem in terms of what it would cost to provide the benefits and services it now furnishes us—for example, the worth of a wetland in terms of the cost of constructing structures that provide the same flood control and storm protection that natural wetlands do.[19] Although conventional economists dismiss the idea of equating the value of some-thing with its replacement cost rather than with what people are willing to pay for it, ecological economists respond that traditional market pricing fails to capture the non-marketed externalities that nature provides, such as the nutrients that a forest recycles. In one study, for example, ecological economists established that a mangrove swamp in Thailand was worth 72 percent more when left intact to provide timber, charcoal, fish, and storm protection than when converted to a fish farm. "In every case we looked at," states Cambridge University biologist Andrew Balmford, "the loss of nature's services outweighed the benefits of development, often by large amounts."[20]

Even putting aside the debate over ecological economics, cost-benefit analyses of rival environmental policies will frequently prove controversial because they inevitably involve making value judgments about nonmonetary costs and benefits. Costs relative to time, effort, and discomfort can and must be introduced. Benefits can take even more numerous forms: health, convenience, comfort, enjoyment, leisure, self-fulfillment, freedom from odor, enhanced beauty, and so on. Benefits are especially difficult to cal-culate in environmental matters because they often take an aesthetic form. Some envi-ronmentalists, for example, may campaign for the preservation of a remote forest visited annually by only a handful of stalwart backpackers, whereas developers wish

---

*Cost-benefit analysis would not, however, prevent other strategies for getting the plant to internalize this external-ity. It could be taxed $1 million or be required to reimburse those who suffer the $1 million loss.

to convert it into a more accessible and frequented ski resort. Should the forest be preserved or should it be converted into a ski resort? Conflicting value judgments are at stake.

With the assistance of an economics consulting firm, the U.S. Department of the Interior asked Americans how much they are willing to shell out for environmental restoration. For instance, what would each consent to pay to restore the ecological balance of the Grand Canyon, even if few of them will actually see or truly understand the improvements: Ten cents a month? A dollar a month? Ten dollars a month? The Interior Department used this technique to justify reintroducing wolves into parts of Montana, Wyoming, and Idaho—a controversial move opposed by some taxpayers, ranchers, and consumers of beef. Some environmentalists applaud this attempt to calculate what economists call "non-use value," but others fear that the attempt to put a monetary price tag on ecosystems belittles the values they champion.[21]

An evaluation of costs and benefits is unavoidably wed to value judgments—to assessments of worth and the ranking of values. Although a cost-effectiveness analysis may be necessary for determining the soundness of an environmental-preservation measure or a pollution-control project, it seems inevitable that any assessment of costs and benefits will be subject to various factual uncertainties and significantly influenced by the values one holds. This is especially true in situations where environmental concerns clash. Windmills, for example, offer a clean, endless renewal source of energy, but they blemish the natural landscape and can chop up migratory birds.[22] Technology that replaces wood fiber with calcium carbonate in the production of paper saves trees, but mining it sometimes despoils bucolic areas.[23]

Who Should Pay the Costs?

The most comprehensive federal study of air pollution rules shows the cost of compliance to be outweighed five to seven times by the economic benefits from reductions in hospitalization, emergency room visits, premature deaths, and lost workdays.[24] In addition, of course, money spent to minimize pollution benefits those paid to clean up or prevent the pollution. Indeed, restoring the environment could become the biggest economic enterprise of our times, a huge source of jobs, profits, and poverty alleviation.[25] Still, environmental protection and restoration do not come cheap, and determining who should pay the necessary costs raises a tough question of social justice. Two popular answers to this question currently circulate: that those responsible for causing the pollution ought to pay, and that those who stand to benefit from protection and restoration should pick up the tab.

Those Responsible   The claim that those responsible for causing the pollution ought to pay the costs of pollution control and environmental restoration seems eminently fair until one asks a simple question. Just who is responsible for the pollution? Who are the polluters? Many people argue that big business is the chief polluter and therefore ought to bear the lion's share of the costs of environmental protection and restoration. Moreover, a policy of making polluters pick up the tab would probably have the desirable social effect of shifting income from the richer to the poorer and thus providing for a more equitable distribution of wealth. In the minds of some persons, the question of who should pay the bill is connected with the fair and just distribution of wealth.

Although business probably has benefited financially more than any other group from treating the environment as a free good, not all corporate wealth or even most of it has resulted directly from doing so. Moreover, consumers themselves have benefited enormously by not having to pay higher costs for products. In fact, some would argue that consumers are primarily to blame for pollution because they create the demand for the products whose production impairs the environment. Therefore, it is the consumer, not business, who should pay to protect and restore the environment. In this way, the argument goes, social costs are not unfairly passed on to those who have not incurred them.

However, both versions of the polluter-should-pay-the-bill thesis, one attributing primary responsibility for pollution to big business, the other to consumers, largely ignore the manifold, deep-rooted causes of environmental degradation.

Two important causes of pollution have been a growing population and its increasing concentration in urban areas. In 1900, Americans numbered 76.2 million; now at the beginning of the twenty-first century our population has more than tripled, to over 292 million. An increasingly urbanized nation, we are a long way from the rural, agriculturally oriented society we once were. Today, for example, the number of college students is more than three times the entire U.S. farm population. More than 70 million Americans live in our ten largest metropolitan areas, and nearly half the country lives in metropolitan areas with populations of a million or more. This tremendous population growth and equally staggering level of urbanization have brought with them an ever-increasing demand for goods and services, natural resources, energy, and industrial production. And these in turn have increased air, water, space, and noise pollution.

Another root cause of environmental problems is rising affluence. As people get more money to spend, they buy and consume more tangible goods, discard them more quickly, and produce more waste, all of which hasten degradation of the environment. Americans today produce 60 percent more garbage per capita than we did thirty years ago, almost 1,600 pounds per person per year.[26] We own more than 221 million motor vehicles[27]—far and away the world record—and are only making matters worse by our growing preference for big, gas-guzzling pickups, minivans, and sports utility vehicles, which emit significantly more carbon dioxide (a principal cause of global warming) and nitrogen oxides (the main source of smog) than ordinary passenger cars do.

Thus, the enemy in the war against environmental abuse turns out to be all of us. No solution to the question of who should pay the costs of pollution control can ignore this fact.

Those Who Would Benefit   A second popular reply to the payment problem is that those who will benefit from environmental improvement should pay the costs.

It's true that workers in certain industries and people living in certain neighborhoods or regions benefit more than other people from environmental controls. The residents of the Los Angeles basin, for instance, gain more from stringently enforced auto-emission standards than do those living in a remote corner of Wyoming. The trouble with this argument, though, is that every individual, rich or poor, and every institution, large or small, stands to profit in some way from environmental improvement, albeit not necessarily to the same degree. As a result, the claim that those who will benefit should pay the costs is not satisfactory, because everyone is touched by pollution. If, on the other hand, this position means that individuals and groups should pay to the degree that they will benefit, then one must wonder how this could possibly be determined. For example, changing the operation of the Glen Canyon Dam has raised electricity bills in the West, but it has reduced ecological damage to the Grand Canyon. Who benefits the most—local residents, visitors to the Grand Canyon, all who value this national resource—and how much should they pay?[28] But perhaps the most serious objection to this thesis is that it seems to leave out responsibility as a legitimate criterion.

Any equitable solution to the problem of who should pay the bill of environmental cleanup should take into account responsibility as well as benefit. The preceding analysis suggests that we all share the blame for pollution and collectively stand to benefit from environmental improvement. This doesn't mean, however, that we can't pinpoint certain areas of industry as chronic polluters. Electric-power plants, for example, are one of the major sources of greenhouse gases, but not all plants are equally dirty. Rather, old coal-burning plants that have resisted modernization produce a disproportionate share of the pollution. Likewise, some companies can be singled out as having particularly distressing environmental records. DuPont's eighty-five facilities, for example, release more than a million pounds of toxic material every day, making it the largest singer emitter of hazardous chemicals, and GM releases three times more toxics than either Ford or Chrysler.[29] The EPA lists Dow Chemical as the potentially responsible party in forty-five Superfund toxic waste sites.[30]

Still, the point is that a fair and just program for assigning costs begins with a recognition that we all bear responsibility for environmental problems and that we all stand to benefit from correcting them. But even if we agree that it is only fair that everyone share the cost of environmental improvement, we can still wonder about how the bill ought to be paid. What would be the fairest and most effective way of handling those costs?

COST ALLOCATION

Most would probably agree that environmental pollution cannot be stopped unless business and government work together. The main proposals for protecting and revitalizing the environment conceptualize government as initiating programs that will prod business into responsible action. The moral question that concerns us, then, is the fairest way of allocating costs for environmental renewal.

Three approaches have gained the most attention: the use of regulations, incentives, and pricing mechanisms. Although similar in some respects, they carry different assumptions about the roles of government and business, as well as about what's fair and just. Each approach has distinct advantages and weaknesses; each raises some questions of social justice.

Regulations

The regulatory approach makes use of direct public regulation and control in determining how the pollution bill is paid. State and federal legislation and regulations formulated by agencies such as the EPA set environmental standards, which are then applied and enforced by those agencies, other regulatory bodies, and the courts. An emissions standard that, for example, prohibits industrial smokestacks from releasing more than a certain percentage of particulate matter would require plants exceeding that standard to comply with it by installing an appropriate pollution-control device.

A clear advantage to such a regulatory approach is that standards would be legally enforceable. Firms not meeting them could be fined or even shut down. Also, from the view of morality, such standards are fair in that they apply to all industries in the same way. There are, however, distinct disadvantages in this approach.

First, pollution statutes and regulations generally require polluters to use the strongest feasible means of pollution control. But that requires the EPA or some other regulatory body to investigate pollution-control technologies and economic conditions in each industry to find the best technology that companies can afford. Such studies may require tens of thousands of pages of documentation, and legal proceedings may be necessary before the courts give final approval to the regulation. Moreover, expecting the EPA to master the economics and technology of dozens of industries, from petrochemicals to steel to electric utilities, may be unreasonable. It is bound to make mistakes, asking more from some companies than they can ultimately achieve while letting others off too lightly.[31]

Second, there's the question of both the equity and the economic sense of requiring compliance with universal standards, without regard for the idiosyncratic nature of each industry or the particular circumstances of individual firms. Is it reasonable to force two companies that cause very different amounts of environmental damage to spend the same amount on pollution abatement? In one case, the courts required two paper mills on the West Coast to install expensive pollution-control equipment, even though their emissions were diluted effectively by the Pacific Ocean. It took a special act of Congress to rescue the mills.[32]

Although universal environmental standards are fair in the sense that they apply to all equally, this very fact raises questions about their effectiveness. In attempting to legislate realistic and reliable standards for all, will government so dilute the standards that they become ineffectual? Or consider areas where the environment is cleaner than government standards. In such cases, should an industry be allowed to pollute up to the maximum of the standard? The Supreme Court thinks not. In a case brought before it by the Sierra Club, the Court ruled that states with relatively clean air must prohibit industries from producing significant air pollution even when EPA standards are not violated. In this case a firm is being forced to pay the costs of meeting an environmental standard that, in one sense, is sterner than what competitors must meet elsewhere.

Regulation can also take away an industry's incentive to do more than the minimum required by law. No polluter has any incentive to discharge less muck than regulations allow. No entrepreneur has an incentive to devise technology that will bring pollution levels below the registered maximum. Moreover, firms have an incentive not to let the EPA know they can pollute less. Under the regulatory approach, a government agency may have the desire to regulate pollution but lack the information to do it efficiently. The position of industry is reversed: It may have the information and the technology but no desire to use it.[33]

Finally, there's the problem of displacement costs resulting from industrial relocation or shutdown due to environmental regulations. For example, Youngstown Sheet and Tube Company moved its corporate headquarters and some production lines to the Chicago area, thus eliminating 500 jobs in Youngstown and causing serious economic problems in nearby communities. One of the reasons for the transfer was the need to implement water-pollution controls, which depleted vital capital. Consider also the marginal firms that would fail while attempting to meet the costs of such standards. When air-pollution regulations were applied to a sixty-year-old cement plant in San Juan

Bautista, California, the plant had to close because it was too obsolete to meet the standard economically. The shut-down seriously injured the economy of the little town, which had been primarily supported by the cement plant.[34]

On the other hand, if regulations are tougher for new entrants to an industry than for existing firms, as they often are, then new investment may be discouraged—even if newer plants would be cleaner than older ones. For example, a clause in the Clean Air Act exempts old coal-fired plants from complying with current emissions rules. As a result, much of America's electricity is produced by plants that are well over thirty years old and far dirtier than newer plants would be.[35] Perhaps at the time it was fair not to force existing plants into compliance with new rules. But is it still fair decades later? Clearly, then, a regulatory approach to environmental improvement, while having advantages, also raises serious questions.

Incentives

A widely supported approach to the problem of cost allocation for environmental improvement is government investment, subsidy, and general economic incentive. For instance, government might give firms a tax break for purchasing (and using) pollution-control equipment, or it might offer matching grants to companies that install such devices. A different example is the "FutureGen" project, launched in 2003. It commits the federal government to underwriting 80 percent of the $1 billion or so cost of industry's developing a cost-effective new generation of coal-fired plants that emit no greenhouse gases into the atmosphere.

In its "33/50 Program," the EPA tried a novel approach. It asked 600 industrial facilities to reduce voluntarily their discharges of seventeen toxic contaminants, first by 33 percent, then by 50 percent. The incentive for firms to commit to the reductions was simply the public relations opportunities afforded by EPA press releases and outstanding performance awards—along with, perhaps, the firms' desire to stave off future regulatory action.[36] The advantage of an incentive approach is that it minimizes government interference in business and encourages voluntary action rather than coercing compliance, as in the case of regulation. By allowing firms to move at their own pace, it avoids the evident unfairness to firms that cannot meet regulatory standards and must either relocate or fail. In addition, whereas regulated standards can encourage minimum legal compliance, an incentive approach provides an economic reason for going beyond minimal compliance. Firms have a financial inducement to do more than just meet EPA standards.

But incentives are not without disadvantages that bear moral overtones. First, as an essentially voluntary device, an incentive program is likely to be slow. Environmental problems that cry out for a solution may continue to fester. Incentive programs may allow urgently needed action to be postponed. In addition, government incentive programs often amount to a subsidy for polluters, with polluting firms being paid not to pollute. Although this approach may sometimes address the economics of pollution more effectively than the regulatory approach, it nonetheless raises questions about the justice of benefiting not the victims of pollution but some of the egregious polluters. In addition, incentive programs are open to abuse, and determining their cost-effectiveness can be problematic. In particular, when it comes to tax incentives, unscrupulous firms may be able to distort the true costs of their anti-pollution expenditures when filing their tax returns.

Pricing Mechanisms

A third approach to the cost-allocation problem involves programs designed to charge firms for the amount of pollution they produce. This could take the form of pricing mechanisms, or effluent charges, which spell out the cost for a specific kind of pollution in a specific area at a specific time. The prices would vary from place to place and from time to time and would be tied to the amount of damage caused. For example, during the summer months in the Los Angeles basin, a firm might pay much higher charges for fly ash emitted into the environment than it would during the winter months. Whatever the set of prices, they would apply equally to every producer of a given type of pollution at the same time and place. The more a firm pollutes, the more it pays.

One advantage in this approach is that it places the cost of pollution control on the polluters. Pricing mechanisms or effluent charges would penalize, not compensate, industrial polluters. For many persons this is inherently fairer than a program that compensates polluters.

Also, because costs are internalized, firms would be encouraged to do more than meet the minimal requirements established under a strict regulatory policy. Under this approach a firm, in theory, could be charged for any amount of pollution and not just incur legal penalties whenever it exceeded an EPA standard. In effect, pollution costs become production costs.

Pollution Permits   Instead of imposing a tax or a fee on the pollutants released into the environment, the government could charge companies for pollution permits. Or it could auction off a limited number of permits. An even more market-oriented strategy is to give companies permits to discharge a limited amount of pollution and then to allow them to buy and sell the right to emit pollutants. With pollution permits, companies with low pollution levels can make money by selling their pollution rights to companies with poorer controls. Thus, each firm can estimate the relative costs of continuing to pollute as opposed to investing in cleaner procedures. The government can also set the precise amount of pollution it is prepared to allow and, by lowering the amount permitted over time, can reduce or even eliminate it.

The EPA successfully experimented with this strategy in the 1970s when it gave oil refineries two years to reduce the allowable lead content in gasoline. Refineries received quotas on lead, which they could then trade with one another. Later, the 1990 Clean Air Act Amendments adopted this approach with respect to the sulfur dioxide (SO_2) emissions of electric utilities. Although controversial at the time—the power industry insisted the SO_2 cuts were prohibitively costly while environmental groups derided the measure as a sham—the scheme has surpassed its initial objectives and at a far lower cost than expected.[37]

Although pricing mechanisms and pollution permits may not work in all situations and for all environmental problems, economists generally favor using them wherever possible. However, they trouble many environmentalists. For one thing, the price tag for polluting seems arbitrary. How will effluent charges or permit prices be set? What is a fair price? Any decision seems bound to reflect debatable economic and value judgments. Moreover, environmentalists dislike the underlying principle of pricing mechanisms and pollution permits and view with suspicion anything that sounds like a license to pollute. They resent the implication that companies have a right to pollute and reject the notion that companies should be able to make money by selling this right to other firms. In fact, Michael J. Sandel, professor of government at Harvard, argues that it's immoral to buy the right to pollute. "Turning pollution into a commodity to be bought and sold removes the moral stigma that is properly associated with it," he says.[38]

In sum, although each of these approaches to cost allocation has decided advantages, none is without its weak points. Because there appears to be no single, ideal approach to all our environmental problems, a combination of regulation, incentive, effluent charges, and permits is probably called for. Any such combination must take into account not only effectiveness but also fairness to those who will have to foot the bill. Fairness in turn calls for input from all sectors of society, a deliberate commitment on the part of all parties to work in concert, a sizable measure of good faith, and perhaps above all else a heightened sense of social justice. This is no mean challenge.

Still, environmental protection is not always a static trade-off, with a fixed economic price to be paid for the gains we want. One reason is that higher environmental standards and properly designed regulatory programs can pressure corporations to invest capital in newer, state-of-the-art manufacturing technology; this both reduces pollution and enhances productive efficiency. In addition, international data in a range of industrial sectors show that innovation can minimize or even eliminate the costs of conforming to tougher environmental standards by increasing productivity, lowering total costs, and improving product quality.[39] The reason is that pollution is evidence of economic waste. The discharge of scrap, chemical wastes, toxic substances, or energy in the form of pollution is a sign that resources have been used inefficiently.

Consider some examples.[40] Environmental regulations forced Dow Chemical to redesign the production process at its complex in California to avoid storing chemical waste in evaporation ponds. Not only did the new process reduce waste, but the company found that it could reuse part of it as raw material in other parts of the plant. For a cost of $250,000 Dow is now saving $2.4 million each year. Likewise, when new environmental standards forced 3M to reduce the volume of solvents to be disposed of, the company found a way to avoid the use of solvents altogether, which yielded it an annual savings of more than $200,000. Most distillers of coal tar opposed regulations requiring them to reduce benzene emissions; they thought the only solution was to cover tar storage tanks with costly gas blankets. But Aristech Chemical Corporation found a way to remove benzene from tar in the first processing step. Instead of a cost increase, the company saved itself $3.3 million.

A broad array of economists, led by Nobel laureates Kenneth J. Arrow and Robert M. Solow, have urged that with regard to global warming, measures to reduce greenhouse gas emissions need not harm the economy and "may in fact improve U.S. productivity in the long run." This is because many innovative, energy-efficient technologies are just waiting for the right financial incentives to enter the market. And in many of these fields, U.S. industry is the leader.[41]

DELVING DEEPER INTO ENVIRONMENTAL ETHICS

So far the discussion of environmental ethics has focused on business's obligation to understand its environmental responsibilities, to acknowledge and internalize its externalities (or spillovers), and to avoid free riding. It has stressed the extent to which environmental protection is in our collective self-interest, and it has looked at the operational and moral dilemmas involved in dealing with the costs of pollution.

The subject of environmental ethics can be pursued more deeply than this, and many moral theorists would advocate doing so. In particular, they would insist that we also consider our obligations to those who live outside our society. The United States has 4.6 percent of the world's population but uses 30 percent of the world's refined oil. Similar figures hold for other nonrenewable natural resources. Moreover, the United States must depend on foreign nations to supply its needs.

The average amount of energy consumed per year by a person in the United States is 3.3 times that of the average Hungarian, 5.2 times that of a Chilean, 12.1 times that of a Chinese, and 27 times that of someone in India.[42] The birth of a baby in the United States imposes more than a hundred times the stress on the world's resources as a birth in, say, Bangladesh. Babies from Bangladesh do not grow up to own automobiles and air conditioners or to eat huge quantities of grain-fed beef. Their lifestyles do not require large inputs of minerals and energy, and they do not undermine the planet's life-support capacity.[43]

Tropical rain forests are of special concern. They are the earth's richest, oldest, and most complex ecosystems. Tropical forests are major reservoirs of biodiversity, home to 40 to 50 percent of all types of living things—as many as 5 million species of plants, animals, and insects. At least 50 million acres of tropical rain forest are destroyed each year, or 100 acres every minute. And already half the globe's original rain forest has disappeared. Tropical forests are often cleared in an attempt to provide farms for growing Third World populations, but the affluence of people in rich nations like the United States is responsible for much forest destruction. Central American forests are cleared in part for pasture land to make pet food and convenience food slightly cheaper in the United States. In Papua, New Guinea, forests are destroyed to supply cardboard packaging for Japanese electronic products. Thus, an affluent American living thousands of miles away can cause more tropical forest destruction than a poor person living within the forest itself.[44]

Our bloated levels of consumption, our dependence on foreign resources to satisfy our needs, and the impact of both on the economies and environments of other nations raise a variety of moral and political issues. This section mentions briefly just two of those problems.

First is the question of how the continued availability of foreign resources is to be secured. Will our need for resources outside our territory lead us to dominate other lands, politically and economically, particularly in the Middle East, Asia, and Latin America? To do so is morally risky, because political and economic domination almost always involves violations of the rights and interests of the dominated population, as well as of our own moral ideals and values.

Second is the question of whether any nation has a right to consume the world's irreplaceable resources at a rate so grossly out of proportion to the size of its population. Of course, we pay to consume resources like oil that other nations own, but in the view of many the fact that other nations acquiesce in our disproportionate consumption of resources does not resolve the moral problem of our doing so. Are we respecting the needs and interests of both our present co-inhabitants on this planet and the future generations who will live on Earth? This question is particularly burning now that scientists believe that human demand for natural resources has outstripped the biosphere's regenerative capacity.[45]

Obligations to Future Generations

Almost everybody feels intuitively that it would be wrong to empty the globe of resources and to irreparably contaminate the environment that we pass on to future generations. Certainly there is a danger that we will do both of these things. But the question of what moral obligations we have to future generations is surprisingly difficult, and discussion among philosophers has not resolved all the important theoretical issues.

Even though most of us agree that it would be immoral to make the world uninhabitable for future people, can we talk meaningfully of those future generations having a right that we not do this? After all, our remote descendants are not yet alive and thus cannot claim a right to a livable environment. In fact, since these generations do not yet exist, they cannot at present, it seems, be said to have any interests at all. How can they then have rights?

Professor of philosophy Joel Feinberg argues, however, that whatever future human beings turn out to be like, they will have interests that we can affect, for better or worse, right now. Even though we do not know who the future people will be, we do know that they will have interests and what the general nature of those interests will be. This is enough, he contends, both to talk coherently about their having rights and to impose a duty on us not to leave ecological time bombs for them.

Feinberg concedes that it doesn't make sense to talk about future people having a right to be born. The child that you could conceive tonight, if you felt like it, cannot intelligibly be said to have a right to be born. Thus, the rights of future generations are "contingent," says Feinberg, on those future people coming into existence. But this qualification does not affect his main contention: "The interests that [future people] are sure to have when they come into being . . . cry out for protection from invasions that can take place now."[46]

Even if we are persuaded that future generations have rights, we still do not know exactly what those rights are or how they are to be balanced against the interests and rights of present people. If we substantially injure future generations to gain some small benefit for ourselves, we are being as selfish and shortsighted as we would be by hurting other people today for some slight advantage for ourselves. Normally, however, if the benefits of some environmental policy outweigh the costs, then a strong case can be made for adopting the policy. But what if it is the present generation that receives the benefits and future generations that pay the costs? Would it be unfair of us to adopt such a policy? Would doing so violate the rights of future people?

An additional puzzle is raised by the fact that policies we adopt will affect who is born in the future. Imagine that we must choose between two environmental policies, one of which would cause a slightly higher standard of living over the next century. Given the effects of those policies on the details of our lives, over time it would increasingly be true that people would marry different people under one policy than they would under the other. And even within the same marriages, children would increasingly be conceived at different times:

Some of the people who are later born would owe their existence to our choice of one of the two policies. If we had chosen the other policy, these particular people would never have existed. And the proportion of those later born who owe their existence to our choice would, like ripples in a pool, steadily grow. We can plausibly assume that, after three centuries, there would be no one living in our community who would have been born whichever policy we chose.*

This reasoning suggests that subsequent generations cannot complain about an environmental policy choice we make today that causes them to have fewer opportunities and a lower standard of living. If we had made a different choice, then those people would not have existed at all. On the other hand, it can be claimed that we act immorally in causing people to exist whose rights to equal opportunity and an equally high standard of living cannot be fulfilled. But if those future people knew the facts, would they regret that we acted as we did?[47]

Perhaps it is mistaken to focus on the rights and interests of future people as individuals. Annette Baier argues that the important thing is to "recognize our obligations to consider the good of the continuing human community."[48] This stance suggests adopting a utilitarian perspective and seeking to maximize total human happiness through time. But a utilitarian approach is also not without problems. If our concern is with total happiness, we may be required to increase greatly the earth's population. Even if individuals on an overcrowded earth do not have much happiness, there may still be more total happiness than there would be if we followed a population-control policy that resulted in fewer but better-off people. This distasteful conclusion has led some utilitarians to modify their theory and maintain that with regard to population policy we should aim for the highest average happiness rather than the highest total happiness. But this, too, is problematic because in theory one could, it seems, increase average happiness by eliminating unhappy people.

John Rawls has suggested another approach to the question of our obligations to future generations, an approach that reflects his general theory of justice (which was discussed in Chapter 3). He suggests that the members of each generation put themselves in the "original position." Then, without knowing what generation they belong to, they could decide what would be a just way of distributing resources between consecutive generations. They would have to balance how much they are willing to sacrifice for their descendants against how much they wish to inherit from their predecessors. In other words, the device of the original position and veil of ignorance might be used to determine our obligations to future generations—in particular, how much each generation should save for use by those who inherit the earth from it.[49]

The Value of Nature

A more radical approach to environmental ethics goes beyond the question of our obligations to future generations. It challenges the human-centered approach adopted so far. Implicit in the discussion has been the assumption that preservation of the environment is good solely because it is good for human beings. This reflects a characteristic human attitude that nature has no intrinsic value, that it has value only because people value it. If human nature were different and none of us cared about the beauty of, say, the Grand Canyon, then it would be without value.

---

*Derek Parfit, *Reasons and Persons* (New York: Oxford University Press, 1986), 361. Parfit adds: "It may help to think about this question: How many of us could truly claim, 'Even if railways and motor cars had never been invented, I would still have been born'?"

Many writers on environmental issues do not recognize their anthropocentric, or human-oriented, bias. William F. Baxter is one who does. In discussing his approach to the pollution problem, Baxter mentions the fact that the use of DDT in food production is causing damage to the penguin population. He writes:

My criteria are oriented to people, not penguins. Damage to penguins, or sugar pines, or geological marvels is, without more, simply irrelevant. . . . Penguins are important because people enjoy seeing them walk about rocks. . . . In short, my observations about environmental problems will be people-oriented. . . . I have no interest in preserving penguins for their own sake. . . .

I reject the proposition that we *ought* to respect the "balance of nature" or to "preserve the environment" unless the reason for doing so, express or implied, is the benefit of man.[50]

Contrast Baxter's position with what Holmes Rolston III calls the "naturalistic ethic." Advocates of a naturalistic ethic contend, contrary to Baxter's view, "that some natural objects, such as whooping cranes, are morally considerable in their own right, apart from human interests, or that some ecosystems, perhaps the Great Smokies, have intrinsic values, such as aesthetic beauty, from which we derive a duty to respect these landscapes."[51] Human beings may value a mountain for a variety of reasons—because they can hike it, build ski lifts on it, mine the ore deep inside it, or simply because they like looking at it. According to a naturalistic ethic, however, the value of the mountain is not simply a function of these human interests. Nature can have value in and of itself, apart from human beings.

Some defenders of a naturalistic ethic contend that we have a particularly strong obligation to preserve species from extinction. This attitude, shared by many, was one of the factors behind the controversial legal efforts to prevent construction of the Tellico Dam on the Little Tennessee River in order to save the only known population of snail darters. But do species really have value above and beyond the individuals that make them up? Scientists have formally identified 1.8 million species (including, for example, 6,700 kinds of starfish, 12,000 species of earthworm, and 400,000 types of beetle), and recent studies suggest that the number of species inhabiting the planet may be much, much higher—with perhaps as many as 30 million kinds of insects alone. Species are always coming into and going out of existence.[52] How valuable is this diversity of species, and how far are we morally required to go in maintaining it?

Adopting a naturalistic ethic would definitely alter our way of looking at nature and our understanding of our moral obligations to preserve and respect the natural environment. Many philosophers doubt, however, that nature has intrinsic value or that we can be said to have moral duties to nature. Having interests is a precondition, they would contend, of something's having rights or of our having moral duties to that thing. Natural objects, however, have no interests. Can a rock meaningfully be said to have an interest in not being eroded or in not being smashed into smaller pieces?

Plants and trees are different from rocks and streams. They are alive, and we can talk intelligibly about what is good or bad for a tree, plant, or vegetable. They can flourish or do poorly. Nonetheless, philosophers who discuss moral rights generally hold that this is not enough for plants to be said to have rights. To have rights, a thing must have genuine interests, and to have interests, most theorists contend, a thing must have beliefs and desires. Vegetative life, however, lacks any cognitive awareness. Claims to the contrary are biologically unsupportable.

Even if the plant world lacks rights, can it still have intrinsic value? Can we still have a moral obligation to respect that world and not abuse it? Or are the only morally relevant values the various interests of human beings and other sentient creatures? These are difficult questions. Among philosophers there is no consensus on how to answer them.

Our Treatment of Animals

Above a certain level of complexity, animals do have at least rudimentary cognitive awareness. No owner of a cat or dog doubts that his pet has beliefs and desires. Accordingly, a number of philosophers have recently defended the claim that animals can have rights. Because they have genuine interests, animals can have genuine moral rights—despite the fact that they cannot claim their rights, that they cannot speak, that we cannot reason with them, and that they themselves lack a moral sense. Animals, it is more and more widely contended, do not have to be equal to human beings to have certain moral rights that we must respect.

Rather than talking about animals' rights, utilitarians would stress that higher animals are sentient—that is, that they are capable of feeling pain. Accordingly, there can be no justifiable reason for excluding their pleasures and pains from the overall utilitarian calculus. As Jeremy Bentham, one of the founders of utilitarianism, put it: "The question is not, Can they *reason*? nor, Can they *talk*? but, Can they *suffer*?"[53] Our actions have effects on animals, and these consequences cannot be ignored. When one is deciding, then, what the morally right course of action is, the pleasures and pains of animals must be taken into account too.

Business affects the welfare of animals very substantially. One way is through experimentation and the testing of products on animals. Critics such as Peter Singer contend that the vast majority of experimentation and testing cannot be justified on moral grounds. Consider the "LD 50" test, which until recently was the standard method of testing new foodstuffs. The object of the test is to find the dosage level at which 50 percent of the test animals die. Nearly all test animals become very sick before finally succumbing or surviving. When the substance is harmless, huge doses must be forced down the animals, until in some cases the sheer volume kills them.[54]

In principle, utilitarians are willing to permit testing and experimentation on animals, provided the overall results justify their pain and suffering. Not only is this proviso frequently ignored, but human beings typically disregard altogether the price the animals must pay. Consider the actions of the pharmaceutical firm Merck Sharp and Dohme, which sought to import chimpanzees to test a vaccine for hepatitis B. Chimps are an endangered species and highly intelligent. Capturing juvenile chimps requires shooting the mother. One analyst assessed the situation this way:

> The world has a growing population of 4 billion people and a dwindling population of some 50,000 chimpanzees. Since the vaccine seems unusually innocuous, and since the disease is only rarely fatal, it would perhaps be more just if the larger population could find some way of solving its problem that was not to the detriment of the smaller.[55]

Business's largest and most devastating impact on animals, however, is through the production of animal-related products—in particular, meat. Many of us still think of our chicken and beef as coming from something like the idyllic farms pictured in storybooks, where the animals roam contentedly and play with the farmer's children. But meat and egg production is big business: Every year in the United States ten billion birds and mammals are raised and killed for food.[56] Today most of the animal products we eat are from factory farms. In 1921, the largest commercial egg farm had a flock of 2,000 hens that ran loose in a large pasture; today the largest commercial flock contains 2.5 million birds, and 80 percent of the 440 million laying hens are housed in 3 percent of the known chicken farms. These birds live in small multitiered wire cages.[57]

Laying hens that are stuffed into tiny cages with several other chickens now produce over 95 percent of our eggs. In these cages, hens are unable to satisfy such fundamental behavioral needs as stretching their wings, perching, walking, scratching, and nest building. Unsuited for wire cages, they suffer foot damage, feather loss, and other injuries. Birds are "debeaked" to prevent pecking injuries and cannibalism from overcrowding.[58]

Of the 95 million hogs born each year in the United States, 80 percent spend their lives in intensive confinement. Piglets are weaned after only three weeks and placed in bare wire cages or tiny cement pens. Once they reach 50 pounds, they are moved into bare 6-foot stalls with concrete-slatted floors. Veal calves have even worse lives. To produce gourmet "milk-fed" veal, newborn calves are taken from their mothers and chained in crates measuring only 22 inches by 54 inches. Here they spend their entire lives. To prevent muscle development and speed weight gain, the calves are allowed absolutely no exercise; they are unable even to turn around or lie down. Their special diet of growth stimulators and antibiotics causes chronic diarrhea, and the withholding of iron to make their meat light-colored makes them anemic. The calves are kept in total darkness to reduce restlessness.[59]

The individuals involved in the meat and animal-products industries are not brutal, but the desire to cut business costs and to economize routinely leads to treatment of animals that can only be described as cruel. Philosopher and animal-rights advocate Tom Regan describes their treatment this way:

> In increasing numbers, animals are being brought in off the land and raised indoors, in unnatural, crowded conditions—raised "intensively," to use the jargon of the animal industry. . . . The inhabitants of these "farms" are kept in cages, or stalls, or pens . . . living out their abbreviated lives in a technologically created and sustained environment: automated feeding, automated watering, automated light cycles, automated waste removal, automated what-not. And the crowding: as many as 9 hens in cages that measure 18 by 24 inches; veal calves confined to 22 inch wide stalls; hogs similarly confined, sometimes in tiers of cages, two, three, four rows high. Could any impartial, morally sensitive person view what goes on in a factory farm with benign approval?[60]

Moral vegetarians are people who reject the eating of meat on moral grounds. Their argument is simple and powerful: The raising of animals for meat, especially with modern factory farming, sacrifices the most important and basic interests of animals simply to satisfy human tastes. Americans eat, per capita, a phenomenal amount of meat, by some estimates more than twice as much as we ate in the 1950s. Chicken production alone is now five times what it was in 1960. Many people eat meat three times a day. Our preference for a Big Mac over a soybean burger is only a matter of taste and culture, but it accounts for many of the 100,000 cows we slaughter every day.[61] The extra pleasure we believe we get from eating the hamburger cannot justify the price the animals must pay.

Would it be wrong to eat animals that were raised humanely, like those that run around freely and happily in children's picture books of farms? Unlike the lives of animals that we do in fact eat, the lives of such humanely raised animals, before being abruptly terminated, are not painful ones. Some philosophers would contend that it is permissible to raise animals for food if their lives are, on balance, positive. Other moral theorists challenge this view, contending that at least higher animals have a right to life and should not be killed.

This debate raises important philosophical issues; but it is also rather hypothetical. Given economic reality, mass production of meat at affordable prices dictates factory farming. The important moral issue, then, is the real suffering and unhappy lives that billions of creatures experience on the way to our dinner tables. This aspect of environmental ethics is often overlooked, but it raises profound and challenging questions for business and consumers alike.

There are hopeful signs that human attitudes toward animal suffering, in general, and factory farming, in particular, are changing. In Florida voters recently amended their state constitution so as to ban the confining of sows to cages so narrow that they cannot turn around. And McDonald's now requires its egg suppliers to provide each hen with a minimum of 72 square inches of living space.[62] Other fast-food chains are following suit. For most American hens this is a 50 percent increase, but it falls well short of the European requirement that by 2012 all hens have at least 120 square inches as well as access to a perch and a nesting box to lay their eggs. In general, other countries are ahead of the U.S. with respect to their treatment of animals. In Britain now (and in the rest of Europe by 2007) it is illegal to treat pregnant sows or veal calves the way American companies do.[63] In New Zealand, one cannot experiment on great apes unless the research actually benefits the apes and this benefit outweighs their discomfort or suffering. And in 2002 the German constitution was changed to include the right of animals to be treated decently.[64]

SUMMARY

1. Business functions within a global ecological system. Because of the interrelated nature of ecosystems, and because intrusion into ecosystems frequently creates unfavorable effects, business must be sensitive to its impacts on the physical environment.

2. Traditionally, business has regarded the natural world as a free and unlimited good. Pollution and resource depletion are examples of situations in which each person's pursuit of self-interest can make everyone worse off (the "tragedy of the commons"). Business must be sensitive to possible disparities between its private economic costs and the social costs of its activities (the problem of externalities or spillovers).

3. Companies that attempt to be free riders in environmental matters or that refuse to address the external costs of their business activities behave unfairly. Some philosophers maintain, further, that each person has a human right to a livable environment.

4. Pollution control has a price, and trade-offs must be made. But weighing costs and benefits involves controversial factual assessments and value judgments. Any equitable solution to the problem of who should pay must recognize that all of us in some way contribute to the problem and benefit from correcting it.

5. Cost allocation requires a combination of regulations, incentives, and charges or permits for polluting. Such an approach must not only consider what is effective but must also seek a fair assignment of costs.

6. A broader view of environmental ethics considers our obligations to those in other societies and to future generations. Some philosophers argue that we must respect the right of future generations to inherit an environment that is not seriously damaged, but talk of the rights of future people raises puzzles.

7. Philosophers disagree about whether nature has intrinsic value. Some, adopting a human-oriented point of view, contend that the environment is valuable only because human beings value it. Those adopting a naturalistic ethic believe that the value of nature is not simply a function of human interests.

8. Through experimentation, testing, and the production of animal products, business has a very substantial impact on the welfare of animals. The meat and animal-products industries rely on factory-farming techniques, which many describe as cruel and horrible. Because of these conditions, moral vegetarians argue that meat eating is wrong.

CASE 11.1

Hazardous Homes in Herculaneum

Twenty-five miles or so outside of St. Louis, Missouri, lies little Herculaneum, a town of only 2,369 people. Looming over the town's economy and the local environment is the Doe Run Company's lead-smelter, which dates back to 1892 and is the largest in the United States. For over twenty years now federal and state regulators have been after the company for polluting. In 1991 they required Doe Run to replace the topsoil in the gardens of about ninety houses in the vicinity of its smelter. In 2001 a study found that 24 percent of the children under six living within a mile of the company's plant had dangerously high levels of lead in their blood. As a result, Doe Run has agreed to clean up the site and has started installing new pollution-control devices to prevent further contamination.[65]

In the meantime, however, environmental investigators have found lead levels as high as 300,000 parts per million on a road used by the plant's trucks. Because of the health hazard that lead contamination poses, the state government and the company want to move local residents temporarily from their homes, replace the topsoil in their lawns and gardens, and clean their houses of lead dust. The state has put up signs warning residents of Herculaneum not to let children play outside, and the federal government is helping out by advising people to alter their diets to resist lead poisoning (the gist: don't drink tea but eat more liver, eggs, whole-grain bread, and ice cream). Not so surprisingly, many residents of Herculaneum find this sort of assistance insulting. Instead, they want the federal government to step in, declare Herculaneum a Superfund cleanup site, and use federal funds to buy up the whole town. The Environmental Protection Agency (EPA), however, believes that adding Herculaneum to the long list of places seeking a Superfund buyout will only delay a solution.

The EPA is right not to exaggerate the speed with which Superfund projects move. When Congress created Superfund in 1980, sponsors of the legislation believed that the program could mop up the nation's worst toxic dumps and other dangerously polluted sites within five years and do so for a relatively modest $1.6 billion, to be covered by sales taxes on chemical and petroleum-based products. Superfund was authorized to recover its costs from the polluters themselves and to use this money to pay for future cleanup efforts. In this way, Superfund would become self-financing, with industry, not the taxpayers, picking up the tab. But the hopes of Superfund's sponsors have yet to be realized. Congress has repeatedly had to pour money into the program to keep it going; there are continual complaints about inefficient, top-heavy administration, and to date only a portion of the country's most environmentally damaged sites have been restored.

Moreover, Superfund has grown increasingly and staggeringly expensive. Its cleanup efforts have become mired in lawsuits, with the resulting litigation costs climbing to the stars. The problem, many observers believe, goes back to the initial Superfund legislation, which permits the EPA to penalize companies for dumping and polluting that was not illegal at the time it occurred. In addition, it makes individual polluters liable for the entire cleanup costs of toxic sites that may have been used by many other firms. Not only do corporations dislike these liability principles; they find it less expensive to resist the EPA in court than to pay up. "From the individual corporation's perspective," says David Morell, a toxic removal consultant and an expert on Superfund's history, "lawyers' bills are still cheaper than paying for an entire cleanup." And he adds: "The longer you can stall—and convince yourself that you may never have to pay at all—the more the legal fees seem like a bargain."

As a result, a flood of lawsuits has slowed Superfund's cleanup efforts to a crawl while the costs of those efforts have ballooned. "The idea [behind Superfund]," Morell says, "was supposed to be 'shovels first and litigation later.' Instead, it has become 'litigation first and shovels never.'" Many experts agree that Superfund has become a financial black hole. Legal fees, transaction costs, and administrative overhead associated with its cleanup projects are projected to exceed $200 billion. Others put the bill as high as $2,000 per person—paid in price increases on countless everyday chemical- and petroleum-based products. And this sum doesn't pay for the removal of hazardous wastes; it covers only litigation-related costs.

According to critics, Congress had done little to solve the problems with Superfund, except to keep digging deeper into the national coffers to keep it going. However, in 2001 Congress did exempt small businesses from Superfund liability if they contributed only a relatively small amount of hazardous waste to a targeted site, and it required the EPA to consider a company's ability to pay when negotiating a settlement. For its part, the EPA contends that it is making good progress. It reports that 760 of the 1,509 toxic waste sites now designated as National Priorities List Sites have been cleaned up and that work has started on over 400 more. Still, every day of delay increases the cleanup costs as waste from untreated sites seeps into the groundwater and increases the size of the polluted area. "These sites are not like fine wine," John O'Connor, director of the National Campaign Against Toxic Hazards, has explained. "They get worse with age, and they get more difficult and costly to clean up."

Meanwhile back in Herculaneum, the state of Missouri and Doe Run have come up with a plan to purchase the homes of twenty-six families who live within a half mile of the plant and have children under six years old and then later to buy up another 134 homes in the same area. Although the plan is voluntary, residents are questioning it for several reasons. First, two schools are within the half-mile zone. What is to be done with them? Second, the plan does nothing for the rest of

Herculaneum, where contamination, though less dangerous, is still serious. And finally there is no guarantee that the company will give the homeowners more than the fair market value of their homes—which is, unfortunately, practically nothing. Residents want pre-contamination prices.

Discussion Questions

1. Identify the values and describe the attitudes that have contributed to pollution problems like those at Herculaneum. How would you feel if you lived in Herculaneum?

2. Do individuals inside the company, now or in the past, bear responsibility for causing the environmental damage at Herculaneum, or is it only the company as a whole? Is that responsibility shared by anyone outside the company? Should families who moved to Herculaneum have known better?

3. Who should pay the costs of cleaning up Herculaneum—the company? The town? The state? The federal government? What if the cost of restoring Herculaneum exceeds Doe Run's resources? In general, whose responsibility is it to clean up the country's hazardous pollution sites and waste dumps?

4. What exactly should be done for residents living near the smelter? Are they entitled to receive the original cost of their homes from either the government or Doe Run? What about the rest of the town—should Superfund purchase all of it?

5. Is it fair for Superfund to fine polluters for dumping or polluting that was legal at the time? Is it fair that each individual polluter have full liability for cleaning up environmental damage to which others may have also contributed? How might Superfund be made to work better?

6. With regard to pollution in general and the disposal of toxic wastes in particular, what are the obligations of individual manufacturers and of society as a whole to future generations?

CASE 11.2

Poverty and Pollution

It is called Brazil's "valley of death," and it may be the most polluted place on Earth. It lies about an hour's drive south of São Paulo, where the land suddenly drops 2,000 feet to a coastal plain. More than 100,000 people live in the valley, along with a variety of industrial plants that discharge thousands of tons of pollutants into the air every day. A reporter for *National Geographic* recalls that within an hour of his arrival in the valley, his chest began aching as the polluted air inflamed his bronchial tubes and restricted his breathing.[66]

The air in the valley is loaded with toxins—among them benzene, a known carcinogen. One in ten of the area's factory workers has a low white-blood cell count, a possible precursor to leukemia. Infant mortality is 10 percent higher here than in the region as a whole. Out of 40,000 urban residents in the valley municipality of Cubatão, nearly 13,000 cases of respiratory disease were reported in a recent year.

Few of the local inhabitants complain, however. For them, the fumes smell of jobs. They also distrust bids to buy their property by local industry, which wants to expand, as well as government efforts to relocate them to free homesites on a landfill.

One young mother says, "Yes, the children are often ill and sometimes can barely breathe. We want to live in another place, but we cannot afford to."

A university professor of public health, Dr. Oswaldo Campos, views the dirty air in Cubatão simply as the result of economic priorities. "Some say it is the price of progress," Campos comments, "but is it? Look who pays the price—the poor."[67]

Maybe the poor do pay the price of pollution, but there are those who believe that they should have more of it. One of them is Lawrence Summers, who was chief economist of the World Bank and subsequently Secretary of the U.S. Treasury, and is now president of Harvard University. He has argued that the bank should encourage the migration of dirty, polluting industries to the poorer, less-developed countries.[68] Why? First, Summers reasons, the costs of health-impairing pollution depend on the earnings forgone from increased injury and death. So polluting should be done in the countries with the lowest costs—that is, with the lowest wages. "The economic logic behind dumping a load of toxic waste in the lowest-wage country," he writes, "is impeccable."

Second, because pollution costs rise disproportionately as pollution increases, it makes sense to shift pollution from already dirty places such as Los Angeles to clean ones like the relatively underpopulated countries in Africa, whose air Summers describes as "vastly *under*-polluted." Third, people value a clean environment more as their incomes rise. If other things are equal, costs fall if pollution moves from affluent places to less affluent places.

Critics charge that Summers views the world through "the distorting prism of market economics" and that his ideas are "a recipe for ruin." Not only do the critics want "greener" development in the Third World, but also they are outraged by Summers's assumption that the value of a life—or of increases or decreases in life expectancy—can be measured in terms of per capita income. This premise implies that an American's life is worth that of a hundred Kenyans and that society should value an extra year of life for a middle-level manager more than it values an extra year for a blue-collar, production-line worker.

Some economists, however, believe that Summers's ideas are basically on the right track. They emphasize that environmental policy always involves trade-offs and that therefore we should seek a balance between costs and benefits. As a matter of fact, the greatest cause of misery in the Third World is poverty. If environmental controls slow growth, then fewer people will be lifted out of poverty by economic development. For this reason, they argue, the richer countries should not impose their standards of environmental protection on poorer nations.

But even if economic growth is the cure for poverty, other economists now believe that sound environmental policy is necessary for durable growth, or at least that growth and environmental protection may not be incompatible. First, environmental damage can undermine economic productivity, and the health effects of pollution on a country's workforce reduce output. Second, poverty itself is an important cause of environmental damage because people living at subsistence levels are unable to invest in environmental protection. Finally, if economic growth and development are defined broadly enough, then enhanced environmental quality is part and parcel of the improvement in welfare that development must bring. For example, 1 billion people in developing countries lack access to clean water while 1.7 billion suffer from inadequate sanitation. Economic development for them means improving their environment. Still, rich and poor countries tend to have different environmental concerns: Environmentalists in affluent nations worry about protecting endangered species, preserving biological diversity, saving the ozone, and preventing climate change, whereas their counterparts in poorer countries are more concerned with dirty air, dirty water, soil erosion, and deforestation.

Update:
According to a World Bank report, environmental conditions have improved in Cubatão, where, thanks to state action and an aroused population, pollution is no worse today than in other medium-sized industrial cities in Brazil. True, it's no paradise, but some days you can see the sun, children are healthier, and fish are returning to the river (though their tissues are laced with toxic metals).[69]

Discussion Questions

1. What attitudes and values on the part of business and others lead to the creation of areas like the "valley of death"?

2. Should the Third World have more pollution, as Lawrence Summers argues? Assess his argument that dirty industries should move to poorer and less-polluted areas.

3. Some say, "Pollution is the price of progress." Is this assertion correct? What is meant by "progress"? Who in fact pays the price? Explain both the moral and economic issues raised by the assertion. What are the connections between economic progress and development, on one hand, and pollution controls and environmental protection, on the other?

4. Do human beings have a moral right to a livable environment? To a nonpolluted environment? It might be argued that if people in the "valley of death" don't complain and don't wish to move, then they accept the risks of living there and the polluters are not violating their rights. Assess this argument.

5. Assess the argument that people in the Third World should learn from the errors of the West and seek development without pollution. Should there be uniform, global environmental standards, or should pollution control standards be lower for less-developed countries?

CASE 11.3

The Fordasaurus

Before Ford publicly unveiled the biggest sport-utility vehicle ever, the Sierra Club ran a contest for the best name and marketing slogan for it. Among the entries were "Fordasaurus, powerful enough to pass anything on the highway except a gas station" and "Ford Saddam, the truck that will put America between Iraq and a hard place." But the winner was "Ford Valdez: Have you driven a tanker lately?"[70]

Ford, which decided to name the nine-passenger vehicle the Excursion, was not amused. Sales of sport-utility vehicles (SUVs) exploded in the 1990s, going up nearly sixfold, and the company sees itself as simply responding to consumer demand for ever larger models. Although most SUVs never leave the pavement, their drivers like knowing their vehicles can go anywhere and do anything. They also like their SUVs to be big. The Excursion is now the largest passenger vehicle on the road, putting Ford far ahead of its rivals in the competition to build the biggest and baddest SUV. The Excursion weighs 8,500 pounds, equivalent to two mid-sized sedans or three Honda Civics. It is more than 6½ feet wide, nearly 7 feet high, and almost 19 feet long—too big to fit comfortably into some garages or into a single parking space.

Although the Excursion is expensive ($40,000 to $50,000 when loaded with options), it is, like other SUVs, profitable to build. Because Ford based the Excursion on the chassis of its Super Duty truck, the company was able to develop the vehicle for a relatively modest investment of about $500 million. With sales of 50,000 to 60,000 per year, Ford earns about $20,000 per vehicle.

Most SUVs are classified as light trucks. Under current rules, they are allowed to emit up to several times more smog-causing gases per mile than automobiles. In 1999, the Clinton administration proposed tighter emissions restrictions on new passenger cars, restrictions that new vehicles in the light-truck category would also have to meet by 2009. However, these rules would not affect the Excursion, which is heavy enough to be classified as a medium-duty truck.

Ford says that the Excursion, with its 44-gallon gas tank, gets 10 to 15 miles per gallon, and that its emission of pollutants is 43 percent below the maximum for its class. By weight, about 85 percent of the vehicle is recyclable, and 20 percent of it comes from recycled metals and plastics. The company thus believes that the Excursion is in keeping with the philosophy of William Clay Ford, Jr. When he became chairman in September 1998, he vowed to make Ford "the world's most environmentally friendly auto maker." He added, however, that "what we do to help the environment must succeed as a business proposition. A zero-emission vehicle that sits unsold on a dealer's lot is not reducing pollution."

The company, however, has failed to win environmentalists to its side. They believe that with the Excursion, the Ford Company is a long way from producing an environmentally friendly product. Daniel Becker of the Sierra Club points out that in the course of an average lifetime of 120,000 miles, each Excursion will emit 130 tons of carbon dioxide, the principal cause of global warming. "It's just bad for the environment any way you look at it," he says. John DeCicco of the American Council for an Energy-Efficient Economy agrees. He worries further that the Excursion is clearing the way for bigger and bigger vehicles. "This is the antithesis of green leadership."

Stung by criticism of the Excursion, William Clay Ford, Jr., has vowed to make the company a more responsible environmental citizen. Worried that if automobile producers don't clean up their act, they will become as vilified as cigarette companies, in August 2000 Ford promised it would improve the fuel economy of its SUVs by 25 percent over the next five years, smugly inviting other automakers to follow its green leadership. To this GM responded that it was the real green leader and "will still be in five years, or 10 years, or for that matter 20 years. End of story." When they aren't bragging about their greenness, however, both companies continue to lobby Congress to forbid the Department of Transportation from studying fuel economy increases.[71]

Update:
Ford is planning on phasing out the Excursion after 2004. The company has also admitted that it will be unable to keep its promise to improve SUV fuel economy by 25 percent by 2005. Meanwhile, with the average fuel economy of new vehicles sold in the U.S. no higher than it was in 1983, the backlash against SUVs is growing—even as the Hummer H2 and other new models of gas-guzzlers roll out of the assembly plants.

Environmentalists have now been joined by conservatives, who in the aftermath of September 11, 2001, are worried about supporting the Middle Eastern oil producers who fund terrorism, and by Evangelical groups, whose bumper stickers ask, "What would Jesus drive?"

Discussion Questions

1. Are environmentalists right to be concerned about the environmental impact of SUVs? How do you explain the growing demand for ever larger passenger vehicles?
2. In developing and producing the Excursion, was the Ford Motor Company sacrificing the environment to profits, or was it acting in a socially responsible way by making the Excursion relatively energy efficient for its vehicle class? If you had been on the board of directors, would you have voted for the project? Why/why not? Do Ford's stockholders have a right to insist that it produce the most profitable vehicles it legally can, regardless of their environmental impact?
3. Assess William Clay Ford's claim that he wants to make his company the "world's most environmentally friendly automaker"? What are the environmental responsibilities of automakers?
4. Is Ford Motor Company simply responding to consumer demand for large vehicles, or is it helping to shape and encourage that demand?
5. Should there be tighter pollution restrictions on SUVs? Should the government try to discourage the production and use of SUVs?

CASE 11.4

The Fight over the Redwoods

Dense forests of coastal redwood trees once covered 2.2 million acres of southern Oregon and northern California. Today, only about 86,000 acres of virgin redwood forest remain. Most of this is in public parks and preserves, but about 6,000 acres of old-growth forest are privately owned—nearly all of it by the Pacific Lumber Company, headquartered in San Francisco.

Founded in 1869, Pacific Lumber owns 220,000 acres of the world's most productive timberland, including the old-growth redwoods. For years the family-run company was a model of social responsibility and environmental awareness. Pacific Lumber paid its employees well, supported them in bad times, funded their pensions, and provided college scholarships for their children. It sold or donated nearly 20,000 acres of forest to the public, and instead of indiscriminate clear-cutting, the company logged its forests carefully and selectively. Throughout its history, the company harvested only about 2 percent of its trees annually, roughly equivalent to their growth rate. After other timber firms had logged all their old-growth stands, Pacific Lumber had a virtual monopoly on the highly durable lumber that comes from the heart of centuries-old redwood trees.[72]

Because Pacific Lumber was debt free and resource rich, its potential value drew attention on Wall Street, where the firm of Drexel Burnham Lambert suspected that the company was undervalued—and thus ripe for raiding. In 1985 Drexel hired a timber consultant to fly over Pacific Lumber's timberland to estimate its worth. With junk-bond financing arranged by its in-house expert, Michael Milken, Drexel assisted Charles Hurwitz, a Texas tycoon, and his firm, Maxxam, Inc., to take over Pacific Lumber for $900 million. After initially resisting the leveraged buyout, the timber company's directors eventually acquiesced, and by the end of the year Hurwitz and Maxxam had control of Pacific Lumber. At the time, Hurwitz was primary owner of United Financial Group, the parent company of United Savings Association of Texas. In exchange for Milken's raising the money for the takeover of Pacific Lumber, Hurwitz had United Savings purchase huge amounts of risky junk bonds from Drexel. Three years later, the savings and loan failed, and taxpayers were stuck with a bill for $1.6 billion.

The takeover of Pacific Lumber left Maxxam with nearly $900 million in high-interest debt. To meet the interest payments, Maxxam terminated Pacific Lumber's pension plan and replaced it with annuities purchased from an insurance company owned by Hurwitz. Worse still, Maxxam tripled the rate of logging on Pacific Lumber's lands, and it was soon clear that Hurwitz intended to log the now-famous Headwaters forest, a 3,000-acre grove of virgin redwoods—the largest single stand of redwoods still in private hands. The value of the grove is astronomical: Milled into lumber, some of the trees are worth $100,000 each.

The potential lumber may be worth a fortune to Hurwitz, but environmentalists consider the Headwaters grove to be priceless as it is, and they have stepped in to do battle with Hurwitz. They see the Headwaters forest with its 500- to 2,000-year-old trees as an intricate ecosystem that took millions of years to evolve, a web of animals and plants that depend not just on living trees but also on dead, fallen redwoods that provide wildlife habitat and reduce soil erosion. Some of these activists—including Darryl Cherney, a member of the environmental group Earth First!—have devoted their lives to stopping Hurwitz.

Earth First! is not a mainstream conservation organization; it has a reputation for destroying billboards, sabotaging bulldozers and lumber trucks, and spiking trees with nails that chew up the blades of saws. "Hurwitz is a latter-day robber baron," says Cherney. "The only thing that's negotiable . . . is the length of his jail sentence."

Other environmental organizations have opposed Hurwitz in court. The Sierra Club Legal Defense Fund and the Environmental Protection Information Center have filed sixteen lawsuits against Pacific Lumber, giving the company's legal experts a run for their money. One of these suits bore fruit in 1995, when a judge blocked the company's plan to harvest timber in a smaller old-growth forest known as Owl Creek Grove. The legal reason was protection of the marbled murrelet, a bird about the size of a thrush, which breeds in the forest and is close to extinction. The judge also noted that "after the logging of an old-growth forest, the original cathedral-like columns of trees do not regenerate for a period of 200 years."

Pacific Lumber appealed the Owl Creek decision, but the ruling was upheld a year later. However, at the same time, the company won the right to appeal to another court to be allowed to harvest timber in the larger Headwaters forest. Meanwhile, both conservationists and a number of public officials are making strenuous efforts to acquire Headwaters and nine other surrounding redwood groves of about 200 acres each from Hurwitz. Although Hurwitz continues to fight both environmentalists and the government in court, he has quietly taken some steps to facilitate a sale, both through an indirect public relations campaign and by refinancing his takeover debt so that if the grove is sold, the proceeds would flow to Maxxam free and clear. Hurwitz has never named a price, but his deputies claim that the U.S. Forest Service has appraised the Headwaters forest at $500 million.

Some environmentalists balk at paying Hurwitz what amounts to ransom. They point to the fact that several government agencies, including the Federal Deposit Insurance Corporation, have filed suit against Hurwitz; they want $250 million from Hurwitz and $500 million from United Financial Group for their role in the $1.6 billion crash of United Savings. The environmentalists argue that Hurwitz should be forced to swap the forest in exchange for being forgiven the federal government's claims against him: The public gets Headwaters; Hurwitz gets off. Hurwitz, however, says that the lawsuits are without merit and denies any wrongdoing in the failure of the savings and loan.

Other environmentalists worry that too much attention is being directed toward saving the 3,000-acre Headwaters grove while leaving Pacific Lumber free to log the rest of its land with abandon. They are less concerned about the murrelets in particular or even the redwoods themselves; rather, what disturbs them is the dismantling of an ancient and intricate ecosystem—an irreplaceable temperate rain forest, home to some 160 species of plants and animals. Their aim is to build a new style of forestry based on values other than board feet of lumber and dollars of profit. They seek sustainable forest management and a new resource ethic devoted to rebuilding and maintaining habitats for coho salmon, the murrelet, the weasel-like fisher, and the northern spotted owl. As a first step, these conservationists call for protection, not just of the 3,000 Headwaters acres, but for an area nearly twenty times that amount, called the Headwaters Forest Complex. This tract includes all the ancient redwoods that Hurwitz owns and large areas of previously logged forest. "We have a vision that's bigger than Headwaters," says Cecelia Lanman of the Environmental Protection Information Center.

Her vision is definitely more sweeping than that of the Pacific Lumber workers in Scotia, California, a village containing 272 company-owned homes. Because Hurwitz has instituted stepped-up logging, which has meant more jobs, his employees tend to side with him, not the environmentalists. Workers say that Hurwitz has reinvested more than $100 million in modernizing his mills and has kept up the tradition of paying college scholarships for their children. The environmentalists are the real threat, says one employee. "You've got a group of people who hate Mr. Hurwitz, and they're using the Endangered Species Act and anything they can to hurt him. And we're caught in the middle."

Update:
In March 1999, Hurwitz signed a deal that a federal team led by Senator Dianne Feinstein and Deputy Interior Secretary John Garamendi had begun negotiating with him several years earlier.[73] In exchange for a 7,500-acre tract that includes the Headwaters grove and 2,500 additional acres of old-growth forest, the U.S. government and the state of California agreed to pay Pacific Lumber $480 million. The agreement also bans logging for fifty years on 8,000 other acres of company land in order to safeguard the murrelet, and it sets up buffer zones to protect the river habitats of

endangered coho salmon and steelhead trout. A Habitat Protection Plan regulates how and where Pacific Lumber harvests timber on the rest of its land. However, because Hurwitz transferred the $868 million debt that still remains from his original hostile takeover of Pacific Lumber from Maxxam to Pacific Lumber itself, the company will need to log as much as it can to make its interest payments.

Feinstein and Garamendi defended the deal as the best that they could get, and President Clinton and California Governor Gray Davis called the pact that saved Headwaters "historic." But Darryl Cherney and other activists have criticized the agreement as a sellout. They would like to see Pacific Lumber more closely regulated, claiming that the company still engages in overharvesting, clear-cutting instead of thinning, and various other poor logging practices. They also note that for 10,000 acres the government is paying Hurwitz half of what he originally spent for the entire company with its 220,000 acres of timberland.

Pacific Lumber, for its part, contends that state and federal agencies are so rigidly enforcing the habitat conservation plan that it can't cut enough lumber to keeps its mills running, and in late 2001 it closed down Scotia's 104-year-old mill. "We are being strangled by the operating restraints," said Robert Manne, current president of Pacific Lumber, which are "not working to meet the company and its employees' economic needs." To this complaint, conservationists and governmental officials respond that Pacific Lumber, which will continue to operate two smaller and much newer mills in neighboring towns, is scapegoating them for problems stemming from falling timber prices and the company's depletion of its old-growth redwood groves by clear-cutting. According to Paul Mason, president of a local environmental organization, "The lumber market is right in the tank, and that takes a bite out of your profit margin. The company has been operating at an unsustainable level for a number of years."

Discussion Questions

1. Does an ancient redwood forest have value other than its economic one as potential lumber? If so, what is this value, and how is it to be weighed against the interests of a company like Maxxam? Are redwoods more important than jobs?

2. Is it morally permissible for private owners to do as they wish with the timberland they own? Explain why or why not. What's your assessment of Hurwitz? Is he a robber baron or a socially responsible businessperson, or something in between?

3. Are mainstream environmentalists right to try to thwart Hurwitz, or are they simply trying to impose their values on others? Does a radical group like Earth First! that engages in sabotage go too far, or do its ends justify its means?

4. Do we have a moral obligation to save old redwood forests? Can a forest have either moral or legal rights? Does an old-growth forest have value in and of itself, or is its value only a function of human interests? How valuable is a small but endangered species such as the murrelet?

5. Before its takeover by Hurwitz, did Pacific Lumber neglect its obligations to its stockholders by not logging at a faster rate? What would be a morally responsible policy for a timber company to follow? Do we need a new environmental resource ethic?

6. How would you respond to the argument that there is no need to try to save the Headwaters (or any other private) forest because there are already tens of thousands of acres of old-growth redwood forest in parks and preserves?

7. Is the deal that the U.S. government and the state of California struck with Pacific Lumber a fair and reasonable one? Are taxpayers having to pay too much, as environmentalists think? Is Pacific Lumber being squeezed too hard? What about Scotia and its laid-off workers?

Notes

1. Eugene Linden, "Condition Critical," *Time* (Special Edition), April/May 2000, 19, 20.

2. Tom Regan, ed., *Earthbound: Introductory Essays in Environmental Ethics* (New York: Random House, 1984), 3.

3. See John Wargo, *Our Children's Toxic Legacy: How Science and Law Fail to Protect Us from Pesticides* (New Haven, Conn.: Yale University Press, 1996). See also "Group Names Most Contaminated Produce," *New York Times,* October 21, 2003, A18.

4. "From *Silent Spring* to Barren Spring?" *Business Week,* March 18, 1996, 42.

5. "Kids Need More Protection from Chemicals," *Los Angeles Times,* January 28, 1999, B9.

6. "Study Links Air Pollution, Heart Defects in Newborns," *San Jose Mercury News,* December 31, 2002, 17A.

7. "U.S. Reveals How Much Industry Pollutes the Air," *San Francisco Chronicle,* March 23, 1989, A1. See also *New York Times 2003 Almanac* (New York: Penguin, 2002), 774.

8. "Clinton Sharply Tightens Air Pollution Regulations," *New York Times,* June 26, 1997, A1.

9. See Michael D. Lemonick, "How to Prevent a Meltdown," *Time* (Special Edition), 61; Bill McKibben, "Acquaintance of the Earth," *New York Review of Books,* May 25, 2000, 48–49; and "Special Report: Global Warming," *Time,* April 23, 2001, 46–55.

10. Ken Silverstein, "Meat Factories," *Sierra,* January–February 1999; "Group's Surprising Beef with Meat Industry," *San Francisco Chronicle,* April 27, 1999; A1; and "Big Farms Making a Mess of U.S. Waters, Cities Say," *New York Times,* February 10, 2002, sec. 1, 20.

11. "U.S. Response to Air Pollution at Animal Farms Is Criticized," *Wall Street Journal,* December 18, 2002, B4; "Huge Farm Cesspools Blamed for Creating Noxious Clouds," *San Jose Mercury News,* May 11, 2003, 9A.

12. See the report by the OECD's Nuclear Energy Agency, "Chernobyl: Assessment of Radiological and Health Impact 2002," 81–98 (available at www.nea.fr).

13. "The Dead Zone," *Economist,* August 24, 2002, 26.

14. "*Playboy* Interview: Dr. Paul Ehrlich," *Playboy,* August 1970, 56.

15. John Steinbeck, *America and Americans* (New York: Viking Press, 1966), 127.

16. Garrett Hardin, "The Tragedy of the Commons," *Science* 162 (December 13, 1968): 1243–1248.

17. "The Tragedy of the Oceans," *Economist,* March 19, 1994, 21–24; John McQuaid, "Reaching the Limit," *San Francisco Examiner,* July 7, 1996, A10; Linden, "Condition Critical," 18.

18. William T. Blackstone, "Ethics and Ecology," in William T. Blackstone, ed., *Philosophy and Environmental Crisis* (Athens: University of Georgia Press, 1974).

19. Sharon Begley, "Furry Math? Market Has Failed to Capture the True Value of Nature," *Wall Street Journal,* August 9, 2002, B1.

20. Ibid.

21. "Would You Pay More to Let Nature Thrive?" *San Jose Mercury News,* October 4, 1994, 1A. For the doubts of an economist, see Amartya Sen, "The Discipline of Cost-Benefit Analysis," *Journal of Legal Studies* 29 (June 2000): 946–950.

22. "Windmills Sow Dissent for Environmentalists," *New York Times,* June 5, 2003, A28.

23. "In Vermont, a Mine Pits 2 Green Goals Against Each Other," *Wall Street Journal,* October 7, 2003, A1.

24. "Clean-Air Rules Worth It, Says White House Study," *San Jose Mercury News,* September 27, 2003, 7A.

25. Mark Hertsgaard, "A Global Green Deal," *Time* (Special Edition), 82–83.

26. *Business Horizons* 39 (January–February 1996): 67; *Time* (Special Edition), 87; "Waste Not," *San Francisco Chronicle,* July 9, 2000, "Sunday," 1.

27. U.S. Bureau of the Census, *Statistical Abstract of the United States 2002* (Washington, D.C.: U.S. Government Printing Office, 2003), Table 1065.

28. "Would You Pay More?" *San Jose Mercury News.*

29. *Business and Society Review* 84 (Winter 1993): 22–23.

30. Molly Ivins, "America's Corporate Hall of Shame," *San Francisco Chronicle,* April 9, 1999, A23.

31. "Grime and Punishment," *New Republic,* February 20, 1989, 7.

32. Ibid.

33. Ibid., 8.

34. Keith Davis and Robert L. Blomstein, *Business and Society* (New York: McGraw-Hill, 1978), 440.

35. "Environmental Enemy No. 1," *Economist,* July 6, 2002, 11.

36. James Lis and Kenneth Chilton, "Limits of Pollution Prevention," *Society* 30 (March–April 1993): 53.

37. "How Many Planets? A Survey of the Global Environment," *Economist,* July 6, 2002, 16. See also "Companies Trade the Right to Emit Greenhouse Gases," *Wall Street Journal,* January 3, 2003, A1.

38. Michael J. Sandel, "It's Immoral to Buy the Right to Pollute," *New York Times,* December 15, 1997, A19.

39. Michael E. Porter and Claas van der Linde, "Green and Competitive: Ending the Stalemate," *Harvard Business Review* 73 (September–October 1995): 120, 122, 125; Hertsgaard, "A Global Green Deal."

40. Porter and van der Linde, "Green and Competitive," 125–126, 128–129.

41. "Yes, Global Warming," *International Herald Tribune,* February 2, 1997, 8; Hertsgaard, "A Global Green Deal."

42. U.S Bureau of the Census, *Statistical Abstract of the United States 2002,* Table 1350.

43. Paul R. Ehrlich and Anne H. Ehrlich, "Population, Plenty, and Poverty," *National Geographic,* December 1988, 917.

44. Ibid.

45. Mathis Wackernagel et al., "Tracking the Ecological Overshoot of the Human Economy," *Proceedings of the National Academy of Sciences* 99 (June 27, 2002): 9266.

46. Joel Feinberg, "The Rights of Animals and Unborn Generations," in Tom L. Beauchamp and Norman E. Bowie, eds., *Ethical Theory and Business,* 2nd ed. (Englewood Cliffs, N.J.: Prentice Hall, 1983), 435.

47. Derek Parfit, *Reasons and Persons* (New York: Oxford University Press, 1986), 365.

48. Annette Baier, "The Rights of Past and Future Persons," in Joseph R. DesJardins and John J. McCall, eds., *Contemporary Issues in Business Ethics* (Belmont, Calif.: Wadsworth, 1985), 501; and Robert Elliot, "The Rights of Future People," *Journal of Applied Philosophy* 6 (1989).

49. See John Rawls, *A Theory of Justice* (Cambridge: Harvard University Press, 1971), 284–293.

50. William F. Baxter, *People or Penguins: The Case for Optimal Pollution* (New York: Columbia University Press, 1974), Chapter 1.

51. Holmes Rolston III, "Just Environmental Business," in Tom Regan, ed., *Just Business: New Introductory Essays in Business Ethics* (New York: Random House, 1984), 325.

52. See W. Wayt Gibbs, "On the Termination of Species," *Scientific American,* November 2001.

53. Jeremy Bentham, *An Introduction to the Principles of Morals and Legislation* (1789), Chapter 17, sec. 2.

54. Peter Singer, "Animal Liberation," *New York Review of Books,* April 5, 1973.

55. Quoted by Rolston, "Just Environmental Business," 340.

56. Peter Singer, "Animal Liberation at 30," *New York Review of Books,* May 15, 2003, 25.

57. Tom L. Beauchamp, *Case Studies in Business, Society, and Ethics* (Englewood Cliffs, N.J.: Prentice Hall, 1983), 118–119.

58. Bradley S. Miller, "The Dangers of Factory Farming," *Business and Society Review* 65 (Spring 1988): 44; "What Humans Owe to Animals," *Economist,* August 19, 1995, 11.

59. Miller, "Dangers of Factory Farming," 43, 44.

60. Tom Regan, "Ethical Vegetarianism and Commercial Animal Farming," in Richard A. Wasserstrom, ed., *Today's Moral Problems,* 3rd ed. (New York: Macmillan, 1985), 463–464. See also "Also a Part of Creation," *Economist,* August 19, 1995, 19.

61. Jeremy Rifkin, "Hold Your Nose at the Steak House," *International Herald Tribune,* March 25, 1992, 4.

62. Singer, "Animal Liberation at 30," 26.

63. Ibid.

64. "Animal Attraction," *Economist*, February 15, 2003, 75.

65. This case study is based on "At War with a Lead-Smelter," *Economist*, April 6, 2002, 30; front-page reports on Superfund in the *San Francisco Chronicle*, May 29 and May 30, 1991; and Michael Wines, "Waste Dumps Untouched, Survey Says," *Los Angeles Times*, September 7, 1984, 1–5, See also *www.epa.gov/superfund*.

66. See Noel Grove, "Air: An Atmosphere of Uncertainty," *National Geographic*, April 1987.

67. Ibid.

68. The following paragraphs are based on "Let Them Eat Pollution," *Economist*, February 8, 1992, 66; "Pollution and the Poor," *Economist*, February 15, 1992, 18; "Economics Brief: A Greener Bank," *Economist*, May 23, 1992, 79; and "A Great Leap Forward," *Economist*, May 11, 2002.

69. David R. Wheeler, *Greening Industry,* (New York: Oxford University Press, 1999), Chapter 5.

70. This case study is based on Donald W. Nauss, "Ford About to Unveil 4 Tons of Controversy," *Los Angeles Times*, March 11, 1999, A1.

71. Margot Roosevelt, "How Green Was My SUV," *Time* (overseas edition), August 14, 2000, 34.

72. The primary source for this case study is Elliot Diringer, "Cutting a Deal on Redwoods," *San Francisco Chronicle,* September 4, 1996, A1.

73. This update is based on news stories in *San Francisco Chronicle,* March 3, 1999, A1; *New York Times,* March 3, 1999, A1, and March 6, 1999, A7; *Economist,* March 6, 1999, 30; and *San Jose Mercury News,* December 8, 2001, 21A.

Further Reading for Chapter 11

Robin Attfield, *The Ethics of Environmental Concern,* 2nd ed. (Athens: University of Georgia Press, 1991), **Joseph R. Des Jardins**, *Environmental Ethics*, 3rd ed. (Belmont, Calif.: Wadsworth, 2001), and **Holmes Rolston III**, *Philosophy Gone Wild: Environmental Ethics* (Buffalo, N.Y.: Prometheus, 1990) are good introductions to environmental ethics.

Dale Jamieson, ed., *A Companion to Environmental Ethics* (Malden, Mass.: Blackwell, 2001) and **Andrew Light** and **Holmes Rolston III**, eds., *Environmental Ethics: An Anthology* (Oxford: Blackwell, 2003) are valuable, although philosophically advanced, reference works.

Lisa H. Newton and **Catherine K. Dillingham**, *Watersheds: Classic Cases in Environmental Ethics,* 3rd ed. (Belmont, Calif.: Wadsworth, 2002) offers ten detailed and insightful environmental case studies.

Joel Reichart and **Patricia H. Werhane**, eds., *Environmental Challenges to Business* (Bowling Green, Ohio: Philosophy Documentation Center, 2000) collects new and insightful essays on business and the environment by prominent business ethicists.

Mark Sagoff, *The Economy of Earth* (New York: Cambridge University Press, 1990) is an informed discussion of environmental policy.

Peter Singer, *Animal Liberation,* 2nd ed. (New York: Random House, 1990) is a seminal work advocating a radical change in our treatment of animals. **Gary L. Francione**, *Introduction to Animal Rights: Your Child or the Dog?* (Philadelphia: Temple University Press) offers a provocative but very readable critique of our treatment of animals.

James Sterba, ed., *Earth Ethics: Introductory Readings in Animal Rights and Environmental Ethics,* 2nd ed. (Upper Saddle River, N.J.: Prentice Hall, 2000) is an excellent, wide-ranging collection of essays, representing different environmental and philosophical approaches.

Timothy S. Yoder, "Corporate Responsibility and the Environment," *Business and Society Review* 106 (Fall 2001) takes up the topic of corporate responsibility for environmental malfeasance.

 InfoTrac College Edition: For further information or to conduct research, please go to www.infotrac-college.com.

Index